A BATTLE TOO FAR

ARRAS 1917

Don Farr

Arras Restored: the Hôtel de Ville (Town Hall). (Photo Gerald Farr)

A BATTLE TOO FAR

ARRAS 1917

Don Farr

Helion & Company

This book is dedicated to my good friend and counsellor, Vic Sayer.

Helion & Company Limited
Unit 8 Amherst Business Centre
Budbrooke Road
Warwick
CV34 5WE
England
Tel. 01926 499 619
Fax 0121 711 4075
Email: info@helion.co.uk
Website: www.helion.co.uk
Twitter: @helionbooks
Visit our blog http://blog.helion.co.uk/

Published by Helion & Company 2018
Designed and typeset by Farr out Publications, Wokingham, Berkshire
Cover designed by Farr out Publications, Wokingham, Berkshire
Printed by Gutenberg Press Limited, Tarxien, Malta

Text © Don Farr 2018
Black and white maps by George Anderson © Helion & Company 2018
Colour maps © Barbara Taylor 2018
Photographs © as individually credited

Front cover image: A British Military Band playing in the town square in Arras, 30 April 1917.
© IWM (Q6407)
Rear cover image: German prisoners captured at Vimy Ridge, 9 April 1917. (Open source)

ISBN 978-1-912174-92-8

British Library Cataloguing-in-Publication Data.

A catalogue record for this book is available from the British Library.

For details of other military history titles published by Helion & Company Limited contact the above address, or visit our website: http://www.helion.co.uk.

We always welcome receiving book proposals from prospective authors.

Contents

List of Illustrations

Black and white illustrations

Colour photographs in colour section

List of Maps

Acknowledgements

Appropriately I begin in Arras, a city with which I have become very familiar over years of visiting the Western Front battlefields. It has never palled as a place to visit and, oftentimes, as a base for wider ranging purposes. As soon as it had been determined that I would try to write the story of the Battle of Arras, I made contact with Alain Jacques, *Directeur du Service Archéologique de la Ville d'Arras*. We met shortly thereafter and he was most helpful in recommending books and collections that I should consult for background on Arras's suffering during the First World War.

Despite the attractions of Arras, most of my research has been carried out at the National Archives in Kew and on their on-line site. There were occasional frustrations when War Diaries disappeared for weeks on end to be digitised, but the staff were invariably most helpful with their advice and guidance during the long periods I spent at Kew. Unlike when I was researching earlier books, there has been little need to visit the Imperial War Museum this time around. I have however been in touch with the Museum's Photographs' Licensing Department regarding the use of a photograph from one of the Museum's collections on the book's front cover. Within the constraints under which the Museum must now operate, the staff of the Department, notably Neera Puttapipat, have been very courteous and helpful.

I must thank Jonathan Walker, the author of *The Blood Tub: General Gough and the Battle of Bullecourt*, for smoothing the way for me to use three maps from his book in mine. I am grateful to Lori Jones of Pen and Sword Books Limited for giving formal permission for me to do so with the following acknowledgement:

> Maps copyright of Pen and Sword Books, as appear in *The Blood Tub: General Gough and the Battle of Bullecourt 1917* by Jonathan Walker.

I should like to offer a very special thank you to a military history buff and great friend, Vic Sayer. Vic has been unstinting in his encouragement to me during the years of research and writing. He has been an excellent sounding board and has plied me with relevant newspaper cuttings. He has also loaned me books from his large collection. I am very grateful.

I am, too, greatly beholden to Barbara Taylor. In addition to being Chairman of the Thames Valley Branch of the Western Front Association, where I am a member of the committee, she is also a cartographer of some distinction who has provided me with most of the coloured maps in the book. In addition to being very informative, they are a great adornment.

Two other fellow members of the WFA Thames Valley Committee I must mention are Mike Lawson and Nigel Parker. Mike has loaned me a number of relevant books and has also always been very ready to track down useful pieces of information at my request. He has also provided some of the coloured photographs from his extensive collection. Nigel has been very helpful in tracking down maps and photographs and guiding me through the NA's archive of trench maps.

With regard to the black and white maps, these have been expertly crafted by cartographer George Anderson from some pretty scruffy raw material. I am much indebted to him.

It was Duncan Rogers of Helion & Company who suggested some years ago that my next book might usefully concentrate on a single First World War battle. It was my idea that it should be the Battle of Arras which, apart from Jonathan Nicholls' ground-breaking *Cheerful Sacrifice: the Battle of Arras 1917,* had been largely ignored by British military historians. The centenary of the battle has changed this to some extent but there is still little sign that Arras will ever receive the attention paid to the Somme or Passchendaele. I hope Duncan's endorsement of my choice of the Battle of Arras will prove to be of benefit to future students. I am grateful for his steadfast encouragement over years when it must have begun to seem that the book would never be completed.

Last but not least my grateful thanks are, as always, due to my wife, Ann, without whose expertise in the technical aspects of readying a book for publication, this book would never have got this far. I am forever in her debt.

Glossary

AIF	Australian Imperial Force
ANZAC	Australian and New Zealand Army Corps
BEF	British Expeditionary Force
BGRA	Brigadier General Royal Artillery
Bn	Battalion
CIB	Canadian Infantry Battalion
CB	Canadian Brigade
CGS	Chief of General Staff
CIGS	Chief of the Imperial General Staff
C in C	Commander in Chief
CO	Commanding Officer
CRA	Commander Royal Artillery
CT	Communications trench
FM	Field Marshal
FOO	Forward Observation Officer
FSC	Field Survey Company
GAC	*Groupe d'Armées du Centre* (French Central Army Group)
GAN	*Groupe d'Armées du Nord* (French Northern Army Group)
GAR	*Groupe d'Armées de Réserve* (French Reserve Army Group)
GHQ	General Headquarters (Headquarters BEF)
GOC	General Officer Commanding
GOCRA	General Officer Commanding Royal Artillery
GQG	*Grand Quartier Général* (French Supreme Headquarters)
GSO1	General Staff Officer, First Grade
HE	High Explosive
HQ	Headquarters
Km(s)	Kilometre(s)
KNA	Kitchener New Army
Kriegsakademie	German Army Staff College
LAC	Light Armoured Car
LHCMA	Liddell Hart Centre for Military Archives
MC	Military Cross
MGRA	Major General Royal Artillery
NCO	Non-Commissioned Officer
OB	Order of Battle
OH	Official History of the Great War
OHL	*Oberste Heeresleitung* (German Supreme HQ)
ORs	Other Ranks
Regt	Regiment
RFC	Royal Flying Corps
RNAS	Royal Naval Air Service

SA	South Africa(n)
SAA	Small arms ammunition
SPAD	*Société pour l'Aviation et ses Dérivés* (French Aircraft Manufacturer)
TNA	The National Archives
WO	War Office

Regiments

Argylls	Argyll and Sutherland Highlanders
Bedfords	Bedfordshire Regiment
Borders	Border Regiment
Buffs	The Buffs (Royal East Kent Regiment)
Camerons	Cameron Highlanders
CMR	Canadian Mounted Rifles
DCLI	Duke of Cornwall's Light Infantry
Devons	Devonshire Regiment
DLI	Durham Light Infantry
Dorsets	Dorsetshire Regiment
Duke's	Duke of Wellington's (West Riding) Regiment
East Lancashires	East Lancashire Regiment
East Yorks	East Yorkshire Regiment
Gordons	Gordon Highlanders
Green Howards	Yorkshire Regiment (Green Howards)
HAC	Honourable Artillery Company
Hampshires	Hampshire Regiment
HLI	Highland Light Infantry (Glasgow Regiment)
King's	King's (Liverpool) Regiment
King's Own	King's Own (Royal Lancaster Regiment)
KOSB	King's Own Scottish Borderers
KOYLI	King's Own Yorkshire Light Infantry
KRRC	King's Royal Rifle Corps
KSLI	King's Shropshire Light Infantry
Leicesters	Leicestershire Regiment
Lincolns	Lincolnshire Regiment
Loyals	Loyal North Lancashire Regiment
Manchesters	Manchester Regiment
Middlesex	Middlesex Regiment
Norfolks	Norfolk Regiment
Northants	Northamptonshire Regiment
North Staffs	North Staffordshire Regiment
Northumberlands	Northumberland Fusiliers
Ox & Bucks LI	Oxfordshire and Buckinghamshire Light Infantry
PPCLI	Princess Patricia's Canadian Light Infantry
Queen's	Queen's Royal (West Surrey) Regiment
QVR	Queen Victoria's Rifles (9th London Regiment)
RA	Royal (Regiment of) Artillery
RB	Rifle Brigade
R Berks	Royal Berkshire Regiment
RCR	Royal Canadian Regiment

RF	Royal Fusiliers
RFA	Royal Field Artillery
RGA	Royal Garrison Artillery
RHA	Royal Horse Artillery
RIF	Royal Irish Fusiliers
R Scots	Royal Scots
RSF	Royal Scots Fusiliers
R Sussex	Royal Sussex Regiment
RWF	Royal Welsh Fusiliers
R West Kents	(Queen's Own) Royal West Kent Regiment
SAI	South African Infantry
Seaforths	Seaforth Highlanders
Sherwoods	Sherwood Foresters (Notts and Derby Regiment)
SLI	Somerset Light Infantry
South Staffs	South Staffordshire Regiment
SR	Cameronians (Scottish Rifles)
Suffolks	Suffolk Regiment
SWB	South Wales Borderers
Warwicks	Royal Warwickshire Regiment
West Yorks	West Yorkshire Regiment
Wilts	Wiltshire Regiment
York & Lancs	York and Lancaster Regiment

Introduction

The employment of the term 'too far' to indicate biting off more than can comfortably be chewed was notably and memorably used by Lieutenant General Browning in the phrase ' ... a bridge too far'. Browning was expressing his concern that, in seeking to take and hold the Rhine Bridge at Arnhem, the most distant bridge of five, the planners of Operation Market Garden in September 1944 might be overreaching themselves. His concern was to prove well founded.[1] I make no apology for adapting the phrase to describe the Battle of Arras, fought a generation earlier than the Battle of Arnhem. Here was a battle that the British Army would have been content not to have fought. The imperatives of inter-allied cooperation and political considerations determined otherwise. The British doubts about the allied strategy of which the Arras campaign formed a part were to prove just as well-founded as Browning's would later prove to be. The Battle of Arras was, in general but with some exceptions, a tragic disappointment with little significant ground gained to compensate for the serious losses suffered. Inevitably, however, this crude balance sheet does not tell the whole story.

The town that gave its name to the 1917 battle can trace its origins back to the Roman occupation of Gaul. Like many other places near France's modern borders it was only in relatively recent times that it could regard itself as permanently French. By the Middle Ages the town was a prosperous industrial centre, its most celebrated product being the tapestries which took their name from the town.[2] Politically it was only finally incorporated into France during the reign of Louis XIII in 1640 having successively been part of Flanders, the France of Philip-Augustus, Burgundy, the France of Louis XI from 1477, and the Spanish Netherlands from 1492. For many years it was the capital of the Artois region. Unsurprisingly, given that its most famous son is Maximilien de Robespierre, Arras played its full part in the excesses of the French Revolution. While Robespierre was directing the reign of terror in Paris, the Mayor of Arras, Joseph Le Bon, ensured that those who allegedly offended against the Revolution in the region found their way to the guillotine which, in Arras, was set up in the Place du Théâtre. Like Robespierre, Le Bon eventually fell victim to the guillotine himself.

Arras does not appear to have played a very prominent part in the political upheavals which periodically rocked France in the nineteenth century as it mutated from Empire to Kingdom, to Republic, to Empire and again to Republic. Although there was much fighting in the area of the town during the Franco-Prussian War of 1870-1, Arras itself was not seriously invested by the Prussians even though French troops sought refuge in its fortifications.

Only a few days after the outbreak of war in 1914 Arras found itself very close to the fighting, where it would remain for all but the last few weeks of the war. In the critical days of the first German onrush, the enemy actually took possession of the town on 6 September. Only three days later, however, they were forced to withdraw and retreat in the face of the Franco/British counteroffensive

---

1   Lieutenant General Frederick 'Boy' Browning (1896-1965) achieved prominence as an Airborne commander in the Second World War. He was appointed to the command of 1st Airborne Division in 1941 and took over 1 Airborne Corps in April 1944. He was Deputy Commander of the First Allied Airborne Army, organised in August 1944, which formed the airborne part of Operation Market Garden, best remembered for 1st Airborne Division's failure, against overwhelming odds, to hold Arnhem Bridge until Land Forces could relieve them. Although no blame was officially attributed to Browning for the Operation's failure, he received no further promotion. He was married to the celebrated author, Daphne du Maurier.

2   Famously, in Shakespeare's Hamlet, Polonius was run through by the eponymous hero as he hid behind the 'arras'.

Arras in ruins.

on the Marne. When this ended with the Germans securely entrenched along the *Chemin des Dames* north of the River Aisne and neither side able to break through the others' defences, the period known as 'the Race to the Sea' ensued as each side sought unsuccessfully to outflank the other to the north and west. As the Germans moved north from the Aisne and brought in new formations which advanced westward from Alsace through the Cambrai area, Arras was once more menaced. The French countered this fresh threat by bringing in General Ernest Barbot's 77th Infantry Division from Alsace where it had distinguished itself under its commander's forceful leadership. The Division arrived in Arras on 1 October where, five days later, it became part of the newly formed Tenth Army. General Barbot[3] immediately received orders from Army HQ to hold a line running from Monchy-le-Preux to Neuville-Vitasse via Wancourt against German troops approaching from the southeast along the axis of the Arras-Cambrai road. It proved to be too late to prevent the Germans occupying Wancourt and part of Monchy-le-Preux. Despite strenuous French efforts, it was the Germans who finally prevailed in the fighting for the latter village and the French were pushed out.

The fighting over the next six days was characterised by heavy German pressure which slowly

---

3 General Barbot assumed command of the 77th Infantry Division in August 1914 following the deaths in action in Alsace of its two previous commanders within three days of each other. After his success at the head of the Division in Alsace and in the defence of Arras, he was in turn mortally wounded on 10 May 1915 while in action near Souchez during the Second Battle of Artois. In 1937 a memorial to the dead of the 77th Division was unveiled in Souchez, quite close to the spot where General Barbot suffered his wounds. At the front of the memorial is a striking bronze statue of the General in his soldier's beret. General Barbot is buried in the national Necropolis of Notre Dame de Lorette in the nearest grave to the main entrance.

drove the French back. The 77th and 20th Divisions, which were assigned the task of holding the Germans on a line between St-Laurent-Blangy and Beaurains by way of Tilloy-lès-Mofflaines, were unable to hold Beaurains and Tilloy, although they exacted a heavy price from the advancing Germans for their success in capturing them. The defenders were pushed back to the Saint-Sauveur and Ronville suburbs of Arras, situated behind the two lost villages, while at the same time they clung on in St-Laurent-Blangy and Roclincourt.

On 7 October the Germans launched a major assault with the intention of finally taking possession of Arras. Until the 26th the struggle against a determined French defence raged back and forth. The German pressure forced the evacuation of St-Laurent-Blangy, but in general, aided by the blowing of the bridges across the River Scarpe, the French held on. The 26th October marked the last day of the German effort to subdue Arras. By then the focus of their efforts was moving north where they were about to launch the First Battle of Ypres. But even though the Germans had been stopped outside Arras, and were never to breach its defences, they were sufficiently close to the town centre to be able to bombard it at will; they would do so to destructive effect for the next four years.

The train of events which led to the Battle of Arras being fought was set in motion at an inter-allied military conference held in mid-November 1916 at the French Supreme Headquarters (*Grand Quartier Général* (GQG)) at Chantilly. It was summoned and chaired by the French Commander in Chief, General Joseph Joffre. That it apparently took place in an atmosphere of sober optimism is remarkable, even if the days preceding the opening of proceedings had seen a slight upturn in allied fortunes in the still ongoing Battles of the Somme and Verdun. Overall, as the generals and their staffs assembled, they could only look back on 27 months of heavy fighting on the Western Front characterised by appalling losses with very little positive to show for them.

From the outset the ground war in France and Belgium had gone badly for the Allies. The principal reasons for this were the French Army's philosophical attachment to *attaque à outrance*, and the serious flaws in the French Army's blueprint for victory, the notorious Plan XVII. *Attaque à outrance* (all out attack) appears to have paid little regard to the advent of the powerful defensive weapons of the machine gun and quick-firing artillery and the effect they would have on the French formations charging across open ground with their visibility enhanced by the red pantaloons and *képis* of their outmoded uniforms. The consequences for the French armies seeking to liberate the lost provinces of Alsace and Lorraine and push on into Germany proper had been catastrophic. Their losses had been huge as they were pushed back to their start lines, and sometimes beyond, by the well organised and equipped German armies facing them.

A major fault of Plan XVII was its misreading of German intentions. The French were well aware of the details of the Schlieffen Plan, the German blueprint for victory in the West, but discounted its advocacy of a wide sweep through Belgium on the grounds that the Germans would not use reserves to bring their right wing armies up to the strength required for the manoeuvre. Even if they did, they would have to strip out troops from their right wing to meet the threat of the French advance through Alsace-Lorraine. In fact, as the French belatedly realised, the Germans intended to stick very closely to their Plan. The British Expeditionary Force (BEF) and the French Fifth Army, which had advanced into Belgium as quickly as they could once that country's neutrality had been violated by Germany, soon found themselves assailed by the vastly superior numbers of the German First and Second Armies and were forced into full retreat, despite inflicting temporary checks on the enemy at the Battles of Mons, Le Cateau and Guise.

Allied prospects of turning the tide were looking bleak until German overconfidence and concerns at the gap opening up between their First and Second Armies began to erode the full implementation of the Schlieffen Plan. As the First Army turned eastward north of Paris (and not south of the capital as planned) to close the gap, it offered its flank to a French advance from Paris. General Joffre and the Military Governor of Paris, General Joseph Galliéni, were quick to take the opportunity offered, with the former creating a new Sixth Army (and the latter rapidly reinforcing it), which went over to the attack on 5 September 1914. With the other French armies and the BEF ending their retreats and also attacking, the Germans were soon in full retreat, and the First Battle of the Marne had been won. Had the Allies succeeded in driving a wedge between the two German armies, the German retreat might have become disastrous for them. But they managed to close the gap just in time and halted their retirement in prepared positions on and near the River Aisne, from which it proved impossible to dislodge them in the First Battle of the Aisne. Both sides dug in and the war of movement began to be replaced by trench warfare. The master plans of both sides for winning the war had become so much waste paper.

With both sides realising the futility of trying to batter their way through well-entrenched defences a last period of mobile warfare, the so-called 'Race to the Sea', took place over the last weeks of 1914. There was no race to the sea as such, merely a series of attempted outflanking manoeuvres where there were still enemy flanks to exploit and which ended, inconclusively, when the sea was reached in Belgian Flanders. The most intense fighting of this phase took place when the Germans made strenuous attempts to break through the attenuated allied defences around Ypres. The First Battle of Ypres eventually ended with the allied defences intact, but only just. Sadly the fighting here nearly completed the destruction of the pre-war British Army, which had begun at Mons. Until the divisions of the Kitchener New Army (KNA) could be trained, the BEF would be heavily reliant on the Territorial Army, the Indian Army and some regular army battalions being brought back from the Colonies to maintain and increase the size of their presence on the Western Front.

In 1915, the first full year of the war, the Germans decided to adopt a defensive posture in the west while they sought to settle matters in the east with the Russians. Such an approach was not seen as an option by the French with important areas of their country now occupied by the invader. Major offensives were undertaken in Artois and Champagne, resulting in heavy casualty lists for negligible gains. The BEF played a significant supporting role in the Second and Third Battles of Artois having, in March 1915, conducted their first offensive at Neuve Chapelle to prove to the sceptical French that they could attack as well as defend. The offensive took the Germans by surprise and could have achieved a breakthrough had inexperience and artillery deficiencies not intervened and led to a stalemate.

Despite their main focus being on the Eastern Front the Germans decided to test a new weapon, 'asphyxiating' gas, by using it in an assault on the Ypres Salient. The Second Battle of Ypres could have resulted in a major German breakthrough had they had the reserves available to exploit the unanticipated success of their new weapon. Even so, it took desperate fighting by the allies to contain the German threat. The battle, which began on 22 April, ended with a much reduced Ypres Salient still in allied hands, on 25 May.

The Second Battle of Artois was launched on 9 May. It began auspiciously with the French taking possession of Vimy Ridge. But they were very quickly driven back. The fighting was to last intermittently until 19 June but no breakthrough was achieved. The British supporting actions consisted of the Battles of Aubers Ridge and Festubert. They were inconclusive engagements which never remotely threatened the German hold on Aubers Ridge despite heavy British losses. The Third Battle of Artois, for which the main objective was again Vimy Ridge, was a further dire experience for the French resulting in heavy losses to show for the capture of a few destroyed villages. In support the British launched on 25 September an offensive known as the Battle of Loos. The biggest British attack of the war thus far was to end with serious casualties and little to show for them. The failure was to lead to the end of Field Marshal Sir John French's tenure as Commander in Chief of the BEF. His inept handling of the reserves and his attempts to place the blame elsewhere in his official dispatch led in December to his recall and his replacement by General Sir Douglas Haig. Two of the badly mishandled reserve divisions were the 21st and 24th, two of the first divisions of the Kitchener New

Army to reach the front.

With the running down of the 1915 campaigning season in October attention focused on 1916 at an inter-Allied conference convened at Chantilly on 6 December. There it was agreed that the main allied effort in the summer of 1916 should be a joint Anglo-French offensive in the Somme *département* where by then the junction between the two nations' forces would be situated. The offensive would be predominantly French but with a large British input consisting mainly of KNA divisions that by then would, it was hoped, be adequately trained and prepared for their role.

However the Germans threw the allied plans into disarray when they launched an offensive against the fortress city of Verdun on 21 February 1916. This was the brainchild of the German Chief of Staff Erich von Falkenhayn who contended that Britain had become Germany's main enemy and advocated a two-pronged strategy to weaken Britain's appetite for the struggle. One prong was unrestricted submarine warfare; the other, the knocking of France out of the war by attacking a place, Verdun, she would feel obliged to defend to the last man. The purpose of the offensive would be not so much to capture Verdun as to draw the French army into a cauldron where it could be 'bled white' in the Verdun 'mincing machine'. When the Germans assaulted in overwhelming strength the French reacted as von Falkenhayn had predicted and a bitter struggle ensued that was to last into December. The Germans mounted a series of attacks between February and July during which the important forts of Douaumont and Vaux were captured to the great embarrassment of the French. When the Germans decided to go onto the defensive in July the initiative passed to the French who had in any case begun to recover from their early shocks in the battle. The restoration of their morale was achieved by General Philippe Pétain. No sooner had he turned things around than he was promoted to Army Group Commander and replaced as Commander of the Second Army at Verdun by General Robert Nivelle, who was subsequently to play a crucial role in allied fortunes in the first half of 1917. Nivelle and one of his corps commanders, the thrusting General Charles Mangin, launched a series of attacks which gradually pushed the Germans back and finally recaptured the lost forts. Despite the heavy casualty lists which accompanied these successes, the enormous fillip they gave to French national morale paved the way shortly thereafter for Nivelle's elevation to the pinnacle of the French Army.

The life and death struggle consuming the French army at Verdun had inevitable consequences for the planned allied Somme offensive. It would perforce become a mainly British campaign with as much assistance as the French could spare. It would, too, need to be launched as soon as possible, and much sooner than General Haig wished, to relieve some of the pressure on the French at Verdun. Joffre's unremitting efforts persuaded Haig to agree to a start date of 29 June (later delayed by two days by bad weather). Following a week-long artillery bombardment elements of 12 British divisions of the newly created Fourth Army (plus two from Third Army) and five divisions of the French Sixth Army went over the top on 1 July 1916. What ensued was the most disastrous day in the history of the British Army as 30,000 troops became casualties in the first hour and nearly 60,000 over the course of the day. Only at the eastern end of the assault were any permanent gains recorded and it was on these that subsequent attacks would seek to build. Offensive action north of the Albert-Bapaume road was temporarily suspended. Over the course of the period up to 18 November, when the Somme campaign closed down, a series of attacks were launched which gradually pushed the British lines forward, captured some important German strong points but never achieved the breakthrough that Haig had been seeking. The more modest ambitions of the Fourth Army Commander, General Sir Henry Rawlinson, were achieved when the Pozières Ridge, the highest point of the battlefield, was secured in September.

Although it is outside the scope of this book to dwell for long on the Battle of the Somme, which had drawn to a close less than five months before the Nivelle Plan began to unfold with the launching of the Battles of Arras, it cannot be put to one side entirely because of the influence it exercised on the methods employed by the French in the Nivelle offensive.

The popular British perception of the French participation in the Somme campaign, that it was a marginal and peripheral one, probably derives from the fact that the French only employed five divisions on the first day compared to the 14 committed by the British. The uncomfortable fact that the French captured a greater area of enemy ground than the British, not only on that first day but over the campaign as a whole, as even a cursory glance at a map of the campaign shows, is usually rationalised as the consequence of the French attacking weak German defences manned by indifferent troops, whereas the British were up against almost impregnable defences manned by highly competent enemy units. Such a rationalisation has been comprehensively demolished by a recently published book on the battle.[4] The British were indeed confronted by formidable defences and opponents; but so were the French. While the British were suffering the most disastrous day's casualties in the nation's military history for negligible gains, the French quickly occupied and consolidated their objectives with minimal losses by Western Front standards.

The explanation for these contrasting fortunes can be summed up in the word 'experience'. By mid 1916 the French had absorbed the skills involved in fighting trench warfare, which the British were only just beginning to learn. The majority of the British divisions on the Somme were Kitchener New Army, many of them seeing action for the first time. The French divisions may have been few in number but they were among the best, if not the best, in their army. Their generals, notably the future Marshals of France, Foch and Fayolle, had quickly learned to place their reliance on overwhelming concentrations of artillery firepower, intended both to pulverise the enemy's defences and defenders and to offer protection to the advancing infantry. Not only were they fortunate in having the right calibre and number of guns and adequate supplies of ammunition, but they ensured this by not taking on tasks beyond their means. The contrast with the British situation is telling. Although the British commanders may have convinced themselves that they had adequate artillery resources for the tasks in hand, they lacked a sufficient number of heavy calibres, the guns were too thinly spread over the length of front to be covered and the ammunition was notoriously defective. The guns signally failed to achieve any of their principle objectives and the infantry paid the price.

General Ferdinand Foch, whose Army Group encompassed the Somme, had long since put to rest the reputation he had somehow unfairly earned when pre-war Commandant of the *Ecole Supérieure de la Guerre* that he was a single-minded *attaque à outrance* leader. An intellectual soldier of the highest calibre he had been one of the first to recognise that the advent of the machine gun and quick-firing artillery had handed the initiative to the defence and new methods would be required for attacks to succeed. He quickly became an advocate of the application of various forms of artillery firepower to the problems confronting the attack. In advocating these to General Fayolle, his subordinate in command of the Sixth Army, he was pushing at an open door as Fayolle was a Gunner with a ready appreciation that the conflict was becoming an artillery war.

On 1 July 1916 the French artillery fulfilled all that was required of it. Quite apart from almost total success in suppressing the German defences, the field guns, the famous seventy-fives, fired what the French called a *barrage roulant*, essentially a form of creeping barrage, which offered greater protection to the advancing infantry than they had been accustomed to in earlier stages of the war.[5]

General Nivelle, also a Gunner, would have been aware of the developments in artillery technique

---

4   William Philpott, *Bloody Victory: the Sacrifice on the Somme.*

5   It is probably no coincidence that one of the few British successes of that day was XIII Corps' achievement of all its objectives, including the capture of the fortified village of Montauban. The Corps' stretch of the line was immediately to the left of the French XX Corps' positions. At least one of the British Corps' gunnery officers, Major Alan Brooke of the 18th Division (later Field Marshal Lord Alanbrooke, the Second World War CIGS) contrived a meeting a few weeks before the battle with a Colonel Herring, a French Gunnery Officer, who described to him the barrage roulant. As a result a form of this was successfully employed by 18th Division on the first day of the battle. Combined with a preliminary bombardment that was more effective than most, especially in cutting the German wire, the ground was laid for the Corps' success.

being practised on the Somme as he conducted operations at Verdun designed to recover the lost forts and eliminate all the German gains of the earlier stages of the battle. He employed methods essentially similar to those of Foch and Fayolle, and with even more striking success as he and his subordinate, General Mangin, drove the Germans back.

The performance of the French Sixth Army during the Somme campaign as a whole continued to outshine that of their British allies, even though the latter were learning fast. The French might well have made even greater inroads into German-held territory had they not been constrained by a need to keep in step with the British units who were covering their left flank.

The last week of the Somme campaign consisted mainly of a British attack known as the Battle of the Ancre. It was fought in deteriorating weather from 13-18 November. Its positive effect on the state of mind of the generals gathering at Chantilly could be accounted for by the overall success of the attack in meeting its limited objectives, which included the capture at long last of the fortified village of Beaumont Hamel, an objective of 1 July. The French contribution to the generals' sense of wellbeing came from recent successes at Verdun where Fort Douaumont had been recaptured on 24 October during a French offensive which had netted 6,000 German prisoners and recovered much of the ground lost in the earlier months of the battle. Fort Vaux had also been retaken on 3 November. As the generals gathered for their conference at Chantilly and the allied political leadership convened in Paris on the same day the sober optimism of the former was certainly not shared by the latter. The two governments were extremely unhappy with the way the war was being conducted by their military commands, especially in the main theatre of the Western Front. The appalling losses of the Somme campaign, coming on top of not insignificant losses in the previous two years, had led to a rapidly growing sentiment on the part of some leading British politicians that the generals were not to be trusted with the prosecution of the land war. Despite their seeming incapacity to put in place and maintain an administration for more than a few months at best in the face of a refractory Parliament, the leading French politicians, with little to show for the horrifying sacrifices their soldiers had been called on to make, were becoming equally anxious to wrest back the strategic direction of the war from the generals, and even beginning to contemplate the unthinkable, the removal of General Joffre from supreme command.

The British concerns were largely articulated by the Secretary of State for War, David Lloyd George. As he had only occupied that position since the death of Lord Kitchener in June 1916, he had been little more than a helpless spectator as the carnage of the Somme unfolded. According to Edward Spears 'his gorge rose at the massacre'.[6] When he learned of the plan for the Chantilly military conference he persuaded the War Committee to seek to have the conference postponed until after the politicians had met, with the clear aim of enabling the latter to agree an overall strategy for the military prosecution of the war which could then be imposed on the generals. He submitted a statement of his views on the military situation to Prime Minister Herbert Asquith that he hoped might form the basis of discussion at the political conference. As submitted, it urged that there should be a follow-up allied conference in Petrograd to coordinate allied efforts in east and west. It scathingly criticised the military failures of the war to date and the apparent inability of the generals to come up with solutions to end the stalemate. The statement was intended to prepare the ground for a search for alternative ways to pursue the war which would marginalise the Western Front. Prime Minister Asquith could not bring himself to submit the statement as drafted to his allied colleagues for fear that its trenchant criticisms of the French and British higher commands would give offence. As finally submitted, Lloyd George complained, all the sting had been taken out of the document.[7] To add to his frustration, General Joffre declined to postpone the Chantilly conference.

In advance of Chantilly, and presumably in anticipation that there might well be political

---

6   E.L. Spears, *Prelude to Victory*, p. 21.
7   David Lloyd George, *War Memoirs Vol I*, pp. 544-55.

pressure for other options to be considered, Haig and General Sir 'Wully' Robertson, the Chief of the Imperial General Staff, had met at Boulogne and reaffirmed their complete agreement that the main military focus should continue to be the Western Front and not the Balkans or elsewhere. They also thought that a tentative proposal of General Joffre's that a general offensive should not take place until May 1917 was quite unsound, even if that was the earliest that the Italians and Russians would be ready to advance.[8]

The decisions reached at Chantilly on 15 November reflected the continuing pre-eminence of the French in allied councils. In Lloyd George's rather jaundiced view the conclusions that the generals had reached, and presented the following day to the allied statesmen gathered in Paris, bore all the hallmarks of having been settled in advance of Chantilly by the staff of GQG.[9] In essence the pre-eminence of the Western front was reaffirmed as was the intention to pursue offensive operations there and elsewhere through the winter as opportunity offered, to the maximum extent permitted by climatic conditions. In a bid to forestall a German attempt to seize the initiative, as they had done so effectively at Verdun early in 1916, the allied armies on all fronts would be ready to undertake joint offensive operations from the first fortnight of February. (That such a commitment displayed a great deal of wishful thinking was implicit in the woolly wording of how and if these operations would be synchronised. Almost certainly only the French had a realistic chance of being ready in early February. Even Haig, earlier so critical of Joffre's now discarded proposal to wait until May, had already warned his French *confrère* of the difficulties such an early start would give him.) The allied commanders tried to sound positive about the Balkan front but again attached so many qualifications that it must have been apparent to more than just a cynical Lloyd George that little effort would be made in that theatre. In the absence of any agreed strategy of their own, the statesmen had little option but to endorse the allied commanders' conclusions which, as Lloyd George railed, would lead in 1917 to a repeat of 'all the bloody stupidities of 1915 and 1916'.[10]

While the wider stage was distracting Joffre and Haig, their staffs had been busy devising an agreed plan of operations for the joint Western Front offensive. On 1 November Joffre was able to write to Haig with detailed proposals. He pointed out that what he was proposing did not affect their joint intention to pursue the current offensive operations, climatic conditions permitting. But it was desirable to put in place an overall plan for 1917. He proposed accordingly that the British should attack with two armies north of the Somme, one on each of the two flanks of the salient between Vimy Ridge and Bapaume. The French Northern Army Group (*Groupe d'Armées du Nord* (GAN)) would attack with three armies between the Somme and Noyon, and the French Fifth Army of the Central Army Group (*Groupe d'Armées du Centre* (GAC)) would launch a surprise attack from between Soissons and Reims two weeks after the main attack. A second surprise attack would also be launched in Upper Alsace.[11]

Haig was broadly content with these proposals subject to agreement on how much of the French front would need to be taken over by the British, and when. He had already envisaged the possibility of a British offensive around Arras and, in late September, had ordered General Edmund Allenby, the Third Army commander, to draw up plans accordingly. He reaffirmed these instructions on 6 November, when he assured Allenby that even if the attack he had been ordered to prepare did not take place in 1916, it would in the coming spring. In this context Haig emphasised to Allenby the importance of upgrading railway communications serving the Arras area.[12]

The apparently clear cut military strategy outlined and agreed for 1917 was potentially thrown into disarray by two significant developments during December, one on each side of the Channel. In

8   Haig d, 22.10.16.
9   Lloyd George, op. cit., p. 566.
10   Ibid, p. 573.
11   Robert A. Doughty, *Pyrrhic Victory*, p. 315.
12   Haig d. 30.9.16 and 6.11.16.

London on the 6th, David Lloyd George replaced Herbert Asquith as Prime Minister of the coalition government. In Paris, over the course of the month, General Joffre was manoeuvred out of office as Commander in Chief of the whole French Army and partially replaced by General Robert Nivelle as Commander in Chief of the French forces on the Western Front.

Prime Minister Asquith's downfall – he certainly did not wish to go – can be mainly explained by a growing, if almost certainly erroneous, impression on the part of the public and some of his coalition colleagues that he was not wholeheartedly committed to the prosecution of the war until victory was achieved. No such accusation could be levelled at his successor, whose commitment to victory was unquestioned, even if his ideas on how to achieve it would prove questionable and divisive.

General Joffre ultimately paid the price for the failure of the allies to make any significant impression on the German hold on a significant area of France in spite of intolerable losses. Not even his legendary status as victor of the Marne could save him from the consequence of his subsequent failures, the most recent of which were his lack of preparedness for the German assault at Verdun and the disappointments of the Somme campaign. The nature of French politics, weak governments frequently at the mercy of a fractious Chamber of Deputies, meant that Joffre's departure was anything but straightforward. But there was little disposition by his nominal political masters to come to his rescue as the pressures against him mounted, and on 26 December he formally requested to be relieved of all his responsibilities. He was consoled in his departure by his appointment to the rank of Marshal of France.[13] His successor would waste little time in seeking to recast the allied plans for 1917.

---

13 Doughty, op. cit., pp. 318-21.

Part I

Politics, Personalities and Plans

1

Politics and Personalities

The arrival of David Lloyd George and Robert Nivelle at the pinnacle of their respective professions in the last month of 1916 would have a major impact on Allied military strategy in 1917 and the framework in which it was conducted. The Joffre blueprint, thrashed out and agreed by the allied generals at Chantilly and endorsed the following day by the politicians meeting in Paris, had its shortcomings as even the generals must have acknowledged privately to themselves. It seemed to offer little more than a further round of the tried and failed approach of the previous two years, the only refinement being that every effort would be made to synchronise the offensives on every front. (As has been noted, this question of timing had begun to unravel almost as soon as the ink was dried on the Chantilly document.)

Despite the growing feeling by members of the French government and National Assembly that the replacement of General Joffre was long overdue, it might well not have happened had it not been for the emergence of General Nivelle onto the national stage. The Army Group Commanders, Foch and Pétain, and Joffre's Chief of Staff, Castelnau, were senior to Nivelle and better qualified, in terms of experience in the exercise of high command, for the role of supreme commander. But, as Haig noted in his diary, they were up against the anti-clerical prejudices of their political masters. Foch had a Jesuit brother and was a churchgoer; Pétain had been brought up by Dominicans and was also a churchgoer, if rather less zealous than Foch; Castelnau, who attended Mass and was 'Very Catholic', was the least acceptable of all.[1] Robert Nivelle was thus chosen to replace Joffre, his selection made easier because he was Joffre's preferred choice to succeed him.

As he assumed the responsibilities of supreme command, Nivelle could look back on two years of unbroken success in the war so far. He had begun it as a colonel in command of an artillery regiment in which role he had distinguished himself at the First Battles of the Marne and the Aisne. At the Marne Nivelle saved an infantry unit from collapse by leading his artillery regiment through them to engage the enemy over open sights. Thereafter his rise through the ranks was rapid, no doubt inadvertently assisted by Joffre's ruthless sacking of general officers at all levels whose performance he deemed inadequate, thereby inevitably creating vacancies for ambitious and competent junior officers such as Nivelle. By 1916 he was a Lieutenant General commanding III Corps at Verdun.[2] As soon as Pétain had sorted out the administrative and strategic chaos he had found on being given the Verdun command, and restored French morale, he was kicked upstairs to take over the Central Army Group (*Groupe d'Armées du Centre*). On 1 May 1916 Nivelle replaced him in command of the Second Army. The French were still very much on the defensive at Verdun and Nivelle showed imagination and inventiveness in the handling of the artillery in containing the German assaults. In an Order of the Day he coined the memorable phrase, *Ils ne passeront pas*, often mistakenly attributed to Pétain. When the Second Army went over to the offensive Nivelle concentrated on achieving overwhelming local artillery superiority, the use of deception, and sophisticated infantry tactics. He was an early, possibly the first, commander to employ the rolling (or creeping) barrage to offer some protection to

---

1 Haig d. 13.12.16. Castelnau was a lay member of the Capuchin order who enjoyed the nickname *Le Capucin Botté* (The Fighting Friar).
2 Anthony Clayton, *Paths of Glory*, pp. 250-1.

the infantry, a concept he had been refining since mid-1915. Notable successes were the recapture of the *Fort de Douaumont* on 24 October and *Fort Vaux* on 3 November.

The politicians were not only impressed by Nivelle's well-publicised successes at Verdun, which had done wonders for French national morale, but also by his claim that he could achieve a massive and war-winning victory in short order on the wider stage of the Western Front as a whole. It was a beguiling alternative to the prospect of more of the same that Joffre seemed to be offering. Furthermore, unlike Joffre, Nivelle was a persuasive advocate in his own cause. He was as charming and charismatic as Joffre was saturnine and uncommunicative. He seemed to offer the politicians the prospect of a genuine duologue on his proposed plans, something which had seldom, if ever, been on offer from Joffre. His Protestantism, which was known to embrace anti-Catholicism, may also, paradoxically, have seemed less of a threat to anti-clerical Republican politicians, than the Catholicism of Foch, Pétain and Castelnau.

In December 1916 Robert Nivelle was in his 61st year. Although his career had been in the artillery he had the dash and élan of a cavalryman, reflected in his love of horses and skill as a rider. Unusually for a French senior officer, and importantly for what was to follow, he was a fluent English speaker; his mother was English, the daughter of an officer who had served under the Duke of Wellington. Although not outstandingly so, he was impressive in appearance and gave off an air of vigorous energy.

Nivelle formally took over as Commander in Chief of the Armies of the North and Northeast on 17 December. With his responsibilities thus essentially confined to the Western Front he did not fully replace Joffre, who had enjoyed virtually dictatorial powers in a generously defined 'Zone of the Armies'. The new C in C wasted little time in making it clear that the war-winning offensive he had been advocating would involve significant modifications of the plans agreed at Chantilly and endorsed in Paris a month earlier. On 20 December he paid his first call on General Haig. It was the first time they had met and Haig recorded that Nivelle had made a very favourable impression on him, describing him as alert in mind and having had much practical experience at divisional, corps and army command levels. Nivelle told him he was unable to accept Joffre's plans for the French and that he was confident of breaking through the enemy's front now that their morale was weakened. The blow would have to be struck by surprise and go through in 24 hours. Haig thought this chimed with his own concepts.[3]

Over the course of further meetings and exchanges of letters Nivelle fleshed out the details of his plan for his offensive to an increasingly cautious Haig. Essentially Nivelle proposed to repeat, on a far grander scale, the tactics which had achieved his successes at Verdun. The efficacy of these were in his eyes finally proved by the last attack mounted under his command at Verdun on 15-16 December involving four infantry divisions. He told a fellow officer, 'We now have the formula'[4]. What took place between 10 and 16 December was a repetition of a formula used successfully in the previous two months. A massive five day artillery bombardment, concentrated on a narrow front but saturating the German defences in depth, was followed by an infantry advance behind the curtain of a rolling barrage. The method had proved effective against tired German troops who had lost whatever enthusiasm they had once had for the Verdun campaign. Whether it would translate to a grander stage, as Nivelle clearly believed it would, would be a question which would increasingly preoccupy not only the British, but also some French politicians and generals.

One of the first actions Nivelle took as Commander in Chief was to stop preparations for the implementation of Joffre's plans for 1917. His own proposals were conveyed by letter to Haig two days later. He envisaged the Germans would be pinned to the Arras-Bapaume and Oise-Somme lengths of front by, respectively, British and French attacks. Simultaneously, a surprise French attack

---

3   Haig d. 20.12.16.
4   Robert A Doughty, *Pyrrhic Victory*, p. 324

on another part of the front would seek to achieve a breakthrough of the German defences, which, after it had been sufficiently enlarged, would be rapidly exploited by a French Reserve Army Group (*Masse de manoeuvre*) of 27 divisions. The allied success would ultimately be exploited by all available French and British forces. To enable the French to create the Reserve Army Group, Nivelle sought Haig's agreement to take over the French part of the line between Bouchavesnes and the Amiens-Roye road by 15 January. Rather more palatably for Haig, he confirmed that he would honour Joffre's commitment to support a British-led offensive to clear the Belgian coast[5], should his own offensive, the Nivelle Plan, not achieve this.[6]

The exchanges that ensued between GQG and GHQ focused on the extent and timing of the British takeover of French line, the question of railway supply arrangements, the extension of the British offensive to include Vimy Ridge, the duration of the main offensive and if and when it would be perceived to have run its course and the French commitment to support Haig's Belgian offensive to become operative. Haig was worried that Nivelle no longer seemed to be talking about an offensive which would achieve its aims in 48 hours, but a battle of prolonged duration (*'une durée prolongée'*), with its obvious implications for Haig's Belgian plans. Nivelle sought to reassure Haig, but insisted that the main battle should fully engage both armies until it ended.[7]

With regard to the takeover of French line, Haig told Nivelle at their second meeting on 31 December that the operation could begin on 15 January and be completed as far as the Amiens-Villers Bretonneux road, a length of line of approximately 13 kilometres, by early February. The further takeover of French line to the Amiens-Roye road would be dependent on the BEF receiving further divisions; it was currently six divisions short of requirements. Nivelle's reaction to this slippage in his timetable is not recorded by Haig, who did, however, note that Nivelle, in a later informal conversation on the same day, was relaxed about the timing of the extension of the British line to the Amiens-Roye road; the end of March or early April would suffice for his purposes.[8] (Haig almost certainly misunderstood Nivelle's position on timing. According to Edward Spears's account of a meeting he and another British officer had with Nivelle in mid-January, the latter was insistent that the takeover of the 32 kilometres of French line to the Amiens-Roye road would have to be completed by the end of February. Unless the British complied with this requirement there would be insufficient French divisions available to bring the Reserve Army Group (GAR) up to its planned size of 27 divisions.)[9]

Nivelle may have been less relaxed about Haig's warning that, although he believed that the Nivelle Plan would succeed, it might not be as successful as Nivelle hoped. Still less would Nivelle have wanted to listen to Haig reverting to his own project for 1917.

> In the event of [Nivelle's offensive] being held up, a rapid decision was required and every effort must be made to pierce the enemy's front in the North. In this case could I rely on the French Army to take over sufficient of the British front to set free the necessary number of British Divisions to ensure success. [Nivelle] said certainly that that was his firm intention.[10]

One of the reasons Haig thought that Nivelle's ambitions for his offensive might be disappointed was because of the comparative advantage the Germans enjoyed in railway infrastructure – a complete

---

5   Haig d. 10.12.16.
6   E.L. Spears, *Prelude to Victory*, pp. 527-9. The wish of the British to launch an offensive to clear the Belgian coast had been conveyed to Joffre by the CIGS, General Robertson, in early December. It was driven by the perceived vital need to deny the Germans the use of their submarine bases at Zeebrugge and Ostend. Joffre responded positively by including a joint British, French and Belgian offensive under British command in his Plan of Operations dated 7 December.
7   Doughty, op. cit., pp. 327-8.
8   Haig d. 31.12.16.
9   Spears, op.cit. p. 69.
10 Haig d. 31.12.16.

system compared with one that would have to be repaired as the allies advanced. This was not Haig's only concern over railways. A much more pressing one was the difficulty the BEF was having in obtaining the 200,000 tons of supplies it required per week in the build up to the offensive. The French railways were only delivering 150,000 tons, a serious shortfall.

Nivelle was soon complaining about Haig's obsession (*idée fixe*) with his Belgian operation which he, Nivelle, regarded as a sideshow and potential distraction from his own offensive. Nivelle was also worried about Haig's reiteration of his warning that his armies would not be ready to attack before 1 May. Although the chance of the allies adhering to Joffre's original concept of a February offensive had already virtually disappeared, Nivelle still wanted to attack as soon as possible so as not to lose maximum benefit from the relative inferiority of the enemy forces opposing the allies. At this time, when the detailed planning of joint operations made close cooperation and understanding between the French and British Headquarters more important than ever, the replacement of Joffre by Nivelle was having the opposite effect on the relationship. Despite the huge preponderance in French numbers on the Western Front, Joffre had always been punctilious in his dealings with the British, seldom seeking to assert authority inappropriately. By contrast Nivelle, and even more his staff, seemed determined to boss the show, even though by now the British presence on the Western Front was significant and growing, if not yet on a par with France's. GQG's assertive attitude may well have been bolstered by the perception that the War Office in London and GHQ at Montreuil did not enjoy the full confidence of the new British Prime Minister. There can be little doubt that one of Nivelle's ambitions from the outset was to bring the BEF under his direct command. Not only would achieving this set him apart from Joffre, who had never managed it, but it might well inhibit Haig's perceived inclination to raise difficulties and indulge in foot dragging at every opportunity.

David Lloyd George became Prime Minister only three weeks after the Paris conference where his efforts to promote an alternative strategy to that agreed by Joffre and Haig and the other allied commanders for 1917, had foundered in the face of the lack of drive and determination (in Lloyd George's estimation) of then Prime Minister Asquith and his French counterpart, Briand. The only satisfaction Lloyd George had been able to derive from the conference was an agreement that a further conference would be held in Russia to address the question of the general conduct of the war and decide on a common line of action. He hoped that this second occasion might finally wrest the strategic initiative, with its focus on the Western Front, away from the generals.

Haig and Robertson viewed the arrival of Lloyd George in 10 Downing Street with some misgiving. It was not the depth of his commitment to the prosecution of the war to a successful conclusion that caused them concern; there could be no doubting that. It was the military strategy that he would seek to impose on them to achieve his aim. They had good reason to fear that this would involve a diminution of concentration of effort on the Western Front in favour of enhanced activity elsewhere, notably Italy and Salonika. What they did not for a moment expect was that the Prime Minister would also seek to place the BEF under the command of the French Commander in Chief.

If they had harboured any hopes that Lloyd George would be supportive of a military strategy based on the primacy of the Western Front, Haig and Robertson would have been disabused by his interventions at the Paris conference. Despite these however, Haig must have emerged from a lunch he had with Lloyd George and Lord Derby a few days later with some hope that the former would accept the confirmation by the Paris conference that the Western Front was the decisive theatre of war. Haig had appealed to his fellow diners to agree that the British should comply with the consequences of that decision, which would mean moving troops and guns to France from Italy and elsewhere and not in the opposite direction. Lloyd George told Haig he was much struck with his appeal and, at a later meeting, 'was most pleasant and anxious to help the army in every possible way'.[11] It was a false dawn. At his first meeting with Lloyd George as Prime Minister, which took place in London

---

11   Haig d. 23.11.16 and 25.11.16.

on 15 December, Lloyd George told him that he wanted to send two divisions from France to the Middle East and 200 heavy guns to Italy, the latter to be returned to the Western Front in the spring. Robertson had already warned Haig that this was what the Prime Minister had in mind and, for good measure, that he also wished to send heavy guns to Russia. In explanation of his apparent change of heart regarding the primacy of the Western Front, the Prime Minister assured Haig that there had been none. But he could not believe that it would be possible to beat the German Armies there in 1917.[12]

Haig had had time to marshal his arguments in rebuttal of Lloyd George's plans. He told the Prime Minister that he could see little point in sending guns to Russia until it was certain she could use them. As regards guns for Italy, those theoretically available were worn and their crews needed rest after their exertions on the Somme. Furthermore there would be little chance of them returning in time to participate in the spring offensive. (The Italian Commander in Chief would later confirm that heavy guns would be of little use to him until the campaigning season of the following year.) Finally, divisions drawn from the Western Front would be of little use in Egypt as they were in no state to fight and were in any case already being trained for their roles in the spring offensive. Haig sensed his arguments had made some impression on Lloyd George.[13]

The Prime Minister's next attempt to 'obtain release from the fatal net in which we were enmeshed by the Chantilly plans' was a conference convened in Rome at his request on 5-7 January 1917. As was his wont Lloyd George distributed a lengthy memorandum as the basis for discussion. It reviewed the largely adverse developments in the Balkans and more generally deplored the fact that, despite their infinitely greater resources, the Entente Powers had been unable to impose themselves on the Central Powers. It identified as a root cause of this the failure to coordinate allied efforts, a problem which the Chantilly conference's decisions would go some way to address. The memorandum stated that the planned conference in Russia should seek answers to the question of how best to support the Russians with heavy guns and other equipment and how they might be delivered. With regard to Salonika, the memorandum declined with regret to meet France's request for two more British divisions to join two French divisions in reinforcing the front, ostensibly because the necessary shipping was not available. The Prime Minister's hand, and the lack of any serious consultation with CIGS General Robertson and the War Office, could be clearly seen in the memorandum's advocacy of an offensive on the Italian Isonzo front. This would require heavy guns to be supplied by Britain and France on a temporary basis; they would have to be returned to the Western Front in time for the planned offensive there.[14] The Italians' own infantry resources would be more than adequate for the task. The memorandum painted a very optimistic picture of what could be achieved on the Italian front, summarised by the claim that the Allies could put the Germans out of action just as well on the Italian as on the Western Front.[15]

The newly-promoted Field Marshal Haig was not present in Rome, but he must have been disappointed to learn that the Prime Minister remained wedded to his enthusiasm for the Italian front. Fortunately for the Nivelle Plan, the French government offered no support for Lloyd George's proposals, and the lack of a positive reaction to them from the Italian Commander in Chief has already been alluded to. In the face of such a reception Lloyd George had little option but to turn his

---

12   In fact the Prime Minister's memoirs make it quite clear that he did not believe in the primacy of the Western Front. He believed that the Italians had the measure of the Austrians on the Italian front and it was only the lack of heavy artillery that had held them back from driving Austria out of the war. If providing this heavy artillery had left the Western Front commanders too short of it to have mounted the Nivelle Offensive and Passchendaele, reasoned Lloyd George, how would that have been inimical to allied interests? (Lloyd George, *War Memoirs*, pp. 827-9)

13   Haig d. 15.12.16.

14   This stipulation was subsequently withdrawn by Lloyd George insofar as the British guns were concerned. It made no difference to the Italian attitude.

15   Lloyd George, op. cit. pp. 838-43.

full attention to the Nivelle Plan. He had been taken aback by the French government's conversion from the 'way round' strategic approach in tune with his own, to an enthusiasm for, and commitment to, Nivelle and had concluded, by the time he left Rome, that serious damage would be caused to Anglo-French relations by anything short of full-hearted British support for the French C in C and his Plan. Nivelle met the Prime Minister at the *Gare du Nord* in Paris on the latter's return journey from Rome and was invited to London to present the details of his Plan to the British War Cabinet.

Field Marshal Haig also travelled to London for the meeting. He was received beforehand by the Prime Minister and explained to him the details of the Nivelle Plan and the proposed British part in it. Lloyd George responded by making unfavourable comparisons between the performance of Haig's Army the previous summer and that of the French, drawing the conclusion that the latter were better all round and were able to gain success at less cost in lives. Haig responded that in its two and a half years' experience of the French Army, the British Army had come to the conclusion that the French infantry lacked discipline and thoroughness. On a number of occasions the British were aware that they had not attacked though ordered to do so.[16]

Nivelle repeated to the War Cabinet what he had already told the French leaders the day before. He made a further plea for Haig to take over the French line as far as the Amiens-Roye road and in sufficient time to allow his offensive to start on 15 February or as soon as possible thereafter. Haig raised a number of difficulties, but he and Robertson were told subsequently by Lloyd George that the War Cabinet had determined that the BEF should indeed take over the French line as requested and do its best to ensure the success of Nivelle's Plan. The BEF should conform to French timings as the latter were the larger force and were understandably anxious to rid themselves of the invader as soon as possible. A final consideration was that if the French attack at this early date failed, there would be more time available to Haig to launch his Belgian operation. Further discussion resulted in agreement that Haig would receive two further divisions and the requested length of French line would be taken over by the first week of March. At a further meeting of the full conference, Nivelle agreed to amend his paper listing the conclusions he wished the conference to arrive at so that 'the first week in March' was substituted for 15 February for the takeover of French line, and the date of the start of the offensive was settled as not later than 1 April.

A problem which was barely touched on at the London gathering even though Haig had for some time never lost an opportunity to remind all and sundry of its importance was that of the failure of the French railway system to cope with the BEF's build up requirements in the run up to the offensive. A further conference was therefore convened at Calais on 26-27 February ostensibly to consider the railway problem. By now, mindful of the fact that the success of the Nivelle Plan was largely dependent on achieving surprise and that its implementation was already well behind schedule, Lloyd George had determined that a major contributory factor to the delays was the lack of a unified allied command. The Prime Minister also believed that the railway problem was being caused by Haig using rolling stock, which should have been devoted to building up the BEF for Arras, for preparation of his Belgian operation. Once the conference opened, the Prime Minister very quickly delegated discussion of the railway problem to technical experts and steered the meeting towards consideration of a unified allied command.

The Prime Minister offered General Nivelle the floor in apparent anticipation that he would make the case for a unified French-led command. After some prompting he finally did so but not before he had lavishly praised current Anglo-French co-operation (which by implication diminished the case for unified command). Seemingly disappointed by Nivelle's failure to rise wholeheartedly to the opportunity he had been given, the Prime Minister asked him to present his proposals in writing and adjourned the meeting. To say that these proposals, when they were received, came as a considerable shock to Robertson and Haig, would be an understatement. They must also have taken

---

16   Haig d. 15.1.17.

aback the Prime Minister who could have been in little doubt that they would prove unacceptable to the War Cabinet, whose endorsement of his unified command idea had been less than enthusiastic. Lloyd George himself must have been uncomfortable to find that Nivelle's proposals had gone much further towards French control and British subservience than he had envisaged, and have been under little illusion of the reception they would receive from the British military leadership. Nivelle had grossly overplayed his hand. His subsequent protestations that his proposals, if adopted, would merely implement the expressed wishes of the two governments, following consultation, in the British case, with the generals, seem implausible. Fortunately for their future working relationships, Haig and Robertson were satisfied with Nivelle's version of events.[17]

There remained the question of how to modify Nivelle's proposals in a way that would preserve Lloyd George's self esteem and wish for a unified command while at the same time would pass muster with the War Cabinet and secure the acquiescence, however reluctant, of Haig and Robertson. During hours of intense and tense exchanges in the margins of the conference the text of a convention was thrashed out. The final act of the conference was the signature of this document on 27 February. Under its terms responsibility for the general direction of the forthcoming campaign, and for its duration only, was placed with the French Commander in Chief. The British C in C would ensure his plan of operations would conform to the French C in C's general strategic plan unless in his view this might compromise the safety of his army. In these circumstances he would have the right to report his reasons for not conforming with the French C in C's instructions to the CIGS for communication to the British War Cabinet. In conforming with the French C in C's instructions the British C in C would be free to choose the manner and means of their implementation. Each C in C, in regard to his own army, would remain judge of when the operation could be considered to have terminated. (Ironically, the railway problem, which had been the ostensible reason for the convening of the conference, was dismissed in a couple of sentences, with the Prime Minister concluding that the problem could be dealt with in the framework of the unified command.)[18]

17   Spears, op. cit., pp. 141-6.
18   Lloyd George's reasons for springing his proposals for a unified French-led command on his Generals in Calais are worthy of examination even if, once the question had been settled, it had very little bearing on the conduct of the Battle of Arras. The Prime Minister's motivations for acting as he did were based on the conclusions he had drawn from the military conduct of the first couple of years of the war. Like any right thinking person his humanitarian instincts had been appalled at the carnage and loss of life on the Western Front. The last straw had been the horrendous losses of the Somme campaign and the apparent bankruptcy of British generalship they had demonstrated. As he took over as Prime Minister all the generals seemed to be offering was more of the same for the foreseeable future. Thus his search for an alternative strategy which would marginalise the Western Front and somehow bring about the collapse of the Central Powers in relatively short order. Lloyd George was fully aware that he had become Prime Minister partly because it was believed that, unlike his predecessor, he would prosecute the war vigorously to ultimate victory. He believed that politically he needed to chalk up a notable success quickly. It was obvious to him that there was little possibility of this emerging from the Western Front in 1917. His favoured option was a version of the 'way round' strategy, an offensive on the Italian front. As has been seen, this found no favour with the French or the Italians, still less with his own military advisers. In the apparent absence of a viable acceptable alternative, he claimed he had no option but to accept the Nivelle Plan and offer it his full support. Lloyd George had clearly been taken aback by the rapidity with which the French political leadership had thrown in their lot with Nivelle and abandoned their previous sympathy with the 'way round' approach. He justified his adoption of Nivelle in terms of Anglo-French relations; a failure to have done so would have led to a major crisis in inter-allied councils. He was especially influenced by the espousal of Nivelle by Albert Thomas, the French Minister of Munitions, whom he greatly respected. He was also clearly influenced by the charismatic Nivelle himself, whose claims to have found the formula for the delivery of a rapid victory were presented in near perfect English. The Prime Minister chose to ignore the cautionary note struck by Haig and, by the time the French War Minister and the senior French generals responsible for implementing the Nivelle Plan began to express similar doubts, it was too late.
It is more difficult to rationalise the Prime Minister's determination to subordinate Haig and the BEF to Nivelle. He was certainly convinced that Haig, left to his own devices, was unlikely to achieve more than further horrendous casualty lists. Feeling unable for political reasons and because there was no clear cut successor, to take the obvious step of dismissing him, he was therefore looking for a means of limiting the damage Haig could do. He presumably felt that

What seems to have been lost in all the toing and froing about overall allied strategy, the questions of unified command and the inadequacies of the French railways was the vital need for the success of the Nivelle Plan for it to be launched at the earliest possible moment. By now the initial hope that it would begin in mid- February had given way to a possible date two months later. There had been two main reasons for wanting an early start; a concern that the longer it was delayed the more likely it would be that the Germans would seize the initiative, as they had the previous year with their Verdun offensive; and a concern that the opportunity it offered to avoid security leaks and take the Germans by surprise, with the area of the main assault only lightly screened, would be squandered. Both these concerns would prove to be more than justified.

Any hope that the signature of the Calais convention would put an end to issues relating to the implementation of a unified command structure was very quickly dissipated. The first problem to surface was the high-handed way in which the French General Staff sought to assert their authority over Haig and GHQ. Two instances of this were the request that General Henry Wilson should be appointed to Nivelle's HQ as Head of the Liaison Mission between the two Headquarters and Nivelle's Chief of Staff's criticism of the British plan to assault Vimy Ridge in the upcoming offensive, as a waste of time and energy. These and other examples of high-handedness were initially blamed on insensitive staff officers with Nivelle successfully persuading Haig and Robertson that he was not to blame. Nivelle's cloak of innocence was however beginning to look increasingly threadbare by the time it was deemed necessary to hold a further high level conference, this time in London, to try once again to sort things out. The French Prime Minister got off on the wrong foot by sending a telegram to his opposite number in which he clearly thought he was reflecting Lloyd George's views in, among other things, urging Haig's recall and replacement for his failure to implement the Calais accord. Not even Lloyd George, and still less his War Cabinet colleagues, were prepared to accept such interference from the French. Matters were made worse when Nivelle, showing signs of the pressure he was under, abandoned his usual attempts to charm his British audience. This, coupled with his unpalatable words, made a poor impression at the conference. Of particular concern to the British side was his failure to acknowledge that a German retirement to the Hindenburg Line, of which there was increasing evidence, might necessitate changes in the Nivelle Plan. Perhaps fortunately for relations between Haig and Robertson on the one side and Nivelle on the other, the former still accepted the latter's assurances that he had been instructed by his government to put forward at Calais the scheme for a unified command.

The final result of the London conference was an agreed protocol which, while still accepting that the forthcoming offensive would be commanded by Nivelle, made it quite clear that the extent to which he could interfere in the British plans and operations was limited and would only last for the duration of the offensive. So confident was Haig that he had successfully seen off French ambitions to achieve permanent unity of command that he felt able to add a couple of sentences to the protocol before signing which insisted that Nivelle should regard the BEF and himself as allies and not subordinates.[19]

The timing of the London conference, 12 March, showed how badly the original timetable was slipping. To the allies' self-inflicted problems which had led to delays could now be added the difficulties caused by the worst winter weather for years and the German retirement, the precise scope and intentions of which would remain uncertain until after battle was joined. Despite the continuing

---

subordinating him to Nivelle would also overcome the delays in mounting the offensive which seemed to be emanating from Haig. Perhaps surprisingly he had also persuaded himself that the French army was more competent and efficient than the BEF, an opinion hardly supported by their overall performance in the war thus far. The conclusion must therefore be that the Prime Minister was driven by a desire to marginalise Haig in whatever way this could be achieved. In the end, the main consequence of the Prime Minister's machinations was a complete breakdown of trust between himself and the Army, which was to persist until the Armistice.

19   Spears, op.cit., pp. 189-97.

bad weather the BEF First and Third Armies began their infantry assaults on 9 April with Fifth Army joining in on the 11th. The main French infantry attack by the Reserve Army Group began a week later on the 16th with the Central Army Group joining in a day later.

2

Planning for 1917

As 1916 gave way to 1917 the Germans could be reasonably certain that at some early date in the new year the Allies would launch a further major offensive or offensives on the Western Front. No other inference could be drawn from the replacement of General Joffre by General Nivelle, especially given the latter's somewhat carefree attitude towards security which had made his broad intentions the common currency of Parisian gossip. By a combination of good fortune with regard to their defensive dispositions and the continuing shortcomings of French security, the Germans would find themselves well placed to deliver a serious rebuff to Allied ambitions.

At the end of August 1916 the German Army Chief of Staff, Erich von Falkenhayn, paid the price of German shortcomings at Verdun and the Somme and was relieved. He was replaced by the partnership of General Paul von Hindenburg, as Chief of the General Staff, and General Erich Ludendorff, as First Quartermaster-General. Recognising that the German Army, still fighting and mired in the mud of Verdun and the Somme, would be in no state to resume the offensive for the foreseeable future, the two Generals quickly decided to look to their defences. Within days earth was being turned in the construction of the *Siegfried Stellung* (known to the Allies as the Hindenburg Line). At this early stage the work on a defensive line between 10 and 25 miles east of the current front line was in all likelihood purely precautionary. It was however quickly apparent to the new commanders that an eventual withdrawal to it would go some way to rectify the growing imbalance between the relative strengths of the two sides on the Western Front. It would eliminate at one stroke the two German salients between Arras and Bapaume in the north and Péronne and Vailly further south, thereby shortening the front line by 25 miles and reducing by 13 or 14 divisions the number required to man it.

The Allies first became aware that something odd was happening behind the German lines in September 1916 when aerial photo reconnaissance detected the first signs of earth being turned at two places well behind the current battlefield. Further investigation confirmed that the enemy were indeed constructing trench works on a line between Quéant and Neuville-Vitasse by way of Bullecourt. The ultimate extent of the new system did not become clear until well into the new year as the appalling winter weather and an unusual spell of enemy control of the air made photo reconnaissance very difficult. It was late February before the full course of the Hindenburg Line opposite the whole length of the British front was established. Even then important detail of the southern part, including progress on both sides of the River Scarpe, was still lacking. Despite the very unwelcome attentions of the legendary Red Baron, Manfred von Richthofen, and his unit flying out of Douai, photo reconnaissance had also confirmed by mid February the construction of another system of trench works called the *Wotan Stellung* (known to the British as the Drocourt-Quéant Switch (or Line)). The French were less successful in establishing the course of the Hindenburg Line opposite their front.[1]

Neither ally at this stage had any clear idea what use, if any, the Germans planned to make of their new defensive systems. It seemed scarcely conceivable that they would make a voluntary retirement to them, involving the giving up of ground they had fought so tenaciously and at great cost to retain only

---

1   OH 1917, Vol 1, pp. 87-93.

a few weeks earlier. In February, the French General Staff declared the notion of an enemy retirement to be 'tempting in principle but liable to encounter grave difficulties in execution'. According to the French Official History, General Robertson told General Nivelle on 24 February that 'it is pretty evident that the enemy has decided to maintain the integrity of the Western Front obstinately'. In his reply of 4 March, Nivelle concurred, adding that he believed the enemy retirement from the British Fifth Army front (then underway) was 'not the beginning of a more extended withdrawal'.[2] The Allies' inaccurate interpretation of German intentions, as voiced by Robertson and Nivelle, may have been to some extent assisted by the German construction of three intermediate defensive lines (R1, R2 and R3 from west to east), which had become the main focus of allied interest.[3] In fact, whatever the purpose of these intermediate lines, the detailed preparations for a retirement all the way to the Hindenburg Line were already well in hand.

It was not just considerations of shortening the line and economising on divisions that swung the German High Command in favour of retirement to the Hindenburg Line. The German Army had been very badly damaged by the attritional battles at Verdun and the Somme in 1916 and, in the view of its new commanders, was in no state to fight a further defensive battle on similar lines in 1917, especially against a significantly numerically superior enemy. It was however the unremitting pressure being exerted on them by the British on the River Ancre that finally tipped the balance in favour of retirement. The Commander in Chief of the group of armies with responsibility for the front from the River Lys to north of Reims, a distance of nearly 170 miles containing the whole length of a potential retirement operation, was Field Marshal Crown Prince Rupprecht of Bavaria. He had already been instructed to draw up a detailed scheme for a withdrawal. On 28 January, with no sign of the British pressure letting up and his troops showing increasing signs of exhaustion, he demanded urgent permission to put the scheme into operation. With considerable reluctance the High Command acquiesced and on 4 February the Kaiser signed the order for the implementation of Operation *Alberich*, the code name given to the retirement.[4]

Whatever satisfaction Crown Prince Rupprecht derived from the granting of his wish to pull back his armies was severely tempered by the methods he was ordered to apply in implementing the operation. Everything of military value which could be moved back, from artillery to the contents of military depots, stores and stockpiles, would be moved back. What had to be left behind would be rendered unusable for the advancing allies. This not only extended to cratering roads, tearing up railway tracks and setting booby traps, but also to destroying as far as possible all the buildings in towns and villages, including houses. In addition all trees were to be felled or ringed, and wells polluted (if not actually poisoned). The French civilian population would be transported to the rear. In effect this aspect of *Alberich* was a scorched earth operation and Crown Prince Rupprecht took strong exception to it on both moral and material grounds. He foresaw, quite correctly, the international opprobrium such behaviour would attract on Germany. He also thought the destruction of buildings would offer very little military benefit and might even help the allies by giving them a ready source of rubble to use in filling up road craters. The pressure he exerted probably saved the towns of Nesle, Ham and Noyon from the destruction visited on nearly everywhere else in the evacuated area, as it was decided to spare them. Many of the women, children and old men in these towns were also spared transportation to the rear, not out of any humanitarian considerations, but because there would thereby be fewer useless mouths to feed in the German area.

There were two separate parts of Operation *Alberich*. The first, during which the material of military value, including the bulk of the artillery, would be moved to the rear and the infrastructure

2   Lt Col Beaugier and others, *Les Armées Françaises dans La Grande Guerre, Tome V, Premier Volume*, pp. 379-80.
3   The Army Quarterly No. 28, p. 224.
4   In the *Niebelung Saga* of Teutonic mythology the dwarf *Alberich* was the guardian of the treasure of King *Niebelung*. *Alberich* was vanquished by Siegfried, who appropriated the treasure and demanded an oath of fidelity from the dwarf. In Wagner's *The Ring Cycle*, *Alberich* is an altogether more sinister character, being portrayed as evil and loveless.

being left behind prepared for destruction and destroyed, would last for 35 days. The second part would be a marching period, lasting from two to four days, depending on the distance to be covered, during which the troops would move to their new positions either screening or behind the Hindenburg Line. The first part would last from 9 February to 15 March; the marching period would begin the following day. In general these dates were observed, although continuing British pressure in the Ancre sector led to an earlier withdrawal of troops of the German First Army in two stages, on 22 February and 11 March.[5]

Both aspects of the operation were carried out with great efficiency. At the beginning of March, slight adjustments to the distribution of armies within the German army groups operating on the Western Front left Crown Prince Rupprecht in overall command of the Fourth, Sixth, First and Second Armies, the last three named of which, in part or in whole, participated in the retirement behind the Hindenburg Line. The exhausted First Army hurried early departure to the rear has already been noted. (They would soon be restored to the line, but in a new area east of Reims.)

Caught up in the pressure in the Ancre sector was the 73rd Hanoverian Fusilier Regiment one of whose company commanders was Lieutenant Ernst Jünger, author of the celebrated post war memoir, *Storm of Steel*. In the book he describes how difficult it had been to disengage to move back in the face of numerous English attacks apparently motivated by a suspicion of German intentions. As his regiment marched back after being relieved, it passed through several villages which

> had the appearance of lunatic asylums let loose. Whole companies were pushing walls down or sitting on the roofs of the houses throwing down the slates. Trees were felled, window-frames broken, and smoke and clouds of dust rose from heap after heap of rubbish. In short, an orgy of destruction was going on. The men were chasing round with incredible zeal, arrayed in the abandoned wardrobes of the population, in women's dresses and with top hats on their heads. With positive genius they singled out the main beams of the houses and, tying ropes round them, tugged with all their might, shouting out in time with their pulls, till the whole house collapsed. Others swung hammers and smashed whatever came in their way, from flowerpots on the window ledges to the glass-work of conservatories.
>
> Every village up to the Siegfried Line was a rubbish-heap. Every tree felled, every road mined, every well fouled, every water-course dammed, every cellar blown up or made into a death-trap with concealed bombs, all supplies or metal sent back, all rails ripped up, all telephone wire rolled up, everything burnable burned. In short, the country over which the enemy were to advance had been turned into an utter desolation.

To Jünger's credit, he shared the outrage of Crown Prince Rupprecht at this wanton vandalism, especially the destruction of the homes of peaceful people.[6]

Allied realisation that the Germans were undertaking a major redeployment involving their newly constructed lines was slow in dawning. The first indication came on 20 and 21 February when the British intercepted radio messages ordering two wireless stations in the area of Bapaume to dismantle their equipment and prepare to retire. These intercepts were not accorded the significance they perhaps should have been, but they were soon to be reinforced by the disclosures of newly captured German prisoners and the increasing very visible evidence provided by a series of explosions and incinerations behind the German lines not caused by allied guns or bombing. There was still uncertainty however about the extent of the planned German retirement. Confusion was sown in British minds by the partial retirements made by the German First Army ahead of the planned schedule as a result of the British pressure on the Ancre. On 22 and 23 February front line units of the Fifth Army gradually

---

5   OH 1917, op. cit., pp. 110-16.
6   Ernst Jünger, *The Storm of Steel*, p. 126.

became aware that the enemy were no longer in occupation of a roughly ten mile stretch of their line between the villages of Le Transloy and Serre by way of Miraumont. Almost disbelievingly, patrols reported making significant advances into previously German-held territory without being fired on. It soon became apparent that the enemy in this north Somme area had withdrawn to their line R1, which ran from Le Transloy via Loupart Wood (*Bois Loupart*) to Achiet le Petit.[7] Once contact was re-established with the enemy in their new positions there remained the uncertainty of whether this represented the full extent of a German voluntary retirement. It would be some time before the answer to this question became clear. What the German move did make immediately clear was that they were now prepared to make retirements without being forced to do so.

With the enemy now in occupation of R1, and Grévillers Trench and the village of Irles in front of it, and with no clear indication that any further retirement was planned, the next operations undertaken by Fifth Army would be attacks to capture these positions. The first stage, the capture of Grévillers Trench and Irles, took place on 10 March. It was a complete success and left the way open for an assault on R1 itself. Preparations for it began immediately, but it seemed increasingly probable that the enemy would not wait to be attacked, but would retire. This proved to be the case; the enemy evacuated the central stretch of R1, between Bapaume and Achiet le Petit, during the night of 11/12 March, and moved back to R2.[8] In the abandoned Loupart Wood an enemy document was found which revealed some of the details of Operation *Alberich*. Although the actual date on which the marching days would start was not specified it could be inferred that it was 13 March (rather earlier than, unknown to the allies, it had been initially planned). It was soon clear that from 14 to 17 March the enemy had withdrawn wholly or in part from their positions in front of part of the Fourth Army, the whole of the Fifth Army and the right wing of the Third Army. The enemy retirement to eliminate the Arras-Bapaume salient was fully underway.[9]

The German retirement described above had obvious implications for the British plans to implement their part of the Nivelle Plan, most notably for the Fifth Army. The enemy's simultaneous retirement from their positions opposite the French lines from which Nivelle was planning to launch the various elements of his offensive had even more important implications for his strategy, given that most French units involved would be directly affected. Nivelle was slow to accept the growing evidence that emerged from late February onwards that the Germans were intent on straightening their line between Arras and Soissons. As late as 7 March he still believed that the German retirement would only affect the stretch of line opposite the British between Arras and Bapaume. At this stage therefore Nivelle saw no reason to change the plans he had drawn up for the French offensive. These were not greatly different from those he had inherited from General Joffre, but whereas the latter had foreseen a continuation of the attritional approach characterised by Verdun and the Somme, Nivelle was planning an overwhelming assault designed to penetrate and break through the German defences in short order beyond hope of recovery. The basis would be unparalleled concentrations of heavy artillery fire which would eliminate both the first and second German lines without the need to reposition the guns before taking on the second line. This would be followed up by rapid infantry penetration of the devastated enemy defences. The French Northern Army Group of General Louis Franchet d'Espèrey[10], consisting originally of three armies (Third, Sixth and Tenth), but reduced to just one (Third) during the run up to the battle, was tasked to attack between the Rivers Avre and Oise in a preliminary offensive intended, like the British one further north, with which it was planned to converge, to pin down the German defenders opposite them. The area between the two rivers, while suitable for an assault, was not considered wide enough for the full scale offensive Nivelle was aiming for. This would fall to a newly created Reserve Army Group (*Groupe d'Armées de Réserve* (GAR)).

---

7   OH 1917, op. cit., pp. 94-7.
8   Ibid., pp. 105-7.
9   Ibid., pp. 109-10.
10   Memorably nicknamed 'Desperate Frankie' by the British troops.

Command of the GAR was entrusted to General Alfred Micheler, who had come to prominence during the Somme campaign. He would be given the Sixth and Tenth Armies, on transfer from the GAN, and the Fifth, already *in situ* on the Aisne front. Nivelle's first plan was that one of these armies, consisting of 15 divisions, would achieve the breakthrough (*la rupture*) of the German defences between Reims and Vailly, which would then be exploited by all three armies, totalling 30 infantry and seven cavalry divisions. This was subsequently amended so that two of the armies, totalling 28 divisions, would be used to make the breakthrough, leaving the third, with 12 infantry and five cavalry divisions, to join in for the exploitation. The overall intention was no less than the destruction of the main body of the enemy's forces on the Western Front.[11]

Franchet d'Espèrey had been quicker than GQG to draw the correct conclusions from the enemy's preparations to withdraw from in front of him. He proposed to Nivelle early in March that, within 10 days, he should mount a surprise attack, to include a large number of tanks. Such an attack might well have played havoc with the German arrangements for an orderly withdrawal. But the still sceptical Nivelle turned down the proposal. Instead the much reduced GAN was merely ordered to maintain energetic and continuous pressure on the retiring enemy. But as the evidence of the planned full extent of the German retirement became too compelling for Nivelle to ignore or discount in mid-March, he did recast his plans somewhat. General Pétain's Central Army Group (*Groupe d'Armées du Centre* (GAC)), which previously, probably due to Pétain's scarcely concealed doubts about the feasibility of Nivelle's strategy, had been excluded from the original Plan, was ordered to participate by mounting an attack east of Reims, some 50 kilometres from Micheler's main thrust.

Nivelle may have been discomfited as the true intentions of the Germans became clear, but he put a brave face on it, pointing out that the new enemy dispositions would also give him an additional 16 divisions with their artillery to deploy. Some of these would be used to strengthen the GAC for their newly arranged participation in the battle. In the meantime those troops manning forward positions who were not required for training or deployment for the battle were ordered to move forward to maintain contact with the retreating enemy. This they did very cautiously, the inherent difficulties of the operation being compounded by the very effective job the Germans had done in laying waste to, and booby trapping, the areas through which they had to move.[12]

As the much delayed time for the launching of the offensive approached, doubts about Nivelle's Plan, and his proposals for its successful completion, were surfacing among his fellow generals, especially those directly responsible for its implementation. To add to what must have been Nivelle's growing sense of isolation, the French government of Aristide Briand, which had selected Nivelle to replace Joffre, fell on 16 March. It was replaced, 4 days later, by one whose War Minister, Paul Painlevé, had reservations about Nivelle, and had been unhappy about his appointment as Commander in Chief. So well known had his concerns been that the new Prime Minister, Alexandre Ribot, had felt it necessary to obtain an undertaking from Painlevé that he was willing to work with Nivelle, an undertaking that would be honoured more in the breach than the observance.

In very short order the new War Minister established that both Generals Pétain and Micheler were very doubtful that the planned large scale offensives would succeed. Both felt that it would be beyond the capacity of the French artillery to deal with more than the first and second German defensive positions; the third and fourth would not be seriously affected. Micheler reiterated what he had already expressed to Nivelle in writing, that circumstances had changed since Nivelle's strategy had been conceived. Then, there had been perhaps only eight enemy divisions holding the Aisne front. Now, as a result of their retirement to the Hindenburg Line, the Germans had found the troops to reinforce significantly and in depth their Aisne defences. Furthermore, the downgrading of the GAN's contribution to the strategy left only the British offensive at Arras offering a serious attempt to

---

11   OH 1917, op. cit., pp. 46-9.
12   Robert Doughty, *Pyrrhic Victory*, pp. 335-6.

divert enemy troops from the Aisne sector in advance of the start of the offensive there. At a meeting of senior politicians and generals, chaired by the President of the Republic at Compiègne on 6 April, Painlevé made a last ditch attempt to persuade Nivelle to delay, or at least scale down, the offensive. He made much of the American declaration of war that day, suggesting in effect that France should conserve its remaining military strength and wait for the Americans to arrive. In response, Nivelle made a persuasive case that unrestricted submarine warfare and developments in Russia, where the effectiveness of the army had been further undermined by the political events of the previous month, would hand the military initiative to the enemy long before American power would make its presence felt in France. Only his offensive would prevent this happening and offer the hope of an allied victory in 1917. Despite their overall opposition, both Pétain and Micheler opposed cancelling the offensive at this late stage although they both repeated their doubts about the possibility of a breakthrough. Franchet d'Espèrey reminded the conference that the British were due to assault in three days' time and their preliminary bombardment was already well under way. Cancelling the offensive in such circumstances would be folly.

To general surprise and dismay, Nivelle dramatically offered to resign. His move persuaded the waverers that there was no alternative to going along with the Nivelle Plan. The only stipulation that was laid down was that the offensive should not be continued beyond the point where it had become clear that the desired results were unattainable.[13]

The conclusions of the conference might have been different if all the participants had been aware that the essential secrecy of Nivelle's Plan had been seriously compromised. It had been recognised from the outset that a vital element in the successful fulfilment of the Nivelle Plan would be surprise. The main contribution to achieving this should have been reducing the time between conception and execution to an absolute minimum, thus minimising the danger that secrecy would be compromised. Ideally the offensive should have begun no later than mid February, the timing originally envisaged in Joffre's strategy for 1917. Instead the wrangling between the allies over railway timetables, the British takeover of French line and, most harmfully, the question of unified command, combined to push back the earliest practicable date to mid April. Not only did this delay enable the Germans to complete their redeployment to the Hindenburg Line and to strengthen their defences along the Aisne, but it also fortuitously allowed them to learn in advance the full details of the French plan.

Although the German retirement to the Hindenburg Line was to be a major factor in the failure of the Nivelle Plan, it had not been carried out with this purpose in mind. It had been forced on a reluctant General Ludendorff, almost as loath as his French opponents to give up ground voluntarily, by the new reality of the Western Front, the growing preponderance of the allied artillery, no longer seriously constrained by shortages of ammunition. This unpalatable fact had also led to the conception of a new defensive strategy known as elastic defence-in-depth, which would soon be the norm for both sides.[14] Its successful application by the Germans on the Aisne front was to be a further significant contributor to the failure of the Nivelle Plan.

The German decision to strengthen the Aisne front and introduce elastic defence-in-depth there as a matter of urgency may well, however, have been intelligence led. As has been previously remarked, General Nivelle himself was his own worst enemy when it came to maintaining secrecy. His openness and fluency, which were such great assets when he was exercising his charm and charisma on colleagues and politicians on both sides of the Channel, were a distinct liability when they led to a readiness to describe his plans in great detail in the presence of listeners who had no need of, or right to, such information. Perhaps unsurprisingly, when the German commanders on the Aisne got to hear of

---

13   Ibid., pp. 336–44.

14   Not all Generals became devotees of the new system. Notoriously the Commander of the French Sixth Army, General Denis Duchêne, refused to employ it along the *Chemin des Dames* in May 1918, committing the bulk of his infantry to hold forward trenches. Three British divisions under his command were among those of his Army consequently overwhelmed by the surprise German assault of 27 May (the first day of the Third Battle of the Aisne).

Nivelle's plans, their initial reaction was that it was part of a deliberate plot to deceive them and they continued to discount the possibility of a French offensive. Their scepticism had however disappeared by the time Operation *Alberich* was completed. New divisions were accordingly moved into the Aisne sector and labour units were put to work reinforcing and extending their defensive lines. Their artillery coverage of the area was also greatly enlarged. These developments became known to French army intelligence but were only reported in detail a couple of days before the French offensive was due to begin. Nivelle had known earlier than this of the large increase in the number of enemy divisions but declined to alter the details of his Plan, commenting somewhat flippantly that it would mean that there would be more Germans to be made prisoner. Nor was he dissuaded by the news that reached him two days before the British were due to launch the Battle of Arras that on the night of 4/5 April a sergeant of 3rd Zouaves, Second Army, had disappeared from his front line post during a German attack. It was known that the sergeant had been carrying a document giving general information on his Army planned part in the Aisne offensive. The fear was that this was now in the hands of the Germans, as indeed proved to be the case. The document was sufficiently detailed to indicate to the Germans that the main French offensive was to be mounted on the Aisne. It confirmed what had been deduced by them from a document captured in the headquarters of the French 2nd Division during a local attack on 15 February. This leakage of information would do little to enhance French hopes of success in the forthcoming battle. It contrasted sadly with the generally effective measures the French had taken to conceal their physical preparations for the battle from their enemy.[15]

Nivelle's final instructions to his army group commanders confirmed that little had changed from the plan and methods for carrying it out he had outlined in December and January. General Micheler's GAR would still be making the main attack, using the Sixth and Fifth Armies to achieve the breakthrough after which the Tenth Army would join in. Nivelle urged on Micheler the importance of violence, brutality and speed in carrying out his orders. General Pétain's GAC would make an 'auxiliary'[16] attack, the GAN would play a minor role commensurate with its reduced size and the British would play a supporting role with their Arras offensive.[17]

There may have been some justification for French doubts about the British commitment to the Nivelle Plan while its details were being thrashed out in an atmosphere dominated by disagreements over railway supply, the takeover of French line and unified command. But there can be no question that once these problems had been sorted out or papered over, the British commitment to their role in the Plan was wholehearted. The Nivelle Plan was unlike that originally conceived by General Joffre, and agreed in broad outline by Field Marshal Haig, in that the British role would no longer be that of an equal partner, but would be designed to attract to it the German reserves, thus reducing the numbers that could be deployed to meet the French offensive. Haig was not altogether happy with this subsidiary role for his armies, but it was going too far to imply, as the French did, that his disagreements with Nivelle were born out of pique at being deprived of the opportunity for glory. The first role foreseen by Nivelle for the British operation was the elimination of the Bapaume salient in co-operation with the French GAN. The German retirement to the Hindenburg Line rendered this nugatory, not entirely beneficially for Haig. Although only the right wing of the Third Army was directly affected, the Fifth Army ability to offer the planned support to its northern neighbour would be seriously affected by the area between it and the enemy having been laid waste by the latter. With the GAN's role reduced almost to passivity by the disappearance of the Bapaume salient, a much

---

15   Robert Doughty, op. cit., pp. 344-6. OH 1917, op. cit., pp. 115-6 and 491-2.

16   Meaning not just a supporting attack putting pressure on the enemy but one intended to make penetrations into, and possibly through, the enemy defences. Not even the Commander of the Fourth Army, charged with making the 'auxiliary' attack, understood what the term was intended to convey, until it was spelt out to him in detail by Nivelle's staff.

17   Robert Doughty, op. cit., p. 346.

greater importance attached to the Third Army offensive. The planning of this had begun as long ago as late September the previous year.

3

Planning for Arras

The idea of a British offensive at Arras was first mooted when the fighting on the Somme was still at its height. It was originally conceived as a means of trapping the German armies which would be driven north from the Somme by General Sir Henry Rawlinson's Fourth Army, if all went according to plan. The Third Army Commander, General Allenby, was instructed in late September 1916 to draw up a plan for the offensive. In the event the Fourth Army never achieved the northward momentum required to justify a Third Army intervention, but Allenby was nevertheless told by General Haig on 6 November to continue with his preparations. The possibility of mounting the offensive later in the year, or early in 1917, was now on the cards in the context of the agreement between Haig and General Joffre to maintain pressure on the enemy throughout the winter with attacks when the circumstances were propitious.[1]

At the same time as Allenby was first told to begin planning, the newly appointed Commander of the First Army, General Sir Henry Horne, was ordered to plan to assault and capture Vimy Ridge. In addition to the advantages possession of this dominant ridge would confer on the allies, and the corresponding difficulties its loss would inflict on the Germans, its seizure would protect the left flank of the Third Army advancing from Arras. The other BEF army which was foreseen as participating in an Arras offensive was General Sir Hubert Gough's Fifth. Its main role would be to protect the Third Army right flank.

General Sir Edmund Allenby, the officer who had been given the main responsibility for the planning and execution of the Arras offensive, had been in command of Third Army since October 1915, when he took over the four months old army from General Sir Charles Monro.[2] Allenby had arrived on the Western Front in August 1914 as a 53-year old Major General in command of the Cavalry Division. He was soon promoted to command of the Cavalry Corps, and this was followed by a short stint in command of V Corps before he took over Third Army. He had been an effective commander of the Cavalry Division during the Retreat from Mons. It was his warning to General Sir Horace Smith-Dorrien that the Cavalry were too fragmented and exhausted to cover the next day's planned continuation of II Corps retreat that contributed to the latter's momentous decision to turn and fight at Le Cateau. The cavalry were also to be heavily engaged in the desperate First Battle of Ypres, generally being used as mounted infantry to plug gaps in the line, actions evocatively described as 'puttying up'. As Commander of Third Army Allenby's main challenge prior to Arras had been to carry out the diversionary attack on the fortified village of Gommecourt on the first day of the Battle of the Somme. That it was a near disaster which achieved nothing and resulted in nearly 7,000 casualties in the two territorial divisions involved, compared to only 2,000 German, was probably a reflection of its ill-conception rather than faulty generalship on Allenby's part. It did not however leave him with an enhanced reputation although he continued to enjoy Haig's confidence.

Allenby had a volcanic temper that had earned him the nickname of 'The Bull'. Although it does not appear to have affected his relationships with his loyal and efficient staff, it did not endear him to the officers and men under his command. But perhaps a greater problem was his chronic

---

1   Gary Sheffield and John Bourne (eds.), *Douglas Haig: War Diaries and Letters 1914-1918*, pp. 235 and 253.
2   The vacancy arose when Monro was sent to take over command in Gallipoli from General Sir Ian Hamilton.

inability to articulate his thoughts, especially in discussions with his Commander in Chief. With Haig notoriously similarly afflicted there was clear scope for mutual incomprehension which could have proved disastrous. However, Brigadier General John Charteris, Haig's Chief of Intelligence, noted with some amusement that the two men appeared to understand each other perfectly despite their shared affliction. It was their respective staffs, often only able to understand their own Chief's contribution to the discussions, who were left floundering until they could compare notes with their opposite numbers.[3]

When the Arras offensive had been seen as supporting a Fourth Army breakthrough northwards from the Somme, it had been visualised by Haig as taking the form of an attack by Third Army from south of Arras to capture the Monchy-le-Preux Ridge, supported by First and Fifth Armies on either flank.[4] The advent of General Nivelle, entailing the need for the BEF to take over additional line from the French, called for a recasting of the details of Haig's strategy, which then had to be further modified to take account of the German retirement to the Hindenburg Line. The basis on which the plans for the offensive were finalised was that the Fourth Army would take over the stretch of French line to the Amiens-Roye road, leaving it too stretched to make any meaningful contribution to the offensive apart from artillery support. To Fourth Army north, the Fifth Army, which would have attacked towards Achiet-le-Grand had not the German retirement left that town about 12 kilometres inside allied territory, would attack towards the village of Bullecourt. The Third Army main objective would remain the high ground dominated by Monchy-le-Preux whence it would advance southeast towards Croisilles and Bullecourt. It would also advance eastwards along the southern bank of the River Scarpe. Its ultimate objective would be to break through towards Cambrai where, if the French offensive succeeded, the advancing allies would link up. The River Scarpe would form the boundary between the Third and First Armies. The latter's main objective would remain the capture of Vimy Ridge. It would then continue to protect the Third Army left flank by advancing north of the Scarpe.

As the pivotal army in the British strategy, it was the Third Army detailed planning which came under the closest scrutiny by Haig and his staff at GHQ. The Commander in Chief had from the outset laid great emphasis on the importance of General Allenby securing a marked improvement in the railway supply services to his Army (which was in the end, as has been seen, only to be partially achieved by getting the problem addressed at the highest political level). When the two officers met on 23 December Allenby offered Haig his first ideas. Haig recorded in his diary:

> [Allenby] is anxious to push the Cavalry right through to Monchy-le-Preux, and then at once Eastwards to Écourt[-St-Quentin] and the Canal du Nord. I agree to the capture of Monchy-le-Preux but instead of moving so far Eastwards at once, I consider that the Cavalry should first cooperate with the Infantry in widening the gap in the line Southwards and joining hands with Gough's Vth Army North of Bapaume.[5]

Allenby's response, if any, is not recorded.

On 7 February Allenby submitted more detailed proposals for the offensive to GHQ.[6] According to one of his biographers, GHQ was profoundly shocked by his revolutionary ideas.[7] But when Haig saw him a week later he confined himself to addressing two of the more mundane concerns he had with Allenby's proposals, the need to mount simultaneous attacks to capture the hill 1,000 yards north of Plouvain and Monchy-le-Preux ridge, and the bringing forward of reserves through Arras. Haig later discussed these concerns with his Chief of Staff, Lieutenant General Sir Launcelot Kiggell,

---

3   J. Charteris, *At GHQ*, p. 210.
4   Haig d. 30.9.16.
5   Ibid., 23.12.16.
6   OH 1917, Volume I, Appendices. Appendix 14.
7   Archibald Wavell, *Allenby, a Study in Greatness*, p. 174.

Field Marshal Sir Douglas Haig,
Commander in Chief BEF.

General Sir Henry Horne,
GOC in C First Army.

General Sir Edmund Allenby,
GOC in C Third Army.

General Sir Hubert Gough, GOC in C Fifth Army.

on 10 February and subsequently noted the outcome in his diary.

> I directed that arrangements be made for concentrating and bringing forward Reserves N. of the Scarpe as well as on the S. bank. I did not like depending solely on the routes through Arras town for the passage of Reserves. Also before the Reserves are sent forward, [Allenby] must be in possession of the following front. (On right) Chat Maigre – Mercatel – Neuville Vitasse and high ground E.S.E. of it. (Centre) Monchy-le-Preux ridge with Boiry-Notre Dame Village. (Left) Plouvain Village, with hill on North of it – Gavrelle Village – Thélus. These points constitute a kind of Bridgehead behind which Reserves can move up and deploy. Kiggell is to draft instructions to Allenby on the above lines.[8]

It was not the matters mentioned above that gave the greatest concern to GHQ however; that privilege was reserved for Allenby's plan to limit his preparatory artillery bombardment to 48 hours. Since the allied failure at the Second Battle of Artois in May 1915 the received wisdom had become that a lengthy and intense bombardment lasting around 6 to 7 days was a necessary preliminary to major offensives if they were to have any hope of achieving their aims. That such prolonged bombardments would vitiate any hope of surprise had become accepted as a price that had to be paid if the artillery were to carry out fully successfully its tasks of destroying the enemy's forward defences and killing their occupants, cutting their wire and suppressing their artillery's capacity to react. It was Allenby's MGRA, Major General Arthur Holland, whose idea it was to limit the preliminary barrage to 48 hours. An outstanding Gunner, he had conducted tests which had confirmed his belief that a hurricane bombardment could be sustained for 48 hours despite the wear and tear on the guns and their crews. He was also satisfied that the impact would be similar to a much longer, but less intense, bombardment. Its short length would restore the element of surprise to the battlefield. While the enemy would be well aware from the outset that an offensive would inevitably follow the bombardment, they would be expecting more time to plan their deployments and reactions in response.

GHQ's response to Allenby's proposal offered a lot more substance than simple outrage at the temerity of such heresy. In Major General Noel Birch, Haig had a Chief Artillery Adviser who was also a Gunner of the first rank. In his view Third Army had seriously underestimated the strain upon guns and personnel which the 48 hour barrage would entail, as well as the gun crews' lack of adequate training for such an operation. Furthermore it would take longer to cut the wire satisfactorily, especially as the bombardment's intensity would make it impossible to gauge the results from land and air observation. Finally a short barrage would do less damage to enemy morale than the longer option and it would not in any case achieve the desired amount of surprise.[9] Allenby did his best to refute these criticisms, but was placed in an impossible position when General Holland was promoted and sent off to command I Corps. His replacement, Major General R. Lecky, professed himself in agreement with GHQ's assessment of Allenby's proposal, leaving the latter with little option but to drop the idea of a 48 hour bombardment. It was replaced by one lasting twice as long, a concession of sorts from GHQ, which would have preferred somewhat longer.[10]

The Third Army for the offensive would consist of three corps containing a total of 13 infantry divisions. In addition, the Cavalry Corps, containing two cavalry and one infantry divisions, would be under command. VII Corps, on the right, would attack with four divisions in line. VI Corps in

---

8   Haig d. 10.2.17.
9   It has to be said, in defence of GHQ's apparently tepid reaction to Allenby's proposal, that the technical developments in gunnery (such as instantaneous fuzes, flash spotting and sound ranging) and tank employment which, within a few months, would enable attacks to achieve full surprise, were not fully perfected at this stage. Nor were all of Allenby's subordinate commanders enamoured of his proposal. Another distinguished Gunner, Major General H. Uniacke, who covered the interregnum between Holland's departure and Lecky's arrival, was also sceptical.
10   OH 1917, Volume I, pp. 176-9.

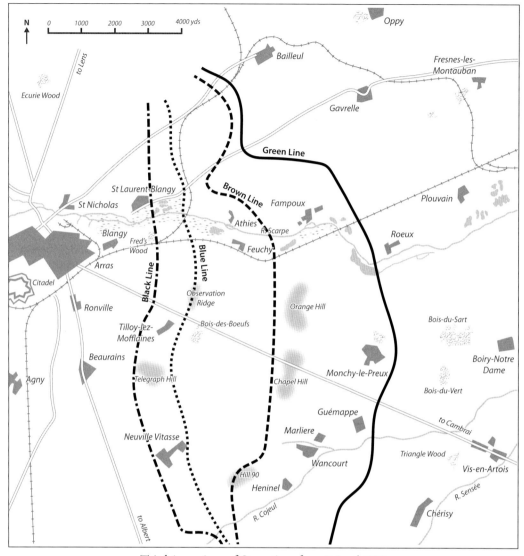

Third Army Area of Operations from 9 April 1917.

the centre and XVII Corps on the left would each advance with three divisions in line. One division in each corps would be held in reserve. The aim of the attacking corps would be to break through the enemy front between Croisilles in the south and the boundary with First Army just southwest of Farbus Wood in the north. Once the enemy defences had been breached the Hindenburg Line was to be assaulted in flank and rear and the advance continued towards Cambrai.[11] The lines of German trenches, the capture of which would form the objectives of the first day, were colour coded. The first, the Black Line, was to be taken by Zero plus 36 minutes, where the assaulting troops would halt until Zero plus 2 hours. The second, the Blue Line, would then be captured by Zero plus 3 hours where the assault would pause until Zero plus 6 hours 40 minutes. The third trench line, the Brown Line (the enemy Wancourt – Feuchy – Point du Jour line), would be attacked and taken by Zero plus 8 hours. Finally the Green Line, which would call for the capture of the villages of Guémappe, Monchy-le-

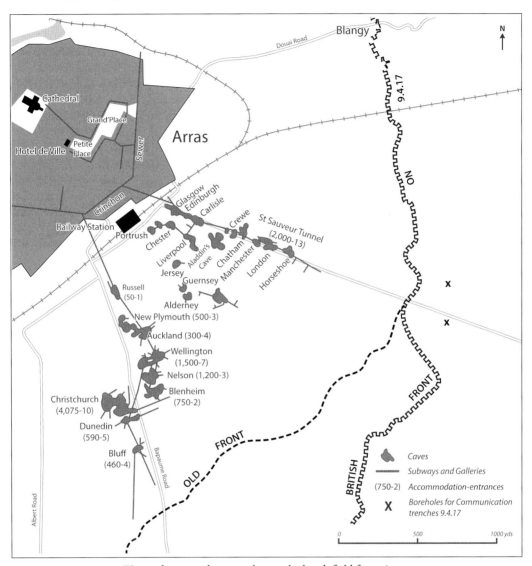

The underground approaches to the battlefield from Arras.

Preux and Fampoux, would be reached before nightfall. If the Third Army reached and captured all these objectives it would have achieved an advance of four and a half miles at its furthest point during the day.

The means by which many of the assaulting infantry would reach their jumping-off points were transformed by the chance discovery in October 1916 of a series of caves under Arras's southeastern suburbs of Ronville and St. Sauveur. When levelled and cleared they could shelter 11,500 fully equipped men. The existence of cellars under the two main squares of Arras, capable of sheltering 13,000 men, was already well-known, and it proved practical to link these cellars with the caves through tunnels constructed to take full advantage of the city's Crinchon sewer which followed the eastern and southeastern edge of Crinchon. Tunnels were also driven from the caves into no man's land and to enable the troops to debouch from shafts constructed for the purpose. The exits from the St Sauveur tunnel worked perfectly. Those from the Ronville were less useful as the German retirement meant that the exits emerged about 1,000 yards short of the new front line. There was no time to drive the tunnel further forward.[12]

The eruption of the new British secret weapon, the 'Tank', during the Battle of the Somme had convincingly demonstrated its future potential as well as its initial mechanical and technical deficiencies. It was hoped that significant numbers of the new weapon, in the form of the newly developed armour-plated Mark IV, would be available for deployment in the Battle of Arras. But production delays meant that all that could be made available were 60 machines consisting of Mark Is, which had survived the Somme, and Mark IIs which had been manufactured solely for training purposes. Neither Mark was adequately armour-plated and was therefore highly vulnerable to anything more significant than enemy small arms fire. Nevertheless the decision was taken to use them. Forty were allocated to Third Army where eight were assigned to XVII Corps and 16 each to VI and VII Corps.[13]

The task of General Horne's First Army was the ostensibly straightforward one of protecting the advancing Third Army left flank. It did however call for the capture of Vimy Ridge, a formidable challenge. The ridge was a tactically important part of the Western Front running north to south for about 12 kms to the northeast of, and overlooking, the town of Arras. Sloping gently upwards from the west to its crest, the highest point of which was 145 metres above sea level, it then fell sharply away to the Douai Plain, which it completely dominated. Allied possession of it would provide matchless observation to the east and seriously limit German freedom to exploit the mines, railways and other industrial assets of the overlooked area. The Germans had occupied the ridge in September 1914. Since then, they had made it a pivotal point in their Western Front defences, linking their northern defensive line, running north from here to the sea, with the new Hindenburg Line system to the south. They had taken advantage of the chalky soil to dig artillery-proof tunnels and storage facilities under the ridge.

The capture of Vimy Ridge was the first major challenge to confront General Horne since his promotion to the command of an army at the end of September 1916. In terms of rapidity of promotion Horne would prove to be one of the most successful senior British officers of the war. A Gunner, he had been selected by Haig to be Brigadier General Royal Artillery (BGRA) of his I Corps on the outbreak of war, thus demonstrating the very high regard in which Haig had held him since their time together in the Cavalry Division during the South African War. He rose further in Haig's esteem with his conduct in command, for short periods, of the Rearguard and Flank Guard of I Corps during the Retreat from Mons. At the end of 1914 he was promoted to Major General and given command of 2nd Division. Its main active involvement in operations during his tenure was at the Battles of Festubert in May and Loos in September, 1915. In a frustrating year marked by shell shortages, equipment deficiencies and inexperience in the arts of trench warfare, Festubert was a tragic failure for the 2nd Division with only heavy casualties to show for its efforts. Loos was, if anything, worse. In an effort to overcome the difficulties presented by 'the most unfavourable ground'[14] over which the battle had to be fought, the then Commander of the First Army, General Haig, decided that his divisions should employ 'asphyxiating' gas, the first time this weapon had been used by the BEF. It would be released from cylinders 40 minutes before Zero Hour. In the 2nd Division sector the wind required to carry the gas clouds over to the German trenches was at best fitfully weak and at worst downright perverse. Horne nevertheless ordered the valves to be opened. Unsurprisingly, little of the gas reached the German lines, and then only slowly, and large quantities blew back into the British trenches. Those battalions still capable of advancing did so to be met by machine gun fire from the untroubled enemy defenders. The 2nd Division thus made its contribution to what the Official

12   OH, op. cit., pp. 192-3.
13   Jonathan Walker, *The Blood Tub*, pp. 36-44.
14   Description attributed to then Lieutenant General Sir Henry Rawlinson.

History described as 'a day of tragedy, unmitigated by any gleam of success'.[15]

Following a brief period in the Near East, firstly as Lord Kitchener's Senior Military Adviser, as the Secretary of State for War wrestled with the problem of what to do about the faltering Gallipoli campaign, and subsequently in command of XV Corps in the Suez Canal zone, Horne was recalled to the Western Front. By now a Lieutenant General he was placed in command of a reconstituted XV Corps for the Battle of the Somme. Although on the disastrous first day of that battle his was one of only two of the five corps involved that could derive any satisfaction from its performance, Horne did not enjoy a particularly successful Somme campaign. His Corps artillery performed well and can claim to have fired the first genuine creeping barrage of the war by the BEF (thus ensuring, certainly erroneously, that Horne is often credited with its invention). But his innate caution caused him to forego opportunities to occupy Mametz and High Woods when they were empty of Germans, mistakes that would take precious time and many casualties to rectify. Nevertheless Haig's faith in him remained unshaken and when the Commander of First Army, General Monro, was appointed Commander-in-Chief of the Indian Army and Haig's first choice to succeed him, Lieutenant General Sir Richard Haking, was firmly vetoed by the War Office[16] he had no difficulty in settling on Horne. He would prove to be an eminently suitable choice.[17]

During the fighting of 1915 the French had made strenuous efforts to capture Vimy Ridge. On 9 May, General Philippe Pétain's XXXIII Corps had launched an assault. The famed Moroccan Division broke through the German lines and took the ridge, having advanced four kilometres in just a few hours. But their effort had exhausted them and they desperately needed reinforcements, which were too far back to reach them before the next day. The Germans retook the ridge that evening. A further attempt on the ridge was made during the Third Battle of Artois, which began on 25 September. Despite great bravery in the face of heavy losses, the French troops did not advance as far as they had in May. When the French handed the area over to the BEF in March 1916, they had sustained over 200,000 casualties in their unsuccessful efforts to expel the Germans from the ridge.[18]

On 22 December 1916 Haig briefed Horne on the results of his first meeting with Nivelle and confirmed that First Army would need to capture Vimy Ridge.[19] Allenby considered possession of the ridge essential to the security of his army's left flank as it advanced east from Arras. Horne had already warned Lieutenant General Sir Julian Byng that his Command, the Canadian Corps, would be assigned the task of taking the northern half of the ridge, with a British corps taking the remainder.[20] When he had assumed command of the Canadian Corps, Byng had already had a very active war. A cavalryman, he commanded the 3rd Cavalry Division at Ypres in 1914. He then briefly commanded the BEF's Cavalry Corps in 1915 before being transferred to Gallipoli to take over IX Corps, although too late to make any difference to the outcome of that campaign. It was on his return to the Western Front in May 1916 that he took over the Canadian Corps. Following their highly unsatisfactory experiences as part of General Gough's Fifth Army during the latter stages of the Somme campaign, the Corps was transferred to what was to prove to be the more congenial environment of the First Army.

In mid-January 1917 Byng was told that his Corps would now have to take the southern part of Vimy Ridge as well. Horne had suggested that Allenby's concerns about his flank might be eased

15   OH 1915, Volume II, p. 251.
16   The reason why Lieutenant General Haking found disfavour in the eyes of the War Committee and the War Office was his increasing reputation for being careless with men's lives. His XI Corps had suffered grievously at Loos and his conduct of the Battle of Fromelles, fought only two weeks before the First Army command vacancy arose, had been disastrous.
17   Don Farr, *The Silent General*, pp. 41-135 passim.
18   OH 1915, Volume II, pp. 267-70.
19   OH 1917, Volume I, Appendix 6. Haig d. 22.12.16
20   J. Williams, *Byng of Vimy: General and Governor-General*, p. 143.

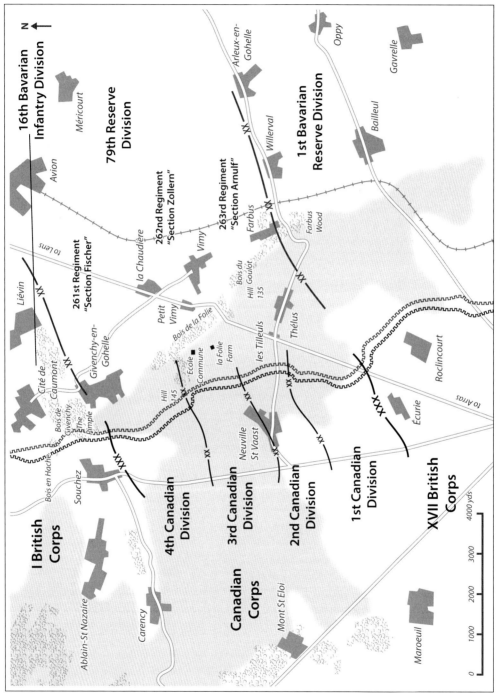

Canadian and German dispositions on Vimy Ridge.

by the capture of the southern part of the ridge, leaving its more northern portion and the village of Thélus out of the operation. But Allenby was adamant that the area thus captured would be so shallow and so overlooked from the higher ground to the north that it would be very difficult to hold if counterattacked by the Germans. Furthermore, the northern part of the ridge, if left in German hands, would give them a jumping-off point from which to launch an attack towards Arras, thus threatening the Third Army flank and lines of communication. Called upon to adjudicate, Haig supported Allenby and confirmed his order that the whole of Vimy Ridge should be assaulted and captured by First Army.[21]

One aspect of General Nivelle's notional command of the BEF for his offensive, which might have had significant consequences, was his attempts to dissuade Haig from mounting the assault on Vimy Ridge. These could have had the power of a veto on the operation had Nivelle succeeded in completely subordinating the BEF to his command. Haig's partially successful defence of his territory meant that, while he conceded overall strategic control of the allied offensive to Nivelle, he retained the right to determine how Nivelle's strategy should be implemented tactically on the British front. Nivelle's objections to the Vimy Ridge plan appear to have fluctuated between a belief that the Germans would evacuate the ridge as part of Operation *Alberich*, thus making planning for its capture a waste of time and effort, and a belief that the ridge was as impregnable as the Germans claimed and attempts to take it would consume men and matériel disproportionate to any possible gain. Nivelle certainly feared that the inclusion of Vimy Ridge in the British offensive would shift too much effort away from where he wanted it focused, on an expanded front south of the River Scarpe.

It is not entirely clear when Nivelle became aware of Haig's intention to assault Vimy Ridge. He would have known that it had been agreed between Haig and Joffre as part of the latter's allied strategy for 1917. But that it still featured in British plans was probably not confirmed until the Chief of the French Mission at GHQ reported the fact to Nivelle in late January 1917. When Nivelle and Haig met at Beauvais a few days later, the subject was discussed, with Haig apparently sticking firmly to his guns in the face of Nivelle's attempts at dissuasion. Nothing daunted, the French C in C reverted to the subject at the Calais conference on 26 February when, in response to promptings from Lloyd George, he said that his only disagreement with Haig was over Vimy Ridge.[22] Haig took the opportunity to clarify his thinking to the conference, as he later recorded in his diary.

> I now explained in French why I rejected Nivelle's suggestion regarding the Vimy ridge. My left must either be in the S. side of Monchy-le-Preux ridge (S. of the Scarpe) in which case my right would extend towards Gommecourt. If we pierced the front in this position we entered a pocket formed by the Hindenburg Line.
>
> On the other hand with my left on the Vimy ridge, I had a secure flank and my attack would bring me in rear of the Hindenburg Line. I therefore decided for the latter plan.
>
> Lyautey said my explanation was quite clear and sound.[23]

Although this seems to have put an end to any hope the French GQG may have had of persuading Haig to change his mind, it did not stop them from continuing to make clear, to the detriment of relations between the two Headquarters, that they still considered the planned operation to be a mistake. The most outspoken voice on the French side was that of a Colonel d'Alenson who occupied a position which theoretically did not exist in the military hierarchy, that of *Chef de Cabinet* (Head of the Private Office) of the C in C. D'Alenson was a dying man, in the late stages of phthisis (pulmonary tuberculosis), who was obsessed with a burning desire to play a significant part in bringing about the

---

21   OH 1917, Volume I, p. 302.
22   Ibid., pp. 53-6.
23   Haig d. 26.2.17.

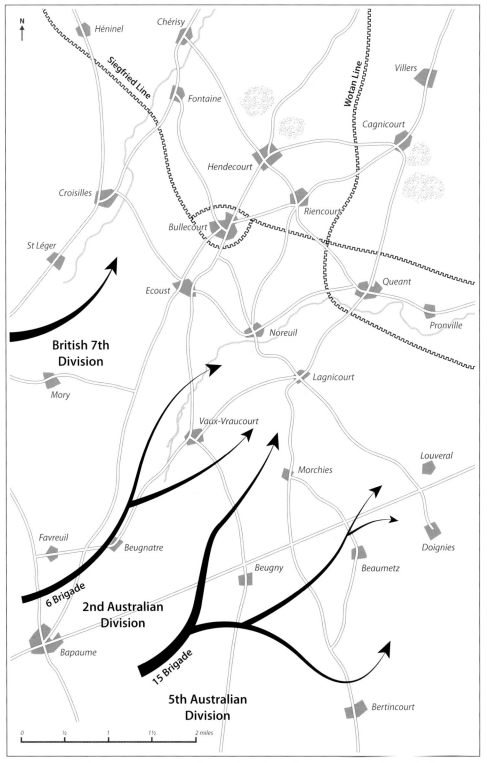

The Fifth Army advance to Bullecourt March/April 1917. (© Pen & Sword Ltd)

defeat of the enemy before his own demise. He saw the Nivelle Plan as the means of achieving this and one of his tasks as dispelling any doubts that Nivelle may have felt in the ultimate success of his offensive plans. He was well placed to do this as Nivelle's most influential adviser with the power of granting or denying access to him, even by his senior commanders. He was no friend of the British, an attitude warmly reciprocated by most British officers he had dealings with. In the margins of the London conference of 12 March D'Alenson made clear his belief, reflecting that of his Chief, that attacking Vimy Ridge would be a waste of time and energy.[24] The British remained unmoved.

The task given to General Gough's Fifth Army was essentially to attack northeastward in support of the Third Army planned thrust southeastwards. The main objective would be the village of Bullecourt, situated between Croisilles and Quéant and equidistant from both. The task would be greatly complicated by the uncertainties introduced by the voluntary German retirement. Of the three British armies participating in the upcoming battle it was on Fifth Army front that the withdrawal was proving to be most marked and was offering the least indication of whether or where it would stop. By the last week in February it had become clear that the scope of the withdrawal was significant. It was described by Haig at that point as being on a front of 18,000 yards and so far involving the enemy's abandonment of the villages of Warlencourt, Pys, Irles, Miraumont and Serre. The assumption had to be that the withdrawal would take the enemy all the way back to the Hindenburg Line. As the Fifth Army sought to press forward and maintain contact with the German rearguards it found itself severely hampered by the logistical problems created for it by the enemy's scorched earth policy, which necessitated repairs to roads and rail lines and the need for extreme caution over the ever-present danger of booby traps. In addition the tired troops frequently found themselves running up against strong German rearguards seemingly determined to hold on in certain places. The reason behind this was that completion of the Hindenburg and Drocourt-Quéant Lines had fallen behind schedule because of the severe winter and other problems, and more time therefore needed to be bought by a slowing up of the Allied progress towards the Lines. The element of unpredictability as to where the Germans would stand and fight and where they would quietly evacuate compounded the uncertainties of the Fifth Army advance. It nevertheless remained essential that the Fifth Army should push right up to the Hindenburg Line in time to be in a position to support the Third Army offensive when this was launched. With General Gough in command there was little doubt that, whatever the constraints, the maximum pressure to achieve this would be called for. In the early hours of 2 April Gough's Headquarters despatched a telegram to V and I ANZAC Corps emphasising the need for urgency.

> Preparations for the attack on the Hindenburg Line must now be taken in hand with the greatest energy. Every available heavy gun must be pushed up without further delay and got into action at suitable range. All risks must be accepted. Infantry must work forward to assaulting positions and any necessary trenches must be prepared.[25]

General Sir Hubert Gough was one of the most controversial officers to exercise senior command on the Western Front. At the outbreak of war he was a 44 year old Brigadier General in command of 3rd Cavalry Brigade, part of the BEF's Cavalry Division. He was fortunate still to be a serving soldier. As an Irish Protestant in command of the Brigade when it was based at the Curragh, outside Dublin, in early 1914, he had been a prime mover in the threat by the Brigade's officers to resign their commissions rather than take part in the feared coercion of the Protestants of Ulster into a largely Catholic Ireland that was about to be granted Home Rule. The crisis that the so-called Curragh Mutiny engendered resulted in the forced resignations of the Secretary of State for War and the

---

24   Edward Spears, *Prelude to Victory*, pp. 130-1 and 191.
25   OH 1917, Volume I, Appendix 34.

CIGS[26] and might have had further repercussions had it not been for the outbreak of the war and a political consensus that the implementation of Home Rule should be shelved until the war was over.

Gough was born and raised in a family steeped in military tradition. No fewer than four of its members were recipients of the Victoria Cross. Commissioned into the 16th Lancers in 1889, his rise through the junior ranks had been unusually rapid and by the age of 34 he was a lecturer at Sandhurst. Two years later he was the youngest Lieutenant Colonel in the British Army and CO of his Regiment. He combined this appointment with that of Chief of Staff to the Inspector General of Cavalry, one Douglas Haig. Haig clearly saw in Gough the true embodiment of the dashing cavalry officer imbued with offensive spirit, and, as one of his protégés, would protect him and secure his preferment whenever possible. By the time he arrived on the Western Front Gough had already been a Brigadier General for four years. Thereafter his rise was even more rapid than Horne's. Within a few weeks he was a Major General commanding the newly created 2nd Cavalry Division. In April 1915 he was given temporary command of 7th Division. By the summer of the same year he was a Lieutenant General commanding I Corps in Haig's First Army. In May 1916 Haig selected him to command the Reserve Army for the Somme offensive, seeing Gough as the ideal choice to lead the Army three cavalry divisions which were intended to exploit the Fourth Army breakthrough of the German defences. The breakthrough failed to materialise but, after the tragic first day of the Battle, the Reserve Army, still under Gough's command, was given two of the Fourth Army five infantry corps. On 30 October 1916 the Reserve Army was renamed the Fifth Army.

It was as Commander of a predominantly infantry Army that the disadvantages of possession of an offensive cavalry spirit, with its tendency towards impetuosity and a sometimes casual approach to meticulous planning, began to come to the fore. The attritional actions which Gough found himself having to fight in the Somme campaign, and later, hardly suited his temperament and it is perhaps unsurprising that, first the Australians and subsequently the Canadians, who were called upon respectively to lead the assaults on Pozières and Pozières Ridge and Courcelette and Regina Trench, emerged from their Somme ordeals highly disenchanted with Gough's generalship.[27]

Although Gough had, as a divisional and corps commander, shown a readiness to disregard orders he regarded as impractical, and had got away with it, he showed no tendency to forgive subordinates who acted similarly when he had given the orders. He became notorious for his sackings and most Corps, Divisional and Brigade commanders were distinctly unhappy at the prospect of being assigned to Fifth Army. Even if a subordinate commander got away with a perceived failure to implement Gough's orders with the utmost aggression once, it was made quite clear that their card was marked and a second lack of sufficient aggression would not be forgiven. Career officers could find themselves confronted with a choice between obedience to orders they considered suicidal and disobedience and probable dismissal. Not surprisingly some chose the former and their soldiers paid the price.

It had been determined, at a meeting on 29 March of Haig and the three army commanders who would fight the Battle of Arras, that the Fifth Army would not attack simultaneously with the Third and First Armies, but would do so about 24 hours later, which should be about when Third Army

26   The CIGS was Field Marshal Sir John French, who never forgave Gough for the near terminal damage he had inflicted on his career.

27   Although Australian divisions continued to fight under Gough's command until mid-1917 (I ANZAC Corps was one of the two corps of Fifth Army that fought at Bullecourt, the other being V British Corps) their experiences on the Somme brought appreciably closer their desire to be officered and led solely by Australians as soon as suitably trained and experienced candidates were available. The Canadians made it known after the Somme that they would not be prepared to serve under Gough again. Haig's Chief of General Staff (CGS), Lieutenant General Kiggell, reminded his boss of this when the Canadian Corps were preparing to be drafted in to fight the concluding phases of Third Ypres (Passchendaele). He recommended that they should be placed in General Sir Herbert Plumer's Second Army, and not under Gough. In acquiescing, Haig speculated that it was Major General Neill Malcolm, Gough's Chief of Staff, who was at least partly the cause of the Canadian disenchantment with Gough. So, as late as October 1917, Haig was still strongly supportive of Gough. Haig d. 5.10.17.

would be carrying the enemy third line. The 21st Division on the extreme right of the Third Army front, and therefore alongside Fifth Army, would assault first followed shortly thereafter by Gough's troops. The main reasons for delaying the entry into battle of 21st Division and Fifth Army was that their assaults would in all likelihood be confronted by thick and largely uncut wire and there would be no time to dig starting trenches. Unless Allenby's troops got forward to distract the enemy, the assaults could result in a check and serious losses.[28]

On 5 April Haig met Nivelle at Montdidier. He was told that General Micheler had asked for a further 48 hours to complete his preparations. Haig said that it would be best to attack before the enemy could retreat further, but he would welcome a 24 hour delay as the wire cutting results were not clear. Micheler was granted his 48 hour delay and the British offensive was postponed from 8 to 9 April.[29] On the same day as Haig's meeting with Nivelle, Gough issued his detailed orders for the Fifth Army attack, provisionally scheduled at this stage for the 10th. This is not to suggest that there was any cessation of fighting in the lead up to the opening of the offensive. V Corps and 1 Anzac Corps were both heavily engaged in attacking and clearing villages leading up to the Hindenburg Line. It was not until 9 April that this task was largely completed. It had involved some heavy fighting and significant casualties, even though the fighting generally consisted of overcoming strong rearguards.

Gough's orders for the battle envisaged attacks on a front of 3,500 yards in the centre of which was the village of Bullecourt, the first objective. The second and third objectives were respectively the villages of Riencourt and Hendecourt, both about a mile behind Bullecourt and half that distance from each other. Tempting though it would have been to widen the offensive to include the pivotal village of Quéant,[30] Gough recognised that this would entail breaking through four lines of trenches, a forbidding task twice as daunting in numbers of trench lines as an attack launched west of Quéant with Bullecourt as its objective. It would be wiser to leave Quéant to one side in the hope that progress elsewhere would enable it to be taken without a direct frontal assault. There were contrary indications of what sort of a fight the Germans would put up in defence of Bullecourt. Fifth Army Intelligence were receiving frequent reports of fires in the villages of Pronville, Cagnicourt and Riencourt, which seemed to indicate that the Germans were planning to continue their pullback to well behind Bullecourt. On the other hand prisoners were almost unanimous in their disclosures that the village's fortifications were being feverishly strengthened and extended to assist the defenders in their assigned task of holding the village at all costs. That the defenders would be the outstanding 27th Württemberg Division lent credence to the prisoners' claims.[31] The successive orders issued by Fifth Army seem however to have assumed that the capture of Bullecourt would be a relatively simple task.[32]

Gough's attack would be carried out by I Anzac and V (British) Corps. The 4th Cavalry Division would pass through the breach in the German defences, once Hendecourt was taken, to join up with the rest of the Cavalry Corps advancing from Arras. Gough had been allotted 12 tanks. Five each were assigned to the two corps with the remaining two kept in Army reserve.

The decision on the timing of Fifth Army attack was beset with several problems. Gough hoped that it would be synchronised with the Third Army assault on the Wancourt-Feuchy Line which, in effect, should have meant early on 9 April. The postponement of the start of the main battle from 8 to 9 April, as belatedly agreed between Nivelle and Haig, put back Fifth Army entry into the battle to the 10th. But Gough learned on the 8th that the enemy wire in front of I Anzac Corps remained substantially uncut, a situation that would not be adequately rectified until the 14th. Gough warned the Australians that it would be unlikely the attack could be put back any further than the 12th.

28   Haig d. 29.3.17.
29   Ibid., 5.4.17.
30   Pivotal because it formed the junction of a particularly formidable section of the Hindenburg Line and the Drocourt-Quéant Switch.
31   Jonathan Walker, op. cit., pp. 76-7.
32   Fifth Army Orders 50, 51 and 52 of 5, 7 and 8 April respectively.

The problem of the uncut wire had been largely a direct result of the German destruction of the infrastructure during their retirement which had delayed the bringing up of the guns and ammunition required for the wire cutting. It had consequently only really got under way on 5 April.

In the event Gough's warning to the Australians regarding the time available to them to complete wire cutting was to prove optimistic. The Third Army striking successes on 9 April would leave Gough champing at the bit and desperate to attack in its support. He would seize the opportunity offered to him by proposals from the Commander of the Tanks attached to his Army to bring forward its entry into the battle.

Part II

First Battle of the Scarpe: Vimy Ridge

First Battle of Bullecourt

4

VII Corps

In common with most of the major offensives of the war, the Battle of Arras was in fact a series of engagements interspersed with relatively quiescent periods during which the armies involved drew breath, took stock, and were re-equipped, resupplied and redeployed in preparation for the next bout of heavy fighting. It should not be inferred from this that the battlefield ever fell silent. Actions on a relatively small scale were daily occurrences as commanders sought to improve their tactical situation by, for example, pinching out enemy salients, improving the defensibility of their positions, or establishing more viable assembly points for the next big attack. The major actions that took place under the catchall name of the Battle of Arras were also individually termed 'Battles'. The Third Army First Battle of the Scarpe (9-14 April) was to be followed by the Second (23-24 April) and Third (3-4 May) battles of the same name. Fought simultaneously with the first of these battles was the First Army Battle of Vimy Ridge. Both the First and Third Armies were involved in the Battle of Arleux (28-29 April). The Fifth Army launched the First Battle of Bullecourt on 11 April. The main, Second Battle of Bullecourt, lasted from 3 to 17 May. Its end signified the imminent closure of the Arras campaign.

The unusually severe and prolonged winter of 1916-17 showed no sign of relenting as Zero Hour approached on Easter Monday, 9 April. Most of the battlefield was being swept with blizzards or, at best, heavy rain or sleet as 0530, Zero Hour on the First and Third Army fronts, arrived. Fortunately for the attackers, the snow or sleet was driving straight into the eyes of the Germans, which hardly helped them to detect any signs there may have been that the British assault was imminent.

The Third Army three infantry corps (from right to left VII, VI and XVII) were deployed on a front totalling eleven and a half miles from Croisilles in the south to the Commandant's House, a building southwest of Farbus Wood and still in German occupied territory, that marked the boundary between Third and First Armies.

VII Corps was commanded by Lieutenant General Sir Thomas D'Oyley Snow. At the outbreak of the war Snow had been in command of 4th Infantry Division for three years. In accordance with Henry Wilson's agreement with the French, Snow's command should have been one of the six infantry divisions participating in the BEF's initial deployment to France. In the event it was one of the two divisions held back in England at the last moment by the newly appointed Secretary of State for War, Field Marshal Lord Kitchener, to meet an illusory threat of German invasion. Kitchener's excessive caution was however quickly seen for what it was and 4th Division embarked for France on 22 August 1914, only a week or so late. It nevertheless arrived too late to participate in the Battle of Mons and the start of the Retreat therefrom, but was in time for Snow to place it at the disposal of General Sir Horace Smith-Dorrien for the Battle of Le Cateau. Relatively fresh, the Division acquitted itself well and then joined the continuing Retreat. On 9 September, during the Battle of the Marne, Snow broke his pelvis in a riding accident and was shipped back to England. When he was able to return to active service he was given command of the newly formed 27th Division and took it to France in December 1914. On the basis of his performance at the Second Battle of Ypres in April-May 1915 he was promoted to the command of VII Corps. In this role his reputation was badly affected by his Corps' catastrophic diversionary attack at Gommecourt on the first day of the Battle of the Somme;

he was lucky not to have been sent home. It would probably be fair to say that, partly because of the lasting effects of his riding injury and possibly because of the problems he had in adjusting to the difficulties of command on the Western Front, his promotion to Lieutenant General had been a step too far.[1]

The sector of Third Army front from which VII Corps would launch its assault was that most affected by the German voluntary withdrawal. As the extent of the German move became increasingly apparent in the latter half of March, General Snow was ordered to close towards the Hindenburg line so as to be ready to advance on it on Z Day, and generally to push his line forward, especially to the east and northwest of the village of Hénin-sur-Cojeul.[2] By 28 March the C in C himself had become sufficiently concerned at the apparent lack of progress in implementing these orders for him to pay Snow a visit at his Headquarters at Fosseux. In answer to Haig's questions,

> Snow explained that all the roads had been destroyed at important junctions, that the difficulties in pushing forward guns had been great. Ample guns were now in position but owing to the bad state of the roads it was not possible to send forward adequate supplies of ammunition.
>
> While agreeing that the difficulties of getting forward over the broken ground of the enemy's original front line system had been great, I called Snow's attention to the manner in which the Fifth Army had pushed forward over much greater distances and had been able that morning to gain a foothold in Croisilles.[3]

Haig did not record what, if any, reaction Snow offered to this scarcely veiled warning that he should up his game. Despite the pressure from both Haig and his army commander, he initially planned only to attack frontally with his left and centre divisions, leaving his right Division, the 21st, which was already close to the formidable obstacle of the Hindenburg Line, to push forward in small groups as and when opportunity offered. Allenby demurred, insisting that the 21st, should also mount frontal attacks. It was agreed that, as reaching the Brown Line in this sector would entail crossing the Hindenburg Line, it would be adjusted so that Snow's Corps would not have to tackle the Hindenburg Line until at least the German wire protecting it had been adequately destroyed.

A further effect of the German retirement on VII Corps plans was that each unit was dependent on the one on its left making progress before it made sense for it to start its own move forward. For this reason the normal practice of describing events as they unfolded from right to left, will be reversed and be dealt with from left to right.

Occupying the left of the VII Corps sector was 14th (Light) Division. The 42 Brigade was on the Division left with the 43rd on the right. The two lead off battalions of the 42 Brigade were 9th King's Royal Rifle Corps (KRRC) on the left and 5th Oxford and Buckinghamshire Light Infantry (Ox and Bucks LI) on the right. Following through would be 5th King's Shropshire Light Infantry (KSLI).

The 14th (Light) Division was a Kitchener New Army (KNA) formation into which service battalions bearing the names of illustrious light infantry regiments had been brigaded. Commanded from the outset by Major General V. A. Couper, it had arrived on the Western Front in mid 1915 and found itself in the Ypres Salient. In June 1916 it participated in the fierce and inconclusive fighting around Bellewaarde and Hooge. In February of the following year the Division transferred from Second to Third Army in preparation for Arras.[4]

---

1   John Bourne, *Who's Who in World War One*, p. 270.
2   The National Archives (TNA) WO 95/361 of 24.3.17: Third Army War Diary.
3   Haig d. 28.3.17.
4   Subsequent to Arras, the Division was in Fifth Army when that formation was overwhelmed by the full force of the German 1918 Spring Offensive. After two weeks of desperate defensive fighting the Division was withdrawn so badly mauled that it was decided not to reconstitute them as a fighting force. Major General Sir Victor Couper (as he had become) remained in command to the end.

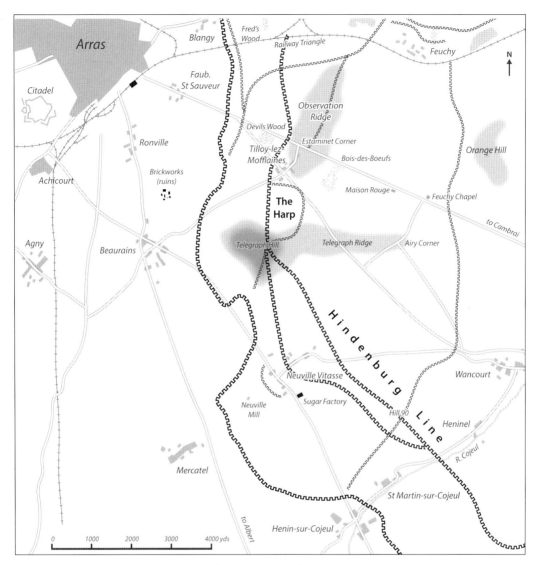

VII Corps battlefield for First Battle of the Scarpe 9-14 April 1917.

To the left of the Division at Zero Hour on 9 April was VI Corps 3rd Division. To give this Division the necessary time to capture the Black Line and come up into line with the 14th, the latter's attack was launched at Zero plus 2 hours 4 minutes. Confronting it was one of the more challenging tasks of the day, the capture of an enemy redoubt known, from its shape as The Harp, the seizure of a trench line running north-south through it known as The String, and the Cojeul Switch. Much of the preparatory work done in digging trenches and by the artillery had been rendered nugatory by the enemy's voluntary withdrawal. The 42 Brigade found itself confronted by 1,000 to 1,500 yards of open ground from what had been the enemy front line, thus necessitating the urgent digging of fresh trenches to bring the assaulting troops to within 400 to 800 yards of The Harp's front line. The artillery had been very effective in its wire cutting, except for some of that protecting The String, and in the destruction of enemy machine gun posts.

The two hour period between Zero Hour and 14th Division's assault beginning was predictably one of great tension in 42nd Brigade's assembly trenches. A ration of hot tea and rum was issued to all ranks. There was great apprehension that the enemy would shell the newly dug trenches as they were in view from the enemy's positions in The Harp and the village of Tilloy. Moreover, two tanks that were manoeuvring over them were a tempting target for enemy fire. But in fact there was only sporadic shelling from 77mm guns. A captured German officer was subsequently asked why he had not ordered the shelling of the assembly trenches. He said he himself had never noticed them and their existence had never been reported to him.

The 42 Brigade's account of the events of 9 April indicates that a total of five tanks had been deployed on the Brigade front. They had escaped the attention of the enemy artillery in the run up to the Brigade's assault, but nevertheless proved to be of very doubtful value, arriving at any given point too late to be of any real use to the infantry; the ground was apparently too soft for them especially in and around The Harp where it had been churned up and softened by repeated bombardments. (This was the Brigade's second experience of tank support; the first had also been considered a failure.)

According to the Brigade account, the two assault battalions left their assembly trenches at 0734 and advanced behind an 'excellent' artillery barrage firing half high explosive (HE) and half shrapnel. Eleven minutes later, despite heavy hostile machine gun fire, they were passing through gaps in the wire in front of The Harp and a few minutes later were into The Harp itself. On the left 9th KRRC then entered The String at either end of the stretch of it assigned to them. They bombed inwards to clear it of two machine guns that, with the inadequately cut wire in front of the trench and the attentions of snipers firing from Noisy Work, a strongpoint to the rear of The Harp, had caused significant casualties to the Battalion.

On 9th KRRC's right, 5th Ox and Bucks LI, after some heavy fighting in which their Lewis guns eliminated three enemy machine guns, also entered and cleared their assigned sector of The String. By 0830, Telegraph Work, a German strongpoint south of The Harp, and the southern third of The String, the first objectives of the Brigade, were secured (the northern two thirds of the trench was 3rd Division's responsibility). The response of the enemy artillery during the period leading to the capture of The String was described as 'thin' except for a heavy bombardment of Telegraph Hill, southwest of The Harp. Its capture evoked a heavy hostile barrage targeted on it.

Within minutes, 5th KSLI passed through the lead battalions and by 0845 had taken the Brigade's second objectives, the rear face of The Harp (the Blue Line) and part of the Cojeul Switch running southeast from the redoubt. By 1330 the Brigade had achieved all its objectives for the day when two companies of 9th Rifle Brigade (RB), the Brigade's reserve battalion, secured positions close to the Tilloy-Wancourt road.

The Brigade could take great satisfaction from its successful achievement of its objectives. Nearly 300 prisoners had been taken including the CO of a *Sturm* Battalion. Many of the defenders had seemed only too eager to surrender, although the machine gun crews and the snipers had fought stubbornly and well. The rifle grenade had demonstrated a gratifying effectiveness against machine gun emplacements. The day was not however entirely a success story. The disappointing performance of the tanks has already been noted. The artillery had failed to blow in the entrances to German dugouts.[5] Casualties too were not light. 9th KRRC, for example, had lost six officers killed and four wounded and 69 Other Ranks (ORs) killed and 135 wounded and missing.[6]

One of the wounded officers was Lieutenant Victor Richardson, who would achieve posthumous fame as one of the four junior infantry officers whose lives and deaths were movingly recounted in Vera Brittain's autobiographical study *Testament of Youth*. Richardson was a close friend of Vera's fiancé, Roland Leighton, and her brother, Edward, dating from their days at Uppingham School, where they were known collectively as the 'Three Musketeers'. Like so many of his contemporaries

---

5   TNA WO 95/1898: 42nd Brigade War Diary.
6   Ibid.

Richardson had volunteered on the outbreak of war and secured a commission in the 4th (Territorial) Battalion of the Royal Sussex Regiment. In September 1916 his agitation for a more active role in the war paid off when he was transferred into 9th KRRC, already on the Western Front. Arras was his first major action and it was to be tragically brief. A platoon commander in B Company, one of the two lead off companies, he was slightly wounded in the right arm, probably as he reached The Harp. He had the wound dressed and carried on. As he advanced on The String he was shot through the head and seriously wounded, probably by a round from one of the machine guns situated in the trench. Not expected to live he was evacuated to London where it was confirmed that he had lost his sight. Although he seemed to be coping well with his loss and was otherwise recovering well, he had a sudden relapse and died on 9 June, exactly two months after his wounding.[7]

The 43 (Light Infantry) Brigade, on the 42's right, also began its assault on a two battalion front at 0734, 2 hours and 4 minutes after Zero Hour. On the left were 10th Durham Light Infantry (DLI), on the right 6th King's Own Yorkshire Light Infantry (KOYLI). In support were 6th Somerset Light Infantry (SLI) and in reserve 6th Duke of Cornwall's Light Infantry (DCLI). The first objective of the day for the lead off battalions was the enemy's Red Line (Pine trench). The troops kept up well with the creeping barrage and the line was successfully secured with only slight losses within 20 minutes. The Brigade's report, like that of 42 Brigade, noted the almost complete absence of enemy artillery fire except for the heavy barrage directed at Telegraph Hill.

The capture of the Blue Line, the Brigade's next objective in effect involved the overrunning of the Hindenburg Line, as the Blue Line was situated behind it on the Brigade front. As the advance got under way it was found that the enemy's Fir Alley redoubt, half way to the Hindenburg Line, had not been adequately neutralised by the artillery bombardment. The problem was overcome by 6th KOYLI with the aid of three tanks, which dealt with the wire. The two lead off battalions, with 5th KSLI on their left, then successfully completed the taking of the Hindenburg and Blue Lines (Telegraph Hill Trench and the Cojeul Switch) in their sector by 0900. It had not however been without cost. 10th DLI had suffered heavy losses in their progress from the Red to the Blue Line. For their part 6th KOYLI had had to contend with the failure of 56th Division on their right to protect them from enfilade machine gun and shellfire from Neuville-Vitasse during their advance to the Blue Line. Their first task on securing the Blue Line was therefore the necessary one of setting up a protective flank. One of their Second Lieutenants followed this up by going into Neuville-Vitasse and securing the services of two companies of the London Scottish and some London Rangers, 56th Division troops, whom he successfully used to drive out the enemy in possession of the gap between the two British divisions.[8] By now it was 1530 and the Brigade's support and reserve battalions, respectively 6th SLI and 6th DCLI, were already involved in the battle, having been ordered to capture the Brown Line.

As they crossed the brow of Telegraph Hill on their way up, their objective, the Brown Line near Wancourt, was pointed out to all of 6th SLI's platoons. The attack began at 1230 with a leading line of skirmishers following closely behind a creeping barrage. It soon became apparent that the Battalion was advancing with little or no support on either flank. The lack of support on the left was not entirely unexpected as the companies of 9th Rifle Brigade on that flank were echeloned slightly to the rear. On the right however the anticipated support from 56th Division had not materialised. The Battalion CO sent a pigeon message to Brigade informing them that he was detaching two platoons to clear the high ground on their left in 42nd Brigade's sector. The remaining two companies would push on to the Brown Line.

The high ground was successfully cleared and handed over to a platoon of 9th RB that arrived at around 1310. A second message to Brigade confirmed these events, but also warned that both the Battalion's flanks were still in the air, although the situation was improving on the left with increasing

7   Don Farr, *None That Go Return*, pp. 128-32 and 144-5.
8   TNA WO 95/1906: 6th KOYLI War Diary.

numbers of 9th RB moving up.

Some leading troops of 2nd Royal Scots (R Scots) belonging to 3rd Division appeared at this stage to the north and, clearly having lost direction, became mixed up with the supporting companies of 6th SLI. The latter Battalion's leading company was by now suffering the full effects of enfilade and reversed machine gun fire from its exposed right flank, which forced it to slow down and, as a consequence, fall behind the creeping barrage. But seeing the 3rd Division troops coming up on their left rear they pushed forward and by 1330 were within 600 yards of their objective. They had however suffered very heavy casualties and were forced to fall back 400 yards to the shelter of a recently dug enemy trench. A company of 6th DCLI arrived in support, the remainder staying in reserve.

At around 1715 6th SLI and 6th DCLI received warning orders for a fresh attack on the Brown Line beginning at 1830. Heavy artillery would begin its bombardment of the Brown Line immediately, with the Field Artillery joining in at 1822. Two minutes later, a creeping barrage would be laid down beginning 300 yards west of the Brown Line. It would start creeping forward at 1834 at a rate of 100 yards in 2 minutes. The main barrage would lift off the front trench of the Brown Line at 1900 and off the second trench 5 minutes later.

The CO of 6th SLI did his best to conform with the demands imposed by the timings of the creeping barrage. He ordered his reserve, about one company, to push up at once to attack, and the Battalion's other three companies to advance with their right on Wancourt Tower, situated on high ground a little over 1,000 yards southeast of Wancourt. Two companies of 6th DCLI were also ordered to advance with their left on Wancourt Tower so as to attack on 6th SLI's right. The DCLI's third company received orders to advance in support with a view to forming a defensive flank. The fourth company would also move up but remain in reserve. Unsurprisingly however none of 6th SLI's companies reached their planned starting points in time to follow the barrage. The message ordering the attack did not reach the officer in command of three of 6th SLI's companies until 1855. By then the barrage was too far advanced to offer any protection. Consequently only the left company was able to make any appreciable advance as enfilade machine gun fire from the high ground to the right of Wancourt, on the Battalion's southern flank, took toll of the advancing troops. The two advance companies of 6th DCLI also took heavy casualties from the same source as they moved forward; they were forced to fall back to the shelter of a former German communication trench. The support company, which did not come under such heavy machine gun fire owing to the configuration of the ground, pushed forward and occupied a German trench, which they held for the night as a defensive flank. As soon as this trench was occupied, bombing parties were sent along it in the direction of Wancourt towards which the enemy were retreating.

At 2140 all companies were ordered to consolidate their present positions. Following a personal reconnaissance by the CO of 6th SLI a message was sent to Brigade describing the situation and pointing out that the enemy were still holding positions in strength in front of their Wancourt-Feuchy Line.[9] One position that the enemy sought to defend was a large dump in the sunken road, which formed part of the Wancourt-Feuchy Line. They barricaded the approach to this with wire and about 100 boxes. Fire from a Lewis gun pushed them back and a Lewis gun position was set up to deny the enemy access to the dump and an ammunition dugout containing a large quantity of small arms ammunition and other material. The dugout was evidently one of the enemy's chief sources of supply for, during the night, four parties of men made attempts to get into it. They were all driven off. The next morning the dump and dugout were completely cleared of the enemy with bombs.

At 0800 on the second day of the battle the CO of 6th DCLI received orders to take command of a composite 6th SLI/6th DCLI Bn. The SLI was reformed into two companies, one of which was ordered to mop up a strong point in the sunken road. Two platoons of this company crept forward and drove over 100 enemy out of the strong point and back behind the Brown Line.

---

9   TNA WO 95/1904: 43rd Brigade War Diary.

The CO of the new composite Battalion also ordered his Lewis guns and machine guns to fire barrages to the front and right to keep down hostile machine gun fire. This was in support of 10th DLI and 6th KOYLI who had been ordered to pass through to mount an attack on the Brown Line (Wancourt Line). Following a 30 minute postponement, the attack began at 1230 under the protection of a creeping barrage that had begun 30 minutes earlier. DLI were on the left and KOYLI on the right. Further to the right 56th Division were tasked with attacking the high ground from which enemy enfilade fire would otherwise threaten 43 Brigade's attack. The 6th KOYLI War Diary here adds its voice to a number of complaints emanating from 14th Division at the apparent failure of 56th Division to achieve what was required to protect them from enfilade fire from this source. It claims that no move had been made by 56th Division thus leaving the KOYLI flank entirely exposed. The fire on them from their right caused KOYLI to veer to the left where they mingled with 10th DLI. Nevertheless the Wancourt Line was reached northwest of the village, where the wire was found to be strong and almost undamaged apart from a single gap. Two other gaps were successfully cut under fire and by 1330 the Trench was taken with little resistance from its enemy occupants. The main cause of the casualties continued to be from the enfilade fire. Belatedly, at around 1500 the 56th Division were seen to be advancing slowly towards the high ground. Ninety minutes later elements of 41 Brigade began the relief of 6th KOYLI. This had barely started when, 30 minutes later, 5th Cavalry Brigade arrived on their left. Their unavailing attempts to get through the wire in front of the Wancourt Line attracted hostile enemy shellfire not only on themselves but also on 6th KOYLI. They were nevertheless very shortly on their way back to the rear, part of the journey being accomplished by a night march through a blizzard. Their casualties in their two days fighting totalled 169, including two officers and 26 ORs killed.

Meanwhile, at about 1225, orders had been received for the SLI/DCLI composite Battalion to advance with their right flank on the sunken road and to get in touch with 10th DLI on the left. As the company covering the right hand flank of the Battalion pushed up the hill with their right flank on the sunken road they came under heavy machine gun fire which prevented them, and consequently the rest of the Battalion, from getting further forward. This was still the situation when, at about 1600, elements of 41 Brigade passed through on their way to attack the Brown Line. In the light of the situation on the SLI/DCLI right flank the initial intention that the newly arrived Brigade should come up and pass on the right was abandoned in favour of their passing through on the left and through the centre of the composite Battalion's positions. Shortly thereafter the SLI/DCLI were ordered to withdraw and return to their quarters in the Dunedin caves in Ronville.[10]

In his report on 43 Brigade's involvement in the battle, Brigadier General Wood called attention to the lack of support his Brigade had received from 56th Division on their right. He reckoned that 75 percent of the Brigade's casualties had been caused by machine gun and sniper fire emanating from the high ground on the right, which should have been taken by the 56th. The unsuccessful attacks on the Brown Line on 9 April had been entirely unsupported from the right. Although the attacks the following day were successful this was despite the continued absence of support from 56th Division. For good measure Brigadier General Wood was also critical of the artillery support his infantry received in their last attack. He described it as weak. 'Parties of Germans moving in the open were not fired on. There seemed to be practically no FOOs with telephone forward of Telegraph Hill. I met several artillery officers who were looking for observation stations. They had no means of communicating with their battery.'[11]

Throughout the first day of the battle the 14th Division 41 Brigade had remained in reserve. On the second day they were ordered to relieve 43 Brigade and take up the assault on the enemy Brown Line and, if the circumstances were propitious, to push on beyond. The relief was carried out

---

10   Ibid.
11   Ibid.

as opportunity offered when 41 Brigade's lead battalions (7th Rifle Brigade (RB) on the left and 7th KRRC on the right) moved up as described above. They found the German front line to be on the sunken road with 43 Brigade holding positions running from half a mile west of Wancourt village north towards Feuchy Chapel. There was however a stretch of this line that was still strongly held by the Germans, because 6th KOYLI's swing to the left had caused the stretch to be overlooked.

As 7th RB completed their part of the relief, two cavalry brigades came up on their left and the final moves were made in conjunction with them. It was fortunate that the moves were largely screened from the enemy by a heavy snowstorm blowing into their faces. Nevertheless the enemy were sufficiently aware of British activity involving cavalry to put down the heavy artillery and machine gun barrages from Wancourt and Hill 90 which had so inconvenienced 6th KOYLI, and which also inflicted casualties on the relieving battalion. The worst sufferers were however the cavalry who were only able withdraw to safety after dark having lost heavily.

7th KRRC's part in the relief was complicated by the fact that 6th KOYLI were not where they were supposed to be, in the Brown Line in front of Wancourt. Instead the Germans were still holding in strength this stretch of line, consisting of the sunken road, about 150 yards ahead. They were also clearly visible along the crest of Hill 90 from where they were directing rifle and machine gun fire on the KRRC. Under cover of the same snowstorm which had been of such help to 7th RB two of KRRC's companies rushed the German positions in the sunken road and seized them, killing or capturing the garrison. The cost was heavy, particularly among the British Battalion's officers.

For both relieving battalions the night passed relatively quietly, but at 0330 orders were received for them both to launch an attack to capture Wancourt and the troublesome high ground behind. Zero hour was 0630. The war diaries of both battalions graphically and sorrowfully described the disaster that ensued. 7th RB's diarist recorded, 'Our artillery barrage entirely failed and the advance was checked from the very beginning by heavy machine gun fire from the front and in enfilade from right and rear.' After considerable confusion the Battalion was reorganised under fire and the Lewis guns effectively managed to silence the enemy rifle and machine gun fire.[12]

The 7th KRRC attack was supported by 8th RB but nevertheless was a total failure. The Battalion's diarist noted that they protested about the impossibility of the task they had been set but were told to carry out their orders. The diarist also complained that, '56th Division never left their trenches or made any attempt to take Hill 90'. But he reserved most of his venom for the Staff.

B Company made a most gallant attempt to push forward but from the start it was an impossible task and the Staff who had ordered the attack, if they had come near enough to look at the ground, would have realised it too and would never have ordered the attack. Whitley[13] was also killed, gallant soldier that he was, and his body was found nearest the German wire, which was totally uncut. The artillery preparation that had been ordered in a great hurry never materialised and in fact the orders in many cases never arrived in time and the whole show was a complete failure from want of preparation and organisation on the part of the staff. The rest of the day was spent in our original positions and towards evening heavy snowstorms set in and before long there were two inches of snow on the ground. It was impossible to get in the wounded until after dark so that their sufferings were very much aggravated by the cold. That night we were relieved by 8th KRRC and moved back to the old Cojeul Switch line, where a bitterly cold night was spent in the open, without any dugouts and with fresh snow showers all night.

The 12th was spent in these trenches and 8th KRRC and 8th RB occupied Wancourt without a casualty as Hill 90 had been evacuated during the night. The whole Division was relieved by the 50th Division and the Battalion marched back to Arras. It was an awful march in

---

12   TNA WO 95/1896: 7th KRRC, 7th RB War Diaries.
13   Captain C. Whitley, MC. He is buried in Hibers Trench Cemetery, Wancourt (C.15).

the dark – the mud was very deep and men had to be dug out of it at times but by 2 am we reached the town and went into billets.[14]

On the right of 14th (Light) Division was 56th Division, otherwise known as the 1st London Division. Commanded by Major General C. P. A. Hull, it was considered to be a very good quality Territorial division, a view perhaps not currently shared by its neighbouring division. At the time of the Battle of Arras it consisted of 10 battalions of the London Regiment and two of the Middlesex Regiment. The Division was formed in France at the turn of the year 1915/1916 and assigned to VII Corps. It was one of the two Third Army divisions involved in the unsuccessful diversionary attack on the village of Gommecourt on the first day of the Battle of the Somme. The southern arm of a pincer movement designed to surround the village, it succeeded in reaching, or getting very close to, the point at which it should have linked up with the northern arm, the 46th (North Midland) Division. Sadly this latter division could make little impression on the formidable German defences confronting it and did not reach the rendezvous. The few of its men who succeeded in reaching the German front line were either killed or captured. Running out of ammunition and bombs, the isolated 56th Division were obliged to withdraw.

This was not to be the end of the Division's involvement in the Somme campaign. Transferred to the Fourth Army XIV Corps it participated in the Battles of Ginchy, Flers-Courcelette, Morval and Ancre Heights. In November 1916 it moved to First Army and from there returned to VII Corps of Third Army in mid-March 1917, in time to participate in the Battle of Arras. The Division was inserted between the 14th and 30th Divisions. It was immediately caught up in following up the German voluntary retirement and by 17 March was occupying what had been, until a few hours before, the German Second Line. The enemy were now holding the line Tilloy-The Harp-Telegraph Hill-Nice Trench-Pine Lane-Neuville-Vitasse village and trench. Further back they were holding the Cojeul Switch. The task assigned to 56th Division was the capture of a 350 yard length of the Brown Line (Wancourt-Feuchy Line). It would entail capturing the village of Neuville-Vitasse, then getting through the Hindenburg Line. Once this was achieved there would follow an advance of nearly a mile over open ground to reach the densely wired Wancourt-Feuchy Line. The Division would attack with 168th Brigade on the left and 167 Brigade on the right. 169th Brigade would be in divisional reserve. To allow for the divisional front narrowing to only 350 yards, 168 Brigade would only advance as far as the Hindenburg Line leaving one battalion only of 167 Brigade to carry out the final assault on the Brown Line.

In a preliminary action 1st London Regiment of 167th Brigade tried to capture Neuville mill with attacks on the night of 6/7 April and the evening of the 7th. They were repulsed by heavy enemy machine gun fire. The Division's main infantry assault was launched at 0745, 11 minutes after 14th Division and two hours 15 minutes after Zero Hour. 168 Brigade's lead battalions were 12th London Regiment (The Rangers) on the left and 13th London (Kensingtons) on the right. In support were 14th London (London Scottish) and in reserve 4th London (less one company assigned as moppers up). On their right 167 Brigade's attack would be led by 8th Middlesex Regiment on the left and 3rd London on the right. In support would be 1st London and in reserve 7th Middlesex. The objective of the lead battalions of both Brigades was the capture of the Blue Line after which the support battalions would pass through and attack the Cojeul Switch. Once this was secured 7th Middlesex would pass through and assault the Brown Line.

When the divisional attack was launched at 0745 the lead battalions had mixed fortunes. The Kensingtons met only light opposition as they made their way through the German front line and occupied Moss Trench. The Rangers also had little difficulty with the German front line but were held up by uncut wire in front of Pine Lane, a trench running north from Neuville-Vitasse. They

---

14   TNA WO 95/1896: 7th KRRC, 7th RB War Diaries.

took heavy casualties before a tank arrived and successfully flattened sufficient of the wire to enable a company to get through and take possession of the trench, helped by a second company which found and exploited a small gap in the wire. The other two lead battalions, 8th Middlesex and 3rd London, had to capture the southern part of Neuville-Vitasse before 1st London would pass through. A preliminary operation led by a tank and involving two platoons of 3rd London, completed the unfinished business of the capture of Neuville mill. The Battalion's subsequent progress through Neuville-Vitasse went like clockwork despite some enemy opposition. By contrast 8th Middlesex found themselves involved in hard fighting before they were able to overcome a German strongpoint which had escaped the attention of the artillery. They consequently lost their artillery cover and were delayed in reaching the Blue Line until 1600. This might have led to a delay in 1st London passing through, but the latter had been able to work their way round the hold up and no overall time was lost.

The second phase of 56th Division's attack, the attack on the Cojeul Switch, began at 1210. On their left 14th Division attacked at the same time; on their right 30th Division attacked four minutes later. Well before 56th Division's attack the artillery support had moved up to its planned positions. Of the four tanks which had been assigned to the Division at the start of the battle, the two which had been ordered to bypass Neuville-Vitasse to the north had become casualties, but the two which had passed round the south side of the village were still in action.

Before 7th Middlesex could pass through on their way to attack the Brown Line the Cojeul Switch had to be secured. On the left of the divisional sector the left hand company of the London Scottish managed this with little difficulty. Indeed they were so successful that they passed right through their objective and advanced about 600 yards beyond without however leaving sufficient troops behind to mop up. They had also lost direction and strayed onto 14th Division ground. The Battalion's centre and right hand companies were by contrast held up by the front trench of the Hindenburg Line where they were soon joined by the recalled left hand company. The Battalion was ordered to clear the trenches with the bomb.

Further to the right 1st London Regiment cleared their sector of the Neuville-Vitasse trench but suffered losses in doing so. They were then held up by the front trench of the Hindenburg Line which obliged 7th Middlesex to abandon any thought for the time being of the Brown Line and instead come to 1st London's aid by twice assaulting a Hindenburg Line support trench. But machine gun fire from their right, where the enemy were still in full possession of the Hindenburg Line, not having been dislodged by 30th Division, prevented their making any progress. All along the divisional front the night would be spent in a series of bombing and bayonet attacks. The main objective was the junction of the Cojeul Switch and the Wancourt Line. German resistance was found to be spasmodic and disorganised, but the situation was almost as confused for the attackers. An enemy strongpoint known as The Egg, just south of Lion Lane, proved particularly troublesome. It was garrisoned by enemy machine gunners and snipers and took some time to clear.

To maintain the momentum of the first day of the battle it was important that the unfinished business of that day, the securing of the Brown Line, should be completed as soon as possible on the second day. Third Army HQ accordingly issued orders for the offensive against the Line to be resumed at 0800 by all three of the Army corps. VII Corps HQ had already anticipated these orders in those issued late on the 9th to its four divisions. In response the GOC of 56th Division quickly made it clear that his command would be in no position to assault at 0800. Major General Hull told Corps HQ by telephone that there was little prospect that the night's bomb and bayonet attacks would have ended with the enemy cleared out of the Hindenburg Line before daylight. The assault was accordingly postponed to 1200, even this revised time being conditional on the situation on the 14th and 56th Divisional fronts being cleared up satisfactorily.

During the night orders were issued by 56th Division HQ confirming that responsibility for the capture of the Brown (Wancourt) Line and Nepal Trench would remain with 167 Brigade. 3rd

London were ordered to take the lead with 7th Middlesex and 1st London in support. The 169th Brigade's 9th London Regiment (Queen Victoria's Rifles) would additionally be attached to the 167 for the operation.

By mid-morning on the 10th it was clear that 167 Brigade were in undisputed possession of virtually all of the Cojeul Switch as far south as Lion Lane. The London Scottish on 168 Brigade's left were in contact with 14th Division and had established positions along the Wancourt Line. VII Corps issued further orders that the troops assaulting the Brown Line should, once it was captured, continue their advance to the Green Line, with 56th Division tasked with occupying Hill 90, the high ground northwest of Héninel, the possession of which by the enemy was a persistent source of trouble for 14th Division. Responsibility for carrying out this operation was added to those which had already been given to 167th Brigade. Beginning at midday the Brigade had made steady progress bombing down the Neuville-Vitasse trench and the Cojeul Switch, but efforts to reach the Wancourt Line were held up by the open ground which had to be traversed, especially on the left. The day was one of confusion but there could be no question of clearing Hill 90 or completing the capture of the Wancourt Line between its junction with the Cojeul Switch and 14th Division's sector of it, before the following day.

The early part of 11th April saw 167 Brigade complete the clearance of the Cojeul Switch and the Hindenburg Line as far south as the Cojeul River by bombing. In addition The Cot trench and part of Nepal trench, both east of the Cojeul Switch, had been cleared by similar means. Late in the afternoon 167 Brigade learned they were to be relieved by 169 Brigade, who received orders at 2115 that they were to make good the whole of Hill 90 and push patrols into the village of Héninel. One of 169 Brigade's battalions, the 1/16th County of London (Queen's Westminster Rifles) had already relieved 168 Brigade's London Scottish Battalion. The rest of 168 Brigade would stay put.

The above reliefs did not mean that a divisional withdrawal from the front line area was underway. Although 56th Division were being placed in Corps reserve, this was in anticipation of their making a further advance. In preparation for this, battalion COs were ordered to reconnoitre the ground as far forward as possible themselves and ensure that all company commanders did likewise. The fresh advance got under way at 0515 on the 12th. 169 Brigade led off with 2nd City of London (Royal Fusiliers) and 5th City of London (London Rifle Brigade) bombing along trenches towards Hill 90 from the northeast and south of the hill respectively, where they successfully linked up. At this point the enemy were seen to be withdrawing from Héninel and 2nd City of London quickly pushed a company into the village meeting only slight resistance. Patrols from 5th City of London Regiment and their 41 Brigade neighbours established that Wancourt had also been vacated by the enemy, except for a few snipers; by 1115 posts had been established in the village.

It was initially planned that the advance should soon be continued to the Sensée river but these orders were modified to ones instructing 56th Division to consolidate and send forward strong reconnaissance patrols with a view to resuming the advance the following day. Shortly after midnight on the night of 12th/13th, VII Corps HQ ordered 56th Division to prepare to move on the village of Chérisy in step with the divisions on either flank, taking advantage of the latters' anticipated progress over the high ground in their sectors. However by 1300 it was apparent that 50th Division[15] on the left were held up by machine gun fire from west of Guémappe and 30th Division on the right were making no progress at all. With progress stalled VII Corps issued fresh orders for a general advance on 14 April that would be coordinated with VI Corps. The objective would be the line of the Sensée river. The 169 Brigade were detailed to carry out 56th Division's share of the operation.

The day proved to be a serious disappointment with virtually no progress to record. It demonstrated that the Germans were by no means the beaten enemy that General Allenby had claimed them to be

---

15   The 50th (Northumbrian) and 33rd Divisions were assigned to VII Corps on 11 April and the former were quickly in action.

48 hours earlier. Theirs was the first move of the 14th when, in the early hours of the morning, they blew up the Wancourt tower, that had become, and the ruins of which would continue to be, a focus of bitter contention between the two sides.

The British attack began at 0530. It was immediately subjected to a counterattack, which struck 169 Brigade's exposed left flank, exposed because of a gap of about 500 yards between them and the right of 50th Division. The gap had probably opened up because the latter had lost direction in their advance from the line of the Cojeul river. The counterattack was sufficiently strong to push back the first wave of 169th Brigade's advance. Supporting waves came under heavy enfilade fire which, coupled with their falling behind the protection offered by the creeping barrage, prevented them from making ground. Neither of the flank divisions was any more successful. With the British attack stalled dispositions were put in place to deal with an anticipated further enemy counterattack that did not in the event materialise. HQ VII Corps decided not to resume the attack that day and the opportunity was taken for 168 Brigade to relieve the 169 with 167 moving up in support.

The 15 April was spent in consolidation. On the following day the London Scottish attempted to push the line forward into some German practice trenches, but found them to be too shallow and waterlogged to be of use. In the evening a heavy German barrage appeared to indicate an imminent German attack that again did not materialise. A German attack that same evening did succeed in wresting possession of Wancourt tower from 50th Division. It was retaken the next day during which notification was received that no further offensive operations would be undertaken before 22 April. Between 18 and 20 April, 56th Division were relieved by 30th Division. During their 12 days in the line the Division had suffered casualties totalling 94 officers and 2,048 men.[16]

Although 30th Division relieved the 56th between 18 and 20 April, it was on the latter's right in the early days of the battle. The 30th Division were raised as part of the fifth tranche of the KNA. Originally the divisions in this tranche were numbered 37 to 42 but were renumbered when the KNA fourth tranche was broken up, so that the 37th became the 30th. The future Secretary of State for War and pillar of Lancastrian society, the Earl of Derby, was the driving force behind the recruiting campaign that resulted in the 30th Division. Hence the number of Liverpool and Manchester Pals battalions in the Division. By the time of the Battles of Arras its 91 Brigade had been exchanged with 7th Division 21 Brigade as part of the War Office's scheme to instil Regular Army experience into New Army divisions. Under the command of Major General John Shea, the 30th arrived on the Western Front in November 1915. Their first major action was on the first day of the Battle of the Somme when, as part of XIII Corps, they captured the village of Montauban, one of the very few British successes on that grim day. They continued to play a part in the Somme campaign, failing in their attempts to capture Trônes Wood, and at the Battle of the Transloy Ridges. By late 1916 the Division were in the Third Army where they would remain throughout the Battle of Arras.

The Division would initially attack with two brigades in line, 21 on the left and 89 on the right. Their attacks would not be launched simultaneously. 21 Brigade's advance would be timed so that the assaulting battalions would enter the Hindenburg Line at 1255, with the proviso that 56th Division on their left had completed the capture of Neuville-Vitasse. The 89 would attack at 1615 at the same time as 64 Brigade of 21st Division on their right. Both brigades would attack on a two battalion front. The 21 led with 18th King's (Liverpool) Regiment (King's) on the left and 2nd Wiltshire Regiment (Wilts) on the right. The 19th Manchester Regiment (Manchesters) were in support and carrying, and 2nd The Yorkshire Regiment (Green Howards), much depleted by previous operations, provided two lines of moppers up. The 89 led with 20th King's on the left and 19th King's on the right with 2nd Bedfordshire Regiment (Bedfords) in support and 17th King's providing carrying parties and moppers up.

The two assaulting battalions of 21 Brigade assembled in trenches averaging 2,000 yards from

---

16   TNA WO 95/2933: 56th Division War Diary.

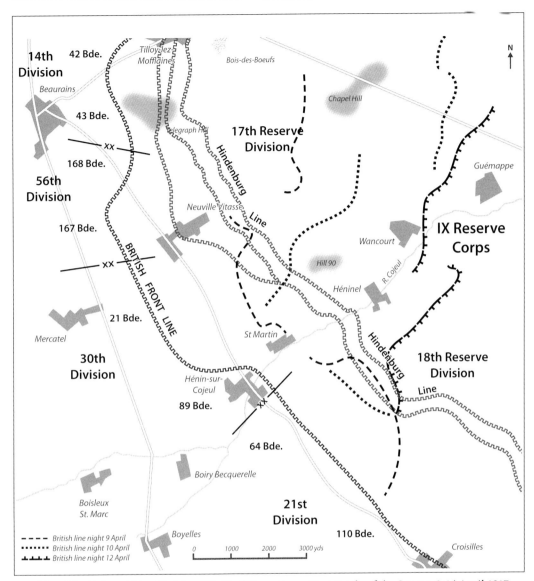

14th, 56th, 30th and 21st Divisions' Field of Operations, First Battle of the Scarpe, 9-14 April 1917.

the German front line. In between the two front lines were two sunken roads between Neuville-Vitasse and respectively Hénin and St-Martin-sur-Cojeul. At a mill about half way along the first of these roads, was a German machine gun post and at least 60 infantry. The Brigade had been ordered to eliminate this potential threat to the success of the main assault during the night of 8/9 April. The raid was to be synchronised with one by 89 Brigade on St-Martin-sur-Cojeul and a second mill. At 0145 three officers and 100 men of 2nd Wilts crawled forward. Tragically many of them got too close to the German position and were hit by their own supporting artillery barrage, taking serious casualties amounting to a third of their number. The survivors withdrew without achieving their objective. It was subsequently discovered from prisoners that the Germans had doubled the size of their presence in the machine gun post in anticipation of an attack.

Despite their overnight losses, 2nd Wilts were still one of the lead battalions for the main advance, which began at 1138 when news was received from 56th Division that they had completed the capture of the Blue Line in their sector. The leading waves of the two battalions were subjected to an enemy artillery barrage and the close attention of machine guns and snipers from the sunken roads, despite which they made satisfactory progress. The first sunken road was successfully crossed with the enemy retiring precipitately before the British advance. Many of them were caught by the British barrage as they tried to reach the shelter of the second sunken road. Between the two roads the attacking battalions came under heavy machine gun fire from their left and right and began taking serious casualties. They nevertheless managed to cross the second road, but then came under an exceptionally heavy barrage as they moved on the German front line which, they quickly realised, was still heavily protected by largely intact wire. The assaulting battalions no longer had sufficient strength to overcome this last formidable obstacle. A small bombing party of 18th King's tried to enter the German trenches on the left but were all killed, except for the officer, while trying to get through the German wire. The remnants of the two battalions not pinned down in shell holes in front of the German wire were consequently ordered back to the second sunken road (the Neuville-Vitasse – St. Martin road), where they dug in. They were joined there by the support battalion, 19th Manchesters, who likewise dug in to await further orders. When received, these ordered them to push forward a strong bombing party by way of Natal trench to support the right flank of 2nd Wilts who were believed to have penetrated the German front system. The orders were countermanded when reconnaissance confirmed, if further confirmation were needed, that the German wire was entirely uncut. Any attack before the wire had been dealt with would have been tantamount to suicide.

Following a report by the CO of the Manchesters to the Brigade Commander, received at around 1800, the decision not to attempt anything more ambitious than a bombing raid until the wire had been dealt with was confirmed. The first essential was for the Brigade to maintain their hold on the second sunken road despite the heavy losses of the two assault battalions which, in the case of the Wilts, amounted to 14 officers and 328 ORs, these in addition to those suffered in the earlier attack on the mill. It was decided that the Manchesters should send strong bombing parties to the left through 167 Brigade's sector. There, with the readily given approval of that Brigade's Commander, they would bomb southwards from Lion Lane, with appropriate artillery support. At 1940, twenty minutes after the orders for this operation were dispatched, the relief of 21 Brigade by 90 Brigade began. It was completed without incident during the course of the night. The Manchesters nevertheless sought to carry out their bombing raids but discovered that Lion Lane was not in British hands and was indeed being shelled intermittently by friendly artillery. Their first task therefore became to clear and consolidate Lion Lane; this was successfully achieved in an attack launched at 0230. Further progress was impossible because of the danger from friendly artillery fire. When this slackened at around 0500, a further raid was launched from Neuville-Vitasse trench. It captured a dugout and some prisoners. The bombing parties then withdrew and rejoined their battalion.[17]

Although 89 Brigade, on 21 Brigade's right, were not scheduled to launch their attack until the late afternoon of the 9th, they had been in position to do so since midday the previous day. The assaulting battalions' initial objective would be a 1,300 yard long sector of the Cojeul Switch immediately southeast of the junction of the switch with the German Wancourt-Feuchy line. Its pivotal position for the enemy meant that it was very likely to be strongly defended. The two lines of trenches, 250 to 300 yards apart, were heavily protected with wire, the destruction of which had been a priority target of the preliminary artillery bombardment. Because of the difficulty of getting short range direct observation of the effects of the bombardment there was understandable anxiety that it might not have been sufficiently effective. As the Brigade Commander's concern was shared by the commanders of the Field Artillery Groups supporting the Brigade the Divisional HQ were urged to do everything feasible to cut the wire using heavy artillery. By midday on the 9th the infantry

17   TNA WO 95/2327: 21st Brigade War Diary.

commanders were more confident that the state of the wire was manageable.

In order for the two assaulting battalions to have a good chance of achieving their objectives, the village of St-Martin-sur-Cojeul would have to be captured and neutralised beforehand. The task, the timing of which was synchronised with 21 Brigade's attack on the German strong point already described, was given to 2nd Bedfords. The Battalion attacked, with six platoons and two machine guns, under a creeping barrage at 0130 on the 9th. The attackers quickly established themselves on the edge of the village where they left three platoons to clear up the relatively light opposition that had been encountered. A simultaneous attempt by a strong patrol of 20th King's to eliminate a German strong point based in a mill midway between Neuville-Vitasse and Hénin-sur-Cojeul was thwarted by the unexpected strength and alertness of the enemy post.

The assaulting battalions for the first day's main attack, 20th and 19th King's, on left and right respectively, began their approach at about 1330 (Zero plus eight hours). As they advanced it became clear that 21 Brigade had been held up and 89 Brigade soon came under hostile artillery fire which inflicted 40 casualties in one company alone of 20th King's. Enemy machine guns, mainly located in a strongpoint northeast of St-Martin-sur-Cojeul known as The Cot, joined in as the attackers got closer to the enemy front line. Undeterred, they reached the enemy wire, which was found to have been practically untouched by the British artillery bombardments. It effectively prevented any possibility of reaching the enemy front trench and forced the attackers to begin digging in an average of 200 yards short of it. It was some time before the exact situation of the assaulting battalions became clear to Brigade HQ. It was eventually realised there that the German front line had not been reached, let alone captured, and that a gap of 400 yards had opened up between the right of 21 Brigade and the left of 20th King's, leaving the latter's flank exposed. A company of 17th King's was sent up to cover the gap. Before another bombardment of the enemy front line and protecting wire could take place, the troops dug in close to it had to be ordered back to positions where they would be less vulnerable to their own artillery. The night was passed in these new positions.

In the late morning of 10 April patrols of 19th and 20th King's and 2nd Bedfords were ordered out to try to ascertain what effect the still ongoing artillery bombardment was having on the German wire. 19th King's spotted two partial gaps in the wire opposite them, one on either side of the Cojeul River, but the other two battalions found no evidence of gaps. Nevertheless 2nd Bedfords advanced towards the German trenches at 1500. They came under heavy machine gun and sniper fire, which, with the lack of exploitable gaps in the enemy wire, forced them to withdraw. Apart from patrols that again came under heavy machine gun and sniper fire when they were spotted, no further offensive operations were undertaken that day.

At Zero Hour, 0546, on the 11th, two companies of 2nd Bedfords, one on each side of the river, moved off with the aim of passing through the German wire at the gaps that had been spotted the previous day. The northern thrust would be followed up by two companies of 20th King's who would enter the Cojeul Switch and bomb down it to the river. The remaining two companies of the 2nd Bedfords would then pass through, one on each side of the river, and attempt to seize Héninel village. The operation would receive full artillery support and be synchronised with an attack by 21st Division on the right, but the offer of two tanks to the Brigade came too late for them to be integrated into the artillery plan. They would instead assist 90 Brigade who would be bombing down the Cojeul Switch from the divisional junction with 56th Division to the Brigade junction with the 89.

From the start things did not go well. Heavy enfilade machine gun fire directed at the gaps in the wire on both sides of the river that 2nd Bedfords were seeking to exploit pinned the two assaulting companies down. Their situation was not helped by the battalion on their right also being held up and by the withdrawal of 21st Division within an hour of the attack starting, leaving the Bedfords' flank exposed. Their orders were hastily changed; the plan to seize Héninel was abandoned but they were still to get into the German trench system and consolidate. The German trenches would be seized by reinforcing the bombing attack on them from the north with two companies of 20th King's and the two tanks. These orders were based on the false assumption that some men of 20th King's were already in the German trenches. In fact, they, like the Bedfords, were pinned down by heavy machine gun fire emanating from a source that neither they nor the tanks could pinpoint. Having made five separate attempts to get into the German trenches, the CO of 20th King's at around 1000 ordered his 'dead beat' men to withdraw to their start line.

For the next four hours 89 Brigade's situation remained unchanged. At that point there were signs that the Germans might be withdrawing, raising the possibility of 2nd Bedfords being free to advance and occupy the high ground. Before this could be put to the test however they, along with the rest of 89 Brigade, were relieved by 33rd Division 19 Brigade.[18]

The 90 Brigade had begun the battle in divisional reserve but, as has been noted, they relieved 21st Brigade in the front line during the course of the night of 9/10 April. They were expecting to attack the following morning but the attack was cancelled when the enemy withdrew voluntarily. On the following day they were under orders to follow up any forward movement resulting from an attack on the Hindenburg Line by 89 Brigade and 21st Division. But the attack failed. The Brigade did, however, become involved in the fighting that morning, when 18th Manchesters entered the Hindenburg Line and Panther Lane to clear the trench system of enemy as far as the Cojeul River. The operation was successfully completed by darkness in cooperation with 56th Division troops. One company of 16th Manchesters also became engaged in trench clearing operations that morning when they were ordered to bomb down the Hindenburg Line from northwest of Natal trench to The Cot strongpoint on the southeast side of the same trench. In conjunction with 1st/9th Londons and 7th Middlesex The Cot was fully secured by 1400. During the night, 18th Manchesters, under the temporary command of 89 Brigade, continued their task of clearing the enemy trench system. By dawn on the 12th, they had cleared it of enemy from the Cojeul River to the High Ground situated about half way between Hénin-sur Cojeul and Fontaine-lès-Croisilles.[19] That same afternoon the Brigade were relieved by 98 Brigade and made their way by stages to billets in the rear.

The 21st Division were situated on the extreme right of VII Corps and consequently of the Third Army. The Division was established as part of the third tranche of the KNA in September 1914. The three brigades, 62, 63 and 64, contained an eclectic mix of battalions mainly from the northeast, Yorkshire and Lincolnshire, but also one battalion each from the Somerset Light Infantry and the Middlesex Regiment. When 63 Brigade moved to 37th Division in July 1916 in a swap with 110 Brigade the last two-named battalions departed. The 110 brought four battalions of the Leicestershire Regiment into the Division giving it a more homogeneous Northern and East Midlands character.

The Division suffered a horrendous baptism of fire. It began its move to the Western Front on 2 September 1915 and completed its concentration a few miles from Calais on the 13th. It was placed in XI Corps, which was to form the reserve for the Battle of Loos. A series of lengthy forced marches had to be undertaken to enable it to get somewhere near the battlefield in time. In the event, when it was committed to the battle on the second day, it and the other two divisions of XI Corps, were too late to exploit the opportunity that had probably been there on the first day. Exhausted, hungry and ill-briefed, as well as inexperienced, the Division was sent into action and hardly surprisingly suffered over 3,800 casualties with virtually nothing to show for its losses.

The Division's next major engagement was on the opening day of the Battle of the Somme. By now it was in XV Corps and under a new Commander, Major General David Campbell.[20] Even though its new Corps had overall a rather better first day than most, 21st Division suffered

18   TNA WO 95/2332: 89th Brigade War Diary.
19   TNA WO 95/2339: 16th, 17th, 18th Manchesters War Diaries.
20   A distinguished cavalry officer, General Campbell had achieved early fame by winning the 1896 Grand National as an amateur. His nickname was, forever after, the name of his winning horse, Soarer. He would remain in command of 21st Division for the rest of the war.

even more badly than it had at Loos, recording 4,256 casualties. One of its battalions, 10th West Yorkshire Regiment (West Yorks), suffered the worst losses of all the battalions engaged on that day. Only one officer and 40 Other Ranks emerged unscathed, a loss rate of over 90 percent.[21] Despite its mauling at the outset of the Somme campaign, the Division remained in the thick of the fighting almost throughout, participating in the Battles of Bazentin Ridge, Flers-Courcelette, Morval and Le Transloy. The Division was transferred to First Army (I Corps) towards the end of the Somme campaign and from there to Third Army at the beginning of April 1917 as VII Corps was enlarged in preparation for Arras.

On 9 April the 21st Division were holding 4,500 yards of front running from the River Sensée at Croisilles northwestwards to the River Cojeul at Hénin-sur-Cojeul. They attacked however on a front of only 2,700 yards, using three battalions of 64 Brigade in line. The other front line Brigade, 110, stood fast in its positions on the Division's right. The 64 Brigade's assaulting battalions were, from left to right, 9th KOYLI, 15th DLI and 1st East Yorkshire Regiment (East Yorks). The 10th KOYLI were in support. The assaulting battalions faced the exceedingly dangerous challenge of advancing across 1,000 yards of rising and open ground before they reached the enemy's wire that they well knew remained relatively intact despite the attentions of the artillery. The enemy wire was backed by concrete machine gun emplacements, numerous protected sniper posts and very strongly built dugouts. In the circumstances it was important that the protective creeping barrage should be highly effective and elaborate plans had been drawn up involving not only the divisional artillery but also the guns of 58th Division and a Heavy Artillery Group.

It was not certain until the last minute that the advance would take place as it was dependent on success on the VI Corps front. With this achieved, the assault battalions began their advance at 1554. The weakness of the German defensive barrage coupled with the effectiveness of the British barrage and the fire of a machine gun section, which had been positioned under cover of darkness where its enfilade fire could keep the enemy garrison's heads down, enabled most of the attackers to reach the enemy wire in good order and with few casualties. On the left 9th KOYLI, who had begun to take casualties in the last 150 yards before reaching the wire, found some gaps in the first section of the double belt of wire, through which they were able to pass without undue difficulty, only to be severely checked by the second section, which lay untouched in front of the first objective. The Battalion incurred heavy losses from machine gun and rifle fire in their efforts to find ways through with the aid of wire cutters. The survivors took what shelter there was in shell holes. There they would have to stay until the cover of darkness might offer the opportunity to regroup and reorganise. The Battalion's second wave, unaware of the difficulties that the first wave had run into, and with all their officers casualties, advanced with considerable dash, but were soon pinned down.[22]

The centre and right battalions, confronted with largely unbroken wire, called down fire from their accompanying Stokes mortars. This enabled them to get through both belts of enemy wire and partially capture the enemy front trench, about 1,000 yards in all. 15th DLI's efforts to clear the enemy trench northwards by bombing were however unsuccessful. The next phase of the attack called for the supporting companies of the lead battalions, supplemented by one company each from the Brigade reserve battalion, 10th KOYLI, to pass through and assault the enemy second trench. When they attempted this they found the wire protecting their objective to be impenetrable. They were forced to fall back to the first trench. Subsequent German counterattacks, although pressed very hard, especially against the right flank of 1st East Yorks, were effectively beaten off. The day ended with 21st Division in possession of roughly two thirds of the front trench of the Hindenburg Line in their sector, a not inconsiderable achievement.[23]

21   Don Farr, *The Silent General*, pp. 88-9.
22   TNA WO 95/2162: 9th,10th KOYLI War Diaries.
23   OH 1917 ,Vol 1, pp. 204-6.

By contrast, the following day was one of frustration for 21st Division. Along with 30th Division they were given orders to support if possible 56th Division in their attempt to secure the high ground beyond the Cojeul river. Again the timing of 21st Division's participation would depend on developments north of them, in particular completion of the capture of the Wancourt-Feuchy Line. In the event fighting for this took up the whole day. While this was going on 64 Brigade found themselves having to repulse a series of bombing attacks emanating from the German second line. The Brigade's right hand Battalion, 1st East Yorks, came under particular pressure from frontal attacks as well as on their exposed right flank, which forced them out of the front trench of the Hindenburg Line and back about 200 yards, where they rallied and stood fast. The rest of the Brigade had to retire to conform with the new positions of the East Yorks. Two companies of 10th KOYLI were under orders to counterattack promptly in the circumstances described above, but the Battalion CO feared that they might fall victims to their own artillery and decided to wait until the artillery had been warned. The time taken for this to happen was however judged to be too long to catch the enemy still disorganised after their recapture of the trench. General Campbell decided to pass the task to the fresh 62 Brigade who were already under orders to relieve the 64.[24][25]

Despite the ongoing efforts of the artillery to cut the wire protecting the Hindenburg Line, patrols during the night of 10/11 from the two battalions of 62 Brigade that had been ordered to attack that morning, found that it remained a most formidable obstacle. The 1st Lincolnshire Regt (Lincolns) on the right found only three cut lanes in their sector. On their left 10th Green Howards were even worse placed, with only one entirely and one partially cut lanes in front of them. Nevertheless at 0548, only five hours after completing the relief of 64 Brigade and 12 minutes before Zero, the two battalions advanced in excellent order and with great steadiness, following their barrage up to the enemy wire. Essentially their objective was to recover the ground from which 64 Brigade had been forced to withdraw. A second objective would be to use patrols to occupy the German second line if it were found to be only lightly held. On reaching the enemy wire they found the few cut lanes available to be completely dominated by enemy machine guns largely located in concrete emplacements with narrow firing slits in the front line, where they were almost immune from any countermeasures available to the attackers, such as rifle grenades. In addition snipers were active from the flanks and from the densest portions of the enemy wire. Despite gallant efforts to overcome the obstacles confronting them, neither battalion could make any effective progress and the survivors were pinned down. They were eventually ordered to withdraw to enable the heavy artillery to conduct a further bombardment of the wire. By dusk the survivors were back in their starting positions and contemplating the total failure of their attack and its heavy cost in casualties.[26] The very high proportion of NCOs among these reflected the determination with which they had led their sections forward on what had clearly been an impossible task.[27] The Lincolns and Green Howards were relieved that evening by 12th and 13th Northumberland Fusiliers (Northumberlands) respectively.

On the 12th 21st Division still faced the challenge of capturing the enemy Green Line. Arrangements were accordingly made to renew the attack that day. It proved to be unnecessary, as a bombing attack by 18th Manchesters of 30th Division had forced the Germans to abandon the 1,000 yards of the Hindenburg Line which would have been 21st Division's objective. The 62 Brigade were consequently able to occupy the Line as far south as a point equidistant between Hénin-sur-Cojeul and Fontaine-lès-Croisilles. On the night of 12/13, 12th Northumberlands bombed their way a further 2-300 yards along the Line.

On the evening of 12th orders were distributed for a further attack by 21st Division, in cooperation with 56th Division on the left. The objective would be to advance in a southeasterly direction to a line

24   Ibid p. 247
25   TNA WO 95/2159: 64th Brigade War Diary.
26   OH, op. cit., p. 260.
27   TNA WO 95/2154: 1st Lincolns War Diary.

running from a point about a mile southwest of Fontaine-lès-Croisilles round the eastern edge of the village to the eastern and northeastern edges of Fontaine Wood. The task was assigned to 62 Brigade with two companies of 6th Leicestershire Regiment (Leicesters) from 110 Brigade attached. At Zero, 0955 on the 13th the attack began, ushering in two unproductive days. The 56th Division on the left made no forward movement and the attacks northeast of the Hindenburg Line made little progress. The attack along the Hindenburg Line did however make some progress. The 6th Leicesters were on the right, southwest of the Line, and 12th Northumberlands on the left. There were supposed to be two tanks in support. One was completely immobilised, the other also had mechanical problems but managed to fire off 400 rounds before retiring. At Zero the two attacking battalions advanced, but heavy enemy machine gun fire and an accurate and strong artillery barrage prevented any movement by most of the attackers. Bombing squads from the Northumberlands did manage to drive the enemy a certain distance along the Hindenburg Line's front and support line trenches . At midday the order was received to break off the attack except for the effort to make ground with the bombing operations along the Hindenburg Line. By 1600 the Northumberlands had reached a point in both the front and support lines about a mile due west of Fontaine village. Here they were held up by a machine gun in a concrete emplacement which not even a Stokes mortar could neutralise. By this time the men were much fatigued by 'deep pudding mud' filling the trenches. The bombing operations were consequently suspended.[28]

During the night of 13th/14th 62 Brigade were relieved by 33rd Division 19 Brigade. This Brigade resumed the attack at 0530 on the 14th but made little progress. The attack was broken off in the early afternoon.

On the 15th 21st Division's relief by 33rd Division was completed.

By the end of 11 April it had become apparent to Third Army HQ that attempts to exploit on a grand scale the great successes achieved on the first day of the battle would have to be replaced by a more measured approach to continuing the advance in the light of the increasingly stubborn defence of the enemy and the difficulties of moving across the churned up battlefield by men, horses, guns and tanks. Two fresh divisions each were assigned to the two corps south of the River Scarpe so that some at least of the tired troops of the initial assaulting divisions could be relieved. In VII Corps, 50th (Northumbrian) Division relieved the 14th, and 33rd Division the 30th. As the 30th had, after their capture of the 1,000 yards of the Hindenburg Line, been squeezed out of contact with the enemy by the divisions on either side, the 33rd Division became Corps reserve. The relieved divisions replaced their successors in XVIII Corps.

---

28   TNA WO 95/2152: 62nd Brigade War Diary.

5

VI Corps

The Commander of VI Corps was Lieutenant General Sir James Haldane, a very competent professional soldier. After an adventurous South African War he had begun the Great War as a Brigade Commander. He was soon promoted to the command of 3rd Division and in August 1916 took over VI Corps where he remained for the rest of the war. Living an austere life himself, he achieved some notoriety for banning the issue of rum in units under his command.[1]

The Corps sector of the front was manned from right to left by the 3rd, 12th (Eastern) and 15th (Scottish) Divisions, with 37th Division initially in reserve. The Brigades which would be involved early on in the battle began moving up to their frontline positions on 5 April. Within 24 hours they were mounting trench raids which proved generally abortive in the face of heavy enemy machine gun and artillery fire and some uncut wire.

The situation facing the Corps was more straightforward than that confronting VII Corps. Whereas the latter had to adjust to a wholesale voluntary enemy withdrawal in their sector, only a few hundred yards on the right of VI Corps sector had been affected, approximately half of the stretch of front facing 3rd Division. This had been confirmed by the Corps' only productive trench raid, which had found the enemy trenches it had entered to be empty.[2] The Corps was therefore largely able to use its well-established trenches as the jumping off point for its initial assault. Its orders were equally straightforward, to capture the enemy's Wancourt-Feuchy Line (the Brown Line) carrying the Black and Blue Lines on the way. This entailed an advance of about 3,500 yards for each of the three attacking divisions as the German line ran broadly parallel to that of VI Corps. Once the Wancourt-Feuchy Line had been secured the 37th Division would pass through to capture the Green line, which in this area constituted the Monchy spur and Guémappe village.

The 3rd Division had arrived in France in mid-August 1914 as one of the original four infantry divisions of the BEF. It was to remain on the Western Front right through to the Armistice and took part in most of that theatre's major engagements. By early 1917 its regular army composition had been diluted by the loss of its 7 Brigade, in exchange for the KNA 25th Division 76 Brigade, and the arrival of other non-regular battalions in its 8 and 9 Brigades. The Division was commanded by Major General C.J. Deverell, who by the mid-1930s would become Field Marshal Sir C.J. Deverell and Chief of the Imperial General Staff.

The Division had its first sight and taste of the sector of the front from which it would be assaulting, on 12 February. At Zero Hour on 9 April it was occupying a frontage of approximately half a mile which would about double in breadth by the time it had achieved its objectives. The initial assault would be undertaken by a single battalion, 1st Gordon Highlanders (Gordons) of 76 Brigade, assisted by B Company of 8th King's Own (Royal Lancaster Regiment) (King's Own)), even though this Company had been caught by an enemy barrage while being issued with bombs, and had suffered 30 casualties.[3] The attackers were to capture the first four German lines. Their task was slightly eased by the fact that from the point where the Germans had begun their withdrawal and abandoned their

---

1   John Bourne, *Who's Who in World War One*, p. 119.
2   TNA WO 95/770: VI Corps War Diary.
3   TNA WO 95/1436: 8th King's Own (Royal Lancasters) War Diary.

front trench (about half way along 1st Gordons' frontage) they had made little attempt to man their second, third and fourth lines of trenches. This confirmed information provided by an enemy prisoner that only rearguards would offer the attackers any resistance until the Brown Line was reached. This line would be found to be held in strength. Preceded by hurricane bombardments by trench mortars and machine guns, and with the enemy wire well cut on their line of advance, the Gordons had little difficulty in completing the capture of the four German lines on schedule, at the relatively light cost of 60 casualties. Passing through, 10th Royal Welsh Fusiliers (RWF) had equally little problem in taking their objectives of Devil's Wood, just northeast of Tilloy-lès-Mofflaines, and the enemy's Black Line, which in this area followed the eastern edge of the wood. Opposition was negligible or non-existent as the enemy rearguards had either been killed by the preliminary barrages or had beaten a hasty retreat.[4]

It was now the turn of 9 Brigade which had been given the task of capturing the enemy Blue Line. In their sector this included the village of Tilloy-lès-Mofflaines from where it ran down the eastern side of The Harp redoubt. It will be recalled that 14th (Light) Division of VII Corps had been made responsible for the capture of the southern half of the Harp. The 9 Brigade would deal with its northern half. With scarcely any pause following the successful completion of 76 Brigade's tasks, 9 Brigade passed through at 0742, 12 minutes behind schedule. Four of its five battalions (the 76 Brigade's 2nd Suffolk Regiment (Suffolks) had been temporarily attached) would be involved from the outset. The two on the Brigade's right, 4th Royal Fusiliers (RF) and the Suffolks, had furthest to travel and ostensibly the hardest tasks. The 4th RF were ordered to take String trench within The Harp and the sunken road to its east whereupon the Suffolks were to pass through and take the eastern side of the redoubt, thus securing the Blue Line. The two battalions on the Brigade's left, 12th West Yorks and 13th King's, would secure the enemy Blue Line having, with the aid of tanks, taken possession of Tilloy on their way.

The Brigade's intervention met with almost total success. The RF, the Suffolks and the West Yorks secured their objectives on schedule. Less fortunate were the King's, on the Brigade's extreme left. They began their advance on a two company front behind a creeping barrage at 0746. Unlike the right hand company, which took Harfleur Trench with ease, the left hand company immediately began to take casualties from shelling and machine gun fire, the latter emanating from the other side of the Arras-Cambrai road in 12th Division's sector. The Battalion nevertheless made progress except for the company on the left which was initially held up for a time by a trench covering the approaches to Tilloy. Once this had been successfully dealt with, they were further delayed by the wood in the grounds of Tilloy Château in the centre of the village, and the Quarry just beyond the village's eastern limits. But with some assistance from 12th West Yorks and 1st Northumberlands (also 9 Brigade) and by placing a Lewis gun on the roof of the Château, they were able to drive the enemy back and move on. The Lewis gun was particularly effective in dealing with enemy snipers, the main cause of the Battalion's losses. It also broke up attempts by German bombers to mount counterattacks. The original plan had envisaged a company of 10 tanks helping 13th King's efforts to deal with these obstacles. Regretfully however the machines nearly all became bogged down on their way up from Arras and none reached the scene until the infantry had largely completed the operation. One did however assist in securing Tilloy. In contrast, another tank company had proved very helpful in the capture of The Harp, although even here only one tank made it through to the eastern side of the redoubt.

It was now the turn of 8 Brigade. Just before noon their two leading battalions, 2nd Royal Scots (R Scots) and 7th KSLI passed through 9 Brigade. Its two remaining battalions, the 8th East Yorks and 1st Royal Scots Fusiliers (RSF) were respectively in support and reserve. The two leading battalions were subjected to heavy shelling prior to coming level with Tilloy. They also suffered some

---

4   TNA WO 95/1433: 13th King's (Liverpool) Regiment War Diary.

casualties from machine guns and sniping from the village despite which, declining to be drawn into the fire fights still going on there, they continued to work their way round it. The realisation that these fresh battalions were on their way to surrounding and cutting them off seemed to be too much for the remaining enemy in Tilloy; some threw down their arms in surrender, others retired hastily to the Quarry and the Bois des Boeufs. There was to be no respite for them there however as the KSLI attacked and captured the Quarry that had given 13th King's such trouble, and also the Bois des Boeufs. It was not until the R Scots and KSLI, experiencing growing difficulty with uncut wire and increasing enemy fire, had crossed a sunken road and got to within 600 yards of the Wancourt-Feuchy Line that their progress was finally halted by heavy enfilade machine gun fire, largely from the direction of Feuchy Chapel redoubt but with some from the sunken road at Wancourt. They were forced to go to ground with little immediate prospect of resuming their advance.

A fresh attack was ordered for 1900 after a lengthy bombardment which would end 15 minutes earlier. Two battalions of 76 Brigade, 1st Gordons and 8th King's Own, the latter making what would have been, for three of the Battalion's companies, their first entry into the battle, were ordered to mount it. Unfortunately the King's Own did not receive their orders to advance until 25 minutes before Zero, when they were still well over a mile back from where they needed to be. Consequently, only the Gordons passed through 8th Brigade and attacked on schedule. After some initial progress they too were pinned down by machine gun fire from Feuchy Chapel and their right flank, which the artillery bombardment had failed to deal with, and were forced back to the Neuville-Vitasse – Feuchy Chapel road, where they dug in.[5]

At 2050 divisional orders were issued calling for a resumption of the attacks on the Wancourt-Feuchy Line the next morning, the 10th. During the night, the Gordons and 8th King's Own were withdrawn and the 8th East Yorks, 2nd R Scots and 7th KSLI dug in 600 yards west of the enemy line. They had been joined by the 1st RSF who entered the newly dug line between the R Scots and the KSLI. Originally scheduled for 0815 the attack was postponed to 1200 in order to synchronise with actions by VII Corps on the right and 12th Division on the left. Following a lengthy artillery bombardment which lifted at 1145 the four battalions of 8 Brigade attacked, with covering fire from their Brigade Machine Gun Company and erratic artillery support which had made no impression on the undamaged German wire. Their assault was nevertheless completely successful and the Wancourt-Feuchy Line was taken by 1230 with only light casualties. The captured position was consolidated and Lewis gun patrols were pushed forward to command the valley leading towards Guémappe.[6]

Shortly after midnight during the night of 10/11 April, 76 Brigade were ordered to take over the line in front of Guémappe and mount an attack to capture the village starting at 0500, later postponed to 0700. The 8 Brigade were placed on standby to offer support if required. The attack went in on schedule with 2nd Suffolks (who had returned to 76 Brigade late on 9 April) on the right and 8th King's Own on the left. The 1st Gordons and 10th RWF were in support. The attack was quickly brought to a standstill near a sunken road about 500 yards from the village by heavy machine gun fire from the high ground north and south of it, which hit the attackers as they moved over the crest of a hill into full view of the enemy. The attack was renewed at 1430 by the two battalions originally in support, with 2nd Suffolks now in support. It failed for the same reason as the earlier effort. The Brigade dug in and consolidated 500 yards west of the sunken road. There they remained throughout the following day (the 12th). Any attempt on their part to advance would have been doomed to failure in the light of the failure of the divisions on either side to move forward during the course of the day.

On the following day the resumption of the attack was ordered, this time with 9 Brigade assaulting Guémappe once attacks by VII Corps on the high ground southeast of Guémappe and by 29th Division on the high ground to the village's north had achieved their objectives. At 1311,

5   OH 1917, Volume I, pp. 216-7.
6   TNA WO 95/1421: 7th King's Staffordshire Light Infantry War Diary.

before Zero Hour, 29th Division indicated that their attack was being postponed which in turn put 9 Brigade's action on hold. But 50th Division of VII Corps still attacked, took the high ground east of Wancourt tower and were keen to advance further. They were, however, unable to do so until VI Corps had taken Guémappe. They accordingly proposed a joint operation with 9 Brigade to start at 1900. Their plan, involving a sophisticated artillery programme, was agreed by VI Corps, and, as a result, 9 Brigade began to advance at 1844 with 1st Northumberlands on the right and 12th West Yorks on the left. Despite the attention of some heavy artillery fire, the two battalions got 200 yards beyond the sunken road before being held up by heavy machine gun fire from the slopes surrounding the village. To this point there had been no sign of the 50th Division's attack, nor of any covering fire from 29th Division, and they were forced back to the sunken road. (It later emerged that 29th Division had had no idea that 9 Brigade were in fact attacking.) During the night they and the rest of 3rd Division were relieved by 29th Division and marched back to Arras where they arrived at 0800 the following morning in a thoroughly exhausted state.[7]

Since the start of the Battle 3rd Division had suffered 2,767 casualties of which 31 officers and 390 ORs had been killed.[8]

On 3rd Division's left were 12th (Eastern) Division. They were one of the first six divisions that made up the first tranche of the Kitchener New Army (informally known as 'The First Hundred Thousand'). As their name indicates their infantry battalions bore the names of regiments largely based in East Anglia and Southeast England. By the end of May 1915, the Division found themselves in France, one of the first KNA units to be dispatched abroad. They first saw serious action in the middle and later stages of the Battle of Loos and remained in the area until April 1916. By then they had been commanded for about six months by Major General A.B. Scott. He replaced the Division's original Commander, Major General F. D. V. (Freddie) Wing, who was one of three divisional commanders killed during the Battle of Loos. General Scott would remain in command of the Division through the Battle of Arras and until the last months of the war.

The Division's next major campaign was the Somme. Although not closely involved on the tragic first day of that battle they were soon handed the unenviable task of capturing the fortified village of Ovillers. Despite three frontal assaults they never achieved this and the village only fell on 16 July when it was effectively surrounded. The Division's seven days opposite Ovillers and two subsequent spells of intense fighting in the Somme campaign resulted in casualties totalling nearly 11,000. With the need to replace these and the earlier losses at Loos the Division had, by the time of Arras, ceased to be the all-volunteer formation they had originally been, and instead contained many conscripts. The makeup of their personnel may have changed but their notable fighting spirit remained intact. The Division moved from Fourth to Third Army in November 1916.

In contrast to the usual experience of units preparing to assault, 12th Division had found themselves very well sheltered from any enemy artillery searching out assembly areas by their use of the caves and tunnels under, and leading out to the front line from, Arras. In his subsequent report on his Brigade's operations during the First Battle of the Scarpe, Brigadier General A.B.E. Cator, pointed out that not a single man had been lost by any of his battalions in the dugouts and caves during the bombardment prior to the battle, which he believed to be a record for any battle in the war. An additional benefit was that the men of the assaulting battalions started out both 'morally and physically fresh'.[9]

The Division's first tasks were to capture the enemy's Black, Blue and Brown Lines. They would attack initially on a two brigade front with 37 on the right and 36 on the left, charged with capturing the first two lines after which 35 Brigade, initially in reserve, would pass through and attack the

7   TNA WO 95/1417: 8 Brigade War Diary; WO 95/1430: 1st Northumberland Fusiliers War Diary.
8   TNA WO 95/1427: 9 Brigade War Diary.
9   TNA WO 95/1858: 37 Brigade War Diary.

Brown Line. The 37 Brigade would lead with 6th Queen's (Royal West Surrey Regiment)(Queen's) on the right and 7th East Surrey Regiment (East Surreys) on the left, and 6th The Buffs (East Kent Regiment)(The Buffs) and 6th (Queen's Own) Royal West Kent Regiment (R West Kents) in support. The 36 Brigade would have 7th Royal Sussex Regiment (R Sussex) on the right, 11th Middlesex on the left and 8th and 9th RF in support. The 35 Brigade, when it passed through, would lead with 7th Norfolk Regiment (Norfolks) on the right and 9th Essex Regiment (Essex) on the left. They would be supported by 7th Suffolks and 5th Royal Berkshire Regiment (R Berks).

The Division's assault would be well supported by their own and 29th Division's artillery and part of VI Corps Heavy Artillery. They had done a very good job in cutting the enemy wire and destroying their trenches over the course of the four day preliminary bombardment. Equally effectively, they would protect the assaulting troops with a creeping barrage that would advance 100 yards every four minutes.

The leading waves of the assaulting battalions formed up in no man's land under cover of the bombardment and, at Zero Hour, advanced to the assault of the German first system, the Black Line. All six trenches which formed the enemy line were carried with very little opposition and on schedule. The attacking battalions halted to consolidate the line and allow the support battalions to pass through on their way to attack the Blue Line. Their advance began at 0700, following a prolonged bombardment of the enemy second system. The attackers soon found themselves under serious fire. The 6th Buffs and 6th R West Kents (37 Brigade) were targeted by snipers and machine gun fire from both flanks and were held up for a time. There was some stiff hand to hand fighting as the Kentish battalions pressed forward, taking advantage of such shelter as was afforded by shell holes. By 1030 6th Buffs had carried their objective, Houlette work, although there were still Germans in the trench between Houlette work and Cambrai Road. The Buffs were still troubled by enfilade fire from machine guns from ruins near Estaminet corner. They managed to silence them with a combined use of Lewis guns and rifle grenades. They then bombed down from Houlette work to gain touch with 3rd Division on their right.[10] On their left the R West Kents, still partially held up in front of Hangest trench, had got into Hamel, Holt and Hotte works and Henley lane and were bombing up the lane to re-establish contact with 36 Brigade on their left who were bombing down from Habacq trench, which they had carried.[11] Enemy resistance in the R W Kent's sector was, however, only finally overcome as the third stage of 12th Division's assault was getting underway. The R West Kents were materially assisted in the final phase of their involvement by the bravery of Sergeant H. Cator of 7th East Surreys who, even though he should not have become involved, took it upon himself to eliminate a machine gun that had been causing heavy loss. He was awarded the Victoria Cross.[12]

The 36 Brigade had also had some serious fighting to do since the 8th and 9th RF had passed through 7th R Sussex and 11th Middlesex on the Black Line. The two Fusilier battalions launched their attack at 0750 and initially kept up closely with a creeping barrage described as 'excellent' in 8th Battalion's War Diary.[13] However, they came up against an enemy seemingly determined to make a stand in Hamel, Heron and Holt works on the Heilly trench. The hostile fire had inevitably forced the two battalions to slow down as a consequence of which they fell behind the barrage. They nevertheless pressed on. Held up in front of Hamel work the 8th Battalion worked their way up the Feuchy switch in conjunction with 8/10th Gordons of 15th Division, on their left. They encountered many Germans in the switch whom they quickly overcame, taking 200 of them prisoner. The 8th Battalion pushed on and secured Hem trench. The 9th Battalion, held up by Heron and Holt works, managed to work some of their men past the enemy strongpoints, and on to the capture of Habacq trench. When they tried to advance further towards Hulst trench however, they were subjected to

10   TNA WO 95/1860: 6th The Buffs War Diary.
11   TNA WO 95/1858:37 Brigade War Diary.
12   OH op. cit., p. 219.
13   TNA WO 95/1857: 8th and 9th Royal Fusiliers War Diaries.

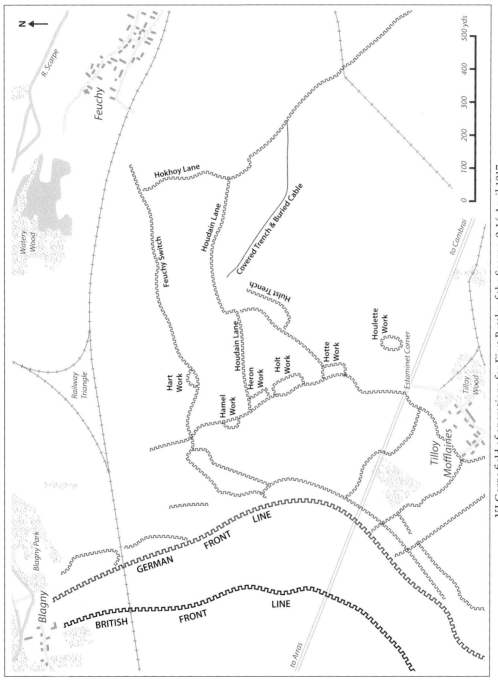

VI Corps field of operations for First Battle of the Scarpe, 9-14 April 1917.

heavy barrages of machine gun and artillery fire. Behind the leading troops the Heron and Hamel works were finally cleared. The capture of the Blue Line was finally completed between 1220 and 1305 and its consolidation was begun.[14]

The third stage of 12th Division's attack had started at 1215 when 35 Brigade passed through 37 Brigade on their way to attack the enemy Brown Line. The 35's move forward to their jumping off points had begun at 1005. As they advanced to the junction of Haucourt trench and Havant lane it became evident to 7th Norfolks that the Blue Line had not yet been entirely taken; Houlette work and the trenches running north and south from it were still in enemy hands. The Battalion took some casualties, mainly from fire from ruined houses in Tilloy. They pressed on however and captured about 100 Germans in Haucourt trench. The Norfolks and 5th R Berks then successfully pinched out Holt work, Havant lane and Observation ridge. As final distractions in their busy morning prior even to reaching their jumping off point, the Norfolks completed the capture of Houlette, Holt and Heron works, assisted in the last two cases by 9th Essex and 5th R Berks. With the Blue Line still not entirely in British hands, 35 Brigade were therefore forced to start their advance on the Brown Line from positions about 400 yards west of the Blue Line.

The 7th Norfolks began their advance at 1205. They found Estaminet corner and the Bois des Boeufs to be clear of enemy and reached *Maison Rouge*. Such opposition as there had been from sniper and machine gun fire had been quickly silenced. They were joined at *Maison Rouge* at around 1300 by 7th Suffolks and 9th Essex and for the next 30 minutes or so had to suffer being shelled by their own artillery.[15] For the 9th Essex this was the unwelcome culmination of what had been a very busy start to their involvement in the fighting. Very early on they had come under fairly heavy machine gun fire from Hotte work and from the direction of Tilloy to their right. This had forced them to seek such shelter as there was in shell holes. They were able to resume their advance only when one of their junior officers, Second Lieutenant Barker, worked his way round the flank of Hotte work, threw a few bombs into it and took its 30-strong garrison prisoner. Thereafter the Battalion's advance continued unchecked until Observation ridge was reached. Further progress down its eastern slope was impossible until the point blank enemy fire from Battery valley was suppressed. This was achieved by a combination of Lewis gun fire and the efforts of 5th R Berks described below.

Despite the inevitable confusion caused by the ill-directed shelling of their own artillery, the attack on the Brown Line itself began at 1335, about 40 minutes late. The 7th Suffolks reached Church redoubt at about 1430 by which time the British artillery barrage had died down so that not a single gun was firing at just the time they were needed to support the infantry in their attack. The Suffolks found the wire around the redoubt fully intact and those who tried to get through were ruthlessly machine gunned and sniped. The survivors took shelter in shell holes.

Meanwhile the right hand company of 9th Essex pushed forward to Feuchy Chapel and the Wancourt-Feuchy Line despite fairly intensive enemy machine gun fire. They managed to get a footing in Feuchy Chapel work and took complete possession of it including both quarries. The Battalion took heavy casualties in unavailing attempts to work their way along Tilloy lane to its junction with the Brown Line. The German front line here was very strongly held. Several attempts to work up communication trenches from the redoubt were frustrated by machine gun and sniper fire against which the trenches were too wide and shallow to offer much protection. The Battalion's left hand company remained still tied down in Battery valley by sniper and machine gun fire. By now it was 1700 and no further action was practicable. After nightfall 9th Essex consolidated the ground gained.

For their part 5th R Berks, with 7th R Sussex in support, had advanced on the left from Hem trench, with their left on Houdain lane. Their advance was unopposed as far as Heilly trench, but they then came under fire from Heron work. They successfully outflanked this redoubt and captured

14   TNA WO 95/1854: 36 Brigade War Diary.
15   TNA WO 95/1853: 7th Norfolk Regiment War Diary.

its garrison of 35 men and a machine gun at the cost of a 45 minute delay. The R Berks resumed their advance at 1145. An hour later they crossed the ridge and entered Battery valley where four enemy batteries were found to be in action. The batteries were rushed and the valley was cleared of the enemy. For good measure the serviceable captured guns were turned on their recent owners. The R Berks then sought to attack the Brown Line by advancing up Hirson lane, thereby assisting the Suffolks and Essex. But their attack was held up on the Feuchy Chapel-Feuchy road because of uncut wire and machine gun fire.[16]

The 35 Brigade made a further effort to capture the Wancourt-Feuchy Line with the assistance of 37th Division 63 Brigade. This Division had moved up behind the 12th with the planned intention of passing through once the German line had been captured to carry out their assigned role of capturing Monchy-le-Preux. Instead they found themselves committing one of their brigades to the struggle to secure one of 12th Division's objectives. Despite 63 Brigade's support, the renewed attempt on the enemy line was as unsuccessful as the earlier one, thwarted mainly by uncut wire. As night fell the two brigades extended themselves along the Feuchy Chapel-Feuchy road. During the night they sent out patrols which confirmed that the enemy were still in full occupation of the Brown Line and that, for the 9th Essex in particular, the wire remained impenetrable.

The prospects for the capture of the Brown Line in 12th Division's sector were improved by the 15th (Scottish) Division's success in getting into the German line on the late evening of the 9th. From their positions on the left of 12th Division they set about bombing their way down the line getting, during the course of the night, to the point in the line roughly due west of Orange Hill. At daybreak on the 10th the artillery of 3rd and 12th Divisions opened a barrage on the Brown Line and at 1200 the 35 Brigade renewed their assault. The Brigade Commander had ordered that no assault against uncut wire should be undertaken. The attack was instead made by bombing up communication trenches, thus making a turning movement. The 5th R Berks, assisted by six companies from 36 Brigade, and the 9th Essex, who had also attacked at 1200, succeeded in outflanking and capturing the German positions. Casualties were light. Patrols were immediately pushed forward to Chapel and Orange Hills and the consolidation of the Wancourt-Feuchy line put in hand.

The 35 Brigade completed the consolidation of the Wancourt-Feuchy line on 11 April. Tragically, during the course of the day, the CO and Brigade Major of 9th Essex were killed by shellfire only shortly before 12th Division were placed in Corps reserve. During 12 April 12th Division were relieved and moved back to billets in Arras.[17]

The northernmost Division of VI Corps participating in the initial assault were the 15th (Scottish), a second tranche KNA Division formed in September 1914. Arriving in July 1915, they were one of the earliest New Army divisions to reach the Western Front. They did so in time to play a major part in the Battle of Loos in September 1915. Under the command of Major General F W N McCracken (who would remain in command until shortly after the Battle of Arras) the Division became part of Rawlinson's IV Corps and were given the important tasks of capturing the village of Loos itself, then, further to the east, the vital Hill 70, the capture and retention of which would spell the difference between the success or failure of the battle as a whole. Despite some initial problems with their own gas, the Division came frustratingly close to pulling off their tasks. Loos was captured within 90 minutes and Hill 70 would have followed suit had not heavy officer losses left the battalions almost leaderless, resulting in the majority of the surviving rank and file losing their way and veering off to the south when Hill 70 was there for the taking. The Division's losses were very heavy.

The 15th (Scottish) did not get involved in the Somme campaign of 1916 until early August. Their main contribution was the capture of the village of Martinpuich the following month during the Battle of Flers-Courcelette. This was their last major operation before Arras, although they did

16   TNA WO 95/1850: 5th Royal Berkshire Regiment War Diary.
17   TNA WO 95/1851: 9th Essex Regiment War Diary.

not leave the Somme area until February 1917. On their departure from Fourth Army they received a particularly fulsome farewell message from their erstwhile Army Commander, General Sir Henry Rawlinson, which read in part as follows: 'I know no Division in which a higher standard of discipline and morale exists, nor one to which I would entrust a difficult undertaking with greater confidence'. The message may well have been greeted with the odd hollow laugh in a Division that was in a poor, run down state when it joined VI Corps and Third Army on 14 February. The nearly two months available before the Arras offensive began would be devoted to intensive training to bring the Division back to a high standard of efficiency. Their performance on the first day of the Battle demonstrated that the time had not been wasted.[18]

In the days leading up to Zero Hour the Division had taken full advantage of the protection afforded by the cellars and tunnels between Arras and the front line, so much so that it was deemed unnecessary to have the reserve battalions of the assaulting brigades pass through once the first objective had been secured. For the initial assault, 44 Brigade on the right would lead with 8/10th Gordons and 9th Black Watch, with 7th Cameron Highlanders (Camerons) in support and 8th Seaforth Highlanders (Seaforths) in brigade reserve. On the left, 45 Brigade would lead with 7th RSF on the right and 11th Argyll and Sutherland Highlanders (Argylls) on the left, with 13th R Scots in support and 6th Camerons in brigade reserve. The 46 Brigade would form the divisional reserve.

That there would be no need for the reserve battalions to pass through once the first objective had been secured proved to be a sound assessment. Even though only one tank out of the four assigned to 44 Brigade had arrived by Zero Hour the Gordons and the Black Watch had within 25 minutes reached and captured the Black Line, 500 yards behind the original German front line, against light opposition and with negligible losses. Here the two battalions paused until shortly after 0700, before resuming their advance, their objective now being the Blue Line, 1,000 yards away. The Gordons had only progressed 150 yards when they came under heavy machine gun fire from a redoubt on their right and the Railway Triangle on their left. The latter was a formidable challenge. It consisted of three intersecting railway lines and their embankments which formed a triangular shape just to the north of the Gordons' line of advance. Although it was causing the Highlanders some trouble it was the Black Watch who were tasked with capturing it. The Gordons' principle concern was the need to neutralise the redoubt on their right. Like the Railway Triangle it was not their direct responsibility but that of 12th Division whose 8th RF had however veered slightly off course to the right leaving the redoubt largely unscathed. The Gordons therefore assembled two small groups to storm it in an operation that successfully dealt with it, but at the cost of the lives of the two officers commanding the groups. The problem posed by Railway Triangle was alleviated, if not eliminated, by the arrival of a tank intent on advancing on the complex, thus distracting the enemy defenders and enabling the Gordons to get on and complete the capture of the second objective.[19] On their left 9th Black Watch had also been held up by machine gun fire from the eastern arm of the Railway Triangle. But through the intervention of the tank and the assistance of 7th Camerons, moving up from support, they were finally able to overcome the enemy resistance and gain their objective.[20] From start to finish the effort had taken around 5 hours. Both leading battalions then reorganised and consolidated the ground taken. The 9th Black Watch, which had taken serious casualties in capturing Railway Triangle, were formally superseded as left hand lead battalion by 7th Camerons.[21]

The story of one of 9th Black Watch's company commanders has been well documented and can be considered typical of the risks facing assaulting infantry on the Western Front, especially the junior officers. They were expected to lead by example, which frequently resulted in them being in full view of the enemy. Lieutenant (acting Captain) Ernest Reid was 20 years old in 1917. He had

---

18   Walter Reid, *Arras 1917*, p. 148.
19   TNA WO 95/1938: 8/10th Gordon Highlanders War Diary.
20   TNA WO 95/1937: 9th Black Watch War Diary.
21   TNA WO 95/1941:7th Cameron Highlanders War Diary.

volunteered for the army as soon as he was old enough in 1915 and was commissioned into the Black Watch in June of that year. By the start of the Battle of Arras he had been with the 9th Battalion for nearly nine months and had seen action in the Battle of the Somme, where he had been slightly wounded. At Zero on 9 April he led the Battalion's A Company over the top. Once the Black Line had been secured the Black Watch's objective would be the Railway Triangle. Captain Reid quickly picked up a minor wound when a small shell fragment entered his upper right thigh. His servant, Private Alexander Black, bound up the wound enabling Reid to carry on. The closer the Battalion got to the Railway Triangle the slower became its forward momentum. At about 1000 Reid was hit by a bullet which traversed his right thigh cutting through the femoral artery. Private Black averted the danger of Reid bleeding to death by placing a tourniquet in position and binding up the wound as best he could. Eventually Captain Reid was evacuated and after the customary traumatic process of evacuation found himself in hospital in Etaples. There his hopes of recovery were probably fatally compromised by the efforts made to save his leg, which allowed septicaemia, almost certainly in his system through dirt picked up on the battlefield, to spread uncontrollably. Sadly Captain Reid died on 18 April.[22]

The two leading battalions of 45 Brigade, like those of 44 on their right, reached the Black Line with little difficulty and few casualties. Those that they did suffer were mainly caused by a mine exploding in the enemy front line. A few among the leading waves of attackers were buried under falling debris; others became confused and disorientated. But the most serious problems of the early stages of the Brigade's assault were experienced by A and C Companies of 13th R Scots, who found themselves under heavy fire from the outset. They had been given the task of capturing that part of the village of Blangy, a suburb of Arras, through which the German front line ran. The line was well manned by determined snipers and machine gun crews and the Scots had some hard fighting lasting over three hours until the fire of Stokes mortars and howitzers was brought to bear and the opposition overcome. Even though the problem had taken significant time to resolve and resulted in some casualties, it was essentially a separate operation and did not hold up the overall progress of the Brigade as they moved on towards Railway Triangle.

The German strong point was reached by around 0800 but it would be over four hours before it was captured. The problem was largely enemy machine gun and rifle fire from the railway embankment. The momentum of the attack had been lost when the assaulting battalions had been hit by their own barrage, which had then moved on too quickly for the disorganised attackers to keep up with it. This had enabled the enemy to raise their heads and fire at their attackers with relative impunity. When the situation became apparent to the battalion commanders a further barrage was ordered. Unfortunately the attackers could not be informed in time for them to follow up this new barrage which was fired from 1155 to 1205. It was not until a Stokes mortar and a tank focused on the embankment that the deadlock was broken with the Germans being forced into a hasty retreat. The capture of the Railway Triangle was completed and the Brigade's sector of the Blue Line secured by 1240.

At 1400 the 46 Brigade passed through the two leading brigades on their way to assault the enemy Brown Line. This movement had been planned for 1250 but had been postponed until 1400. News of the postponement did not reach the two leading companies of the Brigade's right hand assaulting Battalion, the 12th Highland Light Infantry (HLI), who moved off in accordance with the original timetable at 1250. They soon sensed that all was not well and that the British barrage would now start by falling behind them before creeping forward towards and through them. They had little option but to seek what shelter they could and wait for the storm to pass. In the event the barrage caused only light losses and the companies were able to get to their feet and follow closely behind it as it crept forward. The Battalion soon found themselves with a much more serious problem as they entered Battery valley and immediately came under fire, at ranges as short as 300 yards, from three

---

22   Walter Reid, op. cit., pp. 156-68.

batteries of German field artillery. Despite taking heavy casualties the Battalion initially captured a battery of four guns and then, by use of a Lewis gun barrage, forced the remaining enemy gunners who had survived the onslaught to abandon their guns. Nine of these fell into British hands.

By 1430 the 12th HLI were in contact with the 10th Cameronians (Scottish Rifles) (SR) on their left and 5th R Berks (36 Brigade) on their right. An hour later their advance had reached Broken mill where it was slowed by hostile machine gun fire from the southeast. Although 5th R Berks' lack of success in suppressing this threat left 12th HLI vulnerable, they were materially assisted in completing their part in the capture of the Brown Line by a tank which, moving south down the line, flattened the uncut German wire and eliminated several machine guns, enabling the Glasgow Highlanders (HLI) to assault and gain their objective.

The Brigade's other two assault battalions, 10th SR in the centre and 7/8th King's Own Scottish Borderers (KOSB) on the left, began their advance as rescheduled at 1400. Despite their leading companies being subjected to a hostile barrage that began as soon as they became visible to the enemy, the 10th SR pushed on as ordered with all possible speed. As a result they did suffer some casualties from their own barrage, fortunately very thin, as they outpaced it. Despite this problem they reached the sunken road east of Battery valley where they halted to wait for 7/8th KOSB to come up alongside.[23] The latter had set themselves a precise timetable for their participation in the attack. They were to assault the Feuchy redoubt at 1400, Feuchy village at 1515 and the Brown Line at 1620. On their way to linking up with the SR, the 7/8th KOSB had also suffered, but much more seriously, from the artillery firing short and had also been pinned down by heavy enemy fire from a railway bridge. A Second Lieutenant Strachan with five men rushed the bridge and seized it, taking 17 prisoners. The Battalion was then able to link up with the SR. The intention was that both battalions would advance in line on the village of Feuchy, situated just north of the Brigade's lines of advance to the Brown Line and therefore, while it remained in enemy hands, a source of potentially damaging enfilade fire. In recognition of its importance as a target, Feuchy had received special treatment from the artillery, in the form of a bombardment by 6 inch howitzers, before the infantry moved in.

The advance through the village progressed relatively smoothly. By around 1600 the two battalions were through the village and out on the eastern side, having captured several guns on their way. Approximately an hour later the SR, taking advantage of gaps in the wire, entered the Brown Line, followed by the KOSB. By 1730 the Line was fully in 46 Brigade's hands and patrols were pushed out several hundred yards to the east onto the northern slopes of Orange Hill, picking up occasional prisoners. Consolidation of the Line was immediately put in hand including the establishment of three posts 200 yards east of it. The KOSB also placed even further forward 25 men and Lewis guns to guard against the possibility of a counterattack from the north. During the night the process of consolidation continued and by dawn on the 10th a new line further forward had been firmly established.

15th (Scottish) Division could look back with great satisfaction on their day's work. They were the only division in VI Corps to have completed the capture of their sector of the Brown Line. They had advanced well over two miles. But there was little time for rest. At 2200 all three assault battalions received orders to advance and consolidate a line on the northern slopes of Orange Hill, about half a mile east of the Brown Line. The 12th HLI moved off without interference before midnight; the other two battalions followed at 0200. The Brigade's reserve battalion, 10/11th HLI began their move forward from their positions in Hokhoy lane to the Reserve Line.

On the afternoon of 10 April 45 Brigade, with 7th Camerons (44 Brigade) attached temporarily in support, passed through 46 Brigade and advanced in support of 37th Division, who were to lead the infantry assault on the village of Monchy-le-Preux. At 0110 the following morning VI Corps received orders from Third Army HQ to advance to the Green Line. Zero Hour would be 0500. The

---

23   TNA WO 95/1954: 10th Cameronians (Scottish Rifles) War Diary.

Green Line ran roughly north-south just to the east of Monchy. 15th Division would attack on a two brigade front. The 45 Brigade, on the left, would attack between Lone Copse and the Scarpe river; 46 Brigade, on the right, would seek to capture the German trenches north of Monchy, between the village itself and Lone Copse. The 44 Brigade would be in support. On 46 Brigade's right, the 37th Division 111 Brigade would deal with Monchy itself.

For 46 Brigade, 10/11th HLI would lead the way with 7/8th KOSB in support. 12th HLI and 10th SR remained in reserve. At 0400 the HLI Battalion formed up in column of route just to the east of the Brown Line and marched southwards along the Line for about 1,000 yards before wheeling left by companies and moving on a compass bearing due east arriving just short of the Terraces by 0500. The Battalion were deployed on a three-company front as day began to break.[24] The attack began on schedule. Whereas the earlier advance over Orange Hill had been concealed by darkness, the new advance would enjoy no such advantage and immediately came under heavy machine gun fire and an artillery barrage from enemy gun positions situated between Monchy and the River Scarpe. Partly because of the enemy machine gun fire coming from northwest of Monchy, which they swung south to meet, and partly because 45 Brigade advanced half right, the 10/11th HLI lost direction southward. They found themselves making straight for an enemy held trench about 400 yards northwest of Monchy. Two of the Battalion's four companies were pinned down for a time and took heavy casualties, including their commanders who were both killed, from the enemy machine guns located in the trench. But they managed to mount a flank attack which drove the enemy out of the trench and back into the village. They then advanced on Monchy, clearing the way as they went, and entered the village from the southwest. By now 45 and 111 Brigades were also in the village. The enemy were quickly cleared out of the village and its consolidation was largely left to 111 Brigade.

Like 46 Brigade, 45 Brigade had been pushed south of their intended course. Their main objective had been Lone Copse on the right. The 6th Camerons were on the right and 6/7th RSF on the left. The 13th R Scots were in support and 11th Argylls in reserve. There was no artillery barrage, as a result of which, when the Camerons were about 700 yards from Lone Copse, they were hit by heavy machine gun fire coming from their left which began to inflict heavy casualties. The RSF were not where the Camerons expected them to be; they had in fact fallen behind the Highlanders. Despite becoming somewhat disorientated the Camerons reached an enemy trench 60 yards east of Lone Copse, by now in British hands. Thirty prisoners were taken and some enemy machine gun teams were bayoneted. But the price had been high. All but four officers had become casualties thus frustrating the possibility of mounting a concerted effort against Monchy. One company did however manage to clear the north end of the village. The Camerons dug in on a line of strong points running northwest from the north end of the village. Here they had to endure a persistent enemy barrage by heavy guns for much of the rest of the day. They received no support from the British artillery which, they were led to believe, was stuck in mud too far back to be of any use.[25]

Aware that they had strayed some distance from their planned line of advance, 10/11th HLI tried to resume their correct line of advance by leaving Monchy village and heading north. They were however checked by heavy machine gun and artillery fire when they then attempted to move east and were forced to take cover in shell holes immediately north of, and to the left of, positions held by 10th York and Lancaster Regiment (York and Lancs), where they remained until the early evening. At 1900 they managed to advance and occupy trenches north of the village that had formed the enemy's main position when the British attack had begun that morning.[26]

The experiences of 7/8th KOSB, in support, essentially paralleled those of the HLI Battalion. They too strayed to the right with their right hand company actually going through Monchy village

24   TNA WO 95/1952: 10/11th and 12th Highland Light Infantry War Diary.
25   TNA WO 95/1945: 6th Cameron Highlanders War Diary.
26   TNA WO 95/1952: 10/11th and12th Highland Light Infantry War Diary.

after taking casualties from within 250 yards of the village, mainly from machine gun fire from houses on the western outskirts. The KOSB were ordered to move north where they eventually dug in precariously in a single line under the unwelcome attention of enemy machine gun fire. To this was added shellfire, seemingly fired as a preliminary to a counterattack. But although the shellfire continued no attack materialised. After what must have been a very uncomfortable and hazardous day and night the Brigade were relieved during the night of 11/12th.[27]

Ostensibly in support for the above attack, 44 Brigade advanced close behind the leading brigades and also suffered from the heavy machine gun and shrapnel fire that greeted them as soon as they reached the crest of Orange Hill. They took shelter in some convenient trenches and received warning that Lone Copse would be bombarded at 1450, 10 minutes prior to them renewing their attack at 1500. Once again they came under exceptionally heavy machine gun and shrapnel fire but succeeded nevertheless in taking up a position roughly between Lone Copse and Monchy. There they remained in a state of heightened alert in expectation of a German counterattack that in the event never materialised.[28][28]

By this time the Division were already on notice that they would be relieved during the course of the night by 17th (Northern) Division. As the relief was not completed during the night it was, at some risk, continued during the following day. Despite high visibility caused by ground covered in snow the relief was finally completed 'without undue loss'. Initially the withdrawal was to an area between the Black and Blue Lines. But at 1130 the march to Arras began and by the evening the Division were safely in billets in the city.[29]

The capture of the entire Brown Line was to be the signal for the 37th Division, which had begun the Battle in Corps reserve, to pass through the leading divisions and advance towards Monchy-le-Preux. It may seem a little odd that such a junior KNA division should have been chosen for a task as important as the capture of the vital villages of Monchy-le-Preux and Guémappe. Originally numbered the 44th Division, it had been established at Andover in March 1915 as part of the sixth and final group of New Army divisions. Unlike other late-forming KNA divisions, however, it was well provided from the outset with an experienced commander, Major General Lord Edward Gleichen, and trained officers and NCOs. Hence it was very quickly adequately trained and readied for active service overseas. It moved to France in July 1915 and joined VII Corps. It was constituted of 110, 111 and 112 Brigades to begin with, but in July 1916 exchanged 110 Brigade for the 21st Division 63 Brigade. The two remaining original brigades participated in the Battles of Bazentin Ridge and Pozières during the Somme campaign and the whole Division fought in the Battle of the Ancre which wound up the same campaign. By the time of the Battles of Arras the Division were in VI Corps and under their third commander, Major General Hugh Bruce Bruce-Williams, who remained in command for the rest of the war.

Formally, the objective of 37th Division was to pass through the three leading divisions, once they had taken the enemy Black, Blue and Brown Lines, capture Monchy-le-Preux and then consolidate a line running roughly north and south 1,000 yards to the east of Monchy and Guémappe, situated further south. This line would be called the Green Line. The importance to 37th Division of the other three divisions completing their tasks successfully and approximately to schedule is self-evident. As reserve division it was not until 1200, Zero plus 6 hours 30 minutes, that it received orders to advance up to the Black Line. Two brigades immediately complied, 112 on the right and 111 on the left. The 63 Brigade for the moment stood fast. One of this Brigade's battalions, the 4th Middlesex, had already suffered significant casualties as they marched towards their assembly positions in the early hours of the 9th. The Battalion were only 200 yards away when an ammunition dump near Arras station

27   TNA WO 95/1953: 7/8th King's Own Scottish Borderers War Diary.
28   TNA WO 95/1941: 7th Cameron Highlanders War Diary.
29   TNA WO 95/1950: 46 Brigade War Diary.

exploded. One of the casualties was the Battalion's CO, who was wounded. This unfortunate event would not affect 4th Middlesex's involvement in the battle.[30]

At 1340 112 Brigade were ordered to continue their advance behind the 12th Division 35 Brigade and halt under cover of Observation ridge. The 111 were told to keep in touch with the advanced troops of 15th Division and to be ready to move further forward as soon as the latter had advanced from the Blue Line. The 63 Brigade were instructed to follow behind 111 Brigade with the proviso that this might subsequently be changed to following behind 112 Brigade. At 1500 the two leading brigades were also ordered to form up on the road between Airy corner to Feuchy Chapel and thence northwards. The 63 were told to move at once and follow the 111 as far as Battery valley where they would form the divisional reserve.

At 1621 a report was received from 12th Division that Chapel and Church works had been taken. On that basis the attack on Monchy was timed for 1900. At this hour the 37th Division brigades were to be in position to cross the Wancourt-Feuchy (Brown) Line. At 1730 the 112 and 111 Brigades were on the line Bois des Boeufs-Battery Valley and still advancing, with 63 Brigade following behind 111. An hour later it was still not clear whether or not the Brown Line was entirely in British hands. The only thing certain was that 15th Division had taken their assigned sector of the line. 37th Division were accordingly told to pass through the 15th on their way to attack Monchy. Orders to this effect reached the three brigades at 1855. With 6th Bedfords and 8th East Lancashire Regiment (East Lancs) leading and 10th Loyal North Lancashire Regiment (Loyals) in support, 112 Brigade immediately advanced in close support of the 12th Division 35 Brigade but came under heavy machine gun fire which stopped them advancing beyond a line from Airy corner to Feuchy road by way of Feuchy Chapel. They dug in on this line. As 111 Brigade's 10th and 13th RF approached the Brown Line they unexpectedly came under fire from the enemy's trench line along the western face of Chapel Hill and took some casualties. Despite this their leading troops immediately extended their line and pushed on as far as Feuchy Chapel and Feuchy road, where they dug in east of the road on 112 Brigade's left. The 13th RB took up supporting positions behind 13th RF and formed a left-facing defensive flank. Neither brigade was in a position to assault the Brown Line until the uncut wire and machine guns protecting it had been dealt with. Notwithstanding this, as soon as it was dark the 112's 8th East Lancs, north of the Cambrai Road, determinedly bombed up Tilloy Lane and managed to get through the enemy wire. But they were driven back, having suffered 20 to 30 casualties, including two officers. Any idea that the 6th Bedfords, south of the Cambrai Road, might also move their positions forward, was thwarted by the impenetrable enemy wire. It was more than a match for the Battalion's attempts during the night to cut a way through.[31][32]

At 1940 63 Brigade were ordered to push forward to a line which would leave them occupying the ground between the left flank of 111 Brigade and the River Scarpe to the north. They were to gain touch with XVII Corps' 4th Division on their left. In accordance with their orders 8th SLI and 8th Lincolns led the Brigade advance with 4th Middlesex in support. Two companies of SLI were soon digging in on Orange Hill; the remainder of the Battalion were in the Brown Line. The 8th Lincolns came up on the SLI's left and at 2400 4th Middlesex were ordered to prolong the line even further to the left. By 1200 on the 10th the Middlesex were in position with their left resting near the River Scarpe. Their patrols did not however manage to get in touch with the cavalry posts believed to be along the Scarpe Valley. Two of 111 Brigade's battalions, 13th KRRC and 13th RB, were ordered to move to Broken mill in support of 63 Brigade under whose orders they would now come. The 10th and 13th RF also received orders to move to the Broken mill area as soon as they were relieved. The moves were completed before daylight.[33]

30 TNA WO 95/2528: 63 Brigade War Diary.
31 TNA WO 95/2513: 37th Division War Diary.
32 TNA WO 95/2537: 6th Bedfordshire Regiment and 8th East Lancashire Regiment War Diaries.
33 TNA WO 95/2531: 111 Brigade War Diary.

There is no indication in the Divisional War Diary that an opportunity may have been lost to exploit the gap opened in the German defence of Monchy by 15th Division's success in breaching the Wancourt-Feuchy line. It seems unfortunate that the task was assigned to 63 Brigade when 111 Brigade, ahead of them, could have been diverted from closing up behind 12th Division to exploit the breach. Alternatively one of 15th Division brigades could have undertaken the task as the Divisional GOC wanted. The consequence of neither of these options being pursued was that the breach remained unexploited and a possibly good chance of capturing Monchy before darkness put an end to the opportunity that day, may have been lost.[34]

The night was nevertheless put to good advantage by 63 Brigade which pushed bombing parties south down the Brown Line and also secured the northern half and the crest of Orange Hill thereby recording the day's greatest advance, nearly three miles, in VI Corps sector. The average was just over two miles.

During the same night 112 Brigade were pulled back. They moved to near *Maison Rouge* where they would be ready to push forward as soon as 12th Division had secured their sector of the Brown Line. As has already been noted 111 Brigade had also retired, in their case to near Broken mill, also in readiness to advance in support of 63 Brigade.

The Division's principal challenge on the morning of the 10th was to repair the lost opportunity of the previous evening by exploiting the gap in the enemy's Brown Line defences created by 15th Division. The 63 Brigade were ordered to advance to Lone Copse valley. They moved off with the four battalions in line abreast. By 1045 one company of 8th SLI had reached the enclosures on Orange Hill. The 111 Brigade were ordered to support 63 Brigade and 'make good Monchy'. The 112, also ultimately aiming to support the 63, were told off to follow closely behind 12th Division 35 Brigade when they launched their attack, and advance as fast as possible through them to a line between the crossroads 400 yards southwest of la Bergère and the road junction 300 yards southeast of Monchy. As 35 Brigade were unable to launch their attack until midday, there was little 112 Brigade could do to cooperate with 63 Brigade until about 1230. By that hour, with 6th Bedfords on the right, supported by 11th Royal Warwickshire Regiment (Warwicks), and 8th East Lancs on the left, closely supported by 10th Loyals, they were over Chapel Hill, south of Orange Hill, before the enemy could put down a barrage, and were able to place machine guns in positions from where they could support the advance of 63 Brigade who had come under heavy enemy artillery fire from the direction of Fampoux. The fire was so well directed that only elements of the four battalions had reached Lone Copse valley. Nevertheless by 1105 the 8th SLI and the 8th Lincolns considered they had done well enough to create an opening for exploitation by cavalry. VI Corps HQ were so informed.

The supporting brigades were enjoying mixed fortunes. The leading battalions of 112 Brigade reached a line running north to south through Les Fosses Farm, southwest of Monchy. The 8th East Lancs were hit by heavy enemy enfilade fire from the direction of the village which prevented them making any further advance. The 6th Bedfords got on still further on the right until they too were hit by enfilade fire from both flanks, forcing them to retreat 200 yards or so before they could dig in. The advance of 111 Brigade was led by 10th and 13th RF with 13th KRRC in support and 13th RB in reserve. Their orders were to advance on Monchy. Their first objective was a scattered group of plantations and enclosures northwest of the village. They came under heavy shellfire as they crossed Orange Hill. As they reached the enclosures, heavy machine gun and sniper fire also struck them. Patrols did excellent work in suppressing the enemy small arms fire, but the leading battalions were finally forced to halt about 500 yards west of Monchy and dig in, in some cases only a few yards from the enemy trenches. All further attempts to reach the village failed, hampered as they were by an absence of artillery support. The leading troops were eventually withdrawn to a line west of the enclosures. The bulk of the artillery fire that had been the main contributor to bringing 111 Brigade

---

34   OH, op. cit., p. 225.

to a halt appeared to emanate from Greenland Hill, north of the River Scarpe and therefore in XVII Corps sector. Even if available, counter battery fire could not have been used to deal with it for fear that it might hit 3 Cavalry Brigade, who were somewhere in the area. This was just one cause of the inadequate artillery support that 37th Division's attempts to capture Monchy that day received. The other was that there were insufficient guns available until 1430 because of the physical difficulties in getting them forward once they were relieved of the unanticipated task of supporting the attempts to complete the capture of the Brown Line, prolonged from the previous day.

By 1700 it had become evident that the whole divisional advance had been brought to a standstill. In an effort to resume forward momentum arrangements were made to bombard Guémappe and Monchy again for 30 minutes from 1900. All available field guns were ordered to support an advance through Monchy beginning at 1930. A creeping barrage was organised, but there were still too few field guns sufficiently far forward to make it really effective. Repeated attempts by 63 and 111 Brigades to advance in spite of the inadequate artillery support resulted in predictable failure in the face of heavy hostile rifle and machine gun fire. The line was consolidated for what for many must have been an appalling night of suffering. There was virtually no shelter from the heavy snowfall. The many wounded lying out in the open suffered particularly, not only from exposure to the weather but also to the unrelenting hostile shellfire.

At 2320 orders were received from Corps for the advance to be resumed on a three divisional front at 0500 the following morning, the 11th. The 3rd Division would be on the right, the 37th in the centre and the 15th on the left. Four tanks were ordered to co-operate. The 37th would have 112 Brigade on the right attacking to the south of Monchy, and 111 on the left attacking the village itself. The 63 Brigade would be in reserve.

The advance began on schedule at 0500, even though this meant that 112 Brigade would lack the cover of 3rd Division 76 Brigade on their right as this formation would not be ready to advance until 0730 at the earliest. In the lead for 112 Brigade were 11th Warwicks and 10th Loyals. With great dash and gallantry, and despite heavy casualties, mainly caused by enfilade fire from Monchy and inadequate to non-existent artillery cover, the Loyals pushed on. They established themselves on a ridge just east of *la Bergère* on the northern side of the Arras-Cambrai road. They set up posts over the crest after some further hard fighting in which they were greatly assisted by the opportune arrival of one of the tanks. South of the Arras-Cambrai road the Warwicks, unable to make any progress, moved north of the road by short rushes behind La Fosse Farm and then advanced about 50 yards east of the Monchy-La Bergère Road.[35] By midday the Brigade had succeeded in establishing a line along the sunken road between the crossroads south west of la Bergère and a point about 600 yards south of Monchy. They were in touch with 3rd Division on their right and, on their left, with 3rd Dragoon Guards, who had moved up to fill a gap which had opened up between 112 and 111 Brigades.

The 111 Brigade had begun the attack with 13th KRRC on the right and 13th RB on the left. Like 112 Brigade they suffered from much delayed artillery support; their advance began without any artillery cover at all. They were initially slowed by a series of natural obstacles and heavy and effective enemy shellfire coupled with machine gun and rifle fire which swept the level ground in front of Monchy causing heavy casualties. But the arrival of four tanks at about 0530 proved of great assistance in dealing with the machine guns, and the assaulting battalions were able to push through the village in time to use their Lewis guns to great effect on an enemy retreating across open ground. By 0900 the whole of the village had been cleared of the enemy and about 150 prisoners had been taken. Ten minutes later the Third Cavalry Division 10th Hussars, 3rd Dragoon Guards and 1st Essex Yeomanry came up. With their Hotchkiss machine guns they greatly strengthened the defences of Monchy against any threat of counterattack, which the unremitting hostile bombardment of the village seemed to presage. The Hussars and Essex Yeomanry established a line between the two roads

---

35   TNA WO 95/2538: 10th Loyal North Lancashire Regiment War Diary.

which ran northeast from the village to Pelves. They also filled in some gaps in the defensive line east of Monchy.

At 0655 information had been received at Divisional HQ that 15th Division 45 Brigade were well east of Monchy. The 63 Brigade had immediately been ordered to support 111 Brigade with a view to securing the high ground in the Bois des Aubépines, which would provide the necessary cover to 45 Brigade's right flank. The 63 Brigade were assembled in the southern arm of Lone Copse valley, but heavy enemy shelling prevented them from forming up immediately to begin their advance. A further message from 15th Division had been received at 0800 indicating that their leading infantry were now just west of Pelves, making it all the more necessary and urgent that 37th Division should push forward to offer protection to 15th Division presumably exposed right flank. However, when 63 Brigade's leading Battalion, the 10th York & Lancs, finally reached the high ground northwest of Monchy they immediately came under enfilade machine gun fire from Roeux, northeast of them. It was clear from this that 15th Division were not in fact east of Monchy as had been reported. The York & Lancs nevertheless pressed on but were finally checked around some old trenches having made little progress. Moving further south to avoid the troublesome enfilade fire from Roeux, 4th Middlesex and 8th Lincolns established contact with 111 Brigade in Monchy. While some of their number took shelter in cellars in Monchy, which was now under heavy bombardment, the remainder established posts on the line of the road running north from Monchy. Advancing behind the Middlesex, 8th Lincolns established a line southeast of the old trenches, where they unfortunately found themselves pinned down by machine gun fire from their northeast. They nevertheless managed to establish contact with the 15th Division 46 Brigade.

For the rest of the day no advance was possible. The lines gained were consolidated. A planned attack by 12th Division 36 Brigade and 111 Brigade was cancelled when it became know that 3rd Division had not succeeded in taking Guémappe. The expected German counterattacks took place beginning at 1630 and 2100. They were launched from the direction of Guémappe and fell on the right flank of 112 Brigade. They were successfully dispersed by rifle and machine gun fire before they reached the British line. Repelling these counterattacks proved to be the last serious actions involving the Brigade before they were relieved. Their losses during the course of the four days amounted to 45 officers and over 800 Other Ranks. The 10th Loyals had lost over 60 percent of their fighting strength (13 officers and 289 men).[36] [37]

Orders for the relief of the Division by 12th Division were received during the course of the day. It was successfully concluded without incident during the night of 11/12 April except for the 8th Lincolns and 10th York & Lancs. The battalions relieving these two units did not reach them in time to enable them to withdraw before daylight. They therefore had to remain in position until the following night.[38]

---

36   TNA WO 95/2536: 112 Brigade War Diary.
37   TNA WO 95/2538: 10th Loyal North Lancashire Regiment War Diary.
38   TNA WO 95/2513: 37th Division War Diary.

6

XVII Corps

XVII Infantry Corps came into being on the Western Front on 9 January 1916. Its first Commander was Lieutenant General Sir Julian Byng, but after only five months he was moved sideways to the Canadian Corps and replaced by Lieutenant General Sir Charles Fergusson, who would remain in command of the Corps until the end of the war.

Sir Charles was a career professional soldier. He was commissioned from Sandhurst into the Grenadier Guards in 1883. At the outbreak of the war he was a Major General and GOC of 5th Division, which he took to France in August 1914 as one of the first four infantry divisions of the BEF. After a brief period as GOC of 9th (Scottish) Division in late 1914 he was promoted to Lieutenant General in January 1915 and placed in command of II Corps, where he remained until he was transferred to XVII Corps in May of the following year.[1] Sir Charles's new command did not become involved in the Somme campaign. Its first serious engagement was the Battle of Arras where its infantry component initially consisted of the 4th, 9th (Scottish), 34th and 51st (Highland) Divisions.

On 9 April the Corps front ran from the north bank of the River Scarpe, on the right, to the line of the Commandant's House, southwest of Farbus wood and still well behind the German lines, on the left. On their right were VI Corps' 15th (Scottish) Division and on their left, the First Army Canadian Corps. The Corps' objectives were the enemy's Black, Blue, Brown and Green Lines. To reach the last-named line would entail the capture of the village of Fampoux. Further north, where the Brown and Green Lines ran closely together, the attackers would find themselves on the southern end of Vimy ridge and faced with the *Point du Jour* Line, which had been dug by the Germans during the winter that was showing such reluctance to loosen its grip.

The Corps would attack with three divisions in line and one division, the 4th, in reserve. From right to left the divisions in line were 9th (Scottish), 34th and 51st (Highland). The 9th (Scottish) were formed as part of the first tranche of the Kitchener New Army in the first month of the war and by May 1915 they were on the Western Front. Their first major action was the Battle of Loos where they, along with most of the units engaged, suffered heavy losses, especially among the officers. The GOC, Major General Thesiger, was one of three divisional commanders to lose their lives at Loos. The Division were also heavily involved in the Somme campaign. As part of XIII Corps they took part in the capture of Bernafay Wood and in the heavy and costly fighting required to loosen the German hold on Trônes wood, Longueval village and Delville wood[2] during and following the Battle of Bazentin Ridge. Later on in the campaign, by now part of III Corps, they fought in the Battle of

---

1   The Fergussons are an old Scottish family, but perhaps their most striking aspect is their close association with New Zealand. Sir Charles's father, Sir James, was the sixth Governor of the Colony. Sir Charles himself would become the third Governor-General of New Zealand from 1924 to 1930. In turn, his son, Sir Bernard (later Lord Ballantrae), was the tenth and last British appointed Governor-General, serving from 1962 to 1967. Unlike his distinguished ancestors, Sir Bernard's son, George, decided not to pursue a military career. Instead he chose diplomacy with the Foreign and Commonwealth Office. Perhaps inevitably, this led to him being appointed British High Commissioner to New Zealand for a four-year term in 2006.

2   Not for nothing is the South African National Memorial located in Delville Wood. Their tenacity in capturing and clinging on to it in July 1916 in the face of horrendous casualties is the stuff of legend.

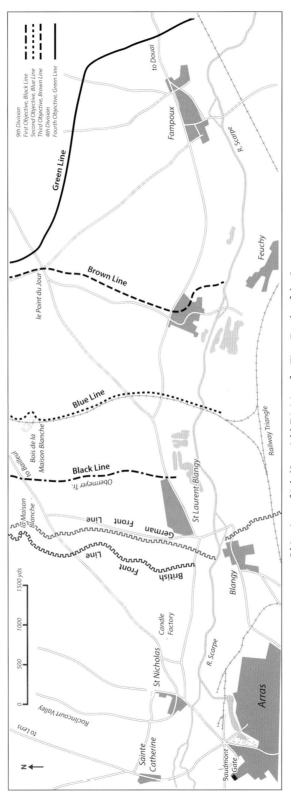

Objectives of 9th (Scottish) Division for First Battle of the Scarpe

the Transloy Ridges. By late 1916 the Division were in XVII Corps in preparation for the Battle of Arras. At about the same time Major General Sir Henry T. Lukin, a South African of British birth, took over the Division on promotion from his previous position as Commander of the South African Brigade. He would remain at the head of the Division until March 1918.

The Division's objectives on 9 April were, firstly, the Black Line from the River Scarpe to Chantecler, including the St Laurent half of the twin village of St Laurent-Blangy: secondly, the Blue Line, which consisted of the German second system resting on the Arras-Lens railway track: and thirdly, the Brown Line, the German third system from, and including, the village of Athies, to *Point du Jour*. When the third objective had been captured the Corps plan was that the 4th Division, initially in reserve, would pass through 9th Division and capture the Green Line, consisting of the German fourth system, including Fampoux village.

In 1914 the 4th Division were one of the six all regular infantry divisions based in Britain. It expected to be part of the BEF's immediate deployment to France on the outbreak of war but was one of the two divisions held back at the last minute in deference to Lord Kitchener's concerns about a possible German invasion of England. However it embarked for France only a few days late and, newly arrived, was in time to participate in the Battle of Le Cateau, the subsequent continuation of the Retreat from Mons and the Battles of the Marne, the Aisne, and First Ypres. In 1915 and 1916 it was engaged in Second Ypres and the Somme campaign. By the time of the Battle of Arras the Division had been commanded by Major General the Hon W. Lambton since 1915.

Air reconnaissance and patrols had established prior to the start of the assault that, whatever the German intentions might be south of the Scarpe, they had no plans to retire voluntarily north of the river; their lines were strongly held. Before the assault, St Laurent-Blangy was consequently subjected to bombardment by Livens Gas Projectors and 4 inch Stokes mortar shells in addition to the general preliminary artillery bombardment. Four tanks would also be assigned to 9th Division, which would assault at Zero on a three-brigade front. From right to left these would be the 26th, the South African and the 27th.

The creeping barrage that was fired in support of the six infantry battalions that led the divisional assault, a mixture of HE and smoke, was described as most effective in the divisional war diary. According to this document it enabled the troops to follow it up very closely throughout the attack suffering only 'tolerable' casualties from it as they did so.[3] Some of the war diaries of individual battalions paint a different picture that indicates that possibly a majority of the casualties suffered in the early stages of the advance were caused by friendly fire. The 26 Brigade's right hand battalion, 7th Seaforth Highlanders, in particular suffered significant casualties from the barrage; they were not alone. On the Seaforths' left 8th Black Watch suffered losses which they described as 'not great' but amounted to between 60 and 70. A contributory factor to these may have been their loss of direction to some extent and their veering left. To compensate, the industrious Seaforths had to stretch their line leftwards to maintain contact.

In the centre of the divisional line, the South African Brigade's initial assault was led by 3rd Regiment South African Infantry (SAI) on the right and 4th Regt SAI on the left, closely supported by 1st and 2nd SAI respectively.[4] The first wave of assaulting troops had moved forward from their front line into shell holes prior to Zero. At Zero proper their advance began, closely following the barrage which, contrary to the expectation of the South Africans that its cadence would not alter, had opened with 'a tremendous roar'.[5] It dwelt for four minutes on the enemy front line before beginning to creep forward. The 3rd Regiment's war diary described the barrage in fulsome terms, saying that its accuracy and intensity afforded perfect cover and inspired the greatest confidence in the men.

3   TNA WO 95/1738: 9th (Scottish) Division War Diary.
4   In South African parlance the terms 'regiment' and 'battalion' seem to be interchangeable, but the formal term for an infantry battalion was 'regiment'.
5   TNA WO 95/1785: 4th South African Infantry (SAI) Regiment War Diary.

Nevertheless, as the assaulting waves crossed no man's land, they suffered a considerable number of casualties, including 10 officers, from machine gun and rifle fire. When they reached the Black Line they set about clearing and consolidating it.[6]

The South African 4th Regiment were also pleased with the support and protection offered by the artillery barrage, although they did suffer casualties from men following it too closely. When they reached the first objective their moppers up were so close behind the assault battalions that they were able to bomb the German dugouts before the occupants had time to emerge and offer resistance. Those Germans who did survive the onslaught and offered no resistance were taken prisoner. Those who did try to resist were dealt with. The Regiment regrouped in preparation for their advance to the second objective.[7]

On the South Africans' left, 27 Brigade led with 12th R Scots, right, and 6th KOSB, left. They were supported respectively by 9th SR and 11th R Scots.

The enemy's artillery response had begun eight minutes after Zero but never became significant. The main early problem came from an enemy machine gun firing from the Parrot's Beak, a very well protected and manned strong point that had resisted all attempts to destroy it over the weeks prior to the battle. It caused casualties among 7th Seaforths and was one of the machine guns which contributed to the losses suffered by 3rd Regt SAI. The Seaforths quickly overran the strong point and its machine gun emplacement, killing the crew.

The bad light of an overcast early April morning and the obliteration of landmarks by the artillery meant that there was some confusion on the part of many troops as to their precise whereabouts. Some moppers up passed by dugouts which had not been cleared. This led to instances of enemy troops emerging and firing into the backs of assaulting troops, particularly the South Africans. It could have been much worse had not the opening barrage killed significant numbers of defenders with many of the survivors being only too glad to put up their hands. The problem was subsequently explained as having arisen from there being too few moppers up to cope with the very large numbers of enemy troops occupying their front trenches, not all of whom had been looking to surrender. The South Africans recorded that the moppers up in their sector, the supporting 1st and 2nd Regiments, suffered severe casualties to the extent of using up much of their fighting strength.[8]

As had been foreseen, the enemy strongly resisted the British attempts to drive them out of St Laurent, launching bombing raids on their attackers from houses and cellars in the village. Their resistance was gradually overcome by 7th Seaforths, who also succeeded in capturing the island in the River Scarpe located between the two villages, even though its capture had been an objective of 15th (Scottish) Division. The Seaforths' war diary described this action in some detail.

> Second Lieutenant Brash with 4 men observed enemy on the island holding up the attack of our troops south of the river. Three of the enemy were at once shot and this party crossed the bridge and attacked the Germans from the rear. Twenty prisoners were taken on the island which was cleared by 0630 and which was gained with the 13th Royal Scots on the mainland.[9]

By 0630 most of the Black Line was in British hands.

At 0736 the second phase of the attack began on schedule with, in 26 Brigade's sector, assaults on the railway cutting and the railway embankment on the Arras-Lens railway (the Blue Line). Almost immediately, the two companies of 8th Black Watch involved, supported by two companies of 10th Argylls, began to suffer casualties from their own barrage falling short. When the barrage at last moved on and they were able to resume their advance they came under heavy machine gun and rifle

6   TNA WO 95/1784: 3rd SAI Regiment War Diary.
7   TNA WO 95/1785: 4th SAI Regiment War Diary.
8   TNA WO 95/1777: South African Brigade War Diary.
9   TNA WO 95/1765: 7th Seaforth Highlanders War Diary.

fire from both flanks. On the right it was coming from the south side of the River Scarpe. Once again the attackers lost direction and veered northwards, away from the enemy guns they could do little about. But the fire from the left was quickly seen to be largely from machine guns clearly visible to them. They were dealt with by keeping the crews' heads down with Lewis gun fire and rifle grenades until they could be rushed and eliminated. German losses were high. Many defending the railway line surrendered including one regimental commander. By 0845 the assaulting troops were moving about freely on the Blue Line as the ridge just to its east was being consolidated. The 8th Black Watch confirmed they had captured their sector of the Blue Line despite their errant route and heavy losses (only two officers had not become casualties). The Seaforths, who had also completed the capture of their sector of the line, despite being peppered by enemy gas shells, were initially prevented from working down it to the river by heavy machine gun and sniper fire from the southern bank of the river. With the Black and Blue Lines now being consolidated by the Brigade's lead battalions, the remainder of the Argylls and the 5th Camerons moved through to continue the advance.[10]

In common with 26 Brigade the South African Brigade entrusted the assault on the Blue Line to the same regiments used in the attack on the Black Line. As these regiments moved forward from the Black Line the two supporting regiments moved up and took the vacated line over. There the 1st Regiment found itself under fire from an enemy machine gun situated south of the River Scarpe and suffered some casualties. The assaulting regiments encountered little opposition until they reached the valley to the west of the railway cutting. There they came upon large quantities of uncut wire. Tempting though it might have been to use the paths left through it by the enemy it soon became apparent that anyone doing so was almost certain to become a casualty.[11] As they moved forward, the assaulting troops came under heavy fire from machine guns located on the western side of the cutting and visible to the South Africans. They were engaged by Lewis guns, which quietened them down. Their crews were then killed by an artillery barrage. For the final advance to the Blue Line all four companies were committed by the 3rd Regiment, which had suffered heavy casualties. The railway cutting sector of the Blue Line was successfully taken by the Regiment, which then pushed out a line of Lewis gun outposts as far forward as could be managed without coming under their own barrage.[12]

During the advance a gap had opened up between the South Africans and the 8th Black Watch on their right. The latter had been slowed down by some determined enemy opposition. The South Africans were able to offer sufficient support to enable the Highlanders to overcome their difficulty.

In the 27 Brigade sector the 9th SR and 11th R Scots passed through the 12th R Scots and 6th KOSB at about 0730 for the assault on the Blue Line. The last two named battalions had probably lost some of their edge through the casualties suffered in taking the Black Line, many of which had been inflicted by their own artillery barrage falling very short. They nevertheless had captured *Obermeyer* trench (the Black Line) by 0640, and many men had pushed on and occupied the sunken road east of the line.[13] They now became the support for the two new leading battalions. As these advanced into the valley on their way due east they in turn were ill-served by their artillery barrage, being unfortunately held up for 30 minutes waiting for it to lift off the second objective. This proved to be too much for the patience of some of the troops who tried to push on, some paying the ultimate price for their intemperance. The attackers were also met by some hostile artillery fire and by machine gun fire from the Arras-Lens railway line in front of them and the Bois de la Maison Blanche on their left, which caused heavy casualties to the 11th R Scots, particularly among the officers and NCOs. At least two of these machine guns were effectively preventing 34th Division, on 27 Brigade's left, from advancing in their sector. By dint of bringing enfilade Lewis gun fire and rifle grenades to bear on them 11th R Scots were able to silence them, enabling their neighbours to resume their advance.

10   TNA WO 95/1766: 8th Black Watch War Diary.
11   TNA WO 95/1785: 4th SAI Regiment War Diary.
12   TNA WO 95/1784: 3rd SAI Regiment War Diary.
13   TNA WO 95/1772: 6th KOSB and 9th Scottish Rifles War Diaries.

With the assistance of a company from 6th KOSB the machine guns targeting them from the railway were rushed and eliminated as the enemy railway positions were overrun. Those Germans not taken prisoner were killed; none escaped. For their part the right hand assaulting battalion, the 9th SR, appear to have enjoyed a relatively trouble free advance. By 0810 they had secured their second objective.[14] The Brigade pushed forward 200 yards beyond the railway and dug in. Lewis gun patrols pushed even further forward.

At 1030 a message from Corps HQ stated that two battalions of the enemy 25th Bavarian Regiment had effectively been eliminated and, if a prisoner were to be believed, a third battalion which had been due to move up on 8 April, may well also have been wiped out. It seemed possible that there remained few enemy to hinder further advances by 9th (Scottish).[15]

The four tanks allotted to the Division had not enjoyed a good day. Two of them had quickly been put out of action by artillery fire. A third broke down 200 yards short of the railway line. The officer commanding the fourth was killed and it consequently failed to reach the railway. Fortunately they were not greatly missed.[16]

In accordance with the timetable the Division's advance on the third objective, the village of Athies and the Brown Line, began at 1215. The hostile barrage was weak and the threat from south of the river was alleviated to a large extent by the putting down of a smoke barrage along the river. The first wave of attackers which, in the case of 26 Brigade, now consisted of 10th Argylls on the right and 5th Camerons on the left, found that the wire in front of them was almost entirely untouched but fortunately incomplete. They were therefore able to force passages through it, probably materially assisted by the demoralisation of the enemy facing them, many of whom were in full flight, helped on their way by Lewis guns which had been brought forward. Several enemy guns were captured[17] in and around Athies, which fell without opposition.[18] By 1345, the 26 Brigade, which had been strengthened by the support of a brigade from 4th Division, were entering the Brown Line. Even though their advance was a little slower on the eastern edge of Athies they were soon reporting that both the Brown Line and Athies were in their hands.[19] The 4th Division 12 Brigade, which had suffered 150 casualties as a result of being held up in the open by the slowness of 26 Brigade's advance ahead of them,[20] thereupon passed through on their way to attack the Green Line. The Argylls then retired from the Brown Line to the Blue Line, to be followed during the evening by 5th Camerons. For the remainder of the battle, until being relieved on 15 May, the Brigade's battalions alternated periods in the front line with time in the support lines, without becoming involved in any serious offensive action.

For their advance on the Brown Line the South African Brigade replaced their initial two assaulting regiments with their 1st and 2nd Regiments. Their advance went exactly as intended. There was little opposition except for some artillery fire which caused a few casualties. Although the dense enemy wire was uncut, two passages left through it by the enemy were found and used by the South Africans to pass through and enter the Brown Line. There they found many of the enemy were taking advantage of occasional breaks in the British barrage to surrender in small groups. Those that did try to get away by fleeing to the rear, leaving behind arms and equipment, were ruthlessly cut down by Lewis gun fire. By 1500 the South Africans were relieved by 4th Division. They withdrew to the Black

14   Ibid.
15   TNA WO 95/1738: 9th (Scottish) Division War Diary.
16   John Ewing, *The History of the Ninth (Scottish) Division*, p. 196.
17   Most of the gun crews were captured including their Commandant and his dachshund dog. The latter was expropriated by 26th Brigade's GOC.
18   A Sergeant MacLennan of the 10th Argylls was credited with personally killing 15 of the enemy with rifle and bayonet on this day. He was awarded the DCM.
19   TNA WO 95/1762: 26 Brigade War Diary
20   TNA WO 95/1502: 12 Brigade War Diary.

Line which they consolidated and from where they sent out Lewis gun patrols.

(The South Africans subsequently commented very favourably on the artillery support they received throughout the course of the day. They described it as excellent and a great boost to morale. This despite the fact that casualties were caused among some troops who followed the barrage too closely. These losses were deemed by the South Africans to be an acceptable price to pay for the protection afforded by the barrage. In their view its absence might well have resulted in much heavier losses from unhindered enemy action.)

At 1417, 27 Brigade reported that their 9th SR and 11th R Scots had passed through the Brown Line and were now entering the Green Line. The CO of 11th R Scots again expressed exasperation at the difficulty in getting their barrage lengthened from its accurate concentration on the third objective, preventing his Battalion from occupying it. It also made it impossible to send patrols forward. The CO lamented the absence of Forward Observation Officers (FOOs) in his Battalion sector, who might have had more success than he in getting the barrage to lift. By around 1500 the 4th Division 11 and 12 Brigades were passing through the 9th Division troops in the Brown Line. In accordance with their designated objectives, the two brigades were on their way to capture Fampoux village and the Hyderabad redoubt and to pierce the Green Line, which at this point consisted of a fourth German trench system on a reverse slope of the *Point du Jour* ridge. On the right 12 Brigade advanced with three battalions in line. From right to left these were 1st King's Own, 2nd Lancashire Fusiliers and 2nd Essex, with the Brigade's fourth battalion, 2nd Duke of Wellington's (West Riding) Regiment (Duke's), following close behind 1st King's Own. They found the wire in front of the German fourth system virtually untouched but met very little opposition when they entered and took possession of it. The 1st King's Own took about 70 prisoners and captured several guns that were later turned on the enemy using ammunition they had failed to remove.[21] The rest of the opposition was dealt with by Lewis guns. The majority of the enemy fled eastwards; the remainder surrendered. The advance of 2nd Lancashire Fusiliers closely mirrored that of 1st King's Own in its incidents and outcomes. But two of the Battalion's companies advanced further, to the line of the Fampoux-Gavrelle road where they came under heavy machine gun fire which forced them to dig in just east of the road.[22] The 2nd Duke's at this point moved through 1st King's Own on their way to capture Fampoux. Their advance was initially held up by the slowness of their supporting barrage to lift. They then suffered a few casualties at the hands of enemy shellfire when they entered the village from the west. As they progressed through the village some enemy holding out in houses had to be bombed out. When the Duke's reached the eastern side of the village they came under heavy machine gun fire, largely emanating from the slopes on the southern side of the River Scarpe, preventing any further advance to the Green Line 500 yards further east.[23] Instead they consolidated the village and placed machine guns in the upper stories of buildings still standing. These were able to pour withering fire on Germans trying to shelter in shallow trenches. The 9th Division meanwhile were ordered to reorganise in the Black and Blue Lines and be prepared for the possibility of enemy counterattacks.

On the left, on schedule at 1510, the 11 Brigade's 1st SLI and 1st Hampshire Regiment (Hampshires) advanced towards the German fourth system. The SLI were unable to get closer to their own barrage than 100 yards because a number of shells were falling short. They found the system's thick protective wire had been practically untouched by artillery, but some of the attackers found gaps left by the Germans, cut others and passed through protected by supporting fire from their comrades. As they entered the front trenches, most of the Germans they found there surrendered. Those in the support trenches fled to the rear, but many were shot down. The 1st East Lancs, following up behind the Hampshires, formed a defensive flank between the *Point du Jour* and the fourth German system.

---

21 TNA WO 95/1506: 1st King's Own (Royal Lancaster) Regiment War Diary.
22 TNA WO 95/1507: 2nd Lancashire Fusiliers War Diary.
23 TNA WO 95/1508: 2nd Duke of Wellington's Regiment War Diary.

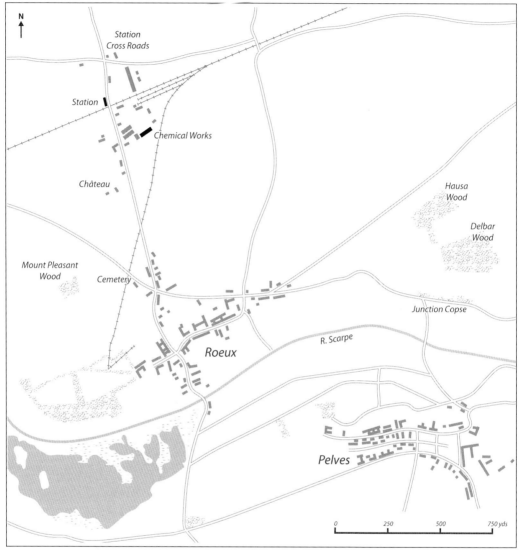

N

Station
Cross Roads

Station

Chemical Works

Château

Hausa
Wood

Delbar
Wood

Mount Pleasant
Wood

Cemetery

Junction Copse

Roeux

R. Scarpe

Pelves

0   250   500   750 yds

Roeux and the Chemical Works.

They took Effie trench and consolidated it for use as a support line. The Battalion encountered considerable opposition in the vicinity of the *Point* from determined enemy gunners who kept their guns in action until the East Lancs were closing in on them. Their attempts to withdraw their guns were unsuccessful. With the German fourth system in British hands patrols were pushed out and the digging of a double line of strong points put in hand, despite the close attention of enemy shellfire, one of the victims of which was the Battalion's CO, who was killed outright.

The Brigade's remaining Battalion, 1st RB, following up 25 minutes behind 1st SLI, suffered some casualties from enemy guns getting through the German fourth system wire. They also took losses in the sunken road. Both these positions had evidently been previously registered by the enemy artillery. The wire protecting the Hyderabad redoubt was found to have been practically untouched by the British artillery. The strong point was nevertheless rushed by the RB's leading platoon, who induced its occupants to surrender. When patrols were immediately pushed forward they came under heavy machine gun fire from the direction of the Inn to the east and from riflemen lying down in the open between the redoubt and the Gavrelle-Roeux road. The patrols were forced to abandon their plans to dig posts east of the redoubt and instead concentrated their efforts on consolidating the redoubt itself. It is probable that the stiffening of enemy resistance at this stage came about through the arrival of the troops of a fresh division from reserve. They, and those of the original defenders who had been persuaded to abandon their flight from the 4th Division advance, were subjected to heavy rifle and machine gun fire and suffered significant losses. Notwithstanding, two enemy battalions counterattacked just before dark. They were stopped in their tracks by an artillery barrage and rifle and machine gun fire from the Hampshires and the RB. After dark the enemy began digging in about 400 yards from the northeastern and southern sides of the redoubt.

During the night preparations were begun to continue the Division's advance with an attack by 12 Brigade on Roeux village, the station and the Chemical Works on the right of the Brigade's line of advance. Its aim was to support an attack by VI Corps south of the River Scarpe. Zero Hour was set for 1500, the earliest possible time by which all the preparations could be completed. However, orders were received at 1325 from XVII Corps cancelling the attack and instead ordering the Brigade to support an advance of 1 Cavalry Brigade towards Greenland Hill and the Plouvain-Gavrelle road by pushing out strong fighting patrols to try to gain ground and clear a passage for them. Unfortunately this order reached the front line too late to prevent one of the Brigade's assaulting battalions, 1st King's Own, from attacking in accordance with their original orders. Their attack failed in the face of heavy machine gun fire as they attempted to emerge from the relative shelter of Fampoux. So too did that of 11 Brigade, whose 1st SLI and 1st Hampshires were ordered to broaden the front for the cavalry by sending out strong patrols and bombing up the fourth trench system in an attempt to reach the line of the Roeux-Gavrelle road. They were met by heavy machine gun and rifle fire that inflicted significant losses before they had progressed 200 yards. Two enemy counterattacks mounted during the evening were successfully stopped by machine gun and artillery fire. The cavalry, on whose behalf these infantry battalions had suffered such great losses, advanced as far as Fampoux where they were heavily shelled. By now, knowing what awaited them in the form of concentrated enemy machine gun fire, they were forced to recognise reality and abandon their plans to gain ground to be consolidated by the infantry following behind. They instead, after dismounting to help the infantry fend off an anticipated German counterattack, which proved to be half-hearted, removed themselves to the western outskirts of the village.

The 4th Division's operations on 11 April would be much influenced by the difficulties in launching attacks over the open ground between Fampoux and the railway station just to the north of Roeux Chemical Works. The ground was commanded to the south by the enemy held railway embankment and Mount Pleasant wood and to the north by enemy strong points grouped round the Inn. There was no scope for assembling troops under cover or for deploying them without their coming under converging machine gun fire. The only option, if heavy infantry casualties were to be avoided, would be first of all to reduce the enemy strong points by artillery barrage and then give full artillery support to the subsequent infantry assault. The first priority was therefore to get XVII Corps heavy artillery and the field artillery batteries into position with adequate ammunition for these tasks. In reasonable weather conditions it was reckoned that, for the heavy artillery, it would take the six hours of darkness before dawn on the 11th, to enable it to begin its bombardment of the station, Inn, Roeux Château and other known strong points at daybreak. For the field artillery it would be midday before its preparations were complete. Unfortunately the weather was far from ideal; heavy snowstorms began at 1800 on the 10th and persisted throughout the night, making artillery movements extremely difficult. The orders for the attack, as first conceived, were nevertheless issued.

There could be no question of calling on 11 and 12 Brigades to lead the infantry assault. They were exhausted from 36 hours of fighting and digging in dire weather. The 10 Brigade, which would take over the lead, had been in reserve until this point, although it had provided the two assaulting brigades with help in the form of carrying parties and stretcher bearers over the first two days of the battle. Only two of its battalions could therefore be deemed to be fully fresh. They were relieved in the Brown Line at 0700 on 11 April and moved forward to their assembly positions in the sunken road. Despite their exhausted state 11 and 12 Brigades would also have to play significant supporting roles in the action.

Unsurprisingly, given the circumstances, the artillery preparation was to prove inadequate. In particular it failed to eliminate enemy batteries that had pre-registered on the only possible places of assembly for the attacking infantry. These were the outskirts of Fampoux, the sunken road running north to the Hyderabad redoubt, and the redoubt itself. The entrance to the sunken road was in full view of the enemy. The route to it through Fampoux was under constant heavy enemy shelling. The Brigade's advance from its assembly positions on the western edge of Fampoux began at 1000 and was led by 2nd Seaforths, followed by 1st Royal Irish Fusiliers (RIF). The two battalions formed up for their attack by turning east on the sunken road between Fampoux and Hyderabad redoubt. The Brigade's other two battalions, the Household Battalion (HB) and 1st Warwicks formed up behind the Seaforths and the RIF respectively. Elements of 12 Brigade assembled south of the two lead battalions which were in position by 1100. So far their progress had apparently been unnoticed by the enemy. But this changed when they were spotted by a hostile aircraft; soon thereafter the sunken road came under shellfire.

At Zero Hour, 1200, the two battalions advanced and immediately came under very heavy machine gun fire from the Inn, the Chemical Works, the station, Roeux Château and the railway embankment. At the same time the enemy put down an artillery barrage on Fampoux and east of the sunken road where 10 Brigade's remaining two battalions were still trying to assemble. Despite the hostile fire the assault battalions struggled forward. One platoon of the RIF managed to get within 200 yards of the station before being forced back for fear of being surrounded and cut off. A party of the Seaforths managed to get into a new trench about 150-200 yards from their first objective, where they maintained themselves for some time before being forced back by a counterattack which they had no ammunition left to deal with. Very few got back to their own lines. The two support battalions, the HB and 1st Warwicks, advanced at Z plus 10 minutes, having already lost many men to the enemy bombardment of the sunken lane. They made hardly any progress as the enemy machine guns in turn took their toll.[24]

The 12 Brigade's 1st King's Own, reinforced by companies from 2nd Lancashire Fusiliers and 2nd Duke's, also attacked with a first objective of Roeux village to be followed by a second objective of Delbar wood. Because of the marshy state of the ground to be traversed, a circuitous route had to be followed. This, coupled with the height of the railway embankment to be crossed, meant that the assaulting troops fell behind the creeping barrage which, in any case, was considered to be 'thin'. The

---

24   The assault led by 10th Brigade's 1st Royal Irish Fusiliers and 2nd Seaforth Highlanders was sadly a not untypical example of the demands placed upon the infantry during the Arras campaign. According to the Official History, 'it was pressed with extraordinary gallantry and determination by the two first-line battalions, which went forward regardless of withering fire from the château, the Chemical Works, the station and the embankment'. A 21 year old Lieutenant Donald Mackintosh of the Seaforths led by outstanding example. The citation for his posthumous Victoria Cross reads in part as follows.

> ... during the initial advance, Lieutenant Mackintosh was shot through the right leg, but although crippled, continued to lead his men and captured the trench. He then collected men of another company who had lost their leader and drove back a counterattack, when he was again wounded and although unable to stand, nevertheless continued to control the situation. With only 15 men left he ordered them to be ready to advance to the final objective and with great difficulty got out of the trench, encouraging them to advance.
> He was wounded yet again and fell. The gallantry and devotion to duty of this officer was beyond all praise.

The impossibility of the task confronting the two battalions is reflected in the Seaforths' casualties. They lost all 12 officers and 363 Other Ranks out of 420.

attackers experienced great difficulty in getting over the embankment as enemy machine guns firing from Mount Pleasant and Roeux were in action. To overcome their threat, three machine guns and every available Lewis gun were placed on the embankment. They provided satisfactory covering fire. Unfortunately the whole operation was compromised by the failure of 10 Brigade to deal with the enemy occupying the Chemical Works and the trenches in front. Without these being neutralised there was no prospect of 12 Brigade getting further forward. They found themselves extended along the railway embankment where they were to spend a bitterly cold and snowy night under shellfire, without greatcoats or the prospect of any hot food.[25]

At 1400 Divisional HQ ordered 10 Brigade to mount a new attack immediately to secure their first objective. Zero would be 1530 after the artillery had carried out a 30-minute bombardment directed mainly at the Chemical Works and Roeux Château. The 2nd Seaforths and 1st RIF, who were supposed to carry out the attack, did not in fact receive their orders until 1600. Both battalions were still disorganised from the heavy losses they had suffered earlier and were in no condition to mount a further assault, a fact immediately conveyed to the Brigade Commander by the Battalion COs. In the case of the Seaforths their losses amounted to all 12 officers and 360 out of 420 ORs engaged.[26] All of the RIF's' officers had also become casualties.[27] The Brigade GOC concurred in this assessment by the Battalion COs and ordered them instead to continue digging in where they were.[28]

The 11 Brigade had been given the role of supporting the 4th Division's left flank by forming a defensive flank between the Hyderabad redoubt and the Inn and linking up with the left of 10 Brigade. The necessary attack to achieve this was entrusted to 1st SLI. The enemy immediately reacted with heavy machine gun fire followed by artillery barrages on the redoubt and sunken road. The SLI were consequently unable to advance far and suffered heavy casualties in their attempts to do so. By contrast 1st Hampshires successfully bombed their way up the Fourth German System as far as Honey trench and the 1st East Lancs advanced their line 400 yards down the Gavrelle road.[29]

Since their exertions on the first day of the battle 9th Division's involvement had been confined to placing a brigade at the disposal of 4th Division. The choice fell on the South African Brigade, which was however only required to act as a reserve. But as a consequence of the failure of 4th Division's attack on the 11th, the 9th Division were ordered to make the same attack the following afternoon, passing through 4th Division on their way up. The first phase would consist of an attack north of the Feuchy-Plouvain railway by the South African and 27 Brigades. Assuming the first phase was successful, 26 Brigade would deploy under cover of the railway embankment and advance south capturing Mount Pleasant wood and Roeux village with special details to attend to the houses south of the railway, the Chemical Works and Roeux Château. A machine gun barrage would support the attackers and heavy artillery would bombard known enemy machine gun positions, the sort of support that might have achieved a different outcome the previous day. The 4th Division were ordered to support the 9th's attack. They accordingly mounted two minor operations involving 1st Hampshires and 1st RB. The former tried to bomb up the Fourth German trench system and the latter sought to form a defensive flank between the Inn and the same trench system. Both operations started at 1330 but the battalions immediately came under heavy flanking machine gun and rifle fire. In the case of 1st RB this was compounded by heavy frontal fire which led to the loss of two officers and 51 men before the attackers had advanced 200 yards.

On the morning of the day of the attack 9th Division HQ received a message from South African Brigade that the men had had no sleep for four nights and no hot food since 8 April. It was doubtful if they were fit for any severe fighting. When informed of this message the Corps Commander warned

25 TNA WO 95/1506: 1st King's Own (Royal Lancaster) Regiment War Diary.
26 TNA WO 95/1483: 2nd Seaforth Highlanders War Diary.
27 TNA WO 95/1482: 1sr Royal Irish Fusiliers War Diary
28 TNA WO 95/1479: 10 Brigade War Diary.
29 TNA WO 95/1446: 4th Division War Diary.

that if the attack were delayed there would be no guarantee that it would enjoy heavy artillery support when it was eventually mounted. He specified that the Corps' ultimate objectives were Greenland Hill and the spur southwest of Plouvain. If further objectives were attainable they should be secured, saving the need to attack them later. The South Africans decided to attack on a two battalion front, with the 1st on the right and the 2nd on the left, each reinforced by two companies of the 4th Battalion. The 3rd Bn would be in reserve.

At 1200 the South African and 27 Brigades, on the right and left respectively, began their advance towards the jumping off points for their attack, east and north of the village of Fampoux. There was no artillery protection as the two brigades deployed for their attack, which in its later stages involved a 30 minute advance from their forming up positions to the point where they would reach the front line held by 4th Division at Zero, when the British bombardment and their assault proper would begin. The enemy could not have failed to observe these movements and brought down a heavy artillery barrage on Fampoux which caused severe South African casualties. Even the 3rd Regiment, who were in reserve for the attack, suffered severely as they moved to the west side of Fampoux. As 27 Brigade's attack would involve an advance of 1,700 yards in full view of the enemy, they requested that smoke should be fired from Zero minus 45 minutes. Instructions were accordingly sent to the CRA but were unfortunately received too late for any action to be taken.

Zero Hour was 1700. The British barrage, described by the 1st South African Regiment as 'very thin', opened. Immediately it passed over the leading line the men started to follow it, but it travelled much too fast for them to keep up. For the South Africans, their objective was the road running north from Roeux, through the Chemical Works to the railway station. It involved crossing 700 yards of open ground under a destructive enemy barrage. The South African advance was almost immediately held up, partially by the very accurate enemy artillery concentrated on them, but mainly by heavy machine gun fire, which the British barrage had failed to suppress, unsurprisingly as it seemed to be targeted on a line some 500 yards east of the 4th Division front line, which put it well behind the enemy's first line of defence.[30] There was also no sign of any attention being paid to the Chemical Works and the station by the heavy guns.[31]

The 27 Brigade's two assaulting battalions, 11th and 12th R Scots, both of which attacked on a three company front, suffered heavy casualties from the enemy barrage. Not even the concentrated fire of the 11th Battalion's machine guns could compensate for the lack of a supporting artillery barrage in those minutes prior to Zero. The shaken Scots nevertheless advanced but within 300 yards were under intense machine gun fire. The British barrage, which in any case from the Scots' perception lacked the required intensity, began by falling much too far ahead and then crept even further forward, thus offering little or no protection to the unfortunate infantry, whom it outpaced from the start; without its cover the casualty toll mounted even further. The 11th Battalion were to record 11 officer and 160 OR casualties and the 12th 13 officer and 250 OR losses stemming from the action. The 9th Division's History described the action of 12 April as calamitous with little that could be said in defence of it. 'Preparations and arrangements were hurried to a culpable degree. The Corps heavy artillery might as well have remained silent for all the assistance they gave.' The time reconnoitring the enemy's positions, particularly by the artillery, was miserably inadequate, and defeat was practically inevitable when 27 Brigade had to be formed up in full view of the enemy. The History assigned much of the blame for the undue haste forced on Divisional HQ by their being too far back, thus lengthening the time for orders to be conveyed to their recipients.[32]

Both brigades sent back messages around two hours after Zero that they were held up and their attacks had failed, thus negating earlier reports that their first objective had been reached.[33] At 2045

30   TNA WO 95/1781: 2nd SAI Regiment War Diary.
31   TNA WO 95/1780: 1st SAI Regiment War Diary.
32   John Ewing, op. cit., pp. 203-5.
33   TNA WO 95/1777: South African Brigade War Diary.

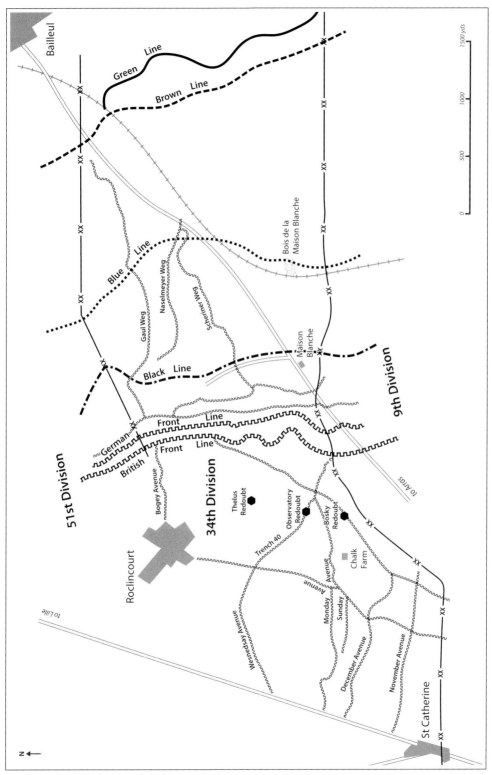

Objectives of 34th Division for First Battle of the Scarpe.

both brigades were informed that 26 Brigade would take over the line from the River Scarpe to the Hyderabad redoubt, thus relieving them both and enabling them to move back to the former German Fourth Line trench system where they would be in support. The relief took place during the night of the 12th/13th. Two nights later the Division were relieved by 51st Division and moved back into billets.[34] The 4th Division had to wait much longer for relief. Their time was spent from 14 April onwards in preparing for the next major action due to be launched on the 23rd. This involved generally unsuccessful attempts to gain ground by individual battalions and a great deal of digging. The Division was finally relieved on the night of 20th/21st April by 37th Division and withdrew to rest in the XVIII Corps area.[35]

The 34th Division was in the centre of XVII Corps attack on a three divisional front on 9 April. The Division's formation was authorised in December 1914 as part of the 5th Tranche of the KNA. Originally designated the 41st Division it was renumbered the 34th in April 1915 when the KNA Fourth Tranche was broken up. The Division became home largely to 'Pals' battalions, most notably the four battalions each of the Tyneside Scottish and Tyneside Irish badged into the Northumberland Fusiliers (Northumberlands). The Division arrived in France in January 1916 and would spend the rest of the war on the Western Front. It first saw intense action on the first day of the Somme when, as part of III Corps, it attacked at La Boisselle and suffered horrendous casualties even by the standards of that tragic day, appreciably the worst of the 16 divisions involved. A small body of Tyneside Irish had the distinction of making the largest advance recorded that day, 4,000 yards. But none survived.

The Division was led on the Somme by Major General E.C. Ingouville-Williams (irreverently known as 'Inky Bill'). He survived that terrible first day, but was killed soon thereafter, on 22 July, by a stray shell. After the Somme the Division moved into II Corps. From there it transferred to XVII Corps and Third Army in February 1917. It would be commanded for the Battle of Arras by General Ingouville-Williams' successor, Major General C. L. Nicholson, who would remain in command for the rest of the war.

On 9 April the Division attacked with all three brigades in line. From right to left these were the 101, 102 (consisting of the four Tyneside Scottish battalions, 20-23 Northumberlands) and 103 (the four Tyneside Irish battalions, 24-27 Northumberlands). Each brigade would attack on a two-battalion front, with their remaining two battalions in each case assuming the lead once the first two objectives (the enemy Black and Blue Lines) had been secured. When the enemy Brown Line had been captured, strong patrols were to be pushed out eastward to reconnoitre for a line east of the Brown Line, between *Point du Jour* and *Maison de la Côte*, which would best serve for observation. In all probability this would roughly conform with the Green Line. Once selected, it was to be dug out and become the British front line. The divisional orders emphasised the need for the leading waves of the assault to follow the creeping barrage closely. Four tanks were allotted to the Division.

At Zero the assault was launched. Within very short order Divisional HQ was receiving only scraps of information concerning its progress. It was noted that, largely in common with the experience along the whole length of the Third Army advance, the enemy counter barrage, which began seven or eight minutes after Zero, was weak and generally ineffective. A positive piece of information received at 0715 indicated that the whole of *Maison Blanche* ridge had been taken, signifying that at least the Black Line had been secured. During the course of the day Divisional HQ received further sketchy indications of their brigades' progress, usually pointing to hold-ups.

The 101 Brigade had launched its attack with 16th R Scots (2nd Edinburgh) leading on the right and 11th Suffolks on the left. The 15th R Scots (1st Edinburgh) were in support of their sister battalion and the 10th Lincolns (the 'Grimsby Chums') were in position on the left and rear of the Brigade. Such was the enthusiasm of 15th R Scots that they advanced so quickly that they became

---

34   TNA WO 95/1738: 9th (Scottish) Division War Diary.
35   TNA WO 95/1446: 4th Division War Diary.

in effect part of their sister Battalion's assault on the enemy Black Line, which had been taken by Zero plus 35 minutes after an advance of 550 yards. The advancing troops had found that although the artillery barrage had done its work in dealing with the enemy wire and trenches it had left their dugouts relatively undamaged. Many of the enemy troops had taken refuge in them but had been killed or captured as they emerged.

At 0936 the advance to the Blue Line, 750 yards away across difficult ground, began. It included traversing a thickly wired valley, a sunken road and a 20 foot high embankment. The wire proved less of an obstacle than anticipated and the enemy artillery fire continued to be feeble. The main problem was rifle fire from railway cutting and the Bois de la Maison Blanche. This was overcome by their capture less than 20 minutes into the advance. The 16th R Scots and 11th Suffolks then set about consolidating them. The latter had had a relatively easy time in their advance through the Black Line to the Blue Line and had suffered few casualties.[36] The 15th R Scots and 10th Lincolns, the latter somewhat belatedly, then prepared for the assault on the Brown and Green Lines. The sector of the Brown Line that they would be attacking appeared from aerial photographs to be a track running north from a ruined farmhouse on the *Point du Jour*. The overenthusiastic support of the 15th R Scots for their sister Battalion during the attacks on the first two objectives may partially account for their apparently depleted strength following completion of the capture of the Blue Line. Because of their numerical weakness the Scots asked the Lincolns to take over part of their sector. The Lincolns were unable to do so, as a result of which there was a gap of fully 100 yards between the two battalions. The attack moved off at 1220, the Scots in one thin line, the Lincolns tending to edge right because of the gap but nevertheless maintaining direction fairly well. The covering artillery barrage was thin and ragged as the guns were firing at the extreme end of their range. As they closed in on their objective, the Scots saw a large body of enemy infantry advancing from the east. They promptly engaged them with rifle fire forcing them to make a hasty retreat, leaving about 50 dead behind. It was surmised later that the enemy body had intended to mount a counterattack on the railway cutting and had been taken by surprise by running into the Royal Scots so far to the east of where they had believed them to be.[37]

The Lincolns' leading companies reached Joke line where they came under point-blank fire from an enemy field gun battery and some sniping from their front and their left rear which caused a number of casualties. They nevertheless pushed on to Jemmy line. The uncut and untouched enemy wire that confronted both battalions, had to be dealt with by the use of wire cutters by parties of men as the rest lay down and waited. Despite the delay that this imposed, which lost them the protection of the barrage, and the close attention of the enemy field gun fire, the near absence of any serious infantry opposition, apart from snipers, enabled the attackers to overrun the *Point du Jour* and to enter, and take full possession of, the Brown Line by about 1430 with only relatively light losses. The line was found to be a trench covered in corrugated iron, making it comparatively easy to consolidate. Outposts were set up about 300 yards in front of the line. They would form the basis of the Green Line. Patrols were pushed out half a mile beyond; they found no sign of the enemy.[38]

The assault of 102 (Tyneside Scottish) Brigade was led by 22nd Nothumberlands on the right and the same regiment's 21st Battalion on the left. The 20th Battalion was in support and the 23rd in brigade reserve. The assaulting battalions encountered little opposition from an enemy apparently demoralised by the Brigade's machine gun barrage and a most effective artillery barrage, and by 0850 they were in, and patrolling beyond, the Blue Line, the second of their objectives. It would however be well over three hours before news of their success reached Divisional HQ. The 20th and 23rd Battalions took over at this point. The 23rd Battalion's left flank was in the air owing to 103

36   TNA WO 95/2458: 16th Royal Scots and 11th Suffolk Regiment War Diaries.
37   TNA WO 95/2457: 15th Royal Scots and 10th Lincolnshire Regt War Diaries.
38   Peter Bryant, *Grimsby Chums*, pp. 86-95.

Brigade's difficulties in the Blue Line. There were casualties from their own artillery barrage, which had become thin and scattered. A thick belt of wire in front of the western section of the Brown Line was found to be uncut requiring lanes to be cut through it by hand by men under sniper fire. Despite these difficulties the western section of the Brown Line was soon taken. The eastern section proved to be a greater challenge as the delays forced on the assaulting battalions by the difficulties described above had enabled the enemy to reorganise and meet the attack with heavy rifle fire. The attackers nevertheless managed to get themselves within charging distance of their objective, which they then rushed and took at the point of the bayonet. They then pushed posts forward to the Green Line.

The 103 (Tyneside Irish) Brigade's four Northumberlands battalions had deployed for their part in the attack with the 24th and 25th leading on the right and left respectively, the 26th in close support and the 27th in divisional reserve. Thirty minutes before Zero the leading waves left their trenches and formed up in no man's land. The trench mortar barrage was very effective and as it lifted the first enemy line was carried by the first wave; moppers up were left in it. The second wave then leapfrogged through and took the German support trench. By Zero plus 34 minutes the Black Line had been occupied. The German dugouts were cleared and many prisoners taken. Although the operation so far had gone apparently smoothly, all the officers in the first wave had become casualties. The advance to the Blue Line nevertheless began on schedule. At 1015 Divisional HQ learned that the Brigade were suffering heavily from machine guns located in this line and from enfilade fire from the Pump and *Zehner Weg* on their left flank. The existence of this enfilade fire was the result of difficulties being experienced by 51st Division 152 Brigade around the Black Line which had prevented them from coming up into line on 103 Brigade's left. When the Highlanders did come up they advanced half right across 25th NF's front and there came under machine gun fire that forced them to retire and become thoroughly mixed up with the Tyneside Irish in the *Mittel Weg*. Sorting this out was no easy job with only two officers still standing to exercise control, but eventually the situation was cleared up by the Highlanders advancing and getting into the Blue Line. At the same time two companies of the 25th, taking advantage of the protection from the enfilade machine gun fire afforded by the lie of the land, also got into the Blue Line but further south than they should have been, thanks to the loss of direction by the Highlanders. The two officers and 80 troops who had not become casualties worked their way left up the Blue Line towards their objective. On the Battalion's extreme left 13 men found themselves with two officers of other regiments and some Highlanders. They moved up *Gaul Weg* and *Zehner Weg* to deal with an enemy machine gun and get into the Blue Line. The line finally fell to 103rd Brigade when 26th and 27th Battalions took over the attack in co-operation with elements of 51st Division. Attempts to get further forward were thwarted by enemy machine gun fire from the *Gavreller Weg*. Although the Brigade had only taken two of the four lines that were its first day objectives, the Brigade Commander considered his men had done exceedingly well considering their heavy losses of officers and sergeants. Only two officers and five sergeants remained unhurt after the day's fighting.

At the end of the first day of the battle the situation appeared to be that the Division's assault had achieved virtually all its objectives on the right and in the centre, but not on the left. In the 101 Brigade's sector on the right, the 15th R Scots and the 10th Lincolns were holding the Brown and Green Lines and had pushed out patrols in front of the latter. In support, the 16th R Scots were in the Brown Line and 11th Suffolks in the Blue Line. Four machine guns had been brought up to the Brown Line and strong points were being constructed by teams of Royal Engineers and Pioneers. On the 101's left, the 102 Brigade's 20th and 23rd Northumberlands were in the easternmost trench of the Brown Line and in touch with the 10th Lincolns on their right. Their left was about on the junction of the *Gavreller Weg* with the Brown Line. In support, the 22nd Northumberlands were holding the westernmost trench of the Brown Line astride the Gavreller Weg and had set up posts along the Weg. The 21st Northumberlands were in the Blue Line where their left was in touch with the 103rd Brigade's furthest forward Battalion, the 26th Northumberlands. Both the 26th and the 27th Northumberlands were in the Blue Line where the latter's left was in touch with the 51st Division's right hand brigade. The two battalions had established posts in *Gaul* and *Muiden Wege*. The two supporting battalions, the 24th and 25th Northumberlands, had been pulled back to the Black Line. During the night two strong points were constructed and occupied, one at the junction of *Gaul Weg* with the Blue Line and the other at the junction of *Zehner* and *Kurzer Wege*.

The divisional orders for the second day of the battle reflected the relative lack of progress that had been made on the first day in 103 Brigade's sector. The Brigade were ordered to attack the enemy's *Gavreller Weg* line and advance and capture a section of the Brown Line including *La Maison de la Côte*. The Brigade's two assaulting battalions, the 26th and 27th Northumberlands, would be reinforced by the 102nd Brigade's 21st Northumberlands. On their left the right hand battalion of the 51st Division would cooperate by advancing to the Brown Line simultaneously with their extreme right directed towards *La Maison de la Côte*. The place of the assaulting battalions in the Blue Line would be taken by three companies of the divisional Pioneer Battalion, the 18th Northumberlands. Zero was set at 0500 to ensure sufficient time for the Brown Line to be taken before daylight. Artillery support would consist of the shelling of roads and railway tracks between *Gavreller Weg* and the Brown Line and a barrage placed east of the Brown Line. There would be no bombardment of the *Weg* and line themselves. The guns would open up just prior to Zero.

By 0930 Divisional HQ had learned that the Brown Line had been captured and patrols sent out towards the Green Line. One of these patrols overreached itself and was cut off with the loss of one officer and 15 men killed. Organised resistance had been encountered mainly at *La Maison de la Côte* and prisoners had been taken. At 0950 Divisional HQ sent a message to the brigades emphasising that it was essential that the Green Line should be completed and occupied on this day. At the same time the consolidation of the Blue and Brown Lines should be continued. Patrols were to be pushed out towards Gavrelle to regain touch with the enemy and secure any abandoned enemy guns. Finally every effort should be made to reorganise the brigades so as to be ready to make a further advance when required.

At 1010 a message was received from Corps HQ informing Division that 51st Division were to take over that part of the 34th Division's front immediately to the 51st's right. This involved the relief of 103 Brigade by 152 Brigade that night. The operation was completed by 0800 on the following morning, the 11th.

Still in the front line, 101 and 102 Brigades continued to push out patrols beyond the Green Line. At 1304 the former Brigade reported that patrols of the 16th R Scots had travelled 1,200 yards east of the Green Line without meeting any enemy. They observed that the enemy seemed still to be working on their Bailleul-Gavrelle line, about 5,000 yards east of the British front line. The workers on the line had been dispersed by artillery. At 1545 patrols from both brigades confirmed a complete absence of enemy for a significant distance beyond the Green Line. The main problem, apart from the dreadful weather, which caused the death of at least two men from exposure and exhaustion,[39] was the enemy artillery which focused its attention throughout the day and the next on the *Point du Jour* and nearby trenches and caused many casualties.

At 2355 on 12 April the Division received notification that it would be relieved on the night of 14th/15th by XIII Corps 63rd (Royal Naval) Division. Their last full day in the line proved to be relatively quiet. The relief was completed in the early hours of the 15th and the Division withdrew to Arras.[40]

The XVII Corps left-hand and northernmost Division on 9 April was the 51st (Highland) Division. By the time of the Battle of Arras, the Division was well on the way to overcoming the

---

39   TNA WO 95/2458: 16th R Scots and 11th Suffolks War Diaries.
40   TNA WO 95/2433: 34th Division War Diary,

slight hint of the second rate that attached to all territorial units and was establishing its legendary reputation, with friend and foe alike, as one of the best British infantry divisions on the Western Front. As 1/1 Highland Division it was one of the 14 territorial divisions established under the Haldane army reforms of 1908. It was mobilised on 5 August 1914 and, almost to a man, quickly signed the Imperial Service Obligation, thus waiving their right not to be sent overseas. After a period of training in the Bedford area the Division moved to France in April/May 1915. A few days later they lost their original designation of 1/1 Highland Division and became the 51st (Highland) Division. Their initial blooding was in the last desperate days of the Second Battle of Ypres. This was quickly followed by their participation in the last phases of the Battle of Festubert. Neither of these operations had offered much scope for distinction. Nor did the Division's involvement in XV Corps' prolonged efforts to capture High Wood during the Somme campaign do anything to help them bury the nickname 'Harper's duds' by which they had become known. It derived from the 'HD' of their stylised divisional flash and the name of their GOC since September 1915, Major General G. M. Harper. But in virtually the last action of the Somme campaign, the Battle of the Ancre, which opened on 13 November 1916, the Division demonstrated that it had become a formidable fighting machine by capturing the German Y Ravine salient and the fortified village of Beaumont Hamel. Both had been objectives for the first day of the Battle of the Somme, 136 days earlier.

On 11 February 1917 the Division became part of XVII Corps and took up positions in the front line running from east of Roclincourt to west of the Arras-Lille road, in an area familiar to them from their early days on the Western Front. The role assigned to them in the forthcoming battle was to capture the southern shoulder of Vimy Ridge in conjunction with the Canadian Corps on their left and 34th Division on their right. The initial assault was entrusted to 152 Brigade on the right and 154 Brigade on the left. Each would assault on a two battalion front; 152 Brigade with 6th Gordons on the right and 6th Seaforths on the left; 154 Brigade with 9th R Scots on the right and 4th Seaforths on the left. Ready to take over for the assault on the day's later objectives would be 8th Argylls and 5th Seaforths (152 Brigade) and 4th Gordons and 7th Argylls (154). The 5th Gordons of 153 Brigade were assigned to 152 Brigade as a reserve. The remainder of 153 Brigade, 6th and 7th Black Watch and 7th Gordons, were in divisional reserve.

The configuration of the battlefield and the enemy's dispositions opposite the Division meant that, while the direction of assault was generally east, one reinforced company of 4th Seaforths on the extreme left would have to attack in a northerly direction in order to capture an enemy position, the Lille road salient, in a joint operation with the Canadians on their left. They would then form a defensive flank. If it were not dealt with, this position would enable the enemy to enfilade the Seaforths and the other assaulting battalions. After some heavy fighting on and in communication trenches, the joint operation ended in total success. Despite stubborn resistance the 50 strong German garrison was overcome by Canadians who had worked round behind them. Elimination of this enemy position materially assisted 154 Brigade's completion of their plan to carry all their objectives as far as the Black Line despite the stiff enemy opposition which resulted in heavy casualties after the first enemy trench had been overrun.

On 154 Brigade's right, 152 Brigade's 6th Gordons, taking full advantage of an effective creeping barrage with which they remained in touch, reached and took their objectives, but not without heavy losses particularly of officers. The 6th Seaforths on their left, despite an accurate supporting barrage[41] that afforded them a relatively trouble free advance to the first German trench, subsequently found themselves being enfiladed by heavy machine gun and rifle fire as they sought to deal with both the second and third German lines. Apparently emanating from positions half right of them, the small arms fire was so intense that all the officers on the Seaforths' right became casualties leaving the

---

41   The barrage was subsequently described as accurate but less intense than the one under which they had advanced at Beaumont Hamel. WO 95/2867.

NCOs to lead. Following the latters' example the men dealt summarily with snipers as they were detected. By 0700, the right wing had a firm footing in the Third line, but it was not until 0900, well behind schedule, that the continuing enfilade machine gun and rifle fire had been overcome and the Black Line secured in their sector. In the centre of the Battalion's advance an officer and 40 men moved up the Switch trench with little resistance and reached and occupied a section of the Black Line by Z plus 34 minutes. On the 6th Seaforths' left the advance was slowed down considerably by the heavy enemy small arms fire. The Black Line was reached by 0750, but there was still heavy fighting, with serious losses, before it was fully secured.

The 6th Seaforths had been so held up that the 5th Seaforths, coming up behind, had had no alternative but to make an early entry into the fight to help clear the ground for their own advance. The Seaforths had not been helped by the two tanks allotted to the Division being put out of action before they could play a part. Unusually for the first day of the battle, the Germans seem to have operated a semblance of the recently devised system of defence in depth in this area. They had evacuated their front line in front of the 6th Seaforths which enabled them to put down an artillery barrage on it as the Seaforths reached it, causing early casualties. A single shell was responsible for 15 of these. The gaps left in the Highlanders' ranks enabled the Germans to bring some of their machine guns, which had been missed by the depleted advancing Scots, into action once the British barrage had passed on. Dealing with them then became a job for the infantry with all its attendant risks. These were reflected in the very severe casualties suffered by the Battalion in capturing the Black Line, estimated to have amounted to 329 officers and men. Only one officer of those who had set off remained both alive and unhurt. Even A Company of the 5th Seaforths, who should not have been involved in fighting at this early stage, suffered 90 casualties before reaching the Black Line.

A further blow was suffered when there was a massive explosion as 6th Gordons, 5th Seaforths and 8th Argylls were traversing the Black Line, causing deaths and injuries and several buried in the three battalions. The cause was attributed to the deliberate detonation of a Minenwerfer bomb store by the enemy; six Germans who tried to surrender just afterwards, and were assumed to have been responsible, were immediately killed.[42]

It was not until 1418 that the Blue Line was reported captured on the 152 Brigade front. They were in touch there with 154 Brigade who had also completed the taking of the Blue Line after severe fighting. This Brigade's battle plan had envisaged the initial assault battalions, the 9th R Scots on the right and the 4th Seaforths on the left, taking the Black Line before the 4th Gordons and 7th Argylls moved through to attack the Blue Line. Although the R Scots' war diary gives no hint of any difficulty having been experienced by the Battalion in completing their task, that of the 7th Argylls indicates that it was only with their assistance that the R Scots were able to take the Black Line in the face of heavy machine gun fire. Even though they were also seriously affected by the enemy machine guns, which caused them to lose the protection of the barrage, the Argylls managed to move on to the Blue Line and secure it. The next phase of the attack, the advance to the Brown Line, began at 1125. As they left the Blue Line they realised that 152 Brigade on their right were held up and that they were coming under heavy machine gun fire from the direction of *Zehner Weg*. They swung round to the right to meet this threat, attacked, took three trenches and captured two machine guns and 70 prisoners. They had however inevitably lost direction, were further right than they should have been and no longer in a position to capture the Brown Line.[43]

The 4th Gordons' initial objective was the Blue Line. As they advanced they suffered casualties, from enemy artillery as well as machine guns. It was only by committing the whole Battalion that their Blue Line objectives were secured. They had suffered particularly seriously in their ultimately successful efforts to capture the *Zwischen Stellung* strongpoint. Officer losses had been severe.

42   TNA WO 95/2866: 5th Seaforth Highlanders War Diary.
43   TNA WO 95/2886: 7th Argyll & Sutherland Highlanders and 4th Gordon Highlanders War Diaries.

On leaving the Blue Line in their advance to the next objective, the Brown Line, the leading two companies began to lose direction to the right, probably as a result of 7th Argyll's rightward move. One platoon, which did manage to follow its prescribed route, managed to reach the Brown Line and establish contact with the Canadians on their left.

The remnants of 152 Brigade's battalions lost no time in pushing on towards the Brown Line. The enemy were holding *Regiment Weg*, but by 1515 it was in British hands along with a number of prisoners who included a high ranking officer. Posts were pushed forward from *Regiment Weg* and the position itself was consolidated. The Brown Line however remained in enemy hands. This would remain the case for the rest of 9 April in 51st Division's sector except for the small intrusion made by the 6th Seaforths' platoon.

The first priority for the following day was to complete the capture of the Brown Line. Orders were issued for 5th Gordons, on detachment from 153 Brigade, to capture 152 Brigade's sector of the line in a predawn attack. The initial assumption that 154 Brigade's sector of the line had been secured and only two companies would therefore be needed for the attack proved false and it was stepped up to an attack involving the whole Battalion. There would be no artillery support. The assault would take place in conjunction with 34th Division on the right. The joint first objective was Elect trench.

At 0430 the 5th Gordons formed up in, and in front of, *Regiment Weg* and advanced. The frontal opposition was comparatively light but there was heavy enfilade machine gun fire. The trench was nevertheless taken within 10 to 15 minutes and enemy troops were observed withdrawing hurriedly to the northeast. The second wave companies then passed through to assault the Brown Line. The attack was pressed with such resolution that the Germans began to evacuate their positions enabling the Gordons to deal with the wire in front of the Brown Line with comparative immunity. There were nevertheless losses from German fire from the north, the direction of the enemy retreat. The Brown Line was occupied. Two companies pushed beyond to take up a line along a sunken road. The other companies remained in support in the Brown Line. Although the right flank was secured by 34th Division, the Gordons' left flank was exposed by the absence of 154 Brigade from their planned position. Hostile machine guns were active and troublesome and efforts to suppress them resulted in all those involved becoming casualties. The sunken road was held throughout the day despite heavy hostile artillery and machine gun fire. This diminished the following day, but an effort by a patrol to seize the railway line was stopped by a hostile barrage which forced the patrol to withdraw.[44]

In the 154 Brigade sector, early morning patrols on the second day of the battle had established that the Brown Line was still strongly held by the enemy. Two attempts to dislodge them were made by 7th Argylls who bombed up Tommy and Ouse trenches in conjunction with a flank attack to the right of the latter trench. The attempts failed in the face of heavy resistance and uncut wire. The 4th Gordons were equally unsuccessful in their attempts to bomb in from the left flank by way of Toast and Tired trenches. Their difficulties were compounded by the continued bombardment being placed on the Brown Line by the British artillery. Plans to resume the attack by both battalions the following day were cancelled when patrols established that the enemy had evacuated the Brown Line during the night. It was quickly occupied and consolidation began.

Apart from 5th Gordons the participation in the first phase of the battle by 153 Brigade, was largely confined to activities such as providing carrying parties and taking over the vacated positions of units advancing to the attack. On 11 April 7th Black Watch and 7th Gordons were due to attack a section of the Brown Line and the sunken road, but their orders were cancelled when the enemy withdrawal was discovered.

The Division was relieved on the night of 11th/12th and moved out of the line.

---

44   TNA WO 95/2881: 5th Gordon Highlanders War Diary.

7

The Cavalry

The planning for the Battle of Arras foresaw a significant role for the Cavalry. Early exchanges between Allenby and Haig, both cavalrymen, had focused on how the mounted arm should be used. In his diary Haig recorded that Allenby was keen to use it rather more aggressively than Haig deemed prudent. But neither had any doubt that it should play a pivotal part in the battle. To this end the Cavalry Corps Headquarters, the 2nd and 3rd Cavalry Divisions and the 17th (Northern) Infantry Division were placed at the disposal of Third Army. The 4th Cavalry Division (consisting of three Indian Army Cavalry brigades) were allocated to Fifth Army. The 1st Cavalry Division had initially been placed at the disposal of First Army. But on 5 April it was withdrawn into GHQ Reserve, although the expectation was still that if they were to be employed during the battle it would be in support of the First Army Canadian Corps.[1]

The C in C and the commanding generals of the three armies envisaged using the cavalry in one of its traditional roles of exploiting the anticipated success of the infantry in creating gaps in the enemy defences. The 17th Infantry Division had been assigned to the Cavalry Corps to follow behind the cavalry and take over and consolidate any gains the latter might make so as to free them to move on with minimal loss of momentum. In the light of the cavalry's involvement on the Western Front since the advent of trench warfare these aspirations might be construed, in the familiar words of Dr. Samuel Johnson, as representing the triumph of hope over experience.

The cavalry were in the war from the very beginning. An enlarged division consisting of five brigades formed part of the BEF which disembarked in France in mid-August 1914. One of the constituent regiments, the 4th (Royal Irish) Dragoon Guards, was the first BEF unit to see action in the war when it skirmished with German cavalry just northeast of Mons on 22 August. During the Retreat from Mons and the subsequent Battles of the Marne and the Aisne the cavalry fulfilled another of their traditional roles, keeping the enemy at arm's length and in the dark while at the same time gathering information about their dispositions and strength. They carried out these tasks with consummate skill and established a gratifying tactical superiority over their opposite numbers, not least because of their readiness to dismount and engage them with their well-honed skills with the rifle. During the First Battle of Ypres the Cavalry found itself largely fighting in a dismounted role shoring up parts of the line as the BEF fought desperately, and ultimately successfully, to stop a German breakthrough to the Channel.

Although the advent of trench warfare in late 1914 left the cavalry with no clearly defined role, their presence on the Western Front increased in the first year of the war to a Corps of three divisions. During the Somme campaign there were fleeting opportunities for it to make effective interventions but they were missed. The Fourth Army Commander, General Sir Henry Rawlinson, an infantryman, found it hard to overcome his doubts about the cavalry's capacity to prevail in modern battlefield conditions. In large part because of these doubts, the cavalry were never quite in the right place at the right time. Significant opportunities were thereby lost on two occasions.[2]

---

1   G.W.L. Nicholson, *Official History of the Canadian Army in the First World War: Canadian Expeditionary Force 1914-1919*, p. 258.

2   As GOC Fourth Army General Rawlinson was in overall command for the opening days of the Battle. Thereafter he and General Sir Hubert Gough (GOC Reserve (later Fifth) Army) conducted the campaign jointly. The significant

Field Marshal Paul von Hindenburg,
German Army General Chief of Staff.

General Erich Ludendorff, First Quartermaster-
General of the German Army.

By the time of the Battles of Arras the Cavalry Corps, consisting of four divisions, had been under the command of Lieutenant General Charles Kavanagh for eight months. He would remain at its head until the end of the war.

The mission of the Cavalry Corps in the Battle of Arras was, in broad terms, to seize and hold the line Riencourt – Cagnicourt – Dury – Etaing with a view to further operations towards Cambrai. Two scenarios for fulfilling the mission were drawn up, depending on whether or not the Corps would be in a position to make their move on the first day of the battle or at some time subsequently. If the former, the Corps would advance through Arras onto and along the Arras-Cambrai Road in the order 2nd and 3rd Cavalry and 17th Infantry Divisions. The 4th Division would come into Corps Reserve about Croisilles. If the latter, the Corps would advance through the gap that had been opened up on the Third Army front, with 4th Division leading followed by 2nd Division, with 3rd Division taking over as Corps Reserve. The 17th Infantry Division would follow as closely behind as the situation permitted.

In more detail, the task of 2nd Division would be to take and hold the high ground on the right bank of the River Sensée between Fontaine-lès-Croisilles and Vis-en-Artois, their right flank to rest on the general line Wancourt – Fontaine-lès-Croisilles and their left on the Arras-Cambrai road. Their line of advance thereafter would cross the road at La Brioche Farm and pass through Sauchy-Lestrée and Haynecourt, thence north of Cambrai to Ramillies. For their part 3rd Division would take and hold the line from Vis-en-Artois north to Boiry-Notre-Dame and thereafter follow the same

---

opportunities referred to occurred on the first day of the Battle and on 14 July (the first day of the Battle of Bazentin Ridge). In the former case the cavalry might well have exploited XIII Corps early success in capturing Montauban. In the latter, had a successful charge by two squadrons of cavalry, which gave the British a toehold in High Wood, been mounted earlier in the day in much greater force, it might well have completely undermined the German defences in Delville Wood, Longueval and High Wood, which were going to give the British so much trouble over the succeeding weeks.

Crown Prince Wilhelm of Germany,
Army Group Commander

Crown Prince Rupprecht of Bavaria,
Army Group Commander

route as 2nd Division from La Brioche Farm to Ramillies. If at any stage the enemy's retirement became a disorderly retreat the two divisions would need to ensure their readiness to follow up the enemy at once.

At 1440 on 9 April the Cavalry Corps received orders from Third Army HQ that the 2nd and 3rd Divisions should advance immediately from their First Positions of Readiness at Ronville to their Second Positions west of The Harp just southwest of Tilloy-lès-Mofflaines. The 2nd Division moved off with 3 Brigade leading followed by the 5th. By 1630 the two brigades were concentrated on their Second Positions and were sending out patrols to clarify and report on the situation ahead. An hour later, the Division 4 Brigade had joined them. It did not prove practical to make any further progress before nightfall. The Division were ordered to withdraw to overnight bivouacs between Wailly and Agny in the Crinchon Valley. Because of road congestion it was not until 0200 that most of the Division reached their bivouacs. For one of their RHA Batteries it was 0530.

The 3rd Division began their move forward at 1530 using a dedicated cavalry track running from the eastern outskirts of Arras parallel to and north of the Arras-Cambrai road. The track proved to be very heavy going, especially for the guns and limbered wagons, once they began crossing the British and enemy trench lines. It was however passable for cavalry and the leading squadrons of 8 Cavalry Brigade were soon in position and sending out patrols. Their reports and other sources made it clear by 1810 that the Brown Line was not wholly in British hands as had been supposed. The Divisional Commander ruled out any question of moving further forward until the line and especially Orange Hill, which would afford the enemy good observation of the Cavalry's movements, had been secured. By nightfall the situation had not changed, and at 2040 the Division were ordered to water at the river south of Athies and then bivouac north of Tilloy-lès-Mofflaines. At 0130 they were ordered back to Arras racecourse, west of the city, where water, forage and rations were available.

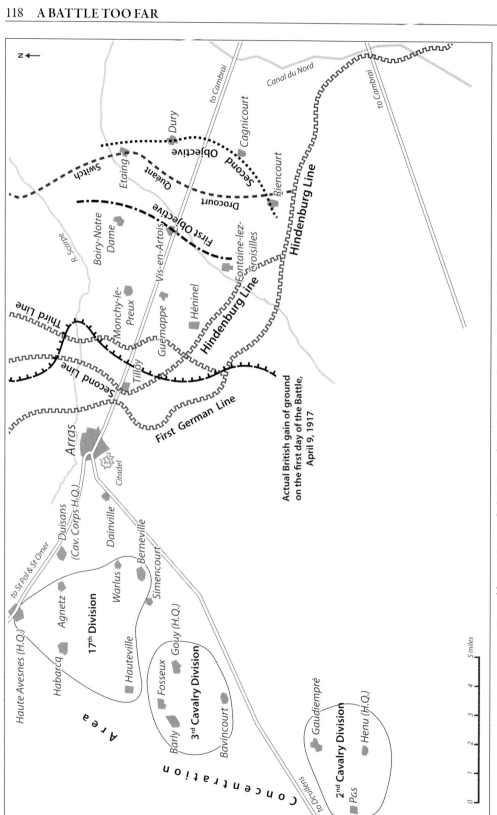

N

to Cambrai

Canal du Nord

to Cambrai

Dury

Cagnicourt

Switch

Second Objective

Etaing

Quéant

Riencourt

Drocourt

Hindenburg Line

R. Scarpe

First Objective

Boiry-Notre Dame

Vis-en-Artois

Fontaine-lez-Croisilles

Monchy-le-Preux

Héninel

Hindenburg Line

Third Line

Guémappe

Tilloy

Second Line

First German Line

Arras

Citadel

Actual British gain of ground on the first day of the Battle, April 9, 1917

to St Pol & St Omer

Duisans (Cav. Corps H.Q.)

Dainville

Berneville

Simencourt

17ᵗʰ Division

Warlus

Habarcq

Agnetz

Hauteville

Gouy (H.Q.)

Haute Avesnes (H.Q.)

Fosseux

3ʳᵈ Cavalry Division

Barly

Bavincourt

C o n c e n t r a t i o n   A r e a

to Doullens

Gaudiempré

2ⁿᵈ Cavalry Division

Henu (H.Q.)

Pas

0 1 2 3 4 5 miles

Assembly positions and objectives of Cavalry Corps for First Battle of the Scarpe.

During the night Cavalry Corps HQ received orders for the divisions to be prepared to move in the morning, initially by 0700. This was later changed to 1100, by which time the divisional advanced guards were to be ready to move at 30 minutes' notice and the rest of the divisions at 60 minutes. When firm orders were received these were for the 2nd and 3rd Divisions to be at their 2nd Positions of Readiness by 1200 and 1230 respectively.

At 1115 GHQ placed 1st Cavalry Division, less its 9 Brigade, back under the orders of the Cavalry Corps. GHQ had already the day before put 9 Brigade at the disposal of First Army. Cavalry Corps HQ lost no time in ordering the Division 1 Brigade to move along the north bank of the River Scarpe against Greenland Hill. The Brigade duly reached Fampoux with 2 Brigade moving up in support. At 1540 the Division were ordered to push on and occupy Plouvain and Greenland Hill, then send out reconnaissance patrols to Vitry-en-Artois, Fresnes-lès-Montauban, Gavrelle and further north to a line running from Izel-lès-Equerchin to Oppy by way of Neuvireuil.

At the same time the 2nd and 3rd Divisions were to advance broadly astride the Arras-Cambrai Road ready to exploit any success achieved on the VI Corps front. By 1430 squadrons of the 3rd Dragoon Guards (6 Brigade) and 1st Essex Yeomanry and 10th Hussars (8 Brigade) were on Orange Hill. The Essex and 10th Hussars pushed out patrols towards Pelves who quickly reported that the slopes and spurs north of Monchy were still held by the enemy who had targeted the patrols with their machine guns. The 10th Hussars suffered serious losses in both men and horses. Although taking fewer casualties, an Essex patrol found themselves cut off. They were only able to get back under the shelter of darkness and a blinding snowstorm. The 3rd Division ordered their brigades to bivouac where they were for the night. The day had been bitterly cold with frequent snowstorms. The horses would suffer severely from exposure and lack of water. To make matters worse for 8 Brigade, they were to pass the night at Feuchy Chapel under continuous and heavy shellfire which inflicted further losses particularly among 10th Hussars' horses.

At about 1600 2nd Division were close to The Harp and were ordered to push on through 14th Light Division towards their first objective. It was at about this time that confirmation was received from 37th Infantry Division that the Brown Line was wholly in British hands. Elements of the same Division had also been seen moving into Monchy-le-Preux. A telephone message from the Cavalry Corps Commander, timed 1550, told 3rd Division that the Infantry on the south side of Monchy were pushing on well. The Division should therefore push on rapidly, taking risks if necessary. The attackers believed that the enemy were holding Monchy with only two battalions and they were confident of dislodging them fairly soon.

By 1720 however it was clear to Cavalry Corps HQ that the infantry had not completed the capture of the village. Cavalry patrols reported that 37th Division were held up at the western exits from Monchy and in a sunken road northwest of the village. A message from 37th Division a few minutes later confirmed that some of the 8th Lincolns and 8th SLI were being held up by heavy machine gun fire. To assist them, 8 Brigade were ordered to gallop the ridge running northeast to Pelves Mill as it was essential to secure their objectives before dark. The squadron of 10th Hussars which attempted to make the gallop were however stopped by heavy artillery and machine gun fire. They were only saved from annihilation by a sudden snowstorm under cover of which they managed to extricate themselves. Two other squadrons of 8 Brigade were also held up by heavy machine gun fire, emanating from the area between the north of Monchy and the River Scarpe.

At 1830 37th Division, in contrast to their earlier optimism, assessed their situation west of Monchy as not rosy. On the telephone to 3rd Division, the Cavalry Corps commander, General Kavanagh, said that he and General Allenby had agreed that the Cavalry should make a determined effort to get Monchy that night; they attached great importance to its rapid capture. General Kavanagh considered there was an opportunity for the cavalry to achieve important results by working wide round the enemy's flank in co-operation with the infantry. It soon became clear that this assessment was unrealistic as the infantry were held up by artillery and machine gun fire all along the front. At 1900 the 6 Cavalry Brigade reported that they could not get forward because the two brigades of 37th Division ahead of them were being held up by machine gun fire coming from Monchy. The opportunity for cavalry-infantry co-operation simply did not exist. The 6 Brigade's orders were modified; they were to offer every possible support to the infantry in the event of a counterattack, but not to take part, dismounted, in any attack launched by the infantry.

A cavalry light armoured car (LAC) was sent forward towards Les Fosses Farm on the Arras-Cambrai road. It got beyond the farm and was close to La Bergère and engaging enemy troops crossing the road when it ditched in a shell hole.

Earlier, at 1845, Cavalry Corps HQ had been told by Third Army to co-operate with the infantry in their attempts to capture Monchy. In conformity with this order the three cavalry divisions were instructed by Corps to have a brigade each ready to move at 0500 the next morning (the 11th) with the rest of each division ready to move an hour later. All three infantry corps were to attack the enemy's defences, running from Wancourt through Guémappe, Monchy, Pelves, Mount Pleasant wood to a point about 3,000 yards just west of north of the wood, with the cavalry to be prepared to take advantage of any success achieved by pushing forward through them should opportunities occur. Each cavalry division would therefore need to ensure that it had one brigade close behind the infantry and in close touch with them. The overall aim of the offensive was to capture the Quéant-Dury line south of the River Scarpe. At the same time the Fifth Army would be attacking at Bullecourt. Zero Hour for the infantry attacks was 0500.

The 2nd and 3rd Cavalry Divisions moved forward during the night and were both in position by 0500 on the 11th. The 2nd Division 5 Cavalry Brigade were however forced to withdraw to an area about half a mile south of Tilloy-lès-Mofflaines when they came under heavy shellfire. When the Division began to move forward, they reported at 0930 that they were held up unable to advance further because the infantry they were following had been stopped in front of Wancourt. Two hours later they reported that both Wancourt and Guémappe were still in enemy hands, making it impossible for them to push further forward; they remained in positions northeast of Neuville-Vitasse. Their only contribution to the day's attack was the firing by three of their RHA batteries of barrages supporting an infantry assault on Wancourt and 3rd Division 8 Cavalry Brigade at Monchy. At 1540 the decision was taken to order the immediate withdrawal of the 2nd Cavalry Division back to their bivouacs between Wailly and Agny, just south of Arras. The withdrawal was completed, except for the RHA batteries, by 1850. Their War Diary expresses clearly the frustrations of their three days' involvement in the Battle of Arras.

> During the whole three days the cold had been intense; high winds with heavy snowfalls. The difficulty of watering horses was extreme, many only got what they could from shell holes between the forenoon of 10 April and their return to bivouacs on the night of 11 April. The going on the cavalry track from Ronville forward was so deep as to be nearly impassable and many horses were unable to struggle through it. The result is that a large percentage of the horses, especially in 5 Brigade which had the hardest time, were for the present quite unfit for active operations. The 4 Brigade, which was the greater part of the time in reserve suffered least and will only require a few days rest to recover.
>
> The Division casualties for the three days, 80 percent of which were suffered by 5th Brigade, were 11 officers (1 killed), 161 ORs (15 killed) and 668 horses.[3]

The 3rd Division were to achieve much greater forward momentum during the course of the day, even though they were to suffer some frustration as the infantry they were following made only fitful

---

3   TNA WO 95/1118: 2nd Cavalry Division War Diary.

progress on occasions. Fifty minutes after their attack started 37th Division reported that their centre brigade were held up by machine gun fire which was preventing them from entering Monchy. Six tanks had been told off to support the infantry attack. Two of these, assigned to the northern side of the village, did not make it to the start line. That left one to deal with the north and the other three to look after the south. Two of the latter very quickly became casualties, leaving just one tank on either side of the village to make a contribution to the action. This was nevertheless significant in enabling 111 Infantry Brigade to overcome German resistance. Indeed, if one German report is to be believed, their involvement may have been decisive in persuading them to abandon the village. (Ironically, two of the tanks were knocked out by the British artillery, virtually the only impact that arm had on the action.)[4]

By 0710, 8 Cavalry Brigade patrols were reporting that the left-hand battalion of the Infantry Division 112 Brigade were in the western outskirts of Monchy and probably in possession of half the village. Fortyfive minutes later 6 Brigade passed on a message from 112 Brigade that Monchy had fallen, and probably La Bergère too. The 8 Brigade partially confirmed the news about Monchy although their message indicated its eastern edge was still in enemy hands. On the basis of the claims that Monchy had fallen, however incompletely, 8 Brigade's Essex Yeomanry and 10th Hussars were ordered to move forward at 0830. The Royal Horse Guards would act as brigade reserve. The objectives of the lead squadrons were to seize and hold the high ground, villages and woods on the eastern spurs facing the River Scarpe about 4,000 yards east and northeast of Monchy. But there should be no question of any attempt being made to seize these objectives until information had been received that the village of Monchy and the sunken road leading northeast from Monchy to Pelves were both in British hands.

The lead squadron of the Essex Yeomanry, followed by that of 10th Royal Hussars, each accompanied by a section of machine guns, advanced over the southern end of Orange Hill. As they did so they were met by a severe artillery barrage between that point and the enclosures on the northwest side of Monchy. At the same time they also came under machine gun fire apparently coming from north of the Scarpe Canal. In an attempt to deal with this situation Cavalry Corps HQ requested that a barrage should be targeted on the southern corner of Mount Pleasant wood. The original intention of the leading squadrons of the Essex Yeomanry and 10th Hussars was to pass north of Monchy, but they were authorised, if the threat posed by the enemy's defensive fire was sufficiently serious, to make instead for Monchy itself. This was clearly the case. The Essex, who were leading, therefore galloped into Monchy through the village's northwestern entrance. The Hussars, following behind and relatively unscathed, immediately wheeled to the right and entered the village by the same route. Both squadrons made for the square in the centre of the village where they were joined by the rest of their regiments and an intensifying enemy artillery barrage.

Both regiments were intent on resuming their planned route as quickly as possible, especially as the effect of the artillery barrage was intensified by its high explosive shells crashing down on the hard surface of the paved main street, exploding instantaneously and causing serious losses, especially amongst the panic stricken horses. The Essex sought to take the sunken road northeast towards Pelves and the Hussars a slightly more northerly road towards Roeux by way of Pelves Mill. It soon became apparent that there could be no question of attempting to leave the village by these two routes in the teeth of enemy machine gun fire.

It was during this period that 8 Cavalry Brigade's Commander, Brigadier General Charles Bulkeley-Johnson was killed. He probably fell victim to a sniper as he made a reconnaissance on foot on the northern edge of Monchy to ascertain the prospects for getting the Brigade out of Monchy and on its way again. (With more imagination than adherence to the facts, his death was written up in the press as having occurred when he was leading his men in a cavalry charge which resulted

---

4   Colin Fox, *Monchy le Preux*, pp. 25-37.

in the capture of Monchy.)[5] He was succeeded in temporary command by Lieutenant Colonel Lord Tweedmouth, the CO of the Royal Horse Guards, whose Regiment had been ordered by General Bulkeley-Johnson to follow him in support to a hollow northwest of Monchy. When the Horse Guards crossed the summit of Orange Hill in obedience to the GOC's order they came under a heavy artillery barrage which forced them back to their starting positions some distance from Monchy,[6] leaving Lord Tweedmouth in no position to exercise operational command of the Brigade. Effective command therefore devolved on the Essex Yeomanry's CO, Lieutenant Colonel Francis Whitmore.

With their planned routes out of the village effectively barred by hostile fire Colonel Whitmore, after taking stock, decided to put the village into a state of defence. He found that the infantry, which had preceded the cavalry's entry into the village and were theoretically in possession of it, consisted of isolated small groups of men mainly sheltering in the cellars of houses. They had suffered heavy losses in fighting their way into the village, almost without artillery support, and were largely leaderless as virtually all their officers had become casualties. These scattered remnants of battalions of 111 and 112 Brigades, and possibly some belonging to 15th Scottish Division, who had found their way into Monchy from the north, were deployed by Colonel Whitmore, along with his own men, dismounted and reinforced with the regimental machine guns and Hotchkiss automatic rifles, on the northern, eastern and southern edges of the village and at two strong points in the Château garden and at the northeastern village exit. These deployments broadly conformed to the orders he and the CO of 6 Brigade had received, that they were to make no further attempt to advance until the hostile guns located behind the Bois du Sart and the Bois du Vert had been dealt with. Any forward movement was to be confined to patrolling in the hope of keeping a close eye on enemy movements.

In the meantime the concentrated enemy artillery barrage, which seemed to be increasing in intensity in a way that often presaged a counterattack, continued to inflict heavy losses on men and equipment and particularly on the unfortunate horses. The consequent losses in machine guns were partially replaced by retrieving abandoned Lewis guns.[7] In the early afternoon 8 Brigade reported on their situation. Essex Yeomanry were holding the northern, northeastern and southern exits of Monchy. They and the 10th Hussars were suffering heavy casualties, especially of horses, and had requested reinforcements of men and machine guns, and artillery support. In response, 6 Brigade ordered up one squadron of 1st North Somerset Yeomanry and 4 machine guns. The Royal Horse Guards also dispatched a squadron which was however unable to get into Monchy, taking serious losses in the attempt. They did however, when darkness fell, provide men to carry ammunition into the village on foot, and act as stretcher bearers. At 1400 the Germans were observed to be digging a new defence line running well to the east of Monchy from St Rohart Factory in the south to Pelves in the north by way of the eastern side of the Bois du Vert and the western side of the Bois du Sart.

By 1700 the village was considered to be in a fair state of defence but there were no reserves or supports to call on. Nor were there ready means available to the Essex or Hussars of communicating with Brigade HQ as their signalling equipment had been destroyed. To add to their problems they appeared to be at the mercy of German aircraft which seemed to have complete control of the air and used it to machine-gun ground targets, especially horses, with relative impunity.

Another 3rd Division regiment to be heavily involved in the battle for Monchy was 6 Brigade's 3rd Dragoon Guards. On 11 April they were the lead regiment of the Brigade. They maintained close touch with 112 Infantry Brigade, who were charged with taking la Bergère and getting into Monchy from the south. A report received by 6 Brigade from the 112th claimed that it was 'practically certain' that both objectives were in British hands. The report proved over-optimistic as it soon became evident to 3rd Dragoon Guards that heavy fighting was still taking place at both places following German

---

5   Ibid., pp. 36-7.
6   TNA WO 95/1156: 1st Essex Yeomanry War Diary.
7   Ibid.

counterattacks. Nevertheless, on the basis of 112 Brigade's claim, 6 Brigade, like the 8th, were ordered to advance. The Dragoon Guards moved forward with the Essex Yeomanry on their left in parallel. They advanced east to cross the road running south from Monchy to la Bergère on the Arras-Cambrai road to occupy their first objective, a ridge south of the village on the 100 metre contour. When the leading squadron advanced further the mounted troopers immediately came under fire from enemy artillery and three machine guns sited to sweep the valley between Feuchy Chapel and la Bergère. Despite serious losses, especially among the horses, the Monchy-La Bergère road was reached at the southern exit from Monchy. There the men dismounted and took cover in positions which closed the gap between the Monchy defences and 112 Brigade. In their respective positions both formations were subjected to heavy shell and machine gun fire, and an order was received from Brigade HQ at about midday for the RHA guns and the horses to be sent back to the Brigade's reserve positions. Observing this, the enemy intensified their shelling for the next two hours. But although some casualties were suffered during the withdrawal it was at least largely completed before the enemy aircraft began the strafing which caused so many casualties to 8 Brigade.

For the rest of the day the 3rd Dragoon Guards, reinforced at about 1530 by a section of machine guns and a dismounted Squadron of the 1st North Somerset Yeomanry, manned their trenches and shell holes, and observed the evident German preparations for a counterattack.[8] At 1700 3rd Division HQ received orders from Cavalry Corps to withdraw one brigade west of Arras immediately and the remaining two when the situation permitted. The 7 Brigade were ordered back at once. With no enemy counterattack having manifested itself, at around midnight on the night of 11th/12th the relief of the other two brigades, by the 12th Infantry Division 36 and 37 Brigades, began. With the exception of two squadrons of the 10th Hussars, who could not be relieved in time, the two brigades withdrew during the night in freezing and snowy conditions which caused great distress to both men and horses. Unfortunately many wounded, whom it was impossible to get out of Monchy, had to be left behind in cellars and dugouts. All but a handful of them were evacuated the following night, as were the two squadrons of 10th Hussars.[9]

Third Army HQ seem to have concluded during the course of 11 April that the role of the Cavalry as an attacking force in the Battle of Arras should be terminated. Therefore the role which had been envisaged for 17th Division as the infantry component of the Cavalry Corps should also be brought to an end. The Division's immediate transfer to VI Corps, and normal infantry duties, was ordered. The following night they relieved 15th Scottish Division.

8   TNA WO 95/1153: 3rd Dragoon Guards War Diary.
9   TNA WO 95/1141: 3rd Cavalry Division War Diary; TNA WO 95/1156: 8 Cavalry Brigade War Diary.

Vimy Ridge: the Canadian Corps

The principal ingredient in the stunning success the Canadians were to achieve at Vimy Ridge was undoubtedly the painstaking and detailed preparation. While the First Army Commander, General Sir Henry Horne, would certainly have insisted on this, he was pushing on an open door given the nature of the Corps Commander, Lieutenant General Sir Julian Byng. When he assumed command of the Corps in May 1916, Byng had already had a very active war. A cavalryman, he commanded the 3rd Cavalry Division at Ypres in 1914. He then briefly commanded the BEF's Cavalry Corps in 1915 before being transferred to Gallipoli to take over IX Corps, although too late to make any difference to the outcome of that campaign. Having returned to the Western Front and assumed command of the Canadian Corps, his first challenge arose when the Corps replaced the Australians on the Somme, as part of General Gough's Reserve Army, in time for the Battle of Flers-Courcelette.

The Canadian attack on Courcelette went well. It was in the subsequent fighting which began on 26 September, as the Canadians pressed north from Courcelette as part of Reserve Army efforts to take the Thiepval Ridge, that they came under severe pressure from well-organised German defences and artillery bombardments. In truly attritional style they slogged forward until, on 1 October, they were in a position to attack the heavily fortified German line known as Regina Trench. In bitter fighting over the next week, with interruptions dictated by bad weather, the Canadians sometimes occupied, but never managed to hold, the trench. When three of the divisions were relieved at the end of the second week of October, the trench was still in German hands. It was finally largely taken by 4th Canadian Division, left behind on temporary attachment to II Corps, on 21 October. The Division attempted to complete the job four days later but failed. They were to be involved intermittently on the Somme up to and including the final British attack of the campaign.[1]

Their involvement in the Somme battle had left the Canadians with a sour taste in the mouth. They had suffered over 17,000 casualties. Neither the senior officers nor the rank and file blamed Byng for the ordeal they had undergone. Their admiration of, and liking for, him, which was warmly reciprocated, remained undimmed. Rather, they laid their misfortunes at the doors of General Gough and his staff at Reserve Army. The Canadians were to refuse to serve ever again under Gough.[2]

If Byng had not already been convinced of the value of detailed and thorough planning for an attack, the experiences of his Corps on the Somme would have persuaded him of the need for it. Confronted with Vimy Ridge, which the Germans regarded with some assurance as an impregnable obstacle, Byng and Horne and their staffs quickly identified the areas where new thinking and solutions would be required to shatter German complacency. The attackers would be faced with three main lines of defences consisting of trenches, machine gun strong points, barbed wire and dugouts capable of sheltering entire battalions at a time, all linked by connecting tunnels. They were manned by the three divisions of *Gruppe Vimy*. The *Gruppe* would, by now, have preferred to have had in place the rather more flexible defence system of defence in depth but, in addition to the practical difficulties of operating it given the physical features of Vimy Ridge, they had not yet been able to start work on

---

1   OH 1916, Volume II, pp 452 and 514-6.

2   Haig d. 5.10.17.

it. Part of the reason for this was the pressure they had been put under by an intense programme of trench raiding instituted by the Canadians not long after they had come into the line. Apart from stretching the nerves of the defenders to near breaking point, these raids were of value in probing the enemy defences and acquiring more detailed information on their layout and strength. Some of these raids were mounted in considerable force and most were highly successful. But some failed and were costly, notably that of 1 March. In the two weeks ending 5 April, the Canadians sustained 1,653 casualties, most suffered as a result of the raids.[3]

Much of the new thinking that went into the planning of the attack would focus on its two main ingredients, the infantry and artillery. But the favourable geology of the area for underground activity also offered opportunities that the planners were quick to seize on. The British had begun to mine assiduously as soon as they had taken over the area from the French, and during the rest of 1916 the British and German miners sought to blow up the others' positions and frustrate their countermining efforts. Gradually the British gained the upper hand and, by the time the Canadians arrived, were in a position to undertake the extensive construction of a network of subways designed to allow the assaulting troops to move to their front line trenches, and sometimes into no man's land, fully protected. Over 5 kms of subways were excavated, the work being done largely at night to maintain secrecy and enable the spoil to be removed undetected. The subways were constructed to a high standard with adjoining chambers included for brigade and battalion HQs, communications centres, dressing stations and ammunition stores. They were illuminated by electric light and fresh air was pumped through. Fully equipped soldiers could pass along the passages comfortably upright, and passing areas facilitated two-way traffic. In addition to the subways, a series of tunnels were driven under the German front lines and 21 mines laid and primed.

As regards infantry tactics, Byng was of the view that the army had lost its way in employing the rigid tactics seen on the first day of the Somme. In this he was reflecting the conclusions of GHQ itself, which had issued two pamphlets (SS143 and SS154) on the subject. Like GHQ, Byng favoured a reversion to the methods of mobile warfare in which the infantry would operate in highly mobile platoon sized groups acting independently. They would be assigned natural features as their objectives rather than, for example, a trench that might be obliterated by the artillery. If an enemy strong point could not be quickly overrun the troops would be instructed to bypass it, throwing up a defensive flank towards it. Reserves coming up would be fed into the parts of the line where there was no hold up thus reverting to the tried and true, but sometimes neglected, doctrine of reinforcing success and not failure. On the assumption that officers and NCOs could well become casualties, the troops were trained to become interchangeable with them and each other. Byng had a full scale replica of the battlefield laid out behind the lines and the troops were thoroughly trained on it in their roles. At Horne's HQ a detailed plasticine model of the Ridge was built which all the officers and NCOs participating in the assault were given time to study and discuss.

Probably for the first time in the war the artillery and shell supply available was more than adequate for the task in hand. In addition to the Canadian Corps own resources, Byng was able to count on the big guns of 11 heavy artillery groups and the artillery of I Corps to his left. The total density this gave him was one heavy gun for every 20 yards of front and a field gun for every 10 yards, proportionately three times as many heavy and twice as many field guns as on the Somme. 42,500 tons of shells were allocated to the operation with a daily quota of 2,465 tons. Although still not readily available, Byng managed to obtain an adequate supply of the new instantaneous '106' fuze, which was proving so effective in a wire cutting role.

The tasks which this profusion of artillery would be called on to perform were the familiar ones of bombarding the enemy strong points and entrenchments, cutting their wire, and providing as much protection to the assaulting infantry as possible. This last task would be achieved firstly by

---

3   J. Nicholls, *Cheerful Sacrifice: the Battle of Arras 1917*, p. 51.

eliminating their worst enemy, hostile artillery, by counter battery work; and secondly, by firing a standard creeping barrage, supplemented by a concentrated line of machine guns firing over the heads of the assaulting troops to keep enemy heads down. What would be different from previous artillery programmes would be the precision with which these tasks would be carried out.

An essential part of the counter battery programme was to be conducted by so called silent batteries. The presence of these batteries would be concealed from the enemy by their not firing to register targets prior to the battle. In many cases their targets were identified for them by aerial reconnaissance; no less than 80 percent of the German artillery was thus spotted. Those that the aircraft missed could well have been pinpointed by the pioneering work of an outstanding Canadian scientific gunner, A. G. L. McNaughton, whose counter battery organisation attached to Byng's headquarters, was the leader in the fields of flash spotting and sound ranging.[4]

The grim weather and resultant mud of a northern French late winter and spring notwithstanding, the apparently intractable problems of getting men and matériel into the right place at the right time were well on the way to being solved, when, on 5 March, Byng put before Horne his detailed plan for the capture of Vimy Ridge. Byng's proposals were based on the Plan of Operations issued by Horne on 31 January. This had called for a Southern Operation to capture the main crest of the ridge dominated by Hill 145, the village of Thélus and Hill 135. If this operation were successful the Northern Operation would be launched to capture the Pimple and *Bois en Hache*. If the enemy lost these last two positions they would be totally deprived of Vimy Ridge. Since mid January, Horne had envisaged the Southern Operation as an entirely Canadian affair, with the Northern Operation entrusted principally to the right flank of I British Corps assisted by the left flank of 4th Canadian Division. As late as 5 April, this was changed to give 4th Canadian Division the full responsibility for the capture of the Pimple. The Divisional Commander gave the task to his reserve Brigade, the 10th.[5]

As all the Canadian divisions would be committed to the battle from the outset, Horne added the British 5th Division to Byng's command as a reserve. One brigade of this, the 13th, would go into action with 2nd Canadian Division. The decision to assign the Northern Operation, except for the *Bois en Hache*, to the Canadians may well have been because the Southern Operation only called for an advance of 700 yards on the left compared with over 4,000 yards on the right.[6]

Byng's plan fully recognised that total surprise could not be achieved. The Germans were well aware that a major allied offensive was in the offing and that Vimy Ridge would be an important objective.[7] Efforts were made to keep the Germans as much in the dark as possible. What remains one of the unresolved mysteries of the war was why the Germans made no more than desultory attempts to interfere with Canadian preparations. This inertia seemed to offer some confirmation of GHQ's belief as late as 19 March that the Germans were planning to abandon Vimy Ridge as part of their withdrawal to the Hindenburg Line.[8] In fact the Germans had no such plans; possession of the ridge was simply too vital for them.[9]

In mid March the date of the attack was set for 8 April. The preliminary bombardment, using only about half of the available batteries, was to begin on 20 March. On 2 April the rest of the artillery were to join in, thus beginning what the Germans were to term 'the week of suffering'. The heavy guns concentrated on the villages and lines of communication behind the lines, the heavy mortars on the German front lines, and the smaller calibres on wire cutting. To deceive the enemy on the precise time of the assault there would be no intensification of the bombardment in the run up to Zero Hour. As this moment arrived a barrage would be laid on the German front line where it would remain for three

4   OH 1917, Volume I, p. 306. J.Williams, *Byng of Vimy; General and Governor-General*, pp. 148-9.
5   Williams, op. cit., p. 150.
6   OH 1917, Volume I, p. 304.
7   Ibid., p. 305.
8   Haig d. 18 and 19.3.17.
9   Horne ls, 20 and 27.3.17.

minutes before lifting 100 yards every three minutes. Gas and high explosive shells would rain down on known German strong points, artillery batteries and ammunition dumps.[10]

Byng's plan called for all four Canadian infantry divisions to go into action together for the first time in the war. They would assault in line abreast on a front of four and a half miles in numerical order from 1st Division on the right to 4th Division on the left. The four stages of the assault were delineated by coloured lines. The Black Line, about 750 yards from the Canadian front lines, incorporated all the German forward defensive line. The Red Line ran north along a German trench called *Zwischen (or Swischen) Stellung* to the crest of the ridge and included La Folie farm and Hill 145. The Blue Line included Thélus, Hill 135 and the woods above the village of Vimy. The Brown Line marked the German Second Line including Farbus wood, Bois de la Ville and the Bois du Goulot. The German Third Line of defences in the area was situated to the east of the ridge and was not an objective of the assault.

The plan called for the capture of the area up to and including the Black Line within 35 minutes of Zero Hour. There would then be a pause of 40 minutes to ensure the synchronisation of the artillery barrage and the infantry advance to the Red Line which would be reached in 20 minutes. At this point 3rd and 4th Divisions would have achieved all their objectives and could consolidate. For 1st and 2nd Divisions there would be a halt of two and a half hours before fresh troops would resume the advance to the Blue Line. There, after a further pause of 96 minutes, the advance would continue to the Brown Line, scheduled to be reached at 1318. The 51st Highland Division of the Third Army XVII Corps would advance in tandem with, and on the right of, 1st Canadian Division.[11]

Unsurprisingly, given the close liaison between their respective headquarters, Horne only felt the need to make minor modifications to the artillery section of the plan presented by Byng. The First Army issued its Operation Order on 26 March and Byng's headquarters sent out detailed orders based on the now finalised plan to all concerned.[12]

In common with Third Army, Zero Hour was 0530 on Easter Monday, 9 April. (It had been postponed by 24 hours only a few days earlier in partial response to a request from the French for a 48 hour delay.) By 0400 thirty thousand men had assembled in the Canadian forward areas, the leading companies within 100 yards of the German outposts, all without raising the alarm. At Zero Hour the planned assault barrage erupted, two mines were detonated under the German positions and the infantry went over the top. A bitter northwest wind and a snow blizzard made conditions unpleasant for the attackers, but more so for the defenders who were partially blinded by the snow driving into their faces, as well as the very dim light of an early spring morning. The attackers' main problem, given the dazed, disoriented state of most of the front line defenders, was to negotiate the pulverised, and glutinously muddy ground in the poor visibility.

Commanded by the highly competent Major General Arthur Currie, soon destined to become the first Canadian national to command the Canadian Corps, the 1st Division advanced at Zero on a two brigade front more than a mile in length, with 2 Brigade on the right and 3 on the left. The 1 Brigade were in reserve. Both assaulting brigades put three battalions in the line and kept one in reserve.[13] On 2 Brigade's right, the 51st Highland Division strove to keep pace with the Canadians as the latter closely followed behind an artillery barrage which fired for three minutes from Zero on the enemy front line before lifting 100 yards every three minutes thereafter. Despite their shocked state the enemy offered what the divisional war diary described as 'considerable opposition'. The 10th (Canadian) Battalion, on 2 Brigade's left suffered so heavily that 3 Brigade's right-hand Battalion,

---

10   OH 1917, Volume I, p. 312 and Appendix 15.
11   Ibid., p. 304.
12   Ibid., Appendix 27.
13   The battalions from right to left were: 2 Brigade; 5th (Western Cavalry), 7th (1st British Columbia Regt), 10th (Canadians) and in reserve 8th (90th Rifles): 3 Brigade; 15th (48th Highlanders of Canada), 14th (Royal Montreal Regiment), 16th (The Canadian Scottish) and in reserve 13th (Royal Highlanders of Canada).

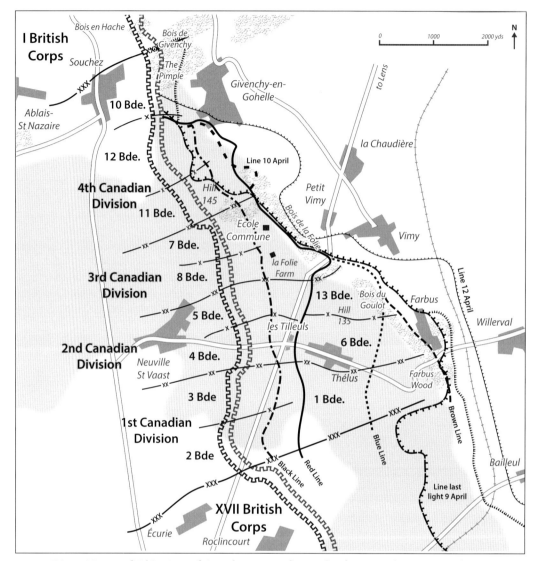

Dispositions and Objectives of Canadian Corps for Battle of Vimy Ridge, 9-12 April 1917.

the 15th (48th Highlanders of Canada), also under heavy fire, in their case from the Argyll Group of craters, were forced to extend right to keep touch. The Brigade's left hand 16th (Canadian Scottish) Battalion were also subjected to heavy machine gun fire, in their case from the Vissec group of old craters.[14] The lines of troops nevertheless pressed steadily on. Some, too impetuous, became victims of their own barrage. A German line, the Eisner Kreuz Weg, was reached on schedule and captured at the point of the bayonet after heavy fighting in which the 14th (Royal Montreal Regiment) Battalion, in the centre of the three Brigade line, suffered severely.

Still the Canadians pressed on, reaching and taking the northern part of the Black Line in the divisional sector. The southern end of the Line had posed a greater challenge. Here an enemy

---

14   Private W J Milne of 3 Brigade's 16th (Canadian Scottish) Battalion won one of the four VCs awarded to the Canadian Corps this day for his action in silencing one of these enemy machine guns. Although he survived this action he was killed later in the day.

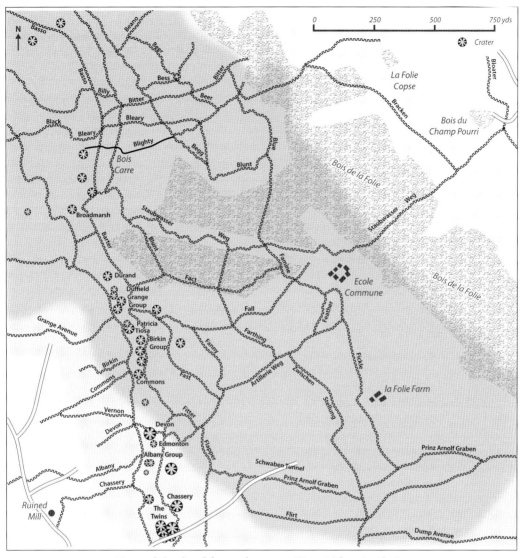

No man's land and forward areas on Vimy Ridge, April 1917.

complex, known as the *Zwölfer Graben*, with its well sited machine guns, inflicted heavy losses on both brigades, before it was overcome, one gun at a time. The Black Line was in 1st Division's hands close to schedule.[15]

Following the planned 40 minute pause there for reorganisation, which involved the original rear companies of the attacking battalions moving through to assume the lead, the advance behind the barrage to the Red Line resumed at 0645. The attackers were favoured by a change of wind direction which not only continued to hamper the enemy by blowing snow across their front but also, perhaps worse, by carrying smoke south from fires in Thélus, which prevented them from observing the attackers' progress until the last minute. As a result the Bavarian defenders were routed with those not killed or captured fleeing as fast as the cloying mud allowed. They were later observed in about battalion strength, if not cohesion, making for the relative shelter of Farbus wood. Within 20 minutes

15   TNA WO 95/3773: 3 Canadian Brigade War Diary.

or so of setting off the Division were in full possession of the Zwischen Stellung, which formed the northern part of the Red Line in the divisional sector. The main opposition had again fallen on 16th Battalion in the form of machine gun fire from their left flank. This was finally suppressed by rifle grenade fire. The southern 500 yards of the Division's sector of the Red Line, involving a sharp turn to the south-east and known as the Lille Road salient, needed a separate attack by 1st (Western Ontario) Battalion of 1 Brigade, up to now in reserve, to effect its capture.[16] Cooperating in the operation was a reinforced company of 4th Seaforth Highlanders of the 51st Division 154 Brigade. As already described in Chapter 6 the operation ended in complete success after some heavy fighting.

The 1st Division's assault paused at the Red Line for a scheduled two hours to enable three battalions of 1 Brigade to take over the lead from 2 and 3 Brigades. These were the 1st Battalion on the right, the 3rd (Toronto Regiment) Battalion in the centre and the 4th (Central Ontario) Battalion on the left. In support 500 yards behind were 2nd (Eastern Ontario) Battalion. The 1st Battalion were warned that they would have to form a defensive right flank if 51st Division were to fail to keep pace with the Canadian advance. When the advance resumed at about 0930 the Blue Line was taken without much difficulty. There was a further 90 minute pause before the advance was resumed with the 3rd and 4th Battalions leading, with the objective now the enemy's Brown Line. This too was taken without undue difficulty and its consolidation put in hand. After a delay waiting for the barrage of Farbus wood to move on, strong patrols were sent into the wood to capture enemy guns and to form and consolidate an outpost line on its eastern edge. The enemy were reported to be retreating towards the village of Willerval. Early in the afternoon the Corps Commander ordered a squadron of the Canadian Light Horse to push on to this village, which was scarcely a mile away. At 1620 two patrols set out from Farbus. Although one patrol took 10 prisoners in Willerval, they both came under enemy machine gun fire and were driven back with heavy losses in both men and horses. The main body of the squadron also came under fire, shellfire in their case, and lost half their horses.[17] Despite this setback, the 1st Division had achieved all its objectives in completing the capture of their sector of Vimy Ridge. Their main concern at the end of the day was that their right flank was in the air. 51st Division had in fact veered off southwards and would not come back alongside until 11 April. Despite occasional indications to the contrary, no counterattack would be mounted by the enemy to exploit the exposed Canadian flank.

On the 1st Division's left, the 2nd Division, commanded by Major General Henry Burstall, had also advanced on a two brigade front with 4 Brigade on the right and 5 Brigade on the left. At 1,400 yards the Division had a shorter length of front to cover than 1st Division (although this would lengthen to 2,000 yards by the time the Brown Line was reached). Consequently the two assaulting brigades would initially have only two battalions each spearheading their advance. From right to left these were 18th (Western Ontario) and 19th (Central Ontario) of 4 Brigade, and 24th (Victoria Rifles of Canada) and 26th (New Brunswick) of 5 Brigade. In reserve for the two brigades and due to take over the lead at the Black Line were respectively 21st (Eastern Ontario) and 25th (Nova Scotia Rifles) Battalions. They would be supported by companies from the 20th (Central Ontario) and 22nd (French Canadian) Battalions, acting mainly as moppers up. When the Red Line was captured 6 Brigade (31st (Alberta), 28th (Northwest) and 29th (Vancouver) Battalions) would take over from 4 Brigade and 13 British Brigade (1st R West Kents and 2nd KOSB) from 5 Brigade. When the Blue Line was taken the 6 Brigade's 27th (City of Winnipeg) Battalion, previously in reserve, would take up position on the right of 29th Battalion for the final push to the Brown Line. In all, 2nd Division's objectives for the day called for an advance of 2,300 yards on the left of their line and 3,000 yards on the right.[18]

---

16   Col G.W.L. Nicholson, *Official History of the Canadian Army in the First World War*, p. 265.
17   Nicholson, op. cit., p. 258.
18   Geoffrey Hayes and Others, *Vimy Ridge: a Canadian Reassessment*, p.172.

The apparent ease with which all four lead off battalions captured their sectors of the Black Line on schedule conceals the fact that German resistance stiffened after their front line had been overrun. Although the German artillery at no stage offered a really serious threat to the assaulting troops, the 19th Battalion came under heavy machine gun fire from Balloon trench which forced them to take cover. Flanking parties worked round both sides of the enemy position and destroyed the machine guns with rifle grenades thereby freeing the Battalion to resume their advance. On several occasions enemy resistance was only overcome and forward momentum maintained or resumed by the initiative and bravery shown by individuals such as Lance Sergeant Ellis Sifton of the 18th Battalion, who was awarded a posthumous Victoria Cross for overthrowing a machine gun causing casualties to his Battalion, and bayoneting the crew. The eight tanks assigned to the Corps, all of which had been allocated to 2nd Division in anticipation that they might be required to deal with the wire in front of Thélus, had soon demonstrated the near impossibility of their coping with the glutinously muddy ground of the battlefield. All had ditched well short of the Black Line.[19]

With the Black Line secured one of the two supporting battalions of each attacking brigade moved through at 0645 for the 500/600 yard advance on the Red Line. In the divisional sector this consisted of the Zwischen Stellung and, just beyond, the Arras-Lens road on which lay the largely flattened hamlet of Les Tilleuls, just west of Thélus. Despite the nominal halving of the numbers attacking, 4 Brigade's 21st (Eastern Ontario) Battalion and 5 Brigade's 25th (Nova Scotia Rifles) Battalion, the latter galvanised by the skirl of the pipes, progressed on schedule, but not without significant losses numbering 215 for 21st Battalion and more than 250 for the 25th. On the plus side the 21st Battalion, who had been given the responsibility for taking and clearing Les Tilleuls found and captured the personnel of two battalion headquarters in a cave under the hamlet ruins as they were clearing out the machine gun nests that had contributed to their losses. Companies of the 22nd Battalion, acting as moppers up for 4 Brigade, also recorded striking successes. Coming under considerable opposition from one spot in *Grenadier Graben*, they outflanked the position and captured one machine gun and 125 men. They then secured *Dump Graben*, capturing three machine guns and 271 men. By 0800 the divisional sector of the Red Line had been fully captured.

At this point the Division 6 Brigade and the British 5th Division 13 Brigade took over the lead. Their joint task would be to take the enemy's Blue Line, about 1,000 yards away, after which they would carry on to capture the Brown Line. By 0930 the three Canadian and two British battalions were in position and ready to follow the barrage. Five minutes later they began their advance on time. The Canadian objective was the portion of the Blue Line just to the northeast of the village of Thélus, the British, the enemy defences in the Bois du Goulot and around Hill 135, the second highest point of the ridge. A major challenge for the British battalions would be Thélus trench which ran northwards from the western edge of Thélus village, about half way between the Red and Blue Lines, and was strongly protected by wire.

In the event the trench proved to be less of an obstacle than had been feared. The wire protecting it had been well cut. The main problem for the Canadians was from some of their own barrage falling short and causing casualties. Nevertheless, by around 1000 the 29th Battalion and the two British battalions were in possession of the trench. A little to the south the other two Canadian battalions met more resistance as they moved into the western outskirts of Thélus village. This was overcome by the use of bombing parties working their way up trenches covered by Lewis guns. The rubble of the village was soon in Canadian hands. At the same time 29th Battalion had moved over the southern slopes of Hill 135 and cleared Thélus wood northeast of the village. Meanwhile the northernmost of the two British battalions, 2nd KOSB, had come under heavy sniper fire from the Bois de Bonval on their left flank. This should have been dealt with by 3rd Division. A bombing party solved the problem and the two battalions moved on to clear the Bois de Bonval and, to the southeast, the Count's wood

---

19   Nicholson, op. cit., p.254.

and the Bois du Goulot.

The 2nd Division's sector of the Blue Line was in Canadian and British hands by around 1100. There was a pause at this point of nearly 90 minutes for reorganisation prior to the advance to the Brown Line which ran from the Bois du Goulot to the east of the Bois de la Ville between that wood and the village of Farbus. Despite a spirited defence by the Germans the 27th and 29th Battalions had secured their objectives by the early afternoon. The 2nd KOSB and 1st R West Kents completed the clearance of the Bois du Goulot and by mid-afternoon the whole of the Brown Line was in 2nd Division's possession. Consolidation in anticipation of German counterattacks was urgently put in hand. Patrols were sent out and advanced observation posts set up.[20]

On the 2nd Division's left, the 3rd Division, commanded by Major General Louis Lipsett, had been assigned the task of attacking the enemy's defences between B4 Crater and La Salle Avenue. Their first objective was the capture of the Black Line which on the right consisted of the *Zwischen Stellung* before continuing north along Farthing trench. The second objective would involve the capture of the Red Line on the reverse slope of Vimy Ridge. The intention was then to consolidate a defensive line on the western edge of the Ridge, with strong points on the Red Line, and push patrols forward through La Folie wood.

The Division deployed on a two brigade front, each with three battalions attacking and one in reserve. The 8 Brigade were on the right and the 7th on the left. In reserve were 9 Brigade. The assaulting troops moved forward three minutes after Zero as the bombardment lifted from the German front line. Although the German artillery reacted within five minutes of Zero and the fire became quite heavy within 10 minutes, it largely fell on empty trenches behind the Canadian front line and failed to prevent the assault overrunning the front and support lines with only light losses. The attackers found the German defences had been practically obliterated by the preliminary bombardment. The German wire had been thoroughly cut by trench mortars. Surprise had apparently been complete and such defenders as had survived were shocked and demoralised and in no state to offer serious resistance. The main problem for the attackers was recognising the points they had reached where trenches had wholly disappeared. This led to some of them getting too close to their own barrage, which caused most of the casualties there were.

By 0625 it was confirmed that both brigades were in possession of the Black Line. Twenty minutes later they were advancing towards their second objective. The 7 were the more heavily engaged of the two brigades as the enemy mounted largely ineffective local counterattacks in orchards, mainly targeting The Royal Canadian Regiment (RCR) on the Brigade's right, at their point of junction with the 4th Canadian Mounted Rifles (CMR) on 8 Brigade's left. One enemy strong point in La Folie wood, which had apparently survived the bombardment relatively unscathed, did prove troublesome to RCR and was responsible for most of their casualties.[21] By 0730 the troops of both brigades had reached the crest of the ridge and occupied the western edge of La Folie wood (Bois de la Folie). Shortly afterwards the consolidation of the Resistance Line west of the ridge was begun and parties were pushed forward to begin construction of strong points on the Red Line. An enemy troop concentration in Bloater, Flower and Fillip trenches was successfully dispersed by artillery fire.

At around 0900 came the first indications to 3rd Division that all was not well with 4th Division's assault on Hill 145. The left of 7 Brigade began to come under heavy fire from the direction of the Hill, a clear indication that it was still in enemy hands. As a consequence, 7 Brigade were forced to establish a defensive flank using 42nd (Royal Highlanders of Canada) Battalion and Princess Patricia's Canadian Light Infantry (PPCLI), respectively their left and centre battalions. For some time both of these units would continue to be plagued by harassing fire from the Hill.[22] They were

---

20 Geoffrey Hayes and Others, op. cit., pp. 181-3.
21 TNA WO 95/3865: Royal Canadian Regiment War Diary.
22 Nicholson, op. cit., pp. 255-6. TNA WO 95/3838: 3rd Canadian Division War Diary.

also bothered by the close attentions of enemy aircraft that, at the very least, would be reporting their movements to the enemy artillery. The RFC were pressed to do something to deal with the enemy's apparent freedom of the skies.

By 1130 3rd Division battalions had achieved all their objectives but 7 Brigade's left and centre battalions were still taking significant losses from sniping and rifle fire from Hill 145. The left flank of 42nd (Royal Highlanders of Canada) Battalion, on the extreme left of 3rd Division's line, was in the air. Although they expressed themselves satisfied with the situation the 4th Division were urged to get their right flank in touch with 3rd Division's left. This link up had been planned to take place on the Red Line, but only 3rd Division had made it that far. Instead, it was eventually achieved further back in Blunt trench. Because of the persistence of the problem of Hill 145 for 3rd Division's left flank, two companies of 9 Brigade's 58th (Central Ontario) Battalion were sent up to support 7 Brigade who, at 1450, were ordered to be prepared to cooperate with 4th Division in an operation against Hill 145 timed to begin at 1630. It did not take long for the 7 Brigade Commander to determine that the proposed operation was not practical. It was therefore cancelled. At about this time there were reports that the enemy were massing on Hill 145, presumably in preparation for a counterattack. The threat was satisfactorily dealt with by the artillery.

In contrast with 7 Brigade the 3rd Division 8 Brigade had a relatively straightforward morning. Typical was the experience of 2nd Battalion CMR,[23] the centre one of the Brigade's three assaulting battalions, the others being 1st CMR on the right and 4th CMR on the left. Their plan had been for B Company to seize the enemy front line system, where C Company would pass through and assault and capture the *Zwischen Stellung*. D Company would in turn pass through and take Fickle trench, a subsidiary enemy Line of Resistance, and La Folie farm. Finally A Company would take over and seize the Red Line and establish a protective outpost system. The plan had worked virtually to perfection. Greatly assisted by a barrage, described as 'curtain fire' by the Battalion War Diary, the assaulting infantrymen were generally upon the enemy machine gunners before they could bring their weapons into action. The heavy bombardment too was found to have done its job. Fickle trench had been virtually obliterated, making it necessary to consolidate *Zwischen Stellung* instead as a defensive trench. The 2nd CMR's D Company found La Folie farm to be a pile of rubble; they passed over it unopposed. By 0750 the Battalion's final objective had been taken and the tasks of mopping up, evacuating the wounded, channelling prisoners to the rear, bringing up supplies and consolidating trenches were put in hand.[24]

At the end of the day 3rd Division could take great satisfaction from the results they had achieved. Apart from one enemy post which they should have taken, but which had instead been occupied by 13 British Brigade and only taken over from them during the night, all their objectives had been completed and, where appropriate, consolidated. Their success had not however been achieved without significant losses; their estimated casualties were 45 officers and 1,500 other ranks killed, wounded and missing. A large number of these were probably caused by some heavy and accurate enemy artillery fire and machine gun fire from north of La Folie farm that, in the latter case, was a by-product of 4th Division's failure to capture Hill 145. The next day added to their casualty list when patrols reconnoitring towards Petit Vimy and Bloater trench found both to be heavily manned by an alert enemy.[25]

In divisional reserve at the opening of the battle, 9 Brigade's role had been confined to supporting the other two brigades by furnishing troops in time of need by battalion or company. At midday on 12 April however, the GOC of 9 Brigade took command of the divisional front, in effect relieving 7 and 8 Brigades with his own troops. Within six hours Flicker, Flit and Flute trenches had been entered

---

23   All four CMR battalions were fighting as Infantry.
24   TNA WO 95/3871: 2nd Canadian Mounted Rifles War Diary.
25   Ibid.

and found unoccupied. The following day, patrols were ordered into Petit Vimy and Vimy against little or no opposition.[26] La Chaudière was also occupied without opposition.

Even though the 4th Division on the Canadian left had the shortest distance to cover of the four divisions, it had been given two of the toughest nuts to crack in the shape of Hill 145,[27] the highest and most important feature of the Ridge, and the 120 metre-high Pimple, a German strong point at the extreme north of the ridge which, situated between Souchez and Givenchy-en-Gohelle, afforded the Germans complete command of the Souchez River valley. Its capture had been foreseen as a joint task for the right flank of I British Corps and the left flank only of 4th Canadian Division but, as has already been noted, the latter were given full responsibility for its capture only four days before the battle was to begin. The Divisional Commander, Major General David Watson, gave the task to his reserve Brigade, the 10th. Provided that they had not been drawn further into the Division's early fighting on the 9th than planned (they were to provide a battalion each to the assaulting brigades) they would assault the strong point during the afternoon of that day. But, in contrast to the other three divisions, 4th Division's initial attack did run into problems which necessitated the commitment of elements of the reserve Brigade.

It was inevitable that a vantage point as important to the Germans as Hill 145 would be heavily defended. The physical obstacles it possessed were augmented by old, deep, shell proof mine workings manned by large garrisons easily reinforced from reserves sheltered in deep dugouts on the reverse slope. The severe challenge its capture would present would have come as no surprise to 4th Division following the disastrous raid in force they had mounted on the Hill just over a month previously, on 1 March. The raid involved about 1,700 troops drawn from 11 Brigade's 54th (Kootenay) and 75th (Mississauga) Battalions and 12 Brigade's 72nd (Seaforth Highlanders of Canada) and 73rd (Royal Highlanders of Canada) Battalions. Its aim had been to reconnoitre and inflict severe damage on the German positions at the top of Hill 145. The preliminary bombardment, which included gas, apparently had little effect on the elements of the two German divisions holding the line, beyond alerting them to the imminence of an attack. When they launched their infantry assault, the Canadians were met by uncut wire and withering fire. The attackers suffered 687 casualties, including two battalion COs who were killed, and achieved nothing.[28]

At Zero on 9 April the 4th Division attacked on a two brigade front. The 11 Brigade on the right were to make a direct assault on Hill 145. On the left 12 Brigade were to attack north of the Hill to secure the Canadians' northern flank and to prevent if possible the enemy garrisons of Hill 145 and the Pimple offering each other mutual support at any stage. The Division's frontage extended 1,950 yards from Broadmarsh crater in the south to opposite Givenchy in the north. In addition to the formidable tasks of capturing Hill 145 and the Pimple, the divisional attack plan required an initial advance of around 700 yards across ground which was much more severely broken up than that confronting the other three divisions. The glutinous mud would slow the advancing infantry's pace to a crawl during which they would be in danger of falling behind the barrage and of being thoroughly exposed to the enemy's view unless the main artillery bombardment and the machine gun barrage succeeded in destroying the German defences and confining any surviving defenders to their dugouts or at least forcing them to keep their heads down. Given this imperative, it is surprising that a 100 yard stretch of trench in the German second line, on the planned line of advance of the right half of 11 Brigade's 87th (Canadian Grenadier Guards) Battalion, was apparently deliberately left untouched.[29] This was to result in the enemy having sufficient time to get their second line properly

---

26   TNA WO 95/3875: 9 Canadian Brigade War Diary.

27   Where the Canadian National Memorial now stands.

28   Geoffrey Hayes and Others, op. cit., p. 216.

29   The generally proffered reason for the failure to deal with this stretch of the German defences is that the CO of 87th Battalion planned to use it as a battalion HQ once it had been captured. It is unfortunate that the matter was not cleared up when those involved in the decision were still around. There is still speculation surrounding it but also a

garrisoned with, as luck would have it, seasoned and well led troops more than capable of inflicting severe disruption and heavy casualties on Canadian attempts to get forward.

Immediately the assault began 11 Brigade's 102nd ((North British Columbians) Battalion on the right, advancing on a front of 500 yards, achieved a measure of surprise and by 0545 had captured the enemy's front dugouts, having passed through the protective wire without difficulty. Fifteen minutes later the enemy's second line of trenches had been successfully stormed. The Battalion then moved on and by 0740 had seized their final objective, the third line of enemy trenches on the southwestern slope of Hill 145, their half of the forward slope of the ridge.[30] An enemy strong point on the left of Broadmarsh crater had also been surrounded and captured in a well executed classic infantry manoeuvre.[31] At this stage the supporting 54th Battalion passed through with the intention of occupying Beer and Blue trenches on the reverse slope, about 500 yards ahead. Initially the opposition had been light as the artillery had destroyed the enemy fixed defences in front of them. But the 54th Battalion were soon to suffer the malign effects of the failure to deal with the 100 yard stretch of trench to their left. They found themselves being enfiladed by machine gun and rifle fire from enemy strong points at Old Boot sap and near Broadmarsh crater. They nevertheless reached their objectives and established communication with 3rd Division 42nd Battalion on their right. But the failure of the 87th and 75th Battalions to their north, left their left flank exposed. This, combined with persistent sniping from enemy troops emerging from dugouts behind them, forced them, as their casualties, particularly of officers, mounted, to retire to the line of Beggar trench, where they had taken over the assault from 102nd Battalion.

The right half of the 87th Battalion, on the brigade left, had made virtually no progress before they felt the effects of the failure to bombard the stretch of enemy defences facing them. As the two lines of the Battalion tried to advance from the jumping-off points they had reached through Tottenham tunnel, they were stopped well before reaching the German line, largely by machine gun fire from a German strong point which commanded the exit from Tottenham tunnel from only 400 yards away. Brave attempts to rush the German strong point were not only frustrated by the machine gun fire but also by its practically untouched protective wire. As a consequence of their misfortune, which resulted in casualties amounting to 60 percent, the right half of the two lines of the 75th Battalion, who should have advanced close behind the 87th, could not even get out of the jumping off trenches, let alone begin to advance.

The left half of the assaulting 87th and 75th Battalions initially enjoyed better fortune than their comrades, and were able to make some progress forward. But they soon came under heavy enfilade machine gun fire emanating from the untaken German line to their right. The leading lines of the 87th Battalion were so severely mauled that those men still capable of movement were forced back, many becoming entangled with the right wing of 12 Brigade's advance.

Any further progress by 11 Brigade was clearly dependent on the elimination of the hitherto untouched German defences in front of 87th Battalion. The close proximity of men of the 87th to the defences precluded the possibility of bombarding them at this stage. Consequently, with only fire from Stokes mortars and a machine gun barrage to support them, the remnants of the 87th Battalion had perforce to storm them making liberal use of bombs. In cooperation with a party from 75th Battalion they assaulted at about 1300 and the defences were soon in Canadian hands. The next

recognition that the true facts will probably now never be uncovered.

30   The account may read as if 102nd Battalion had a relatively easy time of it. But their losses, especially among officers, were so severe that for a time the Battalion was commanded by a Warrant Officer, Company Sergeant Major J. Russell of C Company, until he too became a casualty. Geoffrey Hayes, op. cit., p.218.

31   WO 95/3903. The bulk of the Battalion's casualties came from persistent enemy sniping from Hill 145. The Battalion War Diary, which is generally rich in sarcasm, is outspoken in its criticism of 87th Battalion for having failed to capture the Hill. It reads in part, '... owing to the defection of the 87th, who had failed to carry out orders, our left flank was hanging in the air ... '

priority was to try to make up for lost time by driving the Germans back from the western side of the Hill before dark. At 1515 the Divisional Commander sent forward two companies of the 85th (Nova Scotia Highlanders) Battalion to reinforce 11 Brigade. They were given the task of taking the last two German trenches to the west of the ridge. Even though the earlier attacking waves had passed the trenches they had not been properly mopped up, allowing the enemy to emerge from dugouts and mine shafts and retake possession of them. Despite some delay in orders reaching their intended recipients which resulted in there being no artillery barrage fired in support and no time to amend the orders to take this into account, the 85th advanced at 1845 as fast as the muddy ground permitted. Firing their Lewis guns and rifles from the hip to compensate partially for the lack of artillery support, they soon cleared the enemy from Batter and Basso trenches and established a garrison in Bed Bug trench. They then pushed out outposts as far as Beer trench.[32]

The 12 Brigade were on the left of 4th Division and consequently on the left of the entire Canadian Corps. Their objective on 9 April, after seizing their sector of the enemy front line position, would be to set up a northern defensive flank for the Division, a main purpose of which would be to protect the assault further south from interference from the Pimple. In effect they were being called upon to advance into an area between Hill 145 on their right, which would still be in enemy hands for at least the early hours of the battle and the Pimple, which most probably would not be assaulted until the following day at the earliest. They would therefore be in danger of exposure to enfilade fire from both flanks. On the plus side the distances to be traversed by the advancing battalions were very small. It was only about 200 yards from the Canadian front line to the crest of the Ridge. The threat that the Pimple offered would be to some extent mitigated by the laying down of a smoke barrage to blind the German guns.

The Brigade deployed and advanced on a three battalion front. On the right were the 38th (Ottawa) Battalion; in the centre the 72nd (Seaforth Highlanders of Canada) Battalion; on the left the 73rd (Royal Highlanders of Canada (Black Watch)) Battalion (who were to be disbanded as soon as the battle was over and replaced in 12 Brigade by the recently arrived 85th Battalion). In support, and positioned behind the right hand assault battalion which had the longest distance to cover, were 78th (Winnipeg Grenadiers) Battalion. They were tasked with taking the German Third trench on the reverse slope and establishing outposts further down the slope. Further support to the Brigade would be provided if needed by 46th (South Saskatchewan) Battalion, on attachment from 10 Brigade.

The Brigade's assault began with the detonation at Zero Hour of two mines in Gunner and Kennedy craters, in front of 73rd Battalion's part of the line, that killed a large number of the German garrison. Understandably many of the survivors fled leaving the three Canadian battalions with the relatively easy task of occupying and clearing the German front trench. A German attempt at a bombing assault on the rear of Kennedy crater was easily repelled by 73rd Battalion, who immediately deployed and consolidated to secure the Canadian left flank. Patrols sent out northwards found the enemy front line unoccupied for 300 yards. The patrols nevertheless had to withdraw because of the danger from friendly artillery fire targeting that stretch of line.

The other two battalions found resistance hardening as they attempted to seize the second enemy trench. The 72nd Battalion had little difficulty in taking their first objective in rear of the Montreal group of craters. But they then found the ground further east of the craters to be a mass of water filled shell holes which caused them to fall behind the barrage. They came under heavy machine gun fire from all sides as they moved forward down the slope towards their second objective. Their frontal assault on this having failed, they then mounted a flank attack with bombs that succeeded. The whole of Clutch trench as far north as Clucas trench was captured.

The 38th Battalion were also given severe problems by the state of the ground in front of the

32   TNA WO 95/3909:78th Canadian Infantry Battalion War Diary.

German second trench. Some of the water-filled shell holes they had to negotiate their way round were so deep that several wounded men who fell into them were drowned. They also suffered losses from the unexpected emergence of German troops from deep dugouts in the trench, not having fully appreciated quite how extensive the underground workings available to the enemy were. The trench was finally secured, at least partially helped by the enterprise and courage of Captain T. W. MacDowell who, with only two runners to support him, succeeded in bluffing 77 occupants of a dugout to surrender.[33]

The lead companies of the 78th Battalion, following closely behind the 38th and due to pass through them at the German Second Line, found themselves under severe enfilade fire coming from Hill 145 and nearby trenches, still untaken by 11 Brigade. They were also under fire from the Pimple as by now the protective smokescreen had dissipated. With stubborn determination they reached the Second Line, where the support companies passed through. As these arrived in front of the Third Line in a seriously weakened and scattered state, they were overwhelmed by a German counterattack of at least 200 men. The Germans pressed forward, determined to retake their Second Line, but were forced to take refuge in shell holes by the Winnipeg Grenadiers' Lewis gun and rifle fire. Their losses had been severe, totaling 486 or about 60 percent, some of the worst suffered by a battalion involved in the battle.[34]

It was now about 0830 and the situation was precarious. It was clear that the Germans had effectively prevented the junction of 11 and 12 Brigades by working up Basin trench and obtaining footholds in craters Nos. 1 and 2 and in Basso and Butter trenches. Canadian reinforcements were scraped together and sent up to reinforce the 12 Brigade right flank. This move succeeded in stemming any further German advance but was not strong enough to push them back. In the afternoon the decision was taken to bring forward 10 Brigade's 46th Battalion, temporarily on attachment to 12 Brigade as reserve battalion. The whole Battalion crossed the Zouave Valley without trouble between 1600 and 1700. Their planned attack, using two companies only, would be synchronized with 85th Battalion's on the 11 Brigade front, described above. Its objectives would be to capture the as yet unsecured craters Nos. 1, 2 and 3 beyond the German second trench and establish touch with 11 Brigade to the right of No. 1 crater.

The advance began at 1855 and was carried out 'splendidly', according to the Brigade war diary. The objectives were gained, the enemy dispersed and forced to retreat with heavy losses from the Canadian machine gun fire. The whole situation had been 'cleared up'; certainly the right and left flanks of 78th Battalion were secured. Some prisoners were taken and losses were described as 'not heavy'. The machine guns then materially assisted 85th Battalion's advance across Hill 145 and helped eliminate the threat to the 3rd Division 7 Brigade.[35]

Some accounts seem to regard the actions of the 85th and 46th Battalions as having completed the capture of Hill 145 on the night of 9 April, but in fact there still remained work to be done to wrap up the first day objectives of 11 Brigade, which would then enable 12 Brigade to complete theirs. Although the night of 9th/10th must have been a most unpleasant experience for the men lying out

---

33   TNA WO 95/3905: 12 Canadian Brigade's War Diary records Captain MacDowell's feat as follows:
   A nest of machine guns were encountered near the junction of Cyrus and Baby Trenches. Captain MacDowell, with 2 runners, bombed up Baby Trench and dislodged 2 of the guns, killing some of the crews and capturing 1 of the guns. The remaining crew took their gun into a large dugout at the junction of Cyrus and Baby Trenches followed by MacDowell and his two men. The dugout was very large. The occupants, 2 officers, 75 other ranks and 2 machine guns, surrendered. They were bluffed into thinking MacDowell had a large party with him. As they were brought out 6 at a time, a [Canadian] sniper, unaware of the situation, killed the first 12. MacDowell told the sniper of his error and the rest of the enemy were sent back. Those disposed to change their mind were summarily dealt with.
   Captain MacDowell was awarded the Victoria Cross. He was the only one of the four Vimy Ridge VCs to survive the war.
34   TNA WO 95/3909: 78th Canadian Infantry Battalion War Diary.
35   TNA WO 95/3905: 12 Canadian Brigade's War Diary.

on Hill 145, this was due to the appalling weather rather than from any attempts by the Germans to retrieve their situation by counterattacks or infiltration. At 1800 on the 9th the two fresh battalions of 10 Brigade, which had been held in readiness to attack the Pimple on the 10th, were ordered instead to complete the exhausted 11 Brigade's task by assaulting and capturing the Hangstellung (the extensive system of deep dugouts on the reverse slope of Hill 145, otherwise partly known as Boat and Banff trenches). At 0200 on the 10th the men of the 44th (Manitoba) and 50th (Calgary) Battalions moved to Music Hall line from where they began to advance to their jumping off positions at 1130. There had been no time to prepare written orders. By 1500 all troops were in position.

At 1515 an intense barrage opened on the Hangstellung, a repetition of that fired the previous day. The 44th and 50th Battalions formed up under its protection and assaulted with great dash against strong opposition. By 1615 both battalions had achieved their objectives. 50th Battalion then drove off an enemy counterattack that had initially looked as if it might succeed. The enemy had suffered many casualties and a large number of them were taken prisoner.[36] By late afternoon on the 10th it could safely be said that the crest of Hill 145 and the whole of Vimy Ridge, except for the Pimple, were in Canadian hands. The way was now open for 4th Division 10 Brigade's attack on the Pimple, rescheduled for 12 April.[37]

The assault on the Pimple had been originally scheduled to take place within 24 hours of the main assault on Vimy Ridge to take advantage of the expected disarray of the enemy as a result of the first day's fighting. The planned timing had been based on the assumption that 4th Division 10 Brigade, who had been assigned the task of capturing the Pimple, would not be drawn into the first day's fighting even though they were in divisional reserve for the day. In the event, as has been described, they were drawn into the main battle on both the first and second days, making a postponement of the attack on the Pimple to 12 April necessary to enable them to reequip and regroup. Zero Hour would now be 0500 on the 12th. The attack would be synchronized with an attack on the Bois en Hache by 73 Brigade of I British Corps' 24th Division.

During the course of 11 April the weather deteriorated rapidly and when 10 Brigade's 44th and 50th Battalions and a 46th Battalion, weakened by the absence of two companies, advanced at Zero Hour on a 1,000 yard front they did so with a strong westerly gale at their backs driving a blizzard of snow and sleet into the faces of the enemy defenders. So bad was the weather that the Germans had largely convinced themselves that, despite the inevitability of an early Canadian assault, it was almost inconceivable that it would take place in such conditions. The downside of the conditions for the attackers was that they would inevitably fall behind the barrage which had erupted at Zero because of the heavy mud and the darkness they would have to cope with. This proved to be the case with the attackers only managing to inch forward at an average of 20 yards per minute. This at least ensured that the mopping up was thoroughly carried out.

In general the Canadian assault nevertheless went well especially on the right and in the centre. The unexpectedness of their attack allowed the 44th and 50th Battalions to take the first two German trenches with little opposition although, as they pushed further forward, they met some spirited resistance from small groups of the Guards Regiment which had just come into the front line. On the Canadian left the 46th Battalion came under heavy rifle fire from the outset and suffered 50 percent casualties. But by 0600 the 44th Battalion were on the Pimple, having overshot their objective line by 200/300 yards because of the dreadful visibility and therefore having to pull back most of the way accordingly. The 50th Battalion had in the same timescale taken what remained of the Bois de Givenchy, 500 yards to the north. Two hours later the 46th Battalon, having wiped out a unit of Guards who had imprudently left the shelter of their trenches to confront them in the open,

36   TNA WO 95/3880: 4th Canadian Division War Diary.
37   OH 1917, Vol I, pp. 326-30 and 340-3.

had secured the Brigade's left flank.[38] The following day the 46th, having observed and reported that there appeared to be very little enemy activity in front of them, were ordered to advance to a new line based on Clash, Clannish and Cancan trenches. The move was successfully carried out with the battalions on either side also moving forward to conform. There was no opposition.[39]

The Bois en Hache was a small irregularly shaped wood on the Lorette ridge less than a mile northwest of the Pimple. Its possession, along with tshe Pimple, would give observers oversight of enemy positions in the Souchez Valley. It would also deny observation of movements on the Vimy Ridge to the enemy. The task of capturing the Bois en Hache was given to two battalions of 73 Brigade, the 2nd Leinster Regiment and 9th R Sussex. Each battalion attacked on a 500 yard front with the Leinsters ordered to capture the southern and middle parts of the wood and the R Sussex the northern part and the open slope beyond. The first and second German trenches were the main objectives. When the first one fell it was to be consolidated as the main line of resistance. The second one, 200 yards down the slope, would be used for observation for which outposts would be set up.

At 0500 the barrage opened and the battalions' assaulting companies began their advance, hampered by the near total darkness and the churned up state of the ground, with its water filled shell holes and deep mud which reduced their rate of progress significantly. As they slowly approached the first trench they came under machine gun and rifle fire which was fortunately not as accurate and damaging as it might have been because of the effects of the barrage and the blinding snowstorm on the defenders. Nevertheless the assaulting companies reached and entered the first trench within 10 minutes of their setting off even though 9th R Sussex had suffered 60 casualties in that time. Some Germans surrendered and many fled back to the temporary refuge of their second line.

As it became lighter and the weather improved slightly the two battalions pressed on down the slope towards the second line. The Leinsters encountered severe resistance from the trench and from enfilade machine gun fire from south of the Souchez. All the Leinster officers in the assaulting companies became casualties and it was only by dint of the survivors reorganizing themselves into small bombing groups that they were able to get into the trench at two points and hold on precariously. The Sussex also suffered severely but they too got into the trench at one or two places. Both battalions came under minor counterattack but managed to cling on until they were withdrawn once the consolidation of the German first trench had been completed. Although the Germans might still be in possession of their second trench their positions were now overlooked and completely dominated as were the approaches to their forward positions by which they would have to be resupplied and reinforced. It would only be a matter of time before they accepted the inevitable and withdrew.[40]

By the end of 12 April the Battle of Vimy Ridge had concluded with the Germans having been totally ejected from the ridge and apparently in no mood to seek to reverse their comprehensive defeat, at least in the short term. Their focus would be on damage limitation and making it as hard as possible for the Canadians to build on their success by forcing the Germans into further retreats. Fighting would therefore continue intermittently as the Canadians probed forward, seeking to occupy villages and test the German defences. But with the completion of the capture of the Pimple and Bois en Hache the southern and northern operations to seize the whole of Vimy Ridge had reached a triumphant conclusion. The Ridge's capture would prove to be one of the two high points of the Battles of Arras from the BEF's point of view, although this would not become apparent until the disappointments of the later stages of the battle began to mount up.

Field Marshal Haig recorded in his diary for 12 April what General Horne had told him about the day's events.

---

38   TNA WO 95/3880: 4th Canadian Division War Diary.
39   TNA WO 95/3895: 10 Canadian Brigade War Diary.
40   OH 1917, Vol 1, pp. 347-8.

[Horne] told me that the going this morning (owing to the snow and the shell holes) when the Canadians attacked the Pimple was very bad indeed. Yesterday Horne had visited Thélus and found it difficult to discover where the German front line trenches had been. All had been so terribly destroyed by our shell fire. Horne thought he had used too many shells! It had broken up the soil so frightfully that all movement was made so difficult.

Owing to the amount of Artillery and ammunition now available, the frontal attack on a position had become, Horne thought, the easiest task. The difficult matter was to advance later on when the enemy had organised a defence with machine guns. He also said that many officers in the First Army had said to him that their chief joy in gaining Monday's victory was the knowledge that it would put the stopper on all the disgraceful intrigues which had been going on at home in certain quarters against me. Especially was this feeling marked in the Canadian Corps, who had resented very much the attacks to which I had been subjected by certain politicians and others in England.

... When I think over the fine work of the 4th Canadian Division in taking the Pimple notwithstanding the mud, shell holes and snow, I come to the conclusion that no other people are comparable to the British race as downright hard fighters. This operation of Hilliam's Brigade (ex Sgt Major 17th Lancers) this morning was a fine performance.[41]

The Canadian Corps, with some British assistance, had completed a stunningly comprehensive victory, the most complete to this date by the BEF in the war. It proved to be a real shot in the arm for the Allies, both military and civilian, who were by this time more expectant of news of inconclusive battles and disproportionate casualty figures. The Canadian victory had not been bought lightly. Over 10 percent (10,602) of the 100,000 troops involved had become casualties, of whom 3,598 were dead.[42] Despite their severity these losses were deemed to be fully acceptable in the light of what had become the norm for the Western Front. The intensity of much of the fighting was reflected in the award of four Victoria Crosses.

---

41   Haig d. 12.4.17.
42   Nicholson, op. cit., p.255. TNA WO 95/3758: 1 Canadian Brigade War Diary.

9

Bullecourt: I ANZAC and V British Corps

T he First Battle of Bullecourt marked the advent into the Battles of Arras of General Sir Hubert Gough's Fifth Army. As already noted, General Gough's performance since his elevation to army command had not attracted universal admiration, especially among the Empire troops who had served under him during the Somme campaign. It did not bode well for future Anglo/Australian harmony that one of Fifth Army's two corps would be I ANZAC with its four Australian divisions.

As has already been described the planning of Fifth Army involvement in the Battle of Arras was seriously complicated by the voluntary German retirement to the Hindenburg Line. Initially it had been foreseen that Gough's Army would assist the Third Army thrust southeast from Arras towards Cambrai, by driving northeast from the positions it had found itself in at the end of the Somme campaign into an area known as the Bapaume salient. The German withdrawal from the area in question necessitated a substantial recasting of Fifth Army role, the planning of which was not helped by the uncertainty as to where precisely the German voluntary withdrawal would end. Field Marshal Haig instructed Gough to strive to maintain contact with the German rear guards, to press them back towards the Hindenburg Line, and also prepare to launch an attack on a stretch of the Line known as the Cojeul Switch, between the villages of Quéant and Écoust. When the latter village was captured on 2 April during Fifth Army operations against outposts of the Hindenburg Line, the village of Bullecourt replaced it at the western end of the line to be attacked. Fifth Army plan was subsequently further refined to make Bullecourt the main initial objective, Quéant being deemed too challenging with its four lines of defensive trenches. The second and third objectives would be respectively the villages of Riencourt and Hendecourt. Assuming that by this time a breach would have been made in the German defences, the 4th Cavalry Division would pass through with the aim of driving on to join hands with the rest of the Cavalry Corps advancing from Arras.

It had generally been foreseen that Fifth Army attack would be launched subsequently to those of Third and First Armies. Gough believed that the ideal time would be simultaneously with Third Army assault on the Brown (Wancourt-Feuchy) Line. This seemed likely to mean a Zero Hour 24 hours later than that of the other two armies. Even though on 24 March the whole of the heavy artillery of Gough's two corps had been ordered forward 'as soon as the state of the ground permits' and he had urged that no effort should be spared and any question of risk should be disregarded, Gough learned to his dismay on 8 April that it would be a further eight days before the artillery had dealt adequately with the enemy wire, an essential prerequisite to his assault being launched. Reluctantly Gough put his Army attack on hold until the artillery had completed its wire cutting task. He was therefore in a highly receptive mood when the Commander of D Tank Battalion, to which the company of tanks assigned to Fifth Army belonged, put forward a proposal emanating from the Tank Company Commander that seemed to offer a way of dealing with a sufficient quantity of the enemy wire without the need for a prolonged artillery bombardment. The proposal was that, instead of deploying the dozen tanks in pairs at intervals along the assault line, a configuration that the tank commanders themselves believed would lead to them being picked off piecemeal, all 12 of them should launch a surprise attack on a 1,000 yard front with no bombardment being fired until they had passed through the wire. This would, it was claimed, give them the opportunity to roll up the enemy wire along their whole frontage, thus creating a wide gap.

By the time Gough learned of this proposal early on the afternoon of 9 April he had become even more anxious to intervene in the main battle at the earliest possible moment as the first reports from the Third Army front were indicating that Allenby's Army were heading for a major victory. He not only accepted the Tank Officers' proposal but, less to their liking, ordered that it should be implemented the following morning. This presented major challenges. The tanks were some four miles to the rear and could not move until nightfall for fear of being spotted, and possibly bombed, by enemy aircraft. The weather was bad and getting worse with snowstorms limiting visibility and likely to reduce the speed of the tanks to a crawl. The shortcomings in the projected plan were perceived as so manifest, especially as it became apparent that Third Army offensive had not been as generally successful as first supposed, that Lieutenant General Birdwood, the ANZAC Corps Commander, and his Chief of Staff, Major General White, made separate attempts by telephone calls to Fifth Army HQ to have the operation postponed or cancelled.[1]

The decision was nevertheless confirmed that the attack would take place and start at the time Gough had ordered. It would be carried out on a frontage of 1,500 yards with the aim of penetrating the Hindenburg Line between the villages of Bullecourt and Quéant, which stood on either side of the jaws of a re-entrant into the Line. The infantry element for the operation would be 4th Australian Division. They would be preceded by the tanks, which would have the task of breaking through the wire. Once through the wire and in possession of this stretch of the Hindenburg Line four of the tanks would peel left and enter Bullecourt. They would be followed by one of 4th Division's infantry battalions tasked with clearing the village, an operation in which they would be joined by troops of the 62nd Division of the British V Corps. Once Bullecourt was secured the 62nd Division would advance to attack Hendecourt. At the same time another four tanks and the right wing of the Australian 4th Division would move on Riencourt.

The Fifth Army plan was unfortunately based on a serious misreading of German intentions. Gough's staff had persuaded themselves that once Fifth Army had penetrated the Hindenburg Line the enemy would evacuate it and fall back to the Drocourt-Quéant Switch (or the *Wotan Stellung* as the Germans called it). Optimistically therefore they hoped they would find Bullecourt only lightly defended by rearguards. For the Germans, however, Bullecourt was a pivotal part of their newly organised defensive system that they had no intention of allowing to fall into British hands.

The seeds of Fifth Army Plan's failure were additionally sown by Gough's decision to launch the attack so soon after the Tank Officers' plan had been adopted. Zero Hour was set for 0430 on 10 April which would give the attackers nearly two hours of darkness to achieve their initial objective before the increasing light would expose them to fire from both sides of the re-entrant. The 4th Australian Division Commander decided to attack on a two brigade front. They were in position in good time even though two of the six battalions that would initially be engaged had had a journey of seven miles to reach their positions. With the artillery maintaining a normal rate of fire to give the enemy no inkling of the planned assault, the infantry mainly lay out in the snow-covered open to await the arrival of the tanks, ever conscious of the danger of discovery in their exposed positions. When the tanks failed to appear on schedule, Zero Hour may initially have been postponed (although there is no record of any such decision reaching the attacking battalions). Then came the news that the tanks had been caught in a blizzard on their way up which had slowed their progress to a crawl. With time running short they would need at least a further 90 minutes to reach their jumping-off point. There could be no question of waiting for them. The increasing light would have revealed the Australian infantry positions well before their arrival. The tanks themselves would also have become easy targets without the cover of darkness. The 4th Division GOC therefore made the decision to pull back his

1   OH of Australia in the War of 1914-18 Volume IV, The AIF in France, pp. 277-8

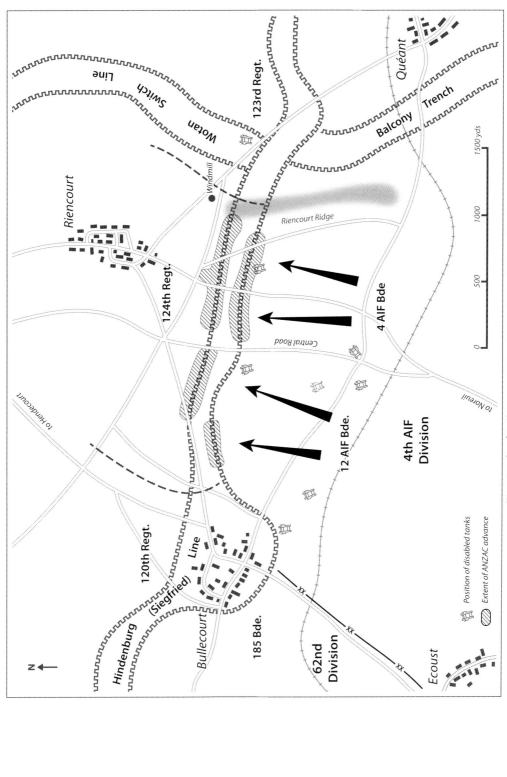

First Battle of Bullecourt, 11 April 1917. (© Pen & Sword Ltd)

men to positions of relative safety, a manoeuvre that was achieved with virtually no loss, partially because of a snowstorm that fortuitously passed over the area just as the darkness began to lift. No serious harm was done except to the tempers of the Australian infantrymen who had endured a night of frayed nerves and exposure to appalling weather for nothing.

The same could not be said for 62nd Division. They were not informed of the failure of the tanks to appear and sent forward strong patrols from three battalions of 185 Brigade to probe the Bullecourt defences in accordance with their planned part in the operation. The patrols were met by unexpected and murderous enemy fire as they sought to penetrate the wire. Realising that something had gone wrong, the patrols retired, but not without suffering the loss of 162 men. The principal sufferers were 7th East Yorks.

Thus ended Gough's first attempt to overcome the delay imposed on his plans by the time required by the artillery to deal with the enemy wire. The second attempt emerged from a meeting summoned by Gough at midday on the 10th at which he told the senior officers present that he intended to carry out the next morning the attack with tanks that had not taken place that morning in the hope that with a little more time for preparation the tanks would be in position by Zero Hour, which would again be 0430. Once again Lieutenant General Birdwood objected, his earlier reservations reinforced by the showing of the tanks that morning. He seemed to be making some headway until Gough received a telephone call from Field Marshal Haig in which the latter ordered the Fifth Army to attack as proposed by Gough. It is not entirely clear how privy Haig was to the details of Gough's plan. His innate caution might suggest that, had he been fully conversant with these, he might have expressed some reservations at the crucial role assigned to the unproven and unreliable tanks. In the light of this intervention, which he had no reason to suppose Haig had made without full possession of the facts, Birdwood did not feel able to continue his opposition, especially as the ANZACs had not had any direct experience of fighting alongside tanks. Gough had got his way.[2]

For the 4th Division infantry the decision meant that they would have to spend most of a further night out in the open on ground covered in even more snow than the previous night. One change in the plan was made. Patrols had established that some damage had been done to the enemy wire by the artillery, possibly sufficient to enable the infantry to get forward without waiting for the tanks to signal that they had completed clearance of the wire. The infantry were therefore ordered to begin their advance 15 minutes after the tanks without regard to the latter's success or otherwise. The orders for the tanks were also refined. Six would form up in front of each infantry brigade, and their individual manoeuvres subsequently were defined in precise detail. The inevitable noise made by them as they moved into position was to be concealed by machine gun barrages. To avoid a repetition of 62nd Division's premature move on Bullecourt the previous day, they were given strict instructions not to begin their advance until they had received a clear signal that the tanks and the Australian 46th Battalion had entered and mopped up the village.

As the performance of the tanks was to loom large in later Australian criticism of the conduct of the battle, it would be as well to record how their participation was perceived by the British Official History, which based its account on three sources, the records of the Tank Corps and Fifth Army and the despatches of Field Marshal Sir Douglas Haig. That the War Dairy of D Battalion of the Tank Corps does not feature in this list is certainly owing to its claim that two tanks had assisted in the capture of Riencourt and two more had led the infantry into Hendecourt. Riencourt was half a mile and Hendecourt twice that distance from the front trench of the Hindenburg Line. Neither tanks nor infantry reached either village. The Australian and German accounts are in agreement on that point. In fact, of the 12 tanks given to Fifth Army, all of which were initially assigned to the Australians, one was already sidelined before battle was joined. Only four of the remaining 11, which had been split into three sections, right (4), centre (3) and left (4), were in position by Zero Hour.

---

2   OH of Australia, op. cit., p.285.

Some of the others, those that had not been disabled or destroyed by enemy fire or succumbed to mechanical failure, joined in later. Overall the tanks' contribution to the battle must be described as disappointing, especially as the whole Fifth Army plan had been built around their involvement. One of them did eliminate a troublesome machine gun; another actually got over the enemy trenches and into Bullecourt in the mistaken belief that it was following behind the Australian infantry. There its engine failed, forcing the crew to abandon it. In general however the tanks demonstrated their mechanical unreliability, their vulnerability to enemy artillery and armour piercing bullets and their penchant for straying off course, with very little positive to show for only two of the tanks surviving. One positive was that the enemy guns and small arms fire tended to focus on the tanks long after they were wrecked and abandoned, thus diminishing to some extent the attention they should have been paying to the infantry. It also demonstrated the German obsession with the tanks' appearance on the battlefield, out of all proportion to the impact they could make, with their mechanical unreliability and lack of adequate armoured protection.

The disappointing performance of the tanks turned the Australian action into an infantry attack against mainly uncut wire largely unsupported by either tanks or artillery. Despite these daunting circumstances it nevertheless came close to succeeding. The 4th Division attacked with two brigades in line, the 4th on the right and the 12th on the left. Each brigade used two battalions in their initial assault. The 4 Brigade's were 16th Battalion on the right and 14th Battalion on the left. Behind them in support were the 13th and 15th Battalions. They jumped off at 0445 and very quickly overtook the tanks. The first and second lines of the German defences were soon captured, the first relatively easily thanks to the partially cut wire, the second, against intact wire and stubborn resistance, only by bombing and with the assistance of companies from the support battalions. Their first objectives in the Hindenburg Line had been gained but their losses in achieving these were too heavy to allow for a continuation of the advance towards Riencourt that had been planned.

The 12 Brigade's assault, which was to be led by 46th Battalion with 48th Battalion in support, made a slightly delayed start as 46th Battalion's orders had not made it clear that their 0445 Zero Hour was not dependent on the tanks beginning their assault at 0430. As a result the Battalion waited. When, by 0510, only one tank had made an appearance they sought orders by telephone and were told to advance immediately. By then the artillery had lifted its barrage on Bullecourt on the assumption that the tanks and the clearing infantry battalion would be entering the village. As a result both battalions came under much heavier fire than that suffered by 4 Brigade's. Nevertheless, by 0650, they had largely gained their objectives in the Hindenburg Line. The right of 46th Battalion had however failed to get through the wire and break into the Line, having fatally followed a tank into a gap in the wire where they were slaughtered. On the brigade left 48th Battalion had failed to extend its left beyond the Riencourt-Bullecourt road. Overall, like their fellow Brigade, their casualties had left them too weak to undertake the planned advance on Bullecourt. It would be tantamount to suicide to try to move reinforcements of men and supplies forward in broad daylight. In the light of this, the main challenge for the Australians was to hold on to what they had gained at least until nightfall. To do this they needed strong artillery support. Sadly they would not receive it.

A request from 4 Brigade HQ for barrages to be put down 200 yards beyond the second Hindenburg Trench and the same distance beyond the Brigade's right flank was made at 0810. Although the true situation at the front was perfectly clear to the Brigade GOC and his artillery liaison officer, the Divisional and Corps HQs chose to put their faith in the two entirely erroneous reports that tanks and infantry had passed through Riencourt and were on their way to Hendecourt, and that British troops were in Bullecourt. The request was refused and the consequent lack of artillery support enabled the enemy to mount a series of co-ordinated counterattacks on the two Australian brigades from 1000 onwards. The 4 Brigade managed to maintain their positions until their supply of bombs began to run out. They were then slowly pushed back along the trenches leaving many of their number to be taken prisoner. When they were forced to withdraw across open ground, the enemy machine guns took a heavy toll. For 12 Brigade matters were, if possible, even worse. The enemy managed to get behind 48th Battalion by, unknown to them, clearing out the handful of 46th Battalion survivors from the first Hindenburg Line. They were effectively surrounded and cut off, a situation they discovered when they began their withdrawal through the trenches and came across enemy where they had expected Australians. Dismissing any notion of surrender, they used their remaining bombs to clear the enemy from the communication trenches and the first line. At this point a belated Australian barrage came down on the Hindenburg Line, making the newly recaptured first line untenable. The withdrawal had perforce to be continued under heavy enemy machine gun fire despite which the Battalion remained remarkably composed. The 48th was the last battalion to withdraw, a full hour behind the rest.[3]

By 1300 the 4th Australian Division's action was effectively over. Losses had been severe. The 4 Brigade's casualties totalled 2,339 out of the 3,000 who were engaged. The 12 Brigade suffered rather fewer at 950. Remarkable was the high number of prisoners in these totals. The Germans claimed to have captured 28 Officers and 1,142 Other Ranks. German casualties amounted to 749.[4]

It is difficult not to share the Australian Official History's view that the First Battle of Bullecourt had been a near total disaster. On the plus side the Australian 4th Division's achievement in penetrating and capturing the First Hindenburg Line, without artillery support and negligible help from the tanks, was an outstanding, if ephemeral, achievement. On the minus side the short-lived achievement had been gained at a huge and unacceptable cost in Australian casualty numbers. The Germans were justifiably in no doubt that they had secured a significant victory. While accepting that there were instances of operational shortcomings for which Australian staff work was to blame, the Australian Official History does not mince its words in laying the major blame firmly at the door of General Gough.

Despite the setback on the 11th General Gough was very soon planning to renew Fifth Army attempts to capture Bullecourt. Reflecting this, the front of I ANZAC had been reorganised so that 2nd Australian Division which, along with 62nd Division on their left, had been selected to carry out the renewed assault on Bullecourt, were concentrated on a frontage of about 2,750 yards south and southeast of that village. Responsible for the continuation of Fifth Army front eastward were 1st Australian Division. Following their advance on 13-14 April to within 1,000 yards of the Hindenburg Line, 1st Division's front was 13,500 yards long. From the point of their junction with 2nd Division north of Lagnicourt, the line described a fan shape as it changed direction south half way along its length. At an average of nearly two miles per battalion in the front line, the Division's length of front was dangerously extended in an active sector; it almost invited a German assault on the overstretched line. The 1st Division were deployed on a two brigade front, 1 Brigade on the right and 3 Brigade on the left. Each had two battalions manning the front line positions. From the right these were the 3rd, 4th, 11th and 12th, the last named having relieved the 9th during the night of the 14th. In close support of the two 3 Brigade battalions were two companies each from the Brigade's two resting battalions. The remaining four battalions were in reserve. In divisional reserve were 2 Brigade.

The enemy were quick to spot the opportunity the Australian deployment offered them. Their XIV Corps hastily drew up a plan to achieve a breakthrough and then exploit it by capturing and destroying the concentrations of Australian artillery in the Noreuil and Lagnicourt valleys between and around the two villages. Most of these guns were temptingly close to the German front line, at about a mile distant. In an Australian attempt not to call attention to themselves, precautions such as setting up protective wire around their gun positions had been foregone. Less understandably the gun crews had not been issued with their rifles. Nor had infantry protection of the guns been put in place.

3   OH 1917 Volume 1, pp. 359-69.
4   OH of Australia, op. cit., pp. 343 and 349

All this despite the fact that the loss of the guns would make it almost impossible for Fifth Army to mount a meaningful attack on the Hindenburg Line for some time. The German attack would involve elements of four divisions. Its main thrust would be southwest through Lagnicourt and between that village and Noreuil. The infantry assault would not be presaged by the sort of artillery barrage that would be interpreted as a sure warning of an attack, thus offering the Germans the possibility of surprise. Zero Hour would be 0430 on 15 April.

The Australians first became aware that something was afoot when a little after 0400 a 3rd Battalion sentry, on the Division's right flank and looking east towards the Canal du Nord, observed a large number of Germans approaching. They were immediately forced into a hasty retreat by Lewis gun and rifle fire. When they made a second attempt to attack the 3rd Battalion's posts, the Australians were greatly helped in dealing successfully with the assault by the bright illumination of the attackers provided by the numerous rockets fired off by the German infantry to warn their own artillery that they were firing short. The attack was driven back in disorder. About 1,000 yards of line, manned by a handful of pickets had been maintained intact. On 3rd Battalion's left, the 4th Battalion were less successful. Although they successfully withstood the initial German assault they were partially undone when the enemy employed a flame thrower against a post on the road running east from the village of Demicourt, overwhelming it. Other posts near the Bapaume-Cambrai road were also driven in. The Battalion's attempts to retrieve the situation by counterattacks using their own reserves were unavailing, but the defence of Demicourt and the neighbouring village of Boursies and the line between them, was assured by the reserve company and three companies of 1st Battalion moving up from Doignies. So confident was the Brigade Commander that the situation was under control that he allowed two companies of his 2nd Battalion to go to the support of the harder pressed 3 Brigade. Unlike 1 Brigade the 3rd were subjected to a short but severe bombardment which began at 0400. Despite this, when the enemy infantry assaulted, initially against the positions held by 11th Battalion, their attacks were beaten off. The enemy nevertheless made progress by infiltrating between posts manned by the Battalion's right hand company and then picked them off one by one despite the great gallantry shown by the virtually surrounded troops. Their sacrifice was not entirely in vain as the delay they imposed on the enemy advance enabled a new line to be formed to the rear by the Battalion reserve and two companies of the 10th Battalion.

For some reason only the right half of the 12th Battalion, on the left of 11th Battalion, was assaulted at Zero Hour. The Battalion's left half was not attacked until nearly an hour later. While the right half had little difficulty in withstanding the enemy attack, the same was not the case with the left, for it was here and against the right of the 17th Battalion of the 2nd Division 5 Brigade, on the left of 12th Battalion, that the enemy made their only significant breakthrough of the day. This became apparent when daylight revealed that a large number of the enemy were already south of Lagnicourt having made rapid progress into and through the village. Both of the battalions covering the area where the breakthrough was made were inclined to blame the other, but the probable truth is that they were both hit simultaneously by overwhelming force. Whatever the precise reasons for the German success were, it had created a very dangerous situation for the Australians. Already the enemy had captured four batteries of field artillery and were probably in possession of another three further west. They were in addition threatening a battery near Maricourt wood and nine batteries in the valley southwest of Noreuil. Disaster was narrowly averted by the stubbornness and aggression of the front line troops who slowed up the German progress, winning two Victoria Crosses in the process, for long enough for the reserves to position themselves to stem the German tide. Valuable assistance was provided by two groups of the 2nd Division's artillery and the heavy artillery despite the danger they were in of being overrun.

The enemy's attempts to advance southwards and southeastwards from Lagnicourt had been contained. An attempt to advance in strength to the west was also halted by a numerically stronger defence. The 5 Brigade's 19th Battalion, which had been called forward to boost the defence of Noreuil, arrived just in time to meet and stop two German attacks. With the enemy stopped the Australians now began to advance cautiously. By about 0700 the 5 Brigade's 20th Battalion had got as far as the Noreuil-Morchies road and the Germans found themselves under fire in broad daylight from three sides of their self-created salient. The mere threat of the inevitable Australian counterattack proved sufficient to bring about a collapse in German morale and little resistance was offered when the counterattack was launched. Many of the enemy surrendered, others were killed and those in less forward positions sought to hurry back to their own lines. The Australians were in no mood to show mercy after their heavy losses and artillery was called down on bodies of the enemy observed making their way through their own wire to safety. With the Australian infantry pressing forward, only slightly delayed by the need to wait for their own barrage on the north of Lagnicourt to lift, the situation was soon restored to that which had prevailed before the German assault had begun. Most of the artillery pieces, even those that had been temporarily taken by the Germans, were recovered undamaged. The Germans had only had time to destroy four 18 pounders and a howitzer. Another had been destroyed by shellfire. The remainder were all back in action once the parts removed by the retiring Australians had been reinstalled.

As the fighting wound down the Australians could take considerable satisfaction from the serious damage they had inflicted on their attackers despite the latters' great superiority in numbers. Among the four officers and 358 other ranks captured and the many bodies of enemy dead were found members of 26 battalions from four divisions. The Australians reckoned the Germans had lost 1,500 in killed alone. More realistically, the Germans computed their losses as totalling 2,313 killed, wounded, missing and prisoners, fewer than the Australians believed, but nevertheless more than twice as many as the Australian total of 1,010, which included at least 300 taken prisoner. Unsurprisingly the losses were suffered mainly by the 11th and 12th Battalions of the 1st Division 3 Brigade and the 17th Battalion of the 2nd Division 5 Brigade. There could be little doubt that, despite their early setbacks, the Australians had given the Germans a bloody nose and dented their morale. It would be some time before it would be seen whether a renewal of the assault on Bullecourt and the Hindenburg Line would be the easier as a result.[5]

---

5   OH, op. cit., pp. 370-6. OH of Australia, op. cit., pp. 393-400.

Part III

Nivelle Offensive. Second Battle of the Aisne (Chemin des Dames)

10

Preparations

On 16 April, exactly one week after the BEF's Third and First Armies had launched their offensives at Arras and Vimy Ridge in its support, the French Armies under the overall command of General Robert Nivelle set in motion their massive offensive usually referred to as the Chemin des Dames, but officially entitled the Second Battle of the Aisne.

The auguries for a French success were not good, still less for the smashing triumph that Nivelle had persuasively offered when he assumed supreme command in December 1916. Since then, confidence in his ability to deliver on his promises had slowly eroded as the timetable, beset by inter-allied differences over unity of command, railway priorities and the British takeover of French sectors of the line, slipped by two months, when speed had been seen as an essential ingredient. Equally damaging to confidence were the advent of a more sceptical French Minister of War, growing concerns about Nivelle's cavalier approach to security and his perceived failure to pay sufficient attention to the German withdrawal to the Hindenburg Line and the massive changes in his Plan that this seemed to call for. These concerns were fully aired at the meeting of 6 April that has already been fully described. Although the Group Army Commanders, whatever their reservations, were in reluctant agreement that it was too late to stop the offensive it was probably only Nivelle's threat to resign and General Franchet d'Espèrey's timely reminder that the British preliminary bombardments at Arras and Vimy Ridge were already well under way that brought everyone to agreement that the offensive should be launched as planned.

The Nivelle Plan had undergone relatively little modification since it had first been outlined immediately following its author's accession to the Supreme Command in mid-December 1916. By the end of that year Nivelle had secured General Haig's agreement in principle to the broad outline of his Plan and had determined that the key role of commanding the soon to be formed *Groupe d'Armées de Réserve* (GAR) would be given to General Micheler rather than General Pétain. The latter was the obvious choice for the role, given that the main initial battlefield was projected to be in the area covered by his *Groupe d'Armées du Centre* (GAC). Pétain had however already made clear his doubts about the wisdom of assaulting the Chemin des Dames, the focal point of Nivelle's Plan. Even though he had posited an alternative plan for an offensive in his area, Pétain's evident lack of enthusiasm for Nivelle's proposed strategy persuaded the latter that he should be looking elsewhere for his key army group commander. Hence General Micheler. Ironically he would, more belatedly and deviously, turn out to be even less enthusiastic than Pétain about their superior's strategy.

The *Groupe d'Armées de Réserve* would consist of three armies, the Fifth (General Mazel), the Sixth (Mangin) and the Tenth (Duchêne). The Fifth would be transferred from the GAC while remaining physically in place where it was on the Aisne. The other two armies would come from the GAN, in the case of the Tenth, once it had been relieved by the British taking over its part of the French line. The main change from Nivelle's original thinking was that two of these armies, rather than one, would be used to achieve the breakthrough. This would leave just the Tenth Army, rather than the two previously planned, to join the battle for the exploitation phase (as '*La Masse de Manoeuvre*',[1] as the French termed it).

---

1   There is no exact equivalent in English. 'Strategic Reserve' has been used.

General Robert Nivelle, French Commander in Chief

General Philippe Pétain, GOC in
C *Groupe d'Armées du Centre.*

General Charles Mangin, GOC
French Sixth Army

General Louis Franchet d'Espèrey, GOC
in C Groupe d'Armées du Nord

General Alfred Micheler, GOC in
C Groupe d'Armées de Réserve

The Nivelle Plan, as formally drawn up, called for nothing less than the destruction of the enemy's main forces on the Western Front, through a decisive battle between Soissons and Craonne towards the Chemin des Dames leading to a breakthrough of the enemy front within 48 hours. Through this breach in the enemy lines, *la Masse de Manoeuvre*, hitherto in reserve, would advance to engage and defeat the enemy forces to hand. At the same time the army or armies that had achieved the breakthrough would expand the breach by fanning out to the left, advancing towards Laon and Saint-Quentin, and to the right astride the River Aisne. The pressure that these manoeuvres would bring to bear on the enemy's lines of communication would oblige them to abandon their fixed positions and accept battle under the most unfavourable conditions for them. In addition to the British offensive at Arras, two supporting French attacks would be launched to pin down the enemy and force them to divide their forces. The GAN would assault between the Rivers Somme and Oise to the southeast of Saint-Quentin on the same timescale as the British. A day after the main attack was launched the GAC would assault east of Reims. The three attacks and that of the British would be sufficiently separated both in place and time to pin down the Germans and sow doubt as to where to feed in their reserves. Once the German defences were overcome the victorious French armies would advance northwards.

The strength of Micheler's Army Group would be significant. The Fifth and Sixth Armies, tasked with making the breakthrough would each have 14 divisions, four of which would be held by Nivelle in reserve. The Tenth Army would have 12 divisions for its exploitative role as *Masse de Manoeuvre*. Five cavalry divisions would also be assigned to this role. General Franchet d'Espèrey's GAN, reduced to the First and Third Armies by the departure of the Sixth and Tenth to GAR, would consist of 24 infantry divisions, five of which would form part of Nivelle's reserve. Two cavalry divisions would complete the Army Group's order of battle. General Pétain's GAC would consist of the Second and Fourth Armies for its secondary role in the French offensive. General Ferdinand Foch's Groupe d'Armées de l'Est would not, as its name suggests, be directly involved in the battle, its Seventh and Eighth Armies being deployed opposite Alsace-Lorraine. Furthermore, concerns about German intentions towards Nancy and Belfort were a continual preoccupation for Nivelle making it impossible for him to contemplate thinning out Foch's order of battle to reinforce the upcoming offensive.

As Nivelle got into the detailed planning of his offensive, his major concern was to maximise the number of infantry divisions he could bring together for the main and supporting thrusts. Distractions such as those that the French feared might erupt in Alsace-Lorraine and the continuing aggressiveness of the Germans on the Verdun battlefield which, by rights, should have become a quiet sector following the French victory of mid December 1916, limited his scope for moving divisions westward. Nivelle's former command, the Second Army, from which he had hoped to take eight divisions, could not in the event be weakened to that extent. More positively, the BEF's taking over of French line to release the French Tenth Army. had proceeded smoothly if tardily. Nivelle made it clear that his armies should avoid as far as possible undertaking actions that were not essential, for fear of them leading to heavy casualties. Instead the emphasis should be on training and rehearsal for the forthcoming offensive.

Into this mix entered the growing evidence that the Germans had, since the latter stages of the Battle of the Somme, been building new defences well behind their current front lines. Could they be intending to withdraw into them? The initial indications of what the Germans might be up to came from deserters, prisoners and repatriated French civilians. The hope that their claims might be verified or disproved by allied air reconnaissance was to a large extent frustrated by the weather conditions the aircrews had to contend with throughout the appalling winter of 1916-17 and, in addition, by the clear determination of their adversaries, currently enjoying a brief period of technical superiority in aircraft, to prevent allied intrusions into their airspace, with the obvious intention of keeping the extent and location of the new defences as secret as possible.[2] The main sources of information would continue to be deserters, prisoners and repatriates. These sources and the visual evidence of large numbers of fires being lit in areas behind the German lines enabled a picture to be put together of the extent of the new defences, if not of if and when the Germans might be planning a withdrawal. By mid March the French were aware that in their sector the new German fortified line extended from Cambrai in the north to Saint-Quentin in the south, largely following, between these two towns, the route of the Saint-Quentin Canal through Vendhuile, Bellicourt and Lesdins. From there it passed to the east of Saint-Quentin before continuing in a southeasterly direction from south of that town to Urvillers and Alaincourt where it entered the valley of the River Oise. Of particular concern to the French planners was that the new and previous fortifications meant that Saint-Quentin was almost completely surrounded by trench works including three lines of them between the town and Ribemont to its southeast.

Signs that the construction of the new defences would be coupled with a German withdrawal multiplied. The increasing number of repatriated civilians showed that the enemy were clearing large swathes of occupied territory of their populations. The German Army Group and Army Headquarters were moving back, in the case of Crown Prince Rupprecht's Army Group HQ as far as Mons in Belgium. Air reconnaissance revealed that many bridges and crossings were being blown up and roads cratered. A captured German officer warned his British captors that should a French advance break through the German lines they would find themselves confronted with mined roads, villages and bridges. Also becoming noticeable was a diminution by about half of German medium and heavy calibre artillery activity, particularly opposite the GAN and the British Fifth Army. While this

---

2   The Royal Flying Corps were rather more successful than their French allies in penetrating enemy airspace, but their efforts were focused on the British sector.

appeared to indicate that a German withdrawal might already be underway the robustness of German front line activity throughout February and into March seemed to indicate no such intention. As late as late February both Allies seemed wedded to the belief that on balance the Germans would have more to lose from a withdrawal than they would gain and that therefore no withdrawal would take place. When it became inescapably evident that the Germans facing the British Fifth Army were indeed withdrawing, reactions among the French High Command varied.

As the nearest French neighbour to the British Fifth Army the reaction of the GAN's Commander Franchet d'Espérey was predictably the strongest and potentially the most enterprising. Based on the information he had received from the British he foresaw the probable extent of the German withdrawal and immediately ordered his troops to seek urgently by all appropriate means, including aggressive patrolling to secure prisoners, and air reconnaissance, to obtain as much information as possible to determine the extent of any German retirement in his sector. He also ordered plans to be drawn up for a possible offensive to catch the Germans in mid retirement when they might well be at their most vulnerable. These orders were issued on 25 February; by 1 March he was reiterating them in even more pressing terms having received further information from the British. Both his remaining armies, the First and Third, reacted energetically. Prisoners taken on 6 March by First Army confirmed that they had received orders the previous day to prepare for an imminent retirement from in front of the French by evacuating villages, moving back supplies and stores, withdrawing artillery and carrying out demolitions. Prisoners taken by Third Army on 9 March and during the night of 10/11 March confirmed what had been learned by First Army, adding that they had been ordered to clear several towns of their civilian populations. They had however still not been given a date for the retirement to begin.

For their part the French air observers, despite the continuing severe weather, had seen enough to indicate that since 1 March there had been daily increasing signs that preparations for withdrawal were well underway. Particularly noticeable, not only to the airmen but also to land based observers, were the large areas covered by fires as homes burned in towns and villages behind the German lines. There were also areas around the town of Noyon, which had been deliberately inundated. Franchet d'Espérey did not wait until he had accumulated overwhelming evidence of German intentions before informing Nivelle. On 25 February he reviewed the situation and evidence as perceived by him and his army commanders in a report to the Commander in Chief. It concluded that the information it contained merited the closest attention but it should not be unreservedly accepted, principally because it contained no indication of the date a German retirement might begin nor the methods that might be employed in carrying it out. On 4 March Franchet d'Espérey sent Nivelle a more wide ranging note reviewing the information accumulated over the past three months and concluding that it was certain that the enemy were preparing to withdraw their front between Arras and Laon by about 20 kilometres to the so-called *Position Hindenburg*.[3] In the light of this the GAN Commander submitted a proposed plan of operations designed to surprise the Germans at the earliest possible moment during the course of their preparations and to compel them through this surprise attack to unveil their intentions and force them into withdrawals before they were ready to make them. Whenever they found forward positions had been abandoned by the enemy the units making the discovery were to follow up immediately in order to maintain contact, without awaiting orders from higher up the chain of command. Franchet d'Espérey concluded his note by repeating the reservations in his earlier report.

In his response of 7 March, General Nivelle accepted that while there was evidence of the possibility of a German withdrawal there was no concrete indication that, if it took place, it would

---

3   To the British, of course, the 'Hindenburg Line'. To the Germans, at various stages of its length, the 'Wotan – Siegfried – Alberich-Stellung'. Unless quoting directly from French or German texts the term 'Hindenburg Line' will be adhered to.

extend to GAN's sector of the front. In his view it remained highly improbable that the enemy would voluntarily give up the prized asset of this French territory without an all out fight. Furthermore strategy could not be determined on the basis of hypotheses. As a result he had decided to make no changes in the overall plan of operations for 1917. Nevertheless, recognising that a German withdrawal on the GAN front appeared to be a distinct possibility, he ordered Franchet d'Espérey's armies to mount an operation to capture the enemy's forward positions and set up a solid base from which might be made a further advance against the enemy's second positions. The attack should be supported by all available artillery resources but only involve the minimum number of infantry necessary to complete the task. As they advanced, a major priority would be to restore to a usable state all the infrastructure and equipment destroyed by the enemy. The operation should begin on 17 March with a 36 hour artillery bombardment.

In a note issued on 16 March Nivelle announced that the enemy were beating a retreat; the war of movement was beginning. This confirmed what the First and Third Armies had been finding, that the enemy were retiring on both sides of the River Avre and on the south side of the River Oise. On the north side of the Oise they were still holding their positions in strength.

Although they were increasingly finding that the enemy had abandoned frontline and sometimes even second line positions, the army commanders, scarcely able to bring themselves to believe that their opponents were just simply withdrawing, were sometimes hesitant in ordering their troops to advance vigorously out of fear that they might thereby be marching them into a trap. Franchet d'Espèrey had to remind them that his orders had to be obeyed, although they should remain on constant guard against the possibility of enemy counterattacks. The tempo of the French advance did thereupon indeed pick up, but it was clear that they were finding it difficult to readapt to a war of movement, especially when movement was inhibited by the obstacles to mobility that the Germans had left in their wake. Once again, on 17 March, General Franchet d'Espèrey urged his armies forward whatever the difficulties. The 1st and 3rd Cavalry Divisions should push forward to the Hindenburg Line and the main bodies of infantry to a line running from Ham to Tergnier by way of Saint-Simon.

The closer the French got to the Hindenburg Line the more resistance there was from the Germans, especially in their defence of river and canal crossings. Bridges and crossing points were destroyed and a full range of artillery deployed to make progress as difficult as possible. Nevertheless by late March the GAN were coming up against the advanced defences of the Hindenburg Line. At this point General Nivelle decided to reduce GAN to one army, the Third, in order to strengthen the forces available for the upcoming main offensive. The length of the GAN's front was consequently reduced from 55 to 35 kms. They would take up a defensive posture along this line as there was no plan to mount an attack on the Hindenburg Line at this stage.

Indications of a possible German withdrawal were also being picked up, as early as the beginning of February, in front of the left wing of the GAR, where XXXVII Infantry Corps were in the line from Pernant Ravine to Chavonne on either side of Soissons. Initially Intelligence picked up that the Germans were planning modifications in their defensive organisation which indicated that they were no longer interested in any territory west of a line between Condé Fort and Vauxaillon but were strengthening their defences further to the east at, and to the north and south of, Laffaux mill. It was in any case prudent to assume that if the Germans were withdrawing from in front of the British and GAN to the north, they would also be intending to do so in front of the left wing of GAR. From 10 March these indications of a planned withdrawal were reinforced by the fires being lit by the enemy mostly west of a line between Vailly and Anizy.

The GAR Commander General Micheler's response to these indications was to put the Sixth Army, of which XXXVII Corps was a part, on heightened alert. He ordered the Sixth Army Commander, General Charles Mangin, to organise fighting patrols with the main aim of taking prisoners from around Soissons, Soupir and the Chemin des Dames. Mangin passed these orders on to his XXXVII and VI Corps. The former, consisting only of one infantry division (the 127th) and two territorial regiments, was immediately reinforced with the 158th Division and a cavalry regiment. Without waiting for these reinforcements to deploy however, the Corps Commander ordered 127th Division to occupy the heights between Pasly and Crouy, which dominated the right bank of the River Aisne, so as to enable an army corps to debouch to the north of the Aisne by way of the Soissons bridgehead and push out patrols to keep in touch with enemy rearguards.

On 19 March the rest of XXXVII Corps crossed the Aisne via the Soissons bridgehead. In the days following, the Corps continued to advance with its two divisions in line. The right of the 127th were on the Aisne and attacking towards Nanteuil-la-Fosse; the 158th were providing cover on the left as they moved via Sorny to the east of Vauxaillon. The enemy opposed these moves much more strongly than they had those of GAN, using infantry units plentifully equipped with machine guns and well-supported by artillery. Not only were they ready to defend their fixed positions, but they readily counterattacked when they deemed the French progress to be too rapid. Nevertheless the French made further progress on 20-21 March despite the vigorous enemy reaction. Missy-sur-Aisne changed hands twice before being finally secured by the French.

At the end of 21 March the XXXVII Corps Commander called a halt to general offensive operations and ordered his troops to go on the defensive, in conformity with Nivelle's order not to attack the Hindenburg Line at this stage. The Corps would instead make preparations for its participation in the Sixth Army role in the forthcoming offensive. These would include actions to secure or improve suitable start lines. The role would be little different from that decided on in January despite the German withdrawal. As the result of the recent success of his left wing, General Mangin did, however, now have the option of complementing his attack northwards with one eastwards.

General Nivelle's response of 7 March to Franchet d'Espèrey had also invited Generals Micheler and Pétain to offer their reactions and proposals in the event that a German retirement to the Hindenburg Line on the GAN front became an indisputable fact and might even become more extensive. Pétain proposed an offensive astride the River Suippe using a force of 15 or 16 divisions. In combination with the GAR the aim would be to encircle and force the surrender of the *Berru Massif,* enlarge the breach thereby made in the enemy defensive system and rapidly clear the loop in the River Aisne, northeast of Reims.

Micheler's proposal called for the bulk of the French resources to be placed at his disposal for the battle aimed at breaking through the German defences and then exploiting the breakthrough. Micheler claimed that all the German forces not tied down by GAN would rush to join in the battle. It was necessary therefore that he should have all possible means to conduct it. He did envisage a possible reinforcement of the left wing of Pétain's Army Group to extend and complete his attack. Neither General's proposals represented a significant departure from what was already being planned. But even though there was much tactical merit in it, Pétain's proposal involved a delay of about 5 or 6 weeks before all would be ready. This would mean putting off Micheler's attack until around 1 May. On top of all the other delays, amounting by now to about two months, this was perceived as completely unacceptable. Micheler's proposal, on the other hand, entailed no further delay. After detailed study at Nivelle's HQ, it was agreed to with the sole reserve that the divisions withdrawn from GAN to reinforce the GAR would be kept under the control of Nivelle, for use either to reinforce Micheler's breakthrough or to meet a German attack elsewhere on the front.

The net effect of all this was that Nivelle's Plan underwent very little modification in the light of the changed circumstances brought about by the German withdrawal. The GAN was marginalised, reduced as it was to one army of three corps charged with maintaining pressure on the withdrawing enemy but otherwise maintaining a defensive posture close up to the Hindenburg Line. All thought of a GAN surprise attack with tanks was discarded.[4] The GAC would mount a secondary attack

---

4   The British Official History considered that this surprise attack might well have resulted in a 'sensational victory'. OH

east of Reims between Nauroy and Aubérive. It would be launched simultaneously with that of Micheler's Army Group and would either take advantage of the latter's success or, at the very least, tie down important enemy forces. The First Army, formerly part of GAN, would form a reserve and be reinforced by units withdrawn from GAN and the Groupe d'Armées de l'Est, should this become a possibility.

At this stage the French offensive was scheduled to begin on 8 April, a date which Nivelle hoped was sufficiently soon to forestall any attempts by the enemy to make any further voluntary withdrawals on the fronts where he was planning to launch his offensive. It was now clear that the German voluntary retirement was in full flow and there was growing unease that it might not stop at the Hindenburg Line. Contingency plans to ensure that contact was not lost with the enemy were drawn up by Nivelle's staff. If the sector of the front affected was limited to a line from Soissons east to Vailly, then the left wing of the GAR would need to advance to a line running from Vailly northwest to Pont-St-Mard. From there the GAN would take over and move forward to a line running northnorthwest to Bray-St-Christophe, where junction would be made with the British Fourth Army. Their right flank was currently resting at Douchy, just north of Bray. The GAN were in addition ordered to make preparations for a surprise attack between the Oise and Somme rivers although permission for this to be launched would be subject to developments on the GAR front.

Until 8 April however, there would be little that the French could do to stop the Germans retiring as they pleased, thus possibly avoiding the battle that Nivelle was anxious to bring about. If this proved to be the case, one way to bring them to battle would be to attack in areas where the Germans would be very reluctant to retire for reasons of security or because the areas concerned were too economically valuable to them. Both the GAC and the GAE were close to such areas and were accordingly ordered to be prepared to launch powerful attacks on them. Nivelle in the meantime continued his planning on the basis that by beginning their attacks on 8 April his armies would still be able to inflict major damage on the enemy's retirement plans. On 21 March he told his Army Group Commanders that the GAR would attack on that date followed two days later by the GAC. General Micheler's response was immediate and must have been a severe disappointment to Nivelle. The GAR Commander pointed out that his plans had been predicated on the assumption that the enemy he would face would have been sitting in their fixed defences, consisting of two lines, for 30 months. Their numbers had not been expected to be great. In these circumstances a brutal and lightning surprise attack by his armies would have had a good chance of succeeding, especially if both the British and the GAN to the north had, by attacking earlier, successfully prevented the Germans from moving troops south to reinforce their defences opposite the GAR. But, Micheler pointed out, these circumstances no longer applied. At least three enemy divisions, and probably more, had moved in to strengthen the German front in the sector due to be attacked by GAR. Behind these were divisions in reserve. In addition the enemy could move more divisions currently in the Laon area to bolster their defences. Furthermore the Germans now seemed to be expecting a French offensive. Surprise had apparently been lost. The enemy now had four lines of defences in depth. It was therefore no longer sensible to reckon on a rapid breakthrough and it had to be questioned whether there would be a successful exploitation.

Micheler continued that the original plan had been for earlier attacks, notably those of the British and GAN, to tie down the Germans. The latest orders seemed to suggest that the British would not attack until 8 April. Furthermore the length of front on which they and GAN would be tying down the enemy had decreased as a result of the German withdrawal. Micheler concluded that in the light of these developments the plans for a rapid and deep exploitation following a breakthrough no longer had the same chances of success especially as the enemy would be able to commit about 30 fresh divisions to the battle. He wrote, "We risk being stopped on the threshold of the breakthrough."

General Nivelle's somewhat muted reaction to Micheler's views was to rejig the starting times of the various elements involved. The BEF would lead off on D Day[55] followed by GAN on D plus 2, GAR on D plus 4 and GAC on D plus 5. D Day would remain 8 April unless very adverse weather conditions forced a postponement. When conveying this to Field Marshal Haig, Nivelle also requested, in the light of the perceived diminution of the British role, that on D plus 2 the BEF's Fourth Army (holding the line between the BEF's Fifth Army and the GAN) should mount a powerful artillery 'demonstration' along its whole front to give the enemy the impression that it was going to unleash an offensive which would oblige them to keep their forces in place in that sector.

A brief scare was raised on 31 March that the enemy were planning a further withdrawal opposite the British. Nivelle asked Haig if he would be prepared to attack sooner than 8 April to take advantage of any such move. He also ordered his Army Groups to prepare for earlier action. However, Haig was able to reassure Nivelle that there was no evidence to back up his fear.

The French Commander in Chief, finding reassurance from all his exchanges that his offensive would not fall on empty enemy defences, issued his last instructions. He wrote, "Nothing is changed in the conditions of the breakthrough; it will still assume the characteristics of violence, brutality and rapidity." In his instructions to the troops under his command regarding the exploitation phase, General Micheler took into consideration the increase in enemy numbers confronting his men. He envisaged a more methodical advance for his infantry, under the protection of close artillery support. Like Micheler, the GAC Commander, General Pétain, no longer foresaw the possibility of a breakthrough by his Fourth Army followed by immediate exploitation. Instead he saw his Army role as one of conducting an attack subordinate to, and dependent on, the success of the GAR and not as an all out and rapid attack intended to ensure the success of the GAR. When Nivelle saw these instructions from two of his Army Group Commanders he immediately ordered them to be revised to take on a more offensive minded character.

In the light of the withdrawal of the Germans into the Hindenburg Line defences, entailing as it did changes in the plans of action of the attackers, Nivelle thought it necessary to issue a general directive summarising the instructions that had been given to all concerned to ensure that they realised how their particular role fitted into the overall plan. A translation of this is at Appendix VI.

The possibility of adverse weather conditions forcing a postponement of D Day, which had been foreseen when 8 April had been decided on, became a reality when General Micheler indicated that his artillery programme was being affected by the weather's interference with aerial observation. Nivelle sought Haig's agreement to a 48 hour postponement. The British C in C pointed out that his preparations were on schedule but reluctantly agreed to a 24 hour delay. He would in addition not object to the French timetable slipping more than that, within reason. In the event, the French finally settled on a 48 hour delay for GAN (co-operating with the British Fourth Army), and 96 hours for GAR and GAC. The revised times were therefore: BEF, D Day (9 April): GAN, D plus 3 (12th): GAR, D plus 7 (16th): GAC, D plus 8 (17th).

There would be no further slippage but there had already been more than enough to have seriously dented the prospects of a French victory, let alone the crushing triumph that Nivelle had been promising to mastermind since December. On leaving the Second Army at Verdun to take over from General Joffre, he had claimed, in reference to the Verdun battle just concluding, "We now have the formula ... our method has proved itself". This may well have turned out to be true had the original timetable been adhered to. Sadly it was not. In mid February, when the offensive should have been launched, the Western Front allies were instead still embroiled, politically and militarily, in arguments over the timetable for extending the British share of the Front, intended to free French troops to take part in the offensive, over share of railway supply facilities and, most debilitatingly, over unity of allied command. It took time to sort these out satisfactorily, not helped by growing inter-allied mistrust and Nivelle's apparent determination, despite the outcome of the row over unity of

---

5   'J-Jour' in French parlance.

command, to treat Haig as a subordinate. Haig's constant harping on about his northern offensive, giving Nivelle the impression that he was scarcely giving his wholehearted support to the Nivelle Plan, did not help either.

There were other factors that ideally needed to be in place to give the Nivelle Plan a reasonable chance of succeeding. One was the maintenance of secrecy concerning the detail and timing of the plan to ensure that the offensive when it came would achieve maximum surprise. The replacement of Joffre by Nivelle meant that the Germans could scarcely have been unaware that a major allied offensive on the Western Front would be an inevitable consequence. Where and when should however have been almost impossible for them to discover. Sadly this would not prove to be the case. Reference has already been made to Nivelle's cavalier approach to security. This was at a personal level; French preparations on the ground for the battle were well, and largely securely, put in hand. Nivelle's problem was his readiness to talk about his plans almost without care as to who might be listening. Even worse than this however were two serious breaches of good practice in the front line, which were sufficiently egregious to merit mention in the French Official History.

The first instance concerned the 2nd Infantry Division which, as part of the Fourth Army in Pétain's GAC, was involved in fighting in the Maisons-de-Champagne area. After initial German success in mid-February 1917, trumpeted by the German press as a great victory, vigorous French counterattacks had negated any German gains by 12 March. During the course of the early fighting, however, the Germans carried out an operation to improve their position that inflicted severe losses on the 4th and 5th Battalions of the 2nd Division 208th Regiment. According to Quartermaster General Erich Ludendorff's post war memoirs, one of the documents that fell into German hands during this operation was a 2nd Division order dated 29 January which contained important information on the timing and whereabouts of the forthcoming French offensive that Ludendorff claimed enabled the Germans not to take seriously, and pay only token attention to, preparations for French attacks in Lorraine and the *Sundgau* (Southern Alsace). While not disputing that the Germans did indeed obtain vital information as a result of their attack on the 208th Regiment, the French Official History appears to doubt that it came from a captured document, no record of the existence of which has been found in the French military archives. The inference which the reader appears to be invited to draw is that the information was obtained from one or more of the more than 750 men of the 4th and 5th Battalions who became casualties, mostly missing in action and probably captured, that day. It is known that 21 officers, including the CO of the 5th Battalion and his *Adjudant-Major*, were taken prisoner.[6]

If Nivelle's staff had no reason to suspect that French security had been compromised by the events described above the same was not the case in the second instance. In the course of an attempted *coup de main* northwest of Reims on 4 April the enemy seized a copy of the plan of attack of one of the battalions scheduled to take part in the offensive. Not only did the document reveal the plan of action of the battalion that was due to assault the Fort de Brimont, but it gave the order of battle of the armies due to attack south of the River Aisne and the objectives of two French army corps north of that river. It was a document of the greatest importance. The French High Command had, on several occasions, called the attention of all concerned to the importance of not taking secret documents into the front line, the latest occasion being as recently as 31 March. Informed by General Micheler of this dereliction, General Nivelle, having satisfied himself that the guilty had been punished, once more reminded everyone on 11 April of the gravity of such behaviour which could reveal to the enemy the details of attack plans, thus putting at risk the prospect of their success. However, despite this recognition of what might well have happened, nothing was done to modify the plan of operations for the imminent offensive.[7]

---

6   Lt Colonel Beaugier and others, *Les Armées Françaises dans la Grande Guerre*, Tome V Premier Volume, p. 362.
7   Ibid., pp. 569-70.

The Canadian National Memorial, Vimy Ridge. (Photo Barbara Taylor)

TheAustralian Digger Memorial, Bullecourt. (Photo Barbara Taylor)

The Seaforth Highlanders Memorial, Fampoux. (Photo Gerald Farr)

The 9th (Scottish) Division Memorial, *Point-du-Jour.* (Photo Mike Lawson)

Newfoundland Regiment Caribou Memorial, Monchy-le-Preux. (Photo Mike Lawson)

37th Division Memorial, Monchy-le-Preux. (Photo Mike Lawson)

The Arras Memorial to the Missing, Faubourg d'Amiens British Cemetery, Arras. (Photo Mike Lawson)

The Flying Services Memorial at Arras. (Photo Mike Lawson)

L'Hôtel de Ville, Arras. (Photo Mike Lawson)

The water tower at Bullecourt (in
its Centenary Commemoration
colours). (Photo Mike Lawson)

The Kingston upon Hull Memorial
at Oppy. (Photo Barbara Taylor)

The 63rd (Royal Naval) Division Memorial at Gavrelle. (Photo Mike Lawson)

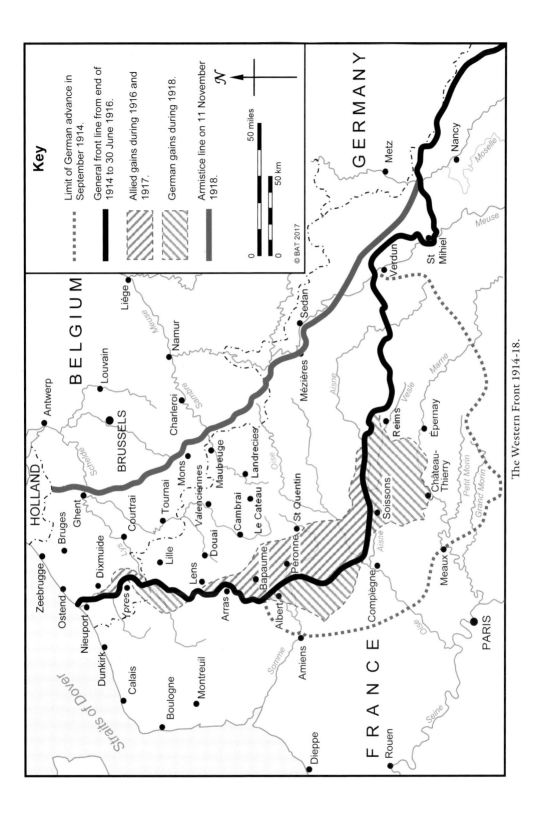

The Western Front 1914-18.

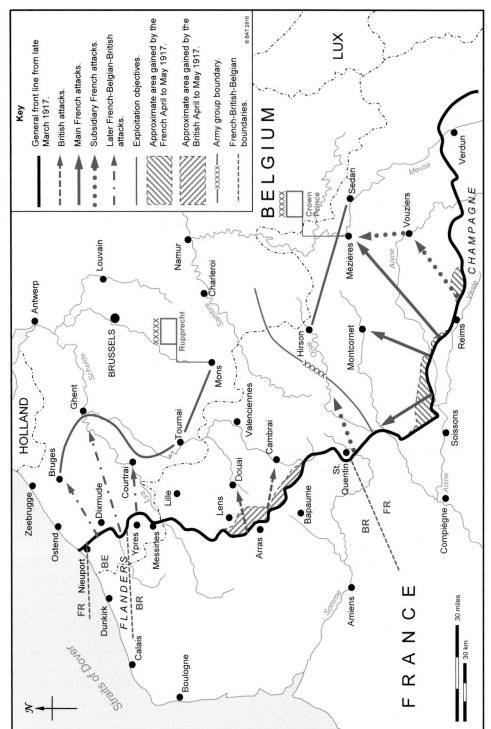

The Nivelle Plan, April 1917.

Key

General front line from late March 1917.	
British attacks.	
Main French attacks.	
Subsidiary French attacks.	
Later French-Belgian-British attacks.	
Exploitation objectives.	
Approximate area gained by the French April to May 1917.	
Approximate area gained by the British April to May 1917.	
Army group boundary.	—xxxxx—
French-British-Belgian boundaries.	

© BAT 2016

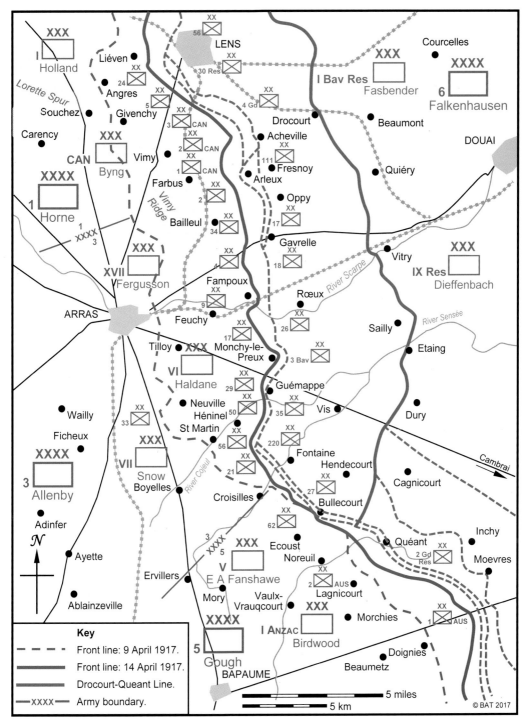

The First Battle of the Scarpe, 9-14 April 1917.

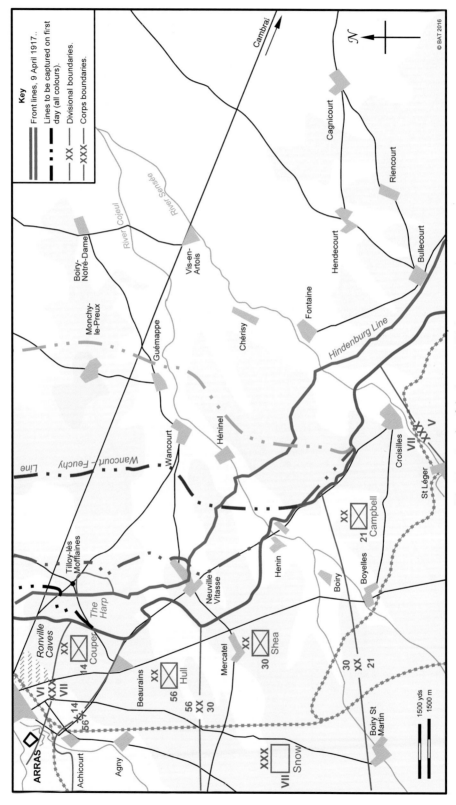

The First Battle of the Scarpe. VII Corps.

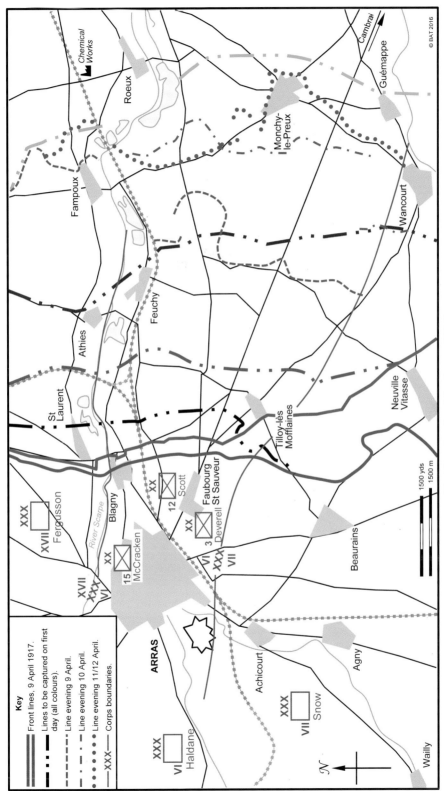

The First Battle of the Scarpe. VI Corps.

Key

Front lines, 9 April 1917.

Lines to be captured on first day (all colours).

Line evening 9 April.

Line evening 10 April.

Line evening 11/12 April.

Corps boundaries.

© BAT 2016

1500 yds
1500 m

Roeux

Chemical Works

Fampoux

Monchy-le-Preux

Cambrai

Guémappe

Wancourt

Feuchy

Athies

St Laurent

Neuville Vitasse

Tilloy-lès Mofflaines

River Scarpe

Blagny

Scott

Faubourg St Sauveur

Deverell

Beaurains

ARRAS

Achicourt

Agny

Wailly

XXX
XVII
Fergusson

XX
15
McCracken

XX
12

XX
3

XXX
VI
XVII

VI
XXX
VII

XXX
VI
Haldane

XXX
VII
Snow

N

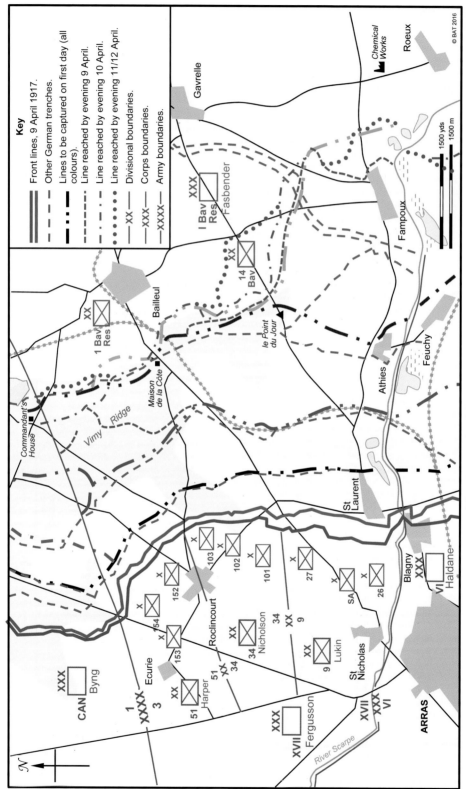

The First Battle of the Scarpe. XVII Corps.

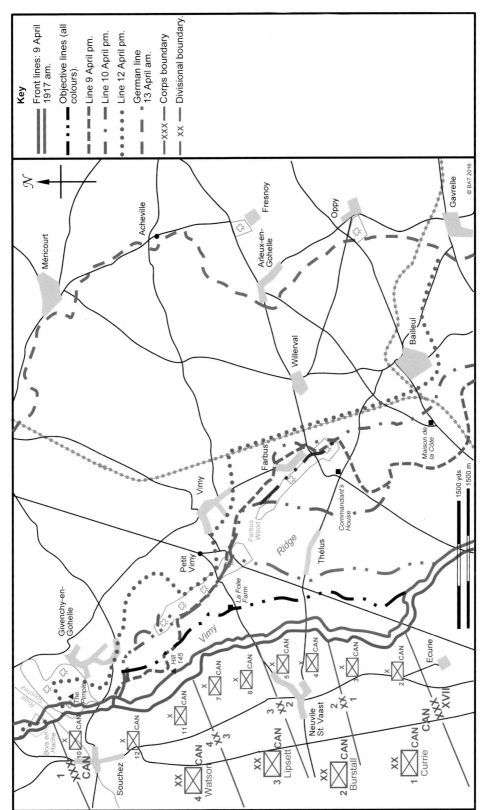

Key

	Front lines: 9 April 1917 am.
	Objective lines (all colours).
	Line 9 April pm.
	Line 10 April pm.
	Line 12 April pm.
	German line 13 April am.
XXX	Corps boundary
XX	Divisional boundary.

The Battle of Vimy Ridge, 9-12 April 1917. Canadian Corps.

© BAT 2016

1500 yds

1500 m

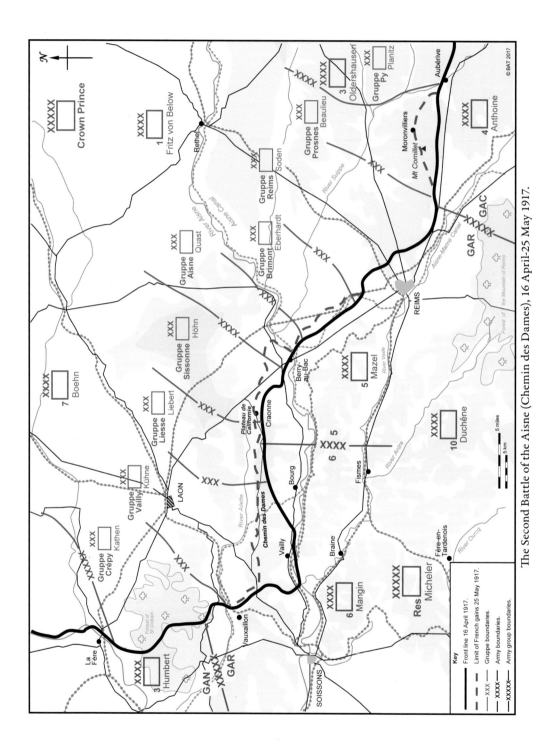

The Second Battle of the Aisne (Chemin des Dames), 16 April–25 May 1917.

Key

- —— Front line 16 April 1917.
- – – – Limit of French gains 25 May 1917.
- XXX Gruppe boundaries.
- XXXX Army boundaries.
- XXXXX Army group boundaries.

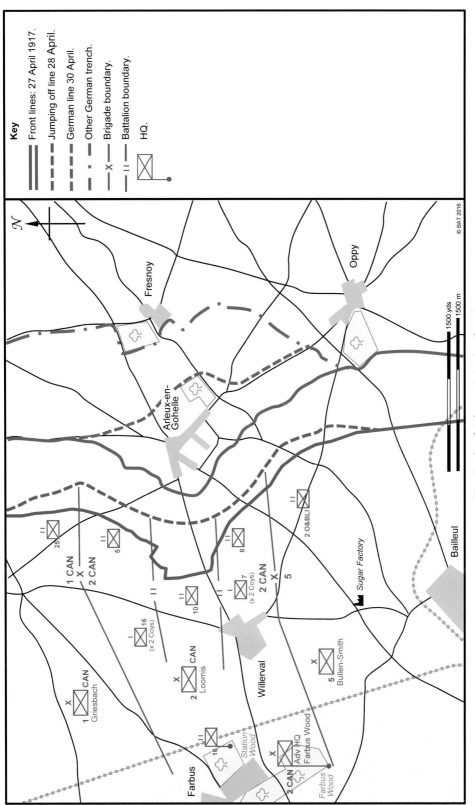

Key

▬▬▬	Front lines: 27 April 1917.
▬·▬·	Jumping off line 28 April.
▬ ▬ ▬	German line 30 April.
▬ · ▬ ·	Other German trench.
──x──	Brigade boundary.
──ıı──	Battalion boundary.
⊠	HQ.

The Battle of Arleux, 28-29 April 1917.

© BAT 2016

1500 yds
1500 m

(xiii)

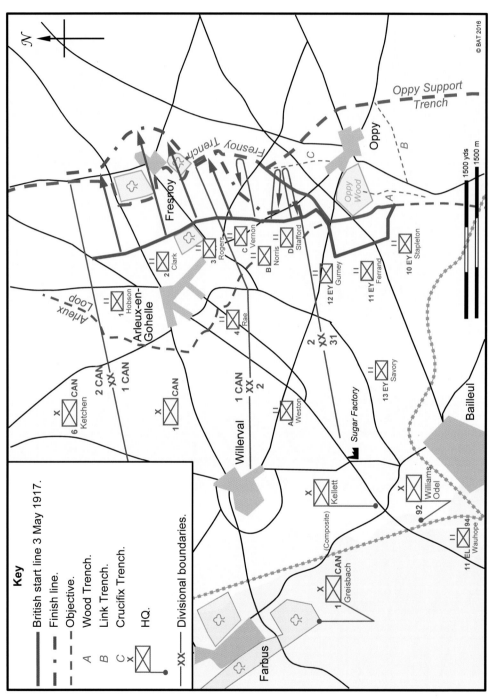

Key

British start line 3 May 1917.

Finish line.

Objective.

A   Wood Trench.

B   Link Trench.

C   Crucifix Trench.

x   HQ.

xx —— Divisional boundaries.

The Third Battle of the Scarpe, 3-4 May 1917. The Capture of Fresnoy.

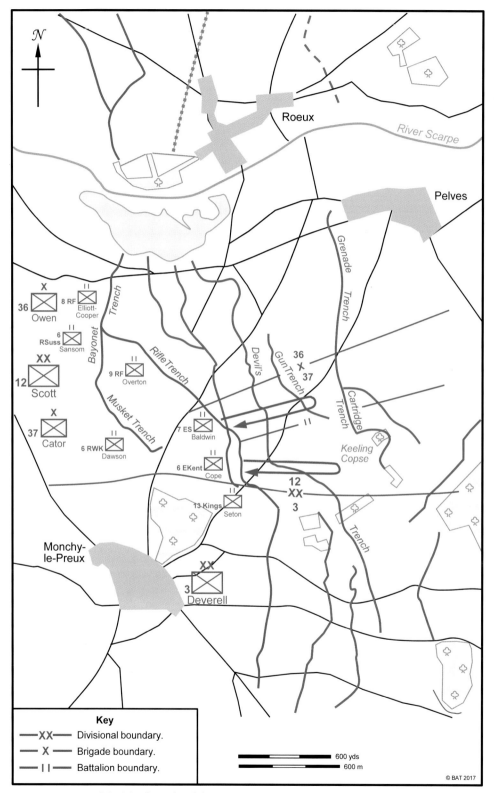

The Third Battle of the Scarpe. The Attack by 12th Division.

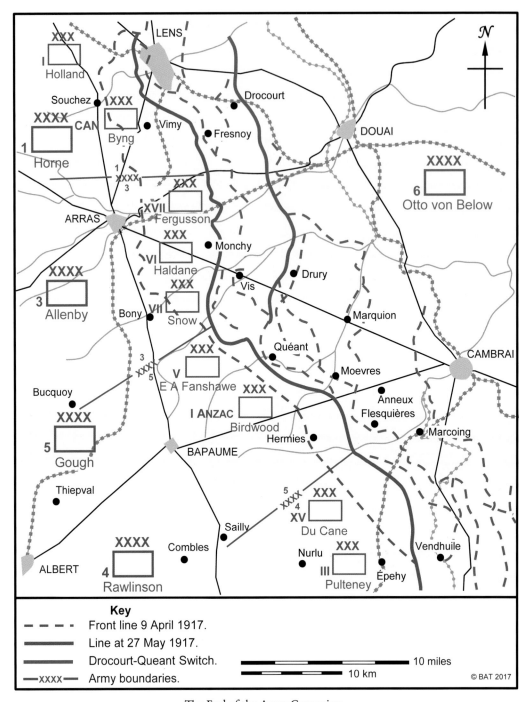

Key

– – – – Front line 9 April 1917.

——— Line at 27 May 1917.

——— Drocourt-Queant Switch.

—xxxx— Army boundaries.

10 miles

10 km

© BAT 2017

The End of the Arras Campaign.

On top of these French and allied own goals, Nivelle scarcely needed the Germans to have regained the strategic initiative in the run up to his offensive, as they did by successfully carrying out Operation *Alberich*, their voluntary withdrawal from the Noyon salient back to the Hindenburg Line. When they arrived from the Eastern Front to take over supreme command of the German Army after General Erich von Falkenhayn's dismissal following the failure of his Verdun strategy, General Paul von Hindenburg and Quartermaster General Erich Ludendorff quickly realised that the salient was very vulnerable to simultaneous attack from both north and south. Withdrawing from it would not only negate this threat but, by shortening their front line, would save around 14 divisions for use elsewhere. Fortuitously, from the German point of view, by implementing the withdrawal from mid March onwards they effectively undermined a major feature of the Nivelle Plan, which was indeed to attack and eliminate the Noyon salient. Almost certainly at the time of making their withdrawal the Germans were thinking only of shortening their line and conserving manpower as well as giving the allies the major problem of advancing through vacated territory left devastated and booby trapped by their departing foe. The effect it would have on Nivelle's strategy and his stubborn refusal to adjust it were uncovenanted bonuses.

The final misfortune for the French was provided by the weather. The worst winter of the war, in a war of bad winters, played havoc with their preparations and was certainly a contributory factor to the delays in launching the offensive. The calendar may have indicated that the offensive was timed for early spring. It made no difference; the winter weather persisted. Only one day in the week prior to the opening of the battle was free of the rain and sleet that otherwise persisted. The effects were felt not only by the airmen and artillery, but its glutinous consequences would also render the assaulting infantry's timetables, which would have been wildly optimistic even in ideal conditions, totally unrealistic. It would also have a deleterious effect on the French attempt to mount a mass tank attack as they deployed this new weapon for the first time.

11

Operations

General Nivelle's Plan initially involved the use of 59 infantry divisions, seven cavalry divisions and two Russian brigades by the Army Groups deployed along and behind the soon to be active front line. They accounted for roughly two-thirds of the total French Army strength on the Western Front. The allocation of weaponry to the attacking infantry had been markedly increased with a doubling to 16 of the number of light machine guns allotted to each company and an increase to eight in the number of machine guns per battalion. In addition one 37mm cannon and 16 grenade launchers were provided to every battalion. The total number of guns placed at the disposal of the assaulting armies was 6,623 field guns, 4,151 heavy calibres, 312 heavy long range pieces and 3,222 trench mortars. In the unlikely event of the enemy deploying tanks the French planned to use 37 and 75mm cannons in an anti-tank role.

The French themselves were planning to use tanks for the first time. 128 of the new Schneider tanks were allocated to the GAR's Fifth Army, and 32 Schneiders and 16 of the equally new Saint-Chamond tanks were allotted to the GAC's Fourth Army. That General Nivelle was convinced of the potential of this new weapon is evident from his request in mid March 1917 that 2,500 tanks should be built. However his instincts as a gunner would come to the fore when there was a question of the allocation of scarce resources between the competing claims of the artillery and tanks.

Nivelle had similarly ambitious plans for his aviation arm (*le Service Aéronautique*). He had requested an increase in the number of aircraft available to him from 1,950 to 2,665. This would allow the number of fighter squadrons to be augmented from 40 to 60, each with 15 machines instead of the previous 10. Bomber squadrons would similarly be increased from the previous 27 with 10 aircraft each, to 30 with 15 aircraft each. This programme had been approved but was still in the process of implementation when the offensive began.[1] As has already been noted, however, the effectiveness of the French aviation's contribution to the battle would be much reduced by the adverse weather, the current German technical superiority and the greater skill and experience of their pilots.

The massive French build up for the offensive, which included much attention paid to ancillary services such as pre-battle training, resupply arrangements, communications, health and sanitary services, and transport, persuaded the average *poilu* that this time things were truly different from the slapdash *Système D*[2] that had usually prevailed in the past. Morale was accordingly very high, boosted by news of the entry of the United States into the war and not discernibly damaged by the problems in Russia and Italy that meant there would be no synchronised supporting offensives on those fronts. The offensive would therefore be a major French undertaking, with significant British support (that had already manifested itself with the triumphant recapture of Vimy Ridge).

The build up to the French offensive on the GAR front started on 2 April with the artillery beginning its registration and counter battery fire. The artillery activity was intensified from 8 April but its effectiveness was diminished by the weather conditions and the lively reaction of the enemy artillery and aircraft. These combined to prevent French observation of fall of shot. It quickly became apparent that the enemy artillery had been significantly reinforced since mid February and was able

---

1   Lt Colonel Beaugier and others, *Les Armées Françaises dans la Grande Guerre*, Tome V Premier Volume, pp. 576-9.
2   A shorthand reference to *se débrouiller* meaning roughly 'to muddle through'.

to direct persistent harassing fire on the French rear areas paying particular attention to observation points, troop concentrations, ammunition dumps, crossroads and artillery positions. Both Reims and Soissons were subjected to bombardments, day and night, which included gas shells. Enemy air activity was also stepped up with an approximate doubling of the number of aircraft operating in the area. Not only were there more enemy aircraft, but the fighter squadrons among them became much more aggressive. There was a marked increase too in bomber raids. The Germans also put to good use the time available to them by importing German workers to strengthen the first three lines of their defences and create a fourth.[3]

The enhanced activity of the German Army in the days leading up to the French offensive indicated that it was not just the preliminary French and British bombardments that had alerted them to allied intentions. From the beginning of April large numbers of German troops moved in to reinforce their forward defences. Coups de main were launched on a virtually daily basis. These operations focused mainly on the right wing of the GAR. The most devastating one began around 1500 on 4 April between Berry-au-Bac and Loivre, a distance of roughly 10 kilometres, where the French defences formed a bridgehead on the eastern bank of the Aisne-Marne canal. These defences were subjected to a violent bombardment, similar to one normally preceding a major attack, by *minenwerfers* and shells of all calibres. It lasted four to five hours, destroyed the French trench works and cut off their garrisons by firing a box barrage that destroyed almost all the canal crossings. At around 1930 German stormtroopers assaulted on a 4.5 km front. Supported by flamethrowers they captured nearly all the French first and second lines and reached the east bank of the canal. Although French counterattacks on the following two days managed to regain some of the lost ground, and by 12 April all of it, the French had suffered heavy losses in both men and equipment. It was also as a result of this operation that the Germans got hold of the 'document of the greatest importance' described in the previous chapter.[4]

During the first half of April German activity was also stepped up opposite the GAC's Fourth Army. Coups de main were launched almost daily against the Army XII Corps. The intention behind them was evidently to establish what the exact intentions of the French were in the light of their manifest preparations for an offensive. The GAC's Second Army was not one of those due to attack on 16 April. It was nevertheless kept busy by an aggressive enemy in what were almost the last convulsions of the Battle of Verdun. As April progressed however, enemy activity in Second Army area began to die down. But enemy strength, particularly opposite the left wing of the Fourth Army, continued to grow in the numbers of artillery batteries and aircraft, indicating that they expected a major French offensive to be launched by GAC. This expectation must have been reinforced when the Army Group's artillery began registering on 3 April.

General Franchet d'Espèrey's by now inappropriately named Groupe d'Armées du Nord, consisting as it now did of only the Third Army, was the first Army Group to launch its offensive. At daybreak, 0500, on 13 April the Third Army XIII Corps began their assault against the German defences of Rocourt salient, Tous Vents mill, and Pire-Aller, all outposts of the Hindenburg Line west of Saint-Quentin. The attackers would have to advance between 600 to 1,000 metres to reach the enemy forward positions, hopefully before daylight would reveal their movements to the excellent observation posts the enemy enjoyed in Saint-Quentin.

On the Corps left, the 25th Division were very soon halted by only partially cut wire and enemy machine guns firing from concrete emplacements that had survived the French bombardments. Violently counterattacked they were forced back to their start line. On the right the 26th Division captured the First German Line astride the Route Nationale 44 in the area of Pire-Aller and successfully repulsed two German counterattacks. During the afternoon they consolidated the position gained

3   Lt Colonel Beaugier, op. cit., p. 586.
4   Ibid., pp. 586-8.

and resisted enemy attempts to outflank them. At 1545 the Army Commander, General Humbert, ordered XIII Corps to resume the attack before 1800. The heavy French and British artillery support of the attack seemed to have little effect on the German defences. A further problem was that the enemy air force (*Luftstreitkräfte*) wrested back control of the air from the French, who had held it during the morning. After severe hand to hand fighting the sorely tried 25th Division troops were once more forced back. For their part the 26th Division's attempts to build on their modest earlier success by capturing a small fort east of Pire-Aller proved nearly fruitless, with only the capture of a 100 metre length of the German Brandenburg trench to show for their efforts. They were thwarted by the enemy's artillery and machine gun fire, their own artillery's ineffectiveness when deprived of the assistance of air spotting and their lack of a sufficient quantity of trench mortars to destroy the enemy wire on reverse slopes. Although the enemy had taken heavy casualties, the French attackers too had suffered severely with losses of 1,350 men, 1,000 of them by 25th Division. Humbert's second attack had unquestionably failed, and to such an extent that the order that XXXV Corps should resume the assault the following morning was cancelled. Instead both Corps were told to make or continue their artillery preparations for a future assault.

On the extreme right of the Third Army line were the XXXIII Corps 77th Division. They had very rapidly captured three enemy strong points, the defences of Hill 169, le Bois Carré, and Cranne farm. During the rest of the day they pushed on slowly further east. Over the next few days the 77th Division, together with the 70th, succeeded in pushing further forward, but generally speaking the period was one of consolidation of meagre gains while the heavy artillery continued its counterbattery fire, evoking a lively reaction from the Germans. The GAN's operations since 13 April were now being described as a reconnaissance in strength aimed at forcing the enemy to evacuate ill prepared positions. The operations had established that the Hindenburg Line was a formidable obstacle with garrisons intent on maintaining their hold on it. Consequently General Nivelle ordered the GAN to halt its attempts to press on towards Saint-Quentin until possibly 19 or 20 April by when its artillery might have been sufficiently reinforced and resupplied. General Humbert had pointed out that in his view his army's lack of success could be blamed on a shortage of heavy guns and the shells they required.[5]

At 0600 on 16 April, three days after the GAN, the GAR's Sixth and Fifth Armies launched their assaults on which the hopes of a breakthrough of the German defences rested. Exploitation of the breakthrough, assuming one had been achieved, would be the task of the Tenth Army which would advance northwards between the other two armies. The front line from which the GAR armies would be advancing was approximately 40 kms long. On the right the Fifth Army share ran for 25 kms from east of Reims on a gentle northwest curve past the German held Fort Brimont, Berry-au-Bac and Craonne to Hurtebise Farm. From that point the Sixth Army 15 kms of front began. It continued broadly in a westward direction to near Fort de Condé where it turned north past Laffaux linking up with GAN at Coucy-le-Château.

All five corps of the Fifth Army were present in the front line. On the right were XXXVIII Corps (151st Division and a Russian brigade). Their objective was to capture les Cavaliers de Courcy and make progress towards Fresne Fort. To their left were VII Corps (41st, 14th and 37th Divisions and 1st Russian Brigade) whose objective was a line between Brimont Fort and Mount Spin. One brigade of 41st Division was held back in corps reserve. To VII Corps left were XXXII Corps (40th Division on the south side of the Aisne and 42nd and 69th Divisions north of the river). They would be attacking astride the river in the general direction of Prouvais with the support of 80 tanks. V Corps (9th and 10th Divisions) were next in line. Their objective was to advance in the general direction of Juvincourt and Amifontaine. They too would be supported by tanks, 48 of them. Finally, on the left of Fifth Army, were I Corps (2nd, 1st and 162nd Divisions, with 51st Division in corps reserve). Their

---

5   Ibid., pp. 608-11.

objectives were the Bove Plateau and Corbeny.[6]

The Sixth Army also consisted of five infantry corps together with 5th Cavalry Division and the 97th Territorial Division. On the Army right were II Colonial Corps (10th and 15th Colonial Divisions). Attacking by way of the Vauclerc Plateau their objectives were the Martigny Line, and the western part of Ployart Wood (the eastern part being the responsibility of Fifth Army I Corps). To the left of II Colonial Corps were XX Corps (153rd and 39th Divisions) whose objective was a line between Monampteuil and Presles Château. Between XX Corps and the next in line, VI Corps (127th and 56th Divisions), the front line made its 90 degree turn to the north. Advancing east, their objective was to advance in the direction of Chavignon with, on their left, a 'special Aisne detachment' charged with mopping up enemy units in the Aisne valley west of Chavonne. On the Sixth Army left were I Colonial Corps (2nd and 3rd Colonial Divisions). Their objective was to attack in the direction of Pinon.

Between H plus 4 and H plus 6 the remaining Corps of Sixth Army, XI Corps, were scheduled to move up to the front between II Colonial Corps and XX Corps. The latter's 153rd Division would thereby be relieved by XI Corps' 133rd Division.

Despite his strenuous efforts, the Sixth Army Commander, General Mangin, had been unable to persuade General Nivelle's staff to let him have any of the available tanks, all of which had been assigned either to Fifth or Fourth Armies.[7]

The mission of the GAR's Tenth Army was to exploit *la rupture* (or breakthrough) of the German defences once this was achieved by the Fifth and Sixth Armies. For this reason it was deployed south of the two breakthrough armies ready to advance between them when the call came. It was confidently anticipated that this would be three hours into the first day of the battle. Made up of four infantry (XVIII, II, III and IX) and one cavalry corps they expected to pass through the breach in three bounds and have advanced 25 kms beyond the original French front line by the end of the second day of the battle. Behind the Tenth Army, around Château-Thierry and Épernay were the eight divisions, grouped into X and XXI Corps, of the First Army which General Nivelle retained under his direct control. His intention was undoubtedly to use them to reinforce the Tenth Army progress.

The last army to be actively engaged in the planned early stages of the Nivelle offensive would be the GAC's Fourth Army. Theirs was to be an auxiliary attack beginning 24 hours after GAR's. The use of the term 'auxiliary' rather than 'supporting' indicated that the attack would involve a serious attempt to penetrate the German defences on a 12 km long front some 20 kms east of Reims.

General Nivelle's confidence that he was on the verge of a smashing victory was seemingly undented by the growing evidence that the enemy had taken advantage of the delays in the launching of the offensive and the foreknowledge they had obtained of the French plans, to reinforce and redeploy their defences, to such an extent that the pivotal figure of General Micheler, for one, no longer believed that the planned breakthrough and exploitation by his Army Group were achievable. Despite this dose of reality, formidable targets remained in place for the distances to be covered by the assaulting troops in the early stages of the battle. By the norms of the Western Front these were almost unprecedented in their ambition and seem to have paid little heed to the state of the ground over which the infantry would have to advance, churned up as it had been by the appalling winter weather, artillery barrages and the scorched earth legacy of the German voluntary retirement to the Hindenburg Line.

The extent of the German reinforcement of their defences was impressive. The retirement to the Hindenburg Line, with its consequent saving of manpower, had left them with the necessary resources to add significantly to the challenges facing the French. Had the battle begun in February as originally planned, General Mangin's Sixth Army would have been faced by four enemy divisions.

6   Ibid. pp. 641-2
7   Ibid. pp. 631-2.

They would now find themselves confronted by seven, possibly eight, divisions. The number of enemy artillery batteries ranged against them had similarly increased by 100 percent over the same timescale. There had also been a marked augmentation in the number of aircraft squadrons, all of which were described as being 'extremely active'.[8]

French intelligence pieced together a similar story on the Fifth Army front. On 1 March 53 artillery batteries had been identified. By 15 April this figure had risen to 392. The number of enemy divisions in place in the zone to be attacked had risen from five on 15 February, to nine or ten two months later. Behind them, situated in the areas of Laon, Rethel and Pont-Faverger, from where they could intervene rapidly, were a further 12 to 15 divisions. Five or six more were located in the sector between Reims and Berry-au-Bac, and a further three between there and Ailles. The number of enemy aircraft had quadrupled over the same period.[9]

At 0600 on 16 April the Sixth and Fifth Armies began their assault. Their last minute preparations, as the troops moved into their positions for jump off, had not been helped by the blackness of the night, the constant rain and the very poor state of the trenches and saps. As the advance began conditions were heavily overcast and misty. On Sixth Army's right II Colonial Corps moved off smoothly and advanced steadily against relatively light enemy artillery fire. Despite enemy machine gun fire the first waves of the assault advanced through the enemy lines and reached the Chemin des Dames ridge between 0700 and 0800. Problems were however building up. The battalions on the right of 10th Colonial Division were stopped and scattered north of the Foulon valley on the western side of the Vauclerc forest. To their left machine gun fire prevented any progress north of the Hurtebise Monument[10] and La Creute Farm. A Senegalese battalion that reached the edges of Ailles was virtually wiped out. The second wave of the assault became mixed up with the remnants of the first and took severe losses as they tried to retire.

On the Corps left the 15th Colonial Division was largely stopped in front of Cerny-en-Laonnais, although some elements did manage to get into the village. Within an hour the fighting had settled down. Both divisions, but especially the 10th, had suffered heavy losses. Virtually all the latter's officers had become casualties including all the brigade commanders and three regimental commanders. The morale of the rank and file of the black battalions had also been seriously affected, mainly by the cold and rain and exposure. They were to spend the night on the crest of the Chemin des Dames, panicking at the least sign of a German counterattack.

On II Colonial Corps left, XX Corps' assault met only relatively light opposition from the enemy artillery. On the right the 153rd Division reached the Cerny Sugar Factory after only 30 minutes. Their Regiment of Moroccan Infantry (*Tirailleurs Marocains*) reached the southern edge of the Bois du Paradis (Paradise wood) after which further progress became difficult. The 39th Division to their left advanced initially more slowly until they were brought to a stop about 300 metres north of Le Moulin Brûlé and in Bois de Brouzé (Brouzé wood) where they had gained a foothold. The indifferent progress was by no means to the taste of General Mangin who urged the Corps Commander to try to make up for lost time, reminding him that strong points should be bypassed. Clearing them up was nevertheless to take the whole day and would require much effort involving large numbers of the available troops to overcome the tenacious German resistance.

By 1100, and despite their losses, the Moroccans had passed through the Bois du Paradis and crossed the Chemin des Dames ridge towards L'Arbre de Cerny (Cerny tree) where they were ordered to stop as they were too far ahead of the units on either side of them. The 39th Division captured Chivy and at 1500 the two divisions linked up on *Saale* trench. The fighting died down with the front

---

8   Ibid., pp. 632-3.

9   Ibid. pp. 642-3.

10   The monument was erected in August 1914 to mark the centenary of the Napoleonic Battle of Craonne. It was destroyed during the Great War fighting and replaced in 1927 by the present monument linking the fighting of 1814 and 1914-18.

line running from Cerny Sugar Factory to the *Moulin de Braye* (Braye mill) by way of Misaine, Deva, du Pirate, and de la Saale trenches and Brouzé wood.[11]

On XX Corps left, VI Corps' assault initially went well. On the right 56th Division passed through the enemy first line and climbed the slopes on which stood the *Bois la Bovette* (La Bovette wood) and disappeared over the ridge. Their momentum was then stopped by a machine gun barrage that inflicted heavy losses. A little further to the left, in the Bois des Gouttes d'Or, the infantry were stopped by intact wire in front of a heavily garrisoned enemy trench. There they fought off a counterattack. Artillery was called down on the obstacles preventing further progress. Typically when General Mangin learned of this development, he issued orders very critical of the reversion to the use or artillery at this stage. Claiming that it had already created gaps in the enemy's continuous line of machine guns, he urged the attacking units to take advantage of these and if necessary bypass intact strong points. Uncut wire should be dealt with by hand by the infantry. It was essential to gain ground. Despite Mangin's urgings, and two attempts to comply with them, further progress was minimal.

The objectives of 127th Division, VI Corps left hand division, were the German occupied villages of Soupir and Chavonne and *La Cour Soupir* farm. Capturing them would necessitate attacking three rocky outcrops honeycombed with caverns (*le Balcon, Mont Sapin* and *Grinons*). The fighting, which went on throughout the day, was intense and progress was slow and painful. By nightfall *le Balcon* and *Mont Sapin*, and parts of *La Cour Soupir* and Chavonne had been captured.[12]

The left hand corps of Sixth Army was I Colonial Corps. The assault divisions were 2nd Colonial on the right and 3rd Colonial on the left. H Hour for both of them was three hours behind the rest of the Army at 0900. 2nd Colonial quickly passed through the first German line but as they approached the outskirts of Laffaux, the enemy opposition stiffened and by 1000 they had been stopped. In the meantime the 3rd Division had entered *Bois Mortier* (Mortar wood), with its prepared defences, and from there the 7th Colonial Infantry Regiment, at the cost of heavy losses, briefly took possession of the *Mont des Singes* (the capture of which was assisted by British Fourth Army artillery fire).

In response to General Mangin's reminder that units should press forward regardless of the progress of neighbouring units, a few got as far as Laffaux mill. There they were subjected to violent counterattacks which forced them back to their start lines. Orders were issued for preparations to be made for a further attack at 1800. It was duly launched but failed in the face of heavy machine gun fire. The areas gained earlier in the day were evacuated by the retreating troops. The Mont des Singes, taken at such cost so recently, was recaptured by the Germans taking advantage of hail, snow and thunderstorms to overcome distraught Senegalese troops.[13]

The Fifth Army assaulted simultaneously with the bulk of Sixth Army from its positions on the right of the GAR sector of the line. All five of its infantry corps would be engaged from the outset. On the right was XXXVIII Corps. Two regiments of its 151st Division, the 403rd and 410th, attacked respectively the Neufchâtel road salient and the Cavaliers de Courcy. With only light resistance from the enemy to overcome they were both captured by 0800. Thereafter enemy machine guns became more active and progress slowed to a stop just north of the Cavaliers de Courcy, preventing the two attacking regiments from linking up reliably and from liaising with 1 Russian Brigade on their left. Nevertheless the French retained their hold on their gains of the day, in the case of 403rd Regiment despite 19 counterattacks during the night.

1 Russian Brigade was the right hand formation of VII Corps. To their left on the Corps front were 41st, 14th and 37th Divisions. The Russian objective was the village of Courcy, that of the rest of the Corps the village of Brimont with its fort. After heavy fighting and serious losses the Russians

---

11   Lt Colonel Beaugier, op. cit., pp.635-6.
12   Ibid. pp. 636-7.
13   Ibid. pp. 637-8.

completed the capture of Courcy, including strong points Tête de Cochon and Carré, at midday. They completed their advance on the line of the railway and the Aisne-Marne Canal where they established contact with 41st Division. Apart from using a fresh battalion to clear up some enemy resistance between Courcy and their right hand neighbours, 151st Division, they remained where they were, successfully fighting off two counterattacks.

The 41st Division captured the village of Loivre at 1400, then crossed the Aisne-Marne Canal canal and reached the railway east of Loivre. At this point their advance was halted by the Corps Commander who ordered them instead to consolidate the captured ground because the situation of the 37th Division to their left made a further advance inadvisable. The 14th Division, between the 41st and 37th Divisions, was also to be adversely affected by the latter's difficulties. Their assault had made excellent and rapid progress. They had captured a series of objectives and were doing so well that the Corps reserves were ordered to follow them. The failure of 37th Division in front of Mount Spin meant however that their left flank was left uncovered and they were obliged to halt. At 1500 a violent counterattack pushed part of their line back. A second forced them out of the Bois du Champ du Seigneur.

It was the left of 37th Division which suffered severely from the intact machine guns firing from Mount Spin. The Commanders of VII and XXXII Corps, on the former's left, decided to resume the attack, after preparation, on Mounts Spin and Sapigneul.[14] The Army Commander declined to commit any reserves to the action until the two corps had made progress using their own resources. By midday the attack had failed with serious losses. The exhausted 37th Division would make no further progress during the day.[15]

The XXXII Corps 40th Division, reinforced by a Russian battalion, had flung itself into the battle and, despite partially losing its barrage, had passed through the enemy front line, reached part of the crest of Mount Sapigneul and encircled Hill 108. Their momentum was stopped by enemy machine guns and counterattacks. In co-operation with VII Corps an unavailing attempt was made to resume the advance, but the Division crumbling formations were, except for Hill 108, forced back from their gains to their starting trenches.

The same Corps 42nd Division likewise made a good start. On the north side of the River Aisne they quickly took the enemy's first line, the first trenches of their second position as well as Caesar's Camp strong hold in between. However they were brought to a halt by nests of machine guns in Bois des Consuls (Consuls wood) and concealed in clumps of trees along the Aisne as far as Condé-sur-Suippe. Before attempting a further advance they awaited the arrival of the five groups of tanks commanded by Commandant (Major) Bossut which were intended to lead the assault on the enemy's third position. Their progress forward had been slowed by the shell holes around Caesar's Camp and it was not until midday that they were more or less in position. They began their advance at 1430, some to the north and some to the east, but still sufficiently concentrated to offer a very visible target to the enemy artillery. Many, hit by shellfire burst into flames. Commandant Bossut was killed. The remaining tanks made heroic but generally fruitless efforts until nightfall. They did however lead the entry into the enemy positions before Juvincourt, which led to their capture. On this, the first appearance of French tanks in action, they had demonstrated that there was a place for their form of mobile artillery on the battlefield.

On 42nd Division's left and closely liaising with them, the 69th Division quickly captured the enemy's first and second positions, By 1300 the new front line ran in front of Bois des Béliers (Rams wood) and Mauchamp farm. But much weakened by the attentions of the German heavy artillery

14   The use of the word 'Mont' (mount, mountain) to describe Spin and Sapigneul and many similar pieces of high ground might seem somewhat flattering when, for example, the summit of Mont Spin was only 102 metres above sea level and 42 metres above the surrounding land. 'Butte' (mound) might be a more appropriate description. But there can be no denying the advantage their height offered to their defenders.

15   Lt Colonel Beaugier, op. cit., pp. 643-6.

they could advance no further. In the absence of reinforcements the Corps Commander proposed a retirement to their jump off trenches. This was rejected by the Army Commander who instead made available two Russian battalions and 165th Division from Army reserve to 'pursue the success of 69th and 42nd Divisions'. To these units were soon added the dismounted 8th Cuirassiers. Large concentrations of enemy troops, observed in the direction of Amifontaine, *Claquedent* wood and Prouvais, were effectively dealt with by the Fifth Army artillery. Enemy counterattacks were broken up on the fronts of 42nd, 69th and 165th Divisions.[16]

V Corps were the next corps in line with 9th and 10th Divisions. The objective of the 9th Division was Juvincourt. They quickly took the enemy's first position, the *Ouvrage de Vallon*, and reached the RN44 main road. They then captured the enemy second position south of Juvincourt that included an old mill farm. Three attempts were then made to capture Juvigny itself, but the best that could be achieved was to reach the southwest edge of the village. A counterattack drove them back to the mill farm. A second very strong counterattack emanating from Juvigny pushed back the Division left behind the enemy's former second position before their front could be stabilised. At 1630 a third counterattack of brigade strength was successfully stopped and thrown back with heavy enemy losses.

The 10th Division made only slow progress as they fought their way forward through two woods (the Bois des Buttes and the Bois des Bosches) while being enfiladed by machine guns from enemy positions at la Musette and on the RN44. They reached and surrounded la Ville-au-Bois but could not get into the ruins of the village. Orders were given for the capture of La Musette and the RN44 making use of the three groups of tanks assigned to 10th Division. These proved to be of no help to the infantry, as they were unable to cross the enemy's first position. Immobilised and targeted by ever increasing artillery fire the tanks were gradually put out of action. Only eight out of 48 managed, despite being damaged, to get back to their starting point. The air squadrons attached to V Corps suffered almost as badly, many of their machines sustaining damage and requiring urgent replacement.

By evening the situation had changed somewhat. Although the Bois des Bosches had not been completely surrounded and continued to hold out, as did la Musette, the Bois des Buttes had been captured and several advance units had reached the RN44. The 125th Division, which had been held back to form part of the army reserve, was returned to V Corps which also retained full use of Tenth Army artillery.[17]

The I Corps was on the left of the Fifth Army line and had three divisions in the line, the 2nd, 1st and 162nd from right to left. The 2nd Division quickly seized Chevreux Wood, Bastion and Marteau trench. Next to them the 1st Division had the very difficult task of seizing the village of Craonne and the surrounding area, including the Californie plateau, which, from its situation above Craonne, offered the Germans superb observation over the French positions. The Division made a promising start by gaining footholds in the Tyrol and Jutland salients and the Balcon trench. On their left the 162nd Division passed by Vauclerc mill and Luttwits trench. But coming under murderous machine gun fire from Chevreux and the Californie plateau, the attacking units were stopped. Further artillery preparation, including heavy guns, neutralised the active enemy guns and denied the use of the crossings over the Ailette river to enemy reinforcements. The attacking divisions were then ordered to complete the capture of the Marteau Trench in order to resume the advance towards Corbeny, to capture the Californie Plateau by enveloping it, and to seize the whole of the Vauclerc plateau. But all progress was stopped by the still active enemy machine guns joined by others firing from Hurtebise, still in enemy hands.

The Corps Commander ordered further efforts from his divisions. As a result the 162nd Division captured the Abri trench at 1400. In the centre the 1st Division made a further attempt on the Californie plateau. This time, despite the machine gun fire poured on them from Craonne they

---

16 Ibid. pp. 646-7.
17 Ibid. pp. 648-9.

managed some infiltration into the village at the cost of heavy losses. On the right 2nd Division were violently counterattacked and forced to commit their last reserves. There was, however, little they could do in the face of the murderous machine gun fire from the plateau. The 208th Regiment were virtually wiped out.

Nothing daunted, the Corps Commander sent 2nd Division a battalion taken, contrary to orders, from the army reserve for another attack on the plateau. Once again the attack failed except on the left where the Tourillon de Vauclerc and the western part of the Balcon Trench were captured, the latter by bombing. Thereafter there would be little change in the overall situation on the I Corps front.[18]

At the end of a day of fierce fighting, both breakthrough armies had to face up to the fact that the results had not been up to expectations. The Sixth Army, probably the less successful of the two, nevertheless regarded the day as having been far from a failure. Believing that they had inflicted severe losses on the enemy, and knowing they had taken 3,500 prisoners, they consoled themselves that they had forced the enemy to fight on ground of their, Sixth Army's, choosing, which would suck in more and more of the enemy's available manpower resources, tie them down, and thus prevent them being deployed elsewhere. The enemy's offensive operations would thereby be confined to counterattacks of limited scope. At the same time the Sixth Army Command had to own that their own losses had been heavy and that the Army was in no state to launch another major offensive in the near future. General Mangin's orders for the night and the following day were to continue the artillery barrages to hinder German efforts to relieve their forward troops and stop reserves from moving up. Gas, which had been effective on the first day, should continue to be used. The infantry should attack at an hour to be determined later with a view to completing the occupation of the Chemin des Dames at the very least.

The Fifth Army day had also been marked by serious losses; three divisions (37th, 40th and 2nd) had been very badly mauled and others had lost heavily. The tanks had been a major disappointment. On the plus side more than 7,000 prisoners had been taken and air reconnaissance had detected no sign of enemy troop movements behind the lines, suggesting that all available enemy forces had already been committed. By nightfall the front line ran from the Neufchâtel road salient to the RN44 north of Ville-au-Bois, by way of Cavaliers de Courcy – the canal between Courcy and Loivre – the railway west of Berméricourt – the southwest edge of Champ du Seigneur wood – the French first line east of Neuville – the first enemy line east of Sapigneul – Hill 108 – the River Aisne up to the west of Condé-sur-Suippes – the second German position between the Rivers Aisne and Miette – south of Juvincourt – the southern half of Bois des Bosches – and Bois des Buttes.

Orders for the following day were to complete the capture of the Craonne Plateau while maintaining occupation of the ground already gained south of the Aisne. Preparations were to be made to resume the attack on Mount Spin and Brimont.

The best indication of how far short of expectation had been the French achievements of the first day of the battle was that Tenth Army, which was supposed to begin its advance between the Fifth and Sixth Armies at H plus 3 hours to exploit the breakthrough, did not move at all during the day except for some minor adjustments to avoid bunching up. General Nivelle had told all who would listen that the breakthrough and exploitation would be achieved in 48 hours. The prospect of the failure of his entire strategy was now very real.

The second day of the battle saw the entry into it of General Pétain's Groupe d'Armées du Centre. As has already been noted, given that it had finally been determined that the GAC's participation would be in the form of an auxiliary attack, rather than a full out offensive or a supporting attack, only one of its armies, the Fourth, would be fully committed. Two corps, XVII (Moroccan, 33rd and 45th Divisions) and VIII (34th and 16th Divisions, with 128th and 169th Divisions behind) would lead the attack, supported on the eastern flank by XII Corps 24th Division, temporarily on detachment

---

18   Ibid. pp. 649-50.

to XVII Corps. VIII Corps would be supported by 48 tanks.[19] Although the total frontage of Fourth Army ran to about 45 kms between Ville-sur-Tourbe to Ferme des Marquises (Marchionesses farm) about 5 kms south of the village of Beine, the attack would be mounted on a 12 kms front at the western end of the Army sector with the intention of capturing the high ground due north known as the Massif de Moronvilliers. It was a formidable challenge. The five peaks in the Massif averaged over 230 metres. French intelligence had established that there were four German divisions belonging to their Third Army in position to oppose Fourth Army assault.

At 0445, H-Hour, the Fourth Army infantry began their advance behind a creeping barrage. The weather was appalling, a combination of freezing rain and flurries of snow, that at least made the early stages of their progress more or less invisible to the enemy. It also however effectively grounded their air support. At the end of what must have been by any standards an immensely trying day for the unfortunate infantry the results can best be described as patchy. What is certain is that the main objectives which might have led to a breakthrough had not been attained. The French line had been advanced between 500 metres and 2.5kms. On the plus side the village of Aubérive had been captured by 126th Division which, having taken the enemy by surprise, reached all its objectives. The 7th Tirailleurs (Colonial Infantry) of the Moroccan Division 2 Brigade overcame strong resistance to take the Levant trench strong point, while the 8th Zouaves from the same Brigade rapidly climbed the southern slopes of Mont Sans-Nom to reach and secure the summit by 0555. The 1 Brigade's regiments, the Foreign Legion and the 4th Tirailleurs, were less successful, but after hard fighting and some setbacks captured parts of enemy held trenches and woods.

The 33rd Division found reaching the German positions relatively easy and, having done so, progressed further, capturing le Grand Bois and Bois du Chien (Dog's wood). Thereafter enemy resistance, notably machine gun fire from the edges of woods, increased markedly, and further progress would be dependent on prior artillery preparation the following day. The Division had nevertheless achieved one of the furthest advances of the day. On their left the 45th Division made slow progress against machine gun nests that had to be reduced one at a time by bombing.

The 34th Division was the main beneficiary of the cloak of invisibility provided by the early H-Hour and the weather. The two attacking regiments, the 59th and 83rd, crossed two lines of partially destroyed trenches and passed through a zone of concrete machine gun emplacements, and reached with only light losses the area surrounding the crests of Mont Blond and Mont Cornillet, the two westernmost peaks of the Massif de Moronvilliers. By then they were so far in advance of their neighbours that they were in danger of being enfiladed, particularly from the enemy held Konstanzlager on their right. This strong point was holding back the left of 45th Division. On 34th Division left, 16th Division were in retreat. Battalions were brought up on either side of 34th Division to bridge the gaps that had opened up between the 34th and their neighbours.

The 16th Division's three regiments in line abreast were the 85th, 27th and 95th. The last named were to form a defensive left flank while the other two dealt with enemy machine gun nests in Bois de la Grille and Leopoldshöhe trench. They were decimated before they even reached the trench and fell back to Wood 92 and Wahn trench where they clung on. The 95th Regiment met less resistance and tried, with remnants of the 27th, to deal with Leopoldshöhe Trench. But they were violently counterattacked and fell back slowly to Skoda trench with heavy losses.

Around midday a battalion of the 34th Division, 13th Regiment was sent forward to support the 83rd Regiment, who were closest to the summit of Mount Cornillet. There they were being subjected to heavy artillery and machine gun fire. The 13th linked up with 16th Division 85th Regiment on their left, who were stalled and disorganised. By this time units had become thoroughly mixed up and tired out.

Given his scepticism over General Nivelle's plans it would have come as little surprise to General

---

19   Ibid. pp. 663-4.

Pétain when he learned during the course of the morning that he could expect no help from the Fifth Army moving up on Fourth Army left as had been planned. The former's attack on Brimont had failed and their plans would have to be recast on the basis of a methodical operation which would require time to draw up and mount. Some of the plans for Fourth Army would accordingly have to be put on hold. There was however the unfinished work of the day to be attended to. The Fourth Army Commander reiterated at 1300 that XVII and VIII Corps should be in occupation by the end of the day of the five crests running from Mount Téton to Mount Cornillet. Attacks were duly mounted but made no progress.

General Pétain meanwhile had telegraphed Nivelle that his five attacking divisions were in urgent need of relief after their exertions of the day. As he only had two fresh divisions available from his own resources he asked for a fresh corps of three divisions to be made available to him.[20]

During the night of 16/17 April the GAR Commander, General Micheler issued orders for the following day to his two breakthrough armies. Those to Sixth Army offered a more realistic assessment of what might be achieved after the disappointed ambitions of the first day. The Army should confine itself to the capture of the region Ailles, Courtecon, Froidmont Hilltop farm and Chavonne. Once these had been taken preparations should be made for a later attack on the heights north of the Ailette river. On the left I Colonial Corps should capture the Fruty quarries, Allemant, Hill 154 (southwest of Pinon) and Locq Château. Micheler also took the opportunity to tell General Mangin that he could not have the Tenth Army 35th Division which he had asked to be place under his command.

Overnight there was little change in the situation of Sixth Army. The rain was incessant, adding to the misery of the troops and the difficulties of the artillery's preparations. Both VI Corps and I Colonial Corps were subjected to violent counterattacks. VI Corps successfully fought them off inflicting heavy casualties on the attackers. I Colonial were less fortunate and were forced to evacuate little by little the Mont des Singes and Moisy farm leaving them only in possession of the *Aviatik* and *Les Trous* Trenches of their gains of the previous evening.

On the morning of the 17th General Micheler received a telegram from General Nivelle. In translation it said, 'Yesterday's battle has clearly shown that the enemy intend to stand firm on the Sixth Army front and consequently to make it difficult and costly for your Army Group to make progress northward. Therefore it is towards the northeast that you must make your effort, building on the progress made by the Fifth Army. On the Sixth Army front you should limit yourself to completing and consolidating the capture of the heights south of the River Ailette, in order finally to ensure that we establish ourselves north of the River Aisne'.[21]

The role of Sixth Army would thenceforth be to provide cover on the left of the main offensive, led by Fifth Army. Its main role would therefore be defensive, except for the completion of the capture of the heights south of the Ailette. This would involve the taking of the ridge between Froidmont farm and Chavonne and the enemy's observation points overlooking the Aisne river crossings. These were termed local actions, designed to improve GAR's current situation.

The so-called local actions were Sixth Army main preoccupation on 17 April along with reconstituting as much as possible the units that had suffered severely the previous day. The II Colonial Corps spent the day trying to deal with fresh enemy troops probing for weak points in the French lines that might be exploited. They made little progress. XX Corps, seeking to extend its start line for future operations, needed to capture Salzbourg trench between Cerny and Cerny Sugar Factory, still in German hands. The first attack failed with significant losses; the second was more successful, enabling the left of 39th Division to get a foothold on the eastern spur of Braye-en-Laonnais and to move closer to Grélines farm. An attempt on the Sugar Factory was fixed for the next day when it would be postponed because of the weather.

---

20   Ibid. pp. 663-70.
21   Ibid. p. 655.

The 56th Division of VI Corps were ordered to capture the enemy's second position (the Courant trenches and the southern slopes of *la Croix-sans-Tête* plateau). This was achieved at 2000 after a two hour battle. The Corps' other division, the 127th, repulsed a dawn counterattack mounted by fresh enemy troops who were punished heavily. On their right the old quarries south of *Cour Soupir* farm were captured. On the left a Senegalese battalion, overcoming the torment of snow, captured Grinons ridge after three attempts.[22]

General Mazel's orders to his Army for the 17th were very ambitious. He was to receive IX Corps (17th, 18th and 152nd Divisions) from Tenth Army to help him build on his Army modest gains of the day before. The attack would be resumed all along Fifth Army front with the principal effort being over the plain between the River Aisne and Corbeny with the aim of seizing Prouvais Massif. I Corps would continue with its initial objective of capturing the Californie plateau and the heights of Corbeny. The 66th Division, brought up from army reserve and deployed on I Corps right, would outflank Corbeny to the east in co-operation with V Corps. This Corps would attack astride the River Miette in the general direction of Amifontaine, which had been a first day objective. The 125th Division would be brought forward from its first-day role in corps reserve. They would co-operate south of the Miette with XXXII Corps who would push forward in the general direction of Prouvais, making use of 165th Division brought up from Army reserve and in liaison with the right of V Corps. XXXII Corps would be strengthened north of the Aisne by IX Corps' 18th Division. South of the River Aisne, VII Corps, reinforced by 40th Division (XXXII Corps) and 152nd Division (IX Corps), would organise a first attack on Mount Spin and, if possible, Brimont. XXXVIII Corps' 151st Division would consolidate the ground already occupied and link up with 1st Russian Brigade. The 17th Division (IX Corps) would constitute the Army reserve.

The attacks of the 17th April were to be prefaced by comprehensive artillery preparation. Unfortunately however, the dire weather failed to relent, not only largely preventing artillery operations but also delaying the moving up into position of the assaulting units. The planned attacks on Mount Spin and Brimont, as well as the combined operation involving 66th Division and V and XXXII Corps were therefore delayed for a day. The only operations to go ahead would be the attack on the Californie plateau by I Corps and the clearance of Bois des Bosches by V Corps. Neither operation achieved anything of note at the cost of significant losses.

Throughout 17 April the weather remained very bad with strong winds bringing on gusts of rain and hail. Low lying cloud reduced flying operations virtually to nothing. The joint operations of IX, V and XXXII Corps were postponed for a further day with preparation only to take place on the 18th. The attacks on the Californie plateau and the heights north of Craonne by I Corps would continue, because their possession was vital if further progress were to be made. Likewise V Corps would continue the efforts to capture Bois des Bosches.[23]

When issuing his orders for 18 April to his Corps Commanders, Sixth Army Commander General Mangin emphasised the need for close co-operation between them if progress were to be made. II Colonial Corps should lend their support to XX Corps in their effort to capture Cerny Sugar Factory by pushing round it to the east. VI Corps should advance their right by taking advantage of the advance of the left of XX Corps in the operations currently taking place east of the Oise-Aisne Canal. General Mangin urged the complete elimination of enemy formations by increasingly severe interdiction barrages. The use of air-burst shells would help protect the infantry from machine guns. Gas shells should also be widely used.

After a fairly uneventful night the attacks on the following day, notably those by XX and VI Corps, led to some positive results. The two Corps advanced uphill to the plateau and occupied the northern edge of Braye-en-Laonnais and La Creute farm. They then took Vautour Trench and got

---

22   Ibid. pp. 656-8.
23   Ibid. pp. 659-60.

men into l'Aigle Trench. Leaving a great deal of materièl behind the enemy retreated rapidly before VI Corps advance back to the Chemin des Dames ridge. By 0815 the Corps 56th Division had seized Coblentz quarry, and 127th Division la Cour Soupir farm. The advance continued right along the Corps front and at 1300 56th Division passed la Croix-sans-Tête and Brody and le Courant trenches in co-operation with 127th Division. As they evacuated the villages of Vailly, Aisy, Sancy and Jouy, and Rochefort farm, the Germans set them on fire. The planned attack on the Cerny Sugar Factory by II Colonial Corps and XX Corps 153rd Division was prevented by the adverse weather conditions.

The other notable event of the day was that a strong patrol sent out by I Colonial Corps made its way to the Fort de Condé, which it found unoccupied. On Sixth Army right the exhausted II Colonial Corps stayed put during the day. Likewise, on the Army left there was no change in the situation between Laffaux and the Oise-Aisne Canal.

The Army orders for 19 April aimed to build on VI Corps success the previous day. Assisted by the right of I Colonial Corps, the Corps would press the enemy back towards Malmaison and attempt to reach a line Ostel – Aizy – Volvreux. On their right XX Corps would aim to reach the stretch of the Chemin des Dames between the Cerny Sugar Factory, which would be taken, and the Oise-Aisne Canal. Apart from assisting XX Corps in their attempt to take the Sugar Factory, II Colonial Corps would consolidate the ground already gained and prepare the way forward for XI Corps, who would relieve them. I Colonial Corps, on the Army left, would remain on the defensive on their left, except on the Moisy plateau. On their right they would push forward to a line Volvreux Farm – Sancy – Nanteuil-la-Fosse.

The results of the day were considered disappointing with relatively little change on the fronts of XI, XX and VI Corps. The 38th Division, forming the right of XI Corps, which had completed the relief of II Colonial despite the delays caused by a heavy enemy bombardment and the muddy state of the ground, had completed the capture of the ground around the Hurtebise monument by 1615. However, they lost Bonn trench southwest of Ailles, with one of their regiments, the 8th Tirailleurs, suffering heavy losses in the process. The 153rd Division's capture of Cerny Sugar Factory proved only temporary; by 1800 they had been forced back to their starting trenches.

On VI Corps left the 127th Division made progress towards Aisy, Jouy and Colombe farm (*Ferme de Colombe*). (The divisional artillery, ordered to push forward one of its batteries to Cour Soupir farm in the morning only succeeded in reaching the plateau with the greatest difficulty. It took 18 horses to move each gun carriage.) The 44th Territorial Regiment occupied the smoking ruin of Vailly and tried to link up with I Colonial Corps further west near Celles-sur-Aisne. A regiment of 166th Division was placed at the disposal of 127th Division to extend the latter's front towards the west, also with the intention of liaising with the Colonial Corps, and later with XXXVII Corps of the GAN's Third Army near Colombe farm.

For its part I Colonial Corps managed to occupy Celles-sur-Aisne and the outskirts of Nanteuil-la-Fosse to the northwest. But any further advance was held up by enemy machine guns and particularly stubborn resistance to the east of *Ferme Chimy* (Chimy farm). At 1800 2nd Colonial Division succeeded in seizing Laffaux and trenches east of the village, taking a number of prisoners.

The situation at the end of 19 April persuaded General Mangin that XXXVII Corps should be given command of the sector of the front between Laffaux and Colombe farm and should accordingly position themselves between VI and I Colonial Corps by midday on the 21st. The German retirement on the French left raised the possibility of spearheading an advance by GAN, but General Nivelle considered the situation still too uncertain to order such a move. Instead, he told General Micheler that for now constant and heavy pressure should be maintained on the enemy until the situation became sufficiently clear to enable decisions on future strategy to be made. The Sixth Army should be ready to take advantage of any indication of an enemy retirement.

Because of the extension of the battle beyond the foreseen 48 hours the consumption of ammunition, particularly of artillery shells, was exceeding all expectations. General Micheler ordered economies to be made so that all units had no more than three or four days' supply in hand. Nivelle also weighed in by ordering a limit on the length of heavy barrages in stationary sectors. Assaulting troops must on the other hand be fully supported by creeping barrages and all other available measures to suppress the enemy machine gun fire.

During the course of 20 April, the Sixth Army made only minor gains west of the Oise-Aisne Canal. General Mangin sought the agreement of Micheler to his proposal to launch a renewed attack on the 23rd, in the meantime undertaking only the most necessary local actions. Micheler warned Mangin that he would be largely dependent on his own resources to carry out his proposal. He could not hope for two fresh replacement divisions or the tanks he wanted. He would not even be able to retain his present artillery strength; he would be losing an army corps' field artillery and four groups of tractors for 155mm guns. Nor was there hope for any further resupply of shells as all those available were going to Fifth and Tenth Armies. Micheler explained that these constraints were due to Nivelle's decision to focus mainly on GAR's drive to the northeast. He warned Mangin to establish what his artillery requirements would be and then decide if he would have to postpone his plan.[24]

Nearly all the operations planned for the Fifth Army on 18 April were deferred as a result of the appalling weather of that day. Only V Corps launched a major attack which successfully captured Bois des Bosches and la Ville-au-Bois during the morning, taking 1,300 prisoners, several guns and a great deal of matériel. In the afternoon *le Bois en L* (L wood), 1,700 metres southwest of Juvincourt, was taken. On the Army right, the Russian Brigade took the *Ouvrage Carré*. During the afternoon the Germans launched a counterattack of at least two division strength between the River Aisne and Juvincourt. It was quickly targeted by French heavy and field artillery and suffered heavy losses. Those who reached the French positions were dealt with by rifle and machine gun fire. A second attempt by the Germans failed completely.

The Army programme for the 19th called for the completion of the capture of Californie plateau by I Corps, and the heights of Mounts Sapigneul and Spin by VII Corps, all after comprehensive artillery preparation. The IX, V and XXXII Corps would be brought forward to the line *Tranchée du Marteau* (Hammer trench) – Bois de l'Enclume (Anvil wood) – Corbeny (if possible) – *Bois en T* (T wood) – Juvincourt – *Wurzbourg* trench. This operation would be supported by concentrations of fire on enemy centres of resistance where machine gun nests had been detected.

The 19th dawned fine with some mist but insufficient to affect visibility. After prolonged and intense artillery preparation the right-hand VII Corps (14th and 37th Divisions) moved forward at 1500. On the extreme right 14th Division entered Bermericourt but were thrown back at the railway and the northeast edge of the *Bois en Potence* (L-shaped wood). On the left 37th Division, reinforced by the 3rd Russian Brigade and a regiment of 152nd Division, attacked Mounts Sapigneul and Spin but made no progress. In the centre the Russians reached Bois de la Chenille (Caterpillar wood) and Bois en Dentelle (Lace wood) on the northern slopes of Mount Spin, and appeared to be gaining full control when a counterattack forced them back to their start line and inflicted significant losses. As on 16 April it was the failure to eliminate all the enemy machine guns that led to the failure of the attack.

The I Corps launched their attack at 1600. Its objective was to complete the capture of Vauclerc and Californie plateaus. At first good progress was made and by 1700 the objectives appeared to have been secured. But an enemy counterattack forced the French back to their starting trenches after a violent and bloody struggle. Only 162nd Division on the left managed to cling on to some trenches on Mount Sapigneul. Possession of Craonne village continued to be violently disputed and was contributing to the increasing exhaustion of I Corps, so much so that the Corps Commander felt obliged to call the state of his command to the attention of General Micheler. More generally the day

---

24   Ibid. pp. 673-82.

had achieved little for Fifth Army.

The following day became one of relative calm for Fifth Army as the planned offensive operations were placed on hold. Only a handful of minor actions and reorganisations took place, the main ones stemming from the entry of Tenth Army into the line between Hurtebise and the River Aisne. This development would have an effect on the make-up and orientation of Fifth Army.

The period 16-20 April was regarded as the first phase of the Second Battle of the Aisne. When reviewing the performance of the Fifth Army, its Commander, General Mazel, made the following points.

> The Army did not fully achieve the tasks laid down for it by the Commander in Chief. But it was important to note that at the time of their conception, the actions of GAR were the second phase of an offensive, of which the first phase was to be played out in the north by Franco-British troops and which ought to have attracted and used up the German reserves leaving only a screen of enemy troops in front of us. The German withdrawal to the Hindenburg Line had changed the situation. From 16-20 April our 16 divisions had clashed with 16 fresh German divisions supported by plentiful equipment and supplies, and able to call on readily available reserves.
>
> Evidently from then on our original plan of action had hardly any chance of being implemented to its full extent.
>
> (On 21 April General Mazel pointed out to General Micheler that one of the causes of the failure of the offensive was, in his opinion, the obtaining by the enemy of the French battle plans for operations south of the River Aisne.) Declarations by prisoners specified that the enemy knew the day and the very hour on which our attacks would begin. This very regrettable fact explains in large measure the resistance that confronted us in the region between Berry-au-Bac and Brimont, as well as the power of the counterattacks that had been organised in advance by the enemy.

On a more positive note General Mazel pointed out that Fifth Army had taken 11,000 prisoners, more than 40 guns and 200 machine guns and a huge amount of equipment; had disrupted the forces facing them; taken almost the whole of the enemy's first position; made great inroads into the second position between Juvincourt and the River Aisne; and begun the capture of Brimont and the heights of Craonne.[25]

The GAC's Fourth Army first day of action on 17 April was followed by a night during which the Germans launched three counterattacks with the aim of driving the French off Mounts Blond and Cornillet. They all failed. On the 18th, a day of rain and snow squalls, the Army XVII and VIII Corps would jointly seek to complete the occupation of the Massif de Moronvilliers by taking Mounts Haut, Casque and Téton. These operations would begin at 1830, allowing time for preparations to be completed. These preparations included eliminating the threat posed by the *Konstanzlager* strong point; overcoming other pockets of resistance not dealt with on the first day; and completing the clearance of Aubérive and surrounding areas.

In their attempt to clear the trenches around Aubérive the Foreign Legion, Moroccan Division, met stubborn resistance which had to be overcome by bombing parties. Finally, after changing hands several times, the Legion took full possession of Poznan and Beirut trenches. The Legion and 4th Tirailleurs also occupied Woods 039, 132 and 69. On their left 8th Zouaves completed the capture of their assigned gun batteries by midday. On the Moroccan Division's left, 33rd Division, having cleared pockets of resistance, reached a line from the northern edge of Wood 198 to the northern edge of Wood 320. The Division's right-hand Brigade then took the northwestern part of Wood M50 and all of Wood M52. The left-hand Brigade was however checked by machine gun fire from Rensburg

---

25   Ibid. pp. 683-9.

and Göttingen trenches.

At 0700 a heavy concentration of medium and heavy shells fell on *Konstanzlager* strong point, successfully eliminating it. By 0730 91st Regiment had cleared and occupied the enemy machine gun nests and immediately moved on towards Mount Haut. There they came under heavy machine gun fire but were able to hold on in the shelter of Woods 202 and 203. On the right 90th Regiment gained some ground and their 1st Tirailleurs occupied Mount Haut at around 1400 before falling back to Wood J51.

When the joint attack was launched, 1st Tirailleurs were stopped dead by machine gun fire and only began to move forward after 45 minutes. However 91st Regiment managed to establish themselves on Mount Haut and by 2015 had captured the summit. For VIII Corps the day was largely one of consolidation of the gains of the previous day. The summits of Mounts Cornillet and Blond were completely cleared and prepared to deal with any German counterattack. They also helped XVII Corps 45th Division to capture Mont Haut by launching a supporting attack on it from Mont Blond. On the eastern side of the River Suippe, 24th Division had spent the night of 17/18 April in bombing exchanges as they sought to capture Baden Baden Trench. They then had to fight off two determined counterattacks.

The overall result of the fighting of 18 April was that XVII Corps had at certain points advanced up to 1,500 metres. But VIII Corps, and 24th Division on temporary attachment to XVII Corps, had not gained any ground at all.

The two days of fighting had led to significant losses and exhaustion for Fourth Army troops. As has been noted General Pétain reacted to this by seeking the reinforcement of a fresh Corps from General Nivelle. Perhaps to Pétain's surprise his request was granted and the three divisions of X Corps were added to Fourth Army order of battle. One of these (the 131st) was immediately made available to General Anthoine, the Fourth Army Commander. The other two (the 19th and 20th) were placed in GAC reserve. Anthoine also made a strong plea for more artillery, especially three groups of mountain guns for use in the Massif de Moronvilliers and long range heavy guns. Finally he asked for two territorial regiments to help with resupply and transport. Pétain passed these on with his full endorsement. The territorial troops were rapidly forthcoming. Regarding artillery, Nivelle consulted General Micheler, whom he hoped might be able to make the guns available at the expense of Sixth Army. During the night of 19/20 April Nivelle ordered that Fourth Army should urgently be supplied with four groups of tractor mounted 155 long range guns. No mountain guns were available.

The Fourth Army Commander set the objectives for 19 April as completion of the capture of the Moronvilliers ridge running over the five summits of the Massif eastwards to join up with the northern Golfe trench and thence to a crossing of the River Suippe north of Aubérive. Once the ridge was secured an observation line should be established beyond. The main resistance line should be organised on the reverse slope behind the ridge. During the night of 18/19 massive barrages of gas shells were to be fired with the aim of reducing the trenches of the Golfe region. The XVII Corps Moroccan Division would clear up this area while the Corps other two divisions, the 33rd and 45th would deal with Mounts Haut, Casque and Téton. In VIII Corps sector, 34th Division would consolidate their hold on Mounts Blond and Cornillet, clear up the ground beyond and, in cooperation with 16th Division, push their left forward to the western edge of Bois de la Grille.

Overnight fighting made little difference to the situation. The weather for the 19th seemed set fair with clear skies. The Moroccan Division attempted to clear the Golfe Region by bombing but came up against lively resistance and on their left a violent counterattack struck the 8th Zouaves and 7th Tirailleurs at 0800 forcing the former regiment back. The latter regiment stood firm until a counterattack by 2 Brigade pushed the enemy back at around 1430. The increasing signs that the enemy were abandoning Aubérive were confirmed by a patrol that found it empty. The Foreign Legion pushed forward and reached the southwest small fort of Vaudesincourt where at 2130 they linked up with elements of 24th Division which had managed to cross the River Suippe.

The 33rd Division 11th Infantry Regiment captured Mount Téton at 0530 and moved on towards the northern trench of the mountain. The 20th Infantry Regiment, harassed by machine gun fire from nearby woods, managed to reach Rendsburg and Göttingen woods. While the daylight lasted the Division was subjected to a series of determined counterattacks, which they dealt with successfully. At 1700 their line was unbroken and they were in touch with the Moroccan and 45th Divisions on their flanks. The 45th Division had also suffered badly from the attention of German machine guns but had successfully thrown back numerous counterattacks. The divisional artillery had helped VIII Corps deal with resolute German attempts to repossess Mount Blond.

In VIII Corps sector 34th Division were seeking to clear the ground north of Mounts Blond and Cornillet when it was observed that strong waves of German infantry were advancing from north and south towards the two mountains. The Division was rapidly reinforced by the 29th Regiment. By 1100 the German counterattack had been broken up by artillery and French aircraft. At 1430 General Anthoine issued a reminder that Mounts Blond and Cornillet must be held at all costs. Then, as soon as possible, preparations should be made to complete the capture of the wooded *massif* to the southwest of Mount Cornillet. At about the same time information was received from French aircraft that in the wooded *massif* and trenches to the north were groups of enemy troops and machine guns. The artillery of two divisions was concentrated on these inviting targets rendering them untenable for the enemy.

As a result of the fighting on 19 April, the French had secured Mount Téton and all of Aubérive. Elsewhere however little progress had been made in the last 24 hours. The orders issued by the Corps Commanders for the following day reflected this state of affairs. XVII Corps were ordered to consolidate the occupation of the Moronvilliers ridge; VIII Corps to confine themselves to the orders already in place.

During the course of the night of 19/20 the enemy launched several counterattacks preceded by heavy bombardments on French positions in the region of Moronvilliers. To the west of Vaudesincourt, around Wood M50, on the slopes of Mount Haut and at the Bois de la Grille, these were repulsed. But after a relentless struggle in which the ground changed hands several times, the 33rd Division were forced off the summit of Mount Téton. Fighting involving the Division continued all day. At 1700 66 Brigade attacked both Mounts Téton and Casque. On the right 11th Regiment reoccupied a point known as le Fer à Cheval (The Horseshoe) and the north trench of Téton. On the left 20th Regiment occupied the whole of Göttingen and Rendburg trenches. Advanced elements entered Casque wood, occupied the mountain's summit and advanced into the Boyau du Bois. But with their left flank exposed because of 45th Division's problems, they were obliged to return to Göttingen trench.

Increasingly exhausted, 45th Division nevertheless managed to maintain, and sometimes improve their positions. On the right they reduced the last obstacle separating them from the summits when 90th Regiment's African Battalion cleaned out the shelters on Mount Perthois in hand to hand fighting before pushing forward about 400 metres. On their left the Tirailleurs succeeded in bypassing the Fosse-Froide trench but had to retreat. On the Mount Haut side, 91st Regiment maintained their positions on the Mounts Haut and Blond front despite strong counterattacks preceded by heavy bombardments.

On the XVII Corps right the Moroccan Division's Zouaves had to endure and repulse a violent counterattack in the morning. It was led by two Saxon regiments after a heavy bombardment on Mont Sans-Nom. In the afternoon the Foreign Legion and the Tirailleurs made good progress through wooded areas. At the Labyrinth the Legion cleared out the enemy bunkers with bombs. Despite difficulties over resupply they reached le Grand Boyau and there successfully resisted an enemy counterattack. A further attack by the Germans at 2100 was shattered by artillery fire.

In VIII Corps sector there was less success to report. A major effort was made in the afternoon to attain their objectives. After preparation by heavy artillery on the area of bunkers enveloping the wooded massif southwest of Mount Cornillet, 34th Division 13th Regiment attacked. They were overcome by machine gun fire from bunkers and forced back. There could be no question of resuming the attack until the machine guns had been dealt with. The guns to do this were requested from Army HQ. The 85th Regiment, on the right of 16th Division, which had attacked in cooperation with 13th Regiment were also stopped by machine gun fire, in their case emanating from woods. On their left, in the centre of 16th Division, 27th Regiment made a little progress through some trenches. On the left of the Division, 95th Regiment could not advance at all.

The four days (17-20 April) of fighting by Fourth Army had resulted in the capture of the trenches south of Mount Cornillet, the major parts of Mounts Blond, Haut and Casque, the regions to the north and east of Mont Sans-Nom, the Golfe region and the village of Aubérive. Fifty enemy officers and 3,500 other ranks had been taken prisoner. Twentyseven guns had been captured. In effect this meant that Fourth Army had partially, but not entirely, secured the German Second Position, a disappointing outcome.[26]

By the end of 20 April what can be seen in retrospect as the first phase of the Nivelle Offensive was largely winding down. By the standards of previous major offensives on the Western Front the results were not out of the ordinary. There had been some significant advances but in general little, and in some cases, no progress had been made against a stubborn enemy whose defences, bristling with machine guns which had been well-placed to avoid the attentions of the French artillery bombardments, had taken a heavy toll of the assaulting infantry. What was to make this a major disaster in French military history was its failure to achieve what General Nivelle had proclaimed it would achieve, a war-winning major victory within 48 hours; he had undertaken to discontinue it if this deadline were not met. Already more than twice that length of time had passed without the promised breakthrough of the German defences and its subsequent exploitation. It was increasingly evident that no breakthrough would be achieved by the offensive in the foreseeable future. With Nivelle showing no sign of honouring his promise to break off the battle, the prospect was for a reversion to the usual attritional struggles that had come to characterise the Western Front. The effects that this would have on the morale of the *poilus* would not be long in showing themselves.

---

26   Ibid. pp. 689-701.

Part IV

Second Battle of the Scarpe:

Battle of Arleux

12

VII Corps

The Third Army opening offensive, later to be termed the First Battle of the Scarpe, had clearly almost run its course by 15 April, the day before the much postponed French offensive was due to be launched. Given that the British operation was mainly intended to tie down German divisions and prevent their deployment to oppose the French there could be no suggestion that 15 April signalled the end of the campaign for the BEF. The question for Field Marshal Haig to address was what next. General Allenby had already on the 14th issued orders that his Army should continue to seek to advance to the southeast with the aim of reaching the Sensée river between Vis-en-Artois and Fontaine-lès-Croisilles, on course for a rendezvous with the hopefully advancing French in the area of Cambrai. Haig however countermanded these orders on the 16th in favour of larger-scale operations involving all three of the armies committed to the Arras campaign, to be launched on Friday 20 April. As recorded in his diary entry for 16 April,

> I decided that all three Armies should attack next Friday simultaneously. First Army will break the Oppy Line, take Gavrelle etc, and push advanced guards into the Drocourt-Quéant Line. Third Army to advance towards Boiry, Vis-en-Artois and gain the rising ground on the right bank of the Sensée in cooperation with an attack by Gough (on the right flank) having as objective Riencourt, Hendecourt and the rising ground north and northwest of the latter. As a preliminary operation Allenby is to take the high ground on either side of Guémappe Village, and then a detachment (covered by a creeping barrage) will move down to take the village itself. The object of this operation is to be able to use the valley of the Cojeul for gun positions about Guémappe and Héninel.[1]

In diary entries later that day and the day following Haig recorded his growing concern that the paucity of reports on the progress of the French offensive, always in his experience a bad sign, probably meant that things were going badly. On the 18th he received a letter from General Sir Henry Wilson at Compiègne (French GQG), confirming his worst forebodings. Wilson thought that the French should not have attempted to break through the German defences on the Chemin des Dames, which had been greatly strengthened in the thirty months since the BEF had fought there. Haig described the French Sixth Army attack as a 'dead failure' and the Fifth Army one as having got on much better. Optimistically he thought, sadly inaccurately, that French losses had not been heavy.[2]

As regards Haig's own plans for a resumption of the offensive these had to be modified when, on 17 April, he received a request for a postponement from First Army Commander, General Horne, on the grounds that the continuing bad weather was delaying the movement forward of guns and ammunition. Haig also learned that the VI and VII Corps commanders were not keen on the notion of a preliminary operation on either side of Guémappe and would prefer to take the village during the course of the main operation. The Fifth Army General Gough also made it known that, except for artillery support, he would prefer not to join in the operation until Third Army had reached the

---

1   Haig d. 16.4.17.
2   Ibid., 18.4.17.

Sensée river. Finally General Horne, despite having been accorded his postponement, informed Haig on the 21st that his Army, still behindhand with the movement of guns and ammunition, would not be able to attack the Oppy Line all along, but could take Gavrelle village and so provide the necessary cover to Third Army left flank. Faced with all these concerns Haig decided that the operation should begin on Monday 23 April with the participation of First and Fifth Armies limited as requested by their commanders. In other words, the operation would become almost exclusively a Third Army one.

Preparation for it had already begun with the main focus being intense artillery programmes consisting largely of nightly barrages, with an emphasis on teargas shells, and hurricane bombardments of villages close behind the German front. One particular problem that needed to be addressed was Wancourt tower. Although by this stage the tower had been reduced to a ruin, its possession nevertheless afforded the enemy complete command of the Cojeul valley and a second valley running north between the villages of Wancourt and Neuville-Vitasse. Essential bridging work over the Cojeul river could not be carried out while the tower remained in enemy hands. The task of ejecting them fell to 50th Division which, along with 33rd Division, had just exchanged places with the very tired 14th and 21st Divisions in VII Corps, allowing them to go into reserve with XVIII Corps. The enemy had occupied the tower ruins that lay between the two front lines, on 15 April. That night they were ejected by troops of 1/6th Northumberland Fusiliers of 50th Division 149th Brigade who then successfully fought off four counterattacks that same night. But the following night, when the 1/6th were being relieved in heavy rain by their sister Battalion, the 1/7th, the enemy attacked and regained possession. An immediate counterattack by the two British battalions failed. The following day, after an intense bombardment, riflemen of the 1/7th supported by bombers of 1/6th drove the enemy out. The tower was firmly consolidated that same night.[3]

The 20th April was fine and seemed to hold out the promise that spring might be arriving at last. The state of the roads nevertheless continued to present great problems to those responsible for maintaining a plentiful supply of ammunition to the guns, nearly all of which had been pushed forward. The problem was partially alleviated by a more regular arrival of stone by railway for road repairs. The new challenge facing the gunners was that, unlike in the first phase of the battle, there was little certainty as to where the German guns were now situated, making counter battery work much more problematical. What was certain was that there were significantly more of them in place to oppose the British assault than there had been on 9 April.

Only 19 tanks were still battle worthy enough to take part in Second Scarpe. Of these, eight were allocated to VII Corps. Two pairs were placed at the disposal of 33rd Division and one pair each went to 30th and 50th Divisions. The lack of a meaningful number of tanks would be a signal disadvantage to the attackers who would also be handicapped by being unable to count on taking the enemy by surprise this time.

The VII Corps launched their attack at 0445 on the 23rd with the 33rd, 30th and 50th Divisions all in line. Initially the weather was misty. When combined with the smoke of the guns the effect was to reduce visibility severely until around 0800 when wind and sun dispersed the mist, leaving a clear, fine day. The Corps plan called for the three divisions to advance downhill in a southeasterly direction to the River Sensée. In detail 33rd Division on the right were to employ 98 and 100 Brigades to advance southeast astride the Hindenburg Line. In addition to this, 100 Brigade were to provide a detachment which would make a night march from Croisilles along the eastern side of the Sensée to attack and capture a 500 yard long stretch of the Hindenburg Line on that side of the river. The purpose of this action would be to deny the Germans command of the valley and the opportunity to enfilade the main Corps advance with machine guns firing from across the river.

In the centre of the Corps line, 30th Division would advance on a 1,500 yard front to attack and secure the high ground overlooking Chérisy. On the left, 50th Division would advance from a line

---

3   OH, 1917 Vol. 1, pp. 378-81.

extending from Wancourt tower to a small lake lying between Wancourt and Guémappe with two objectives. The first ran from just south of the crossroads of the Vis-en-Artois – Héninel and Chérisy – Guémappe roads; the second ran from 500 yards west of the northern edge of Chérisy to St. Rohart Factory on the River Cojeul.

The detachment furnished by the 33rd Division 100 Brigade consisted of 1st Queen's supported by two companies of 16th KRRC. The two tanks, which were also supposed to support this action, were unable in the event to take part because of technical problems. The night march from Croisilles went well and the enemy's front trench was captured despite the hindrance of wire that had not been satisfactorily dealt with. However, when 1st Queen's moved on to the enemy's support trench they found the wire protecting it virtually undamaged, preventing any further significant progress. German counterattacks from the middle of the day onwards finally drove the Queen's and KRRC back after two hours of stubborn resistance. Those who did not manage to retire were mainly taken prisoner.

The 33rd Division's second lead off 98 Brigade, attacked with three battalions in line. On the right the 1/4th Suffolks supported by two companies of 2nd Royal Welsh Fusiliers, on detachment from 19 Brigade, and a tank, bombed their way down the two trenches of the Hindenburg Line with such rapidity that they soon reached the Chérisy-Croisilles road, having covered 2,000 yards. They were materially assisted in this remarkable feat by the tank which, travelling parallel to the front line, overcame a number of machine guns in concrete emplacements and induced a large number of demoralised enemy troops to surrender. The Suffolks were however still 300 yards from their objective when their advance was stopped.

The other two 98 Brigade battalions experienced mixed fortunes. Advancing over open ground the right of the 2nd Argylls, the centre battalion, and the left of the 1st Middlesex, the left battalion, reached their objectives. But the left and right respectively of the two battalions were held up by heavy machine gun fire from a small copse that had somehow escaped the attention of the British artillery. The situation had not changed when the Germans counterattacked late in the morning. They managed to get behind, and cut off, the more advanced of the Argylls and Middlesex attackers. Some Suffolks, in danger of a similar fate from Germans bombing their way down a communication trench into the Hindenburg Line, were able to withdraw from their positions in the support line. The Germans did manage to get behind the remaining Suffolks, who held on until 1400 when they made their escape and got back to their own lines.[4]

With the task of capturing the high ground overlooking Chérisy, the 30th Division sought to advance through smoke and heavy mist on a front of 1,500 yards using 17th Manchesters and 2nd Royal Scots Fusiliers of 90 Brigade as the lead-off battalions. A heavy British barrage began at Zero, but it was only two minutes later that a strong German artillery response began. Almost immediately enemy machine guns also opened up with deadly effect on the two advancing battalions causing considerable casualties. Within minutes the RSF CO was dead and nearly all officers either killed or wounded. Although the attack was largely held up, a few NCOs and men took shelter in shell holes and, firing from them, inflicted many casualties on the enemy. But in effect the Battalion had been cut to pieces. The 17th Manchesters fared little better although their right hand company, reinforced by some 16th Manchesters, did manage to push on a little and take some prisoners, despite also suffering very heavy officer casualties. The Battalion's left hand company was practically destroyed. The two tanks assigned to support the Brigade were both quickly dealt with by the enemy artillery when one stuck fast and the other broke down after overheating.

Plans to rectify 90 Brigade's situation by making a flank attack on an enemy position in a quarry that had been responsible for much of the damage to the battalions, were suspended when it became apparent that 50th Division were being strongly counterattacked and troops were falling back to their start lines. Instead a defensive flank was established which enabled an enemy counterattack to

---

4   Ibid., pp. 384-6.

be thrown back.[5]

The 50th Division's attack initially enjoyed much better fortune. Even the two tanks supporting the assault were able to make a significant contribution. The attack was carried out by 150 Brigade, utilising 1/4th East Yorks and 1/4th Green Howards for the first phase, the intention being that 1/5th Green Howards and 1/5th Durham Light Infantry would take over for the second phase. The lead battalions advanced with great dash and captured most of the first objective on schedule. By 0800 the remaining part of the first objective, the copse on the Chérisy-Guémappe road where an enemy group had put up stubborn resistance, was taken by 1/4th East Yorks, who dug in on its eastern side. It was at this stage that the advance should have been resumed by 1/5th Green Howards and 1/5th DLI. Apart from one of the tanks having succumbed to engine trouble there seemed to be no reason for the attack not to be resumed. Even four batteries of guns had crossed the River Cojeul and had taken up positions from which they could offer the attack close support. But an order was received from Third Army HQ postponing the attack until the enemy first line (the Blue Line) was entirely in British hands and had been fully consolidated. Before this order could be implemented the Germans launched a strong counterattack. With their right flank exposed by the failure of 30th Division and their left flank under heavy fire from the other side of the Cojeul, 150th Brigade's four battalions were driven back to their starting line by 1130 having suffered heavy losses, particularly of officers.

Third Army HQ's reaction to this setback was to order that the Blue Line must be taken that day at all costs in an attack involving both VII and VI Corps. After consulting the Commander VI Corps, the attack was set to start at 1800. The 33rd Division were in the event 24 minutes late in launching their attack. It was led on the right by 1/5th Scottish Rifles (on detachment from 19 Brigade) who, as soon as they crossed the barriers in the Hindenburg Line, were driven back by trench mortar fire and bombs. To their left a mixed detachment of RWF, Argylls and Middlesex found themselves trying to advance across open ground in daylight with generally predictable results. To make matters worse some advance companies came under fire from their own artillery barrage, fortunately with only light losses. Having reached the barrier in the Hindenburg Line support trench they were fiercely, but unsuccessfully, counterattacked by the enemy at 1945.[6]

The 30th Division's share of the attack would involve the capture of about 800 yards of the Blue Line consisting of an enemy occupied trench overlooking Chérisy. The 18th Manchesters (90 Brigade) would be on the right and the 19th Manchesters (21 Brigade) on the left. Both battalions had been in reserve for the morning's fighting, but the 19th Battalion had suffered losses when they came under artillery and machine gun fire when moving up into positions with their left resting on Wancourt tower. The various companies had become intermingled as a result and they were still sorting themselves out when the Battalion CO learned of the planned attack less than an hour before it was set to begin.

The 18th Battalion received their orders perhaps 30 minutes earlier and began their advance towards their distant objective on time. They were immediately assailed by machine gun fire from in front and both flanks. Nevertheless they managed to reach their objective despite heavy officer casualties. At around 2000 they were counterattacked by superior enemy forces and were forced to withdraw to their start line where they held on until midnight, when they were relieved. By then every officer had become a casualty. Their total killed, wounded and missing were 15 officers and 339 ORs.[7]

The 19th Manchesters' CO commented subsequently on the task given to his Battalion at only minutes' notice that, "It would have been difficult to carry out an easy operation at such short notice, and this was not an easy operation." On return to his Battalion HQ after having received his orders, his first task had been to brief his company commanders, who were still trying to reorganise and

---

5   TNA WO 95/2337: 90 Brigade War Diary.
6   OH, Ibid., pp. 387-8.
7   TNA WO 95/2339: 18th Manchesters War Diary.

reposition their companies. He told them to discontinue this exercise. They would attack on a three-company front. Unfortunately the Commander of D Company, which was ordered to support the three assaulting companies with a platoon to each, was killed on his way back to his company so that the men never received any orders and made no move when the attack began. The other three company commanders had only about five minutes to explain the plan of attack to their men.

Perhaps surprisingly the advance began on schedule on a front much too wide for three companies to remain in close contact with each other. The first casualties were caused by their own barrage; when enemy machine guns joined in the men rushed forward to get into the comparative shelter of the enemy's front trench despite the efforts of the officers and NCOs to maintain some semblance of order. Two of the companies were able to join up in the trench, but on either side the enemy remained in occupation. There was no sign of the battalion of moppers up which had been part of the overall plan. There could be no further advance, with the certainty that the Germans would fire into the advancing men from behind to add to the machine gun fire that would assail them from the enemy second trench. The men were therefore ordered to cling on to what they had gained. The two companies had been reduced to a total of 35 men; all the officers had become casualties. The third company, on the right, were ordered by an officer of another regiment to retire as soon as darkness offered them some protection; they did so. At about midnight the precarious situation of the remnants of the first two companies was alleviated by the arrival in support of 2nd Green Howards. On the following day the reserve platoons of the 19th Manchesters moved up to occupy the German support line and steps were taken to strengthen the Battalion's situation by the construction of strong points.

It was the 21 Brigade's 18th King's (Liverpool) Regiment which had been assigned to support the two Manchester Battalions and provide them with a company each of moppers up. They appear to have been given as little notice to get themselves organised as the two other battalions with the result that there was no time to report in advance to them and no guides to lead them to where they needed to be. The designated moppers up therefore pushed forward on what they presumed to be the line of attack of the Manchesters, but still failed to make contact. The Battalion's remaining companies, moving forward in support, found themselves under such a heavy enemy barrage that they were forced to take shelter in shell holes. Losses and lack of knowledge of where they should go decided them against pushing further forward.

The CO of 19th Manchesters tells a slightly different story. He relates that 15 minutes after his Battalion began their advance, two 18th King's officers reported to him for instructions. Until that point he had believed that the moppers up had already gone forward behind the Manchesters' leading waves. As by this time it was too late for them to do the actual work of mopping up, he told the two officers to move their men up in support of his, who should by this time be beyond the German front line. One of the officers reported back 90 minutes later that his group had been nearly wiped out; the other officer had been killed and his group had disappeared.[8]

The 50th Division's share of the attack would remain the responsibility of 150 Brigade. Because of the losses they had suffered earlier in the day that had left them with only two battalions, 1/5th Green Howards and 1/5th DLI, with sufficient numbers to play a meaningful part, two battalions of 151 Brigade were placed at 150's disposal. These two battalions, the 1/5th Border Regiment (Borders) and 1/9th DLI, would lead the attack with 1/5th Green Howards and 1/5th DLI continuing in a support role. To avoid unnecessary confusion the artillery barrage replicated that fired in support of the morning's attack. When the advance took place on schedule it proved to be of sufficient determination and steadiness to take advantage of enemy troops wearied from the constant battering they had been subjected to and, in many cases, only too ready to surrender or to retreat under fire. On the left 1/9th DLI captured all their objective. On the right the 1/5th Borders, advancing equally

---

8   TNA WO 95/2329/4, WO 95/2330, WO 95/2327: Respectively 19th Manchesters, 18th King's (Liverpool) and 21 Brigade War Diaries.

successfully, retook the copse on the Chérisy-Guémappe road with less trouble than its first capture that morning had given. But they had to take account of the failure of 30th Division on their right and take measures to avoid exposing their right flank. As a result their line ran overnight from the copse back to 400 yards east of Wancourt tower.

At daylight on 24 April 33rd Division discovered that the Germans had retired to the line of the Chérisy-Croisilles road. They quickly followed up and in the Hindenburg Line they reached the point where the German support trench crossed the Fontaine-St. Martin road. Further north their advance enabled them to come to the rescue of the companies of the 2nd Argylls and 1st Middlesex who had been cut off by a German counterattack the previous day. Their resistance during their isolation may well have played a significant part in weakening enemy resolve. The 30th and 50th Divisions also completed the occupation of the Blue Line. During the night of 24/25 April an enemy counterattack regained the much fought over copse. 50th Division reacted rapidly and retook it. They then established a line 500 yards to its east. With the battle more or less ended the results for VII Corps were decidedly mixed. Both the 33rd and 30th Divisions had gained about 1,500 yards of ground and 50th Division a mile in the centre of their line. Prisoners taken totalled 1,802. Three guns of Russian manufacture were seized.[9] Whether these outcomes were reasonable compensation for the serious losses sustained by the attackers must however be called into question.

---

9   OH, Ibid., pp. 388-9.

13

VI Corps

The length of front from which VI Corps launched their attack ran from the junction with VII Corps in the south at the small lake between the villages of Wancourt and Guémapppe, to the junction with XVII Corps in the north where the Monchy-Fampoux road reached the River Scarpe. The overall direction was almost due north but the salient formed by the British possession of Monchy-le-Preux protruded to the east and made the planning of the advance less straightforward than it otherwise might have been. The three divisions that would initially attack were, from south to north, 15th (Scottish), 29th and 17th (Northern).

The 15th Division's right was on the River Cojeul. On the other side of the river were VII Corps' 50th Division (150 Brigade). On the left, the line that formed the junction between 15th Division and 88 Brigade of 29th Division ran from La Bergère on the Arras-Cambrai road through the southern corner of the Bois du Vert. The 15th would attack on a two brigade front with 44 Brigade on the right and 45 Brigade on the left. The 46 Brigade would form the divisional reserve. The objectives assigned to all three divisions in VI Corps were first to capture and consolidate the Blue Line, which ran north to south through Hill 100 (otherwise known as Infantry Hill and situated about a mile east of Monchy), and then the Red Line, which included the German support trenches east of St Rohart Factory and the Bois du Vert. A third objective, the Green Line, foresaw the possible capture of Vis-en-Artois and Boiry-Notre-Dame. The timetable planned on the attack on the Red Line beginning seven hours after that on the Blue Line. A major challenge for 44 Brigade on the right was the need to capture Guémappe as part of their progress to the Blue Line. It was decided that only one battalion, 8th Seaforths, would actually attack the village, although they would be assisted by two tanks. The other two assaulting battalions, 7th Camerons and 9th Black Watch, would leave their trenches 20 minutes later than the Seaforths, bypass the village to the north and then spread out for their advance to the stretch of Blue Line between the River Cojeul and Cavalry farm on the south side of the Arras-Cambrai road.

The task assigned to 45 Brigade was not quite so challenging, lacking as it did the complication of a fortified village like Guémappe to deal with. Nevertheless, despite the meticulous planning and preparation, it was a demanding challenge, the more so because the enemy, in contrast to 9 April, would be alert, in strength and well prepared. Two battalions, 11th Argylls on the right and 13th R Scots on the left, would lead the attack with 6/7th RSF in support and 6th Camerons in reserve.

The combination of an exceedingly dark Zero Hour, a heavy and accurate retaliatory enemy artillery and machine gun barrage, and loss of direction by 7th Camerons very soon led to both Brigades' battalions becoming mixed up. The Seaforths suffered particularly from enfilade fire from south of the Cojeul until this was finally eliminated by VII Corps' 50th Division at about 0930. The 7th Camerons and some 9th Black Watch managed to work their way round the north of Guémappe, forcing the German garrison to retire to avoid being surrounded and cut off. The Seaforths were then able to advance right through Guémappe and push the brigade line just to the east of the village.

The 45 Brigade's battalions had become mixed up largely because of the intense enemy barrages and the initial slowness of 44 Brigade in getting forward. Progress was made however with the assistance of reinforcements from 6/7th RSF; some enemy trenches were captured. At around

1000 the divisional and brigade commanders secured a reasonably clear picture of the situation of the attacking battalions. This confirmed the presence of parties of Seaforths and Black Watch in Guémappe and that the divisional line had been advanced irregularly from the Cojeul to north of the Arras-Cambrai road. The Divisional GOC, Major General Sir F. McCracken, taking account of this and the success of the divisions on either side, ordered the divisional reserve, 46 Brigade, to make a fresh attack at 1200. Before this could be launched a German counterattack drove back the left of 50th Division and the right flank of 44 Brigade, thus re-exposing 8th Seaforths and 9th Black Watch to enfilade fire from the south. The two battalions were forced back to positions west of Guémappe. North of the village 7th Camerons maintained their hold on positions which, for the four hours until they were ordered back to the former German front line, prevented any further German advance from the Cojeul. Under no direct pressure 45 Brigade maintained their positions. Later in the course of the day the enemy launched further counterattacks, none of which achieved any success.

At 1450 General McCracken ordered a further attack involving all three of his brigades. The 44 and 45 were ordered to capture the southern portion of Shovel trench and Guémappe cemetery, east of the village. This would be followed at 1800 by 46 Brigade passing through the other two brigades, leaving the village on their right, to capture the Blue Line. South of the Cojeul, 50th Division would attack simultaneously. By now 44 Brigade was a motley collection of Camerons, Seaforths and Black Watch. They were reorganised by Captain Morrison of the Black Watch who started them off towards their objective, the cemetery, before he was unfortunately killed. The advance nevertheless continued and reached its objective, thus regaining all the ground taken earlier in the day by the Brigade. The 45 Brigade were already where they needed to be for 46 Brigade to pass through.

The 46 Brigade's advance was led by 10th SR on the right and 10/11th HLI on the left. The 12th HLI were placed in support behind the Scottish Rifles and 7/8th KOSB formed the brigade reserve. The 10/11th HLI had the misfortune not to receive a message that the artillery barrage would halt for an hour (instead of the planned 30 minutes) on a north-south line just west of Cavalry farm. As a result they advanced through the barrage and suffered heavy casualties. These were additional to those inflicted by enemy machine guns firing from the farm. Despite the inevitable disruption the attack maintained its momentum and the Blue Line was reached by 1830. The HLI consolidated and began to inflict severe losses on the enemy with their rifle and machine gun fire. Meanwhile the Scottish Rifles and remnants of 44 Brigade came up level with the HLI and dug in, having established that Cavalry farm was strongly held by the enemy. Had the artillery barrage not stopped short of the farm, its capture would have been perfectly feasible; an opportunity lost. Although the advance of 15th Division had achieved its aims, those of the divisions on either side had not, thus leaving the Scots with their flanks exposed. When it became apparent that the enemy were preparing to exploit this vulnerability with a counterattack, the two battalions withdrew to south and east of Shovel trench where they hastily dug in under constant shellfire.

During the night, 44 Brigade withdrew to become divisional reserve, leaving behind 8/10th Gordons in trenches west of Guémappe in support of 46 Brigade. The night was otherwise relatively quiet as was the next day until mid-afternoon, in the absence of the anticipated enemy counterattack. At 1400 46 Brigade received orders to resume the attack at 1600, leaving very little time for the preparation and distribution of orders. Some company commanders only received theirs five minutes before the attack was due to start. The advance nevertheless began on time with 10th SR on the right and 12th HLI on the left. In close support were respectively 8/10th Gordons and 7/8th KOSB.

The Scottish attack essentially foundered on the strongly held Cavalry farm with its heavy concentration of machine guns. So intense was their fire from the very start that the SR were forced to dig in on a line just west and north of the farm. On their left the HLI lost one platoon to a German counter barrage; the remainder however continued their advance and reached the Blue Line. There they too had to dig in for protection against the fire emanating from Cavalry farm, and could advance no further. The gap that had opened up between the two assaulting battalions was plugged by Lewis guns and platoons sent forward by 7/8th KOSB. An hour after it had begun the entire attack had come to a standstill.

During the day that followed both sides seemed content to catch their breath. It passed relatively quietly and the opportunity was taken to organise the relief of 46 Brigade by 44 and 45 Brigades who would thereby be handed the task of completing the divisional objectives with a further attack. The relief was finalised during the night of 25th/26th and the orders for the attack issued. The whole of 26 April would be spent saturating the enemy positions with a non-stop heavy bombardment. This would be so intense and concentrated that it was deemed prudent to withdraw the troops in trenches very close to those of the enemy in the vicinity of Cavalry farm, for their own safety. The infantry attack itself would be launched during the night. The capture of Cavalry farm would be the main objective of 44 Brigade on the right. The lead off battalions were 9th Black Watch on the right and 7th Camerons on the left. In support were respectively 8/10th Gordons and 8th Seaforths. At 2230 the advance began close behind what was described as 'an exceedingly good and accurate barrage'. The Black Watch, having reached the Blue Line, then established a series of posts on a crest line running northwards from the Cojeul river. The Camerons met only light opposition as they rapidly cleared the farm. But as they advanced beyond it they found themselves confronted by a very strongly held trench about 150 yards east of the farm. Coming under fire from this and enfilade fire from another enemy held trench, they were forced to withdraw leaving a post occupied about 50 yards east of the farm. A German counterattack obliged the occupants of this to retire and the whole Battalion to move back from the farm. At about 0200 two officer patrols were sent out to secure the farm and make contact with the Black Watch. Although neither of these aims was achieved, three posts were established south and south-east of the farm, which effectively denied its use to the enemy. A further enemy counterattack at 0800 managed to seize two of the Black Watch posts. The remaining one stood fast, as did the Camerons' posts, and inflicted heavy casualties on the enemy over the next 24 hours.

North of the Arras-Cambrai Road, 45 Brigade were holding the line with 6th Camerons and 11th Argylls. The 13th R Scots and 6/7th RSF were in reserve. In the light of the murderous fire that could be anticipated from Cavalry farm, there could be no question of attempting an advance from their forward positions until the farm had been fully secured. As this had not been achieved the Brigade spent the time consolidating and improving their defences.

Both brigades were relieved over the course of the period 27th/29th April and the whole Division was withdrawn in view of the fact that the five days it had been in action had left it in no state to undertake any further offensive operations. It required rest, re-equipping and replacements. The timescale for these ensured that it would play no further part in the Battle of Arras. The casualties resulting from its participation amounted to 6,313 out of a total of 11,932, its strength on 9 April. Of these 977 had been killed, including 80 officers. The Second Battle of the Scarpe accounted for about 3,000 of them.[1]

Occupying the centre of the VI Corps line on 23 April was the 29th Division. The 11th[2] and last of the British Army all regular divisions, it was formed largely from infantry battalions hastily summoned back on the outbreak of war from garrison duties in the more distant colonies of the Empire. Some had to wait until Territorial Army battalions had arrived to replace them, but by the early weeks of 1915 the Division was up to wartime establishment and ready for deployment abroad. 11 of its battalions were regular army; the shortfall of one battalion was dealt with by bringing in a TA Battalion, the 5th R Scots. When this unit moved on in September 1915 they were replaced by the

---

1   Stewart and Buchan, *The 15th (Scottish) Division 1914-1919*, pp. 132-41.
2   By the time the last three regular divisions, the 9th, 10th and 11th were established, those numbers and the rest up to 26 had been allocated to the newly created Kitchener New Army divisions, hence the need to give them the numbers 27th, 28th and 29th.

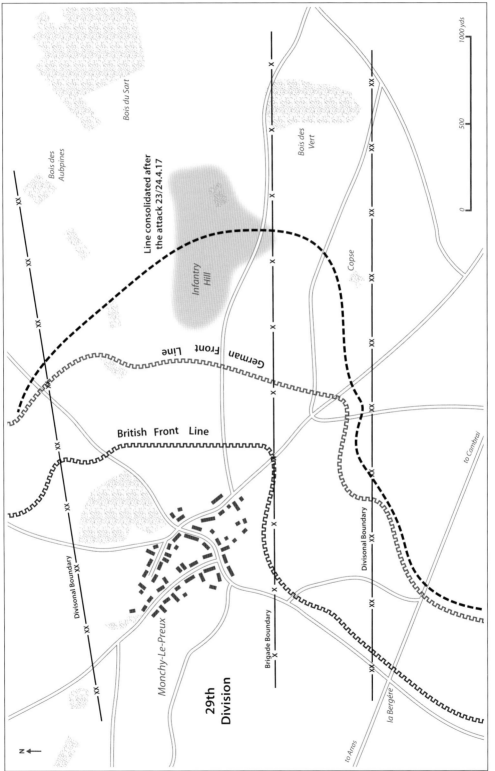

Line consolidated after
the attack 23/24.4.17

Bois du Sart

Bois des
Aubpines

Bois des
Vert

Infantry
Hill

Copse

German Front Line

British Front Line

Monchy-Le-Preux

29th
Division

Divisonal Boundary

Divisonal Boundary

Brigade Boundary

la Bergère

to Arras

to Cambrai

1000 yds

500

0

N

29th Division advance from Monchy-le-Preux during Second Battle of the Scarpe 23-24 April 1917.

Royal Newfoundland Regiment.[3]

The Division's first campaign was Gallipoli. Two of their brigades landed on the first day and began building up their lustrous reputation that was to earn them the nickname 'the Incomparables'. One of their battalions, 1st Lancashire Fusiliers, achieved lasting fame that day by winning six Victoria Crosses 'before breakfast'.[4] When the Gallipoli campaign was closed down the Division quickly found itself on the Western Front in time for the Somme campaign. Like nearly all divisions on the first day of the battle, the 29th suffered horrendous casualties with nothing to show for them. Particularly poignant was the fate of the Newfoundland Regiment, who had the second worst losses (684) of all the battalions engaged that day.[5]

At the beginning of the Battle of Arras the 29th was in XVIII Corps. It did not become directly involved until it transferred to VI Corps on 13 April. The Division took over the line to the east of Monchy-le-Preux from the Cojeul river to a point north of Monchy. Dominating the enemy positions in front of them was the 100 metres high Infantry Hill. Its capture would be an essential first step to making any further progress eastward and fully securing Monchy from the threat of recapture that could be posed by enemy counterattacks. The Division 88 Brigade were accordingly ordered to attack Infantry Hill on 14 April at 0530. The two battalions involved, the Newfoundland Regt and 1st Essex, after a promising start, quickly found themselves under enormous pressure from an almost simultaneously launched enemy assault designed to retake Monchy. It was presaged by a massive bombardment on the village itself and on the British artillery batteries behind Orange Hill. The two battalions were heavily outnumbered and suffered serious losses, but were somehow able to slow down the enemy advance sufficiently to enable some sort of defence of the village to be organised by the Newfoundland Regiment's CO. The German attempt to retake the village was finally thwarted, to the great relief of the British High Command. For 29th Division the time between the events just described and 23 April was largely spent in or close to Monchy or back in Arras for brief periods of rest.

The Division's deployment for 23 April found them on familiar ground, facing east from Monchy itself and from the ground south of the village between it and the hamlet of La Bergère on the Arras-Cambrai Road. Two brigades would be utilised for the initial assault with 86 Brigade in reserve. On the right were the two relatively intact battalions of 88 Brigade, 4th Worcesters supported by 2nd Hampshires, who were to advance in the direction of the Bois du Vert which lay approximately 2,000 yards away. Before reaching this formidable obstacle they were to link up with 87 Brigade's leading right hand battalion, 1st KOSB, with 1st Royal Inniskilling Fusiliers (Inniskillings) in support, to form a north-south line running through a point roughly 200 yards west of Infantry Hill. From here the plan was to renew the advance in the afternoon to capture the three enemy positions of Infantry Hill, Bois du Sart and Bois du Vert, without possession of which there could be very little prospect of VI Corps making significant progress. In broad terms the initial advance went reasonably well. Despite heavy casualties the Worcesters reached their objective and dug in. Behind them, the Hampshires were caught by the German counterbarrage and lost heavily but nevertheless carried out their mopping up duties effectively. 1st KOSB, under the protection of a very effective barrage, reached their objective with only light losses some of which were ascribed to impetuosity causing them to get too close to their own barrage. Further north, 2nd South Wales Borderers (SWB) captured two copses but were then forced to set up a defensive flank to avoid their flank being in the air.

Although 29th Division were reasonably well-placed to fulfil the plans for the afternoon, they had to be suspended because the Division were in positions much further forward than those of the Divisions on either side and vulnerable to the constant threat of counterattack from an enemy which launched its first one, on the SWB, from the direction of Pelves as early as 1000. Largely beaten off they

3   Gillon, *The Story of the 29th Division*, pp. 3-10.
4   Ibid., pp. 19-28.
5   Ibid., pp. 80-3.

nevertheless resulted in the loss once more of Guémappe. When the counterattacks stopped they were replaced by a very heavy barrage that inflicted severe losses on the Worcesters and Hampshires and resulted in some ground being given up. The planned afternoon attack, which had been rescheduled for the next afternoon, was cancelled. The cancellation order never reached 1st Royal Dublin Fusiliers, who attacked and suffered needless and pointless losses as a result. The Division was relieved by 3rd Division during the night of 24th/25th.[6]

The third VI Corps division involved from the outset of the Second Battle of the Scarpe was the 17th (Northern) Division. Formed as part of the second tranche of the KNA they drew their recruits mainly from the counties of Yorkshire and Lancashire with the battalions being badged into regiments largely from those counties. Probably in recognition of the fact that their main training area was centred on Wareham, one southern battalion, the 6th Dorsetshire Regiment (Dorsets), broke the otherwise northern totality of their regimental roll call. In January 1915 Major General T. D. Pilcher assumed command of the Division which moved to France in July of the same year. Their first year was largely spent in the Ypres Salient, but in June 1916 they moved to the Somme as the Reserve Division of XV Corps, whose other two divisions on 1 July were the 7th and 21st. Only one brigade of 17th Division, the 50th, participated on the first day of the battle, on temporary attachment to 21st Division. Fully engaged in the heavy fighting around Fricourt, the Brigade suffered heavy casualties.

The whole Division quickly became involved in the attempts to secure the enemy defences leading up to Mametz Wood. It soon became apparent that the XV Corps Commander, Lieutenant General Sir Henry Horne, was unhappy with the way General Pilcher was handling his Division which, Horne told Haig, would not advance quickly. Matters came to a head over the failure of the joint attempts of 38th (Welsh) Division (released to XV Corps from GHQ Reserve) and 17th Division to capture Mametz Wood quickly. As a result the GOCs of both divisions were relieved and sent home. In General Pilcher's case he may well have been the unfortunate victim of his concern not to risk his troops' lives in ill-conceived operations doomed to fail.

Major General Pilcher was soon replaced by Major General Philip R. Robertson, who would remain in command of the Division for the rest of the war. The Division remained on the Somme until the end of February 1917 when they were moved into GHQ Reserve in preparation for Arras. They began training for a new role as the infantry arm of the Cavalry Corps. 17th Division's role would be to follow behind the cavalry and occupy and secure any objective they captured thus freeing the cavalry to resume their advance. In the event no such opportunity presented itself and on the afternoon of 11 April the Division were transferred from the Cavalry Corps to VI Corps and back to a normal infantry role.

The 17th Division's initial task on 23 April was to clear out enemy positions on the south bank of the Scarpe opposite the village of Roeux. Once this had been achieved the intention was to advance to the capture of the village of Pelves. Two battalions of 51st Brigade, 7th Borders on the right and 8th South Staffordshire Regiment (South Staffs) on the left moved up into assembly trenches which had been dug on a line running north and south through Lone copse. To complete their initial objective the two battalions would have to attack and subdue the enemy held Bayonet and Rifle trenches opposite their assembly positions. They should have had the assistance of two tanks but they both broke down on their way forward. Rather more reliably they had 9th Northumberlands, on attachment from 52 Brigade, to cover their right, 50 Brigade in support and 52 Brigade in reserve. Much use would be made of trench mortars, both to bombard the enemy trenches and to put down a smoke screen to blind enemy guns seeking to fire in enfilade from north of the Scarpe.

Despite the planning and their own covering barrage, when the two battalions went over the top at 0445 they almost immediately found themselves under a heavy enemy artillery barrage and concentrated enfilade machine gun fire from north of the Scarpe. Trying to get forward was difficult

---

6   Ibid. pp. 114-121.

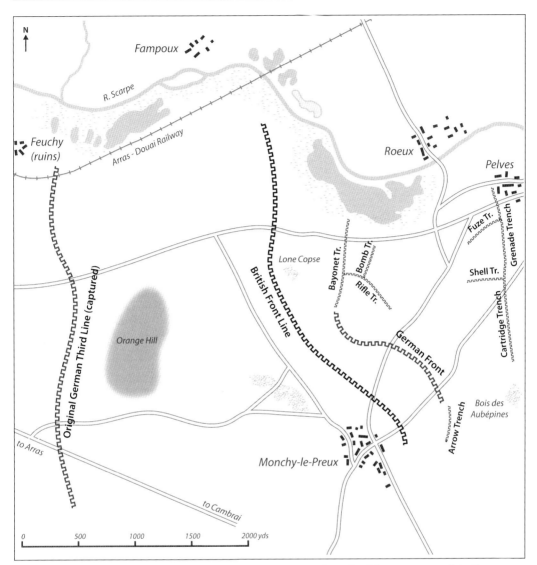

17th Division operations south of the River during the Second Battle of the Scarpe, 23-24 April 1917.

enough in these conditions without the discovery that the German protective wire was almost untouched and therefore uncut. Nevertheless the Borders fought their way into and along Bayonet trench from the south, almost making it to the junction with Rifle trench. An attempt to reach the latter over open ground failed leaving many Borders sheltering in shell holes where they remained until after dark and could retire. The South Staffs mounted two attacks on the north end of Bayonet trench but both were thrown back with heavy losses.[7]

The two remaining battalions of 51 Brigade, 7th Lincolns and 10th Sherwood Foresters (Sherwoods), had meanwhile moved forward to the Lone copse assembly trenches. They were to advance behind the South Staffs and Borders respectively and pass through them to complete the capture of the enemy trenches should this be necessary. In the event the Lincolns were ordered to attack the north end of Bayonet trench once the remnants of the South Staffs had withdrawn.

7   Hilliard Atteridge, *A History of the 17th (Northern) Division*, pp. 210-11.

Although their attack was cancelled because the artillery could not fire the requested supporting barrage the message did not reach the Lincolns until after they had begun their advance at 0800. They got as far as the enemy wire where they were held up. Despite desperate efforts to get through or under this obstacle, it proved impossible to advance further. The Lincolns' attack failed with a loss of nearly 200 all ranks. Their predecessors, the South Staffs, had lost 214.[8]

When 10th Sherwoods advanced they were soon targeted by the German artillery and suffered many casualties. As they approached Bayonet trench they came under enfilade machine gun fire from the north forcing the extreme left of the Battalion to take cover in shell holes. But many in the centre and on the right did reach the trench where they came across remnants of the Borders who had crossed Bayonet trench but then been stopped by machine gun fire from Rifle trench.[9] A proposal by the acting CO of the Sherwoods to bomb north along Bayonet trench was turned down by Divisional HQ in favour of a renewal of the attack on the two trenches by the heretofore supporting 50 Brigade, following intensive artillery preparation.[10]

When 50 Brigade's attack was launched at 1530 it was believed that Roeux was in British hands and that their left flank was therefore secure. The village had indeed been held for a while but had been retaken by the Germans, who were consequently able to target the attackers with machine gun fire from Roeux and from the untaken parts of Bayonet and Rifle trenches. The inevitable failure of 50 Brigade's attack would mark the end of the Division's efforts to achieve their objectives for the day.[11]

The next day, the 24th, was relatively quiet apart from two attempts by 52 Brigade bombing parties to work their way further up Bayonet trench. Both failed in the face of heavy machine gun fire from a fully alerted enemy in Rifle trench. During the afternoon orders were received that a joint surprise attack with 3rd Division was to be launched at 0330 the following morning with the purpose of capturing the enemy front line from Arrow trench east of Monchy, where 3rd Division were in occupation, to the junction of Rifle and Bayonet trenches. The 52 Brigade, on the left of the attack, were ordered to capture Rifle trench with the support of two tanks (which were to be knocked out as they attempted to cross the British front line). The attempt to achieve surprise by not firing a preliminary barrage failed as the Germans were on the alert and established almost immediately what was going on. This resulted in a heavy barrage on no man's land that, in addition to eliminating the tanks, inflicted heavy casualties on the two main attacking battalions, the 12th Manchesters and 9th Duke's. Nevertheless two companies of the Manchesters on the right did get into the right hand end of the trench and consolidated their hold on it during the course of the next day. The Duke's were less fortunate. Although about 60 of them did get into Rifle trench, they were driven out by a counterattack before support could reach them. The possibility of further action to complete the capture of Rifle trench was discussed but rejected in favour of consolidating what had been gained in the light of the planned relief of the Division during the night of 25th/26th by 6th Division. In this last action of the Second Battle of the Scarpe for the Division, the Duke's had lost nine officers and 250 men killed and wounded and the Manchesters four officers and 110 men.[12]

---

8   Ibid., pp. 211-12.
9   A notable casualty during these events was Lieutenant Geoffrey Thurlow, another of Vera Brittain's close friends. Acting Commander of 10th Sherwood Forester's C Company, he was shot by a sniper and died only minutes later. His body was subsequently lost and he is commemorated on the Arras Memorial to the Missing.
10   Hoyte, *10th (S) Battalion The Sherwood Foresters*, pp. 30-1.
11   Hilliard Atteridge, op. cit., p. 213.
12   Ibid., pp. 214-5.

14

XVII, XIII, Canadian and I Corps

The River Scarpe offered a natural boundary between VI Corps and their northern neighbour, XVII Corps. The latter would attack on a two divisional front with 51st (Highland) and 37th Divisions on the right and left respectively. On 37th Division's left was XIII Corps' 63rd (Royal Naval) Division. The GOC in C of XVII Corps, Lieutenant General Sir Charles Fergusson, ordered that his divisions' objectives should be tackled in four stages. The first was to capture the tiny Mount Pleasant wood to the west of Roeux, a newly dug trench running north from the wood to the Oppy Line and the enemy held Oppy Line itself. The second was to take Roeux village, the nearby Chemical Works and the Roeux-Gavrelle road. The third stage was to take a convex curved line between the Chemical Works and the Plouvain-Gavrelle road. The fourth and final stage was to capture a trench covering Delbar and Hausa woods and Plouvain station. The main objective of XIII Corps' 63rd Division was the village of Gavrelle. This was to be taken in two stages, in step with the two XVII Corps divisions, after a first stage that would involve the capture of their sector of the Oppy Line.

Concerned that the above objectives would be beyond the capacity of the already overstretched 51st Division to achieve, General Fergusson had sought to have them amended so that the village of Roeux and the Chemical Works would be the Highlanders' final objectives. His request had however been turned down and the original orders were left unchanged. The Divisional Commander decided to use two brigades in his attack plan with the dividing line between them being the Arras-Douai railway line. South of the line, between it and the River Scarpe, would be 154 Brigade; north of it, 153 Brigade. Both Brigades' tasks would be made significantly more difficult by the number of buildings confronting them, not least those of the Chemical Works, which had already acquired a malign reputation among the many who had already fought in and around that complex of buildings.[1]

The 154 Brigade went over the top at 0445 with 7th Argylls on the right and 4th Gordons on the left. The 9th R Scots were in support of both assaulting battalions and 4th Seaforths were in brigade reserve. The advance of 7th Argylls, the leading two companies of which were to take their sector of the first and second objectives, including Roeux village, was immediately in trouble when the first wave ran into their own barrage and took heavy losses. These were compounded by an enemy barrage, largely of heavy guns, that had quickly come into action. The Battalion nevertheless pressed forward only to find that Mount Pleasant and Roeux woods and the enemy trenches were strongly held, with plentiful machine guns and snipers. Losses continued to mount, especially among officers; the whole attack fell 90 minutes behind schedule. The Argylls' pressure had however begun to tell on the Germans, who were beginning to trickle to the rear from their trenches. The advent of a tank played a significant part in exerting this pressure by shelling houses in Roeux suspected to be concealing snipers and machine guns that were causing great problems, especially among runners and stretcher bearers. Its support enabled the infantry to enter the village from the west. Bombing parties began to clear the houses. It proved to be a very time consuming operation as the enemy seemed to have the means to reoccupy houses supposedly cleared. Machine guns continued to fire from the upper stories of buildings.

---

1   OH, 1917 Vol. 1, p. 394.

To the south the attackers got into Roeux wood and from there into the southern outskirts of the village. By now the supporting companies of 9th R Scots had been drawn into the fighting and had become much mixed up with the assaulting battalions. All the 7th Argyll officers had become casualties. At about 1030 the enemy launched a strong counterattack which pushed out most of the Highlanders who had occupied the northern end of the village. Some scattered parties did manage to dig themselves into shell holes near a light railway, where they held on until relieved that evening. Strong points were also set up in front of Mount Pleasant wood. Overall however the Battalion had become seriously disorganised. Reorganisation was difficult especially under machine gun fire coming from the south side of the Scarpe. When 4th Seaforths advanced to attack on the Argylls' left the latter had no organised parties available to support them.

During the evening the Argylls were relieved by 26th Northumberlands and retired to their start line. The following night they were relieved there by 11th Suffolks and withdrew to Arras.[2]

The 4th Gordons, on the left of the Brigade attack, advanced on a two company front with initially patchy results. Some parts of the German front line were entered with little difficulty. In other parts, the enemy held out for some time, especially on the left near the railway in front of the Chemical Works. By the time the Battalion's third and fourth companies, starting out 10 minutes after the first two, reached the enemy front positions, they found no enemy presence on the right but were, like the preceding companies, held up on the left. Elements of the Gordons' right wing, probably through losing direction rather than by design, passed right through Roeux village before being forced to retire for lack of support. Their progress had been partially helped by the same tank that had supported the 7th Argylls. A small bombing party subsequently worked its way down a communication trench to the road running from Roeux to the Chemical Works and held on there for some time. On the Battalion left progress was finally made when 4th Seaforths came up at around 0830 and worked along the railway, taking prisoners as they progressed.

The Gordons' War Diary was very critical of the apparent inadequacy of the supporting artillery barrage for their attack. They had found the German front line very little damaged. This had allowed the enemy to bring their machine guns into action as soon as the barrage had lifted. Indeed some of them had been active right through the barrage. Partially as a consequence casualties had been high at 325 killed, wounded and missing, including six officers killed and 10 wounded. The Gordons were relieved in similar stages to the 7th Argylls and were back in Arras by the morning of 25 April.[3]

The 9th R Scots, in support of the two assaulting battalions, began their advance 30 minutes after Zero Hour. The two companies on the right quickly found themselves held up by heavy and accurate small arms fire. One company did however manage to take a trench south west of Mount Pleasant wood with a bayonet charge and the assistance of a tank. But when they entered Roeux wood they were stopped from making further progress by enemy holding a sunken road in strength.

The two companies on the left also found progress difficult in the face of heavy machine gun and rifle fire directed at them from a railway embankment and the Chemical Works. Some men who managed to get past the Chemical Works became isolated and were probably mostly made prisoner. Throughout the day snipers firing from Mount Pleasant wood and the Battalion flanks defied attempts to clear them. The snipers and artillery which rapidly targeted places such as Roeux and the Chemical Works when they were entered by the attackers, brought to a halt any hope of further progress. At 2200 the Battalion withdrew to their starting line that morning. Losses for the day amounted to 231 killed, wounded and missing.[4]

The 4th Seaforths had not remained in brigade reserve for long. As has already been recorded they were ordered to move up in support of 4th Gordons who were held up on the left. They received

2   TNA WO 95/2886/1: 7th Argyll and Sutherland Highlanders War Diary.
3   TNA WO 95/2886/2: 4th Gordon Highlanders War Diary.
4   TNA WO 95/2887/5: 9th Royal Scots War Diary.

their orders at about 0800 and sent forward two companies who crossed a small wooden bridge over the Scarpe despite enemy artillery fire, and advanced along the right side of the railway. The main problem that had halted the Gordons was one machine gun and 50 troops holding out at the junction of the German front line with the Arras-Douai railway. As the Seaforths made their plans to deal with this obstacle a tank appeared which quickly ruled itself out of any role in the operation by getting bogged down. A remarkable infantry action then ensued in which the Seaforths captured the enemy position, killing 20 and taking the rest prisoner, all at no cost to themselves. The machine gun had disappeared, presumably carried to the rear.

At 1105 the Seaforths' remaining two companies were ordered to enter the Chemical Works. The left company did so without opposition but the right company could make no progress to the right of Roeux Château because of machine gun fire from the village cemetery. The Battalion formed a defensive flank along the railway. At 1730 the enemy launched a counterattack from Greenland Hill. It was effectively dealt with by rifle and Lewis gun fire. A subsequent counterattack from Roeux was shattered by artillery fire with the remnants being dispersed by small arms fire. At 2100 the Seaforths' forward troops moved back to the former German front line. The Chemical Works were being shelled by the artillery of both sides, making this withdrawal necessary. During the night patrols were unable to advance more than 50 yards because of manned German positions in a house south of the railway and in the Château, and two machine guns lined up on the road between the station and the Château. The enemy continued to be active throughout the night, but their movements were effectively dealt with. They did not help their cause when at one stage they ran into their own barrage and suffered heavy losses. By 0600 on 24 April, all was relatively quiet. The Battalion were relieved by 11th Suffolks and marched back to Arras.[5]

On 51st Division's left, the 37th Division, relatively fresh from their capture of Monchy-le-Preux 12 days earlier, began their assault with 63 and 111 Brigades up, and 112 Brigade in divisional reserve. The 4th Middlesex and 10th York and Lancs formed the first waves of 63 Brigade's advance with 8th SLI and 8th Lincolns respectively in close support. At 0445, when the two assaulting battalions began to advance, the night was still very dark; visibility was further curtailed by the all pervasive smoke. Unsurprisingly there was a tendency to lose direction. Even worse for the attackers was the considerable enemy resistance they met. The 4th Middlesex and 8th SLI nevertheless managed to reach a line about 200 yards east of the Roeux-Gavrelle road, where they were stopped from making any further progress by enfilade machine gun fire. The 10th York and Lancs failed even to reach the German front line, Chili Trench, before their advance was checked. The 8th Lincolns immediately passed through them and maintained the advance. The 50 or so Germans in Chili Trench continued to resist until the Lincolns turned their flank, thus completing the capture of the trench at about 1030.[6]

In contrast to 63 Brigade, the initial advance of 111 Brigade, with 13th Royal Fusiliers (RF) on the right and 13th KRRC on the left, was not checked. But 13th RF found themselves under machine gun fire on their right flank and suffered some losses until they took an officer and 40 men prisoner. They moved on with relatively light losses until the enemy second line, Cuba trench, was reached. The 13th KRRC had closely followed their barrage, carried the first line and, despite suffering from the same machine gun fire as the RF, reached their objective and dug in along the Plouvain-Gavrelle road. There they were in touch with 63rd (Royal Naval) Division on their left. Under the apparent misapprehension that the Battalion were not in contact with any friendly troops, the Brigade Commander ordered his reserve battalion, 13th RB, forward to support 13th KRRC. Having lost heavily, including their CO, when they were caught in an enemy barrage, they positioned themselves on the KRRC's right in Cuba Trench, but had not closed up on them, obliging KRRC to

---

5   TNA WO 95/2888/1: 4th Seaforth Highlanders War Diary.
6   TNA WO 95/2528: 4th Middlesex Regiment War Diary.

dig a defensive trench facing east.[7]

At about 0845 enemy troops were observed massing in the area between Plouvain station and Fresnes village in preparation for mounting counterattacks. Throughout the day a number of these were launched against the fronts of 63rd and 37th Divisions. They were all ineffective and dispersed by artillery and machine gun fire.[8]

Only one of the battalions of 112 Brigade, the divisional reserve, became involved in the early stages of the battle. At 0910 the 6th Bedfords came under the orders of 63 Brigade to provide support to their left. Their support succeeded in pushing forward the advance to about 200 yards east of the Roeux-Gavrelle road. The remainder of 112 Brigade were ordered forward in the afternoon. In an attack scheduled for 1830 they were to pass through 63 Brigade with the aim of completing the latter's objectives set for the day. All three of their remaining battalions would participate. From right to left these were 10th Loyals, 8th East Lancs and 11th Warwicks. At 1800 a barrage was put down 150 yards in front of the line that 63 Brigade had reached. The protection this offered would be used to cover the advance of the three battalions to Chili Trench from where they would jump off at 1830, the intention being that they would thereby be able to keep close under the barrage as it began its creep forward. Unfortunately the enemy seemed to be fully aware of what to expect. As a result they heavily bombarded the open ground that the three battalions had to cross to reach Chili Trench, inflicting substantial casualties. Further losses were suffered from the enemy artillery as the battalions then moved forward to get under the cover of their own creeping barrage. Immediately this barrage lifted and the advance to the east of the Roeux-Gavrelle road began, the leading lines of attackers were hit by an avalanche of machine gun and rifle fire from the Chemical Works and the hedge along the railway embankment. Nonetheless the centre and left battalions managed to reach a line immediately east of Cuba Trench. On the right however 10th Loyals were unable to advance the line at all.

An hour after the infantry attack had begun it was evident that 63 and 112 Brigades were thoroughly mixed up and any further attempt to move forward on the right would be doomed to failure because of the enfilade rifle and machine gun fire coming from the south. Orders were therefore issued for any ground gained during the day's fighting to be organised and consolidated. In recognising and commenting on the disappointing outcome of the 1830 attack, the 37th Division War Diary called attention to the fact that a German counterattack on 51st Highland Division that began at 1700, prevented that Division from co-operating in 37th Division's attack as had been intended. Another problem had been uncertainty about the situation in the Chemical Works. Persistent doubts about who held what had meant that it had been impossible to shell it. In the event, had it been shelled, that might have made the difference between success and failure for the right of the Division.[9]

In effect, as far as XVII Corps and the Second Battle of the Scarpe are concerned, all the really intense fighting had already taken place by the end of the first day of the battle. For the following three days the main activity centred around dealing with an enemy who maintained a high level of artillery and sniping activity and, notably on 24 April, launched a number of counterattacks. The preparations for the first of these were observed at 0445. It was directed specifically against the right flank of 13th KRRC and was met immediately by the massed fire of machine guns and Lewis guns which inflicted heavy casualties and dissipated the threat. Other counterattacks were launched during the day from Greenland Hill and the vicinity of Square wood. They were all easily dealt with by artillery and machine gun fire.

The XIII Corps 63rd (Royal Naval) Division, on 37th Division's left, had been born out of a pre-war appreciation by the Admiralty that in the event of the Fleet being fully mobilised for war there would be a large number of RN reserves, perhaps as many as 30,000, who would be surplus to the

7   TNA WO 95/2533: 13th King's Royal Rifle Corps War Diary.
8   TNA WO 95/2513: 37th Division War Diary.
9   TNA WO 95/2513: 37th Division War Diary.

number needed to crew the fully manned Fleet. Acting on the appreciation, three brigades would be established, one of Royal Marine and two of RN reserves, ready to fight as an infantry division. On the outbreak of war the Royal Naval Division was rapidly mobilised and welcomed by the new Secretary of State for War, Lord Kitchener, as a much appreciated addition to the small number of regular army divisions then in being. It was soon in action in Belgium, briefly at Ostend and then subsequently participating in the abortive defence of Antwerp. It was then one of the first two British divisions to land on Gallipoli and one of the last to leave. When it was decided that the Division should next serve on the Western Front its naval content was perforce diminished by the incorporation of 190 Brigade, consisting entirely of army battalions (1st HAC, 4th Bedfords, 7th Royal Fusiliers and 10th Dublin Fusiliers). At the same time as it arrived in France in May 1916 its designation was changed to 63rd (Royal Naval) Division and its two Naval Brigades became the 188 and 189 Brigades. Their battalions however still retained their Naval names, thus maintaining the essentially naval character of the Division (to the irritation of some senior army officers who had dealings with them, notably Major General Cameron Shute who commanded the Division from October 1916 to February 1917). This naval flavour persisted even when the Division was transferred from Admiralty to War Office control.

The Division's first serious action on the Western Front came in the last convulsion of the Somme campaign, the Battle of the Ancre that began on 13 November 1916. In the first 48 hours of this battle, until it was relieved, the Division achieved all its objectives, but at the enormous cost of nearly 3,000 casualties. These losses contributed to total casualties in the month of November of 100 officers and 1,600 men killed and 160 officers and 2,377 men wounded. Little wonder that the Division was withdrawn from the battle area for two months to rest, re-equip, retrain and absorb reinforcements. Even though it spent time in the front line from mid-January onward, its next major involvement would be during the Second Battle of the Scarpe.[10]

The XIII Corps, which had been in general reserve in the early stages of the Battle of Arras, would, largely through 63rd Division, take a leading role in Second Scarpe. The first elements of the Division moved into the front line during the night of 14th/15th April, taking over a sector west of the village of Gavrelle from XVII Corps' 34th Division. On their left were 2nd Division. Although the Division 189 Brigade, on the right, found their new positions to be within striking distance of the enemy defences, those of the 190 Brigade on the left were not. Considerable effort and not inconsiderable losses were required of the Brigade's four battalions over the next few days and nights to rectify this situation, ultimately successfully, even though there was still the problem that the Division's front positions were on a forward slope in full view of the enemy 3,500 yards away over open ground.

The same two brigades would carry out the initial assault on 23 April. The first objective would be the enemy trench system in front of Gavrelle, the second the road running north-south through the centre of the village and the third, a line between three and six hundred yards beyond the village. After the capture of the first objective, only 189 Brigade would move on to the second and third objectives leaving 190 Brigade to form a defensive flank. The two battalions each from the assaulting brigades were the Drake, the Nelson, 4th Bedfords and 7th RF. The Hood Battalion would start out in close support of the Nelson until the first and second objectives had been secured, after which it would aim to capture the third objective in conjunction with Drake Battalion.

At Zero Hour the four battalions began their advance under the protection of a creeping barrage. Three of them reached and captured their stretch of the first objective in ten minutes, despite the fact that Drake Battalion had discovered prior to Zero that the enemy wire on their right was mostly uncut. This was successfully dealt with by Drake advancing on a one company front while their right flank was covered by intensive Stokes mortar and machine gun fire. On the left of the advance the 7th RF had the most difficult time. They were held up by uncut enemy wire and heavy fire from their left flank, but still managed to gain a foothold in the enemy front line. Although the Hood Battalion

---

10   Douglas Jerrold, *The Royal Naval Division*, pp. 183-222 passim.

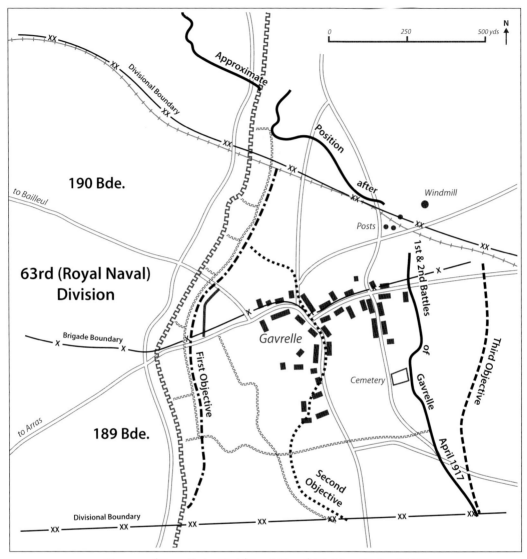

Capture of Gavrelle by 63rd (Royal Naval) Division, 23 April 1917.

had been ordered not to advance until the first objective had been secured, they decided to do so immediately to avoid any enemy defensive barrage that might come down on their position. As a result they were close behind Nelson Battalion when the German lines were reached.

After a 15-minute pause the advance on the second objective began, Drake and Nelson Battalions still leading with Hood Battalion in support. Even though the Bedfords and RF should have stayed on the first objective, in the latter's case to complete its capture, and then set about setting up their defensive flank, a large number of the Bedfords followed Hood Battalion forward and into Gavrelle village, thus assuring that the inevitable mix-up of different units became an even larger problem. As the attackers reached the north-south road through the village, the barrage stopped creeping in order to give the commanders time to reorganise their troops for the advance to the third objective. Any serious reorganisation proved virtually impossible in the unfamiliar conditions of house to house rather than trench fighting. Movement was difficult owing to the threat posed by snipers and machine guns operating at close quarters and both the British and enemy artillery pounding the village. Nevertheless, although unreorganised, the advance resumed on schedule when the artillery resumed its creep forward. There were approximately 600 yards to go.

The first 250 yards of this was covered with only light losses until the main Oppy-Gavrelle road was reached. The road passed through the eastern half of a completely ruined Gavrelle across the line of advance of the attackers, whose left flank was the west-east Gavrelle-Fresnes road. Immediately south of the road were Hood Battalion; further south were Drake Battalion. The former's route to the final objective would be through the remains of the village. Drake Battalion on the other hand would be confronted by open country on which the only feature offering the possibility of shelter or concealment was the walled village cemetery, south of the village, which marked the dividing line between the two battalions. Although Hood Battalion were perhaps fortunate in being inside the village they were nevertheless overlooked by the enemy from a ridge commanding their exposed left flank on their direction of advance. Situated at the ridge's highest point was the Gavrelle windmill. There could be no question of getting any distance beyond the Oppy-Gavrelle road while this strong point remained in German hands.

The capture of the windmill had been one of the objectives of 4th Bedfords, who had planned to use it as the apex of their defensive flank. Unfortunately, although that Battalion had had very little difficulty in completing its first objective, the same was not the case for 7th RF on their left. They had ben forced to seek the assistance of a company of 1st HAC, 190 Brigade's support Battalion, to complete their task. When this reinforcement proved insufficient, the Royal Fusiliers sought the further help of a second HAC company. By now the struggle had become an attritional one with bombing parties disputing every inch of trench. Progress was slow, which meant that the left of the Bedfords could not take the risk of advancing as planned. Their right, on the other hand, were able to continue the advance but lost direction and, as we have seen, followed Hood Battalion into the centre of Gavrelle. The result of the difficulties to their left had now placed Hood Battalion in a very precarious situation with their left flank open and the enemy in trenches in front of them only 300 yards away and able to observe their every move. In anticipation of the inevitable counterattack the Battalion commander [11] made his dispositions, using shell holes and the Gavrelle Mayor's house as the first line, and the former German second line west of the village as a second line to be held at all costs.

The time was roughly 0700. At 1300 the first of the enemy counterattacks was launched, largely on the Drake Battalion front. It was broken up by rifle and machine gun fire and an artillery barrage. The enemy nevertheless persisted in trying to concentrate for further attacks. The Hood and Drake Battalions managed to prevent these concentrations taking place but only at the expense of continuous casualties largely from enemy artillery barrages. At 1630 an order was received by the hard-pressed battalions that they should complete the capture of the day's objectives. It was decided to ignore it. During what turned out to be a surprisingly quiet night, Hood Battalion was relieved by Howe Battalion.

On the following day the enemy mounted its largest counterattack of the battle. The whole 63rd Division front was heavily shelled from noon onwards and the infantry advance began at around 1500. For an hour there were frequent attempts to enter the Division front line. Although suffering heavily from the British artillery the enemy reached the front posts in several places and at one point on the Howe front actually made a penetration. Spirited and well-led defence finally assured that no ground was lost; the enemy were thrown back with heavy losses. This appeared to be the enemy's last attempt to reverse the gains of the previous day. With 1st HAC, having relieved 7th RF, succeeding in setting up the defensive flank more or less as planned, and Gavrelle firmly in British hands, the British objectives for the battle had nearly been fulfilled. However Gavrelle windmill remained in German hands and the Division's advance beyond Gavrelle had been less than hoped, hardly a satisfactory

---

11   Commander Arthur Asquith, DSO and bar, son of the former Prime Minister.

outcome in the light of the casualties suffered.[12]

Further north none of the four Canadian divisions of the Canadian Corps was scheduled to attack the enemy Oppy-Mericourt Line, because the weather had prevented adequate artillery preparation for such an operation. First Army involvement, in addition to 63rd Division already described, would therefore be confined to a two-divisional attack astride the River Souchez designed to capture part of the German Vimy-Riegel Line and the village of La Coulotte. South of the river the attack would be made by two brigades of the British 5th Division, still under the command of the GOC Canadian Corps, as it had been since the build up to the Canadian assault on Vimy Ridge. North of the river I Corps 46th (North Midland) Division would attack, using two battalions, 6th and 8th Sherwoods, of 139th Brigade. The 5th Division 15 and 95 Brigades would each attack on a two battalion front, the leading waves consisting of 1st Northumberlands, 1st Bedfords, 1st Devons and 1st DCLI. Initial reports that the wire had been adequately cut in front of the Vimy-Riegel Line proved to be optimistic. Insufficient gaps had been cut and German machine gun nests in buildings behind the German lines had not been dealt with and immediately opened fire on the leading waves of all four battalions as they began their advance. Their losses were heavy. Only scattered parties succeeded in getting into the German line and these found themselves under attack by bombs. With no reinforcements able to reach them because of the intensity of the machine gun fire over the open ground, they were finally obliged to try to make their way back to their jumping off trenches. The only gain of the day was the capture by the left hand battalion of the railway loop just south of the River Souchez. They managed to maintain their hold on this.

North of the river the objectives of the two Sherwood Foresters battalions were Fosse[13] 3 *bis* de Liévin and Hill 65, a commanding height overlooking the western part of Lens. Although the 46th Division Commander believed that the German voluntary withdrawal was over, the Corps Commander did not; indeed he was of the opinion that Lens would soon be abandoned. He anticipated therefore that the objectives of 139th Brigade would only be lightly held. As a result only one company from each battalion was committed to the attack. It was quickly clear that this had been a serious miscalculation. The 6th Sherwoods came under heavy fire on reaching the Fosse and were then counterattacked by enemy bombers leaving them with only one isolated house and a row of cottages in no man's land in their possession. Their sister Battalion captured the western edge of Hill 65 before they were counterattacked by superior numbers emerging from well concealed dugouts and other vantage points. The few that were able extricated themselves and got back to their starting points. In the light of the failure of the attack south of the river it was decided that capture of the Fosse and Hill 65 would make little difference to the overall situation. Plans to renew 46th Division's attempts to take them were therefore cancelled.[14]

The Second Battle of the Scarpe had been launched with little expectation that it would achieve any sort of breakthrough. Its objectives had been deliberately limited in recognition of this. It had been fought in the context of a growing realisation that the Nivelle offensive had largely failed to live up to its advanced billing. With these considerations in mind and recognising that the possibility of a breakthrough was by now decreasingly likely on the British front, the only really viable option had been an offensive with limited objectives designed to improve the British position in certain places in preparation for a later attempt to break through to Cambrai, but in the short term to keep the Germans in place. With even these limited objectives, the outcome of the battle was nevertheless a great disappointment and its cost in casualties very high.

---

12   Douglas Jerrold, ibid, pp. 227-37 passim.
13   'Pit' in the coalmine sense.
14   OH, ibid, pp. 404-6.

The Battle of Arleux: 28-29 April 1917

With Second Scarpe having run its unsatisfactory course the question confronting Field Marshal Haig was what to do next. The question would have to be resolved in the context of the perceived need to continue to exert pressure on the Germans. There now seemed to be little prospect of a French breakthrough and the hope that a subsequent allied advance north past Cambrai towards Charleroi and Liège would achieve Haig's main ambition of clearing the Belgian coast by forcing the Germans in that area to withdraw to avoid being cut off. Haig was also aware that Nivelle's position as French Commander in Chief was coming under serious threat. Haig had inferred from meetings with French government ministers that not only was Nivelle's replacement by Pétain almost inevitable, but pressure was growing that Nivelle's offensive should be brought to a halt as soon as possible, mainly to avoid further casualties. Although Haig had, in the early days of their relationship, sought assurances from Nivelle that if his offensive had not achieved the planned breakthrough in 48 hours, it would be suspended in favour of Haig's plan to clear the Belgian coast by means of an offensive out of the Ypres Salient, he was now alarmed that he would be called on to implement his plan when his armies had been exhausted in support of a French offensive that had suddenly been stopped. Haig now considered it would be better if the French offensive were to continue in the hope of achieving the planned breakthrough and a subsequent advance into Belgium.

Haig explained his reasoning to General Nivelle in a private meeting with him on 24 April. He warned Nivelle that Prime Minister Lloyd George had been told by the French government that unless there had been a distinct success in the early days of the Nivelle offensive, they intended to stop it. Haig then returned to the submarine threat to Britain and the importance of clearing the Belgian ports before the end of the summer. This would have to be done either indirectly through the Nivelle offensive or by a new offensive from the Ypres Salient. Haig said he was prepared to continue to give full backing to the Nivelle offensive option by making every effort to break through the Hindenburg Line and capture Cambrai, but an essential requisite to this was continuing action by the French Army. He sought and received Nivelle's assurance that neither he nor his Government had any intention of stopping the offensive. Nivelle then described his immediate plans for its continuation. Prudently Haig carried on making his own plans for the Ypres Salient option.[1]

Haig had also decided on the future course of action he would order in support of Nivelle. On 26 April the Commanders of the three armies involved were told that he would fully support the French as long as the latter's offensive continued. He would only fully turn his attention to the Flanders option if and when the French offensive were stopped. On or about 3 May the British offensive would be resumed with all three armies fully engaged. Beforehand, on 28 April, there would be what was described as a secondary operation in which the First Army would capture the villages of Oppy and Arleux (which had been dropped from their objectives on 23 April, through lack of time for preparation caused by the bad weather), and the Third Army, the village of Roeux and Greenland Hill, still frustratingly in enemy hands despite the efforts that had been made against them. In addition VI Corps left flank, south of the Scarpe, would be brought up into line. A major problem for the operations of 28 April and 3 May was that they would have to be largely carried out by tired and

---

1   Sheffield and Bourne (eds.), *Douglas Haig: War Diaries and Letters, 1914-1918*, pp. 286-8.

depleted units, as there could be no question of bringing fresh divisions down from the Second Army in Flanders while the possibility, indeed probability, remained that there might soon be the need for an offensive there requiring those divisions.[2]

Preparations by the artillery for the 'secondary' operation had been put in hand as soon as the Second Battle of the Scarpe had come to an end. The First Army had focused on wire cutting; the Third Army artillery plan was more wide-ranging encompassing counter battery fire, harassing night time fire and gas bombardments. The enemy railway sidings at Brebières, three miles southwest of Douai, were targeted by heavy rail-mounted guns brought up for the purpose to Railway Triangle. Despite the attentions of the British artillery, the German guns were nevertheless able to unleash an intense bombardment astride the Monchy-Pelves road at the junction of the 3rd and 12th Divisions at 2100 on 27 April. The follow up attack was satisfactorily dealt with by 3rd Division 76 Brigade and 12th Division 35 Brigade.[3]

Zero Hour for all the units involved in the Battle of Arleux was 0425 on 28 April. South of the River Scarpe, 35 Brigade of 12th Division had the task of capturing the northern portions of Bayonet and Rifle trenches. A second objective was to capture and consolidate a line running north to south through Pelves Mill. The ultimate aim was to secure the northern flank of the Monchy salient. The main obstacle to the achievement of these objectives was that likely to be presented by enfilade fire from Roeux until that village could be taken and secured. The 35 Brigade attacked with 7th Norfolks on the right and 5th R Berks on the left. Their joint objective was the two trenches. Two companies of the Norfolks advanced to capture Rifle trench. It soon became apparent that the trench had hardly been touched by the artillery and the attackers were subjected to heavy and accurate machine gun fire from the trench itself which virtually annihilated their left hand company. Neither the two leading companies, nor the remaining two following up, succeeded in reaching the enemy lines. By contrast, 5th R Berks, assisted by an effective creeping barrage, quickly took their share of the objective without difficulty, occupying the whole of Bayonet trench up to the Scarpe and 150 yards of Rifle trench. Consolidation was put in hand. The 7th Suffolks, passing through 5th R Berks with orders to take the second objective, were however met and stopped by heavy machine gun fire. Despite two gallant attempts they could not get on. Further attempts to achieve the outstanding objectives on that day and the three days following, notably a night attack by 9th Essex Regiment, which had been in reserve on the first day, all failed.[4]

North of 12th Division, XVII Corps attacked along the full length of their front using 34th Division on the right and 37th Division on the left. Their joint objective was to reach a line running roughly south-north from the River Scarpe just south of Roeux to the junction of the Plouvain-Gavrelle and Fampoux-Fresnes roads and thence to follow the former road to the Corps junction with XIII Corps. To achieve this objective called for an advance of no more than half a mile at any point, and much less in some places, but it nevertheless presented a major challenge for the two severely depleted divisions. The 34th Division had the daunting task of advancing through Roeux village to the Gavrelle-Roeux road. The presence of the village buildings, some sheltering enemy machine guns, complicated the artillery fire plan of the creeping barrage and the infantry's task in keeping up with it. The divisional attack would be on a two brigade front with 101 Brigade on the right using all four of its infantry battalions from the outset. These were 15th R Scots, 10th Lincolns and 11th Suffolks each reinforced by one or two companies of 16th R Scots, whose main task would be to mop up the village buildings. The Brigade would advance on a broad front between the River Scarpe and the Arras-Douai Railway.[5]

On the right of the Brigade line, 15th R Scots had to advance through Roeux wood to the village.

---

2   OH, 1917 Vol.1, pp. 411-2.
3   Ibid., pp. 412-3.
4   TNA WO 95/1850: 5th Royal Berkshire Regiment War Diary: TNA WO 95/1853: 7th Norfolk Regiment War Diary.
5   OH, op. cit., pp. 414-5.

They were almost immediately held up by machine guns, which waited until the main assault and the moppers up had passed, before firing into their rear. Casualties were heavy. Some members of the leading waves had succeeded in passing right through the village, had reached their objective and begun to dig in. But they were heavily counterattacked and were either killed or captured when they ran out of ammunition. At 1000 the enemy counterattack penetrated the Brigade's defences around Mount Pleasant wood. They were driven out by 20th Northumberlands, 102 Brigade, on attachment as reserve battalion to 101 Brigade.[6]

The problems of the centre battalion in the attack, the 10th Lincolns (the 'Grimsby Chums'), began even before Zero Hour. Having suffered heavy losses earlier in the month, they had had virtually no time to absorb and train the replacement drafts which consisted largely of inexperienced junior officers and minimally trained conscripts. Because their orders for the assault did not call for them to advance straight ahead but at an angle to their own trenches – a challenge for even experienced troops to accomplish in pitch darkness without losing direction – it was decided that the troops should form up silently in the open 10 minutes ahead of Zero. Unfortunately the necessary silence was not achieved, the Germans were alerted and the assembling Lincolns came under fire from trench mortars, 77mm guns and machine guns. Despite this, the assaulting waves began their advance on time. They were soon in trouble from machine gun fire taking them in enfilade from positions apparently in Roeux Château and in a house situated along the road to the Chemical Works. It was evident that Clip trench, running parallel to, and to the west of, the Chemical Works road was strongly held by the enemy, as were houses around the village cemetery. The Battalion's losses were severe and included a high proportion of dead. The nearest any Lincolns got to Clip trench was about 20 yards away where a dozen men took shelter in Corona trench which ran at right angles towards Clip trench. A further 20 men were in a half-dug enemy trench to the south, with others clustered in shell holes nearby.

About an hour after Zero the enemy advanced in strength to surround the men in shell holes. About 30 of these, nearly all wounded, surrendered. Those who tried to make it back to their own trenches were shot down. The acting Battalion CO tried to rally his remaining men and concentrate them at the junction of Corona and Ceylon trenches where a junior officer and a small number of men were already established. Lewis guns and Stokes mortars were also sent up and brought into action. These began to inflict serious losses on the enemy sheltering in houses north of the cemetery. Their position was however vulnerable to enemy fire and some of their guns were put out of action. A remnant of 40 Lincolns withdrew westwards along Ceylon trench, from where contact was established with 11th Suffolks on their left. Although the Lincolns were not in touch with 20th Northumberlands on their right they were aware they were in Cusp trench.

At 0800, after shelling Mount Pleasant wood, the Germans launched a counterattack from dead ground near Roeux with the wood as their apparent objective. They advanced under the protection of a machine gun barrage. The attack was met by Lewis gun and machine gun fire from both the Lincolns and the Northumberlands in their respective trenches. Significant damage was inflicted on both flanks of the enemy advance but in the centre more than 200 of them reached and entered the British lines at Care and Colne trenches and Mount Pleasant wood; a few of them even reached Ceylon trench near its junction with Colne. The two British battalions quickly organised bombing parties, which forced the enemy troops not killed to retire hastily to the wood. Some of those who were not cut down by Lewis gun fire were eventually forced to surrender. The situation was completely restored by 1230. The Lincolns then made haste to strengthen their hold on Ceylon trench by pushing forward all the troops that could be found. With a few more straggling back from no man's land after dark, the garrison eventually numbered about 70.

There was no more significant fighting that day or on the two that followed before the 10th Lincolns were relieved. The action was described in the Battalion's Great War history as the most

6   TNA WO 95/2457/5: 15th Royal Scots War Diary.

disastrous ever fought by it. Bearing in mind their terrible losses on the first day of the Battle of the Somme that is saying a great deal. On 28 April they went into action with 18 officers and 626 other ranks. Of these 13 officers and 420 other ranks became casualties, or 67 percent of those engaged. An unusually high proportion of the total casualties, 204, were killed.[7]

On the left of 101 Brigade's assault were 11th Suffolks. They followed their barrage over the top at Zero Hour. On the line of their intended advance were Roeux Château and the Chemical Works. These were to prove unattainable objectives as the Battalion were soon held up and then driven back by very heavy machine gun fire emanating from a trench which had, according to the War Diary, been entirely missed by the barrage. Those that managed to get back unscathed formed up in the trenches from which they had set off. There they were organised for defence against an enemy counterattack. As has already been noted this was duly launched from Roeux and made inroads into Mount Pleasant wood and part of Ceylon trench. Communication was lost between the front line and Battalion HQ, but when the acting CO went forward he found that the Suffolk line was still intact and they had managed to clear the enemy out of Ceylon trench. They were also in retreat from Mount Pleasant wood.

At 2200 that night the Suffolks temporarily moved out of the front line trenches to enable the heavy artillery to bombard the Chemical Works in preparation for a night assault on the complex by 102 Brigade. They returned to the front line trenches at midnight. They were relieved two nights later. Their involvement in the Battle of Arleux had resulted in casualties of 50 percent for no discernible gain.[8]

The last of 101 Brigade's infantry battalions, 16th R Scots, were to act as moppers up for the other three battalions. They were split among them on a company basis, with two going to 15th R Scots and one each to 10th Lincolns and 11th Suffolks. All companies left their jumping off trenches at Zero Hour and soon came under heavy machine gun and rifle fire from Roeux, Mount Pleasant wood and the Chemical Works. The two companies following the Suffolks and Lincolns were quickly forced to stop. For the most part they retired to their jumping off trenches. On the right they followed 15th R Scots into and through Roeux but were later compelled to withdraw for fear of being cut off. At 0730 the enemy attacked the British line in front of Mount Pleasant wood and achieved a temporary lodgement there until driven out by a bombing attack. The rest of 16th R Scots' day passed under artillery and sniping exchanges. They were relieved two nights later. Their casualties were 10 officers and 230 ORs.[9]

To the left of 101 Brigade were 103 Brigade, whose infantry component consisted of four battalions of Northumberland Fusiliers, the 24th, 25th, 26th and 27th, otherwise known as the Tyneside Irish. The relatively fresher 24th and 25th Battalions, on respectively the right and left, would lead the assault with two companies each in the front line with the task of going straight through to the objective. The remaining companies were to follow behind and mop up as required. In support, following closely behind the assaulting battalions, apportioning two of their companies to each, would be the 27th Battalion. Their role would be to support the attack if and when required, and take over mopping up from the attacking battalions. Most of the two companies assigned to 24th Northumberlands were to pay particular attention to mopping up houses and other buildings immediately north of the railway and the railway embankment itself where, if necessary, a defensive flank should be formed on what was the Brigade's right flank.

At Zero Hour the assaulting battalions and the supporting 27th Battalion began their advance and were very quickly out of touch with Brigade HQ, a situation which was to last for some time. Only later could it be established that the 24th Battalion, with their share of the 27th, had been brought to a complete halt by enemy machine gun and rifle fire from the houses north of the railway.

7   Peter Bryant, *Grimsby Chums*, pp. 112-3.
8   TNA WO 95/2458/3: 11th Suffolk Regiment War Diary.
9   TNA WO 95/2458/1: 16th Royal Scots War Diary.

Those members of the two battalions who had succeeded in crossing the Roeux-Gavrelle road were unable to get messages back to Brigade HQ because the road and the exposed areas on either side of it offered no protection from enemy fire to runners trying to cross. On the left the 25th Battalion had the same difficulty in maintaining contact with HQ, but did succeed in getting to within 250 yards of their objective, Cupid trench, despite heavy machine gun fire from an unregistered enemy trench, the Chemical Works and other buildings. Their relative and limited success was at the expense of exposing both flanks, with gaps of approximately 200 yards between them and the railway on the right, and 37th Division on the left. Their situation was also unsatisfactory in that most of the troops that had got furthest forward were scattered in shell holes between the Roeux-Gavrelle road and their final objective where they were under heavy enfilade fire from the right, and also frontal fire. The gap between them and 37th Division 112 Brigade, who were in Cuthbert trench, was subsequently closed by 25th Battalion's share of 27th Battalion, who took possession of the upper reach of Cash trench. During the night contact was also re-established with 24th Battalion by way of Cash trench. In an effort to surround the Fusiliers sheltering in shell holes, the enemy infiltrated men in groups of two or three under cover of darkness. With very few officers left to provide leadership many of the troops under this threat of being cut off, fell back to their original front line.[10]

At Zero Hour 102 Brigade, the infantry component of which consisted of the four Tyneside Scottish battalions (20th, 21st, 22nd and 23rd Northumberland Fusiliers), were in divisional reserve. At 1540 they received orders to prepare to attack the Chemical Works and Roeux starting off from the line of the railway and advancing south. At 1915 these orders were modified so that the attack on the Chemical Works would be launched from Ceylon and Cawdor trenches in an easterly direction. In accordance with these orders 23rd Battalion on the right and south of the railway and 22nd Battalion on the left and north of the railway were to attack at 0300 on 29th. Unfortunately 23rd Battalion only received their final orders at 0030. They entailed assembling in Ceylon trench, which meant that the companies could not be ready until 0400. An order to postpone Zero Hour to this later hour did not reach 22nd Battalion until too late. They therefore began their assault at 0300 from their assembly point of Cawdor trench. Within 100 yards they came under heavy machine gun and rifle fire which was fortunately largely aimed too high and did not prevent them from driving a strong party of enemy out of Calabar trench. Their advance continued until the forward waves found themselves among houses and assailed by machine gun fire from the northeast and south. The only cover readily available was the northern portion of Calabar trench where there was only room for one company. The remainder withdrew to Cam trench and thence back to Cawdor trench.

The 23rd Battalion attacked at the revised Zero of 0400. They were faced with an enemy in occupation of houses, a trench and a number of advanced posts. There were several machine guns situated in and around the buildings. The attackers came under heavy and increasing fire as soon as they left their assembly trench. The two companies on the left lost nearly all their officers and 50 percent of their men. The right hand company however managed to advance along Corona trench driving the enemy before them. But once they ran out of trench and tried to continue to advance they came under intense machine gun fire and were ordered to withdraw along Corona trench. Their experience had left the Battalion exhausted and dispirited at their lack of progress at the cost of so many casualties. By contrast although 22nd Battalion had made little more progress than their neighbours, the casualties they had suffered were relatively light at around 50. This was largely due to the configuration of the ground, which had caused the enemy to fire high. The Chemical Works remained in enemy hands.[11]

The 37th Division, on the left of XVII Corps line, decided to use all three brigades in their

---

10   TNA WO 95/2464: 103 Brigade War Diary; TNA WO 95/2466/4: 24th Northumberland Fusiliers (NF) War Diary; TNA WO 95/2467/1: 25th (NF) War Diary; TNA WO 95/2467/3: 27th NF War Diary.

11   TNA WO 95/2460: 102 Brigade War Diary; TNA WO 95/2463/1: 22nd NF War Diary; TNA WO 95/2463/2: 23rd NF War Diary.

initial assault. From the right these were the 112, 63 and 111. At this stage the brigades were down to an infantry strength of around 800 to 900. Battalions therefore were probably only a little over 200 strong. The 112 Brigade led with 10th Loyals and 6th Bedfords in the front line. In support of the former were 8th East Lancs and of the latter 11th Warwicks. The advance began in bad visibility caused by a combination of ground mist and dust and smoke arising from the creeping barrage. It may have been this that led the assaulting waves to believe that they had reached Cuthbert trench, only just short of their objective and about 500 yards from their starting point, when in fact they had only reached a newly dug trench about 200 yards away from it. Their officer losses may also have contributed to the confusion. It is, in any case, unlikely that the advance would have made much more ground because the assaulting troops were coming under heavy enfilade fire from the Chemical Works, which effectively prevented any further forward movement. They dug in just to the west of what they believed to be Cuthbert trench, and formed a defensive flank in a communication trench facing the Chemical Works.[12]

To 112 Brigade's left, 63 Brigade assaulted with two battalions in line. On the right were 8th SLI with half of 4th Middlesex in support. On the left were 8th Lincolns with 10th York and Lancs in support. The remaining half of 4th Middlesex were in brigade reserve. Initially the two assaulting battalions and the supporting Middlesex companies made remarkable progress, possibly partially because they bore rather to the left of their intended direction of attack. The 8th SLI believed they advanced due east to Cuthbert trench where they mopped up and consolidated. It is more probable that they mistook Whip trench for Cuthbert Trench, which, apart from a few of their number, they missed by having veered left. The majority of the troops of the attacking battalions appear to have moved on, passing round the south end of Hollow copse and actually crossing the front trench of the Fresnes village defensive system, nearly reaching Railway copse. At this point, realising they were too far advanced, parties of all battalions worked their way back to Whip trench and a position about 300 yards east of Cuthbert trench where they dug in and were to remain throughout the day.

Had the attackers realised what they had achieved and had reserves been immediately available to exploit the situation, it might have been possible to capture Fresnes or even outflank the German defences on Greenland Hill. But the fog of war ensured the opportunity was not appreciated. Even had it been there was in any case an absence of adequate reserves and the attackers were much weakened, too weak to have exploited the situation without substantial reinforcement, particularly against defenders growing in strength.[13]

After dark the two companies of 4th Middlesex in reserve were ordered forward to reconnoitre. They soon came under heavy machine gun fire and were forced to dig in in front of the enemy trench from which the machine guns were operating. During the course of the night they were withdrawn to Cuba trench where they were subsequently relieved.

On the left of the 37th Division were 111 Brigade with 13th RF on the right and 13th RB on the left. In support were 10th RF and in reserve, 13th KRRC. The Brigade had the relatively straightforward task of advancing their line up to a maximum of 800 yards to the Plouvain-Gavrelle road north of its junction with the Fampoux-Fresnes road. This would bring them into line with a company of 9th North Staffordshire Regiment (North Staffs), a Pioneer Battalion, which had been put at the disposal of 111 Brigade. They were holding the advanced front on the left and a trench connecting the two roads. The 13th RF reached their objective without great difficulty and were beginning to consolidate it when a mixed body of troops from 63 Brigade, heading northeast towards Square Wood swept through, clearly having lost direction. A large number of Fusiliers joined them despite the attempts of some of their officers to stop them. It was only with the greatest difficulty that

---

12   TNA WO 95/2536: 112 Brigade War Diary.

13   OH, op.cit., p. 417. TNA WO 95/2528: 63 Brigade and 4 Middlesex Regiment War Diaries; TNA WO 95/2529: 8th Lincolnshire Regiment, 8th Somerset Light Infantry and 10th York and Lancaster Regiment War Diaries.

around 150 of them were later persuaded to turn back after about 400 yards to resume consolidating their position. The 13th RB also had little difficulty in reaching their objective and establishing contact with 9th North Staffs on the left. Perhaps because of their following 63 Brigade there was no immediate sign of 13th RF, obliging 13th RB to protect their open flank with a Lewis gun. The Battalion came under fire from their right rear as Greenland Hill was still in enemy possession. The same problem prevented the Battalion from making effective use of a newly discovered trench running in front of the objective.

Even though the success of 111 Brigade was of very modest proportions it was the only part of the Third Army front where the attack of 28 April had achieved anything notable. But even this was largely nullified when the 9th Division, which had relieved the 37th on the night of 29 April, decided, after some limited fighting, to abandon a stretch of the Plouvain-Gavrelle road north of the crossroads, leaving little to show for the efforts of 37th Division despite the heavy casualties suffered.[14]

The First Army part in the Battle of Arleux would involve 63rd (Royal Naval) and 2nd Divisions of XIII Corps and the Canadian Corps 1st and 2nd Divisions. XIII Corps were given the task of capturing the village of Oppy and Canadian Corps the village of Arleux. The former task would also involve the taking of the part of the Oppy Line still in German hands. The 63rd Division's role was to protect the right flank of 2nd Division, which would carry out the attack on Oppy, by forming a defensive flank. This was by no means a straightforward challenge as the salient that had been created by the capture of Gavrelle meant that two battalions would have to advance in echelon, one debouching from the east of the village and advancing 750 yards north of the Fresnes road with its right flank on the road; and the other, having formed up west of the Oppy Line, further to the north, to advance eastward until it came up into line with the first battalion. This meant that the two advances could not offer mutual support and would essentially be two separate operations. Because they were advancing out of a salient, 190 Brigade's 2nd Royal Marines could not progress far without exposing their flanks and so were dependent on those units either side of them making good progress. Until this was seen to be happening the Battalion focused its efforts on securing the ridge northeast of Gavrelle and, in particular, the ruins of Gavrelle windmill with its dominant position. This objective was successfully achieved and a platoon put in place to resist the inevitable enemy attempts to recapture the position. Three times during the course of the rest of the day the enemy launched determined counterattacks, all of which were successfully beaten off. The rest of the Battalion however had suffered heavy losses and were forced to withdraw back to the eastern edge of Gavrelle, beginning as darkness fell.

The northern attack was entrusted to 190 Brigade's 1st Royal Marines. Starting from assembly points west of the Oppy Line and on the right of 2nd Division, their task was to advance eastward and overrun a number of German-held trenches. Unfortunately for them they were held up by uncut German wire. Those that succeeded in getting into the front German trench were mainly killed by enfilade fire from an untaken enemy strong point on the railway to their right. The troops who were supposed to have dealt with it had probably all been killed in the attempt. At 0850 the supporting 1st HAC mounted a company strength attack on the strong point which was successful. But by the time it was taken the remnants of 1st Marines (and the 2nd Division on their left) had fallen back under the heavy enemy pressure. When the enemy counterattacked at around 1000 they quickly re-entered their front trench. They then bombed 1st HAC out of the strong point driving them back for nearly 100 yards before they could be stopped. By noon it was clear that the attack had completely failed; the enemy had even taken 50 yards of the British front line.[15]

The failure of 1st Royal Marines was bad news for 2nd Division whose task was to capture Oppy village and the densely wired part of the Oppy Line still remaining in enemy hands. Between these

---

14   OH, op. cit., pp. 418-9. TNA WO 95/2532/2: 13th Royal Fusiliers War Diary; TNA WO 95/2534: 13th Rifle Brigade War Diary.

15   Douglas Jerrold, *The Royal Naval Division*, pp. 239-40.

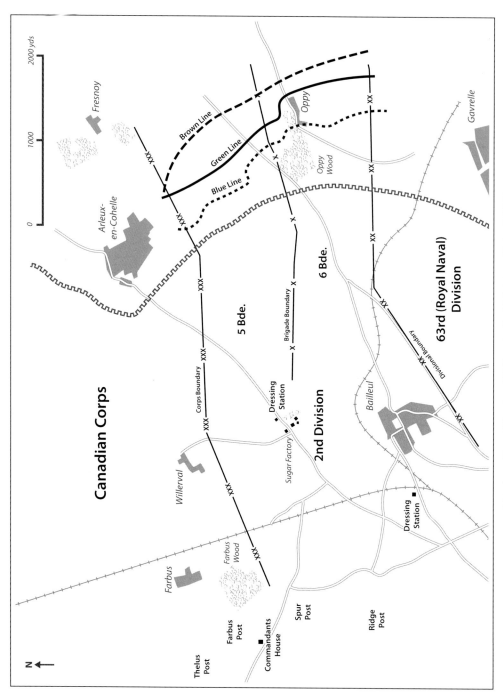

Attack on Oppy Wood and Village by 2nd Division, 28 April 1917.

two formidable challenges lay Oppy Wood that by now was a mass of fallen trees, the last thing that was needed by attackers wanting a clear run at the village. A further problem of concern to the GOC 2nd Division was that his command could only muster about 3,500 rifles, only just over half the number a fully manned division might expect to field. The all regular 2nd Division had been one of the first formations to arrive in France in August 1914 and since then had taken part in most of the major actions involving the BEF. By the time of the Battle of Arras its all regular composition had been diluted by the loss of 4 (Guards) Brigade and the arrival of 99 Brigade, three of whose battalions were New Army formations. Half of the battalions in the original 5 and 6 Brigades had also by now been replaced by New Army formations. The Division would remain on the Western Front for the rest of the war.

The attack would initially involve 6 Brigade on the right and 5 Brigade on the left. For 6 Brigade 13th Essex would assault on the right and 17th Middlesex on the left. As the other two battalions, 1st King's and 2nd South Staffs were given a mopping up role, direct support would be provided by 99 Brigade's 1st KRRC on attachment. When it became clear that all this would consist of would be one company about 120 strong, another company, this time from 1st R Berks of 99 Brigade, were attached to 6 Brigade. Even this only amounted to eight officers and 60 ORs. When further troops were later needed in 6 Brigade's attempts to clear Oppy village, 99 Brigade were once again called upon, this time in the shape of 23rd Royal Fusiliers.

At Zero Hour the barrage, targeting the German front line, opened and the infantry advance began. At first all seemed to go well. The 13th Essex reached the German second line due south of Oppy even though their right was held up by uncut wire. However the failure of 188 Brigade on their right made it necessary for them to deploy a company to form a defensive flank. The 17th Middlesex succeeded in getting through Oppy Wood with 13th Essex on their right. But it soon became clear that the Germans were determined not to lose the village. Both battalions were coming under pressure from an enemy seeking to exploit their exposed flanks. It was around 12 noon that 23rd RF received their orders to move forward and clear Oppy village. But by the time they were ready to act on these orders the enemy pressure, especially on the Brigade's right flank, had forced them back to the former German front line. In these changed circumstances 23rd RF were ordered to establish posts in Oppy Wood. By mid afternoon it was clear that the enemy still held a significant stretch of the Oppy Line and that 6 Brigade were on the defensive. In the evening the former German front line was evacuated. The Brigade handed over command of the sector to the Commander of 99 Brigade, which would be responsible for resuming the attack at a time to be determined early the following morning.[16]

The 5 Brigade attacked with two battalions leading, 2nd HLI on the right and 2nd Ox & Bucks LI on the left. The 17th RF were used as carriers. By around 09h00 2nd HLI were reported as being at the sunken Oppy-Arleux road. But owing to heavy enemy artillery, machine gun and *minenwerfer* fire they were forced to retreat to the former German front line. 2nd Ox & Bucks LI had also reached the sunken road, but with heavy losses from the intense enemy fire that hit them when they reached the German wire, which had not been thoroughly cut, although there were gaps. When they lost contact with 2nd HLI on their right and 6 Brigade were forced back from Oppy Wood, the consequent vulnerability of their right flank forced them too to fall back. In contrast to the problems on their right the Battalion had advanced sufficiently on their left to provide cover to the Canadians as they sought to capture Arleux. The inevitable enemy counterattacks were satisfactorily dealt with and the active sniping and machine gun fire coming from Oppy village and wood were targeted by heavy artillery.

With the results of the fighting of 28 April having been at best unsatisfactory for XIII Corps' two divisions, orders were issued that evening for a further attempt to be made to capture that part of the Oppy Line still in enemy hands. Zero Hour would be at 0400 the following morning with

---

16   OH, op. cit., pp. 419-20. TNA WO 95/1356: 6 Brigade War Diary.

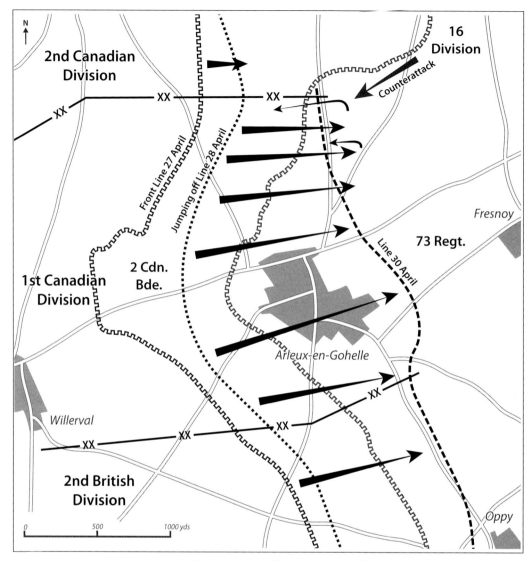

Capture of Arleux by Canadian Corps, 28 April 1917.

preparatory bombardments being fired during the night. Both seriously depleted divisions would be involved. Two battalions of the 63rd, the 4th Bedfords and 7th RF, were made into a composite unit and attached to 188 Brigade for the attack. The 14th Worcesters, a pioneer battalion given an infantry role, were put in charge of defending a stretch of line south of Gavrelle. For 2nd Division, 6 Brigade were relieved by the 99th. Despite the immense bravery and determination shown by the attacking troops, matched by that displayed by the enemy, the results were disappointing with virtually no success to show from the set attack. The 188 Brigade did reach their objective but were almost immediately driven back. The attack of 22nd RF and 1st R Berks of 99 Brigade was not much more successful and certainly not helped by the loss of two of their three forward small arms ammunition and grenade dumps to some very accurate, or fortuitous, enemy shelling. As the two battalions began their advance at 0400 the RF on the right found themselves confronted by uncut wire, which initially stopped them in their tracks. Two parties of roughly platoon strength did eventually find gaps that enabled them to fight their way into the enemy trench. There the right hand party were organised into two groups that bombed along the trench northward and southward. The latter group got 400 yards beyond the divisional boundary before it made contact with men of the 63rd Division who were bombing northward having captured the troublesome strong point on the railway. Reinforced by two companies of 99 Brigade's 23rd RF, who reached them along the railway, the group successfully cleared the trenches of enemy up to a point 200 yards from the southwest corner of Oppy Wood. North of this point up to the Willerval-Oppy road the enemy remained in possession.[17]

The R Berks on the left found there to be plenty of gaps in the wire facing them and, within 15 minutes, had taken the enemy trench. They moved forward into Oppy Wood and captured three machine guns that they turned to some effect onto their previous owners. They were soon however being subjected to a series of counterattacks which became increasingly difficult to fight off as their supplies of ammunition and particularly bombs ran low and could not be replenished. The lack of cover on their right, due to the misfortune of 22nd RF, and the presence of a large gap between them and 5 Brigade on their left, seemed to offer them little choice but to retire. As they did so they came across a cache of German grenades, rearmed themselves, turned round and once more drove the Germans back. But it could not last as the further forward they got, the more exposed they became. Their losses were mounting and they were running out of ammunition. They retired to the old British front line down to less than half their starting strength.[18]

The fact that three Victoria Crosses were earned during the actions described above is testimony to the ferocity and stubbornness of the fighting despite the exhaustion and depletion of the units involved. Although some of the actions fought enjoyed some modest success the fact remained that Oppy village and a reduced part of the Oppy Line remained in enemy hands, an outcome for XIII Corps that was little recompense for the heavy losses that had been suffered.

The First Army objective of capturing the Arleux Loop trenches and the village of Arleux, to reach a line approximately half way between that village and Fresnoy 1,000 yards away, was assigned mainly to the Canadian Corps 1st Division. Their 2 Brigade would carry out the attack, supported by 1 Brigade. A battalion of the 2nd Division would also advance to protect and cover 2 Brigade's left flank. The total frontage of the attack would measure 2,600 yards divided from right to left between 8th, 10th and 5th Battalions of 1st Division and 25th Battalion of 2nd Division. The German defences, featuring an unusually large number of machine guns, formed a protective salient around Arleux.

The preliminary bombardment was fired along the whole Canadian front in an apparently successful attempt to deceive the enemy into thinking that a general attack was imminent, thereby inducing them to spread their response more widely and thinly than necessary. Nevertheless their resistance to the attack was strenuous with heavy machine gun and rifle fire. But the attack was pressed home with considerable vigour. On the right, 8th Battalion were hit by heavy machine gun fire as they breasted a slight rise in front of Arleux. The fire came from the village itself and woods to the south. The two flanking companies nevertheless reached their objective on schedule, that on the right establishing contact with 2nd Ox and Bucks LI. They also set up a strong point in time to break up a counterattack against their British 2nd Division neighbours. The centre company was less fortunate initially as all its officers became casualties. Despite repeated efforts to get forward it was not until they were reinforced by battalion reserves that they were able to complete clearance of their segment of the village and reach their objective.

In the centre of 2 Brigade's front, 10th Battalion were at first held up by two machine guns concealed near their wire. Once they were dealt with by use of bombs, the Battalion found themselves in severe house to house fighting as they attempted to clear their way through the northern outskirts of Arleux advancing astride the road to Drocourt. Despite this and their right being held up for a time

---

17   Ibid., pp. 421-2
18   Ian Cull, *The China Dragon's Tales*, pp. 70-1.

by fire from the village they cleared out the enemy and reached their objective only three minutes late.

On the Brigade's left, 5th Battalion's right and centre companies overcame spirited resistance to take the enemy's front trench and then cross open ground to link up with 10th Battalion. Their left hand company found making progress much more difficult when they came up against uncut wire and were subjected to heavy enfilade machine gun fire that cost them heavily and forced them to retire to the German front trench and there form a defensive flank, clearly well short of their objective. The enemy's ability to lay down this enfilade fire was because the 2nd Canadian Division 25th Battalion, who should have advanced in tandem with, and on the left of, 5th Battalion, had mistaken a trench only 300 yards from their start line as their final objective, and stopped. Had they continued their advance for the necessary further 600 yards to their objective they might well have been in a position to deal with the machine gun threat to 5th Battalion. In the event it was dealt with by the arrival of 5th Battalion's support company who bombed up a trench from the right and dealt with the trouble. It was then possible for the survivors to resume their advance towards the sunken Arleux-Méricourt track just north of Arleux. It would however be the afternoon of the following day before the left of 5th and all of 25th Battalions resumed their advance and reached their objectives, which had been gained by the rest of 2 Brigade by 0600 on the 28th. Unusually for them the Germans decided against mounting any counterattacks seeking to reverse this modest allied success. Their reckoning was that as long as their Fresnoy Line, about 400 hundred yards beyond the new Canadian front line, remained firmly in their hands, it made little sense to sacrifice men in attempting to regain the Arleux Loop trench.[19]

It is difficult not to agree with the British Official History's assessment that the capture of Arleux represented the only tangible success of the operations of 28-29 April.

---

19   OH op. cit., pp. 422-4. Col G W L Nicholson, *Canadian Expeditionary Force 1914-19*, pp. 270-2. WO 95/1049.

Part V

Third Battle of the Scarpe:
Second Battle of Bullecourt

16

The Third Battle of the Scarpe: 3-4 May 1917

The second phase of the plan of action that Field Marshal Haig had outlined to the three Army commanders concerned, at his meeting with them on 26 April, would take place in circumstances even less propitious than those obtaining when it had first been disclosed. Not only had the first phase, the Battle of Arleux, largely been a failure – an inauspicious precursor on which to build – but there was increasing uncertainty about French commitment to the continuation of the Nivelle offensive and indeed their physical and military capacity to achieve their objectives even if the commitment remained. On the same day as the meeting with his generals, Haig travelled to Paris for meetings at their request with the French Prime Minister and the Minister of War. From these Haig had received clear indications that General Nivelle's days as French Commander in Chief were numbered and his almost certain successor would be the Central Army Group Commander, General Philippe Pétain. War Minister Paul Painlevé had always had doubts about Nivelle's strategy. By this time, its evident failure had left him bitterly regretting that he had not prevented it from being implemented. He was also a great admirer of Pétain. On 30 April, Haig's worst fears moved a step nearer when Pétain was appointed Chief of the French General Staff with powers enhanced at the expense of the Commander in Chief. For the time being Nivelle remained in place, but Haig's inference that Pétain's appointment was just a staging post on his way to replacing Nivelle as C in C was only just over two weeks away from being confirmed.

Haig's worst fears were of course that the advent of Pétain as Chief of Staff would mean the immediate cessation of French offensive operations. It was known that he had shared Painlevé's view of Nivelle's plan. (Indeed he may have been influential in the shaping of the Minister's view.) On 3 May, Haig took an early opportunity to visit Pétain. During their meeting and the intergovernmental meeting the next day Haig received full endorsement of his proposals for the immediate way forward. This included the French attacking in support of the British continuation of their Arras offensive. They would also take over part of the British line and endeavour to hold the Germans on their front and stop them moving reserves northwards.[1]

On 30 April at a further meeting with his Army commanders Haig had spelt out precisely what the continuation of the British offensive would involve in the short term, before the question of operations elsewhere would become pressing. He told them that all hope of linking up with the French at Cambrai was now gone. He now planned to reach, by the middle of the month, the line Lens, Acheville, Fresnoy, Greenland Hill, Bois du Vert and Riencourt. When this had been achieved he would consider whether to attack the Droucourt-Quéant Switch or transfer troops elsewhere, a choice of words that belied his evident determination that the next major effort of the BEF would be the Flanders operations to clear the Belgian coast. In the margins of the meeting he told General Gough in strictest secrecy that he would be appointed to command the northern half of these operations.[2]

---

1   An ironic footnote was the behaviour of Prime Minister Lloyd George who proclaimed that he had full confidence in his military advisors and would not dream of trying to interfere in the drawing up of strategy. He also confided to Haig and the CIGS that he was afraid that the French were not going to act offensively. A far cry from his attitudes earlier in the year.

2   OH 1917, Volume 1, pp. 427-30. Sheffield and Bourne (eds.), *Douglas Haig, War Diaries and Letter, 1914-1918*, pp. 287-92.

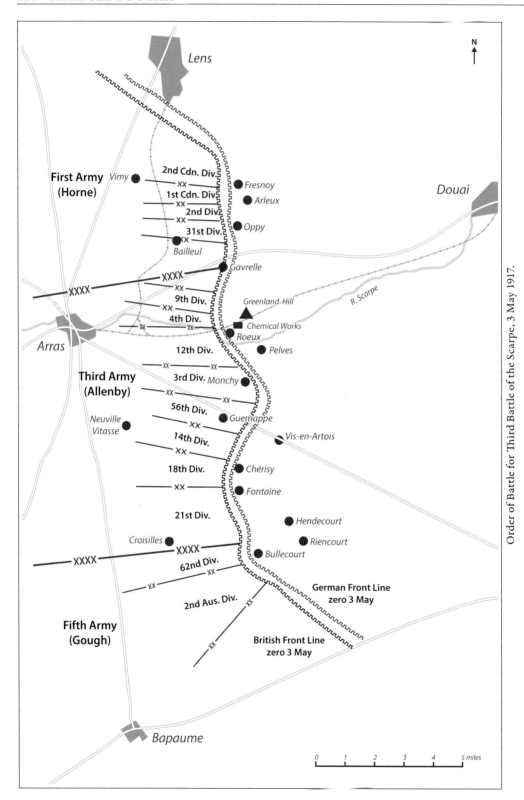

Lens

N

First Army
(Horne)

Vimy

2nd Cdn. Div.
—— xx ——
1st Cdn. Div.
—— xx ——
2nd Div.
—— xx ——
31st Div.
xx
Bailleul

Fresnoy

Arleux

Oppy

Douai

XXXX
—— xx ——
9th Div.
—— xx ——
4th Div.
xx —— xx

Gavrelle

Greenland Hill

R. Scarpe

Chemical Works
Roeux

Arras

XXXX

12th Div.
xx —— xx
3rd Div. Monchy
xx —— xx
56th Div.
—— xx ——
14th Div.
—— xx ——
18th Div.
—— xx ——

21st Div.

Pelves

Third Army
(Allenby)

Neuville
Vitasse

Guemappe

Vis-en-Artois

Chérisy

Fontaine

Hendecourt

Riencourt

Croisilles
XXXX
62nd Div.
xx —— xx

2nd Aus. Div.
xx

xx

Bullecourt

German Front Line
zero 3 May

XXXX

Fifth Army
(Gough)

British Front Line
zero 3 May

Bapaume

0   1   2   3   4   5 miles

Order of Battle for Third Battle of the Scarpe, 3 May 1917.

For the present however the priority was to achieve the objectives laid down for the middle of the month. Their achievement would begin with the Third Battle of the Scarpe and the Second Battle of Bullecourt.[3] The first issue was to settle on a Zero Hour on 3 May for the start of the battles. Haig decided that all three armies involved would need to observe the same Zero Hour as once one began to assault, the enemy would be alerted and in all likelihood lay down a barrage on the entire length of the British front line with serious consequences for the troops waiting there for a later Zero Hour. The problem was that Gough's Australians were required to assault over some open ground, for which they needed, at least initially, the cover of total darkness. They had accordingly decided on a Zero Hour of 0330. Conversely, Horne's First Army, which needed to get through Oppy wood on the way to their objective of Oppy village, required some daylight to negotiate the wood. Ideally this meant that Zero should be 0405. Allenby's Third Army would have to conform with First Army. At a meeting with Allenby and Gough, Haig decided on the compromise time for all of 0345, a decision with which none of the Army commanders was happy, although Gough was marginally less dissatisfied than the other two.[4]

The objectives of Third Army for the battle were the villages of Fontaine-lès-Croisilles, Chérisy and Pelves; St Rohart Factory, the Bois du Sart and Plouvain station. On the right of the Third Army line VII Corps would employ three divisions, the relatively fresh 21st and 18th on the right and in the centre respectively and a tired 14th (Light) on the left. The Corps share of Third Army objectives was, first, to reach a line running from the point where the River Sensée crossed the Hindenburg Line, to the River Cojeul just south of St. Rohart Factory, by way of the southeast corner of Fontaine wood and the crossroads half a mile southeast of Chérisy. A second objective, for 21st Division only, was to cross the Sensée, then capture 500 yards of the Hindenburg Line and the village of Fontaine. With the Fifth Army planning simultaneously to advance north and 21st Division's direction of advance being southeast as far as Fontaine the resultant corridor between the two would be kept under artillery fire until 21st Division were in a position to clear it with the help of tanks, hopefully starting 2 hours 40 minutes after Zero.

To accomplish these challenging objectives 21st Division used all three of their brigades from the outset. The leading role would be played by 110 Brigade on the left, who were given the task of advancing to the Sensée about 1,400 yards distant, and then capturing Fontaine. In the centre, 64 Brigade were to advance down the Hindenburg Line as far as the final objective. The 62 Brigade, on the right, would merely need to keep pace with the 64th and occupy the ground southwest of the Hindenburg Line. The dissimilar tasks assigned to the brigades complicated the timing of the creeping barrage. It was decided that it would creep very rapidly over open ground and only a third as fast when traversing woods, villages and enemy strong points. Two of the four tanks assigned to the Division were allocated to 110 Brigade, one to 64 Brigade and the fourth would be kept in divisional reserve. This proved to be purely academic as none of them was subsequently to play any significant part in the action.

The 64 Brigade's attempts to bomb down the front and support trenches of the Hindenburg Line were a complete failure. The 15th DLI led with 10th KOYLI in close support. 1st East Yorks were in brigade reserve and 9th KOYLI on carrying duties but available for use as reserves if required. No sooner had the advance begun than the enemy put down a heavy barrage that inflicted many casualties on the attackers, particularly among the officers. The DLI's left company were soon reporting that they were held up by wire filling the trench beyond the place where the enemy had positioned a block. They were ordered to bypass the obstacle by advancing in the open. When they did so they fell prey to numerous enemy snipers put in place precisely to counter such a move. The Battalion's right hand

---

3   The Second Battle of Bullecourt will be dealt with in the next chapter.
4   The Official History (pp. 431-3) describes this decision as 'unfortunate, even disastrous' for Horne and Allenby's commands and questions whether anything really serious would have resulted from a decision to allow the three armies their preferred Zero Hours. In the case of the First and Third Armies it would have been the same anyway

company reported that they had overcome the first enemy block, despite it being strongly held. But there was some doubt at Battalion HQ that this was correct as most of the company's officers had become casualties and the company was in a disorganised state. The tank, which might have been able to intervene effectively, had been slow getting forward in the pitch dark that had forced it to advance parallel to the Hindenburg Support Line in order to keep direction. When it reached a British block in the trench placed during earlier fighting, it was put out of action by an enemy trench mortar.

During the course of the day no progress was made up the Hindenburg Support line and only about 200 yards up the Front line. Even this was quickly negated when the enemy counterattacked and drove the mixed group of DLI and KOYLI back to their original positions. At 1230 the Brigade Commander told Division that the whole of 64 Brigade were very tired and fresh troops were needed to take over. Late that night he informed Division that the Brigade were back where they had started the day.[5]

As the involvement of 62 Brigade, on the Division and Corps right, was dependent on progress having been made by 64 Brigade, they passed a quiet day and relieved elements of 110 Brigade during the course of the nights of 3 and 4 May.

The 110 Brigade began the battle on 21st Division's left and were up against the greatest challenge of reaching and crossing the Sensée to take Fontaine-lès-Croisilles. The assault was led by 8th Leicesters on the right and their sister 9th Battalion on the left. The 6th Leicesters were in close support of both assaulting battalions and 7th Leicesters in brigade reserve. Fortunately for the two lead battalions the German barrage, which had opened almost simultaneously with the British one, was rather lighter than had been feared, probably because of the effectiveness of the British counter battery fire. Had it not been, the two battalions might well have suffered severely, as they had been unable to advance their jump off positions because doing so would have placed them too far in advance of 54 Brigade on their left, who were unable to move up. From the off, progress by the two lead battalions was slow because of the intensity of the enemy artillery and machine gun fire. They were not helped either by the profound darkness, serious officer losses and 54 Brigade veering right, forcing them to do the same. The tanks were also of little help, being quickly put out of action by mechanical breakdown or enemy armour piercing fire.

The 8th Leicesters lost direction rather quickly because of their enforced swing to the right. By 0630 it was apparent that their attack had failed. Their right flank was exposed by the failure of 64 Brigade's attempt to bomb up the Hindenburg Line and their left flank was halted in the sunken Héninel-Fontaine road by unremitting machine gun fire. The remainder of the Battalion had advanced scarcely 200 yards. The 9th Leicesters fared little better. No sooner had they begun their advance than they were subjected to a heavy enemy barrage, which caused serious losses, and machine gun fire from both flanks. They nevertheless pushed forward but within 30 minutes were held up in front of the strongly manned trench protecting Chérisy and Fontaine known by its German name as the *Chérisy Riegel*. The Official History suggests that about 100 men of the Battalion may have got beyond this trench where, lacking reinforcement, they were counterattacked and cut off and eventually forced to surrender. There is no reference to this in the Battalion War Diary, but it is certainly the case that 110 Brigade did list an unusually large number of men as missing following the battle. There is a reference to a captain, another officer and 30 men holding a trench with enemy to the front and either side of their position. The captain had no idea where he was and could see no friendly troops on either flank. Possibly this was the group referred to in the Official History.[6]

Reports reaching Brigade HQ indicated that by late morning 54 Brigade on the left had withdrawn and 64 Brigade on the right had made no progress. Communication with the two leading

---

5   TNA WO 95/2159, WO 95/2161, and WO 95/2162: Respectively War Diaries of 64 Brigade; 1st East Yorks and 15th DLI; 9th and 10th KOYLI.

6   OH op. cit., p. 435. TNA WO 95/2165: 8th and 9th Leicesters War Diaries.

battalions was virtually non-existent as telephone cables were constantly being cut and no runners could hope to survive the intense enemy machine gun fire. The situation appeared to be that those troops still alive were sheltering in shell holes about 50 yards in front of *Chérisy Riegel* and organising themselves as best they could to withstand enemy counterattacks. One of these forestalled a planned attempt by the supporting 6th Leicesters to attack Fontaine wood as a means of strengthening the resistance of the two leading battalions to counterattack.

At 1915 the reserve 7th Leicesters co-operated in a renewed attack by 18th Division by working down the sunken Héninel-Fontaine road and a trench running parallel to it. A supporting artillery barrage that began simultaneously was immediately responded to by the enemy with a barrage of heavy howitzers targeted on the trench being used by the Leicesters. The combination of this and the growing vulnerability of the Battalion to machine gun fire brought the advance to a halt. Because of the danger of a counterattack that they would not have had the strength to resist and the fact that 54 Brigade had retired with some of 110 Brigade's leading troops doing likewise, the 7th Battalion were pulled back.[7]

The 18th (Eastern) Division, occupying the centre of VII Corps line, had, at the start of the Third Battle of the Scarpe, only just joined the Corps, having been transferred in from GHQ reserve. The Division arrived with a formidable reputation garnered largely from its performance during the Somme campaign. It had been established under the auspices of Eastern Command in September 1914 as one of the second tranche of Kitchener New Army divisions and had arrived in France in July 1915 under the command of Major General Ivor Maxse. Its rapid success would have owed much to its first Commander, a renowned trainer of men. By the end of 1916, however, Maxse had been deservedly promoted to the command of XVIII Corps. His replacement at 18th Division was Major General Richard P. Lee, who would remain the Division's commander for the rest of the war.

The fact that 18th Division had only been in position since the beginning of May and had had no chance to familiarise themselves with the ground over which they would have to advance was almost certainly a major reason why 3 May became the day on which the Division suffered their first substantial check on the Western Front. Additional reasons were the pitch darkness at Zero Hour and the large areas of uncut German wire confronting them. The assault was mounted by two brigades, 54 on the right and 55 on the left. The 53 Brigade were in reserve. On the right and left for 54 Brigade were respectively 7th Bedfords and 12th Middlesex. The 11th Royal Fusiliers were in support with one company detailed off as moppers up and another to provide carrying parties. The 6th Northants were in reserve. Starting from a line approximately 500 yards west of the ruined village of Chérisy the first divisional objective ran from St Michael's Statue, north of the village, in a curve round the crossroads of the Fontaine – Vis-en-Artois road and the Chérisy-Hendecourt road, thence to a line just northeast of Fontaine wood and north of Fontaine village. The second and final objective largely followed the curve of the first about 7-800 yards further east. The German front line barred the way to Chérisy about equidistant between the British front line and the village itself. In all, the average advance called for to gain both objectives was 2,000 yards. If achieved, this would bring the Division to within 750 yards of Vis-en-Artois. As has already become clear, it was not to be.

The darkness at Zero Hour was so intense that it was impossible to see anyone more than two yards away. It quickly became evident that the enemy were fully alert; their counter barrage, supplemented by heavy machine gun and rifle fire, began only four minutes after Zero. The darkness was made even worse by the curtain of dust thrown up by the shelling. The men of the two battalions struggled forward, trying to maintain open order in the teeth of heavy enemy fire that became even more intense when the Bedfords breasted a slope and found themselves enfiladed from both sides. It is scarcely surprising that direction was quickly lost and the veering to the right complained of by 110 Brigade began to take place. The Divisional History placed the blame principally on the darkness.

---

7   OH op. cit., p. 435. TNA WO 95/2164: 6th and 7th Leicesters War Diaries.

But it also claims that 110 Brigade were also at fault because of inaccurate synchronisation of watches that meant that they were two minutes later than 18th Division jumping off. This was sufficient to mean that they had not cleared the danger zone before the German counter barrage, by then intense, hit them. The 110 Brigade War Diary does confirm without comment that the advance of their two battalions only began at 0347, two minutes late. It is however difficult to see why this should have contributed to making 54 Brigade veer to the right.

Despite all their difficulties with loss of direction and heavy enemy fire, both leading battalions reached the dip in which the enemy front line was located only to find themselves confronted by inadequately cut wire. Those gaps there might have been were impossible to locate in the darkness. The bulk of both battalions were held up in the open in front of the wire. Two companies of the Middlesex and some other small parties of men did find ways through, took them and crossed over the German line, reaching the Sensée, where they linked up with 55 Brigade troops. One of the companies even got into and through Chérisy. Heavy machine gun fire and the exposure of their right flank prevented them making any further progress. Instead they set up a strong point in the south of the village. Lacking officers and NCOs, who had disproportionately become casualties, the men of the two battalions facing the wire were in a state of confusion, which was made worse when a tank assigned to 21st Division, which had lost direction and found itself ahead of supporting infantry, turned round and retired through 18th Division lines. Coincidentally at this precise moment the word 'retire' was passed along the leaderless line. It was sufficient to start a retreat of most of the assault troops of the Bedfords and half those of the Middlesex, which did not end until they were back in their original front line. There they were rallied and pushed forward once again. They had by then lost the protection of the barrage and could only seek what shelter they could in shell holes some distance in front of the German front line. They would remain there for the rest of the day until they were picked up during the attack that evening, launched jointly by 18th and 21st Divisions.[8] Before dealing with this, the assault from Zero Hour onwards of 55 Brigade on 54's left will be described.

The 7th Buffs on the right and the 8th East Surrey Regiment (East Surreys) on the left led 55 Brigade's assault. Despite some initial confusion caused by the darkness, which led to the intermingling of waves, companies and platoons, the lack of serious enemy opposition enabled the two battalions to reach Chérisy from their own front line in relatively quick time. Those enemy that were encountered were either killed, taken prisoner, managed to run away or went to ground in shell holes allowing the assault to pass by them. By the time the attackers, maintaining close contact with their barrage, reached the eastern edge of the village, the light was good enough to see clearly. The left of the Buffs and all the East Surreys reached their first objective, averaging 500 yards beyond the Sensée River, and there took pause to dig in and try to reorganise. The right of the Buffs was held back on the Sensée to wait for some of the 12th Middlesex of 54 Brigade to catch up and come into line. The East Surreys were in touch on their left with 14th Division 8th RB, who had also reached their first objective. By 0545 parties of both the Buffs and the East Surreys had reached their final objective but came under fire from both flank and rear, in the latter case from Germans who had earlier taken shelter in shell holes.

Despite the promising start described above a problem, which would ultimately play a major part in the failure of the action, had become apparent by around 0530. A significant gap had opened up between the two brigades that was never to be closed in spite of the efforts that were made to do so. The gap would enable a resurgent and well organised enemy to push reinforcements along Fontaine trench and trench works known as Chérisy Lane, running east-west just to the south of the village, and finally retake the whole of it. The German artillery played an important part in their successful recapture of the village, systematically bombarding it and, seemingly enjoying excellent observation, pinpointing and targeting concentrations of British troops. By about 1030 large numbers of the

---

8   Nichols, *The 18th Division in the Great War*, pp. 167-71. OH, op. cit., p. 436.

attackers had been forced back to their start line although some were still lying out in front of the *Chérisy Riegel* and others, mainly Middlesex, remained in the village itself, despite it being back in German hands.

The joint 21st/18th Division attack, launched at 1915 after an hour's postponement, has already been referred to in the context of 7th Leicesters' part in it. Its purpose was essentially to extricate those troops thought to have been left stranded and vulnerable in forward positions as a consequence of the failure of the morning's attacks. In fact there were far fewer such troops than the planners of the attack thought, the bulk of them having already made their way back or been taken prisoner. It was therefore questionable whether the attack would serve any useful purpose. The 18th Division's contribution to the joint attack consisted of 6th Northants (54 Brigade) and 7th Queen's (55 Brigade). Both battalions came under heavy rifle and machine gun fire immediately they began their assault. The right company of the Queen's and their support company nevertheless reached Cable trench, where they made contact with 6th Northants. But their left company and their support company failed to reach Chérisy. The two leading companies of 6th Northants also had mixed fortunes. That on the left, keeping well up with the artillery barrage, reached and entered Fontaine trench after only 10 minutes. The right hand company had further to travel to reach Fontaine trench. When they became exposed, moving down a slope to reach their objective, they were heavily machine-gunned from their front and right flank and were forced to take shelter in shell holes about 50 yards in front of the enemy wire where they joined, or were joined by, some 12th Middlesex and 7th Bedfords men who had been sheltering in shell holes since early morning.

The leading 6th Northants company that had reached Cable trench used 30 men to bomb their way down Fontaine trench, clearing about 150 yards of it and recapturing in the process eight Lewis guns which had been lost during the morning's fighting. Some of the enemy managed to slip away and, from a support trench only 40 yards away, bombed the Northants so effectively that they were reduced after 90 minutes to only 10 men. In their attempt to get back to their own lines there were further losses.[9]

The 14th (Light) Division, the northernmost of VII Corps' three divisions, were to share similar experiences to those of their southern neighbour, 18th Division. Both of their assaulting brigades, 41 on the right and 42 on the left, attacked on a two-battalion front. The 41 Brigade deployed 8th RB on the right and 8th KRRC on the left. Despite the pitch darkness at 0345 both battalions made good progress close up to a good creeping barrage and in 50 minutes had successfully reached their first objective, the track running northeast from Chérisy, with only light casualties. They began to consolidate in anticipation of moving on to their second objective, a trench 500 yards further on, at 0545. There was no sign of 42 Brigade that should have been in line with them on their left. After about 30 minutes of their planned stay on the first objective, it became apparent to 8th KRRC that the enemy had succeeded in placing machine guns in Triangle wood despite sustaining heavy casualties in doing so. These guns were soon sweeping the KRRC's front line forcing them to stop digging and lie flat. To make matters worse a German aircraft spotted them and, by means of flares, called artillery fire down on them. Pinned down and with their left flank exposed by the non-arrival of 42 Brigade, there could be no question of setting off for the second objective. By contrast, 8th RB, largely unaffected by the enemy machine gun and artillery fire, advanced and took their second objective. This opened a gap between the two battalions, which was filled by a reserve company of 8th RB. The gap between 42 Brigade and 8th KRRC was also filled by the forming of a defensive flank and the moving up of one of KRRC's reserve companies. To add to the Battalion's problems a heavy German artillery barrage cut their headquarters' communications both with the front line troops and Brigade HQ. Later on in the morning a retirement that began in 18th Division became unavoidable as in turn each unit found its right flank exposed. The retirement was orderly but nevertheless 8th KRRC

---

9   Nichols, op. cit., pp. 185-7.

suffered heavily from enemy machine gun fire during it. Back in the trenches from which they had started that morning, 42 Brigade's rifle and machine gun fire dealt very successfully with the German attempt to exploit their advantage.[10]

As may be inferred from the claimed loss of contact between 41 and 42 Brigades, the latter had a very difficult time from almost the start of their advance on a two battalion front, involving the 5th Ox & Bucks LI on the right and 9th RB on the left. To some extent this was mitigated by the leading waves of the two battalions moving out of their jumping off trench 10 minutes prior to Zero and lying down 250 yards in front of it. They waited here until Zero plus 18 minutes before beginning their advance. During these 28 minutes they suffered no casualties at all. Had they remained in their jumping off trenches they might well have taken serious casualties from an enemy barrage that opened at Zero plus three minutes and targeted these trenches. However, when the two battalions began their advance proper they were immediately subjected to heavy machine gun fire from St Rohart Factory and Village trench, suffering heavy losses. Contact was lost between the attackers and Battalion HQ and attempts to restore it by use of runners resulted in the rapid loss of eight of them.

Despite their losses, 5th Ox & Bucks LI managed to get into New trench from which the enemy quickly retired, moving back to trenches in front of Triangle wood where they set up machine guns and grenade launchers to target New trench. They were eventually silenced by the British Battalion's rifle grenades, but there could be no question of the Ox & Bucks LI resuming their advance. They had been too weakened by their losses and were still under fire from machine guns and grenade launchers to their left. Enemy artillery was also targeting the trench. It was impossible to do very much to consolidate their gains under this concentration of fire. By around 1030 they were down to about 50 men in New trench and 40 others in shell holes 50 yards or so away in front of the trench. Fifteen minutes later it was observed that the retirement begun in the 18th Division's sector was taking place and would soon be followed by a very strong enemy counterattack emanating from Village trench. The Ox & Bucks LI men concentrated their firepower and inflicted serious losses on the enemy especially where they bunched at a point just east of Triangle wood. The enemy nevertheless advanced into Triangle wood and there were subjected to an intense artillery barrage under the cover of which the remnants of the 5th Ox & Bucks LI were able to withdraw to their start line and begin reorganising.

On the Ox & Bucks LI left, 9th RB suffered very badly. Their first wave did manage to enter Hill Side work, a German strong point, but at the cost of losing all their officers and all but seven of their NCOs. Total losses were 68 percent. Their second wave could not enter the German strong point and took shelter in shell holes short of it and tried to consolidate. But they came under intense pressure from machine gun fire and grenade launchers. Their own weaponry was unable to suppress the machine guns. With little prospect of any further progress being made by either of his battalions and the obvious threat of strong hostile counterattacks the Brigade Commander ordered a general retirement to the morning's start line. Under cover of darkness patrols were sent out to convey this order. They found everyone except one group of one officer and 12 men who had established a strong point and seemed prepared to carry on if they could be resupplied. When contact was established they were ordered to retire too and did so the following night.[11]

The three divisions of VI Corps engaged in the Third Battle of the Scarpe were 56th (1st London), 3rd and 12th Divisions. All three had been involved in earlier stages of the Arras campaign; the 56th had been in the First Battle of the Scarpe as part of VII Corps. Now the right hand Division of VI Corps, they would attack with two brigades in line, 169 on the right and 167 on the left. The overall objective set by Corps HQ was to reach a line running to the east of St Rohart Factory, the Bois du Sart and Pelves. The 56th Division Commander designated an intermediate objective for his two brigades of Lanyard trench, which was halfway between Cavalry farm and St Rohart factory.

10   General Sir Steuart Hare, *The Annals of the King's Royal Rifle Corps, Volume V: The Great War*, pp. 204-6.
11   TNA WO 95/1898/2: 42 Brigade War Diary.

The assault by 169 Brigade, led by 5th London Regiment (London Rifle Brigade) and 2nd (City of) London Regiment, progressed well in spite of the pitch darkness. The greater part of Cavalry farm was quickly taken and The Pit, just before St Rohart factory, reached and occupied. Here they would remain for the rest of the day, largely because of the failure of the brigades on either side of them. One of these, 167 Brigade, with 1st (City of) London Regiment and 1/7th Middlesex in the lead, were instantly subjected to a very accurate German barrage. They then found themselves up against the densely packed German front line Tool trench, which, because of its position on a reverse slope, had largely escaped the attentions of the British artillery. Only the shelter of darkness prevented a massacre. Withdrawal was the only sensible option and both battalions fell back to their start line. In the meantime 169 Brigade sought to improve the situation by establishing a bombing post in Tool trench, using 9th London Regt (Queen Victoria's Rifles). Despite their tiredness they made several attempts to achieve this objective but were unsuccessful. In the late evening a German counterattack temporarily pushed back the Brigade but the ground was quickly retaken. At 0200 the Brigade reluctantly retired to their start line of the previous morning in response to an order from Brigade HQ, but only after the local commanders, confident of being able to maintain their positions, had demanded, and received, confirmation of the order. In the start line, Queen Victoria's Rifles (QVR) and 16th London Regiment (Queen's Westminster Rifles) took over the Brigade's front line duties.[12]

The 3rd Division, occupying the centre of VI Corps line, attacked out of Monchy on a two brigade front with 8 Brigade on the right and 9 Brigade on the left. Even prior to Zero Hour it became quite evident that the enemy were expecting the attack when the front was deluged with high explosive and gas barrages, the latter specifically targeting the British artillery positions, forcing the gun crews to don respirators. When 8 Brigade's two leading battalions, 2nd R Scots and 1st RSF began to advance they found themselves under fire from enemy groups who had advanced from their front line to avoid the British barrage by taking shelter in shell holes. The effect of this unexpected attack, coupled with the profound darkness, was to sow confusion in the Scottish battalions leading to bunching and intermingling and the loss of the protection of the creeping barrage. Effectively the attack broke down before it had begun.

The 9 Brigade fared a little better, at least to begin with. They too had endured a heavy enemy barrage of gas, shrapnel and high explosive shell, which had begun at about 2200 on 2 May and was still continuing at increasing intensity at Zero Hour just less than six hours later. The two supporting battalions, 1st Northumberlands and 12th West Yorks, had to run the gauntlet of this barrage as they moved forward to take up their positions. The need to wear respirators added to the confusion caused by the extreme darkness and the inevitable casualties, and led to some loss of direction. Despite the respirators a number of officers and men were sick.

The Brigade's assaulting battalions were 4th RF and 13th King's. At 0345 their supporting barrage opened up, reflecting great credit on the gun crews, who were still being subjected to gas shelling. Nevertheless the barrage did seem thin, especially on the right, in contrast to the very heavy enemy bombardment. Following closely behind their barrage the two battalions advanced until they reached a line roughly 100 yards to the east of the Bois des Aubépines (Hawthorns). They had however failed to deal with several concealed machine guns during their transit of the wood. These began firing into their rear, adding to the machine gun and rifle fire that had assailed them from both sides and in front during the course of their advance. Casualties were high and touch had been lost with 8 Brigade on the right and 12th Division on the left, both of which had been outrun. The two battalions tried to dig in along the line reached by their leading troops but found it impossible as the enemy fire continued unabated. The first enemy counterattack was repulsed, but a second in greater strength, emanating from the east, northeast and southeast, began to work its way round the flanks of the leading companies, forcing them to retire with many men missing. Although by now all the

---

12   OH op. cit., p. 438. TNA WO 95/2958/1: 169 Brigade War Diary.

officers of the leading companies had become casualties and information was consequently difficult to obtain, it was evident that the attack was completely stalled. The few wounded who managed to crawl back spoke of continuing intense machine gun and rifle fire from both flanks. Attempts after dark to get forward to rescue the wounded and clarify the situation were met by heavy gunfire from close quarters and consequently failed.[13]

Occupying the left of the VI Corps line were 12th Division. Their objective was the capture of Pelves village. They were ordered however not to attempt this until Roeux village, on the north bank of the Scarpe and notorious as the source of enfilade fire targeting British units south of the river, had been taken and secured. The difficult task of achieving this would fall to XVII Corps. Until it had been accomplished, 12th Division were ordered to advance only as far as first and second objectives, lines respectively codenamed Brown(Gun trench) and Yellow (Cartridge trench), the former running northwest from Keeling copse. The 37 and 36 Brigades were tasked with the capture of these lines. On the right 37 Brigade's assault was led by 6th The Buffs (East Kents) and 7th East Surreys. On the left 9th and 8th RF were 36 Brigade's assault battalions. The Buffs, East Surreys and 9th RF, advancing behind their creeping barrage, had little trouble in reaching the Brown Line. But in so doing in pitch darkness they failed to mop up enemy troops who had probably been overrun while taking shelter in shell holes. These enemy troops subsequently rapidly congregated in Devil's trench, behind the Brown Line.

In contrast to the other three assault battalions, the left of 8th RF, on 12th Division's extreme left, quickly came under considerable fire from Roeux, and only managed to reach Scabbard trench, well short of the Brown Line. Here they were soon counterattacked and driven back from even this modest gain. The enemy were thus in possession of two trenches on either side of the two brigades' line of advance where they were able to prevent supporting troops from getting forward to link up with the troops in the Brown Line. Uncertainty at Brigade HQs as to the precise whereabouts of the leading troops discouraged any thought of shelling the two trenches. The situation in Scabbard trench became sufficiently clear by 1210, however, to enable two companies of 36 Brigade's 7th R Sussex, to attack under cover of a howitzer barrage and drive the Germans out and back beyond the Brown Line. A counterattack was decisively defeated with a number of prisoners being taken and two machine guns seized.[14]

A group of about 40 men from the leading waves of the Buffs had managed to get beyond the Brown Line and reach the southern end of Cartridge trench, a part of the Yellow Line. They consolidated the position and remained there all day beating off three determined counterattacks, which, however, left them very low on ammunition. Isolated as they were, they decided to fight their way back once they had the cover of darkness. In doing so they reached Devil's trench and found it full of Germans. Only two officers and eight men of the original 40 managed to get past the Trench and regain their own lines, and they were all wounded.

The 6th R West Kents, which had been in 37 Brigade reserve during the day were ordered late in the afternoon to try to clear up the situation on the Brigade front by attacking the southern end of Gun trench and Keeling copse. The attack was launched at 2145 but immediately ran into serious trouble caused by heavy enemy fire from Devil's trench, which barred the way to their objectives. The attack failed with the loss of 12 officers and 250 ORs.[15] By the early hours of 4 May it had become clear that 37 Brigade had no success to report from its efforts of the previous day. Although 36 Brigade's 7th

---

13　Ibid., pp. 439-40. TNA WO 95/1427: 9 Brigade War Diary.

14　While later clearing up the trench a bomb was thrown by a Royal Sussex soldier into a dugout where some 8th Royal Fusiliers, taken prisoner earlier, had been held. One of these, Sergeant G Jarratt, promptly stepped on the bomb to take its impact and prevent harm to his comrades. The bomb exploded and blew off Sgt Jarratt's legs. He died before he could be evacuated. None of his comrades was harmed. Sgt Jarratt was awarded a posthumous Victoria Cross. A tragic instance of 'friendly fire'.

15　TNA WO 95/1861: 6th Royal West Kents War Diary.

R Sussex had successfully driven the Germans back and occupied their front line, they were ordered to retire after dark because their right flank was exposed. They nevertheless remained in possession of 500 yards of enemy territory on a one thousand yard front. This would prove to be the Third Army sole gain from Third Scarpe.[16]

North of the River Scarpe on VI Corps left were deployed the last of Third Army Corps engaged in Third Scarpe. Two divisions would be committed to the attack by XVII Corps, 4th Division on the right and 9th (Scottish) Division on the left. They faced the extremely difficult task of capturing and securing the village of Roeux, the Chemical Works and Greenland Hill, all still in German hands despite the strenuous attempts that had already been made to wrest them permanently from their possession, notably by these same two divisions. In an effort to ensure that on this occasion their endeavours would be successful, an intense artillery programme began early on 1 May. The guns were concentrated into three target groups, Counter Battery, Trench Bombardment and Super Heavy, the last-named focusing on particularly sensitive targets such as the Chemical Works and on enemy machine gun emplacements.

The 4th Division assaulted with two brigades in line, 10 on the right and 12 on the left. The former led off on a three battalion front, from right to left 1st SLI (on attachment from 11 Brigade), Household Battalion and 1st Warwicks. The 2nd Seaforths were in close support on the right and 1st Royal Irish Fusiliers (RIF) on the left. Once again the pitch darkness of a Zero Hour of 0345 proved the undoing of the assault. (The problem it posed was exacerbated for all of XVII Corps by the mass of ruined buildings that would confront them.) The SLI, given the task of capturing Roeux in their own time and acting more or less independently, started their advance 20 minutes after Zero. Despite this additional proximity to daylight they still found it impossible to see anything as they attempted to traverse Roeux wood. Their right company was quickly brought to a halt by machine gun fire. Some of their left company did manage to penetrate into the outskirts of the village, but could not establish themselves there. They were forced to retire to their own front line. Their attack had failed in their view because Roeux wood had not been shelled and had become a shelter for a large number of enemy machine guns, which it had been impossible to locate in the darkness.[17]

The Household Battalion began their assault at Zero Hour. As they advanced they came up in line with a German machine gun concealed behind a wall. They were swept with enfilade fire, which inflicted 'exceedingly heavy casualties'.[18] They were compelled to retire to their original front line trench. Next to them, the Warwicks also found the going very difficult in the darkness against heavy machine gun fire. They too were largely forced back to their start line. The two close support battalions, 2nd Seaforths and 1st RIF left their trenches at respectively 0430 and 0415. The Seaforths sought to advance beyond Delbar and Hausa woods but suffered heavy casualties and were forced back to their original front line. The RIF's two leading companies were held up before the Roeux-Gavrelle road by heavy machine gun fire from the Chemical Works, Roeux Château and individual houses. Some of them veered off-course and became mixed up with 12th Brigade troops. They were reorganised and dug in on a line from west of the Château to the railway embankment. There they stayed until recalled late that night.

The 10 Brigade's War Diary summed up what had been a terrible day for its battalions. 'As far as has been ascertained the only organised party that ever reached the first objective were some 40 men of 1st Warwicks and a few men, who lost direction, of the Household Battalion, The King's Own and the Duke of Wellington's Regiment. This party dug themselves in and probably captured a number of prisoners, but were eventually counterattacked or practically wiped out by our own barrage which opened fire on the German counterattack towards the Chemical Works. No further news has ever

16   Brumwell, *The History of the 12th (Eastern) Division in the Great War*, pp. 110-2. TNA WO 95/1862: 7th East Surrey Regiment War Diary; OH, op. cit., p 440.
17   TNA WO 95/1499/1: 1st Somerset Light Infantry War Diary.
18   In the words of the Battalion War Diary, TNA WO 95/1481/1: Household Battalion.

been received as to what actually happened to them.'[19]

On 10 Brigade's left, 12 Brigade's objectives were to capture the Chemical Works and the German line running north from there towards Gavrelle. A peculiar difficulty this presented was that it called for an advance straddling the Arras-Douai railway that ran diagonally across the battle zone. The 2nd Lancashire Fusiliers, the right hand assault battalion, would therefore have to advance on both sides of the railway which ran partly through a cutting and partly on an embankment. To the Fusiliers' left were 2nd Essex who, jointly with them, were to take the first objective, a stretch of line just to the east of the Roeux-Gavrelle road. There the Essex would form a flank along the railway while the Fusiliers would move on to attack the second objective, south of the railway, with 2nd Duke's, who would have moved up into line on their right. The final objective, the trench north of the railway covering the village of Plouvain, would then be taken by 2nd Duke's and 1st King's Own.

The 2nd Lancashire Fusiliers south of the railway, advancing behind a creeping barrage, passed through buildings in the area of the Chemical Works and Roeux Château with apparent ease and soon reached the Blue Line, approximately 2,000 yards from their start line. The 2nd Bn Duke's were close behind them. For once the darkness had been of some assistance as it had concealed them from the German weaponry in the Château on their immediate right, still untaken by 10 Brigade. Once daylight had arrived, possession of the Château by the Germans would effectively prevent the sort of advance achieved by the two battalions. The implications for their reinforcement were obvious, and not long in manifesting themselves. Isolated well in advance of the rest of the Brigade, the two battalions were helpless to stop the enemy getting behind them and surrounding them. All the officers of both battalions had by now become casualties. Nearly all those not killed were captured; only a few managed to get back. They included 30 brought back by a Duke's Warrant Officer. Eventually the remnants of the two battalions, about 100 men, were collected together, and dug in just in front of what had been their first objective.

North of the railway there was no comparable initial success to report. Almost immediately the 2nd Lancashire Fusiliers, the 1st King's Own and the left of 2nd Essex were held up by machine gun fire from houses not dealt with by the heavy artillery, and suffered heavy casualties. The right of 2nd Essex did capture a couple of trenches (Crook and Crow) and consequently found themselves further forward than the units on either side of them with both flanks in the air. The majority of them became casualties or were taken prisoner.

By 1100 the situation appeared to Brigade HQ to be that the buildings south of the railway, apart from the Château and one or two houses east of the Roeux-Gavrelle road, were in British hands as was the previously unoccupied southern portion of Calabar trench. The reserve 11th Brigade's 1st RB and two companies of 1st Hampshires were ordered forward to trenches east of Fampoux as potential reinforcements. At 1400 the enemy launched a counterattack out of Hausa wood. It was successfully beaten off by artillery fire. In response to an order received during the afternoon to clear up the situation south of the railway, 1st RB were ordered to attack the Château at 2300, to synchronise with a 10 Brigade attack up Corona trench. The RB took over trenches on the western edge of the built up area dominated by the Château but their attack was not launched until 0300 the following morning. It was a failure. The Battalion made no progress and withdrew to Ceylon trench.[20]

The 9th Division were the second of XVII Corps divisions committed to the battle. They assaulted with 26 Brigade on the right and 27 Brigade on the left. On the right of 26 Brigade's front line were 5th Camerons and on the left, 8th Black Watch. The 10th Argylls were in support and 7th Seaforths in reserve. The 27 Brigade had 9th Cameronians (Scottish Rifles) (SR) and 6th KOSB leading, with 11th and 12th R Scots respectively in support and in reserve. In place of the South African Brigade, sidelined until they could replace the losses they had sustained in earlier fighting, were 17th Division

19   TNA WO 95/1479: 10 Brigade War Diary.
20   TNA WO 95/1479: 10 Brigade War Diary; TNA WO 95/1508: 2nd Duke of Wellington's Regiment War Diary.

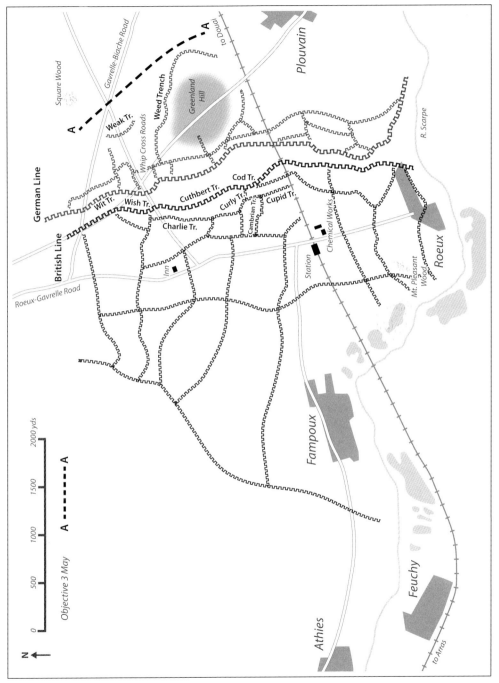

Objective of 9th (Scottish) Division for Third Battle of the Scarpe, 3 May 1917.

52 Brigade on attachment. They would form the divisional reserve.

The divisional objective was to capture a line consisting of Weed, Why and Weak trenches and a length of the Biache-Gavrelle road from its junction with Weak Trench. The attackers would be confronted by a fully alerted enemy in occupation of hastily dug trenches and shell holes on the western slopes of Greenland Hill. In addition to the customary creeping barrage the attackers would be supported by a machine gun barrage that would keep 400 yards ahead of the creeping barrage. The Zero Hour of 0345 would prove disastrous for the attackers. The Division had only been informed of the bringing forward of Zero a few hours previously, too late to make any adjustments that would help to cope with the pitch darkness instead of the early light that had been expected. To make matters worse the bombardment, which erupted at Zero, threw up huge clouds of dust that were blown into the faces of the attackers by the wind. Coupled with the almost immediate German riposte of accurate machine gun fire from trenches and shell holes much closer to the British lines than had been expected, it was small wonder that the assault rapidly lost direction. The Camerons, additionally misled by the alarm lights being fired from the enemy trenches and under heavy machine gun fire from the direction of the Chemical Works, swung so far to the right that they crossed in front of 2nd Essex and, mistaken for enemy, were fired upon by them. On the Camerons' left, 8th Black Watch, short of officers at the outset, also lost cohesion and direction, not helped when their second line was charged by 9th SR firing from the hip. Only a few isolated parties succeeded in reaching the enemy front line. The 10th Argylls, advancing in support and in the right direction if veering slightly leftwards, became heavily involved in the fighting. They came under severe enfilade machine gun fire from the railway embankment and the Chemical Works and were subjected to persistent bombing attacks from the direction of the Gavrelle-Plouvain road. One company nevertheless succeeded in reaching the first objective where, lacking support, they were cut off. Only a few survivors managed to get back. Most of the Battalion were compelled to take cover in shell holes well short of their objective from where they gradually worked their way back to their own line.[21]

The 27 Brigade's 9th SR, on the right, made satisfactory progress for about 200 yards when they suddenly veered from east to south east (some to the extent that they mistook the 26 Brigade's lines for the enemy's and charged them). But the bulk became intermingled with 8th Black Watch, some of whom had veered north east. It was still dark and the enemy's machine gun and rifle fire were inflicting heavy casualties. The Battalion War Diary admits that leadership was at this stage breaking down and was difficult to restore. Nevertheless the attack somehow continued and the troops of one company managed to enter the German trenches. They found them strongly held and were nearly all killed or wounded. Another group encountered an enemy group in the open and inflicted some casualties before being annihilated. By this time the Battalion's attack had completely broken down and it only remained for the small groups able to, to make their way back to the British lines. Those that managed it were reformed in Cuba trench.[22]

The swing right of the SR might have been avoided had they not failed to pick up the light from a lamp being shone from the right flank of 6th KOSB expressly to keep them on course. The KOSB's start line was some way ahead of that of the Rifles and, as a result, they were supposed to wait for 5 minutes until the latter had come up into line before advancing themselves. They had formed up in Clive and Civic trenches, but then moved out into the open under cover of their barrage to await the arrival of the Rifles. After the 5 minutes had elapsed and there was no sign of the Rifles, the KOSB moved off. Their task was to advance half right keeping the road running west/east from just south of Gavrelle on their left until it reached the enemy-held Wobble trench where the Battalion were to swing left and form a defensive flank along the road facing north. Progress was initially good.

21   John Ewing, *The History of the Ninth (Scottish) Division*, pp. 206-9. TNA WO 95/1739: 9th (Scottish) Division War Diary; TNA WO 95/1762: 26 Brigade War Diary.
22   Ewing, op. cit., p. 209. TNA WO 95/1772: 6th KOSB and 9th Scottish Rifles War Diaries.

Three companies crossed the enemy's front trench and pressed on. The problem was that both flanks were becoming exposed because of the failure of the battalions on either side to keep pace. A platoon from the remaining company that was sent to alleviate the situation on the left flank by blocking the southern end of Wit trench was virtually annihilated as soon as they exposed themselves. Some men of the three companies had managed to reach Square wood, but the enemy's occupation of Wit trench meant that all three companies were effectively cut off with little hope of survival unless they were taken prisoner. In the event most were killed. The 6th KOSB had suffered a major disaster. Fifteen officers, including the CO, and 400 NCOs and men had become casualties. The remnants of the Battalion were relieved that evening by 12th R Scots.[23]

The 27 Brigade Commander was unwilling to abandon men who had been cut off without an avenue of retreat and accordingly 12th R Scots were ordered to attack Wit trench. One and a half companies of the Battalion undertook the operation beginning at 2000, when it was still light. They were covered by a barrage of artillery and machine gun fire on each flank. Of the 150 men who charged, some of whom did reach the trench despite heavy enemy machine gun fire, only 30 returned. On the plus side a number of KOSB were able to get back under cover of the raid.[24]

The First Army part in the Third Battle of the Scarpe was assigned to two divisions each from XIII Corps and the Canadian Corps. XIII Corps two were 31st and 2nd Divisions. The 31st was a KNA unit whose infantry component was largely composed of Pals Battalions recruited in Leeds, Bradford, Hull, Accrington, Sheffield and Barnsley. On the first day of The Somme these battalions had been decimated as they attempted, unavailingly, to capture the fortified village of Serre. The communities from which they had come had been left devastated. By the time of Third Scarpe, however, 31st Division were, by the standards of most units involved in the Battles of Arras, comparatively fresh, having only just completed a considerable spell in First Army reserve. The same could not be said for 2nd Division, whose units were so tired and understrength that they were only assigned 1,100 of the 4,600 yards of the Corps front. The right half of 2nd Division's front would have to be covered by 31st Division. By Zero Hour the latter's freshness was largely a thing of the past as the two days they spent in the forward areas prior to Zero were characterised by manual labour, digging or deepening the trenches required for communication or cable burying or for assembly positions. All this work had to be done under heavy enemy artillery barrages of the front lines that led to serious losses.

The 31st Division's unusually long stretch of line ran from the southern end of Gavrelle to just north of Oppy wood and village, both of which remained in enemy hands and were the main objectives of the Division. The hope that the enemy defences would be manned by troops still shaken from the effects of the previous British attack were to prove misplaced; they had been replaced by fresh troops whose morale remained unshaken, and were in greater numbers than 31st Division could muster. The setting of Zero Hour at 0345 came as a very unpleasant surprise for 31st Division as they would have to assemble with a full, if setting, moon behind them, providing the enemy with a clear view of the operation. With the moon having disappeared they would then have to negotiate their way through Oppy wood, by now a formidable defensive barricade of felled trees, in pitch darkness. It was quite clear that, however well the divisional attack might go, there could be no doubting that the advance through Oppy wood would take much longer than the advance over the open ground south of the Gavrelle windmill spur. Separate artillery and machine gun barrage plans would be necessary. The retention of the windmill itself, even if it lay in ruins, was essential, because its possession by the enemy would allow them to take the advances on either side in enfilade. It was consequently ordered that it must be held 'at all costs'.[25]

The Division attacked on a two brigade front, with 93 Brigade on the right and 92 Brigade on the

---

23   Ibid., pp. 209-10. TNA WO 95/1770: 27 Brigade War Diary.
24   TNA WO 95/1770; 27 Brigade War Diary.
25   TNA WO 95/2342/3: 31st Division War Diary.

left. Because of the need to cover such a wide front the spaces between the individual men of the first waves were unusually wide, adding to the problem of maintaining direction in the pitch darkness. Even more of a problem was that presented by heavy enemy machine gun fire from their right flank and a strong point that had been missed in the darkness by the first wave. With their first objective 300 to 400 yards away and their final objective 800 to 1,000 yards away the right half of 93 Brigade's attack, consisting of 15th West Yorks and half its sister Regiment, the 18th Battalion, took heavy losses in partially gaining their first objective. An indication of the difficulties under which the attack was labouring was an incident where German prisoners, being escorted back, saw that the numbers of their captors were much depleted, rounded on and disarmed them and took them prisoner in turn. The enemy then mounted a number of counter attacks, none of which succeeded, being broken up by artillery and machine gun fire. By this stage it was clear that there was little prospect of mounting further offensive action even though there were increasing signs that the enemy troops were moving back to Fresnes. Priority was given to ensuring that Gavrelle did not fall to a counterattack. The troops available were deployed accordingly, reinforced by a platoon from 12th KOYLI (Pioneers) and two companies of the Brigade's 18th DLI.

The left half of 93 Brigade's attack was carried out by the remaining half of 18th West Yorks, and 16th Battalion of the same Regiment. When the former began their advance they almost immediately came under accurate fire from an intense artillery bombardment. Enemy machine fire was also much in evidence. Despite the hostile fire and the extreme darkness, made worse by the smoke and dust thrown up by the barrages of both sides, they nevertheless managed to reach their objectives, but only at the cost of heavy losses. They found the enemy often ready to give up until they realised that the few men seeking their surrender were devoid of support, at which point they took heart and fought on or turned the tables. When a strong counterattack from Oppy wood threatened to cut off the remaining troops and it was apparent that the attack had failed, the men were reorganised into defensive positions so as to be able to offer support to the battalions on either flank, if required, and avoid the threat of being surrounded.

In spite of the problem of darkness and the opening of an enemy counter barrage only four minutes after Zero, 16th West Yorks made good initial progress and reached their first objective in 15 minutes. They found the trench only lightly held and a number of the enemy therein surrendered readily and were sent back to the rear. The first wave was left to consolidate and the remaining waves advanced towards the second objective. At this stage enfilade rifle and machine gun fire from the left became increasingly heavy. Nevertheless, the advance was maintained behind a creeping barrage. As the second objective came closer the enemy were observed abandoning the trench in large numbers and retiring in disorder. Many were shot down in flight. By 0420 the trench was occupied. It was in a poor state and only offered patchy protection. The first enemy counterattack at 0500 was initially mistaken as a mass surrender, But the mistake was quickly rectified and the enemy driven off. Attempts to improve the shelter offered by the trench and some positions further forward were frustrated by the chalky soil. The situation became distinctly uncomfortable when the enemy opened concentrated machine gun and rifle fire from the left and the rear. It became impossible to continue digging. When a further enemy counterattack in strength was launched it soon became apparent that it was only a matter of time before the British positions would be cut off. The decision was taken to withdraw to the original British front line. This was done with the inevitable additional losses caused by the need for the men to traverse open ground on their way back.[26]

It will be recalled that an order had been given to hold Gavrelle windmill 'at all costs', despite which by 0540 it was clear that the ruin was in enemy hands and that the four machine guns and two Stokes mortars that had been deployed to help ensure the mill's retention had been knocked out. The 18th DLI, 93 Brigade's Support Battalion, were consequently instructed to retake the Windmill

26 Ibid.

'at all costs'. Most of the DLI Battalion had by this stage been fed into various sectors of the line to help the original assault battalions strengthen the Gavrelle defences, but C Company were not yet committed. They were accordingly ordered by the Battalion CO to recapture the windmill after due reconnaissance. What little reconnaissance there was time for prior to the Zero Hour of 0645 decided on indicated no sign of enemy occupation. The Company Commander decided on a frontal assault by three waves in three bounds. The first of the latter was from the starting trench to the Gavrelle-Douai road; the second from the road to the railway; the third from the railway to the windmill. The attack was launched on schedule and immediately provoked a flurry of German SOS flares from west and southwest of the windmill that was quickly followed by an enemy shrapnel barrage on no man's land. The attackers nevertheless reached the road without difficulty or loss, but all attempts to progress further were driven back by heavy machine gun fire from three different directions. A final effort, led personally by the Company Commander, got to within 50 yards of the windmill. Just when things appeared to be moving favourably for the attackers with increasing indications that the Germans had decided to withdraw, the DLI Company came under fire from friendly artillery targeting the retreating enemy and suffered serious casualties. They were forced to fall back to the road where it was found that they had suffered 50 percent casualties in the course of their attack. In a final and ultimately successful attempt to capture the windmill, the Company Commander split his remaining men into small fighting patrols who, using the cover provided by shell holes, were able to occupy the ruins and the surrounding ground. The operation had lasted four hours.[27]

The 92 Brigade also attacked on a three-battalion front using, from right to left, 10th, 11th and 12th Battalions of the East Yorks. The 13th East Yorks were on carrying duties and 11th East Lancashires, on loan from 94 Brigade, were in support. All four East Yorks Battalions were Hull Pals Battalions. The objectives of the Brigade were to capture Oppy wood and village. Achieving these in the circumstances created by the belated decision to advance Zero Hour to a time when there would be no light would be a major challenge. The need for the attackers to assemble for their assault with a full moon behind them, thus silhouetting them to a watchful enemy, and then for the moonlight to disappear, with the setting of the moon, just when its light might have become helpful, gave the attackers the worst of both worlds. The consequences would prove disastrous, especially for 11th and 12th East Yorks. As these two battalions sought to take up their assembly positions in the open ahead of their front line they came under an enemy barrage that started at 0140 and lasted for at least 20 minutes. At 0255 a second barrage was apparently triggered by enemy SOS rockets fired from Oppy wood. This continued until just before Zero Hour. The rear waves of 11th Battalion and the whole of 12th Battalion suffered heavily from both these barrages and with some at least of the troops forced to move back to the relative shelter of their own assembly trenches or convenient shell holes, the plan of attack was considerably disorganised. When the British bombardment erupted at Zero the response of the German artillery, and their machine guns, was immediate and intense. The planned advance of 10th East Yorks, which had not been as badly affected by the German bombardments as its sister battalions, was intended to skirt the southern edge of Oppy wood and enter the village from the south. The waves moved forward at Zero behind their creeping barrage. The effort of the barrage to suppress resistance from the enemy front line demonstrably failed. No sooner had the barrage moved on, than heavy machine gun and rifle fire targeted the attackers from this still very strongly held line. The casualties suffered included all four company commanders. Progress was impossible and the survivors took shelter in their assembly trench or shell holes. Despite the artillery pounding they had received and the disruption it and the pitch darkness had caused, the other two battalions did move forward at Zero Hour, 50 yards behind their barrage. The 11th did however find it quite impossible to make out the German front line. Their right-hand company made three attempts in progressively diminishing numbers to find and enter the German line. The remnants finally withdrew to their

27   Kyle Tallett and Trevor Tasker, *Gavrelle: Arras*, pp. 79-81. WO 95/2342/3: 31st Division War Diary.

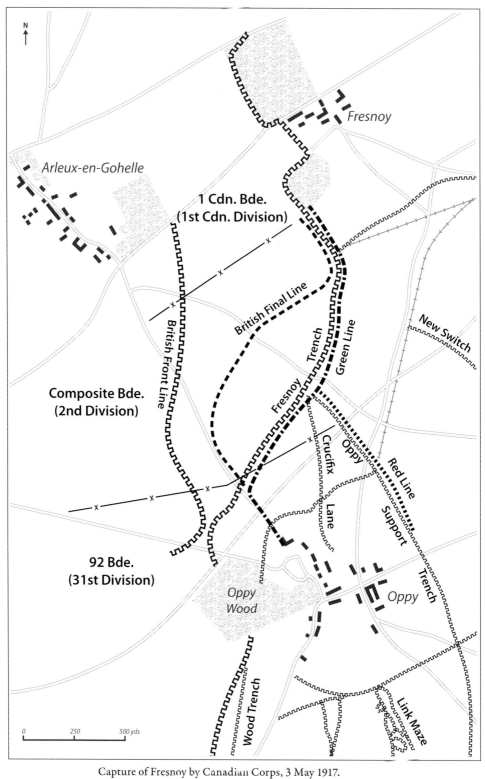

Capture of Fresnoy by Canadian Corps, 3 May 1917.

assembly trench and there consolidated. The two front waves of the centre company did manage to get into Oppy wood. There they were cut off. The left-hand company, the most disorganised, advanced haphazardly and soon lost direction and veered right into the wood. All the officers and 84 ORs were subsequently listed as missing although most of the latter were wounded and were eventually successfully evacuated. The 11th Battalion's last company, initially in close support of the three assaulting companies, were almost as disorganised by the enemy barrages as the leading waves. They did make one attempt to capture the enemy front line, but failed. Their casualties of about 30 were fewer than those of the other companies. In total 92 Brigade's casualties in the attack amounted to 74 percent of the officers engaged and 53 percent of the Other Ranks.[28]

Mention has already been made of the depleted state of 2nd Division. In effect they had been reduced to about half of establishment at 1,800 rifles. Sadly the Division fully merited the description bestowed on it by the Official History as 'a shadow of its former self'.[29] The drastic restructuring required saw it reduced to one brigade of four battalions created out of most of the remnants of 5, 6 and 99 Brigades. The four new battalions were designated by the letters 'A', 'B', 'C' and 'D' with 'A' Battalion drawing on the remnants of 5 Brigade (2nd Ox & Bucks LI, 2nd Highland LI, 17th and 24th RF); 'B' Battalion on the remnants of 6 Brigade (1st King's, 2nd South Staffs and 13th Essex); 'C' and 'D' Bns on the remnants of 99 Brigade (1st R Berks, 1st KRRC, 22nd and 23rd RF). Command of the composite Brigade was given to the former Commander of 99 Brigade, Brigadier General R. O. Kellett. The Brigade was accordingly named the 99th (Composite). Its objectives on 3 May were first to capture the rearward line of the enemy Arleux Loop from the wood south of Fresnoy southwards. Secondly, to take the Fresnoy-Oppy road. Leading for the Brigade would be B Battalion on the right and C Battalion on the left. D Battalion would be in close support of B, and A Battalion would be in reserve.

During the night of 2/3 May the Brigade moved into their assembly positions, for part of the time under heavy shelling prompted, in the optimistic view of 2nd Division HQ, by the enemy's nervousness. Be that as it may the troops moving up suffered significant losses as well as being slowed down by fire directed at crowded communication trenches. Nevertheless most of the leading waves had reached their jumping off positions by Zero hour and were able to begin their advance punctually. Within a minute the enemy artillery responded to the start of the British barrage, concentrating their fire on the front trenches and the railway embankment. For B Battalion only the left made progress and this was quickly negated by a German counterattack from Oppy. C Battalion on the other hand established early contact with the Canadians on their left, reaching their final objective. On their right the Battalion captured the trench that was their first objective. But the enemy, having dealt with B Battalion, were able to enter the trench and begin to bomb northwards. Divisional Headquarters were seriously alarmed at the threat a successful continuation of German progress northwards would offer to the right flank of the Canadians, who had successfully completed the capture of Fresnoy. The threat was finally averted by the joint effort of the Canadians and 2nd Division reserves. The Composite Brigade successfully formed a block 400 yards south of their boundary with the Canadians and posts were established in touch with the Canadian flank at the road fork southeast of Fresnoy. Despite their weary and depleted state the men of the 2nd Division had provided invaluable support to the Canadians in their efforts to maintain their hold on Fresnoy. This had been the main purpose of their involvement in the battle during the course of which they also took 138 prisoners. The Official History was unusually scathing in its comments on what the Division had been put through, stating, ' ... it had been subjected to treatment such as only a desperate emergency could have justified; for the employment of practically all the surviving infantry in this manner bled the division white'.[30]

---

28   TNA WO 95/2342/3: 31st Division War Diary.
29   OH, op. cit., p. 446.
30   Ibid., pp. 447-8. TNA WO 95/1297/1: 2nd Division War Diary; David Bilton, *Oppy Wood*, pp. 115 7.

As they had with the capture of Arleux during Second Scarpe, the Canadian Corps were to provide what little solace that could be gleaned from the calamity of Third Scarpe, with the capture of their objective, the village of Fresnoy.

The task was assigned to the 1st Canadian Division 1 Brigade on the right and 2nd Canadian Division 6 Brigade on the left. The 1 Brigade assaulted on a frontage of 1,400 yards using three battalions in line. With a frontage of only 900 yards, the 6 Brigade used only two battalions. An attack on Fresnoy was the logical continuation of the Canadians' earlier success in capturing Arleux. Consequently the Germans were in no doubt of their intentions and surprise would be impossible to achieve. Only the exact timing of the assault was open to question and this seemed to have been partially solved for the enemy when the moonlight illuminated the Canadian preparations in the early hours of 3 May. The Germans nevertheless did not expect the attack to be launched before first light. For once therefore the choice of a night attack worked partially to the advantage of the attackers by limiting the German ability to identify and engage targets. At the same time it made it difficult for the attackers to find the gaps in the enemy wire that the wire-cutting barrages had very effectively opened.

The German guns were very active in the small hours of 3 May. At 0200 they laid down a heavy barrage as the Canadians were moving into their assembly positions, causing severe casualties. At 0305 they laid down a further barrage. When the British barrage opened up at Zero Hour the Germans were quick to respond. On the 1 Brigade front the three battalions made steady progress despite the losses inflicted by the enemy guns and the difficulties caused by the darkness. On the right the 3rd (Toronto) Battalion were to advance through Fresnoy wood and bypass the objective village to the south. In the centre the 2nd (Eastern Ontario) Battalion were to attack and seize the village itself. On the left the 1st (Western Ontario) Battalion were to advance astride the Lille Road which formed the northern boundary of Fresnoy park. The right of the Battalion were to pass through the park and the left to advance north of, and parallel with, the Lille Road. The final objective of all three battalions was the support trench of the enemy's *Fresnoy-Riegel* (Oppy-Méricourt Line) running about 500 yards beyond the village.

Once they had overcome the problems presented by the German wire and the difficulty of finding the gaps through it, all three battalions made good progress. The 3rd Battalion quickly overran Fresnoy wood, taking 75 prisoners, and by soon after 0500 had reached and captured their stretch of the final objective. Losses had however been heavy; one assault company had been reduced to 25 men. The 2nd Battalion's leading company stormed and seized the German front trench barring their direct route into the village, eliminating three machine guns in the process. Despite rifle fire from outlying houses, two of their companies passed through the leading company and forced their way into the village. They cleaned up small pockets of resistance and by 0600 had reached their final objective. Consolidation and the evacuation of wounded were put in hand. Even though they had had serious difficulties in getting food, water and ammunition to their assaulting troops in preparation for their assault, the 1st Battalion nevertheless moved off on time closely following their barrage. By 0450 the left hand company had gained their objective but found their left flank was in the air. By 0540 the other two assaulting companies had also gained their objectives and, in the absence of 6 Brigade's right hand battalion on their left, measures were taken to prevent any infiltration of their open flank by the enemy.

The 6 Brigade's two assaulting battalions were the 27th (City of Winnipeg) on the right and the 31st (Alberta) on the left. In support were 28th (Northwest) and in reserve 29th (Vancouver) Battalions. The task confronting the assaulting battalions was to protect the left flank of the First Army advance by forming a strong front facing northeast. The 27th Battalion were to capture the junction of the northern end of the former Arleux Loop with the main Oppy-Méricourt Line, approximately 500 yards south of the village of Acheville. The 31st Battalion were to guard the 27th's left flank during the course of this operation. However straightforward the Brigade's ordained role might have seemed, the War Diary found a great deal to complain about. They were by no means reconciled to the earlier Zero Hour that had been ordered and were less than impressed by the effectiveness of the artillery's attempts to cut the wire protecting the trenches that were their objectives, as well as that protecting a newly dug German trench about 300 yards in front of them which was on 31st Bn's line of advance. The wire cutting programme had begun on the afternoon preceding Zero Hour and its results were so apparently inadequate that 6 Brigade raised the matter with Division who in turn raised it with Corps HQ, to little obvious effect.

When the two battalions began their assault at Zero they soon felt the effects of the German counter barrage although they were more slowed down by uncut wire. The 27th Battalion's left hand company nevertheless made good progress, overrunning their first objective, the German front trench. Unfortunately however the mopping up troops behind them lost their way, with the result that German troops, emerging from their dugouts, were not dealt with and were able to take the leading waves from behind. With both flanks open, as they had outrun both their own Battalion's right hand company and the right hand company of 31st Bn, which should have been covering their left, they were forced to turn around and take on the Germans behind them, driving them towards the Canadian lines and taking numbers of them prisoner. With this diversion completed the Battalion dug in, but in positions well short of where they wished to be. The absence of the 27th Battalion's right hand company from where they should have been, on the right of the left hand company, was caused by the very effective enemy barrage halting them about 500 yards short of the German front trench. Only a handful of men, led by Lieutenant R. G. Combe (subsequently awarded a posthumous VC) managed to reach the objective. They took possession of 250 yards of the trench, took nearly 100 prisoners and made contact with 1st (Western Ontario) Battalion on their right. When men of the reserve 29th (Vancouver) Battalion arrived they extended the Canadian hold on the trench by 150 yards and consolidated the position. After dark the 27th Battalion, with help from 29th Battalion, further extended their hold on the trench.

As Brigade HQ had feared, the wire protecting the newly dug, and largely empty, German trench only 300 yards away from 31st Battalion's start line, proved a serious problem. It and heavy enfilade fire from their trench junction objective forced the Battalion to try a two-pronged attack with one group seeking to outflank the objective while the other attacked from the front. Both failed, one with heavy losses. The decision was taken to treat the new German trench as the Battalion's front line and establish a block in the Arleux Loop where the new trench joined it. Touch was established with 27th Battalion and a new communication trench dug linking the two battalions.[31]

By the end of the same day on which it had begun the Third Battle of the Scarpe had effectively ended. From the British point of view the battle had been an almost total disaster. In the words of the Official History, 'many who witnessed it consider [the day to have been] the blackest of the War',[32] its only relieving feature being the Canadian capture of Fresnoy. The two main purposes in ordering the offensive had been to keep the Germans tied down and not free to transfer troops to the French sector of the front and to reach a tenable and defensible line where it would be relatively safe to shut down the Arras campaign prior to launching the offensive in Flanders. On the latter of these objectives virtually no progress was achieved. If the former had been achieved to some extent it is questionable whether the severe losses suffered in distracting German attention from the French sector had been an acceptable price to pay. The causes of the disaster will be examined in detail later, but undoubtedly a major factor was what was probably the worst decision made in the whole Arras campaign, to set a compromise Zero Hour between the preferences of the three Army Commanders which satisfied

31   OH, op. cit., pp. 448-50. Nichols, op. cit., pp. 274-7. TNA WO 95/3827: 6 Canadian Brigade War Diary; TNA WO 95/3760; 1st Canadian Battalion War Diary.

32   OH, op. cit., p. 450.

none of them and, especially for First and Third Armies, frequently led to catastrophe. The effect on the Fifth Army will be examined in the next chapter.

17

The Second Battle of Bullecourt: 3-17 May 1917

Since the German attack on Lagnicourt and the successful Australian counterattack on 15 April, General Gough's Fifth Army had not been more than notionally involved in the Arras campaign. A plan that they should participate in the Second Battle of the Scarpe on 23 April had been shelved in favour of their waiting until Third Army had made some significant progress in tandem with First Army before renewing the assault on the Hindenburg Line about Bullecourt. Although the results of Second Scarpe and the Battle of Arleux could scarcely be described as significant progress it was decided that Fifth Army would participate with the other two armies in the offensive to be launched on 3 May. As has been seen the Third and First Armies' participation in Third Scarpe was brought to an end within hours; the Fifth Army intervention, known as the Second Battle of Bullecourt, would continue for two weeks until the 17th. It was to become a byword for the horrors of fighting on the Western Front, especially among Australians.

The battle was planned in the context of a realisation that the Nivelle Plan had gone badly wrong and that there was a danger that the French would abandon their offensive altogether. Although he was moving towards a decision to close down the Arras campaign and transfer his offensive operations to Flanders, Field Marshal Haig was anxious that the French should keep attacking. A major purpose of the attacks of his three armies on 3 May was therefore to tie the Germans down and thereby encourage the French to continue their offensive. The achievement of an early small penetration of the German defences by Fifth Army was sufficient for Haig to decide to keep them attacking for the next fortnight. The capture of Fresnoy, the only positive result of the endeavours of First and Third Armies on 3 May, was by contrast not perceived as offering scope for exploitation, hence the decision to close down these Armies' parts of the offensive in short order.

The objectives laid down by Gough for 3 May were not dissimilar to those of First Bullecourt; the means of achieving them were. Both I ANZAC and V British Corps would again be involved, but this time they would attack simultaneously rather than V Corps waiting until the Australians had penetrated the Hindenburg Line and then wheeled left to follow the tanks into Bullecourt. The first objective this time would be the Hindenburg Support Trench, to be attacked on a 4,000 yard front. The second objective would be the Fontaine-Quéant Road, which ran parallel to the front line about 1,000 yards behind it. Reaching this would necessitate the capture of Bullecourt. The final objectives would be the villages of Riencourt and Hendecourt. Each Corps would attack on a one division front, I ANZAC using the fresh 2nd Australian Division and V Corps, the 62nd (2nd West Riding), a Territorial Division. The boundary between the two Corps would run along the eastern edge of Bullecourt, about 500 yards further east than for First Bullecourt, with 62nd Division having responsibility for the village's capture as well as 1,500 yards of the Hindenburg Line northwest of the village. V Corps would also be responsible for the capture of Hendecourt. The 2nd Australian Division would repeat the assault on the re-entrant in the Hindenburg Line between Quéant and Bullecourt, which had ended unsatisfactorily when attempted by 1st Australian Division during First Bullecourt. I ANZAC would also be responsible for taking Riencourt. The main difference in the planning for the Australian attacks in First and Second Bullecourt was that there was no place for tanks in the latter. The Australians had been so disillusioned by the tanks in the former battle that they wanted

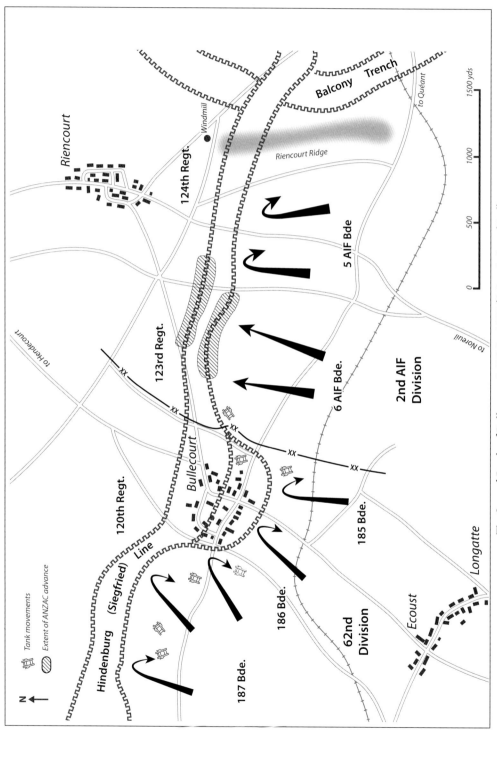

The Second Battle of Bullecourt 3-17 May 1917. (© Pen & Sword Ltd)

nothing further to do with them. As a result all the tanks available were assigned to 62nd Division, which, along with 2nd Australian, were also given much strengthened artillery support, especially in siege and heavy guns. In the run up to 3 May these guns were kept busy reducing the target villages, especially Bullecourt and Riencourt, to rubble. But there were still deficiencies in target selection, which would cause problems later on. The problem of Zero Hour was finally settled by Haig only hours beforehand when Gough got the better of the compromise of 0345 handed down, being forced to accept a 15 minute delay while Horne and Allenby had to accept a start one hour earlier than they had wished, and 20 minutes earlier than the earliest time they considered manageable.

The 2nd Australian Division would attack on a two-brigade front, with 5 Brigade on the right and 6 Brigade on the left. To their left the British 62nd Division would use all three of their brigades, from right to left, 185, 186 and 187. In I ANZAC corps reserve were 1st AIF Division, and for V Corps, 7th and 58th Divisions. Although the plan of attack had been much more carefully thought out and prepared than that for First Bullecourt there were still elements of concern that had not always been fully addressed. One of these was the importance of close liaison between the left hand 6 Australian Brigade and the neighbouring right hand 185 Brigade. Whether this was achievable given the tensions between the two corps that had arisen during First Bullecourt and the fact that the Australian Brigade HQ was established close to the front line and the British HQ some three miles behind it was open to question. The Australian need to advance into a re-entrant with the serious consequent threat from enfilade fire had also led them to narrow their front of attack initially (with the intention of widening it later by bombing outwards along the target trenches once entered). The narrowing would result in a 300 yard-wide gap between the two brigades that there was not even a plan to neutralise by an artillery barrage. A second concern was the state of 62nd Division. Although they would have the support of eight tanks, it was questionable whether these, even if well led, would compensate for a largely inexperienced division given the difficult tasks of capturing Bullecourt and Hendecourt.

The two Australian brigades began their advance at 0345 on 3 May under cover of a creeping barrage that initially crept at the rate of 100 yards every three minutes, and heavy machine gun support providing overhead and flanking fire as well as anti-aircraft protection. Even though they were attacking in darkness from preference, 5 Brigade's infantry began to bunch in front of the German wire despite it having been almost completely destroyed. There they were confronted by heavy German machine gun fire sweeping the ground in front of them. Despite this, some tried to move on; others hesitated. At this stage the order to retire was given by someone who had panicked. It was quickly obeyed and the troops streamed back to the relative protection of the Bullecourt-Quéant road. The Brigade's attack had been a total failure. The 6 Brigade were more successful. They took full advantage of the well cut enemy wire and their 24th Battalion and the right of 22nd Battalion entered the first Hindenburg Line. By 0418 the same units had carried their sectors of the second trench. By contrast the left half of 22nd Battalion enjoyed no success. Coming under heavy enfilade fire from Bullecourt they were forced back.

The extent of the reverse inflicted on 5 Brigade did not immediately become apparent to Divisional HQ, which had received misleading indications of what was unfolding. The first intimation that things had gone badly wrong was when men began coming back. Even this did not conclusively prove that the Brigade's attack had been the total failure that it was. It was the GOC of 6 Brigade, Brigadier General J. Gellibrand, who, from the vantage point of his Brigade HQ established on the railway line very close to the fighting, was the first to assess correctly what was happening and counter the optimistic reports emanating from 5 Brigade HQ. He notified Divisional HQ only an hour or so after Zero Hour that the bulk of 5 Brigade were falling back. He was immediately given a company of the reserve 7 Brigade's 26th Battalion to help rally the troops who had retreated and lead them forward once again in a second effort to capture the first objective. The resultant advance began at 0545 with some 200 men of 5 Brigade becoming the second wave behind the 26th Battalion's company. Once again the attack largely failed to reach the German front line because of the heavy hostile fire. A small number of men who did get into the trench did not have sufficient support to bomb their way eastward as the officer leading them wanted.

At the same time as the events above were unfolding, the units of 6 Brigade that had carried the first two German trenches were advancing on the Fontaine-Quéant road and, on the right, to just beyond the road to the line of a tramway. Parts of the 24th Battalion having reached the tramway line, some members of the 23rd Battalion, who were under orders to take the final objective, Riencourt, moved up on their right aiming to reach the crossroads just southwest of that village. But with their right flank open, through the absence of 5 Brigade, and exposed to fire from untouched enemy trenches, they could do no more than form a defensive flank. Any further advance was out of the question especially given the state of affairs on the Brigade left. An order that the 25th Battalion of 7 Brigade should assist 62nd Division, whose assault was in trouble, by attacking Bullecourt from the southeast across open ground, was countermanded when the first two platoons sent forward were assailed by heavy fire that caused severe losses and pinned the survivors down.

In the places where the Australians had got into the Hindenburg Line trenches they attempted to bomb their way along them. The clashes swayed to and fro, with sometimes the Australians making good progress before being pushed back and vice-versa. On the right, having made progress eastward they were driven back to where the trenches crossed the central road; on the left they could not get beyond the point where the Hindenburg support trench crossed the Riencourt-Bullecourt road.

Another battalion of the reserve 7 Brigade, the 28th, was placed at the disposal of the GOC 5 Brigade for the purpose of capturing those parts of the Hindenburg Line which the original attacks had failed to take. They were able to reach the two trenches in question by way of the central road that largely concealed them from enemy view. At 1400 they began to bomb eastward and on three occasions were able to get as far as the Noreuil-Riencourt road, a distance of about 500 yards, but each time they were driven back, the last being at 2040. Just after the last of these failures two events occurred which led to a serious mistake being made by 28th Battalion. The first was that they came under a heavy bombardment targeting the area south of the Hindenburg Line; the second was that they mistook a group of 5 Brigade men, who had been sheltering out in shell holes all day and were now taking advantage of the growing darkness to move back, for German troops attempting to cut them off. Coupled with the spreading of a false report that 6 Brigade on their left were falling back and the state of exhaustion the 28th Battalion were in after prolonged fighting, the perhaps inevitable happened and an order to retire was given. In fact there had been no retirement by 6 Brigade. Indeed they were to decline to do so even when they received the same order as 28th Battalion. Instead they worked hard to strengthen their defensive situation and await relief where they were.

To the Australian left, the relatively inexperienced 62nd Division would attack on a three brigade front. On the right were 185 Brigade, whose infantry element consisted of four battalions of the West Yorkshire Regiment. Two of these, the 2/6th on the right and the 2/5th on the left, both rather understrength, would lead the assault. The 2/7th would be in support and the 2/8th had been sent on temporary attachment to 186 Brigade. The first formidable challenge confronting the two assault battalions was the capture of Bullecourt. They would first have to take the German front line Tower trench that formed a semi-circle to the south of the village starting and finishing where it joined the Hindenburg Front Line trench west and east of the village. This eastern junction also marked the notional boundary between 6 Australian Brigade and 185 Brigade although, as has been noted, the Australians had deliberately left a gap of 300 yards between the two brigades ending at this point. Once the German front line trench had been taken, the next obstacle would be the Hindenburg Front Line trench running east-west through the centre of the village. The Hindenburg Support Line trench just to the north of the village also added significantly to Bullecourt's defences and would need to be dealt with.[1]

It was belatedly decided that the assault battalions' start line should be about 200 yards behind that originally planned on the railway embankment, because of the bright moonlight. The assembly and forming up were successfully achieved without enemy interference. At Zero Hour the advance began. Within five minutes the enemy's hostile barrage had begun and would continue at an intense level for an hour before decreasing. Enemy machine guns also quickly became very active. The 2/6th West Yorks were planning to break into Bullecourt from the southeast and east of the village, but came under heavy fire from machine guns firing from the shelter of a derelict tank and nearby, as well as from the enemy artillery barrage, resulting in heavy casualties. As they advanced they came up against the wire protecting the enemy Tower trench with little prospect of finding ways through before they lost the protection of their own creeping barrage. By the time they did, the Germans manning the trench had had time to exit their dugouts and engage the Yorkshiremen with rifle and machine gun fire. In their efforts to deal with what confronted them in a darkness compounded by dust and smoke, a number of them veered off to the left where they overlapped the right of the 2/5th Battalion. Despite all their setbacks however they did manage to capture the first German trench, and a small number of one of their companies reached the village church and set up a post close by.

The 2/5th Battalion, although assailed by the machine guns that gave their sister battalion so much trouble early in the assault, did find the wire in front of them well cut and were able to take the enemy front line trench with relative ease. They pressed on towards the Hindenburg Front Line trench running through the centre of Bullecourt and managed to set up a couple of posts. Their follow up waves established contact with 2/6th Battalion's post close to the church. An attempt to reinforce 2/6th Battalion with a company from the reserve 2/7th Battalion failed with heavy losses from enemy machine gun fire. When the survivors saw troops of 186 Brigade on their left retiring in large numbers, they did likewise falling back to the railway embankment. The small British lodgements in Bullecourt came under increasing pressure during the day and were finally eliminated by German counterattacks that drove them out towards the west or forced them to surrender.[2]

Like 185 Brigade, the 186 Brigade's infantry element consisted of four battalions from the same regiment, in their case the Yorkshire based Duke of Wellington's (West Riding) Regiment (Duke's). The two assault battalions on 3 May were the 2/5th and the 2/6th. Supporting the former Battalion were the 2/7th and the 2/8th West Yorks on detachment from 185 Brigade. The 2/4th Duke's were in support of 2/6th Bn. The three objectives of the Brigade were the Hindenburg Front and Support Lines, the Fontaine-Quéant road (partly forming the German artillery protection line), and the village of Hendecourt. The leading waves of the assault battalions were a couple of minutes late in getting under way having veered slightly to the right on their way forward to the start line, a sunken road. But generally the troops had moved forward without losing direction with the assistance of taped lines. The barrages of both sides however soon enveloped the whole area in clouds of dust that, coupled with the extreme darkness, made maintaining direction with any certainty very difficult. Nevertheless on the right of the 2/5th Duke's, the wire was found to be well cut although it did channel the men into the first objective at places separated from each other by pockets still occupied by the enemy. The Battalion's troops on the extreme right came under accurate fire from a solitary enemy machine gun, forcing them to check their advance. They were reinforced by 2/8th West Yorks in an apparently fruitless attempt to get moving forward again. By midday, numbers of the two battalions had been bombed back to shell holes south and southwest of Bullecourt. Other members succeeded in reaching and occupying a factory north of the village. They were sighted there by a reconnaissance aircraft.

On the left of the Brigade front, 2/6th Duke's found the enemy wire to be in good repair with very few gaps. This state of affairs and the accurate hostile shellfire obliged the leading waves to take

---

1   TNA WO 95/3079/3: 185 Brigade War Diary.
2   *OH 1917 Volume 1*, pp. 463-4. TNA WO 95/30/9/3: 185 Brigade War Diary.

shelter in shell holes, thereby losing their artillery cover. The rear waves coming up behind created a deal of congestion and confusion, made worse by their tendency to veer to the right. As attempts were being made to sort out the confusion and cut back the enemy wire, the Battalion were subjected to bombing attacks and enfilade machine gun fire from their left. With the 2/4th Duke's also by now involved, the two battalions were ordered back to the line of the railway embankment to reorganise. A further attempt of the limited numbers now remaining to get forward proved ineffective.[3]

The 62nd Division third Brigade, the 187th, consisted of two KOYLI battalions (the 2/4th and the 2/5th) and two battalions of The York and Lancaster Regiment (the 2/4th and 2/5th). These last two battalions would lead the assault with the 2/4th on the right and 2/5th on the left. The 2/5th KOYLI would be in support. The task of the assaulting battalions was to reach the second objective, the Fontaine-Quéant road, where they were to stop and form a defensive left flank. To achieve this they would have to cross the Hindenburg Front and Support lines. By 0145 the leading waves were formed up on tapes which had been laid with the aid of the bright moonlight that was soon to disappear. While waiting in position they were subjected to shelling that lasted about 20 minutes and caused an appreciable number of casualties. The whole line was supposed to have begun to advance eight minutes before Zero but because they had been ordered to keep touch with the man on the right there was a tendency to wait until he moved off before following suit, thus resulting in there being a period of about five minutes before everyone was on the move. Once moving there was an instinctive tendency, probably caused by the conformation of the ground, to circumvent shell holes to the right; this led to a gradual drift to the right of the prescribed line of advance, and bunching. When the enemy wire was reached it was very difficult to locate gaps in the total darkness. As they tried to find a way through they formed the impression that members of the Brigade on their right had intruded into their sector in their efforts to find gaps in the wire. Whether this was indeed the case must be open to question as 2/6th and 2/4th Duke's had also tended to drift rightwards. What is not open to question is that the situation was becoming increasingly one of confusion, compounded by the arrival of successive waves. Somehow 2/5th York and Lancs, on the left, succeeded in crossing the Hindenburg Front line without recognising it and then entered the sunken Lagnicourt-St Martin road. There they began to be joined by men of other units. Meanwhile some of the men detailed for the attack on the Support Line did in fact reach it; others made no attempt to do so. The 187 Brigade's report on the day's operation highlights the state of confusion reigning at this point. 'Company commanders, owing to the darkness, did not know whether their men had gone on or not, or if so, how many. In fact, many officers and men completely lost their bearings and walked in circles.'[4]

Lieutenant Colonel W, Watson, the CO of 2/5th KOYLI, tried to restore some order to the situation, threatening any men he found trying to retire with his revolver, seeking instead to get them moving forward. Unfortunately he was soon killed and with his death the attack rapidly began to lose any chance of success. Many men, perceiving themselves to be leaderless, either stayed where they were in shell holes or in the sunken road or, in the case of 300 of them, made their way back to the railway cutting. Although at this stage it was by no means clear whether those men who had not retired were sheltering in shell holes in front of the German lines or had in fact reached and entered them it was decided that a second attack should be mounted with artillery and machine gun support using the 300 men who had retired and any others who might be found in shell holes as the attack passed over them. At this stage it was believed that 186 Brigade had taken the two Hindenburg lines and if the second attack by 187 Brigade were launched promptly it would have a good chance of success. This optimism proved ill-founded. The attack was launched at 0825 and almost immediately foundered under a hail of enemy machine gun fire. Some of the survivors of this and the first attack now sought to retire in twos and threes, suffering further losses as they did so. The more prudent clung to their

3   Op. cit., p.464. TNA WO 95/3084/2: 186 Brigade War Diary.
4   TNA WO 95/3088/2: 187 Brigade War Diary.

shelter in shell holes to await a more propitious opportunity.

The Brigade had suffered around 50 percent casualties during the day for what the GOC described as, 'a failure, a costly failure'. He blamed the failure on a Zero Hour which had turned what should have been a dawn attack into a night attack for which his troops were untrained and inexperienced. He was also critical of his troops for their failure to use their own initiative when left to their own devices.[5]

Mention should be made of the eight tanks of Sections 9 and 10, No. 12 Company, D Battalion, Machine Gun Corps Heavy Branch, which were assigned to assist 62nd Division on 3 May. These tanks, all inadequately armoured Mark Ones or Twos, had survived the Battle of Vimy Ridge on 9 April by dint of bogging down in the mud and shell holes before they had offered themselves as targets for the German defenders of the ridge. They were to enjoy mixed fortunes on 3 May as they came up against German defenders who no longer panicked at the merest sight of them and had an effective weapon to deploy against them in the form of armour piercing bullets. The most notable achievements of the day were recorded by Tanks Nos. 793, 596 and 785. Commanded by Second Lieutenant Charles Knight, Tank 793 drove along the western side of Bullecourt before turning into the village itself and driving into the centre. Under heavy fire from enemy armour-piercing bullets, the tank drove back and forth along the German trench defending the southern sector of the village until, with four of his crew and he himself wounded, Knight decided to withdraw to the predetermined rallying point for the tanks. On the way there they came across a broken-down tank with its crew intact. Knight thereupon exchanged his wounded men for four fit men from the other tank and turned Tank 793 back to Bullecourt. There it remained in action until wounds to a further three of his makeshift crew forced him to accept that they could not continue. The tank returned to its starting point after seven hours in action. All its crew had by then been wounded.

Tank 596 was commanded by Lieutenant T. Westbrook. It crossed the British front line at Zero plus 25 minutes. Upon reaching the German trenches Lieutenant Westbrook was told by a British infantry officer that they were having trouble from a German machine gun. Despite the danger from enemy fire Lieutenant Westbrook emerged from the tank and, in consultation with the infantry officer, decided on a plan to deal with the problem. Telling the infantry officer to follow with his men, Westbrook returned to his tank. Although it soon became apparent that the infantry were not following, the tank continued on its way and dealt with the machine gun without infantry support. In moving back to the enemy wire a second machine gun was detected and dealt with. By now, with several of his crew and he himself wounded and the tank severely damaged and disabled, with five of its Lewis guns out of action, Westbrook decided to abandon the tank and try to get back to the British lines. The whole crew successfully made it back.

Tank 785 was under the command of Second Lieutenant Herbert Chick. It left its starting point promptly at Zero Hour. Twenty minutes later it encountered about 600 British infantrymen returning from the German lines. Their commanding officer told Lieutenant Chick they had been unable to get through the thick belts of enemy wire under heavy machine gun fire. Chick believed that he and his tank could help the infantry by penetrating the wire and eliminating the troublesome machine guns by attacking the strong point sheltering them. The infantry could follow 200 yards behind. Tank 785 performed precisely as planned, getting into the strong point and knocking out several machine guns and emplacements. They then waited for the infantry to come up, but they were still held up. With four of his crew wounded Chick decided to return to the British lines and did so successfully.[6]

Most of the remaining tanks also performed creditably, but mainly fell victim to enemy action,

---

5   Ibid.
6   Tank 785 was to survive the battle, and also the rest of the war. It is now the only surviving Mark II in the world and is a major attraction at the Tank Museum at Bovington Camp, Dorset.

mechanical failure or the boggy ground or a combination of them, before they could make a really telling contribution. Nevertheless this was one action where the Battalion as a whole had made a difference. The price paid was high. Of the 64 tank officers and crew who went into action on that first day, 34 became casualties.[7]

It had become apparent by midday on the first day of Second Bullecourt that there was very little positive to show for the efforts of 2nd Australian Division and 62nd British Division. About the only productive outcome of the two divisions' efforts had been the capture by the Australians of stretches of the Hindenburg Front and Support Lines to the east of Bullecourt. Despite casualties amounting to nearly 3,000, 62nd Division had not succeeded in capturing Bullecourt. This failure threatened the Australians' tenuous hold on the Hindenburg Lines as enemy weaponry could enfilade their positions from the village. If the battle were not to be abandoned therefore, there was a clear and urgent need to resume the assault on Bullecourt. 62nd Division were obviously in no fit state to take on this task single-handed, if at all. Nor at this early stage could there be any question of abandonment. Accordingly the V Corps GOC ordered 7th British Division to take over from 185 Brigade and launch an immediate fresh attack on Bullecourt. An all regular division, it was made up originally of battalions shipped back from the Colonies in the early weeks of the war. By early October 1914 it was in Belgium under orders to assist in the defence of Antwerp. Too late to intervene effectively in that lost cause, it moved down to the Ypres area where it participated in the First Battle of Ypres and began to build its reputation as one of the finest divisions in the BEF. By the time of Arras it had seen service in virtually all the actions fought by the BEF on the Western Front. Although its all regular composition had been inevitably much diluted by April 1917 it still continued to enjoy its reputation as a great fighting formation.

At 1245 on 3 May the task of relieving 185 Brigade and carrying out the attack was devolved by the recently appointed GOC of 7th Division, Major General Thomas H. Shoubridge, on 22 Brigade. It would be a two battalion attack with 2/1st The Honourable Artillery Company (HAC) and 1st Royal Welsh Fusiliers (RWF) leading. The former Battalion, due to attack on the right would be reinforced on their right by a company from 2/7th West Yorks, on attachment from 185 Brigade. The Brigade's remaining two battalions, 2nd Warwicks and 20th Manchesters, would form up on the railway, ready to pass through the leading battalions and complete the capture of Bullecourt if required. The plan for the attack, originally scheduled to start at 1830, called for the two battalions to advance on either side of the road leading into Bullecourt from Écoust-St-Mein (the Longatte-Bullecourt road) and make what would be a night assault on Tower trench. Once the trench had been secured they were to advance into the village. Once in the centre, 2nd HAC were to establish contact with 6 Australian Brigade on their right and 1st RWF were to dig in and form a defensive flank facing northwest, based on the western perimeter of the village. It became clear that the scheduled 1830 start was unrealistic given the two battalions' lack of familiarity with the ground over which they would have to advance as well as the layout of the German wire and the whereabouts of any gaps that had been blasted in it. A postponement of Zero Hour to 2230 was therefore ordered so that the terrain could be reconnoitred by officers of both battalions. During the course of this it became evident that the German artillery was targeting the railway embankment in the confident knowledge that it would be there that any attack would assemble. The assembly area of 2nd HAC was therefore moved back 300 yards, and Zero moved forward three minutes, to try to minimise casualties from the enemy guns and any loss of time.

At 2230 both battalions, the HAC having come back into line with 1st RWF, began to cross the 300 yards of open and shell-pocked ground that constituted no man's land. Depressingly the ground was also covered with the bodies of those comrades who had been killed in the day's early fighting. Many of those now advancing with fixed bayonets would soon join them. The creeping

7   Paul Kendall, *Bullecourt 1917*, pp. 227-33.

barrage behind which the leading waves advanced did little to protect them from enemy machine gun fire emanating from Bullecourt and the German trenches. The two main problems for the attackers were the German wire, the thickness of which seemed to have been enhanced rather than diminished by the attempts of the artillery to clear it, and a darkness, exacerbated by the smoke of the barrage, so intense that some of those who had reached the enemy trenches stumbled into them unaware of where they were. Nevertheless both battalions reached and occupied Tower trench after severe hand to hand fighting. Fifty prisoners were taken. The hold of 1st RWF on Tower trench was limited to the remnants of their right hand C Company, A Company on their left having got entangled in the German wire. As they had no apparent support on the right either, they were forced to withdraw. The 2nd HAC's hold on Tower trench was more solid with remnants of both their A and B Companies in possession. Accordingly C and D Companies passed through and entered Bullecourt. As they did so their situation became exposed, especially to fire from both flanks, and from the rear where German infantry emerged from bunkers that had been bypassed, to assail them. Many of the HAC men found themselves surrounded. A German counterattack succeeded in driving C Company out of the village and back to Tower trench.

By now the attack was running short of ammunition, especially bombs, and there were no stocks readily available for resupply. By 0230 on the 4th German counterattacks with bombing parties had managed to drive both the outnumbered British battalions back and out of Tower trench. Machine gun fire pursued them as they tried to get back to the British line. At 0330 the two battalions were ordered to withdraw. Many wounded were left out in no man's land. Some of these would succumb to fire from the British artillery as it searched out enemy positions north of Tower trench. Losses had been heavy, especially those of 2nd HAC. The attack had been a failure; the Germans remained in complete control of Bullecourt.[8]

The first day's fighting came to an end with 2nd Australian Division, by virtue of the tenacity and élan of 6 Brigade, in precarious possession of stretches of the Hindenburg Front and Support Lines (known to the Australians as O.G.1 and O.G.2 respectively[9]), and with 62nd and latterly 7th British Divisions almost completely back to where they had begun the day. Losses in all cases had been heavy. As had been appreciated before the commitment of 7th Division, the key to progress by both the British and Australians lay in the capture of Bullecourt, the British because the village stood in the way of their final objective of Hendecourt, the Australians because their hold on their gains in the Hindenburg Line was very vulnerable to enfilade fire from the village while it remained in enemy hands. As there was no question at this stage of calling a halt to Second Bullecourt the capture of the village would remain the top priority. For the Germans its successful retention was just as important as it was close to where their *Wotan* Line (the Drocourt-Quéant Switch) linked up with the Hindenburg Line.

It would not have been in the Australian nature to adopt a defensive posture and wait for the British to capture Bullecourt. During the early hours of the morning of 4 May the relief of 6 Brigade by the 3rd and 1st Battalions of the 1st Division 1 Brigade was completed despite an enemy counterattack that the relievers and relieved combined to drive off. At dawn the 2nd Battalion of the same Brigade relieved some posts of 5 Brigade.[10] It was decided to use these relatively fresh troops to extend the Australian foothold in the two Hindenburg Line trenches so as to give them more room to absorb the shock of the enemy counterattacks that would inevitably be coming. The 1st Division 3 Brigade, in camp near Bapaume, were told to be ready to move forward at very short notice. To say

8   Ibid., pp. 236-9. TNA WO 95/1662:2nd/1st Honourable Artillery Company War Diary; TNA WO 95/1665: 1st Royal Welsh Fusiliers War Diary.

9   The codes had previously been applied by the Australians to German trenches during the Somme Campaign fighting for Pozières and Pozières Ridge, the 'O.G.' standing for 'Old German'. Kendall, op. cit., p. 37.

10   So unexpected was it that 1st Australian Division would become involved in Second Bullecourt that two of the Brigade commanders had been sent on leave.

that there was a degree of dissatisfaction in Australian circles at the increasing likelihood that growing numbers of their brigades would find themselves drawn into an attritional and profitless battle, would be putting it mildly. Disillusionment with British generalship. and General Gough in particular, went up another notch as, perhaps with a degree of hindsight, it was perceived that had Fifth Army focused all its effort from the outset on taking Bullecourt, it would have been quickly captured.[11]

The Australian attempt to expand the extent of their grip on O.G.s 1 and 2 would take the form of bombing along the trenches in both directions from their current positions. The 3rd and 1st Battalions, temporarily under the command of Brigadier General Gellibrand of 6 Brigade in the absence of their own commander on leave, would attack westward towards Bullecourt. The 2nd Battalion, to be joined as soon as possible by 4th Battalion, and temporarily under the command of Brigadier General Smith of 5 Brigade, would attack eastward, aiming for the point where the Hindenburg Line crossed the Noreuil-Riencourt spur. Before these attacks could be launched the Australians had to fend off enemy counterattacks that featured, for the first time in their experience, flamethrowers. The attacks were nevertheless satisfactorily dealt with and at 1300 on 4 May the Australians belatedly resumed the offensive. The 3rd Battalion bombers moved along O.G.2 finding the going increasingly hard as the enemy resisted with machine gun fire and stick bombs. When several NCOs became casualties the advance slowed but picked up again under the lead of a company commander, and reached a cross trench L linking the two O.G.s. The 1st Battalion's bombers were meanwhile progressing along O.G.1 until they reached the same cross trench and linked up with their comrades. The Australian left flank was now 725 yards west of the Central Road. East of that road was now the responsibility of 2nd Battalion which would have to advance along both O.G.s. Their start was delayed while arrangements for artillery support were put in place. The advance in both trenches eventually began at 1415 and made fair progress even though cross trenches north of O.G.2 were found to be manned by the enemy. The advance paused to enable the artillery to lay down a barrage on both O.G.s further to the east. It resumed at 1540 and evolved into a deadly bombing battle, which was to continue until about 1900. By then the Australians had advanced about 400 yards from the Central Road, less than they had hoped to achieve. But, unlike the previous day, they would not be pushed back from the positions they had reached.

No sooner had the bombing battle died down than it was superseded by a two hour long enemy artillery barrage targeted on the Australian occupied stretches of O.G.s 1 and 2 and the area beyond back to the railway embankment. The O.G.s were wide and offered scant cover. Losses were accordingly significant. It soon became apparent that the barrage was the precursor to further counterattacks launched by the Germans down some of the cross trenches leading to the two O.G.s. These were largely dealt with by the British artillery, but one attack on a 3rd Battalion post near the junction of O.G.2 with cross trench L did succeed in driving the garrison, running short of bombs, out at around 2200. After a couple of barrages that seemed to be as much of a threat to their own side as to the enemy, and some disorganised and half-hearted attempts by the infantry to retake the post it became clear that the 3rd Battalion had shot their bolt offensively. The front line was redrawn to take account of this German intrusion. In the meantime two relatively fresh battalions, the 11th and 12th, had arrived to relieve some of the troops currently under the command of Brigadier Generals Gellibrand and Smith. Both the new battalions were from the 1st Division 3 Brigade. In anticipation that most of the enemy pressure in the immediate future would fall on the section of the Australian line to the right of the Central Road, both the new battalions were assigned to that sector by the Divisional GOC, where they relieved 2nd and 4th Battalions. The trenches to the left of Central Road would continue to be in the hands of the weary 1st and 3rd Battalions. Both Gellibrand and Smith relinquished their front line commands, being relieved by acting brigade commanders from 1st

---

11   *OH of Australia in the War of 1914-18, Volume IV*, p. 491.

Division. Such was the situation as 5 May dawned.[12]

The 5 and 6 May would see a continuation of heavy fighting as the Germans sought, by persistent counterattacks, to throw the Australians out of their hard won gains in O.G.1 and O.G.2, by now about 1,100 yards in width. For their part the Australians would seek, on the right of the Central Road, to complete the capture of the Noreuil-Riencourt spur and, on the left of the road, to recover the lost post and stand firm against an aggressive enemy. The newly arrived 12th Battalion were placed on the right in both trenches with the 11th Battalion on their left ready to pass through if the 12th were held up prior to reaching the crest of the spur. Planning for, and timing of, the Australian advance were complicated, not only by German counterattacks, but also by the intense artillery activity of both sides which led to seriously damaged trenches requiring urgent excavation and repair. A further difficulty was introduced by the close similarity of both sides' infantry signals to their respective artilleries causing the former's requirements to be misinterpreted by the latter, which could and did lead to barrages being fired when none was required or not being fired when one was.

Just before noon on the 5th the Germans began an intense barrage of the whole sector occupied by 3 Brigade. This persisted undiminished throughout the afternoon and after dark intensified into a bombardment that, according to men who experienced both, bore comparison to those suffered by the Australians at Pozières. Many men were buried and had to be dug out. There could be no question of carrying out the planned advance on the Noreuil-Riencourt spur despite orders that 11th Battalion should take over the lead from 12th Battalion and advance. The two battalions could muster only 200 unwounded men between them and there was little doubt, among the officers in the trenches, that the enemy would be following up the bombardment with a counterattack. For the moment however the enemy determined that a further bombardment was required. It began at 0100 on 6 May. Only the extreme right of 12th Battalion, presumably deemed to be too close to German positions, escaped the attention of the enemy guns. The suffering of the rest of the two battalions continued from where it had left off with many men being buried, some more than once. The bombardment continued steadily until 0430 when it intensified. The German infantry made little effort to hide their intentions and at 0330 these provoked an Australian counter barrage. Apparently little discouraged by this the German infantry began to advance at 0500. Unfortunately for them, at the same moment the Australian guns began firing what had been intended to be the supporting barrage for a planned Australian attack. Combined with the rifle, machine gun and Lewis gun fire of the Australian garrison, which had just been reinforced by a company from 10th Battalion, it effectively ensured that the enemy attack was a failure. However a simultaneous enemy attack along both Hindenburg trenches from the right proved much more difficult to deal with. The attack along O.G.1 featured a total of three flamethrowers at various stages, which created a degree of havoc in the Australian ranks. The situation was partially restored by the use of trench mortars, which the Germans tried, but failed, to eliminate or capture. Nevertheless O.G.1 was more or less emptied of Australians right back to the Central Road. Eventually, with the elimination of two of the flamethrowers, a steadying of the ranks of the 11th and 12th Battalions and a notable intervention from 1st Battalion from their positions just to the left of Central Road, the situation was restored, the Germans were put to flight and the Australians recovered all their lost ground.

The CO of 1st Battalion could not but have become aware of the plight of the two battalions to the east, given his Battalion's position. He had in any case been warned by a Corporal G. Howell that the Battalion on their right [presumably the 11th] were retiring. The CO had at once ordered his Signals Officer to take all available men and drive the pursuing enemy back. The two officers leading the Germans had soon been killed and the rest of the 80-strong enemy group had been forced to take shelter in O.G.1 from Australian machine gun fire. At this stage Corporal Howell took it upon himself to race alongside O.G.1 dropping bombs down on the enemy troops forcing them to flee to

12   Ibid., pp. 492-506.

the rear.[13] There could be no question of 1st Battalion following up Corporal Howell's coup de main as this would have drawn them out of position when the evidence was growing that the enemy were waiting for an opportunity to attack in their sector.

For the rest of the day in the Australian sector most of the activity was artillery led with only minor actions involving the infantry. Reserves were moved forward in anticipation of further enemy counterattacks, but these hardly materialised. A relatively quiet night reflected the fact that both sides were worn out from their exertions in the four days since 3 May.[14]

In the early hours of 4 May the 7th British Division 22 Brigade were deploying for their second attempt to capture Bullecourt. The two battalions previously in reserve, 20th Manchesters and 2nd Warwicks, were ordered to recapture Tower trench in an attack scheduled to start at 0400. In order for the preparatory bombardment to be fired the few remnants of 2nd HAC and 1st RWF still forward of the British front line were pulled back from their shell holes in front of Tower trench. The two fresh battalions formed up close to the railway at around 0330 where shortly thereafter they were caught in an enemy barrage which wrought particular devastation on the Manchesters, who suffered 80 casualties (some reports suggest their losses could have been as high as 75 percent). Less affected by the barrage, the Warwicks were still able to begin their advance on schedule. They reached the enemy wire, cut through it and entered the village, but were pushed back by counterattacks. They then received orders to link up with what remained of 1st RWF and send patrols into Bullecourt. About 200 men were involved. They tried to reach the village by way of a sunken road on the southwestern edge but had to dig in. Very little news of what was happening was getting back to HQs. Officers were sent forward to try to clarify the situation. They found that some groups of men were in positions near to the Crucifix, an enemy fortified strong point on the village's western perimeter. An effort was made to push towards it with a bombing attack from the sunken road beginning at 1100. It was met by heavy machine gun fire that drove the attackers back with heavy casualties. The much depleted Manchesters did manage to get into the village from the southeast, but were too weak in numbers to hold on there.

The second attempt to capture Bullecourt was a failure. A survivor from 20th Manchesters remarked cynically in exculpation that 22 Brigade had been called upon to capture an objective that a full division with eight tanks had failed to manage.[15]

By the end of the events described above the Anglo-Australian situation was that very little progress had been made towards completing the objectives which had been ordained. Hendecourt, Riencourt and, above all, Bullecourt remained firmly in German hands as did the bulk of the Hindenburg Front and Support Lines. In the process the 2nd Australian Division and 62nd Division had been seriously used up and 1st Australian and 7th British Divisions were in danger of following suit. Even though Haig's thoughts, and increasingly those of Gough, must have been turning towards the planned Belgian Flanders campaign, there appeared to be no suggestion that Bullecourt should be wound down despite its increasing irrelevance in the overall scheme of things. The rationale for continuing it seemed to have moved on from lending support to the French to it being a means of diverting German attention from the BEF's preparations for the Flanders offensive. Gough was therefore ordered to continue his Army pressure on the enemy. An operation with the limited objective of safeguarding the Australian left flank (which remained very vulnerable while Bullecourt remained in enemy hands) was accordingly planned. It began on 5 May with two days of artillery preparation that included feint barrages, one of which, fired by 62nd Division, would target the Hindenburg Line northwest of Bullecourt. The infantry's part would be a combined operation involving 7th Division 20 Brigade and 1st Australian Division 3 Brigade. 7th Division initially asked the Australians to secure

---

13   Despite being wounded during his exploit, for which he was awarded the Victoria Cross, Corporal G.J. Howell survived the war.

14   *OH of Australia*, op. cit., pp. 514-19.

15   Kendall, op. cit. pp. 245-6.

beforehand the two Hindenburg trenches leading up to the northeastern corner of Bullecourt with an attack to be launched at 2130 on 6 May. At 0345 the following morning the British Brigade's 2nd Gordon Highlanders, supported by 9th Devons would advance from southeast of Bullecourt to seize the triangular area between the Tower trench and the Hindenburg Front Line and the southeastern part of the village, and link up with the Australians. But the 7th Division's plan allowed insufficient time for Australian preparation when it proved necessary to bring in 3 Brigade's 9th Battalion for the operation. (For good measure 1 Brigade at the same time relieved their exhausted 1st and 3rd Battalions, who were holding the left of O.G.s 1 and 2, with their 2nd and 4th Battalions.) It was then agreed that both the British and Australian brigades would launch their attacks simultaneously at 0345 on 7 May.

The 9th Battalion arrived at nightfall on 6 May and made their way through 2nd and 4th Battalions to take up positions on the extreme left of the Australian held stretch of the two trenches, three companies in O.G.1, where the main thrust would be made, and one in O.G.2. The start of the Australian advance along O.G.1 was delayed by 14 minutes to avoid getting too close to their own supporting barrage. When they did advance they clambered over the barricade separating the Australian held sector of trench from that held by the enemy and began bombing along it. The Germans rapidly responded and a fierce struggle ensued with the outcome in doubt for some time. Rifle grenades and Lewis guns played a full part but the German tactic of manning shell holes on either side of the trench with snipers and machine gunners caused the Australians problems as did their running short of supplies of bombs at crucial moments. However, by adopting the German tactic described above and receiving further supplies of bombs in the nick of time the Australians began to prevail and at 0515 established contact with the Gordons.

The single company of 9th Battalion that was to advance along O.G.2 were given the task of setting up four posts, each to be manned by a platoon. They came up against equally fierce opposition as they attempted to advance, but managed to push the Germans back beyond Cross trench L and set up two posts just short of it. The two remaining platoons continued to move forward towards the crossroads 250 yards further on that was their final objective. But increasing enemy rifle, machine gun and rifle grenade fire, and the failure of 7th Division to come up on the left, meant that, even if taken, the crossroads could not have been held. The remaining two posts were therefore set up in Cross trench L.[16]

The attack by 7th Division 20 Brigade, starting from southeast of Bullecourt and heading northwest, had three objectives which were; to secure the length of Tower trench protecting the southeast of Bullecourt (the Blue Line); then to take the section of trench from O.G.1 in the east westward to Bullecourt (the Green Line); finally to secure the Riencourt-Bullecourt road (the Red Line). The overall aim was to link up with the Australian 9th Battalion on the right and enter the village from the southeast on the left. The lead would be taken by two companies of 2nd Gordons, followed by two companies of 9th Devons in a mopping up role. They in turn would be followed by the remaining two companies of the Gordons. Behind them, on the railway, were 9th Devon's two remaining companies. The 8th Devons were in positions on the railway south of Bullecourt having recently returned from attachment to 22 Brigade. In brigade reserve were 2nd Borders.

The hours of darkness before Zero Hour were notable for the very active German artillery. A company of 8th Devons occupying advanced posts north of the railway embankment had been ordered to withdraw to enable the British preparatory bombardment to fire without fear of hitting them. Many of the men were unable to do so because of the intensity of the German barrage and were obliged to stay in place until the following night. The 2nd Gordons also experienced this heavy shelling as they assembled for the attack in bright moonlight. By dint of crawling to the jumping off tapes they successfully escaped detection and were in position 30 minutes before Zero about 300

---

16   *OH of Australia*, op. cit., pp. 520-4.

yards from the village. The advance of the Gordons, followed by the 9th Devons, began on schedule at 0345 behind a creeping barrage fired by Australian guns. Little opposition was encountered and the Gordons soon gained a foothold in Tower trench. Bombing parties then began to fight their way northeastwards with the aim of linking up with the Australian 9th Battalion. By 0515 the Gordons were in possession of their second objective, the Green Line, and in touch with the Australians. Although the German artillery reacted violently and poured down fire on the Gordons they only succeeded in dislodging them from a small portion on the left of their second objective. Their position may have been precarious but, as long as they could cling on, the Australian hold on the Hindenburg Front and Support Lines was relatively secure. But very little, if any, progress had been made in expelling the Germans from Bullecourt. Indeed their hold on the area of the village and its defences known as the Red Patch,[17] had been strongly reinforced. The main focus of future Anglo-Australian endeavour would continue to be on securing the village.[18]

A start on this was made on 8 May. Although a major priority was to achieve a link up of the British with the Australians where the two Hindenburg Lines passed into and north of the northeast of the village, the task given to two companies of 8th Devons was to launch bombing attacks from the south into the village with the aim of driving the Germans out of the Red Patch. This daunting task was made even more challenging by the presence near the southwest corner of the Patch of the heavily fortified Crucifix strong point. At 1100 the two companies began to advance westward from the stretch of the Blue Line (Tower trench) already in their possession. At first they made good progress behind the creeping barrage against relatively light opposition, capturing four dugouts. But about 50 yards short of where the trench crossed the Écoust-St-Mein – Bullecourt road they came under heavy bombing and machine gun fire from the Crucifix, and sniper fire, targeting the officers, from houses in the village. The Devons made two unsuccessful attempts to reach and capture the Crucifix, but were forced to retreat out of range of the German bomb throwers. After about two hours the fighting died down. During the course of the night the Australians brought in 14 and 15 Brigades of their 5th Division to relieve the tired battalions holding the lines east of Bullecourt. The relief was carried out under heavy enemy artillery fire.

Meanwhile 8th Devons received orders to repeat their attack the following day, the 9th, using one of the two companies, C, that had been involved in the first attack, strengthened by a platoon from one of the companies not previously engaged. Given that C Company's losses had been serious, including the Company Commander mortally wounded, and the enemy would this time be waiting for them, it must have been questionable whether an additional platoon would lead to a more satisfactory outcome than the previous day. At 1200 C Company advanced northwest into the Red Patch. Their right flank was protected by a second platoon from the other of the companies not previously engaged. A protective barrage of sorts was fired by two trench mortars; it provoked an immediate response from the German artillery. The assault involved bombers, Lewis gunners and riflemen. But the only two officers soon became casualties and the advance was stopped by fire from the Crucifix that forced the remnants of C Company to withdraw. Scarcely believably these remnants, now led by a Warrant Officer, resumed the attack at 1230. Although they managed to get into the Red Patch they could not cling on. Following behind, one of the previously uninvolved companies did manage to penetrate 200 yards into Bullecourt before being compelled to retire with heavy casualties. It now remained to prepare for the inevitable German counterattack. A Lieutenant Marshall, a platoon commander from B Company, and by now the senior surviving officer, took this in hand. Despite all the Lewis guns being knocked out and running out of rifle bombs, the remnants of 8th Devons, reinforced by the last three uncommitted platoons which arrived at 1315, succeeded in fighting off the German attack.

17   A name given to the area between Tower trench and the Bullecourt-Quéant Road west of the Longatte-Bullecourt Road, not because of any connotation of blood as one might expect, but because the area was shaded red on German maps.

18   Kendall, op. cit., pp. 257-61. *OH 1917, Volume 1*, pp. 472-3.

At this stage a party of 50 men from 9th Devons, complete with fresh supplies of bombs and rifle grenades, arrived. Lieutenant Marshall immediately organised a fresh attack. He and his men bombed their way along the Blue Line until they reached the Ecoust-Bullecourt road on each side of which they formed a defensive flank using bombers and Lewis guns. Soldiers from 2nd Borders, which had relieved 2nd Gordons, supported Marshall's left flank. Caught between the Devon assault and a British artillery barrage, many of the German infantrymen were forced into the open where they fell victim to Lewis guns. At 1600 three columns of German bombers made a concentrated final effort to drive the British out of Tower trench; it failed with enemy losses calculated to have been around 50 percent. Losses on the British side over the course of the two days had also been high, especially those of 8th Devons, at 11 officers and 241 men.[19] The newly installed 5th Australian Division had had two relatively quiet days that would extend through 10 May. They were spent improving their defences. The night of 10/11 May saw the exhausted 20 Brigade relieved by 7th Division previously uncommitted brigade, the 91st. To them would fall the task, with Australian support, of mounting the next attempt to complete the capture of Bullecourt.[20]

The planned means of achieving what, in the light of what had happened previously, was a very ambitious aim, was for 91 Brigade's 2nd Queen's, supported by four platoons of 21st Manchesters to advance northwestwards to link up with 15 Australian Brigade's 58th Battalion, advancing westwards, at the crossroads northeast of the village. At the same time the British Brigade's 1st South Staffs would advance north and northwest and fight their way through the village to the north of the Red Patch. Lastly 62nd Division 185 Brigade would attack and capture the Crucifix strong point at the southwestern edge of the village. The attack was launched at 0345 on 12 May against a background of a distinct lack of harmony in the higher echelons of command. General Gough was becoming increasingly anxious to complete the capture of Bullecourt quickly so that he could concentrate on preparations for his next task in Belgian Flanders. In his impatience, he was piling the pressure on Major General Shoubridge, GOC, 7th Division, to get the job done. Shoubridge was all too aware of what could be in store for him if he did not deliver. His predecessor in command of 7th Division had been relieved by Gough for perceived underperformance, just one of several victims of Gough's ruthlessness in dealing with perceived inadequacies on the part of subordinate commanders. In his turn therefore Shoubridge was unlikely to tolerate any shortcomings, actual or perceived, in the performance of 91 Brigade and its Commander, Brigadier General Hanway Cumming. There was already history between these two officers as General Cumming had reported critically and outspokenly on General Shoubridge's performance during two previous actions involving 91 Brigade. Shoubridge's orders on this occasion that 91 Brigade should capture Bullecourt without delay could, if not successfully implemented, be bad news for one or both of these officers. The auguries were not good. The previous attempts to take the village, one in much greater strength than 91 Brigade could muster, had all been failures and on this occasion the Brigade had been given very little time to prepare. Although theoretically fresh they had been heavily engaged in carrying duties for the previous few days that had left them tired and with losses of over 50.

The attack nevertheless made a good start on the right with 2nd Queen's reaching the ruins of the church in the northeast of the village and making contact with the Australians bombing westward along O.G.2. But the failure of 185 Brigade's 2/7th and 2/6th West Yorks to capture The Crucifix enabled the enemy to continue to funnel reinforcements into the strong point. In contrast to the Queen's, 1st South Staffs, on the left of the Brigade assault, had problems from the start when the German artillery inflicted casualties on them as they prepared to move off. They then came under heavy machine gun and sniper fire from the shelter of The Crucifix as their left flank tried to move into the Red Patch and their right into the centre of the village. Their attempt on the Red Patch became

---

19   Ibid., pp. 267-70.
20   OH 1917, Volume 1, p. 474.

completely disorganised. On the right, despite taking casualties, they did manage to get into and through the village with some of them reaching the northern and northwestern outskirts. Because of the failure to capture The Crucifix, the Germans were able to keep open a lifeline to the Red Patch and were well able to resist any attempt to effect its capture. By this stage virtually all Bullecourt was in British hands except for the southwest corner, which remained stubbornly in German possession and enabled them to prevent any daylight movement by the British in much of the village. There now began a series of attempts by 91 Brigade to eliminate this last vestige of German possession of Bullecourt. The first was an attempt by 1st South Staffs launched at 0800. It was a failure at a cost of 50 per cent casualties.

It was only at 1100 that Brigadier General Cumming gained a clear idea of the situation of his leading battalions. As a result three companies of 22nd Manchesters were ordered forward to reinforce 1st South Staffs on attachment, for use in a further attack on the Red Patch. It quickly became clear however that no forward movement was possible in the face of the German guns and machine guns. In the light of this the South Staffs CO decided that the new attack should not take place until darkness offered some protection for his troops. In the meantime General Cumming decided to see for himself and visited the HQs of all three of his battalions that had been engaged thus far. He concluded that the situation of 2nd Queen's was satisfactory, but that 1st South Staffs and 21st Manchesters, who were disorganised, tired and thirsty, should be relieved as soon as possible by 22nd Manchesters, who would not be ordered to resume the attack until the following day. Operations planned for the rest of the first day would be suspended. On his return to his headquarters General Cumming telephoned General Shoubridge to report on his findings, the decisions he had taken and his proposals for the following day. He quickly discovered that his Divisional Commander did not share his assessment. General Shoubridge considered that 91 Brigade's attack had been a total failure and that it must be resumed immediately by the same battalions that had been engaged up to this point, without relief or reinforcement. After trying in vain to persuade his Commander that waiting for the next day would be the best way forward, Brigadier Cumming declined to implement the orders he had been given. Incensed at his subordinate's disobedience, General Shoubridge ordered him to hand his command over to the CO of 21st Manchesters and leave immediately for England. Perhaps predictably, no sooner had the change of command been implemented, than the next attack was postponed by General Shoubridge to 0340 the following morning.[21]

Mention has been made of the successful link up during the course of the day of 2nd Queen's with the Australian 58th Battalion advancing west along O.G.2. In its early stages the Australian advance had shown worrying signs of running out of steam until its momentum was restored, largely by the actions of Lieutenant Rupert Moon, who was in command of a platoon of about 30 men. Moon's platoon was one of three which had been assigned the tasks of attacking the centres of enemy opposition on the left of the Australian line of advance. These consisted of a substantial dugout; a concrete German pillbox sheltering several machine guns situated between O.G.s 1 and 2; and, further to the left, another German strong point. Belying his reputation as one who was possibly too diffident to command, Moon organised, inspired and led his troops to overcome the stubborn defence of seasoned German troops enabling 58th Battalion to achieve all their objectives. His own platoon forced the surrender of 186 enemy soldiers. Despite being wounded on four separate occasions, twice seriously, during this action, Lieutenant Moon survived and was awarded the Victoria Cross.[22] 58th Battalion bought their success at a heavy price, suffering casualties of 16 officers and 300 men. They were relieved during the course of the night of 12/13 May by the British 58th Division 173 Brigade, thereby almost terminating Australian participation in the Second Battle of Bullecourt. All that remained were 54th Battalion holding O.G.s 1 and 2 east of the Central Road.

---

21   Kendall, op. cit., pp. 277-8.
22   Jonathan Walker, *The Blood Tub*, pp. 167-70. Kendall, op. cit., pp. 274-8. *OH of Australia*, op. cit., pp. 530-1.

The British 58th (2/1st London) Division was a second line Territorial Division composed, as its bracketed name suggests, entirely of battalions of the City or County of London Regiment, badged into the Royal Fusiliers. The Division had fully arrived in France by 8 February 1917, and saw action initially following up the German voluntary retirement to the Hindenburg Line. The relief of the Australian 58th Battalion by 173 Brigade's 2/3rd and 2/4th Battalions London Regiment had resulted in 80 casualties. Nevertheless, when the Germans mounted a full counterattack on the morning of the 13th, in an attempt to reverse the Australian successes of the previous day, they gave a good account of themselves and beat them off. Three days later the Division 175 Brigade relieved 7th Division, meaning that 58th Division were holding the line from Bullecourt in the west to the western side of the Central Road in the east.

For 7th Division 91 Brigade however, whom we left on the night of 12/13 May, there was still work to be done in the hope of completing the capture of Bullecourt before they could look forward to their relief by 175 Brigade. The first operation was that ordered by General Shoubridge for 0340 on the 13th. Brigadier General Cummings' proposal that 22nd Manchesters should attack from the east had been discarded along with him. Instead, the Manchesters would attack from the northeast and 2nd Warwicks, on attachment from 22 Brigade to replace the withdrawn 21st Manchesters, would attack from the southwest. The dangers such a plan posed from errant 'friendly' artillery fire trying to aim in darkness at a diminishing target as the two battalions converged were either disregarded or considered a risk worth taking. The results were disastrous with first the Warwicks being hit by the British barrage falling short and then the Manchesters suffering the same fate as the range lengthened. Very few of the British shells hit enemy positions.

The weather, a mixture of thunderstorms and heavy rain, also played its part in the disaster. Those troops that survived the friendly and enemy artillery fire and attempted to mount bayonet charges were met by heavy machine gun fire. A simultaneous attempt by 186 Brigade's 2/6th Duke's to capture The Crucifix also met with failure. By 1000 the survivors of 2nd Warwicks were withdrawn. The same day, at 1900, 1st South Staffs and 21st Manchesters combined to mount a further attempt to bomb their way into the Red Patch. Once more the result was failure in the face of overwhelming enemy machine gun fire.

During the night of the 13th/14th the 7th Division 22 Brigade were ordered to take over the Bullecourt front from 91 Brigade. They planned to deploy 2nd HAC, 20th Manchesters and 1st RWF. The new plan for the capture of Bullecourt was essentially the one proposed two days earlier by Brigadier General Cumming, that it should be mounted from east of the village. It would be led by two companies of 1st RWF who were scheduled to attack at 0210 on 14 May. The move of 2nd HAC to the start line in support of 1st RWF was delayed by the lateness of receipt of the order to advance and the congestion in the trenches through which they had to pass. As a result they would have been taking over the line when the enemy barrage, responding to the start of the attack by 1st RWF, came down. The 2nd HAC CO accordingly sought a postponement of Zero Hour. When this was refused, with the agreement of all concerned, he withdrew his Battalion[23] temporarily to Écoust-St-Mein.

B and D Companies of the 1st RWF attacked the Red Patch on schedule in the darkness of early morning. They were soon repelled by machine gun fire, regrouped and attacked again at 0400. Once again the attack was halted by machine gun fire before the men could break into the enemy trenches, although they did manage to establish small pockets facing The Crucifix strong point. The two companies then offered fire support with rifle grenades as A and C Companies took over and resumed the attack at 0615. Once more the attack was stopped. After a lengthy pause in which dwindling supplies of bombs and small arms ammunition were replenished, C Company on its own attacked at 1430 and came close to penetrating the German defences. Only the attackers' lack of

---

23 Following their earlier forlorn attempt to capture Bullecourt, 2nd HAC could at this stage only muster 250 officers and men.

bombs enabled the Germans to hold on. When the Battalion CO then received an order to mount a fifth attack later the same day he protested vigorously that his men were too tired after their exertions, and losses, of the day. There should in any case, in his view, be no further attacks until The Crucifix, southwest of the village, had been captured. The attack was cancelled.[24] Although the survivors of 1st RWF had been spared the ordeal of a fifth attack on the 14th, they were not going to be relieved. Instead they were ordered to remain in Bullecourt and await reinforcement by 2nd HAC, and 20th and 21st Manchesters, who were filing forward into the ruins of the village under cover of darkness.[25]

As the Welsh Battalion were preparing in the early hours of the following morning to resume their attack, the Germans struck first at around 0415 with a counterattack which fell largely on 2nd HAC who had completed their deployment, involving the relief of 1st South Staffs, about two hours previously. A patrol which the Battalion had earlier sent into the Red Patch had returned with confirmation that the area was still strongly held by the enemy. Despite their attenuated numbers they were able to hold off the Germans. The counterattack also fell heavily on the remnants of 1st RWF's C Company, who were completely overwhelmed enabling the Germans to drive a wedge into the village that threatened to outflank B Company and overrun 2nd HAC's Battalion HQ. They were stopped only 30 yards away. At 1600 the acting 22 Brigade Commander ordered 1st RWF to stop all further attacks in preparation for the relief of the Battalion as well as the withdrawal of the remnants of 2nd Queen's and 1st South Staffs, to be relieved as necessary by 2nd HAC and 21st Manchesters. The receipt of this message by 2nd HAC coincided with a further counterattack on them from the southwest by enemy infantry backed by artillery and machine guns. B Company bore the brunt and were forced back. But somehow the Germans never achieved a breakthrough as the British units clung on and later mounted a counterattack that retook some of the lost ground. The completely exhausted 7th Division was withdrawn on the night of 15/16 May after 12 days. 58th Division 174 Brigade moved in to replace them.

Further to the east, on the front between the crossroads east of Bullecourt and the Central Road, now defended by two battalions of 58th Division 173 Brigade, and the front east of the Central Road still being guarded by the last remaining Australian unit, the 54th Battalion, the German counterattack was prefaced by a bombardment mainly of large and small trench mortars beginning at 0100 on 15 May. It initially targeted the Australian sector but had spread by 0300 to include big guns and coverage of the whole of the front between Bullecourt and Riencourt. The challenge had quickly been taken up by the Australian artillery and a tense duel ensued in which the Australian gunners found themselves being targeted by enemy counter battery fire. British counter battery batteries were soon in action in response. At 0340 the German infantry began their advance. Those advancing from the direction of Riencourt were cut down by rifle and Lewis gun fire before they were able to reach O.G.2. Two groups that started from a cross trench did succeed in entering O.G.2 but they were quickly ejected. The two British battalions, 2/4th and 2/3rd London Regiment, were fighting their first action of the war, but acquitted themselves well, withstanding the initial onslaught and then successfully counterattacking. They also sent some of their reserves to help 54th Battalion, a gesture that was much appreciated by the Australians.[26]

With the failure of what was to prove to have been the last major German counterattack of Second Bullecourt the situation remained that the British were in possession of O.G.s 1 and 2 and the whole of Bullecourt except for parts of the western half of the village including of course the Red Patch The task of clearing the Germans from these was given to 174 Brigade. It was prefaced at 1830 on 16 May by an attack by 173 Brigade's 2/1st London Regiment which succeeded in capturing the Hindenburg Support Trench (O.G.2) up to its junction with the Langatte-Hendecourt Road. The

24   Kendall, op. cit., p. 280.
25   Jonathan Walker, op. cit., pp. 173-4.
26   Graham Keech, *Bullecourt*, pp. 112-4.

attack by 174 Brigade would be a frontal assault on the Red Patch by a single battalion, the 2/5th London Regiment (London Rifle Brigade). Following a two minute long hurricane bombardment it was launched at 0200 on 17 May from positions in front of the railway where it ran south of the objective. Immediately the bombardment ended the Londoners stormed in and rapidly secured the whole area taking prisoners and capturing five machine guns. As soon as the ground had been properly secured a company of the 2/8th London Regiment (Post Office Rifles) moved in from the west, passed across the front of their sister Battalion and by dint of scrambling through the ruins, secured more prisoners and completed clearance of the village. The relative ease of the operation probably owed a great deal to the fact that it caught the Germans in the midst of preparations for an evacuation of the parts of the village still in their possession.[27]

Although the completion of the capture of Bullecourt was considered by the British High Command as having brought Second Bullecourt to an end, it was still deemed essential not to give the enemy the impression that the British had broken off the battle and were transferring their attentions to elsewhere on the Western Front, as indeed was the case. Isolated actions would therefore continue, but at a much less intense level than heretofore. An exception to this damping down of intensity was an attack launched by 174 Brigade's 2/6th London Regiment (The Rifles) on 21 May that was intended in broad terms to straighten the front line north of Bullecourt by assaulting and capturing Bovis trench, the enemy held continuation of the Hindenburg Support Line (O.G.2) lying just north of the village. With an optimism hardly justified in the light of recent experience of German tenacity, the attacking troops were informed that once the British bombardment had moved on they would enter Bovis trench with ease as the few Germans believed to be holding it would offer little resistance. With similar optimism, the attackers were given a series of subsidiary tasks to achieve in the same operation.

At Zero Hour in the darkness of the early hours of 21 May a four minute long hurricane bombardment was launched targeting enemy front line machine gun emplacements. The two leading companies of The Rifles, loaded down with bombs and grenades that included German egg grenades, began to advance at the slow pace forced on them by the loads they were carrying. The centre of the advancing line in particular soon came under fire from machine guns that had not been affected by the British barrage and which inflicted serious losses, especially among the officers. Enemy artillery quickly joined in, adding to the losses and the consequent growing confusion among the attackers, not just in the centre but also on both wings as they became disorientated by the darkness and the dust kicked up by the barrages, and lost touch with the centre. The left wing failed completely to reach Bovis trench; the right wing, owing to the shell damage to the trench, failed to recognise it in the darkness and confusion, bypassed it and then had to retire, when they realised they were in danger of being surrounded and cut off. The attack had descended into a shambles and was a total failure. Casualties amounted to 13 officers and 226 men, 50 per cent of those engaged. A battalion had been sacrificed for virtually no gain.[28]

It is a tragic fact that, from the Anglo-Australian point of view, there is very little positive to be drawn from the two battles bearing the name Bullecourt that were fought in April and May 1917. Even by the standard of the Arras campaign as a whole the casualties were grim. The three British Divisions principally involved, the 62nd, 7th and 58th suffered respectively (killed, wounded and missing) 191, 134 and 85 officers and 4,042, 2,588 and 1,853 men, a grand total of 8,893. The 1st, 2nd and 5th Australian Divisions together lost 292 officers and 7,190 men at Second Bullecourt, to which should be added the 3,300 officers and men lost at First Bullecourt/Lagnicourt, making a grand total of 10,782. The large number of those who were killed were perforce to lie where they fell for long periods as recovery and burial were not practical propositions in circumstances where attempting

27   OH 1917, Volume 1, pp. 477-8.
28   Kendall, op. cit., pp.311-3.

to do so would have drawn enemy fire from the vantage points they continued to enjoy during the fighting and after it had died down. When the many German dead are added to the numbers above it is small wonder that a major memory of those obliged to man forward positions subsequent to the battles was of the nauseous stench of human decomposition. Unsurprisingly, Bullecourt itself had virtually ceased to exist. It had been reduced to rubble in which only the church could be identified, and that only because it had become a slightly higher mound with a whiter colour than the rest of the ruins.

Another casualty was the blow it dealt to the Australian perception of the competence of British command. This was already at a low ebb following Gallipoli, the Somme and Fromelles. Bullecourt did little to restore a more balanced view. The Australians had not emerged from the fighting at Pozières Village and Ridge with any admiration for their Army Commander, General Gough. It required no stretch for them to see him as a source of their misfortunes at Bullecourt. There is no denying that the failure of First Bullecourt could be put down to Gough's tactical shortcomings and his over hasty adoption of the proposal to rely on tanks. There was however a certain amount of Australian casting around for scapegoats, and assigning that role to Gough, his Staff and the Tanks, when they might well have looked closer to home for the causes of shortcomings in their performance. It was unfortunate that the Australian experience with the tanks at First Bullecourt resulted in a disenchantment with the weapon lasting over a year.

It must be questionable whether the ostensible reasons for fighting at Bullecourt justified the losses of life that it involved. Initially it was intended to support the Third Army advance towards Cambrai and a rendezvous with the French, fully justifiable in military terms if not in the way it was carried out. But its continuation when it became apparent that the Nivelle Offensive had failed, its justification then becoming that it would distract the Germans from noticing and exploiting the French problems and Haig's intention to launch his Flanders offensive, was much more questionable.

Part VI

Nivelle Offensive

18

The End of the Nivelle Plan

It has already been shown that the closer the French armies got to the date for the launch of the Nivelle Offensive the less enthusiasm there was for it among leading government ministers and politicians, and the senior generals who, as Army Group and Army Commanders, would have to implement it. The basic reason for the loss of belief that it could succeed was that the circumstances in which Nivelle had drawn up his plan for the offensive no longer obtained. The offensive had been intended to start in mid-February when surprise might have been achievable and the German defences were thinly stretched. The Anglo-French squabbling over railway access, the British takeover of French line and unity of command, as well as the appalling weather, put paid to that. But also significant in the growing loss of confidence in success was Nivelle's refusal to make significant changes to his plan to take account of the very changed circumstances brought about by the voluntary German retirement to the Hindenburg Line, and the realisation that almost certainly the Germans were in possession of the detailed French plan of attack.

The disenchantment with Nivelle's plan had, by the time of the emergency meeting of the senior politicians and generals on 6 April, reached a point at which it was probably only Nivelle's dramatic offer to resign that won the day for him and his plan. Two weeks to the day later Nivelle was once again in Paris in response to a summons to a meeting with President Poincaré and Prime Minister Ribot. The meeting took place at a time when it had become clear that the Nivelle offensive had completely failed to accomplish its proclaimed aim of achieving a breakthrough within 48 hours. The two politicians told Nivelle that they were greatly concerned at the high number of casualties apparently being suffered by the attacking troops and urged him to minimise further losses.[1] Nivelle assured them that he envisaged for the time being only a series of small operations, all of which would be preceded by heavy artillery bombardments. He had already ordered Tenth Army forward between Sixth and Fifth Armies so that they might relieve some of these two armies' exhausted and depleted divisions and take on operations north of the River Aisne. In the longer term his main objectives would be to drive the enemy back from Reims and complete the capture and occupation of the Chemin des Dames. There might also be operations in Alsace and the Woëvre. He also told his interlocutors that he would be willing to support the proposed British operation to clear the Belgian coast.

On the following day the three participants at the above meeting met Prime Minister Lloyd George and assured him that the French would continue their offensive so as to prevent the Germans from moving reserves towards the British front. Up to this point the reverse had been the case, with the British attacking in no small measure to tie down the Germans and prevent them from moving reserves to confront the French.

On his return to GQG, Nivelle lost no time in visiting Generals Micheler and Pétain in their respective headquarters to apprise them of his decision no longer to go all out for the elusive

---

1   Nivelle's own figures for French losses for the period 16-25 April were 96,125, of whom 15,589 were killed and 20,500 missing (mostly probably also killed). He was not of course in possession of these figures at the time of the 20 April meeting, but neither he nor the politicians were in any doubt that losses had been heavy. A more recent estimate of French casualties for the same period by the French Army *Service Historique* indicates, in round figures French casualties of 134,000, of whom 30,000 were killed, 100,000 wounded and 4,000 captured. With figures like these it could have been of little consolation that German losses had been almost as bad.

breakthrough, but instead to focus on Reims and the Chemin des Dames. Shortly after, Nivelle responded to a ritual message he received from Field Marshal Haig congratulating him on the great success the valiant French armies had already achieved under his command, by affirming his conviction that victory was ever more certain. Nivelle also sent a note to General Sir Henry Wilson in which he offered more specific detail on how he foresaw the joint Anglo-French offensive developing, which Wilson was at liberty to use in briefing Haig. He wrote that although progress had been slower than expected, he had made no changes to his general instructions for the offensive, with which Haig was already familiar. In particular there would be no question of it being abandoned. Both the GAR and the GAC were actively preparing their next attacks along the whole of their fronts and these would be launched very soon. As regards the BEF's offensive operations, Nivelle hoped they could be pursued in the same timescale as those of the French. The British Armies, he pointed out, should be able to profit from the operations on the French front by increasing the extent of their attacks and by aiming to achieve more ambitious objectives.[2]

Unfortunately, despite the positive spin Nivelle had put on the situation, he no longer enjoyed the confidence of Micheler and Pétain and his political masters, not because his offensive had failed – in some respects it had been relatively successful – but because he had manifestly failed to deliver on his self-proclaimed promises. Over the course of the next few weeks there would be a number of meetings and other events far removed from the battlefield that would finally determine the fate of Nivelle and his plan. But for the moment Nivelle remained in charge.

Nivelle followed up his visits of 22 April to GAR and GAC HQs, when he had given verbal instructions to the two Army Group Commanders, with written orders. These confirmed what he had told them, that the current offensive would be pursued through two operations. The first would be to clear the area round Reims by a combined attack by the Fourth and Fifth Armies. The Fifth Army should capture the Heights of Savigneul, Mont Spin and Brimont. The Fourth Army should complete the clearance of the summits of the Massif de Moronvilliers, in accordance with the plan already drawn up by that Army. It might later be possible to expel the enemy from the Heights of Nogent-l'Abbesse. The second operation would be a combined Sixth Army and Tenth Army attack to complete the occupation of the Chemin des Dames plateau. The dates on which these operations would be launched would be determined after consultations between the three Army Group Commanders. GAN would be involved as Sixth Army would be transferred to GAN from GAR with effect from 1200 on 24 April, in order to free GAR to concentrate on operations in a north-easterly direction.

In effect these new orders represented a marked change of approach from that on which the Nivelle Offensive had been launched. In place of an offensive of broad scope intended to rupture violently the enemy front and be followed by rapid exploitation of its success, Nivelle's ambitions had been scaled down to operations with limited objectives of which even the dates would be determined by the Army Group Commanders. Although the dates for the attacks by Fourth and Fifth Armies were quickly settled on as respectively 27 April and 1 May, that for the Sixth and Tenth Armies depended on the completion of the latter Army preparations.

In the meantime the politicians in Paris were, individually and in various combinations, making known their concerns about the way things were going under Nivelle's stewardship. President Poincaré was the first to weigh in when, on 23 April, he sent a message by telephone to Nivelle to express concern about the preparations for a new attack, which, having heard from those charged with carrying it out, he thought was premature. Quite apart from the irritation such an intervention from a politician would inevitably cause to a military commander it was evident that the President was making use of information he could only have obtained from disloyal subordinates of the Commander in Chief. With some justification Nivelle informed the President in response that no decision had yet been made on the dates of future operations.

---

2   Beaugier, *Les Armées Françaises dans la Grande Guerre, Tome V Premier Volume*, p. 704.

The following day, at a meeting involving the President, the Prime Minister, the Minister of War and the Minister for the Navy, the question of Nivelle's future and his possible replacement was discussed. Predictably War Minister Paul Painlevé, opposed from the outset to Nivelle and his plan, was outspoken in his denigration of the Commander in Chief, but the meeting determined that the effect on army morale and public opinion that Nivelle's dismissal would cause, would make it an unwise move at this stage. Rather than take this step they decided to summon Nivelle to another meeting to offer a further explanation of his future operational plans.[3] This took place the next day, the 25th. During it Nivelle described the operations he was planning to undertake at the end of the month. The most important one, on which the whole strategy hinged, was to be an attack by Fifth Army to seize Brimont Fort. The Army Commander, General Mazel, had assured Nivelle that he could capture it, but had also told Painlevé that the operation would fail with 60,000 casualties. The Minister passed on to the meeting Mazel's views on the proposed operation and also those of Pétain, who had similar reservations. The meeting concluded by offering its support to Nivelle's plans but insisted that they should be resubmitted after they had been more fully developed.

Following this meeting matters gathered pace. Painlevé had long wanted to replace Nivelle as Commander in Chief with Pétain and came up with the idea of reviving the post of Chief of Staff of the Army, endowing it with enhanced powers, and giving it to Pétain as a first step in his ultimate replacement of Nivelle. The post of Chief of Staff had been in abeyance since Joffre had combined it with that of Commander in Chief when he had reigned supreme. In its new form the position would have powers similar to the British Chief of the Imperial General Staff. General Pétain assumed his new post on 29 April. His appointment signified that the French government saw the way forward in terms of an end to an all out offensive doctrine in favour of a more defensive one. Pétain was best known for his caution and care for his men's lives by undertaking offensive operations only when they were well planned and implemented, and had strictly limited objectives. His reassuring presence was also a great restorer of morale, as had been demonstrated at Verdun. This attribute was soon to be put to an even greater test. General Pétain's replacement as GAC Commander was General Emile Fayolle, also an officer known for his caution.

For the moment Nivelle remained as Commander in Chief, with his plans for further operations by Fourth, Fifth and Tenth Armies on 4 and 5 May resulting in only very limited success. The single positive achievement was the Tenth Army completion of the capture of the Californie plateau on the Chemin des Dames ridge. In a further blow to his authority, Nivelle's intention to include an attack on Fort Brimont by Fifth Army among the operations of 4-5 May had been ruled out by the Minister of War until it had been fully discussed with Pétain. The first significant casualty of the failure of the Nivelle Offensive was the firebrand General Charles Mangin who had been Nivelle's closest associate in the turning around of French fortunes at Verdun. The Commander in Chief had determined that Mangin had lost the confidence of his subordinates at Sixth Army and relieved him of his command on 2 May at a meeting during which Mangin, not one to go quietly, created a violent scene. At a subsequent equally stormy meeting with Minister of War Painlevé, his dismissal was confirmed. He was replaced by General Paul Maistre, who had built up a good reputation as a successful Commander of XXI Corps since 1914. Whether or not the change of command was a determining factor, Sixth Army performed remarkably well in the fighting up to 9 May. They captured four kilometres of the Chemin des Dames ridge and drove in a salient at Laffaux, reaching the outskirts of the village of Allemant.

Apart from the capture by Fourth Army of Mont Cornillet on 20 May the fighting relating to the Nivelle Offensive had largely died down by this time. French political and military attention turned to dealing with its aftermath. A priority was for the Western Front allies to agree their joint strategy post Nivelle plan. Haig and the CIGS, General Robertson, had been much worried by

---

3   Ibid., pp. 708-9.

Pétain's new appointment, which they feared was the first step towards his replacement of Nivelle as French Commander in Chief, and the consequent abandonment of French offensive operations. They were well aware of Pétain's reputation as a cautious general, and the reasoning of the French politicians behind his appointment. But Haig's first meeting with Pétain in his new role had been generally reassuring. Haig could not fault his professional competence and he had found him ready to give full consideration to Haig's assessment of the current situation and his ideas for taking matters forward. These were, essentially, to keep wearing down the enemy by maintaining pressure with attacks suitably prepared for by the use of artillery. Haig specifically sought Pétain's help by asking him to relieve six British divisions and urging him to keep up the pressure on the enemy and thereby tie them down and prevent them moving large reserves to meet British attacks. The French Chief of Army Staff said in reply that he entirely agreed with Haig's views and plans and would let him have a formal response in writing. He pointed out, however, that his freedom of manoeuvre would be increasingly constrained by a growing manpower problem to which there was no discernible solution unless the Americans could be persuaded to send men over to enlist in French regiments. An unlikely prospect, Haig confided in his diary.[4]

Following their meeting on 3 May, Haig and Pétain were joined at a formal conference the following morning by Generals Nivelle and Robertson. The four officers quickly agreed that, at the plenary session of the conference that same afternoon, they would inform the politicians that both Allied armies were fully intent on continuing the offensive to the full extent of their power. The British would make the main attack with the French supporting them to the utmost of their power, both by taking over some of the British line and by attacking vigorously to wear out and retain the enemy on their front.

At the plenary session, which was co-chaired by Prime Ministers David Lloyd George and Alexandre Ribot, General Robertson read a statement that included the following:

> It is no longer a question of aiming at breaking through the enemy's front and aiming at distant objectives. It is now a question of wearing down and exhausting the enemy's resistance, and if and when this is achieved to exploit it to the fullest extent possible. In order to wear him down we are agreed that it is absolutely necessary to fight with all our available forces, with the object of destroying the enemy's divisions. We are unanimously of the opinion that there is no half-way between this course and fighting defensively, which, at this stage of the war, would be tantamount to acknowledging defeat. We are all of opinion that our object can be obtained by relentlessly attacking with limited objectives, while making the fullest use of our artillery.[5]

With the conference endorsing the Generals' perception of the way ahead, this proved to be a very successful event, especially for Haig. Lloyd George stated in a speech to the conference that Haig had full power to attack where and when he thought best. He (Lloyd George) did not wish to know the plan or where and when any attack would take place. He suggested the French Government might treat their Commanders on the same lines. As Haig commented in his diary, 'Rather a changed attitude for him to adopt since the Calais Conference'. Ironically, Haig and Pétain had agreed at their earlier meeting that, 'Plan to be kept a perfect secret. Governments not to be told any details concerning the place or date of any attack, only the principles ... '.[6] As well as both Allies keeping up pressure on the Germans in their current campaigns, Haig was now able to build up in earnest for his Belgian offensive, with a reasonable hope of full French support, although he still wondered to what extent this could be relied upon. In effect the conference marked the point at which the French lost

4   Gary Sheffield and John Bourne (eds.), *Douglas Haig War Diaries and Letters 1914-1918,* pp. 290-1.
5   Beaugier, op. cit., p. 788. Robert Doughty, *Pyrrhic Victory*, p.357.
6   Sheffield and Bourne (eds.), op. cit., pp. 291-2.

their primacy on the Western Front to the British.

The changes in approach agreed to at the Paris conference were quickly reflected in changes in the French Army high command. Prior to the conference, on 2 May, Nivelle's Chief of Staff, Major General Ferdinand Pont, had been removed and replaced by General Eugène Debeney. (Pont did not suffer unduly as he quickly replaced General Maistre in command of XXI Corps on the latter's departure for Sixth Army.) On 8 May General Micheler's Groupe d'Armées de Réserve (GAR) was broken up, with Tenth Army going to GAN and the Fifth to GAC. General Micheler initially succeeded General Fayolle as Commander of First Army, but on 23 May he moved on again to take over command of Fifth Army in succession to General Mazel (who may have paid the price for his duplicitous behaviour over Fort Brimont and his indiscreet description of his Commander in Chief as a 'criminal'). On 10 May the politicians finally summoned up the courage to call on General Nivelle to tender his resignation as Commander in Chief. After digging in his heels for a while and refusing to comply, Nivelle finally did so on 15 May. Two days later he was formally replaced as C in C by General Philippe Pétain. The new Commander in Chief of the Armies of the North and Northeast was in turn succeeded as Chief of the Army Staff by General Ferdinand Foch. General Nivelle had been partly persuaded to accept his fate by the offer of a position as an Army Group Commander, but as there were no vacancies at that level, Pétain, on 29 June, placed Nivelle at the disposition of the Minister of War and annulled his status as an Army Group Commander. Nivelle was sent on leave. Some time later he was appointed Commander of French forces in North Africa where he was to see out the war.

Despite Haig's private ruminations on whether the French could be relied on to keep their side of the bargain and attack to maintain pressure on the Germans, the early signs were that they intended to do precisely that. Immediately on returning to his Headquarters from the Paris conference Nivelle wrote letters to Pétain, Haig and the Army Group Commanders outlining his plans to keep up the pressure on the enemy by the continuation of attacks by the Sixth, Tenth, Fifth and Fourth Armies and putting in hand preparations for attacks by Third Army, between Saint-Quentin and the River Oise in co-operation with the British Fourth Army; by the Second Army, towards Briey to reduce the St Mihiel salient; by the Seventh and Eighth Armies into Upper Alsace. In addition the XXXVI Corps would operate on the right bank of the River Yser in support of the British Flanders operation.[7] However, worthy though these intentions were, and there is no reason to doubt that General Pétain would have endorsed their general thrust when he succeeded General Nivelle, circumstances were dramatically to change with the outbreak and rapid spread of disaffection in the French Army.

This is not the place to describe in any detail the outbreaks of collective indiscipline that severely damaged the fighting capacity of the French Army from late April to mid-June 1917. The effects extended well beyond the end of the Second Battle of the Aisne and the Battles of Arras. Indeed it could be claimed that the French Army did not fully recover its old offensive capacity and its readiness to use it until the brilliant counterattack of General Mangin, restored to favour and appointed Commander of Tenth Army, on 10 July 1918 during the Second Battle of the Marne. As far as Field Marshal Haig was concerned the first rumours that all was not well with the French Army certainly contributed to his decision that the Arras campaign should be prolonged, but now not only to distract the Germans from the planned British build up in Belgium, but also to distract their attention from the French Army disciplinary difficulties. It was not until 2 June that Haig was directly briefed by the French, in the person of Pétain's Chief of Staff, General Debeney, about the state of affairs regarding indiscipline among the troops. The briefing he received then, and subsequently direct from Pétain on 7 June, did not go into great detail and may have left a lot of questions unanswered, but it was clear that the situation was having, and would continue to have, an effect on the French Army ability to play a full part in operations for the foreseeable future.

---

7   Beaugier, op. cit., pp. 789-90.

The causes of what are termed, perhaps with some exaggeration, the 'Mutinies' (*les Mutineries*) of the French Army in the second quarter of 1917 were wide ranging. The disappointment of the expectations surrounding the Nivelle Offensive clearly played its part; it could hardly have been a coincidence that the outbreaks of collective indiscipline began immediately following the early days of the offensive. The news of the first Russian Revolution in March 1917 and the abdication of Tsar Nicholas II were widely welcomed in France. The Russian Brigades attached to the French Army became sufficiently infused with revolutionary fervour that they had to be sidelined by the French authorities, justly fearing some contagion of their own troops. Domestically too, the political situation was in ferment with the fall of the Briand government in March and its replacement by an administration led by Alexandre Ribot, an octogenarian, which scarcely suggested stability and permanence. But probably the main causes of most of the disaffection were those matters dear to the heart of the *poilu*; the lottery of home leave, constantly cancelled from military necessity and the unfairness of its granting, less often in front line units than in rear area units, and, when it was granted, the amount of it used up in travelling to and from home; the excessive lengths of time spent by some units in the front line; the eroding value of static pay in an inflationary period.

Estimates differ as to how many incidents there were and how many units were affected and to what extent. But there is little doubt that, during the period late April to mid-June, at least half the regiments in key situations were affected to some extent. It has been suggested that there might have been only two divisions during this period that were completely reliable. On the positive side the French authorities were fortunate that General Pétain was in the key position to deal with the situation. As the only top-ranking officer in the French Army with a peasant and infantry background, Pétain was widely known to be protective of his soldiers' lives and welfare, while at the same time being a stern disciplinarian. At Verdun he had restored order out of chaos, improved leave, ensured insofar as possible that supplies of food, water and ammunition reached the front line soldiers as and when required. He had also ensured that the wounded were evacuated efficiently and quickly. These arrangements were made possible by using the only available road into and out of the cauldron from Bar-le-Duc (*La Voie Sacrée*, as it became known). He also introduced a system known as *roulement* (rotation) by which front line troops were relieved after short periods in the front line, thus ensuring that nearly all the French Army infantry divisions did time at Verdun but not for prolonged periods. The challenge he faced during and in the aftermath of the Nivelle Offensive required in his view a carrot and stick approach. Discipline had to be restored. This was done by courts martial at which well over 500 death sentences were handed down, but only just over 50 were carried out. At the same time the troops' grievances were attended to as far as possible. Leave was given priority and made more generous with reasonable travel time added on. It would sometimes happen from now on that units called on to fight had so many men on leave that they were unable to take their place in the line. Recreation facilities were improved, both near the front and at railway stations through which soldiers would pass on their way to and from their leave destinations. Pétain visited as many units as he could, to listen to the troops' grievances. He made it known that there would be no more futile attacks with little prospect of success.

The measures taken by Pétain undoubtedly went a long way towards restoring the French Army morale, and it was soon once more capable of mounting limited attacks. There were three of these during the rest of 1917, including the First Army involvement from day one in the Third Battle of Ypres. The First Army presence on the left of General Gough's Fifth Army honoured the promises of Nivelle and Pétain that the French would support Haig's long cherished ambition to clear the Belgian coast. The First Army performed very creditably during the battle. The other two attacks, at Verdun and at La Malmaison on the Chemin des Dames, were also successful, especially the latter. Casualties in the Verdun attack were heavy, but so were the losses inflicted on the enemy. Although the troops' mail home continued to show signs of disgruntlement, there were no outbreaks of indiscipline during any of the three actions. Haig would nevertheless still have reservations about the reliability of the French until well into the next year.

Part VII

Conclusions

19

The Last Stages 5-17 (24) May 1917

With the conclusion of the Paris conference of 4 May and the near total failure of the British attack, the Third Battle of the Scarpe, the same day, Haig's attention was focusing more and more on his planned Belgian offensive, the precursor to which, an assault on Messines Ridge, was scheduled to take place just over a month later. In the meantime, however, pressure had to be maintained on the Arras front to keep the Germans tied down and constrained from moving any reserves northwards. Second Bullecourt was a major part of this strategy, as has been seen, but First and Third Armies would have to play their part even though they were on the point of losing about a third of their artillery to the Messines Ridge build up, and their divisions were mainly very tired. Consequently their operations would have to be limited in scope and relatively small scale. There were some obvious candidates for what these might be; they were all north of the River Scarpe and centred on Roeux. Not only the village itself, but also the cemetery, the Château and the Chemical Works had all been strenuously fought over, had often changed hands, but were all currently held by the enemy.

The Third Army XVII Corps was given the task of planning and mounting an operation that, while its main focus would be the capture and retention of the Chemical Works, would also encompass the seizure of the other three objectives listed above. Although probably the most tired and depleted of the Corps' three divisions the main responsibility for carrying out the operation was given to 4th Division, which had featured prominently in the earlier attempts to capture the Chemical Works and had paid a heavy price. When he had looked for possible reasons for the failure of the earlier attempts on the Chemical Works the Divisional GSO1, Colonel W. Kirke, had reached the conclusion that there had been two. The first was the insufficiency of the artillery preparation; the second, the lack of surprise inherent in launching the attacks at dawn. Acting on these conclusions Colonel Kirke proposed that the forthcoming assault should incorporate certain changes. First, the artillery barrage should be enlarged to a density of one 18 pounder gun every seven yards by utilising the guns of the neighbouring VI and XIII Corps. In addition all available Stokes mortars should join in. The overhead machine gun barrage should be enlarged by adding to it two of 17th Division's machine gun companies. Some of the machine guns should advance with the infantry. Well prior to the assault the buildings north and south of the Arras-Douai railway in the vicinity of the Chemical Works should be subjected to slow, methodical bombardments to accustom the Germans to them happening. A rehearsal of the main barrage should also be carried out with the aim of gauging the intensity of the German counter barrage. As regards the timing of the assault Colonel Kirke proposed that to achieve surprise an evening Zero Hour should be selected. His proposals were approved by both the Divisional and Corps Commanders. The latter set Zero Hour as 1930 on 11 May.

Although 4th Division's morale was remarkably high, it was nevertheless a fact that their rifle strength was only just over a quarter of full establishment. The GOC therefore decided that all 12 battalions would need to participate in the attack, leaving him with no reserve to fall back on. Accordingly 12 Brigade's battalions were divided between 10 and 11 Brigades, who were to carry out the attack on the right and left respectively. In addition two companies of 6th Dorsetshire Regiment (Dorsets), from 17th Division 50 Brigade, were attached to the Division's left hand battalion, 1st RB. To provide for a reserve, the Corps Commander placed 152 Brigade, 51st Division, at the disposal of the Divisional Commander.[1]

The creeping barrage, thought by some to have been the thickest barrage they had ever seen, opened up at Zero Hour and the two leading battalions of 10 Brigade advanced. On the right 1st RIF's objective was to set up a defensive flank covering Roeux and Roeux wood with their right on the River Scarpe and their left at their planned junction with the Household Battalion. The objective of the Household Battalion was to capture Roeux cemetery and the houses north and east of it. Behind 1st RIF would be 1st Warwicks in support. The 2nd Seaforths would act as moppers up behind the Household Battalion. In brigade reserve would be 12 Brigade's 1st King's Own.

The RIF reached their objective within 45 minutes and began digging in. Their left was not in touch with the Household Battalion but the link was shortly indirectly made through a company of the Warwicks who had been ordered to work round to the right of the cemetery and link up any gaps in the line. The Household Battalion had gone right through to their objectives and were digging in. The losses they had suffered in the centre and right of their line of advance, from enfilade machine gun fire from the houses, may have been the cause of the failure to achieve a direct link up with the RIF. They were reinforced by a company of the 1st King's Own. The main problem confronting 10 Brigade during the course of the night was from German snipers who had been cut off, but not dealt with, by the speed of the British advance. By 0600 the following morning they had all been eliminated by 2nd Seaforths' clearance of the houses that had been overrun. By about the same time the Brigade were holding a continuous line from the Scarpe northwards, including the cemetery and the houses round it. Although there had been no intention to stray into Roeux itself during the operation, some Royal Householders and Seaforths did so and captured the Headquarters of the German 360th Regiment. Their inadvertent action gave the enemy the impression that Roeux was in British hands. On the evening of the 12th some enemy troops tried to retreat from the village. Lewis guns killed some and forced others to surrender.[2]

The 11 Brigade were given two objectives for their attack. The first was to capture and consolidate on the first evening the complex of buildings that made up the Chemical Works. The second, beyond the Works, was to assault and consolidate their sector of the Blue Line, consisting in all of Corona, Cupid, Curly and Charlie trenches. Their sector was Corona trench, mainly south of the Arras-Douai Railway. From right to left the assaulting battalions were 1st Hampshires, 1st East Lancashires and 1st RB, the last-named reinforced by the two companies of the Dorsets. In brigade reserve would be 1st SLI, positioned on the right. Because of the timing of Zero Hour both Brigades had had to spend the day in their assembly trenches at serious risk of being spotted there by one of the frequent overflights by enemy aircraft. Fortunately neither was detected. As with 10 Brigade, the 11 Brigade troops were much impressed with the intensity and effectiveness of the creeping barrage that opened up at Zero Hour and behind which they followed closely, little bothered by the slow to respond enemy artillery. The enemy troops appeared to have been utterly demoralised by the British barrage and surrendered freely. The only downside to the barrage's effectiveness was that it created a great deal of smoke that caused problems for the advancing troops, some of whom overran the buildings they were supposed to capture and ran into their own barrage. But 'friendly fire' losses were light, certainly lighter than the attackers would have suffered had the barrage not dealt effectively with the enemy machine guns. By 2300 the Chemical Works had been taken and was rapidly consolidated. A new trench was dug and covered by Lewis guns set up in shell holes 100 yards or so further forward. There was no enemy counterattack. The general impression was that the assault had achieved complete surprise, which accounted for the muted response of the enemy artillery, machine guns and infantry, and their failure to mount counterattacks. Belatedly the enemy artillery did shell the British positions quite heavily

1   OH 1917, Volume 1, pp. 509-11.
2   TNA WO 95/1479: 10 Brigade War Diary.

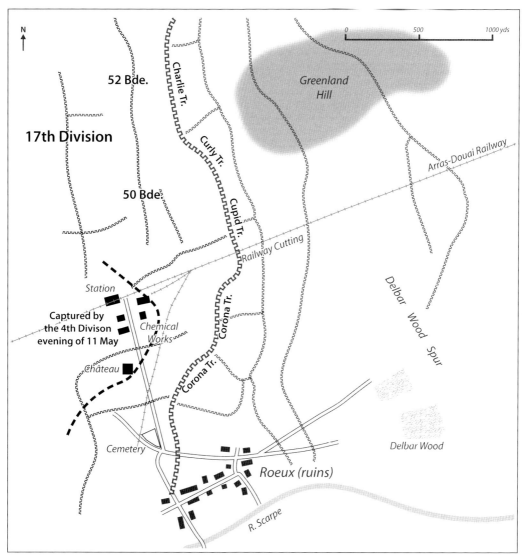

17th Division's advance on Greenland Hill 12 May 1917.

but to little effect.[3]

At 0630 the following morning the advance to the second objective was continued behind a still effective creeping barrage. The Blue Line was assaulted by 1st East Lancashires, 1st SLI and 1st RB and taken with only light losses. The new line was consolidated with no interference from enemy counterattacks, but 1st RB did suffer heavily from enemy artillery during consolidation.[4]

Operating on the left of 11 Brigade in the attack on the second objective were 50 and 52 Brigades of 17th Division. Specifically their objective was the main enemy trench line on the western slope of Greenland Hill. For 50 Brigade, on the right, their share of the objective was Cupid and Curly trenches running south to north from the Arras-Douai railway to Curly trench's junction with Charlie trench (where 52 Brigade took over). In addition to the two trenches, 50 Brigade were also ordered

3   TNA WO 95/1491/3: 11 Brigade War Diary.
4   TNA WO 95/1496: 1st Rifle Brigade War Diary.

to clear the railway cutting running along the south slope of Greenland Hill and to maintain touch with 11 Brigade on the other side of the railway. The two assaulting battalions were the 7th Green Howards and the 7th East Yorks, with 10th West Yorks in support. The remaining two companies of 6th Dorsets, that had not been attached to 1st RB, were in reserve. As the assaulting troops waited for Zero in their front line trenches they were quickly spotted by enemy aircraft in the bright morning light, nullifying any hope of surprise and ensuring that the opening of the British barrage at Zero would be immediately countered by an enemy barrage that, quite apart from the casualties it inflicted, produced a dense fog of smoke and dust that was of no help to the attackers. Nevertheless, on the right near the railway line, 7th Green Howards did succeed in getting into Cupid trench, secured the position and then tried to bomb their way into Curly trench on their left. The 7th East Yorks' efforts to get into the trench from in front had been held up by intense enemy machine gun fire. For the rest of the day there was intermittent trench fighting particularly at the junction of the two trenches. The Germans essayed a few minor counterattacks which posed little threat. Two further attempts at 2200 and 0230 by the two assault battalions to complete the capture of the two trenches made no progress, except for the Green Howards managing to establish a post in Curly trench about 30 yards north of its junction with Cupid trench.

The assault by 52 Brigade to the north of 50 Brigade proved to be equally disappointing. The assaulting battalions were 10th Lancashire Fusiliers and 9th Northumberlands; 12th Manchesters were in support and 9th Duke's in reserve. The objective was Charlie trench. As with 50 Brigade all chance of surprise had been lost and the assault by both battalions was an almost total failure as they came under heavy artillery, machine gun and rifle fire. Only one company of the Lancashire Fusiliers managed to break into Charlie trench, at its southern end. With no support on either side, it took only 20 minutes for an enemy counterattack to drive them out.[5]

During the night of 12/13 May 4th Division were relieved by 152 Brigade of 51st Highland Division. The Brigade immediately occupied the western half of Roeux and the following night, having found the enemy had evacuated the whole village, set up posts on its eastern outskirts. The front line at this point ran from the junction of Cupid trench with the railway, along Corona trench, round the eastern side of the cemetery, and thence through the centre of the village to the River Scarpe. The line was manned by two battalions with one in reserve. Although the enemy artillery was active during the night of 13/14 May, their ground troops appeared to have moved back, which enabled the Scots to move their line slightly forward without opposition. However it soon became apparent that this did not presage any sort of significant enemy withdrawal. At about 0300 on the morning of the 14th the enemy unleashed a heavy hostile barrage on the Highlanders' front-line positions, especially the Chemical Works. During the ensuing day the Works and the ground north of it were subjected to heavy barrages at frequent intervals. At 0700 the following morning the heavy shelling increased markedly in intensity and persisted with very little let up for 18 hours. The GOC 152 Brigade described the bombardment as the most severe he had experienced in 30 months on the Western Front.[6] The British counterbattery fire had little effect on the intensity of the enemy shelling. Although the front line troops had been prudently pulled back from the main enemy target, the Chemical Works, the Brigade nevertheless suffered 450 casualties.

During the night of 15/16 May, 51st Division were to relieve 17th Division by extending their line to the left from the railway along Cupid trench to the junction of Cut and Cuba trenches. Completion of the relief was severely hampered by the enemy artillery which made things doubly difficult by adding gas shells to the mix. At 0345, before the relief had been completed, the enemy opened an intense barrage with guns and howitzers of all calibres on the Highlanders' front line system. At the same time they launched a powerful three-pronged infantry attack that instantly disrupted

---

5   A. Hilliard Attridge, *A History of the 17th (Northern) Division*, pp. 224-8.
6   TNA WO 95/2862: 152 Brigade War Diary.

communications leaving the Division totally dependent on wireless and pigeons. The southern prong of the attack caught 6th Gordons and the Battalion they were relieving, 5th Seaforths, in mid-relief enabling it to overrun the Highlanders' posts east of Roeux. The posts south of the village stood firm although some of the attackers passed between them. The centre prong made for the middle of the village. They entered the western edges of Roeux by making use of a towpath running along the River Scarpe, where they were initially mistaken by the defenders for fellow Scots. The error was however realised in time and rectified with the enemy being dispersed with loss. The enemy northern prong penetrated the British line to the north of the railway at a part of Cupid trench where 17th Division had not yet been relieved. From there they pushed forward, encircled and retook possession of the Chemical Works and reached Calabar trench about 300 yards west of the station. At this point they were counterattacked by a party from the HQ of 8th Argylls led in person by their CO. By 0645 every German had been either killed or taken prisoner. The Argylls continued to advance and established contact with two companies of 6th Seaforths who were holding up another party of Germans. With the Argylls giving covering fire the Seaforths were ordered to advance. Between them the two battalions eliminated the enemy party and carried forward the front line to the Chemical Works.

Early on the same day 153 Brigade's 6th Black Watch and 5th Gordons were ordered forward and placed at the disposal of GOC 152 Brigade. The Gordons were immediately ordered to counterattack the enemy where they had penetrated beyond the Chemical Works. The Gordons were to advance along the northern side of the railway embankment, retake the station buildings and then push on to Cupid and Curly trenches. At 0930 they advanced towards the houses north of the station but were caught in a heavy barrage that inflicted severe casualties and forced them to fall back. They were then ordered to force their way through the barrage. They moved forward with two companies on the right using the railway embankment and two on the left skirting the houses on the northern side of the station. They then reformed having suffered losses of 25 percent. Although they were now clear of the enemy barrage they were coming under fire from rifles and machine guns, but the pressure they were exerting was forcing the enemy to fall back with the Gordons in pursuit. But by 1300 their leading lines came under heavy machine gun fire and were brought to a halt. Stokes mortars were brought up to the embankment from where they targeted Cupid trench with great effect.[7] At 1930 the Gordons mounted a further counterattack on Cupid and Curly trenches intended to eliminate the German presence in the British lines. Advancing behind a barrage that unfortunately fell short and caused casualties, they initially appeared to have achieved their objective, but although they had recovered all the ground lost by 51st Division, they were unable to maintain themselves in Cupid trench. They subsequently ascribed the main reason for this as being the failure of 17th Division to launch their part of what had been planned to be a joint counterattack.[8] There is no denying that 17th Division 51 Brigade did indeed fail to provide the support that the Highlanders were expecting. The Brigade had been in the process of taking over from 50 Brigade but had not completed the relief of 6th Dorsets and 10th West Yorks when the German assault struck, hitting the right of the 17th Division line as well as 51st Division. In the darkness and inevitable confusion the enemy made significant inroads into 17th Division positions, although they did seem to be as disorientated as the British. The one thing that was clear was that the enemy were in Cupid trench and needed to be dislodged. In addition to 5th Gordons this task was supposed to be shared by 51 Brigade's 7th Borders. Unfortunately this Battalion were still some distance away and had been allowed insufficient time to complete their move forward from northwest of Fampoux. Perforce 5th Gordons had to attack unaided with the result already described.

The final result of the German counterattack in force was that the British line remained almost

---

7   TNA WO 95/2881: 5th Gordon Highlanders War Diary.

8   The 152 Brigade War Diary is very critical of the GOC 51st Brigade, not only for not taking part but also for his failure to let the Gordons know of his decision not to. TNA WO 95/2862: 152 Brigade War Diary.

entirely where it had been prior to the counterattack except for the part of Cupid trench lost by 17th Division. In all other respects the British resistance to the German assault had been very satisfactory. The enemy had suffered severe losses during the break up of their assaults, and had been left with very little to show for them.[9] The British, on the other hand, were now at last in full and firm possession of Roeux village and the Chemical Works, for so long objects of frustration and disappointment. For XVII Corps, the Battle of Arras was over and had ended on a largely upbeat note.

To the south of XVII Corps, the Battle of Arras had not ended on 4 May for VI Corps either. Although they did not have unfinished business of the scope of that of their neighbouring Corps to deal with, there were matters still to attend to. At 2030 on 11 May 56th Division 168 Brigade achieved complete surprise in capturing a nearly mile-long stretch of the enemy front line (known as Tool trench) running north from just south of the Arras-Cambrai Road at Cavalry farm. Although there was some heavy fighting, particularly on the left of the Brigade's attack, the capture of the trench was completed with relatively light casualties, mainly because the enemy had not been given the time to bring their machine guns into action.[10]

Much less successful, from VI Corps point of view, was the attack mounted further north the following evening with the object of capturing the enemy's front line, known as Devil's trench, from Bit lane to Harness lane. The task was entrusted to 3rd Division 76 Brigade and 12th Division 36 and 37 Brigades. Each brigade contributed one battalion to the initial assault. They were 8th King's Own (76 Brigade), 11th Middlesex(36) and 6th Queen's (37). The King's Own attacked on a three company front under their barrage but were met by heavy machine gun and rifle fire, on the left from the junction of Devil's trench and Bit lane, in the centre from Devil's trench and on the right from Aubépines wood. Casualties were heavy and the advance was stopped. The survivors had to wait for the cover of darkness before they could make their way back to their front line. The 11th Middlesex also suffered from heavy enemy machine gun and rifle fire from Devil's trench as they advanced and appear to have become rather disorientated. They soon discovered that they had taken cover in Arrow trench on the right and in a line of shell holes level with the trench on the left. Both flanks were in the air, but having received what proved to be false information that the King's Own and 6th Queen's on either side of them had achieved their objectives, they determined that Devil's trench should be carried at all costs. Predictably their second attempt failed for the same reason as the first. On the left 6th Queen's advance progressed quite well until they reached the crest of a hill between their front line and Devil's trench. As they tried to advance further they came under heavy small arms fire and some artillery fire and suffered heavily. A second reinforcing attack fared no better. By 0030 the survivors were back in their own trenches.[11]

During the night of 14 May, 29th Division relieved 3rd Division. Three nights later they also took over 12th Division's sector of the line. An expectation that the Germans facing the 29th might be planning to retire to the Drocourt-Quéant Switch led VI Corps to order all divisions to patrol actively to ensure that such a move did not pass unnoticed. In the meantime plans were finalised by 29th Division for an attack to capture Infantry Hill and Aubépines wood. Protecting their right flank, by assaulting a small sector of Tool trench still in German hands, would be 56th Division. The joint attack was launched at 2100 on 19 May by a total of 23 platoons. The 1/8th Middlesex, 167 Brigade, provided five; 29th Division's contribution of 18 platoons was shared between 1st Royal Inniskilling Fusiliers, 1st Borders and 2nd South Wales Borderers, all from 87 Brigade. The attack was a complete failure even though it was carried out with great gallantry and determination.[12] The enemy were clearly fully prepared for the assault and poured machine gun and shrapnel fire on the

---

9   TNA WO 95/2845: 51st (Highland) Division War Diary.

10   OH 1917, op. cit., p. 516.

11   TNA WO 95/1436/1: 8th King's Own, TNA WO 95/1856/2: 11th Middlesex, and TNA WO 95/1858: 37 Brigade, War Diaries.

12   A Victoria Cross was awarded posthumously to Sergeant Albert White, South Wales Borderers.

attackers within less than a minute of the attack starting. Only two parties of the Inniskillings reached their objective; they were cut off and nearly all killed or captured. Overall about 75 per cent of the assaulting troops became casualties The 29th Divisional History leaves little room to doubt that the plan of attack was betrayed to the Germans by an unnamed British soldier who deserted to the enemy during the night prior to the attack.[13]

The end of the fighting on 4 May had seen the First Army Canadian Corps in possession of the village of Fresnoy, virtually the only positive gain to emerge from the Third Battle of the Scarpe. Unlike Arleux, the loss of which the Germans had accepted with relative equanimity, Fresnoy occupied a pivotal position in the German defences and it would call for every effort to be made by them for its recapture to be effected without delay. If for no other reason therefore the prospect facing the Canadian Corps and XIII Corps was for further fighting before a line could be drawn under the Arras campaign. By early on the morning of 5 May XIII Corps had taken over the front line from northwest of Oppy to north of Fresnoy, with 5th British Division relieving 1st Canadian Division. From north of Fresnoy the 2nd Canadian Division remained in line.

Evidence of German determination to recapture Fresnoy was mounting. Their artillery became very active, firing over 100,000 shells between the evening of 6 May and the early morning of the 8th. Extensive troop movements were also noted on 7 May, a sure sign of an impending counterattack. During the night the enemy shelling intensified with a mixture of high explosive and gas, Casualties were heavy and several guns were hit. At about 0345 the following morning a large body of German infantry blundered, apparently inadvertently, into the extreme right of the Canadian 2nd Division lines just when their 4 Brigade were relieving the 6th. The incoming 19th (Central Ontario) Battalion and the outgoing 29th (Vancouver) quickly ejected the intruders from their part of the line, while 12th Gloucesters and 1st East Surreys dealt effectively with those enemy who had attempted to gain a foothold in the sector of line held by the 5th Division 95 Brigade.

At 0547 the enemy attack proper was launched under a very heavy barrage. Even though it had been anticipated, the British artillery's response was inadequate and largely ineffective. Not only had their capacity been partially weakened by the earlier damage inflicted on their guns and the gassing of some gun crews, but the mist covering the battlefield was so dense that the infantry's distress rockets went unseen. The 12th Gloucesters and the right wing of the Canadian 19th Battalion were completely crushed. But possibly even worse was the fate of 1st East Surreys, charged with the defence of Fresnoy village. Their line was rolled up and, when they abandoned the village and attempted to retire, they were practically annihilated. When the enemy's attack ran out of steam, the British/Canadian line had been pushed back to the eastern outskirts of Arleux.

It is contended, notably in the Canadian Official History, that if a counterattack had been mounted immediately it might well have been successful as the enemy rifles and machine guns had become clogged with mud and were no longer able to fire. Be that as it may it was not until 0230 on 9 May that 5th Division launched the British counterattack. It was to prove a failure even though the 15th Warwicks, who carried it out, did at one stage get back temporarily into Fresnoy. There were three main reasons for the failure. The first was that the Germans had kept Arleux and its environs under heavy bombardment throughout the time in which the attack was being prepared. Secondly, the three Canadian companies that were supposed to have taken part in the operation on the Warwicks' left had not been found by the runners dispatched to find them. Finally it had been mounted by troops who were tired, had been under continuous bombardment, and were often hungry. Having missed the opportunity of an immediate riposte, it might have been better to have waited longer to mount the counterattack with well-prepared and fresh troops. Not that fresh troops were available to First Army. Any such and many guns were already, or would soon be, on their way north.[14]

13   Captain Stair Gillon, *The Story of the 29th Division*, p. 120.
14   OH 1917, op. cit., pp.519-22. Nicholson, OH Canadian Army, pp, 277-9.

With the Arras campaign now effectively over on the Third and First Armies' front, it was a blow to British morale that it had ended with the enemy successfully retaking and holding Fresnoy and giving every indication that they had emerged the stronger and finally got the better of the exchanges that had begun on 9 April.

20

Conclusions and Epilogue

When the Battles of Arras stuttered to a close the main feelings on the part of their British participants must have been a mixture of disappointment at an opportunity lost, relief that the whole tragic episode had at last ended and sorrow at its heavy cost in human terms. The delays in the build up to the opening of the British offensive had not been a happy augury. It had seen postponements caused by the manoeuvrings over unity of command, the sharing of railway capacity, the timing of the British takeover of French line and, last but not least, the appalling weather that dogged the preparations of the French as well as the British. The injection of uncertainty into allied planning caused by the voluntary German withdrawal to the Hindenburg Line was no help either, although it had not of itself led to any additional postponement of the British and French offensives.

Despite the inauspicious build up, the first day of the British offensive had been so successful that it had seemed possible that a corner had been truly turned and the Germans might this time really be about to crack. Vimy Ridge had virtually fallen to the Canadians, some units of Third Army had recorded the longest advances in a day in the war to that date, the German forward defences were in disarray and their reserves too far back to be of immediate aid. The opportunity had been there to press forward urgently, giving the enemy no time to recover their balance. The main area ripe for exploitation in this way was north of the River Scarpe in the zone assaulted by XVII Corps. Unfortunately, too much of Third Army strength had been deployed south of the river, including the mass of the cavalry. Had this arm been reasonably close up behind XVII Corps the opportunity might well have been there to link up with an infantry division and break through the scattered German defences. It was not to be, and not just because of the inappropriate deployment of Third Army, whose Commander, General Allenby, seemed to set more store on success south of the Scarpe than north of it. There was also a mixture of disbelief at what was being achieved, an unfamiliarity with how to deal with a beckoning war of movement and an understandable anxiety to avoid outrunning artillery support, which could in no way be compensated for by the available tanks.

The 24 hours lost before General Allenby issued his exhortation to pursue a beaten enemy were sufficient for the Germans to patch up their defences and get their reserves forward to positions where they could exert an influence on the battle. In retrospect the British Army had lost its one serious opportunity in the Arras campaign to inflict a lasting defeat on the enemy.

It is probably fair to say that despite the lessons learned during the Somme campaign there still remained shortcomings in the performance of all arms of the British Army during the Arras campaign, and at all levels. At the topmost level mention has already been made of General Allenby's focus on the area south of the Scarpe, to the detriment of opportunities north of the river. He could also be criticised for allowing himself to be overridden too easily by GHQ and, it has to be said, the bulk of his peers, over the questions of the length of the preliminary bombardment and the timing of Zero Hour for the Second Battle of the Scarpe. The longer the campaign lasted the less he seemed to be in control of events. Nor can Field Marshal Haig escape criticism, not only for imposing his ill-advised compromise on the Second Scarpe Zero Hour, but also for gradually withdrawing guns and the prospect of relief by fresh divisions, from the three armies fighting the Arras campaign, leaving tired and depleted units to carry on the battle, with predictable results. His decision to appoint General Gough to command the planned Flanders offensive might not have directly affected the Arras campaign, but it must have been something of a distraction for Gough as he continued his efforts to capture Bullecourt. Gough himself had a less than distinguished campaign. He misjudged the German attitude to the retention of Bullecourt. His over hasty introduction of the tanks after his unwise acceptance of their claims that they could be an adequate substitute for the artillery, served I ANZAC ill and reinforced the already intense Australian disillusionment with British generalship.

For the Infantry there were very few redeeming features to be derived from the Arras campaign, particularly if the opening day is discounted. A problem that became more apparent as losses, especially of experienced NCOs and battalion officers, mounted was the lack of adequate training that replacements had received. Many had only been in uniform for three months or even less; they often found themselves pitched into the fighting with no introductory experience of trench warfare in quiet sectors, little notion of infantry tactics and scarcely any familiarity with the weaponry, notably the rifles and bayonets, they were expected to use and on which their lives depended. They were a very long way from matching the '15 rounds a minute' musketry of the professional army that had been decimated in the first few months of the war. The situation was particularly difficult for newly commissioned platoon officers, who were expected to exercise leadership when they had had no time to get to know their men or the tricks of their demanding and very dangerous trade. It could have come as no surprise that the consequent lack of initiative, enterprise and leadership was very soon making itself felt in operations, with troops left leaderless halting or falling back more in a search for further orders than a desire to distance themselves from the enemy. There was no ready made solution, as the time and the personnel were simply unavailable to enable units or individuals to be withdrawn from the line to undertake training away from the fighting. There were of course exceptions to this rather gloomy scenario. Individual acts of great bravery could, and not infrequently did, restore a situation or put an attack back on the front foot. Good morale, courage and endurance remained high. Nevertheless there can be no disputing that inexperience and lack of training must have made a significant contribution to the high casualty lists that emerged from the Battles of Arras.

Although it can hardly be claimed that the artillery had sorted out all the shortcomings that had become evident during the Somme campaign, there is little question that matters had greatly improved by the time of the Battles of Arras. There was by then a more than adequate number of guns of all types together with plentiful ammunition for them that was largely free of the deficiencies that had led to so many 'duds' being fired in the earlier campaign. In addition the 106 fuze, so valuable in its wire cutting role, had become increasingly readily available. Despite the very bad weather the artillery had had sufficient time to position itself for the firing of the preliminary bombardments and to provide full support to the infantry as they advanced on the first day. As for the infantry, the day was a great success for the artillery. The Forward Observation Officers proved their worth especially when they could take up positions with a clear view over the battlefield.

It was not very long however before problems began to surface. Inevitably communication under battlefield conditions was a major one of these. It made it particularly difficult for FOOs or the infantry to get the field artillery, which was invariably firing to a prearranged plan, to switch to a target that was causing serious problems for the attackers. When sometimes the difficulties were overcome, the FOOs were frustrated to discover that far too much ammunition was being wasted firing on a target that did not merit such extravagance. Almost certainly because of the additional distances usually involved, liaison with the heavy artillery for the infantry was much more problematic. It led to tempting targets, such as enemy troops massing for a counterattack, being ignored.

As the British advance inched forward – the best description of it after the first day – the perennial artillery problem of moving the guns forward over ground that they had themselves done much to make impassable, re-emerged. The quality of the support furnished to the infantry inevitably diminished; more barrages were described in war diaries as weak or thin and there were too many cases of 'friendly' fire. A further reason for these outcomes was the often ill considered and over hastily prepared nature of some of these attacks, not something that could be blamed on the artillery.

Both Field Marshal Haig and General Allenby had plans to make full use of the cavalry during the Arras campaign, in its traditional roles of exploiting breakthroughs in the enemy defences to sow confusion and mayhem behind the lines and to conduct reconnaissance missions. In an effort to give them greater latitude an infantry division, the 17th, was made part of the cavalry's order of battle for the start of the campaign and was trained in infantry/cavalry co-operation. Its main role was foreseen as being to occupy ground that had been taken by the cavalry, freeing the latter up to move on. Whether this would have worked was never put to the test as conditions were never deemed suitable to use the cavalry as planned. After only a few days 17th Division resumed its role as a conventional infantry unit.

With its main purpose seemingly denied it the cavalry became largely marginalised in the Arras campaign. Its most significant intervention was in the ultimately successful attempt to capture Monchy-le-Preux on 11 April. Significant roles were played in this event, not only by the cavalry but also by the infantry and tanks. There are claims and counterclaims as to who actually did capture the village with 37th Infantry Division generally regarded as having the strongest claim, which appears supported by their impressive memorial in the village centre (although its inscription makes no specific claim to the Division having captured the village). The 37th were certainly tasked with capturing the village but may have been held up as they approached from the north enabling the 10th Hussars and 1st Essex Yeomanry of 8 Cavalry Brigade, entering from the west, to claim that there were only scattered remnants of two brigades of 37th Division in isolated places in and west of Monchy Château, to be found on their arrival. Therefore, the Essex Yeomanry war diary claimed, the infantry were not holding the village. But both cavalry and infantry quickly had other preoccupations as the Germans, having vacated the village, unleashed a heavy bombardment on it that resulted in the two cavalry units suffering severe losses in both men and horses. A third cavalry unit, 3rd Dragoon Guards, which had advanced along the Arras-Cambrai road to positions south of Monchy, were spotted by an enemy aircraft and also subjected to heavy shelling that caused severe losses of both men and animals. With the withdrawal of the bulk of the survivors, the involvement of the cavalry in the Battles of Arras, other than peripherally, came to an end.

As mentioned above, the tanks also played a significant part in the capture of Monchy. Four of them, from C Battalion, advanced at 0500 on 11 April, one of them taking a route round the northern edge of the village and entering from the east. Its 6 pounder successfully silenced several machine guns before a British shell put the tank out of action and forced the crew to abandon it. The remaining three tanks attacked towards Monchy from the south with mainly tragic results. One of them was hit by the British barrage after clearing an enemy trench. Another was hit by armour-piercing bullets and then a shell, leaving all the crew except the Commander either dead or wounded. The third tank, having exchanged Lewis gun fire with a large number of enemy troops seeking to surround it, was finally hit and set on fire. Only three crew members survived.

The experience of this group of tanks was not untypical of the overall experience of the relatively new weapon during the Arras campaign, except perhaps in the damage inflicted on them by their own artillery. Some failed to make it to their start line because of mechanical breakdown, or soon after crossing the start line fell victim to the same problem. Some were severely damaged or destroyed by enemy armour-piercing or shell fire. Some failed to cope with treacherous ground and became bogged down. But there were some that contributed very useful support to the infantry. Not surprisingly, however, given their limited numbers, their mechanical unreliability and their lack of adequate armour, their performance must at best be deemed to have been disappointing. This is in no way a reflection on the bravery and commitment of the tank commanders and their crews.

Not unlike the tanks, the Royal Flying Corps' unhappy experience could be blamed to a significant extent on inadequate equipment, in their case aircraft which could be outmanoeuvred, outperformed and outgunned by those of the enemy. The other major contributor to their misfortune was the inadequate training that many pilots received before being sent to squadrons – if they survived the hazards of what training they did receive; many did not. Although rather too late to be of assistance during the Arras campaign, new aircraft types that were a match, and in some cases more than a match, for the German machines were soon arriving in adequate quantities that ensured that there would be no repetition of 'Bloody April' during the rest of the war. But the provision of adequate training remained a problem with the insatiable demand for aircrew needed to carry the battle to the enemy.

In view of the fact that the Arras and Second Aisne campaigns ended in disappointment, to say the least, it is scarcely surprising that few of the senior officers involved on the allied side emerged with enhanced reputations. Field Marshal Haig had once again presided over a battle that had produced enormous casualty lists. In normal circumstances Prime Minister Lloyd George might have felt constrained to demand his resignation as he undoubtedly would have done following the Somme campaign had he felt that he had the political strength to do so and there had been an acceptable successor waiting in the wings. But the Prime Minister's position had been weakened by the total failure of his protégé Nivelle, under whose command he had plotted to subordinate Haig and the BEF. Instead he found himself giving his full support to Haig's ambitious plans for the Flanders offensive intended to clear the Belgian coast. These resulted in another bloody failure know to history as Passchendaele. It was not until the 100 Days campaign that ended with the defeat of the German Army and the Armistice that Haig was vindicated and returned to Britain a hero. However Lloyd George saw to it that Haig received no further meaningful government employment and, after the Field Marshal's death, published his war memoirs which contributed to the process of denigrating his reputation. This process continued unabated until John Terraine's publication of his biography of Haig (*Douglas Haig: The Educated Soldier*) in 1963, launched moves to re-establish the esteem in which he had been held prior to his death.

General Sir Edmund Allenby's ambivalent relationship with Haig dated back to their days as students at the Staff College, Camberley, and was not improved by the perceived shortcomings (from Haig's point of view) of Allenby's conduct of the Arras campaign in the weeks following what, Haig readily admitted, had been a triumphant first day. Although Haig never came near removing Allenby from his command of the Third Army, circumstances combined to effect his departure. Lloyd George, still seeking a war winning strategy that would sideline the Western Front, with its enormous casualties for little gain, decided that something needed to be done to galvanise some successful activity into the operations of the Egyptian Expeditionary Force, based in Cairo. The Commander in Chief there, General Sir Archibald Murray, was, probably unfairly, seen as part of the problem and Lloyd George cast about for a successor. He tried to persuade General Jan Christian Smuts to take on the task, but he eventually turned it down. The Prime Minister then asked the CIGS, General 'Wully' Robertson, to recommend a suitable alternative. Aware of Haig's dissatisfaction with Allenby, and anyway believing him to be the best man for the task, he suggested Allenby. Having already formed a high opinion of Allenby, the Prime Minister readily agreed, and the appointment was confirmed on 5 June 1917. Allenby himself was less than pleased; indeed he was devastated, seeing his removal from command of the Third Army as a badge of failure. In some distress he poured out his heart to his successor at Third Army, Sir Julian Byng, before departing for London. There, after seeing the Prime Minister, who demanded he should capture Jerusalem by Christmas, he realised that his appointment was not a demotion, but a challenge.

Allenby more than rose to the challenge. The Turkish Gaza-Beersheba Line was broken and Jerusalem duly captured before Christmas. The following year Palestine and Syria, including

Damascus, were taken and the Turks forced to sue for peace. By the latter half of 1919 Allenby was Field Marshal Viscount Allenby of Felixstowe and Megiddo. He died in 1936.

The Commander of the Fifth Army, General Sir Hubert Gough, was another major figure on the British side whose reputation suffered as a result of the Arras campaign. In his efforts to take Bullecourt and break into the Hindenburg Line he made some ill-judged decisions that have already been described. Nevertheless Haig chose him to command the planned Flanders offensive rather than the eminently more suited General Sir Herbert Plumer, on the probable grounds that Gough was a 'thruster' and Plumer a 'bite and hold' man, and a thruster was what was needed. Events were to prove that Haig had erred in entrusting the Third Battle of Ypres to Gough and prime responsibility for the Passchendaele campaign was soon handed over to Plumer. By the end of the campaign Haig had become fully aware that a significant number of divisional commanders were very reluctant to serve under Gough; the Canadians absolutely refused to. Nevertheless, despite pressure from the Prime Minister, looking as usual for scapegoats, Haig insisted on keeping Gough in place as GOC in C Fifth Army and sacrificed instead GHQ's Director of Intelligence and Quartermaster General. When the German Spring Offensive opened on 21 March 1918, the main blow fell on an undermanned Fifth Army that had only recently taken over their stretch of line from the French. Although forced back for a considerable distance they did not break, with Gough conducting a skilled retirement under immense pressure. Nevertheless Haig, once again under Prime Ministerial pressure, was forced to relieve him and send him home, effectively ending Gough's military career. He spent much of the rest of a long life (he died in 1963) seeking exoneration from blame for the disaster that had initially befallen Fifth Army in the spring of 1918. He had some success and was awarded the GCB in 1937. But he never received what he deemed his due, elevation to Field Marshal rank and to the House of Lords, and a gratuity.

Just about the only senior French Generals to emerge from the Second Battle of the Aisne with their reputations intact were Army Group Commanders Philippe Pétain and Franchet d'Espèrey. The Commander in Chief Robert Nivelle, the Commander of the Reserve Army Group (Groupe d'Armées de Réserve), Joseph Micheler, and Army Commanders, Charles Mangin (6th) and Olivier Mazel (5th) were all damaged by the parts they played in the most disastrous series of events suffered by the French Army in the war. The principal blame for what had gone wrong was quite rightly laid at the door of Nivelle when the recriminations began. Less than four weeks after his eponymous offensive had been launched his resignation was sought by the Minister of War, Paul Painlevé, supported by the Council of Ministers. After 5 days of futile resistance of the inevitable, Nivelle tendered it on 15 May, consoled by the promise that he would be given command of an Army Group with the appropriate rank. But his replacement as Commander in Chief, General Pétain, after a short interval declined to redeem the promise on the grounds that there was no vacancy. Returned to the jurisdiction of the Ministry of War he was appointed Commander in Chief of French forces in North Africa in December 1917. Despite repeated requests he was not allowed to return to active service in Metropolitan France. He was not even invited to participate in the Victory Parade in Paris in 1919. Nivelle retired from the army in 1921 and returned from Algeria to live in Paris. He died in 1924, aged 67.

The military career of General Micheler was damaged by his close involvement with the Nivelle Offensive as Commander in Chief of the Reserve Army Group (GAR) whose three armies were supposed to break through the German defences on the Chemin des Dames and then exploit the breakthrough. It is perhaps ironic that he was damaged in this way as he had quickly formed the opinion that Nivelle's plans were flawed and had conspired unsuccessfully in political circles behind Nivelle's back to get the offensive abandoned or scaled down. When it had clearly failed and Nivelle was on his way out, the GAR was disbanded. Micheler was given temporary command of First Army on 5 May before replacing General Mazel in command of Fifth Army on 22 May. He remained in command of that Army until he was summarily dismissed on 10 June 1918, ostensibly for failing to implement General Pétain's orders to institute defence in depth during the highly successful German offensive from 27 May to 5 June (called Operation Blücher by the Germans and Third Battle of the Aisne by the French). The Fifth Army were relatively unscathed during this battle, the main brunt having fallen on the neighbouring Sixth Army, whose Commander, General Duchêne, had certainly been at fault in not thinning out his forward defences. It is probable therefore that Pétain took the opportunity to get rid of Micheler, who had kept up his conspiratorial habits against his new superior, at the same time as he had Duchêne dismissed. Micheler held no further military appointments. He died in 1931.

General Olivier Mazel commanded the Fifth Army during the Nivelle Offensive until he was relieved of his command on 22 May 1917. Like his Army Group Commander, General Micheler, he was critical of Nivelle's plans for the offensive and even described him as a criminal. He was nevertheless made a scapegoat for the offensive's failure. Following his dismissal he spent some months in the wilderness before being given command of a Territorial military region. He left the army in 1920 and died in 1940.

Perhaps the most controversial of the victims of the failure of the Nivelle Offensive was General Charles Mangin, Commander of the Sixth Army in the GAR. Mangin was a close associate of Nivelle, having shared his triumphs at Verdun. He was a ferociously aggressive General only really happy when his troops were killing Germans. Unfortunately he did not seem to care how many French lives were lost in the process and earned the nickname of 'The Butcher'. The Sixth Army suffered catastrophic losses when attacking, and failing to take, the Chemin des Dames in the early days of Nivelle's offensive. Despite his closeness to the Commander in Chief and his wholehearted support for his offensive, the latter did not spare him when he was casting around for scapegoats. Mangin was an obvious choice for the role after the performance of his Army, which had led to popular calls for his sacking. He was dismissed in early May after famously stormy meetings with Nivelle and War Minister Painlevé. Thereafter he remained in involuntary retirement until he was recalled to active duty in December 1917 by Army Chief of Staff Ferdinand Foch who was looking for aggressive leaders to counterbalance the excessive passivity of Pétain, as he perceived it. By the middle of 1918 Mangin was in command of the Tenth Army and conducted its counterattack on 18 July which broke the German line between the Aisne and Marne rivers, offering an early indication that the tide of the war might at last be turning in the allies' favour. Mangin continued on active operations until the end of the war. He died in harness in Africa in 1925.

There were some military leaders who emerged from Arras and Second Aisne with enhanced reputations. On the British side one of these was the Commander of the First Army, General Sir Henry Horne. His Army capture of Vimy Ridge, and the Third Army first day advance, constituted the only really significant successes of the Battles of Arras. Vimy Ridge was Horne's first major test as an Army Commander and he acquitted himself faultlessly by taking full advantage of his strengths, an excellent staff, the Canadian Corps, a battlefield limited in area that constrained the enemy's freedom of manoeuvre and more than adequate guns and shells for his purposes. The First Army also achieved the main successes of the Battle of Arleux and the Third Battle of the Scarpe with the capture respectively of the villages of Arleux and Fresnoy, again mainly the work of the Canadian Corps. Horne was keen to build on these successes by capturing the town of Lens but had to put his plans on hold as some of his artillery was relocated northward as the build up for the Battle of Messines Ridge and the Flanders offensive got under way.

The First Army next major campaign was the defensive Battle of the Lys which opened coincidentally on 9 April 1918 a year to the day after the Battle of Vimy Ridge. After nearly three weeks of desperate fighting the German assault, Operation Georgette, was contained without them having reached their objective, Hazebrouck. It was Horne's proud boast that he was the only BEF Army commander who had not been forced to move his HQ to the rear by the German spring offensives. The Battle of Amiens, which began of 8 August, 'the Black Day of the German Army', signalled the beginning of the 'Campaign of 100 Days' that concluded with Germany signing an Armistice, its terms amounting to complete surrender. Horne's First Army played a full part in the Allied advance to victory, liberating on the way Cambrai, Douai, Valenciennes and, on the last night of the war, Mons.

In the post war years Horne remained in the Army serving for three years as GOC in C Eastern Command. He then went on the half-pay before finally retiring in 1926. In recognition of his war service he was sent to the House of Lords as Baron Horne of Stirkoke and granted a gratuity of £30,000. Curiously, unlike the other Western Front Army Commanders still in post on Armistice Day, he was not promoted to Field Marshal. General Lord Horne died in 1929.

The other British military leader whose reputation was enhanced was the Commander of the Canadian Corps at the time of the Arras campaign, Lieutenant General Sir Julian Byng. A cavalryman Byng spent the early months of the war with the Cavalry Corps on the Western Front and then commanding IX Infantry Corps in Gallipoli. By June 1916 he had been appointed Commander of the Canadian Corps. He led them during the Somme campaign from where they were transferred to Vimy Ridge. It was Byng's careful and very detailed planning that was largely responsible for the Corps success there and in their subsequent actions during the Arras campaign. In June 1917 he was promoted to replace General Allenby in command of Third Army. He remained in that position for the rest of the war despite criticism arising from his failure to anticipate the German counterstroke at the Battle of Cambrai after the success of the initial British offensive. He was rewarded for his war service by elevation to the peerage as Baron Byng of Vimy and the grant of a gratuity of £30,000. His popularity with Canadians was such that he was appointed Governor General of the Dominion from 1921-6. Just over a year after his return to Britain he was appointed Commissioner of the Metropolitan Police, a position he held until 1931. Just prior to his appointment he was elevated in the House of Lords to Viscount and made a Field Marshal. He died in 1935.

Possibly the only French beneficiary from the disaster that overtook the French Army in April 1917 and the outbreaks of indiscipline that infected it for weeks afterwards was General Philippe Pétain. He began the offensive as Commander of the Central Army Group but very soon found himself Commander in Chief of the French Army as General Nivelle was manoeuvred out of that position during the first half of May. Probably only Pétain could have dealt successfully with the outbreaks of indiscipline that confronted him. His reputation as a stern but fair disciplinarian undoubtedly helped as did his readiness to listen to, and do something about, the *Poilus'* grievances. Most of all it was probably his undertaking not to order attacks unless they were well planned, well supported, limited in scope and duration, and militarily essential. The downside of these commitments was an increasing belief by his British allies that he could not be relied on to support them fully in their offensive operations; he already had a justified reputation for pessimism. Initially it seemed that these fears might be misplaced, but when the Germans launched Operation Michael, the first phase of their spring offensive in March 1918, which impacted mainly on the British Fifth and Third Armies but seemed likely to drive a wedge between them and the French Army, Pétain was found to be more concerned about a possible future threat to Paris, and very reluctant to commit French troops to help close the gap between the French and British armies. Out of this came a sudden readiness by Haig to have an Allied Supreme Commander appointed who, if French, would be well-placed to be able to override Pétain's narrow nationalistic concerns. The choice for Generalissimo fell on General Ferdinand Foch, highly regarded by the British and ideally suited for the task. He and Haig quickly established a good rapport and Pétain was soon made to adopt a less chauvinistic attitude to the Alliance.

Pétain remained in command of the French Army for the rest of the war and, elevated to Marshal, was held in high public esteem as one of the four national heroes who had won the war for France;

the other three were of course Joffre and Foch, and Prime Minister Georges Clemenceau. His prestige was still sufficient for him to be made a member of the French Government following the German invasion in May 1940. His defeatism soon became apparent as the French Army plunged towards defeat. When the Council of Ministers voted to seek an armistice, Prime Minister Paul Reynaud resigned and was replaced by Pétain, who favoured the move. The Armistice was signed on 22 June and once it was ratified on 10 July Pétain became Head of State of the newly established Vichy France with near dictatorial powers. At this stage there is little doubt that Pétain had the support of the vast majority of the French people. But over the course of the next four years disaffection grew. When France was liberated the Marshal and his government moved to Germany and declared themselves a government in exile. In the last days of the Third Reich Pétain returned to France, was arrested and put on trial for treason. Found guilty he was sentenced to death. The sentence was commuted to life imprisonment. Pétain died, aged 95 and senile, in 1951.

The recent centenary commemorations have contributed to a revival of interest in the Battles of Arras. It remains to be seen whether this will be a fleeting revival or whether the campaign has finally escaped from the mischance of having taken place between the Battles of the Somme and Passchendaele, those two outstanding reminders of the futility and horror of war. Although Arras cannot match the duration of those two battles it can certainly compete with them on just about every other measure of ghastliness. On a *per diem* basis, as is frequently pointed out, the British casualty lists comfortably exceeded those recorded for the Somme and Passchendaele. There are probably even fewer positives to be derived from the results of Arras. The argument can certainly be made that German morale was adversely affected by the Somme and Passchendaele, with their heavy losses. At Arras, German morale was almost certainly boosted by the ease with which they coped with all but the first day or so of the British offensive. Although German losses cannot be precisely established it is almost certain that they were notably lower than those of the British, certainly in the latter stages of the campaign. In the opening stages, before they had organised defence in depth, they were probably broadly similar.

Given the imperatives of the Anglo-French alliance there was probably no way in which fighting the Arras campaign could have been avoided entirely or curtailed. It was nevertheless unfortunate that fighting it almost certainly had a very adverse effect on the outcome of the Flanders offensive. Had that been launched a couple of months earlier with a reasonable prospect of weeks of dry weather, there would have been a very good chance that the offensive would have achieved its important objectives and not have become bogged down in autumnal swamps. Perhaps Arras really was 'a battle too far'.

Appendix I

The German Army at Arras

For the German Army the Battles of Arras and the Second Battle of the Aisne were fought in the aftermath of what had been a terrible 1916 for them. The Battles of Verdun and the Somme are frequently thought of in the context of the appalling French losses at Verdun and the equally, if not more, shocking British losses on the Somme. For the Germans these two battles had left them with casualty lists at least as long, if not longer, than the total losses of both their adversaries.

As has already been described, by the end of August 1916 patience with the German Chief of the General Staff, General Erich von Falkenhayn, had run out. He had paid the price for his strategy of 'bleeding France white' that had led to Verdun, and German losses that had shown that bleeding white could be a two-edged sword. On the Somme his insistence that all losses of ground had to be reversed by immediate counterattack had been a major contribution to the mounting up of unsustainable losses. Falkenhayn was replaced by the team of General Paul von Hindenburg as Chief of the General Staff and General Erich Ludendorff as First Quartermaster General. An urgent priority for them was to reduce the bloodletting, which they tried to do by scaling down operations at Verdun and introducing more sophisticated defensive techniques on the Somme. These measures helped to some extent but only a significant reduction in the intensity of the fighting could bring the Germans the relief they needed to strengthen their defences and restore their severely dented morale in anticipation of a resumption of Allied aggression in 1917. To their great relief the onset and persistence of bad weather finally forced the suspension of the Somme campaign in mid November and Verdun a month later.

Another urgent priority was to put in hand the construction of the strong new defensive line some distance in rear of the current front lines in the Arras and Somme sectors. Work began in late September and would continue until early March 1917 on the *Siegfried Stelling*, more familiarly known as the Hindenburg Line. Although when conceived this had been seen as a purely precautionary measure, it rapidly assumed the role of an answer to some of the problems besetting the Army, if it were combined with the Army retirement behind it and its assumption thereby of the role of the new Front Line. The agonising over the voluntary surrendering of ground that had cost so much blood to take, the manner and method of the eventual withdrawal and the confusion it caused in allied headquarters have already been described.[1] Whether or not foreknowledge of the French and British plans for Second Aisne and Arras influenced the German decision to carry out the retirement is a matter for conjecture. There is no doubt it worked very much in favour of the Germans as the British Fifth Army and the French Armies launched their assaults on 11 and 16 April respectively.

The German Army had undergone changes in its command structure since the outbreak of war but in April 1917 the two major components that were to confront the allies were Army Group Crown Prince Rupprecht of Bavaria and Army Group German Crown Prince. Responsible for the northern sector, the Rupprecht Group consisted of four armies, the Fourth, Sixth, First and Second. The principal role in countering the assaults of the British First and Third Armies would fall to the Rupprecht Group's Sixth Army.

Responsible for the southern sector running south and east from St Quentin, roughly the junction

---

1   Ian Passingham, *All the Kaiser's Men*, pp. 102-40 passim.

between the two Groups, the German Crown Prince's Command consisted of Seventh, Third and Fifth Armies. On 16 April, just as the French Army offensive began, First Army were transferred from Prince Ruppprecht's to the German Crown Prince's Group for insertion into the line between Seventh and Third Armies, as the French assault developed. These three armies would have the task of dealing with the French offensive.

Although the two Crown Princes certainly owed their elevated positions in the military hierarchy to the accident of birth, they were both well trained and professional soldiers. Rupprecht in particular took his duties very seriously and carried them out with considerable competence. There was more of the playboy and less intellect in the makeup of German Crown Prince Wilhelm, but he knew his business and was not easily pushed around by senior generals. Although nearly three years of fighting, and especially the Somme and Verdun campaigns, had begun to affect adversely the standards and efficiency of the German Army, it was still a formidable fighting machine, man for man probably still more than a match for their French and British adversaries. The allies would be up against a preponderance of Bavarian units, except at Bullecourt, where one of XIV Reserve Corps' divisions was the formidable 27th, a Kingdom of Wurttemberg unit. Opposing the Canadians at Vimy Ridge were the Sixth Army 1st Bavarian Reserve Corps (*Gruppe* Vimy), commanded by General Karl Ritter von Fasbender. He had under command the 79th Reserve Division, 1st Bavarian Reserve Division and 14th Bavarian Infantry Division.

The battles of April and May 1917 were an opportunity for the German Army to operate the system of defence, known as 'elastic defence in depth' that had been evolving since late 1915 and had been adopted as standard on 1 December 1916, when a training manual, entitled 'Conduct of the Defensive Battle' (*Die Fuhrung der Abwehrschlacht*) was issued to all German divisions. Although the standard method of defence superseded by these instructions, of packing the front line with unbroken lines of rifles and machine guns, had served the German Army well and prevented their adversaries from making any significant breakthroughs, there had been a growing realisation that, as the British and French production of guns and shells increased, front lines would become increasingly untenable. A system of defence needed to be devised that would enable the number of troops in the front line to be thinned out without prejudicing the integrity of the defence overall. The main suggestion that had emerged from the experience of the battles of 1915-16 was that reserve lines should be located on reverse slopes, which not only offered concealment but also made them relatively inaccessible to anything other than plunging fire.

Ironically the first glimmer of light leading ultimately to the solution promulgated in the 1 December 1916 training manual was provided by a seemingly innocuous French document that fell into the hands of the Germans on 10 May, 1915, during a raid on a French trench near La Ville-au-Bois, north of Reims. The document turned out to be the French Fifth Army Commander's proposals for organising the holding of the front trench system by frontline battalions. General Franchet d'Espèrey argued that efforts needed to be made to improve his Army defensive system which had, until this point, consisted of an accumulation of ad hoc arrangements. Some order needed to be instilled. He proposed that sectors of the line in danger of attack should establish three lines of defence. The first line, called the first, or outpost, line of resistance, should consist of groups of sentries or piquets in strongly built but weakly garrisoned dugouts. Pushed out in front of them should be a series of listening posts not necessarily connected with each other by a trench. About 200 metres behind the first line should be the second line, the main line of resistance in the event of the first line being overrun. It should be strongly built and have sufficient dugout space to accommodate the whole garrison. The third line, about 600 metres behind the second, should consist mainly of shell proof shelters to house the reserves. The three lines would be connected by communication trenches and heavily protected by wire.

Although the French document may have been the first airing of the concept of defence in depth

Colonel Fritz von Lossberg, the Architect of Defence

it was still some distance from the finished article as outlined in the German training manual of 1 December 1916. German military opinion on the subject of the optimum defence system seems to have been split between those favouring the status quo and those in favour of some form of defence in depth. The conversion of a certain Colonel von Lossberg from the former to the latter would play an important part in the latter system finally prevailing.

Fritz von Lossberg was born in 1868 into a Thuringian military family. He became its third generation to be commissioned into the 2nd Foot Guards Regiment. After commanding a battalion of the Regiment he spent four years as an instructor at the Army Staff College (*Kriegsakademie*). At the outbreak of the war he was Chief of Staff of XIII Corps. In the first six months he saw action against the French, British and Russians before being appointed, in early 1915, Deputy Chief of the Operations Section of German Supreme Headquarters (*Oberste Heeresleitung* (OHL)), based in Mézières. It was here that he first became exposed to the debate about the relative merits of different defence systems. Perhaps ironically, given his later conversion, Lossberg appeared not to attach any significance to the captured French Fifth Army document; he was to remain formally wedded to the necessity of heavily manned front lines throughout his eight months at OHL. It was only when he was, unexpectedly for a junior Colonel, transferred to the Third Army to assume the post of Chief of Staff, that it was to become apparent that he had been absorbing the ideas of reverse slope positions and lightly held but deep defences during his time at OHL.

Von Lossberg assumed his new post when the Third Army was under attack during the French offensive known as the Second Battle of Champagne. With the approval of the Army Commander he quickly stopped a proposed retirement and went forward to the *Ferme de Navarin*, where there was the greatest danger of a French breakthrough, to assess the situation for himself. What he saw there, and at another vantage point further back, satisfied him of the merits of defence in depth and he immediately began to implement it in his Army sector. As it involved changes of doctrine it required a huge personal effort on his part to get the message across and for the necessary changes to be put in hand. Within two days of his assumption of his new position, the work had been done despite the major battle going on. The new arrangements were to prove themselves in the face of successive French offensives in October 1915. The main improvement on previous practice related to the use of counterattacks. Von Lossberg determined that counterattacks using local infantry reserves, supported by artillery and machine gun fire aiming at identified targets, should only be attempted if they could be mounted before the enemy had had time to consolidate the defence of their gains. If this opportunity had passed then any counterattack should only be mounted after careful and methodical preparation, even should this take several days.

Von Lossberg quickly demonstrated that his visit to the front line on the first day of his new appointment was no flash in the pan. He continued to use every opportunity to visit front line commanders and officers, and ensured that his staff did likewise. He soon acquired a reputation as an officer who cared deeply for the welfare of the front line units in Third Army.

The 1916 Somme campaign would not in normal circumstances have involved Lossberg as it initially fell to the German Second Army to cope with the Anglo-French onslaught. But General von Falkenhayn, still on 1 July Chief of the General Staff, quickly perceived shortcomings in the performance of the Second Army Chief of Staff and offered the job to Lossberg. With some reluctance he accepted, on the understanding that Falkenhayn would immediately cease offensive operations at Verdun so as to make reserves available to bolster the Somme defences. Despite concurring, von Falkenhayn had not fulfilled his undertaking when, on 28 August, he was dismissed and replaced by Generals Hindenburg and Ludendorff, who promptly did what Falkenhayn had failed to do. Not only did Falkenhayn's departure remove his insistence on immediate counterattacks to recover lost ground regardless of its tactical value, but it also had the effect that Lossberg had been seeking of making more troops and guns available to bolster the defences on the Somme. On 17 July responsibility for the Somme had been split leaving Second Army to defend the ground south of the River and First Army the ground to the north. The Commander of the Second Army, General Fritz von Below, and Lossberg were two of many Second Army headquarters staff who transferred over to the newly reformed First Army which would assume the lion's share of the burden of the Somme.

Following the disastrous failure of 1 July the British Army largely abandoned mass attacks with grandiose ambitions in favour of assaults with limited objectives preceded by a battering with artillery of the relevant German defences. In other words 'bite and hold' rather than 'breakthrough'. Using his past experience in Champagne bolstered by numerous visits to the forward areas Lossberg was soon able to refine 'defence in depth' to deal with the changed circumstances. The new defensive positions no longer depended on a line of trenches, but rather on machine gun nests and dugouts concealed around the area to be defended in depth and, in the former case, able to provide flanking and overhead fire to supplement the firepower provided by supporting artillery barrages. It was still regarded as important to retain possession of the front line, but at the first sign of an attack the machine guns were moved forward of the front line to prepared positions usually in shell holes where they could reasonably hope to escape the attentions of the British artillery that habitually focused on German front lines when firing pre-assault barrages. The support troops, no longer confined to the front line, and the local reserves were sheltered in dugouts, situated as far as was practical on reverse slopes around the deep-defended area. Immediately following the conclusion of the Somme campaign, the First Army produced a pamphlet entitled 'Experiences of the First Army in the Somme Battles', the main contributor to which was Colonel von Lossberg. It was printed on 30 January 1917. It encapsulated the idea of a mobile defence in depth and was to provide the basis for the fighting of defensive battles by the German Army for the rest of the war. Its immediate, if patchy, application would be seen in the Arras and Second Aisne battles.[2]

---

2   Wynne, *If Germany Attacks*, pp. 83 et seq.

Given that there is general acceptance that the concept of an elastic or mobile defence in depth, as refined by the time of the Battle of Arras, gave the defence a much enlarged advantage over the attack, it has to be wondered how on the first day of the battle the assaults of the British First and Third Armies inflicted such reverses on the Germans as to amount to a comprehensive, if short-lived, defeat. One reason lay in the German Army reception of the new ideas. There was by no means unanimous endorsement of them, with many senior officers fearing that the term 'elastic', used even in the German document of 1 December 1916, was an invitation to front line troops to retire at the first sign of an advancing enemy. Even von Lossberg deplored the use of the term, insisting that every effort needed to be made to halt or disrupt the enemy advance as far forward as possible. One consequence of the slowness to reach consensus on the implementation of defence in depth was that the Hindenburg Line, construction of which had begun in September 1916, was built according to the old norms. It was only when the decision was taken to begin the withdrawal into the Hindenburg Line on 9 February 1917 that General Fritz von Below and Colonel von Lossberg sought Crown Prince Rupprecht's urgent agreement to begin a programme to modify the Line's configuration in the First Army sector[3] in accordance with the new rules. Rupprecht recognised the force of the arguments put to him and took up the issue with General Ludendorff, who concurred. The work was immediately put in hand and had made significant progress by the time the battle began. It was however by no means complete. When it was realised that Operation *Alberich* would be finished before completion of the work, the First Army sought to have the operation postponed to give more time for completion, but to no avail. The result would be that when the battle began, the modification of the Hindenburg Line, notably the construction of a new line about 2,000 yards forward of the initially planned forward line, and the extension of any changes beyond the First Army sector, had not taken place. There had been other factors at play that had prevented adequate progress being made, besides some senior officers' fear of change. The freezing weather had prevented concrete setting. Labour had been in short supply. There had been a fear that the British would become aware of a thinning out of forward garrisons and would adjust their attack plans accordingly. All this meant that the British would be launching their assault against a work barely in progress rather than one completed.

When the British and Canadian assault began at 0530 on 9 April the novel tactics employed also played their part in overcoming German resistance. The sheer weight of the preliminary bombardment – two weeks long for the Canadians and four days long for Third Army – had done immense damage to the German artillery's powers of resistance. The hurricane bombardment fired in the five minutes immediately prior to Zero Hour, an unusual and therefore unexpected tactic, enabled the assaulting troops to enter the first and second German trenches before their garrisons had had time to exit their dugouts and take up position. Even the garrisons of the third German trench line, often blinded by the snow and sleet blowing into their faces and unable to distinguish friend from foe, were often quickly overrun. As had been feared by some critics of the new defensive system, there was too a readiness to retire, by those in a position to, as seemingly endorsed by the term 'elastic'. Within an hour, possibly one third of the forward battalions had become casualties. There were no reserves close enough to offer support or to counterattack. Holding them too far back was probably the main reason for the German failure on the first day of the battle. Principally at fault for doing so was the Sixth Army Commander, General Ludwig von Falkenhausen, although it was his Army Group Commander, Prince Rupprecht, who had failed to order the reserve divisions forward, despite being begged to do so by General Ludendorff.

As 9 April drew to a close the situation for the Germans was that seven of their forward divisions had been so mauled by the British-Canadian assaults that they had lost the capacity to withstand a renewal of these assaults and were certainly in no position to mount counterattacks. These were

---

3   The First Army sector ran from Croisilles, five miles north of Quéant, to Bellicourt, north of St. Quentin, a distance of about 35 miles.

nevertheless what General von Falkenhausen ordered to be mounted on both sides of the River Scarpe. The *Gruppe* Vimy Commander, General von Fasbender was additionally put in charge of *Gruppe* Arras south of the Scarpe to co-ordinate the counterattack. Fasbender countered with a proposal to withdraw to the original German third line Méricourt-Gavrelle and, south of the Scarpe, to new positions between Roeux lake and Guémappe by way of the high ground west of Monchy. When he was apprised of the two plans Crown Prince Rupprecht came down in support of Fasbender's. It was fortunate for the Germans, as they struggled to retrieve the situation and decide where to place the reserve divisions moving forward, that the British seemed unaware of the extent of their success on 9 April and the need to press forward urgently to keep the Germans off balance. Instead the following day was spent on minor operations intended to clear up local difficulties as realisation slowly dawned on what they had achieved. If General Allenby's order to 'pursue a defeated enemy' had been issued a day earlier, the final outcome of the Battle of Arras might have been very different. Instead a day was wasted determining, at Field Marshal Haig's insistence, to push the cavalry forward against a hardening and reinforced German defence, with predictable results, rather than continuing with the infantry in the van.[4]

A further event took place on 11 April that would have a significant effect on German defensive capacity in the struggle against the British. On that day Colonel von Lossberg was informed by General Ludendorff that he had been appointed Chief of Staff of Sixth Army with immediate effect. Before relinquishing his position with First Army von Lossberg stipulated that he must be given full powers to take whatever actions he deemed fit to deal with the situation he would find at Sixth Army. Ludendorff readily assented. Although as Chief of Staff of First Army, Sixth Army neighbours, von Lossberg was already familiar with the problems they were having, his journey by car to his new HQ was organised so that he could see as much as possible for himself before formally taking over his new duties. What he saw satisfied him that his new army's XIV Corps should well be able to deal with the British Fifth Army onslaught between Bullecourt and Quéant that day. He also saw that there had been no alternative to his new army's withdrawals in the face of the British Third Army and Canadian assaults. His observations that day led him finally to abandon his belief that the foremost position and every foot of ground should be held to the last man, thus bringing him into conformity with the training manual of 1 December 1916.

Almost immediately following his belated arrival at Sixth Army HQ and a conference with General von Falkenhausen and a visiting Lieutenant General Hermann von Kuhl, Chief of Staff of Army Group Crown Prince Rupprecht, von Lossberg was able to inform General Ludendorff that he would organise a new *Wotan* position to a depth of 6,000 yards in front of the *Wotan* Line (Drocourt-Quéant Switch) and operate within this position an elastic defence in depth. The same night he asked Crown Prince Rupprecht to authorise urgent construction of a *Wotan II* Line east of its namesake (which now became the *Wotan I* Line) from the western edge of Douai south to its junction with Hindenburg II Line near Sains-lès-Marquion.

Within 48 hours of arriving at Sixth Army Headquarters Colonel von Lossberg had drawn up the arrangements for his new Army defences against the anticipated renewal of the British offensives. He then spent the next few days on the battlefield ensuring that the defences were being organised in accordance with his blueprint. During this period nine largely fresh divisions moved in to man the 18-mile long sector running south from Loos to the junction with the Hindenburg Line for which Sixth Army were responsible. In accordance with the tenets of mobile defence in depth the front line was situated on reverse slopes wherever possible. In order to conceal the exact whereabouts of the troops from air observation, von Lossberg ordered that as little digging as possible should be undertaken. He also introduced important modifications of the arrangements in place in the Hindenburg Line regarding the positioning of the machine guns. Those belonging to the front line battalions were

---

4   Wynne, op. cit., pp. 191 9.

placed in shell holes a few hundred metres behind the first line. Those belonging to the support and reserve battalions were placed in dugouts or shelters dotted about the intermediate part of the battle zone. Their main purpose would no longer be to help break up the enemy assault, but to provide the essential fire support preparatory to immediate counterattacks. The marksmen machine gun brigades, consisting of 15 to 20 guns, and one of which was allocated to each front line division, would be used to protect the artillery, which meant that they would usually, in future, be deployed at the back of the battle zone, about 1,500 to 2,000 metres behind the front line. They would also be used to provide fire support for the immediate counterattack divisions. The field artillery batteries were, like the machine guns, concealed in dugouts and shelters, and moved frequently to nullify the value of reports of overflying British aircraft that might have spotted them. Once an attack began they would be moved to prepared positions from where they could target advancing British troops and support immediate counterattacks.[5]

Despite the shortness of time available to him before the launching of the French Nivelle Offensive only seven days later on 16 April, General Ludendorff made certain that there would be no repetition of the mistakes of 9 April. He was helped by General Nivelle's strict adherence to his original plan even though he was fully aware that the Germans were in full possession of it in all its detail. With the danger of surprise having been removed from the equation Ludendorff was able to concentrate on the disposition of his forces to best meet the French onslaught. He was helped by the fact that the ground over which the French would have to advance lent itself ideally to an elastic defence in depth. When the French attacked on a front of 25 miles, following a 10-day artillery preparation neither as accurate nor intense as that fired on Vimy Ridge, approximately 400,000 men advanced against the German positions on the Chemin des Dames. The Plan was to break through the German defences in three bounds covering a distance of 8,000 yards over a period of eight hours, which would open the way for exploitation by the cavalry. To meet the French assault the Germans thinned out their foremost lines, so as to take as many divisions as possible out of the line to act as counterattack divisions from positions about 10,000 yards back. This redeployment left 21 divisions in the front lines with 10 counterattack divisions at 10,000 yards distance. A further five counterattack divisions were in position a further 10,000 yards back ready to move forward to replace any of the advanced divisions should they have been committed to the counterattack. In total the Germans deployed approximately 300,000 infantry over a frontage of about 45 miles. It is an indication of French misreading of the German dispositions that, at the point when they planned to release their cavalry to exploit the breakthrough, their assault would still be some distance short of the positions of the first line of enemy counterattack divisions. The outcome of the battle has already been described in all its disastrous consequences for the French army and nation. For the Germans it provided satisfactory vindication of the concept of defence in depth.[6]

The major resumption of the British offensive, the Second Battle of the Scarpe, was much longer coming than von Lossberg and the German High Command in general had expected. Its delay until 23 April, when military logic would have called for an immediate follow up to the stunning successes of 9 April that had left the Germans in complete disarray, had them somewhat puzzled. The main reason for the delay was the difficulty in getting the artillery forward over muddy and self-generated broken up ground was clear for all to see. The German view appears to have been that they would not have allowed such an opportunity to pass regardless of the difficulties involved and ascribed the British procrastination to bad generalship. Not one to look a gift horse in the mouth von Lossberg took full advantage of the delay to refine his defences and dispositions even further, even though, such was his titanic energy, they had already been largely in place by the morning of 13 April. When the British attack was finally launched, it came as a surprise to von Lossberg that the main thrust

---

5   Ibid. pp. 199-210.
6   Ibid., pp. 184-8.

was south of the River Scarpe, where the configuration of the ground strongly favoured the defence, rather than north of the river where the opposite was the case. As a result of his misreading of British intentions, von Lossberg had placed most of his counterattack divisions north of the river. The attack on that side of the river was largely intended to protect the flank of the main attack to the south, but nevertheless resulted in the capture of the western and southern slopes of Greenland Hill and the village of Gavrelle. But it soon became clear that the attack would not be pressed much further unless significant progress south of the river was made. This would not be the case. A series of German counterattacks were launched in attempts to recover Gavrelle and the lost parts of Greeenland Hill, but without success. They revealed the shortcomings of the new system of defence in depth if there was departure from its basic tenets by, for example, unconverted or overenthusiastic generals, or if the configuration of the ground was unsuitable. They resulted in heavy losses for the counterattackers.

It is unquestionable that the Germans could draw more satisfaction from the outcomes of the Arras campaign and the Nivelle Offensive than their foes. Despite their overall numerical inferiority they had, by dint of Operation *Alberich*, their voluntary retirement to the Hindenburg Line, created an adequate pool of reserve divisions. These not only enabled the defence in depth system to be operated extensively but also ensured that front line divisions could be relieved regularly and not left for days at a stretch in action, a great booster for the morale of the troops concerned. It just so happened that the Arras front changed in character at the River Scarpe. To the north the configuration of the ground worked almost entirely in favour of the attacking British, whose artillery observers were able to follow the movements of their own infantry and could clearly see the manoeuvres of the German reserves as they concentrated and advanced to the counterattack. South of the river the reverse was the case; the British forward observation officers generally quickly lost sight of their own infantry as they passed from view over the skyline usually to be confronted by the enemy's machine guns with little hope of accurate artillery support to counter their deadly threat. As has already been noted it puzzled the Germans that the British did not exploit as much as they logically should have done the advantages they enjoyed north of the Scarpe, vis à vis south of the river. Throughout the campaign the Germans greatly feared that the British would come to their senses and re-orientate their strategy. It would not happen.

With the British prepared to launch the weightiest of their attacks on ground south of the Scarpe advantageous to the German defensive battle (*Abwehrschlacht*) as conceived by Colonel von Lossberg, it is little wonder that the German Army grew in confidence as the full effects were observed of the considerable reinforcement of the German artillery, which was now able to bring down rapid, heavy and accurate defensive fire on British preparations for attacks. From the outset the initiative was generally with the usually fresh and well led German infantry who counterattacked very aggressively and very often successfully. The extent of German predominance is most easily demonstrated by the fact that German losses in the Arras campaign were many fewer than those of the British.

Appendix II

Air Operations April-May 1917

The size and importance of the Royal Flying Corps had grown immeasurably since the outbreak of war. Only established in 1912 the fledgling service quickly demonstrated its potential when, at the army manoeuvres that year, the army commanded by Lieutenant General Haig had been soundly beaten by that led by Lieutenant General Grierson, who had made full use of the RFC's ability to see the other side of the hill. By dint of collecting together nearly all available aircraft the RFC managed to assemble four squadrons at Maubeuge by 16 August, only 12 days after the outbreak of war. Two days later the first reconnaissance missions were flown and once again the RFC proved its value by spotting and reporting on German troop movements.

As the war on the Western Front became one of trench warfare, the value of aircraft as a means of assisting the ground forces to overcome some of the problems this new static warfare created was quickly recognised. Aided by rapid technical improvements in aircraft design and performance, the air arms of the belligerents had soon added invaluable photo reconnaissance and artillery spotting to their skills. A need to prevent their opponents conducting these operations without let or hindrance led to the development of specialist scout, or fighter, aircraft with forward firing machine guns that would escort their own larger and slower reconnaissance aircraft and attack those of the enemy. Aerial combat, dogfights and the rise of legendary fighter aces were soon the norm. Ground attack, and day and night bombing roles were also soon to become part of the air war.

Unsurprisingly a major consideration in the relative performance of the three main air arms operating over the Western Front was the quality of their aircraft at any given time compared to those of their opponents. In the roughly 12 months from mid 1915 the Germans enjoyed a measure of superiority largely because, apart from being of high quality, their aircraft were the first to be equipped with a system that enabled a machine gun to be fired forward through the propeller without damaging it. The synchronisation (or interrupter) gear, as the systems were called, simplified aiming the gun at its target and the task of reloading it. This period of German superiority became known as 'The Fokker Scourge'.[1] It was not long before the British and French were able to fit similar equipment to their machines thus nullifying the German advantage. At the same time new improved aircraft began to reach the allied squadrons giving them a lead in the constant battle for pre-eminence. It would not last long.

By the time of the opening of the Battle of Arras the RFC deployment in France and Flanders had grown in size to 50 squadrons. This was fewer than had been hoped, as 12 squadrons had of necessity been held back in England to counter the threat from German Zeppelin raids. Furthermore only half of the 50 squadrons were in I, III and V Brigades RFC, attached respectively to First, Third and Fifth Armies for the battle. In total for the Arras campaign the British had about 365 aircraft available, only about a third of which were fighters. As the RFC Commander in Chief, Major General Hugh Trenchard was only too well aware, they would be up against a German air force which, having reorganised and been supplied with new and superior aircraft, notably the Albatros DII and DIII

---

1   The Fokker factory in Germany was the creation of Anthony Fokker, a Dutchman who designed and supplied a significant number of aircraft to Germany and Austria during the war. Notable among them was the Fokker D1 Triplane, made famous by Manfred von Richthofen, 'The Red Baron'. Fokker also played a leading part in the development of the synchronization gear that gave the Germans air superiority for some of 1915-16.

Scouts, was at the top of its game. Their loss of air superiority the previous year had led the German command to create fighting squadrons known as *Jagdstaffeln* (or *Jasta* for short). By early 1917, 37 of them had been formed. They were manned by well trained pilots anxious to wrest back air superiority from the allies, especially the British, despite their numerical inferiority.

General Trenchard had always been a strong advocate of carrying the air war to the enemy by aggressive patrolling in German airspace. This inevitably meant that most downed British aircraft had historically fallen behind enemy lines. The urgent need for air reconnaissance to find out what the Germans were up to as they constructed the Hindenburg and ancillary defensive lines meant that, appalling weather permitting, intrusions into enemy air space had been stepped up. It is a reflection of the changed circumstance brought about by the reinvigorated German air force that, of the 120 RFC aircraft shot down in March 1917, no fewer than 59 of them fell in or behind the British lines. It was not however just a case of increased German aggressiveness and skill that was to lead to the following month earning the title of 'Bloody April' in reflection of the losses incurred by the RFC that month. To a significant extent the RFC were the makers of their own misfortune. A considerable number of aircraft were lost as a result of being wrecked by their own pilots. As losses mounted, young officers were sent on active operations, often scarcely having learnt to fly and with no combat experience, and sometimes with no previous acquaintance with the aircraft type to which they were being assigned. Inevitably many died before coming face to face with the enemy; others were picked off by the German *Jastas*. But it was not only inexperienced officers who fell victim; experienced pilots also suffered an exceptional number of fatal accidents, many of which were almost certainly brought on by fatigue and stress.

The beginning of 'Bloody April' saw the squadrons of the RFC's I, III and V Brigades equipped with a variety of aircraft types the most common characteristic of which was their obsolescence and unsuitability for the task of overcoming the German *Jastas* and providing the support and protection required by the ground troops. There were some exceptions. The two RNAS squadrons, Numbers 8 (I Brigade) and 3 (V Brigade), were equipped respectively with Sopwith Triplanes and Sopwith Pups. Despite its remarkable success when it appeared on the Western Front in February 1917, the Sopwith Triplane was only seriously adopted by the RNAS and even that Service converted to the Sopwith Camel as soon as it became available. Nevertheless it was a more than adequate opponent of the German aircraft during the Arras campaign. The Sopwith Pup, a single seat biplane, entered into service on the Western Front in late 1916, equipping the four RNAS squadrons and three RFC squadrons, including 3 Squadron RNAS at the time of Arras. Although a pilot-friendly and initially successful aircraft it was quickly overtaken technically by the German machines and would be replaced by the more famous Sopwith Camel as soon as the latter became available later in 1917.

Three of III Brigade's squadrons, the 29th, 60th and 6th RNAS, were equipped with a French fighter, the Nieuport 17. This famous aircraft entered into service with the French air service in March 1916 and quickly became the dominant fighter on the Western Front. By the latter half of 1916 and into 1917 every French fighter squadron was equipped with it. Nearly all the leading French fighter aces scored a significant number of their victories in it. Many British air aces also chalked up a large number of their victories in Nieuport 17s, notably Billy Bishop and Albert Ball.[2] While, by the time of Arras, it no longer enjoyed pre-eminence, it was still one of the most manoeuvrable and fastest-climbing machines available and could still hold its own better than most against the newly arriving German aircraft types.

Apart from V Brigade's 19 Squadron, which in April 1917, was in the process of converting to a new French single seat fighter the SPAD VII (destined largely, along with its stablemate the larger and improved SPAD XIII, to replace the Nieuport 17 as the French mainline fighter), the equipment of

---

2   Less of a household name, the top scoring British Nieuport 17 ace of all was Captain Philip Fullard of 1 Squadron, RFC. All of his 40 victories, achieved between May and October 1917, were accomplished in Nieuports.

the British squadrons required to carry out the tasks involved in supporting the major land offensive about to be launched, was almost entirely obsolescent and no match for the German *Jastas*. No fewer than 9 squadrons (2, 4, 5, 8, 10,12, 13,15 and 16) were flying BE2s, a machine that had been on active service with the RFC since the start of the war. A two-seater initially designed to carry out reconnaissance and observation roles, it had later been fitted out with guns. In 1915, by substituting bombs for the observer, it had undertaken limited bombing missions. Although a steady platform it was also slow and by 1915 was proving its vulnerability to the new forward firing German machines. By 1917 this vulnerability had clearly worsened even though it generally flew with a fighter escort.

Four squadrons (11, 18, 25 and 100) were still equipped with the Royal Aircraft Factory designed FE2b. This machine was conceived as a two-seater fighter specifically designed to overcome the then current problem (1914-15) of providing forward machine gun capacity by virtue of its 'pusher' configuration, which gave the observer a wide field of forward fire from his position in the nose of the nacelle ahead of the pilot. The 'pusher' configuration, by positioning the propeller behind the engine, brought about a loss of aerodynamic performance and quickly became obsolete when the problem of firing forward through the propeller was solved. The FE2b nevertheless remained in service for the rest of the war when it unexpectedly achieved success as a light tactical night bomber.

The remaining six RFC squadrons involved in the Arras campaign were each equipped with a different aircraft type. No. 3 Squadron operated the Morane Parasol, 32 Squadron the DH2, 40 Squadron the FE8, 43 Squadron the Sopwith 1½ Strutter, 48 Squadron the BF2A and 59 Squadron the RE8. The Morane Parasol (or Morane-Saulnier Type P) was the most recent version of a French two-seater reconnaissance monoplane with a light bombing capacity that had been in service with the French and both British air arms in its successive configurations since 1914.

It still enjoyed a good reputation. The Sopwith 1½ Strutter was the first British 'tractor'[3] fighter able to fire safely through its propeller using a synchronised machine gun. It entered service in early 1916 and was very successful until more modern German models came onto the scene. Of the nearly 6,000 built, 75 percent were supplied to the French air force. Both the DH2 and the FE8 were single seat pusher models conceived before the problem of synchronised firing through the propeller had been solved. Given effective armament the DH2 was initially successful when it reached the Front in February 1916. But by September of the same year it was being outclassed by enemy machines. It was not however finally withdrawn until May 1917. The FE8 first flew in October 1915 and by August 1916 it was operating on the Western Front. After a fairly promising start it soon also found itself being outclassed by the new German fighters. Switched to a ground attack role for the Battle of Messines in June 1917 it was withdrawn shortly thereafter. The RE8 was a two-seat reconnaissance and bomber biplane. It began to arrive at the Front in November 1916 and in April 1917 it fell victim in large numbers to the aggressive *Jastas*. It was not until new British fighters were able to restore control of the skies and offer the RE8 effective escort that it was properly able to exercise its primary role as the RFC's standard artillery observation aircraft, a role it fulfilled until the end of the war. The BF2A was a short-lived model on the way to the development of the highly successful Bristol Fighter. Only 52 were built before production switched to the BF2B.

The motley collection of RFC frontline aircraft listed above would have the mission of fulfilling General Trenchard's requirement of a fiercely aggressive approach to taking the battle to the Germans as they sought to carry out the tasks assigned to them in the run up to, and during, the Battle of Arras. Trenchard was acutely aware that the Germans were equipped with better aircraft and agonised at the delays in bringing into operation the new types which would ultimately help restore British control of the skies. The RFC had overcome the 'Fokker scourge' just in time for the opening of the 1916 Somme campaign, by increasing the number of operational squadrons and equipping them with a

---

3   'Tractor' was the term used to describe aircraft whose propeller was situated in front of the engine. 'Pusher' of course described those whose propeller was placed behind. the engine.

number of aircraft types, notably the FE2b, the DH2 and the French Nieuport 17, all of which were capable of dealing with the formerly all-conquering Fokker III *Eindecker*. British control of the skies above the Somme battlefields did not last long, however. By mid-September 1916 the pendulum had swung once again with the German introduction of the Albatros DI Biplane the previous month. Although not especially manoeuvrable the DI was relatively fast and well armed. It quickly made its mark after entering *Jasta* service. It was however superseded only three months later by the Albatros DII, which, by the repositioning of the wings, offered the pilot better upward vision. Otherwise it offered no improvements on the performance of the DI. By January 1917 just over 200 DIIs were in service with the *Jastas*. Although it continued in service well into 1917 and featured in the Battle of Arras, its days were numbered with the arrival of the Albatros DIII at the end of 1916. With improved manoeuvrability and rate of climb the new aircraft was well received by the *Jasta* pilots. Despite being grounded once, in a not altogether successful attempt to deal with a wing failure problem, the Albatros DIII proved to be the principal scourge of the RFC during 'Bloody April'.

It was not only their superior aircraft types that enabled the Germans to impose themselves comprehensively on the RFC during 'Bloody April'. The reorganisation of their air service also played a significant part. It began in the second half of 1916 in at least partial response to the RFC's dominance of the air in July and August of that year. Its inspiration was the German air ace Oswald Boelcke. He and fellow ace Max Immelmann had been the first German airmen to be awarded their nation's highest decoration, the *Pour le Mérite*, when they each reached eight victories. Boelcke is popularly regarded as the Father of the German fighter air force. In mid-1916 he was given permission by the Air Service Chief of Staff to form one of the new fighter squadrons with pilots he had chosen personally. Among the very talented group he selected was the soon-to-be legendary 'Red Baron', Manfred von Richtofen. Boelcke's Squadron, number Jagdstaffel 2, was one of the first three new-style *Jastas* formally established on 10 August 1916. By early spring 1917 there would be 37 of them.[4]

Boelcke was appointed Commander of *Jasta* 2 on 30 August and celebrated by achieving 10 kills in September. Although he did not give up making solo patrols himself he insisted that his pilots should fly in disciplined formations and adopt the tactics he had formulated. By 16 September the Squadron had received its first five Albatros DIs plus a DII for Boelcke's personal use. Although he was to be killed on 28 October as the result of an accidental collision with the machine of a fellow *Jasta* 2 pilot during a dogfight with 24 Squadron RFC, Boelcke's *Jasta* was to become the most successful German unit of the war. By the Armistice 20 of its pilots had become aces and it had recorded 336 victories with a loss of only 44 casualties.

These remarkable figures were achieved despite the fact that, since the reorganisation that had created them, the *Jastas* were no longer content, as their predecessors had largely been, to patrol over and behind their own lines engaging British, French and Belgian aircraft only when they intruded into German airspace. Given the French and especially the British policy of taking the fight to the enemy this had left them with no shortage of opportunities to do battle. The new *Jastas* were keen to exert their advantages over their opponents. They had good aircraft manned by well trained, skilful and brave pilots and the further incentive that it was important to prevent their opponents from gathering information on the extent and state of the new defences, including the Hindenburg Line, that were under construction. Aided by the terrible winter and early spring weather that often grounded their opponents, they made a good job of this.

They were well placed to do so, most of the *Jastas* being based at airfields reasonably close to the front lines. Like the British squadrons, the individual *Jastas* were attached to one or other of the German armies. In April 1917 the Sixth Army, largely confronting the British, had nine *Jastas* attached (Numbers 3, 4, 6, 11, 12, 27, 28, 30 and 33). The Seventh, First and Third Armies, facing the French, had respectively eight, four and four. The late Oswald Boelcke's *Jasta* 2 was one of those

---

4   Franks, Guest and Bailey, *Bloody April 1917*, p. 8.

attached to First Army. His protégé, Rittmeister Manfred von Richthofen, was by now in command of *Jasta* 11 and would add significantly to his kills at the expense of the RFC during 'Bloody April'. (He entered the month with 31 kills to his name. By its end his score was 52, probably all but four of them RFC machines. *Jasta* 11's total for the month was 67 kills.)[5]

Although at no stage of the war after the opening few months did RFC/RAF[6] aircrew losses decline to a level that could be regarded as acceptable, the period between late 1916 and the end of Bloody April was especially grim. July 1916 saw the RFC in control of the skies as the Battle of the Somme opened. Although it is difficult to pin down accurate statistics it is nonetheless clear that this temporary mastery of the skies, which lasted through July and August, was achieved at the cost of 141 men killed or missing and another 90 wounded. The arrival in September of the first reorganised enemy *Jastas* flying improved aircraft made the task that much harder and the cost that much greater. In that month alone the RFC lost 105 men killed or missing. By the end of the year, taking into account the figures for July to September, their casualties amounted to 419 killed or missing and more than 250 wounded or injured. It was perhaps fortunate that there were more than enough volunteers to replace them, especially as a further 250 men had disappeared from squadron rosters without apparent reason, possibly victims of stress or breakdown. By the end of the Somme campaign the RFC had 25 per cent more pilots available than they had had at its start. But the prospects were nevertheless ominous for the RFC. Leaving aside the question of the quality of training their new pilots had received, there was little immediate prospect of them getting new aircraft that were capable of matching, or giving them an edge, over the new German machines. Even though the RFC had about 130 more aeroplanes available than did the German *Jastas* their numerical superiority counted for nothing in the light of the better quality of the German pilots and machines.[7]

The year 1917 dawned with the RFC deficient in all but numbers of aircraft and men compared with its opposition, which had to some extent minimised even these deficiencies by concentrating a disproportionate amount of their strength against the British. The emphasis thus placed on their battle with the RFC, along with the other advantages that they enjoyed enabled them to take the battle to the British in the four months climaxing with 'Bloody April'. Despite the restrictions on flying caused by the weather, the RFC were flying an increasing number of sorties in their attempts to establish what the Germans were up to and in pursuit of Trenchard's policy of aggressive patrolling. It was the slow moving two-seater reconnaissance aircraft that were to suffer most at the hands of the *Jastas*.   Despite increasing recognition that there was little hope for them in German airspace without adequate fighter escort, it was only with reluctance on the part of RFC commanders that the fighters were gradually diverted from their aggressive patrolling to escort duties. Even then the German pilots found ways to penetrate the defensive screens and shoot down the hapless reconnaissance machines. In March RFC losses of dead and missing due to enemy action rose sharply to 143. 120 aircraft were shot down. These figures take no account of the losses in men and machines caused by flying accidents. April was even worse, richly earning its description of 'Bloody'. Best estimates are that the RFC lost 245 aircraft, 211 aircrew killed or missing and 108 taken prisoner, a probably unsustainable rate of loss. By contrast German losses amounted to 66 aircraft.

As April 1917 ended there were signs that the worst might soon be over for the RFC. Although aircrew casualties remained stubbornly high in the latter half of 1917, averaging in the high one hundreds per month, new high performance aircraft were finally reaching the front line squadrons. While not significantly superior to the German machines, they could certainly give a good account of themselves. Apart from the time around the launching in March 1918 of the *Kaiserschlacht* (the Kaiser's Battle), the last desperate German attempt to win the war before the advent of the Americans

---

5   Ibid., Appendix 3.
6   The Royal Air Force (RAF), combining the RNAS and the RFC, came into being on 1 April 1918.
7   Trevor Wilson, *The Myriad Faces of War*, pp. 368-72.

in serious numbers who would assure an Allied victory, there would no longer be a time during the air war when the RFC/RAF would feel at a disadvantage. Quite the reverse, as superior British numbers began to make their presence felt.

There were three main aircraft types that transformed the RFC situation for the better. The soon to be legendary Sopwith Camel, a single seat biplane, entered into service in June 1917 and remained so until the end of the war. Although not as fast as some other aircraft it was exceptionally manoeuvrable. Its main role was as a fighter, but it could also carry a light load of bombs and undertake low level ground attacks. Shortly prior to the arrival of the Camel, the Royal Aircraft Factory-built SE5 and SE5A models put in their appearance. Single seat biplanes mounting a Vickers machine gun and a Lewis gun, they jointly proved to be the most successful British fighter of the war. Like the Camel they too saw it through to the end. The third aircraft was the Bristol Fighter BF2A and BF2B, the latter model almost immediately superseding the former. They arrived on the Western Front at around the same time as the Camel and the SE5s. A two-seater, the BF2B's planned main role was reconnaissance. But it soon became evident that it could, with its manoeuvrability, performance and firepower, more than hold its own as a fighter, and also in a ground attack role side by side with the Camel. The BF2B was probably the most versatile aircraft produced by any nation in the war. It too would see it out; indeed it continued in RAF service well into peacetime.[8]

8   Ibid., pp. 608-13.

Appendix III

The Artillery at Arras

Although not quite as dramatic as the developments that had taken place in military aviation since the beginning of the war, artillery had also undergone striking changes by the time of the Battle of Arras. In 1914 the three branches of the Royal Artillery (the Royal Horse Artillery, the Royal Field Artillery and the Royal Garrison Artillery) were all highly trained to a peak of efficiency. The RA brigades and batteries that arrived in France in August 1914 as part of the one cavalry and four infantry divisions of the BEF were armed mainly with four different artillery pieces. The quick-firing 18 pounder was the principal field gun; the quick-firing 13 pounder horse artillery gun was a lighter, and more mobile, version of the same gun; the 4.5 inch weapon was the principal howitzer and the 60 pounder the heavy artillery gun. The BEF was therefore well equipped with artillery pieces for the sort of colonial war the British Army was used to; it was less so for a European continental war as was quickly to become apparent. In particular it lacked mobile heavy guns and trench mortars of any kind. Nevertheless all four of the guns mentioned were more than adequate enough, in fulfilling their designated roles, to remain in front line service throughout the war. They would be supplemented by other, mainly heavy, guns and trench mortars as these became available.

As the mobile warfare of the early months of the war in 1914 gave way to the more static trench warfare that would persist through the next three years, the means needed to be found to carry out the principal allied war aim, the expulsion of the German invaders from the areas of France and Belgium they had occupied. In 1915 these took the form of major French offensives in Champagne and Artois which, in the latter case, were supported by attacks by the BEF. If the unsatisfactory and disappointing Battles of Aubers Ridge, Festubert and Loos (and the earlier Battle of Neuve Chapelle, fought independently of the French) demonstrated one thing, it was that the British bombardments that accompanied the battles were entirely inadequate to carry out the tasks imposed on them. The number of guns, especially of howitzers and heavy calibres, was insufficient, the weight of shell inadequate and hardly capable of destroying the German wire, trenches and dugouts in even the rudimentary level of sophistication they had attained by 1915. The main problem for the artillery was, however, the lack of sufficient shells of all types and calibres, but especially high explosive, which often led to the rationing of the number of shells the available guns could fire during a given period. The existence of a so-called 'Shell Shortage' was confirmed in leaks to the British Press by the frustrated BEF C in C, Field Marshal Sir John French. The Press elevated the situation, quite justifiably, into the notorious 'Shell Scandal'[1] that led to a full scale political crisis that in mid May brought about the end of the Liberal government and its replacement by a coalition of the Liberal, Conservative and Labour parties, under the continued leadership of Prime Minister Asquith. One of the first acts of the new Government was to create a Ministry of Munitions and appoint as its Minister David Lloyd George, under whose vigorous leadership the production of shells and other ordnance would rise rapidly and significantly.

A lesson that was seen to have emerged from the disappointing results of the 1915 battles was that it would be essential to preface all future battles with a long bombardment lasting several days to

---

1   The Shell Scandal was genuinely that. At the time it erupted in 1915 Britain was producing 22,000 shells a day compared with German and French daily production of 160,00 and 100,000 respectively. Warner, *The Battle of Loos*, p.6.

ensure the suppression of the German defences and the collapse of their morale. The obvious loss of the asset of surprise was a price that would have to be paid. With the increase in the number of available guns and the shells for them, application of this lesson would soon become a practical proposition.

By the time of the Battle of the Somme in the summer of the following year matters were perceived to have so much improved that General Sir Henry Rawlinson, whose Fourth Army was given the main responsibility for conducting the battle, based his strategy on the assumption that the artillery would have succeeded in destroying the enemy wire, in annihilating their front line positions and in neutralising their artillery's capacity to respond meaningfully. Only then would the British infantry advance across no man's land to occupy the German defences and push on further towards Bapaume opening the way for the cavalry to exploit the enemy's disarray. It turned out that General Rawlinson's faith in the artillery's ability to deliver on what was required of it was tragically misplaced. Although there was one gun for every 17 yards of front, a total of 1,436, there were still too few of the heavy calibres required to destroy the very deep and strong German dugouts. The majority of the guns (808) were 18 pounders and there were 202 4.5 inch howitzers and 128 60 pounders. The remainder were heavy howitzers and guns of various calibres from 6 inch to 15 inch. The five divisions of the French Sixth Army that attacked simultaneously with the BEF from their positions straddling the River Somme were supported by a total of 100 guns, 60 of which were the famous 75mm field gun that was used to fire gas shells. The remaining 40 were heavy guns and howitzers.

The supply of shells, even though adequate in number, contained too few of the high explosive variety needed to deal with the wire and too many shrapnel shells that were not particularly suited for the task of wire cutting. Gas shell manufacture was still in its infancy in Britain and few shells of this type reached the guns in time to play a part in the battle. Finally, about one third of the shells by some estimates would prove to be duds. Even those that were not duds had sometimes been inaccurately made in terms of their sizes and dimensions, a probable consequence of Lloyd George's rush to increase the rate of their production. However successful in terms of numbers produced it did little to enhance reliability or consistency.

Rawlinson planned that the preliminary bombardment should last five days. In the event it was extended by two days because of adverse weather, but even then its duration proved inadequate to the task. Although several battalion commanders reported that the wire in front of them was not being adequately cut, the High Command saw no reason to amend their plans to allow more time for this task to be completed.[2] The result was the most disastrous day in British military history with the attacking infantry being mown down in their thousands by German machine gun crews who had emerged from the safety of their impregnable dugouts as soon as the British bombardment had lifted.

The story of the Somme from the artillery point of view was not entirely one of failure however. One development that would save many infantry lives over the remainder of the war was the adoption of the creeping barrage. Probably first used by the Fourth Army XIII and XV Corps only a few days into the battle, its value was quickly appreciated and its adoption rapidly spread throughout the army. By the time of the Battle of Arras the infantry were trained in how to take full advantage of the development by following the barrage closely, but not so closely as to find themselves under it. Its purpose was to keep the enemy defenders' heads down until the assaulting infantry were close enough to enter their trenches and finish off any survivors in hand to hand combat.

Another development introduced for the Somme campaign was the issue of Artillery Operation Orders. They laid down in some detail what the artillery were required to do and when they should do it. At army level they co-ordinated timings with other armies, between corps and, of course, with the French. The GOCRAs' Operation Orders would go into greater detail on implementation. A problem that was to result was that no room was left for flexibility when something unforeseen

---

2   It should be remembered that General Haig was under considerable pressure from the French to launch his offensive at the earliest possible moment to help relieve the pressure on the French Army at Verdun.

happened. When, for instance, there was a need for a barrage to refocus on an objective that had not been properly dealt with the first time around and was still giving serious problems to the infantry.[3]

When exhaustion and bad weather finally brought the Somme campaign to a halt with the conclusion of the Battle of the Ancre on 18 November 1916, thoughts turned to preparation for the battles intended to bring about an allied victory in the war in 1917. Foremost among these from the British point of view would be the Battle of Arras. As far as the Artillery were concerned it was time to absorb the lessons of the Somme campaign and put in hand the necessary measures to ensure that mistakes would be eliminated and the opportunities offered by technical developments fully exploited. There were no easy solutions when it came to the perpetual problem of battlefield communication. The artillery urgently needed a system providing rapid and reliable communication between Forward Observation Officers, artillery spotting aircraft, battalion, brigade, divisional and corps headquarters and individual gun batteries. Mobile radios were still too cumbersome to provide a satisfactory solution. Burying telephone cables at a depth of six feet could help, as could the use of telephone exchanges. Other measures offered some improvement, but it was still often the case that visual signalling offered the only means of communication, with all the problems that was heir to.

Perhaps the single most important technical development was the arrival in growing numbers of the fuze 106. Shells using this fuze would burst instantaneously on any contact, however slight. As this usually meant that they exploded above ground they did not make the craters that could be such a hindrance to advancing infantry and to the artillery when they were trying to move guns forward rapidly. Furthermore, when used in projectiles employed for wire cutting, the fuzes would explode on contact with the wire which the resultant shell splinters would cut very effectively. All in all the new fuzes were a great improvement on shrapnel shells as a wire cutting tool.

Counter-battery work was also becoming a more exact science, greatly helped by improvements in sound ranging techniques. The aim was to plot and register all enemy batteries and observation posts without them becoming aware that they had been pinpointed. They could then be neutralised at any time that suited allied plans. Neutralisation, when it took place, would take the form of a sufficiently heavy concentration of artillery fire to prevent the enemy gunners from manning their guns. By the time of Arras sound ranging crews were able to pinpoint the position of enemy guns to within 50 yards with only one reading of their fire, and 25 yards with several readings. Other valuable information could also be gleaned if several readings had been obtained. By March 1917 the whole British front was covered by fully equipped sound ranging teams.

Planning and preparation for the Battle of Arras followed different courses for the artillery of the three British armies involved. General Allenby's Third Army, whose task it was to break through or drive back the German defences on their way to linking up with General Nivelle's French armies near Cambrai, came up with the novel idea of limiting their preparatory bombardment to 48 hours in the hope that its brevity would catch the enemy unprepared, as they would assume that it would go on for several days more. What the bombardment lacked in duration it would make up for in intensity, a hurricane bombardment of the sort normally fired for the last few minutes before the infantry went over the top. The plan was the brainchild of Allenby's MGRA, Major General Arthur Holland, who had tested his concept and was satisfied that both the barrels of his guns and their crews could withstand the stresses and strains of 48 hours of continuous high intensity fire. His view was shared by his Army Commander but not by GHQ. Field Marshal Haig's MGRA, Major General Noel Birch, criticised Holland's plan on the grounds that it put too much pressure on men and equipment; that it would not complete the necessary wire cutting and other essential tasks in the time available, especially as there would be little opportunity for the necessary observations to be made with the inevitable curtain of smoke that the non-stop bombardment would create; finally, that it would not sap the morale of the German defenders as a prolonged bombardment would. Although Haig was

3   Farndale, *History of the Royal Regiment of Artillery*, pp. 158-61.

in agreement with his MGRA, Allenby and Holland seemed disposed to put up a fight to retain the latter's plan. Whether by coincidence or not, it was at around this point that Holland was promoted to Lieutenant General and given command of I Corps in First Army. His replacement at Third Army was Major General R. Lecky, who supported Haig's and Birch's opinion, leaving Allenby isolated. A compromise was agreed that the preparatory bombardment would last four days, still shorter than the length GHQ would have preferred.

The initial task of General Horne's First Army was the less complex, if no less difficult, one of capturing Vimy ridge in its entirety thereby securing Third Army left flank, and depriving the Germans of a matchless observation point. The ridge's topography, a gradual slope upward from the west to its high point of 145 metres and then a precipitate drop down to the Douai Plain meant that First Army had to capture a relatively limited area of ground to complete their task. They also had the capacity to saturate the enemy held ground with artillery fire if that would contribute to the achievement of their objective. Horne ordered that the four divisions of the Canadian Corps, assisted by 13 British Brigade, should mount the attack. In command of the Canadian Corps was the British Lieutenant General Sir Julian Byng who, although a cavalryman, had a very keen appreciation of the importance of artillery. He was in any case surrounded by some outstanding artillerymen. Horne himself was a Gunner. In charge of the counter battery organisation attached to Byng's HQ was an outstanding Canadian scientific Gunner, A. G. L. McNaughton, a leader in the fields of flash spotting and sound ranging.[4] The senior staff officer on attachment to the Canadian Corps Artillery was Major Alan Brooke RA, also an outstanding Gunner who played a large part in the introduction of the creeping barrage when with XIII Corps' 18th Division on the Somme.

In contrast to previous offensives undertaken during the war, First Army planners were blessed with a more than adequate number of guns of appropriate calibres and the shells to go with them. In addition to the Canadian Corps own resources, General Byng and his staff were able to count on the big guns of 11 heavy artillery groups and the artillery of I Corps on the Canadian Corps left. The total density this gave them was one heavy gun for every 20 yards of front and a field gun for every 10 yards, proportionately three times as many heavy and twice as many field guns than had been deployed on the Somme. 42,609 tons of shells were allocated to the operation, with a daily quota of 2,465 tons. Although still not readily available, Byng had managed to obtain an adequate supply of the fuze 106 for use in its wire-cutting role.

The tasks which this profusion of artillery would be called on to perform were the familiar ones of bombarding the enemy strongpoints and entrenchments, cutting their wire, and providing as much protection to the assaulting infantry as possible. This last task would be achieved firstly by eliminating their worst enemy, hostile artillery, by counter battery work; secondly, by firing what had become by now a standard creeping barrage, supplemented by a concentrated line of machine guns firing over the heads of the assaulting troops to keep the enemy's heads down. What would be different from previous artillery programmes would be the precision with which these tasks would be carried out.

An essential part of the counter-battery programme would be conducted by so-called silent batteries. The presence of these batteries would be concealed from the enemy by their not firing to register targets prior to the battle. In many cases their targets were identified for them by aerial reconnaissance; no less than 80 percent of the German artillery was thus spotted. Those that the aircraft missed could well have been pinpointed by the pioneering work of A. G. L. McNaughton. The preliminary bombardment, using only about half of the available batteries, was to begin on 20 March. On 2 April the rest of the artillery were to join in, thus beginning what the Germans were to term 'the week of suffering' (*Die Leidenswoche*). The heavy guns concentrated on the villages and lines of communication behind the lines, the heavy mortars on the German front lines, and the

---

4   McNaughton rose to the rank of General after the war and was for a time Chief of the Canadian General Staff. In the Second World War he commanded the First Canadian Army until the end of 1943.

smaller calibres on wire cutting. To deceive the enemy on the precise time of the assault there was to be no intensification of the bombardment in the run up to Zero Hour. As this moment arrived a barrage would be laid on the German front line where it would remain for three minutes before lifting 100 yards every three minutes. Gas and high explosive shells would rain down on known German strongpoints, artillery batteries and ammunition dumps.

The British plan fully recognised that total surprise could not be achieved. The Germans were well aware that a major Allied offensive was in the offing and that Vimy ridge would be an important objective. Efforts were made to keep the Germans as much in the dark as possible (the Canadian fighter ace, Billy Bishop, was to win an MC for shooting down a heavily defended German observation balloon over the ridge) but all that could be realistically hoped for was to keep the precise time and date of the assault secret. Judging by the events of 9 April this was successfully achieved.[5]

Whereas Third and First Armies' guns were fully in position and ready to fire their preliminary bombardments and creeping barrages according to schedule, the same could not be said for Fifth Army. In their defence it must be noted that they were by some distance the most affected of the three armies by Operation *Alberich*, the voluntary German withdrawal to the Hindenburg Line. Not only did they have to bring their guns forward over ground frequently reduced to a sea of mud by the appalling weather, but in addition the same ground was also bereft of suitable roads, such as there were having been made unusable as part of the scorched earth policy implemented by the retreating enemy. As a result General Gough was to learn belatedly that the order he had given on 24 March, that the whole of the heavy artillery of his two corps should get forward as fast as the state of the ground permitted, had not resulted in the wire cutting programme being completed in time for his Army assault to be launched on 10 April. It was only on 8 April that he learned that a further eight days would be required. A consequence of his frustration at receiving this news was his ill advised decision to accept and then launch prematurely the proposal that was made to him to use tanks to deal with the wire. It proved to be a complete failure.

Leaving aside the Fifth Army front, the British began the Battle of Arras with more guns than the enemy and greater skill in the new methods of using them. On the Third Army front the guns did well, firing a very effective barrage. The counter battery work was also very successful, all but silencing the enemy guns. The wire cutting programme too went well especially when the distances involved were relatively short. But the longer the range became beyond 2,000 yards, the less likely it was that the cutting would have been carried out effectively. A case in point was on the right of VII Corps front where no man's land was 2,000 yards across; the wire cutting failed because of the consequent long ranges at which it was attempted. One reason for the overall success of the first day of the battle was that all the artillery involved worked to a master plan, the first time this had happened. (On the Somme every corps and division had worked to their own plan and had lost some of their potential effectiveness as a result.) A second reason for the positive outcome of the first day was the success in moving the guns forward if required despite the appalling weather and the ground conditions. Great credit was due to the Engineers for opening up and maintaining passages across no man's land for the guns.

Disappointingly the success of the first day was not repeated on the subsequent days of the First Battle of the Scarpe (as the first phase of the Battle of Arras would become known). The continuing bad weather and ground conditions did not help. Nor did the fact that many of those German guns that had survived the British counter-battery fire of the first day had prudently moved position and were no longer easily locatable. They had also been reinforced by batteries moving up from reserve. When these enemy moves were coupled with the relocation of some of the British batteries it can be of little surprise that the effectiveness of the latter was diminished. The lack of leadership and direction from the top (of the Army) did not help either and uncertainty began to creep in. The main focus of

---

5   Farr, *The Silent General*, pp. 153-5.

the second and subsequent days of the battle was the attack on Monchy-le-Preux by VI Corps, for which there was no artillery fire plan at all. The RFA and RHA Brigades were slow moving forward in the appalling conditions. The attack failed. When 37th Division attacked there was confusion over which artillery brigade should be in support. The 14 Brigade RHA were given the task but then told the attack by 111 Infantry Brigade had been postponed. Unfortunately 111 Brigade were not told of the postponement and attacked, without artillery support. Despite suffering heavy losses they captured Monchy.[6]

With Monchy in British hands but facing strenuous German efforts to recapture it, two cavalry brigades were ordered into the village to bolster its defence, fighting dismounted. They were supported by two RHA batteries, one in the southwest outskirts of the village and the other, concentrating its fire on German infantry concentrations in the Bois du Sart and the Bois du Vert, about 700 yards further to the southwest. Both batteries were forced to withdraw by heavy German counter battery fire but continued to maintain fire on the enemy from their new positions. Their fire was reinforced by that of a heavy artillery group.

Attempts were made over the course of the next four days (11-14 April) to restore forward momentum to the British infantry assault but to little effect. The ineffectiveness of the artillery's efforts to cut the wire facing VII Corps' 21st and 30th Divisions at long range did little to help as did the failure to concentrate gunfire on the commanding German-held Hill 90, possibly because there were not enough guns sufficiently forward. This deficiency included guns used for counter battery work.

In common with most of the rest of the First Army plans to capture Vimy ridge the artillery plan was, as has already been noted, carefully thought out in every detail. Its implementation was deservedly successful. No means of obtaining information that would help identify and pinpoint objectives was neglected. Aircraft, balloons, ground observers, sound ranging and flash spotting all made contributions that were rapidly fed back to those who could correlate the information and take immediate and effective action on it. The objectives singled out for attention were trench junctions, dugouts, concrete machine gun emplacements, strong points and tunnel entrances, ammunition dumps, and light railways within a range of four to five thousand yards behind the German front line. The wire cutting programme did not attempt its total elimination except in the case of that protecting the German front defences. Further back the wire cutting guns concentrated on making lanes through the German defences and keeping them clear of German attempts to repair them. Counter battery work focused first on isolated batteries. Those that were grouped in clusters were subsequently neutralised with high explosive and gas shells. Enemy observation posts were dealt with ahead of the assault by destructive fire. Those that appeared to have survived at Zero Hour were blinded by the use of smoke shells. Close cooperation was maintained throughout with the artillery of XVII and I Corps on either flank, which dealt with any threat to those flanks.

During the 'week of suffering' the villages of Thélus, Les Tilleuls, Farbus, Vimy, Petit Vimy, La Chaudière, Willerval and Givenchy were bombarded, with the first three receiving special attention. By the eve of the assault the artillery programme had saturated the ridge and associated targets with thirty times the amount of ordnance the French had expended prior to their attack two years previously. The state of the German defences and the ground gave ample evidence of this. But the main German dugouts and tunnels, 20 to 50 feet below the surface remained relatively undamaged and their garrisons physically, if perhaps not mentally, unharmed. If these garrisons received sufficient warning to get to the surface and set up their weaponry they could wreak havoc on the Canadian assault. It was essential therefore that the date and time of the assault remained secret to enable the attacking infantry to reach and block the entrances to the enemy deep dugouts and tunnels, most of which were within 700 yards of the Canadian front line.

---

6   Farndale, op. cit., pp. 170-4.

At 0530 on 9 April a comprehensive barrage erupted targeting the German front line, ammunition dumps and artillery batteries. After three minutes the creeping barrage made its first step forward. An area 400 yards ahead was swept by the fire of 150 machine guns. The overall effect was devastating. The counter battery fire was so effective that there was only a feeble response from the German artillery.[7]

The Canadian battalions swept nearly all before them during the course of the day. Only one major objective of 9 April, the highest point of the ridge, Hill 145, remained in German hands at the end of the day. This would fall during the afternoon of the following day, after a fresh artillery barrage on it. As a consequence of this delay, the assaults on the remaining two objectives, the Pimple and the *Bois en Hache* were postponed for a day and mounted on 12 April. They were both successful, bringing to a highly satisfactory end the Battle of Vimy Ridge. It quickly became clear that the Germans were in no mood to attempt its recapture. Vimy ridge would remain in British hands for the rest of the war. The battle had been a triumph for the application of concentrated artillery power. The possible downside to such a weapon was noted by Haig in his diary, recording a conversation he had had with General Horne after the battle. Horne told him that he had visited Thélus the previous day and found it difficult to discover where the German front line trenches had been. All had been so terribly destroyed by the shellfire. Horne thought he had used too many shells! They had broken up the soil so frightfully that all movement had been made so difficult.[8]

The difficulties faced by the Fifth Army artillery as it sought to move into positions within range of the Hindenburg Line to carry out its part in the forthcoming First Battle of Bullecourt were extremely challenging. Such roads and railway lines as there were had been severely damaged by the retiring Germans and, as they were gradually brought back into use, had to be shared between lorries and tractors carrying or hauling road-making material, the guns and the ammunition for them. As a result the guns were late coming into operation and were often restricted in the number of shells available to them. Those guns charged with wire cutting for I ANZAC did not begin their task until 7 April at which point they found themselves further hampered by a shortage of instantaneous 106 fuzes and the fact that many of their targets were on reverse slopes and therefore difficult to pinpoint. Given that the Fifth Army plan called for I ANZAC to advance into a re-entrant between the salients on which Bullecourt and Quéant were located, and the need for effective artillery preparation to avoid the risk of the attackers being enfiladed from both flanks and in front, concern was understandably growing at the tardiness and inadequacy of the artillery programme. Air observation was able to confirm that the wire was only partially and patchily cut with the result that, when informed on 8 April that wire cutting would require a further eight days, General Gough immediately ordered a postponement of Fifth Army attack. This order was only rescinded when Major W. Watson, Commander 11th Company of D Battalion, Heavy Machine Gun Corps, came up with his plan to use his tanks to deal with the enemy wire. The resultant events of 10 and 11 April have been described elsewhere. Suffice it to say here that the performance of the tanks was a major disappointment and in no way compensated for the insufficient artillery support. With great bravery the Australians nevertheless secured lodgments in both the Hindenburg Front (O.G.1) and Support (O.G.2) Lines east of Bullecourt. The village itself remained firmly in German hands.

As long as Bullecourt was held by the Germans the tenuous Australian hold on stretches of O.G.1 and 2 invited counterattacks, particularly against 1st Australian Division, which was responsible for a frontage of over 12,000 yards running east from a point south of Riencourt. By 15 April Australian attempts to move their lines closer to those of the enemy and the resultant skirmishes had extended the 1st Division's frontage by a further 1,000 yards. From midnight onwards on the 15th the Australians became aware by degrees that the Germans were mounting a major counterattack encompassing most of the 1st Division's front and the extreme right of the 2nd Division on 1st Division's left. Their main

---

7   OH 1917 Volume 1, pp. 312-20.
8   Haig Diary 12.4.17.

objectives were the mass of Australian artillery batteries deployed in the shallow valleys between the villages of Noreuil and Lagnicourt. Although the Australian front line infantry fought with great gallantry to try to hold back the German assault, the latter's overwhelming numbers were almost irresistible especially when the defenders ran short of ammunition. The Germans were, however, only able to break through the Australian line north of Lagnicourt enabling them to pass through the village and debouch south of it. They had advanced 1½ miles beyond the Australian front line. In their path now lay the foremost brigade of the 1st Division's artillery. It was practically defenceless having only been issued with 10 rifles for each battery, nine of which had been left behind in Bapaume when the brigade had moved forward. With the fighting moving ever closer and it being impossible in the confusion to fire for fear of hitting one's own infantry, the guns of four batteries of 2 Brigade were abandoned, the breech blocks and dial sights having been removed. Slightly further back three batteries of 1 Brigade, equally devoid of small arms for defence, were also ordered to take the same step.[9]

With the gradual arrival of daylight the Australians began to organise an effective defence that managed largely to stem the German tide. Some batteries were able to bring their guns into action in support of their infantry. One battery, the 43rd, in so doing, was detected by the enemy and came under intense fire which destroyed three 18 pounder guns and killed all the crew of at least one of them. Several ammunition dumps were also hit and exploded into raging fires. Despite the growing inferno, the Battery's remaining two guns were successfully withdrawn, along with the wounded. Over half the Battery's personnel had become casualties.[10] This was, however, to be the high point for the Germans. They would soon find themselves being vigorously counterattacked in turn. As the Germans were pushed back to their own lines, or chose to surrender, the Australians were able to assess what damage had been inflicted on the guns that had either been abandoned or hit by German shells. They found that many guns had not been damaged in any way; the enemy had not had the time to do anything to them before they had been driven back. Of 21 guns that had been in German possession for two hours or so, only five (four 18 pounders and one howitzer) had been destroyed. Others had been prepared for destruction, but the charges had not been fired. Three others had been destroyed by shellfire, as already described. For the most part the Australian guns were in action again as soon as the parts that had been removed had been replaced.[11] By the end of the day's fighting the Germans had suffered a significant defeat, especially to their morale, at the hands of the Australians.

General Robert Nivelle, the new French Commander in Chief whose plan to win the war was launched on 16 April, was a Gunner. It is little surprise therefore that artillery would play a significant part in the Second Battle of the Aisne (or Chemin des Dames, the name more popularly given to the battle). True to his professional expertise, Nivelle had achieved outstanding success by maximizing the use of artillery during the Battle of Verdun. However, his hubristic claim that 'we now have the formula' was to prove sadly mistaken. The formula as he saw it was to employ similar methods on the Chemin des Dames to those that had achieved success at Verdun. They consisted of destroying the German defences with heavy artillery bombardments; neutralising their artillery using predominantly gas shells; using creeping barrages; clearing specified zones with artillery bombardments through which the infantry could advance with relative impunity prior to rolling up what remained of the German defences. Although the French had by now sufficient guns and ammunition to carry out these tasks, the formula did not take sufficient account of changes in circumstances since Verdun. The Germans too had studied the methods used by Nivelle at Verdun and had begun to modify their defensive system to the already described one of defence in depth. Furthermore the ground they would be defending had been carefully selected because of the considerable advantages it would offer to defenders. These were the availability of underground caverns capable of sheltering many troops; the

9   Australian OH Volume IV, pp. 363-79.
10   Ibid., p. 388.
11   OH 1917 op. cit. p. 375.

commanding height of their positions offering observation over the entire battlefield while denying these advantages to the attackers. Partially as a result of the voluntary withdrawal to the Hindenburg Line the Germans also had adequate reserves of men and guns. Finally they were aware of where, when and how the French planned to conduct their offensive thanks to the latters' lapses in security.

Nivelle collected together 5,350 guns of all calibres for the offensive. They were shared between the Fifth and Sixth Armies who would be attacking on a front of 40 kilometres. There were 2,000 field guns (one per 20 metres of front), 1,650 heavy and 160 super-heavy guns (one per 21 metres) and 1,540 trench mortars. Of the heavy guns 700 were modern. Much of the advantage that such a weight of artillery should have given the French was unfortunately lost because of the German readjustment of their defences consequent on their retirement to the Hindenburg Line further north. This put much of them beyond the range of the French artillery and certainly beyond observation when coupled with the German air superiority that prevented the French intruding into their airspace for artillery spotting and target identifying purposes on the relatively rare occasions when the terrible weather would otherwise have allowed such activity. The weather also slowed down preparations for the offensive by slowing up the movement of men, supplies and ammunition, including inevitably shells for the guns. The whole pace of the preliminary bombardment slackened and there was worry that the wire cutting programme would not have been completed by Zero, even though this had been postponed for 24 hours. In the event the preliminary bombardment was to make little impression on the German defences. The German artillery was not neutralised and, among other things, was able to deal effectively with the French tanks introduced for the first time.

A problem for the assaulting infantry was the speed of advance of the creeping barrages. It was set at a pace that might have been suitable for ideal conditions of ground, weather and state of the enemy defences, but was certainly not appropriate for the conditions prevailing from mid April 1917. The consequence was that the infantry all too frequently fell behind the barrage and were exposed to the fire of enemy machine guns no longer suppressed by it.[12]

This is not the place to relate the details of the defeat of the Nivelle plan and the collapse of French morale and discipline that ensued. It should just be noted that the French artillery's shortcomings played a significant part in the failure to deliver the victory that had so extravagantly been promised by Nivelle.

As the evidence grew that the Nivelle offensive was failing, Field Marshal Haig ordered a further offensive by Third and First Armies to begin on 23 April. The British artillery would find conditions for the Second Battle of the Scarpe, as the offensive was later named, much changed from those that had obtained for the First. There could be no question of surprise this time round. It was clear too that the German artillery facing them had been greatly reinforced by batteries whose positions were unknown and not easily locatable to enable counter battery measures to be taken. Although the weather had at last taken a turn for the much better on 20 April, the state of the roads was still sufficiently bad to cause problems to those trying to move forward adequate supplies of shells to the guns.

The preparatory bombardment began on 21 April. For ten hours on that night and the next the guns targeted known German positions and included hurricane bombardments of villages along the German line by the heavy guns. At 0445 on 23 April the infantry assault began behind a creeping barrage that lifted 100 yards every four minutes. Unfortunately for 98 Brigade of 33rd Division, two brigades of the RFA both shelled the same zone leaving a gap containing a copse unattended to. The resultant enemy machine gun fire from the copse caused many casualties among two 98 Brigade battalions, the 2nd Argylls and 1st Middlesex. There was much fighting concentrated around Monchy-le-Preux, which the Germans were still anxious to recapture, and Wancourt tower, which changed hands a couple of times. Two RHA batteries found themselves in very vulnerable positions following the recapture of the tower by the enemy and came under heavy artillery fire from

---

12   Strong and Marble, *Artillery in the Great War*, pp. 130-1.

batteries that could see them clearly. They refused to retire and gave a very good account of themselves despite taking losses of guns and men. Just as it looked as if German infantry might reach them, 50th Division counterattacked and retook the tower, this time for good, thereby saving the gunners from any immediate threat.

The heavy fighting around the village of Guémappe, as 46 Brigade of 15th (Scottish) Division attempted to capture the enemy Blue Line, having passed through the other two brigades of the Division, led to one of those unfortunate 'friendly fire' incidents that would increase in frequency as the Battle of Arras wore on. The 10/11th Highland Light Infantry did not receive a message informing them that their artillery barrage would pause for an hour instead of 30 minutes. As a result they advanced through the barrage suffering heavy casualties.

The First Army main objective was to capture Gavrelle. The task was given to XIII Corp's 63rd (Royal Naval) Division. Despite the firing of a massive bombardment intended to cut the German wire, when the infantry advanced to storm the village they found it only patchily cut. They nevertheless pressed forward and with great difficulty completed the capture of the village. The inevitable counterattack was quickly launched but beaten off by a combination of artillery barrage and rifle and machine gun fire. The following day the Germans tried again with their biggest counterattack of Second Scarpe. The 63rd Division were heavily shelled from noon until 1500 when the enemy infantry assault began. The leading waves of the three attacking battalions were largely dealt with by the guns, the remainder by rifle and machine gun fire. The intensity of the fighting was reflected in the fact that, during the course of the day, the 63rd Divisional Artillery fired 78,000 rounds; one brigade alone of the RFA fired 15,000 rounds.

Following on from the overall disappointment of the Second Battle of the Scarpe, the next attack would not be long in coming. It was later given the name of the Battle of Arleux and was launched and brought to an end on successive days, 28 and 29 April. The intention was to push eastward on either side of the River Scarpe using divisions belonging to VI and XVII Corps. The 34th Division had the difficult task of attacking Roeux on their way to their objective, the Gavrelle-Roeux road. Because of the built up nature of the ground to be covered a special creeping barrage was designed with the 100 yard lifts being separated by varying numbers of minutes according to the perceived nature of the obstacles to be traversed. Despite the weight of the barrage fired, it failed to cut much of the wire or suppress all of the enemy machine guns. Nevertheless the infantry fought their way into the village where they soon found themselves being counterattacked by enemy infantry emerging from nearby woods. They were dealt with by 18 pounders firing shrapnel. Further attempts to move forward by the British infantry came to nothing mainly because of the lack of any planned artillery support. On 34th Division's left, the 37th Division also attacked behind a creeping barrage that worked successfully and saw the infantry onto their objectives, where they consolidated.

Further north the First Army Canadian Corps achieved the only real success of the battle with the capture of the village of Arleux. They were materially helped by a double 18 pounder barrage, some guns firing shrapnel and others HE. Some 4.5 inch howitzers and machine guns also played a part.[13]

The Battle of Arleux was but a curtain raiser for Haig's last serious effort of the Arras campaign. On 3 May all three armies attacked, the First and Third in the Third Battle of the Scarpe and the Fifth in the Second Battle of Bullecourt. The first of these engagements was largely over by 4 May. The second, which will be dealt with separately, would continue until the 17th.

The omens for a successful outcome to Third Scarpe could scarcely have been less auspicious. They had all the makings of a disaster. And so it proved. This is not the place to evaluate the battle except insofar as light might be shed on the contribution of the artillery. The British infantry involved in the battle were either largely tired or inexperienced and therefore even more than usually dependent on strong artillery support and protection. Sadly this would only rarely be forthcoming as the Germans

13   Farndale, op. cit., pp. 177-9.

guns took almost complete control of the battlefield. It was claimed by some in a position to know that the German artillery fire at Third Scarpe was the heaviest ever seen in the whole war; it went on without slackening for a full 15 hours. It was by no means always the British artillery's fault when the infantry lost their barrage. But once they did, they fell victim to massive and concentrated German artillery fire. The loss of the barrage could well have been partly due to the inexperience of the bulk of the infantry and certainly to the very ill advised decision to impose on First and Third Armies a Zero Hour cloaked in complete darkness.

The most serious failure of the British artillery was, however, the ineffectiveness of its counter battery fire. Only in isolated instances was there any indication that the German counter battery fire had been adversely affected by the British guns. For the most part it descended heavily, accurately and very promptly. Given virtually free rein they took full advantage. What were the reasons for this sudden reversal of fortune? There was the obvious one that the British batteries were regularly on the move and could no longer rely on pre-plotting and registering enemy targets as had been the case for 9 April. In addition, both guns and crews were showing signs of wear and tear after a long campaign frequently conducted in appalling weather. Furthermore, with the planned Flanders campaign looming ever closer there could be no question of fresh guns and crews being committed to the dying days of the Arras campaign. Indeed, batteries were already being pulled out to be sent north to join the Flanders campaign. The Germans, by contrast, were still fully focused on Arras and Chemin des Dames and had adequate reserves following the shortening of their front by their recent voluntary withdrawal. The RA History also makes the suggestion that 'there was still a failure in British tactics to weld artillerymen so close to the attack that they would be able to plan ahead and be ready to react quickly to the unexpected'.[14]

As was becoming almost customary, the First Army Canadians provided the one crumb of comfort that could be gleaned from Third Scarpe, with the capture of Fresnoy. This was accomplished by one brigade each from the 1st and 2nd Canadian Divisions despite the fact that the wire cutting programme fired in support of their attack had achieved inadequate results and they were subjected to a heavy German counter barrage.

The Second Battle of Bullecourt was launched simultaneously with Third Scarpe at 0345 on 3 May. It initially involved V British Corps 62nd Division and I ANZAC 2nd Australian Division. The overall objective was to capture the villages of Bullecourt, Riencourt and Hendecourt and to capture stretches of the Hindenburg Main (O.G.1) and Support (O.G.2) Lines on either side of Bullecourt, that were not already in Australian hands. It would have been surprising, given the length of preparatory time that the artillery found itself with, if the counter battery work had not been effective. It duly was. The preliminary barrage was also successful. There was one field gun for every 11 yards of front and one heavy gun for every 20 yards. Much attention was paid to the target villages; Bullecourt and Riencourt were reduced to rubble. In an attempt to minimise the danger of enemy enfilade fire, the Australian attack plan called for the width of their infantry assault to be narrowed compared with First Bullecourt. This resulted in the leaving of a gap of 300 yards between the left of 2nd Australian Division and the right of 62nd Division. No plan was made to neutralise this gap by artillery fire.

The Australian creeping barrage was accompanied by heavy machine gun support providing overhead and flanking fire. It enabled the two attacking brigades to reach the German wire without serious difficulty. One of them successfully navigated the wire and got into the German trenches; the other did not and put the whole attack in peril by retiring precipitately. Although some strong leadership partially restored the situation the net effect was hardly positive. Even worse was the outcome of 62nd Division's attempt to capture Bullecourt. Their attack was slow and cautious against German artillery and machine guns which were quickly recovering from the battering they had been

---

14   Ibid., p. 179.

subjected to from the British guns. Losses were heavy and 7th Division were moved up to relieve the 62nd and take on the task of capturing the village. Their attempts to do during the night of 3/4th May were a total failure. All that Fifth Army had to show for the first day's fighting was the precarious possession by the Australians of stretches of O.G.1 and O.G.2 and long casualty lists.

For the remaining two weeks of the battle the main focus was on the need to capture Bullecourt. The artillery of both sides was heavily and frequently engaged in preparing the way for the numerous British and Australian attacks and against the constant German counterattacks, and firing the accompanying creeping barrages. Several of the attacks and counterattacks were comprehensively stopped in their tracks by artillery barrages, including the German counterattack on the Australians on 6 May. Short, hurricane bombardments became a feature. Despite every effort being made to avoid them there were tragic instances of friendly fire causing significant casualties. One of these was on the night of 13/14th May when yet another attempt was made to capture Bullecourt, this time by 22nd Manchesters, attacking from the northeast, and 2nd Warwicks from the southwest of the village. As the two battalions began to converge disaster struck with both of them being hit in turn by the British barrage.

As Second Bullecourt moved into its final stages news came that the Roeux Chemical Works had finally been captured by 4th Division after what the RA History described as 'a most carefully prepared and brilliantly executed bombardment and attack'.

Bullecourt's capture was finally completed on 17 May enabling the British and Australians to claim victory. There were clearly lessons to be drawn for the Artillery from the whole Arras campaign, which could not realistically be claimed to have been a British victory. With solutions having been found to many of the problems of establishing the precise whereabouts of enemy batteries without giving away the fact that they had been pinpointed, the Arras campaign had demonstrated that the British gunners were masters of the technical aspects of their craft and in their preparations for battle. Where there were still problems was in battlefield communications and how to cope when the enemy moved their batteries from the places that had been pinpointed prior to the battle. An urgent priority was to find methods of finding and then neutralising these guns before they could play an active part in the battle as it was clearly essential to secure and maintain mastery over them for the duration of battles and not just for the opening day or two.

Appendix IV

Underground Warfare at Arras

It can be no surprise that tunnels, subways and caverns featured strongly in the fighting that took place near Arras during the war, and especially during the build-up to the British 1917 offensive. Their exploitation for military purposes would receive a boost when the area was handed over to the BEF by the French in March 1916. The soil of the area was primarily chalk, which readily lent itself to tunnelling and mining operations. During the 18th century large areas of Arraa, both within and outside the town walls, had been exploited as a ready source of hard chalk for use in rebuilding the town. This had resulted in large storage cellars being dug out under the houses of the two main squares in Arras, the Grande Place and the Petite Place (now renamed the Place des Héros). The existence of these cellars was of course well known to the First World War military authorities, who quickly had them cleared out so as to provide shelter and accommodation for 13,000 men. The quarries outside the town walls in the southeastern suburbs of Ronville and St Sauveur were rediscovered by chance in 1916. If they could be extended and linked up they might well be able to provide further accommodation for men and a relatively safe means for men and supplies to reach the front line from Arras undetected and unharmed.

Very conveniently Arras had a sewer, the eight feet high by six feet wide Crinchon sewer, that ran along the course of the ditch forming part of the Arras fortifications. It was quickly decided to drive tunnels from the cellars under the squares to the sewer and then, from the sewer, drive two long tunnels to and through the Ronville and St Sauveur systems of caves, respectively southsoutheast and eastsoutheast from the town, to the British front line. When levelled and cleared the caves were able to accommodate respectively 4,000 and 11,500 men bringing to a total of 24,500 the number who could make the journey from Arras to no man's land without the risk of exposure to German shellfire, which was bound to target assembly places such as the main railway station. The troops using the St Sauveur tunnel were to exit it through five shafts in no man's land. Unfortunately, because of the German voluntary withdrawal, the exits from the Ronville tunnel now found themselves situated 1,000 yards from the new front line. The troops would therefore have to cover the additional distance in the open as there was no time prior to the planned start of the battle to extend the tunnel further.

The tunnelling work was largely carried out by the New Zealand Tunnelling Company to a very satisfactory standard despite the time constraints under which they had to work. Work was not begun until the end of November 1916. The British 184th Tunnelling Company did some of the early work on the St Sauveur tunnel, which accounts for why the various caves along its route are named after British towns. The Ronville tunnel's caves are likewise named after New Zealand towns,[1] the largest one being Christchurch Cave with a capacity of 4,000 troops. When completed the caves and tunnels had electric light, piped water and gas-proof doors fitted to all the entrances. Telephones, telephone exchanges and line testing points were cabled in. In anticipation that congestion in Arras during the battle would hinder the evacuation of wounded needing urgent treatment, a main dressing station (in effect a hospital) was set up in a cave only half a mile from the front line. Advanced dressing stations in the caves, and also in the cellars and basements of buildings in the main squares of Arras, were in

---

1   The *Carrière* Wellington, named after New Zealand's capital, has recently been restored and reopened and is now a major tourist attraction as well as a focal point for local acts of commemoration.

turn upgraded, and equipped and manned to carry out all the functions of main dressing stations. As an aid to the inevitable heavy lifting requirements of an army, a tramline was run from the Crinchon sewer to the St Sauveur caves. Nothing was spared to make the caves and tunnels as user friendly as possible. They must have saved many lives in the early stages of the battle, not only by providing shell proof shelter for assembling troops but also relatively safe passage to jumping off points.[2]

The main impact that tunnelling and mining had on the Battle of Arras was undoubtedly on the successful capture of Vimy ridge by the Canadian Corps. The spring of 1916 saw the British take over the area of the front dominated by Vimy ridge from the French whose best efforts the previous year to capture it had been thwarted by German defences that were heavily reliant on the exploitation of the caverns and tunnels under the ridge, offering them a freedom of movement that the available French artillery had not been sufficiently powerful to neutralise. The underground workings are believed to have been used during the French Wars of Religion in the 16th and 17th centuries. Since their occupation of the ridge the Germans had dug exits from them into their front line positions enabling them to man the latter in strength as soon as any hostile barrage had lifted. Unsurprisingly the Germans had by 1916 convinced themselves that Vimy ridge was impregnable.

When the British arrived in March 1916 they found the Germans holding the upper hand in mining operations. This form of warfare had been growing in intensity in many areas of the Western Front since early 1915 and would continue to do so well into 1916. Although the British had not initiated underground warfare in the war they would soon have an adequate number of well trained and well equipped people to ensure that they would give a good account of themselves, probably more so than their adversaries. The need for such people in the form of specialist battalions had been recognised as early as December 1914. By February of the following year it had been decided to recruit eight specialist tunnelling companies, a figure which by mid 1916 had increased to 25, not counting seven additional ones raised from the Dominions. The early established companies relied heavily on a group of men known in civilian life as 'clay kickers'. The idea of recruiting them for use on the Western Front had been the brainchild of a larger than life character, Major John Norton-Griffiths MP. He had earned the nickname of 'Empire Jack' from his career as an engineering contractor with South African mining experience. Norton-Griffiths persuaded Field Marshal Lord Kitchener to allow him to recruit men he had seen tunnelling a Manchester drainage system. Known as 'moles' as well as 'clay kickers' these men sat in frequently cramped tunnels supported at an angle of 45 degrees by a wooden cross at their backs. They hacked out the clay with a light spade and passed it back with their feet for disposal behind, working very fast. They called it 'working on the cross'. Although they would prove to be more than a match for the Germans in the predominantly clay soil conditions of Flanders, their skills were less applicable around Arras where the soil under a clay cover of only a few feet was largely chalk. They therefore had to be reinforced by skilled miners.[3]

On Vimy ridge no fewer than 70 mines were detonated in the first two months following the British arrival. Most of these were exploded by the enemy. However this apparent German dominance would not last. This was not entirely owing to British aggressiveness on the part of their tunnelling companies overcoming their opposite numbers. It also owed something to the German decision to build their new defensive system, the Hindenburg Line, from September 1916 onwards, and the consequent withdrawal of many of their miners from other areas, including Vimy ridge, to work on the preparation of the new system. German mining activity tailed off discernibly; the Official History suggests, perhaps unfairly, that they 'had virtually abandoned the struggle'.[4] Until their presence had been required elsewhere they had remained very active, combining their exploding of mines with the use of trench mortars to target shaft heads, causing significant casualties among the British tunnellers.

2   OH 1917, Volume 1, pp.192-3.
3   Nigel Cave, *Vimy Ridge: Arras*, pp. 38-40.
4   OH, Ibid., p. 309.

By the time of the arrival of the Canadian Corps at Vimy ridge in October and November 1916 the British were well on top of the Germans underground and were keen to exploit this advantage for the benefit of the four Canadian divisions. In place were the 172nd, 176th, 182nd and 185th Tunnelling Companies, Royal Engineers. A question that was to preoccupy both the tunnelling companies and the Canadians was whether the creation of craters by the exploding of mines under, or close to, the German front line defences was a help or hindrance to the infantry seeking to advance into and through them. From about August 1916 onwards the tunnellers had been refining schemes to lay mines to be blown in support of an attack on the ridge, foreseen for the autumn but subsequently postponed. When the Canadians arrived on the scene they, and especially Major General Arthur Currie, the GOC of 1st Canadian Division (and soon to be the first Canadian Commander of the Canadian Corps), took a close interest in the schemes that were being keenly promoted by the CO of 182 Tunnelling Company, Major Frederick Mulqueen. After a period of consideration Currie told Mulqueen that he feared that the large mines that had already been charged and put in place might prove to be more or a hindrance than a help to the attacking infantry and that they should not for that reason be fired. In elaboration he said that although firing the mines under the German front line position, thereby creating a series of craters, would unquestionably disrupt their defence, it would also hinder the attacking troops by forcing them to advance over extremely difficult terrain. The craters would be at least 50 feet deep obliging the attackers to move around their rims where they would offer sitting targets for machine guns situated in the enemy support trenches. Mulqueen inferred that Currie based this conclusion on his experience at St Eloi in April 1916 where the explosion of the British mines had so altered and damaged the landscape that occupation of the craters by the infantry had been made virtually impossible. Although disappointed, Mulqueen accepted that Currie's conclusions were perfectly soundly based. They were not however shared by all the Canadian Corps senior officers. A group of these had visited the recent battlefields of La Boisselle and Fricourt on the Somme to study the problem of advancing across heavily mine-cratered ground at first hand. They concluded that the craters themselves, with the exception of the newest and largest, did not present an insurmountable obstacle, although the bottoms, which could well be wet and glutinous, should be worked round. They could be negotiated in small parties, equipped with machine guns and readily available Lewis guns, taking advantage of the causeways formed by the lips of the craters. The parties would need to be supported by barrages fired by Stokes mortars and rifle grenades. This method had not been used during the Somme battles, as a result of which troops advancing on either side of craters had been heavily exposed to fire from them. The method had been used subsequently in raids and its viability had been confirmed.

The report produced by the officers who had visited La Boisselle and Fricourt clearly carried less weight than the views of General Currie as eight of the fourteen mines already in position, totalling in all 120,000 pounds of explosive, and mainly situated in the area surrounding Hill 145, were removed. A further three were left in place even though it was decided not to blow them. A decision was taken not to lay any more, especially after the Germans blew a series of mines that created nine craters, called the Longfellow Group, in no man's land. The intention of these enemy mines was apparently to force the Canadians to channel their attack through predictable points and make things difficult for any tanks they might employ.[5] The remaining three of the fourteen British mines were blown as the Canadian assault began on 9 April. They were located beneath the German front line in the 4th Canadian Division's sector. One destroyed an enemy underground gallery loaded with explosives; another destroyed enemy machine guns on the lip of a crater; the third created a crater on the Canadian left flank that might at some stage be needed for defensive purposes.[6]

Despite the decision not to lay any more mines, an exception was made for a mine to be laid under

---

5   Simon Jones, *Underground Warfare 1914-1918*, pp. 133-5.
6   Hayes, Iarocci, Bechthold (eds), *Vimy Ridge: A Canadian Reassessment*, p. 132.

the Pimple strong point. The tunnel was started by 176 Tunnelling Company but by 9 April it was still 70 feet from its target. Even though the Pimple was not captured until 12 April it would have still been too soon for the planned mine to be in position.[7]

One point General Currie made when he was turning down Major Mulqueen's proposals was that the Tunnelling Companies would be much better employed building subways. Subways were part of the Vimy ridge subterranean infrastructure before the arrival of the Canadian Corps, but the work that was put in hand after their arrival would create a network of them that would ensure that troops and supplies could reach the front lines in relative safety and security and casualties could be channelled back on their way to medical care without causing blockages affecting normal traffic. In all a total of six miles of subways would be upgraded or excavated from scratch to support the Corps over the course of the battle. The subways were dug at least 25 feet below ground and sometimes deeper. They were lit by electricity from generators, installed in all the subways by a specialist company, The Australian Electrical and Mechanical Mining and Boring Company. They were fully wired for telephones, and drums of telephone cable were stored adjacent to the subways ready to be used to run lines along enemy trenches as soon as they were captured. Stores and ammunition were also stockpiled in nearby chambers. Some were also equipped with tramways, using wooden rails and rubber tyres in the hope of silent running. They were mainly used to bring forward mortar bombs for heavy mortar positions connected to the subways. Fresh water was on tap from two huge water reservoirs each holding 50,000 gallons of water. Chambers were cut at intervals off the main subways for use as brigade and battalion headquarters, dressing stations and stores. The dressing stations were dug out to a standard size of 34 feet by 9 feet and were well lit and dry.

All this activity taking place in an area overlooked at close quarters by an enemy ensconced on the commanding heights of Vimy ridge made it important to conceal as much as was possible in the circumstances of what was going on underground. It is scarcely conceivable that the enemy did not appreciate that their opponents would be taking advantage of the benign conditions for mining operations, although their still unexplained passivity throughout this period might suggest otherwise. It was nevertheless essential for the British mining companies to keep the Germans as much in the dark as possible. One essential to doing this was to dispose of the very conspicuous chalk spoil from the excavations as unobtrusively as possible. This was achieved by placing the spoil in sandbags that were then dumped in areas where there were abandoned trenches and then covered with earth. This stratagem seems to have worked as the enemy did not single out the exits from the excavations for attention from their artillery.

Much attention was paid to the problem inherent in subterranean works – congestion. As far as possible the subways were excavated to a height of 6 feet 6 inches and a width of 6 feet, which was intended to ensure that two laden men could pass. As a safeguard, passing places were also dug out at regular intervals. An elaborate system of traffic control was also put in place. Direction boards were placed at each junction. Traffic lights were used to ensure that the largely human traffic moved smoothly. At times of great pressure, such as when troops were moving up to their assembly positions, a one way system could thereby be instituted, with only medical personnel, runners and individual officers, allowed to override it. It was enforced by Military Police.

The operations of the tunnelling companies finally resulted in a number of subways that extended the whole length of the Canadian front. From south to north the 185th Tunnelling Company excavated Barricade, Douai, Bentata and Zivy; the 172nd, Grange (1,343 yards),[8] Goodman (the longest at 1,883 yards) and Lichfield (500 yards); the 182nd, Cavalier, Tottenham, Vincent and Blue Ball; the 176th, Coburg and Gobron (both 300 yards long). The 176th Tunnelling Company were

7   Simon Jones, op. cit., p. 136.
8   As visitors to the Canadian National Park at Vimy Ridge will know, the Grange Tunnel has been partially reopened for conducted tours, the only subway that now offers public access.

also responsible for the three mines that were detonated on Vimy ridge on 9 April.[9]

Apart from the three mines already referred to, only one mine was blown by the British on 9 April. As early as January 1917 the Third Army had begun pushing out Russian saps[10] from their front line into no man's land. Despite constant setbacks from them being blown in by shell fire, 'friendly' as well as hostile, and the unfortunate miners being buried and, if lucky, dug out, the saps continued to be pushed forward. One of them inadvertently broke into an abandoned German gallery. The breach was loaded with 2,200 pounds of ammonal and carefully closed. It is believed that it was this mine that was blown at 0530 on 9 April. According to a Lieutenant Neill of the New Zealand Tunnelling Company, the resultant explosion destroyed two dugouts, 50 yards of trench and a concrete pillbox. Less beneficially it also stunned and apparently buried some members of the 13th Royal Scots, 9th Division, and temporarily checked their assault.[11]

---

9   Cave, op.cit., pp. 106-9.
10   Russian saps were galleries excavated at a shallow depth so that the covering earth could subsequently be dug out to allow them to be used as communication trenches.
11   Simon Jones, op. cit., pp. 136 and 232.

Appendix V

The Tanks

During the early stages of the planning of the Battle of Arras, GHQ had hoped that an adequate number of tanks with fully trained crews would feature in the orders of battle of the three participating British armies. The Mark I version of the battle tank that had introduced the world to armoured warfare on 15 September 1916 at the Battle of Flers-Courcelette had shocked and surprised the German army. Its impact had however been limited because of the small number of them that had participated and the mechanical unreliability of those that did. It did not take long for the Germans to recover their poise and identify the main weakness of the Mark I to be its inadequate armour that left it not only vulnerable to shellfire but also to armour piercing bullets. The deficiencies of the Mark I were partially addressed in the Mark II and Mark IV versions. The former was intended to be used only for training purposes and offered only slight improvements on the Mark I. The Mark IV[1] on the other hand was a significant improvement with its more powerful engine, its heavier armour and hopefully its greater reliability. It was this version that GHQ hoped to deploy on the Arras battlefields.

Unfortunately however, even though GHQ placed a significant order for the Mark IV and stressed the urgency, it soon became evident that production delays and other problems would mean that the machines would not start arriving in France in time for the Arras campaign. It had originally been expected that 50 Mark IIs would arrive in France in January 1917 and that Mark IVs would arrive thereafter at the rate of 20 per week from February onwards. In the event neither of these expectations was fulfilled. The Heavy Branch, Machine Gun Corps,[2] would have instead to make do with sixty tanks consisting mainly of Mark I machines that were already in France, plus the few Mark IIs that had recently arrived from England. Forty of these were initially allocated to Third Army, eight to First Army and twelve to Fifth Army.

The conditions for the use of tanks in the Arras campaign were not propitious, and not only because of the shortcomings of the machines themselves. Much of the ground they would have to traverse had been churned up by the inevitable shellfire from both sides. In addition the dire weather of the 1916-17 winter with its heavy bouts of snow and rain, and frozen ground alternating with thaws and mud, had taken its toll. Although the enemy were no longer as fearful of the tanks as they had been on their early appearances and were justifiably confident that they had the means to deal with them, they nevertheless remained obsessive about them. The British infantry had learned very quickly that it was advisable to maintain a healthy distance between the tanks and themselves as the formers' appearance on the battlefield acted as a magnet to every German gun within range, which would continue targeting them long after they had been put out of action and were no longer a threat, thereby incidentally benefitting much more worthwhile targets by their neglect of them.

The forty tanks allocated to Third Army were divided up between the three corps due to assault on 9 April, with 16 each going to VII and VI Corps and 8 to XVII Corps. In general the role given to the tanks for the first day of the battle was the predictable one of offering support to the infantry in capturing the enemy's defensive lines and subduing their strong points. They were expected to carry

---

1   There was a Mark III version. It was produced for experimental purposes and was never used in battle.
2   The regimental name did not become The Tank Corps until July 1917.

out these in groups varying in size from two to ten tanks, and in the case of the attempt to capture Monchy-le-Preux no fewer than twenty. There must have been some raised eyebrows at the demands being placed on the tanks. Not only enemy action, but also their notorious mechanical unreliability, seemed to point to the conclusion that, by the later stages of the day, there were unlikely to be sufficient numbers still operational to meet the demands being placed on them.

The fate of the tanks involved on 9 April is indicative. Of the four tanks assigned to VII Corps' 30th Division, one failed to reach the starting point. The other three made it to the start but became bogged down soon thereafter south of Neuville-Vitasse. The 56th Division were also supported by four tanks deployed in pairs on either side of Neuville-Vitasse. One of these helped 3rd London Regiment capture Neuville mill southwest of the village, a German strong point that threatened to pour enfilade fire onto any advancing infantry. The 12th London Regiment (The Rangers) were also materially assisted by a tank that rolled down sufficient enemy wire to enable one company that had been pinned down and was taking heavy casualties, to get through and take their assigned sector of Pine Line trench. No fewer than 14 tanks were committed to the support of 14th (Light) Division and the right flank of 3rd Division in their efforts to capture Telegraph Hill, The Harp strong point and The String trench that ran through it. Three tanks greatly assisted 6th KOYLI capture a German redoubt half way between the British front line and the Hindenburg Line, the defences of which had hardly been touched by the British barrages, by breaking down its defensive wire.

Of the 22 tanks engaged in supporting the actions described above, twelve were from 10 Company, D Battalion and ten from 8 Company, C Battalion. They had both suffered heavy casualties. Eight of 10 Company's tanks had been put out of action by becoming bogged down or damaged by enemy fire. All of 8 Company's had suffered similarly, seven by becoming bogged down and three by enemy action (two by shellfire and one by bombs thrown under the tracks). The 14th Division found it particularly lamentable that the few tanks that did manage to reach the start point, from where they were supposed to support the attack on The String, arrived too late to be of any help. In their defence the ground across which they had had to travel had been very heavily shelled creating ideal conditions in which to become bogged down.[3]

In common with VII Corps, VI Corps had 16 tanks at their disposal, from C Battalion's 8 and 9 Companies. But 8 Company's machines had in effect been shared by VII Corps 14th Division and VI Corps' 3rd Division, in their joint attack on The Harp. VI Corps had therefore been left with the exclusive support of only 9 Company. Four of this Company's tanks were tasked to encircle Tilloy-lès-Mofflaines, a pair each to the north and south of the village. Of the remainder, two were to sweep down the line of redoubts north of Tilloy and the last two were to attack the Railway Triangle. Those 8 and 9 Company machines still remaining in action would then assist VI Corps in their attack on the Wancourt-Feuchy line and Feuchy Chapel. In general the day went well for the infantry and there were valuable contributions from the tanks. 8 Company performed well in the attack on The Harp, even though only one machine reached the eastern side of the redoubt. The remainder were hit by enemy fire or bogged down. Further north, 9 Company suffered a major misfortune when six of their machines attempting to cross the Crinchon Valley, broke through the surface of the ground and became stuck fast in the muddy morass beneath. By the time they were dug out they were much too late to take any further part in the day's events.

The two tanks that had been ordered to attack the Railway Triangle would be assisting 15th Division. This objective presented a serious and challenging obstacle, with two sides of the Triangle consisting of high embankments carrying the railway tracks that completely dominated the ground between the Triangle and the River Scarpe. The tanks were to attack the obstacle from the rear. They were then to roll up the Wancourt-Feuchy line from the northern end. In the event one of them materially helped 15th Division's two attacking brigades, held up by the Railway Triangle, to complete

---

3   OH 1917 Volume 1, pp. 201-214 passim.

its capture by passing south of the railway and engaging the enemy machine guns in the Triangle. The second tank, named 'Lusitania', did even more valuable work by gaining the Wancourt-Feuchy line, working down it and putting two machine guns out of action. The 15th Division's task of successfully completing the capture of the line was thereby much eased.[4] Lusitania deserved a better fate than that which overtook it. Late in the day its magneto failed leaving it stranded on the edge of an enemy trench. The crew went in a successful search for a replacement magneto, but when they returned the following day to install it they found that Lusitania had been badly damaged by British shellfire.[5]

North of the River Scarpe the Third Army XVII Corps had been allocated eight tanks from 7 Company, C Battalion. They were equally shared between two of the assaulting divisions, the 9th (Scottish) and the 34th. The third assaulting division, the 51st (Highland), received none. Even though this was to be a day on which XVII Corps infantry were to notch up record advances, they were to achieve these without the help of the tanks, all of which either bogged down or were put out of action by enemy fire before they had become engaged.[6]

The First Army, whose Canadian Corps were to assault Vimy ridge, received an allocation of eight tanks. They were attached to 2nd Canadian Division in the hope that they might assist in the Division's advance on, and beyond, Thélus. The planners were, however, realistic enough to accept that the ground conditions the tanks would face could hardly be less conducive to their successful exploitation. The overall plans had accordingly been drawn up independent of any tank participation. This proved to be a wise precaution as all the tanks quickly became bogged down and played no part in the ensuing Canadian victory.[7]

The 9th April had proved to be the British Army most successful and victorious day of the war on the Western Front up to this point. With regard to the performance of the tanks, however, the outcome could at best be described as disappointing. Although some tanks made outstanding contributions to the overall success of the day, there were many instances where they failed to do so, almost always for reasons beyond the scope of the commanders and crews to influence. Despite the following day being largely devoted to strenuous efforts to recover bogged down machines, the ensuing days would see a steady diminution in the number of tanks available to participate in operations.

The second day of the battle was largely one of disappointing progress following the successes of the first. It was not until 11 April that Third Army renewed their attack with determined attempts to exploit the victory and rebuild the momentum of Day One. Inevitably circumstances had changed, one of them being that only 10 tanks were available to Third Army compared with the 40 that had started the battle. Four were attached to VII Corps and six to VI Corps. The two Corps were given the ambitious objective of reaching the Drocourt-Quéant Line. XVII Corps were to capture Greenland Hill and Plouvain village. Perhaps because of the relative closeness of these objectives they were not allocated any tanks.

Both groups of tanks acquitted themselves well during the day's fighting. The four tanks from D Battalion materially assisted 167 Brigade of VII Corps 56th Division as they bombed their way up and down Hindenburg Line trenches and the Wancourt-Feuchy line, finally completing their capture. They then turned northeast and passed through Héninel village and entered Wancourt. Despite urgent signals, the infantry failed to follow up, obliging the tanks, by now running short of fuel, to turn back. An opportunity had been lost, an unfortunate example of the lack of training in infantry/tank co-operation adversely affecting the outcome of events.

Probably the major achievement of the day was the part played by four of the six C Battalion tanks supporting VI Corps, in the capture of Monchy-le-Preux. (The other two tanks had been sidelined, one by mechanical problems and the other by ditching on the way to take up position.) One

4   Ibid., pp. 214-225 passim.
5   Basil Liddell-Hart, *The Tanks*, p. 98.
6   OH op. cit., p. 228.
7   Ibid., pp. 310-1.

of the operational tanks began its advance round the northern edge of the village from the west at the prescribed time of 0500. It reached the eastern edge of the village and eliminated several machine guns with its 6 pounder before it was put out of action by a hit from the British barrage that forced the crew to abandon it. The other three tanks advanced toward Monchy from the south with largely unfortunate results. One cleared an enemy trench but soon came under heavy shellfire from the British barrage, which killed or wounded most of the crew. A second quickly came under fire from armour piercing bullets that wounded all the gunners. It was then hit by a shell of indeterminate nationality. Although surrounded by enemy troops the Commander was able to keep them at bay with Lewis gun fire until British infantry reached them. Only the Commander and one crew member were unharmed. Four crew were dead and two wounded. The third tank engaged a considerable force of enemy troops with Lewis guns until the tank was hit and set on fire by German artillery. Only three crew, one of whom was wounded, survived. Although all four tanks had became casualties, their achievements were gratefully acknowledged in messages from the Commanders of VI Corps and 37th Division to the Commander of the Heavy Machine Gun Corps 1st Brigade.[8] For the remaining three days of the First Battle of the Scarpe there was virtually no tank involvement. Two should have supported 21st Division 62 Brigade in bombing operations down the Hindenburg Line on 13 April, but both broke down before becoming engaged.

The involvement of the tanks in the First Battle of Bullecourt has been described in detail in Chapter 9. To summarise, the 12 tanks of 11th Company, D Battalion had been assigned to General Sir Hubert Gough's Fifth Army. It was planned that they would support I ANZAC in their attempt to break into the Hindenburg Line when Fifth Army assault began 24 hours after that of First Army. When Gough was obliged to postpone his assault because his artillery would not complete their essential wire cutting programme on time he greeted with enthusiasm a proposal by the Tank Company Commander that his tanks, operating *en masse* could deal with the wire without help from the artillery. Gough ordered them to proceed accordingly and restored the planned Zero Hour of 0430 on 10 April, leaving the tanks only a few hours to get themselves organised. In the event they were so late arriving that the Australian infantry only just had time to vacate their exposed positions and retreat to safety when the assault was cancelled. With minor modifications the operation was rescheduled for 24 hours later. Despite the additional time, the performance of the tanks was a major disappointment and such success as there was, was due to the infantrymen of the 4th Australian Division. Only two of the eleven tanks involved survived. The Australians were so disillusioned with the performance of the tanks that they refused to have anything further to do with them until 15 months later.

A total of 19 tanks[9] had been recovered and repaired as necessary, in time for the next major phase of the Arras campaign, the Second Battle of the Scarpe, which was fought on 23-24 April. Eight from D Battalion were allocated to VII Corps (four to 33rd Division and two each to 30th and 50th Divisions), six from C Battalion to VI Corps (two each to 15th, 17th and 37th Divisions), and five from C Battalion to XVII Corps (all to 51st Division in recognition of their difficult dual task of attacking both Roeux village and the nearby Chemical Works). The results of their involvement in the battle were predictably uneven. Two of those assigned to 33rd Division and ordered to support a small detachment from 100 Brigade on a night march from Croisilles along the east bank of the Sensée River, broke down almost immediately and took no part in the action. One of the other two tanks assigned to 33rd Division, on the other hand, provided invaluable assistance to 98 Brigade by sweeping along parallel to the front line, knocking out a number of enemy machine guns in concrete emplacements. The two infantry battalions that were thus supported bombed along the German

8   Liddell-Hart, op. cit., p. 99.
9   It is virtually certain that there were in fact 20 tanks involved, the twentieth being added at the last minute when its repairs were completed in time. It was probably added to the five assigned to 51st Division.

trenches they were attacking with remarkable speed taking large numbers of demoralised prisoners. The two tanks attached to 50th Division also played a significant role in 150 Brigade's advance on a two battalion front, by subduing an enemy party holding out in a copse on the Chérisy-Guémappe road. One of the tanks then succumbed to engine trouble and was forced to turn back.

North of the River Scarpe the 51st (Highland) Division, handed the daunting task of capturing Roeux and the Chemical Works, were faced with the challenge of advancing through an area dominated not only by the buildings relating to their objectives, but also those belonging to the Château and railway station, as well as others. One of the assaulting battalions, the 1st/7th Argyll and, Sutherland Highlanders quickly found themselves slowed to a crawl by heavy enfilade and frontal machine gun fire. Tank No C7, which had been held up on its way to the front, caught up with the infantrymen and helped them to move forward. On entering Roeux, C7 then fired 200 six-pounder rounds through the windows of enemy occupied houses, materially helping the Argylls to clear the village, if only temporarily. Unfortunately it bogged down as it turned back to assist in silencing a machine gun in Mount Pleasant wood. Another tank provided powerful support to 1st/4th Gordon Highlanders as they fought their way into the Chemical Works, only to find themselves isolated and unable to cling on. A third tank from C Battalion gave useful support to the infantry despite suffering heavily from armour piercing bullets penetrating its inadequate armour. Four more of the tanks engaged in the battle suffered similarly, and about two thirds of the remainder broke down at an early stage.[10]

There was no tank involvement in the Battle of Arleux, fought on 28/29 April and conceived as subordinate to the major Third Battle of the Scarpe, involving all three armies, that would be launched on 3 May. For this offensive fourteen tanks were scraped together, ten of which were given to Fifth Army and four to the Third. The First Army, which had hoped to have a few for use in the suburbs of Lens, were left empty handed. Those assigned to Third Army were allocated to VII Corps 21st Division who were ordered to cross the Sensée River and capture a 500 yard long stretch of the Hindenburg Line and Fontaine-lès-Croisilles village. A mile wide corridor that would be left between Fifth Army left flank and 21st Division's right would be secured for two hours forty minutes by an artillery barrage after which it would be cleared by 21st Division making full use of the tanks. The three tanks that took part (one was kept in divisional reserve) made little impact, except adversely in the case of one. One lost its bearings and was 40 minutes late coming into action. When it did it was crippled by a broken track. One suffered radiator trouble caused by armour piercing bullets. The commander of the third could see no infantry as he moved forward and turned back causing serious alarm in the darkness among advancing 7th Bedfords and 12th Middlesex, to the extent that some of them turned back. Although they were rallied they had lost their protective barrage and could not recover their forward momentum.

The Australian disillusionment with tanks as a result of their experiences with them at the First Battle of Bullecourt meant that all ten of those made available to Fifth Army for the Second Battle of Bullecourt were assigned to V British Corps. There was little difference from First Bullecourt in the objectives for Second Bullecourt. As for the method of achieving them the main difference was that both the Australians and V Corps 62nd Division would attack simultaneously, the latter supported by eight tanks of D Battalion with two held in divisional reserve. While the Australians concentrated on expanding their toehold in the Hindenburg Line east of Bullecourt, the British had the task of capturing the village and a stretch of the Hindenburg Line to the northwest of it. When they attacked, three tanks succeeded in breaking into the village and others got into the Hindenburg Line. One of those that entered the village stayed there for 90 minutes. But when returning to the rallying point it was hit and set on fire. A second retired with four of the crew wounded, found some fit replacements from the crew of a broken down tank and returned to the fray. The third tank entered the village where its commander stopped it and emerged to seek to persuade some infantry to follow

---

10   OH op.cit., pp. 384-96 passim.

his tank further into the village. When they declined he returned to his tank to find that a number of his crew had been wounded by armour piercing bullets leaving an insufficient number fit to crew it.

There were other instances of infantry failing to take advantage of opportunities opened up by the tanks. They were to be only fleeting as eight of the tanks had soon been put out of action. Although the battle was to last two grim weeks there was to be no further significant involvement of tanks in it.[11]

French tanks put in their first appearance on the battlefield during the Nivelle Offensive. As with the British the French had recognised early on in the war that a solution to the problems posed for assaulting troops by trench warfare might lie in the development of some form of armoured and caterpillar-tracked vehicle. Their research was only a little behind that of Britain and they were less than pleased when the British squandered the precious asset of surprise by launching the tank on an unsuspecting enemy at the Battle of Flers-Courcelette when there were too few machines available to make the devastating impact they might have had. The generally accepted 'Father' of the French tank was a French artillery officer, Colonel Jean Baptiste Estienne. He and the Chief Engineer of the heavy engineering company, Schneider, pooled their research on the possibility of creating an agricultural tractor-based armoured vehicle, from which emerged the Schneider *Char d'Assaut* (Assault Tank). After trialling two prototypes, the French Ministry responsible for Defence Procurement placed an order for 400. In marked contrast to the dispiriting rate of production of the British Mark IV tank, no fewer than 208 of these were available for deployment for the start of the Nivelle offensive. In addition a second tank was also becoming available. Known as the Saint Chamond it was commissioned and built in-house by the French Army. Essentially it was a scaled-up version of the Schneider, being more than twice as heavy at over 28 tons, better armed and armoured, and faster. 400 were ordered, 48 of which were available by 16 April 1917. In the event both tanks were to prove to be prone to mechanical breakdown and not only vulnerable to artillery fire but also to armour piercing bullets. As a result their impact on the Nivelle offensive was less significant than their numbers might suggest.

Only Schneider tanks took part in the early stages of the French offensive. The major allocation went to the GAR's Fifth Army. Two of the five corps of that Army shared eight groups totalling 128 tanks, with XXXII Corps receiving five groups (80 tanks) and V Corps three groups (48). The 40th, 42nd and 69th Divisions of the former Corps were situated astride the Aisne, the 42nd and 69th north and the 40th south of the river. The 9th and 10th Divisions of V Corps were to their left and therefore also north of the river. The planned broad direction of XXXII Corps advance was northeast in the direction of the village of Prouvais. That of V Corps was towards Juvincourt and Amifontaine villages.

The role of the tanks attached to XXXII Corps was to assist the infantry of 42nd Division to take the German third position. Having made good progress the infantry had to stop before the third position to wait for the tanks, whose advance had been delayed by the churned up state of the ground over which they had had to travel. They were nevertheless in position by 1200 and began their advance at 1430. By this time, however, they were highly visible to the enemy artillery and began to suffer heavily from shellfire, with many of the tanks being set on fire. Those still operational withdrew as soon as possible out of enemy view and from there launched a series of heroic but fruitless attempts to complete their mission while daylight lasted. Despite their tragic losses, both of men and machines, their sacrifice was not entirely wasted. They had, by getting into the enemy's second position in front of Juvincourt, helped significantly in ensuring the village's capture.

The 48 tanks attached to 10th Division, having initially made good progress west of the narrow Miette River found themselves unable to traverse the enemy's first position. Immobilised in full view of the enemy and subjected to increasingly severe shellfire, the tanks were gradually put out of action until there were only eight left capable of moving. Despite also having suffered some damage they

11   Ibid., p. 465.

succeeded in returning to the shelter of the wood clearing from which they had set out. They had nothing to show for their involvement in the day's operation but tragically heavy losses in men and machines.[12]

The GAC's Fourth Army launched its assault on the second day of the offensive. It was to be supported by 48 tanks, two groups (32) of which were Schneider and the balance Saint Chamond. However, when the initial infantry assaults towards the Moronvillers ridge largely failed, the tank attack was cancelled, a decision probably influenced by the outcome of the tanks' involvement in the Fifth Army assault the previous day.

The tanks played no further part in the first stage of the Nivelle offensive, which stuttered to an end on 25 April. Their next opportunity would be on 4 May. By this time it was more than clear that the Nivelle offensive had completely failed to live up to the extravagant promises made for it by its author. Even though it had not been halted as promised if no breakthrough had been achieved in 48 hours, pressure from his political masters and his senior generals, had forced Nivelle to scale back the level of offensive operations to ones seeking essentially to keep the Germans tied down on the Chemin des Dames and in Champagne.

General Nivelle's planned attack on 5 May had been scaled back at the instance of War Minister Painlevé to exclude the proposed attack on the *Fort de Brimont*. What was left were attacks by Fourth, Fifth, Sixth and Tenth Armies, with notable successes being achieved by the last two named. In the case of the Sixth Army the tanks made a notable contribution to the success of the operation, the objective of which was to capture a long stretch of the Chemin des Dames ridge and the German salient east of Laffaux where the Hindenburg Line linked up with the Chemin des Dames. The salient was named after the Moulin (Mill) de Laffaux which dominated it. The same two groups of Schneider, and one group of Saint Chamond, tanks, whose planned attack with Fourth Army on 17 April had been cancelled, were allocated to Sixth Army. They were tasked to participate in the capture of the German salient. They were assisted by an infantry battalion that had been specially trained in combined arms tactics and a fighter escorted observation plane whose job it was to spot German antitank batteries and call down counter battery fire on them.

In the event the tank operation was largely successful in ensuring the infantry completed the capture of the objective. The tanks also assisted in the beating off of the inevitable counterattacks and launched some of their own. Although most of the tanks broke down and had to be temporarily abandoned, only five were destroyed, three of which were Schneiders and two Saint Chamonds. Most of the abandoned machines were repaired and recovered during the night, but only a handful could be deployed the following day.

Notwithstanding the success described above there can be little doubt that the performance of the French tanks during the Nivelle offensive had generally been little short of disastrous. Losses in both men and machines had been very high and, although some good work had been done, very little had been achieved to compensate for the losses. The main problem was quickly recognised as being in the design of both tank models. The placing of an inadequately armoured superstructure on an agricultural tractor-based chassis, which often proved too short to straddle the German trenches, had left many tanks immobilised and sitting ducks for the German artillery. The decision was taken not to seek to improve the design of the Schneider and Saint Chambord, but to find another option. No further orders were placed for the two tanks, although the original orders for 400 of each were allowed to run their course. Instead, the French authorities turned to the newly designed Renault FT 17 light tank, which proved to be an inspired choice. Although it weighed only 6.5 tons it had a fully revolvable turret that housed either a 37mm cannon or an 8mm machine gun. It was powered by an upgraded car engine that gave it a speed of 6 mph. To compensate for its lack of weight it was conceived as a machine that would fight in swarms to overcome the enemy by sheer weight of numbers. It first

---

12   Lt Colonel Beaugier and Others, *Les Armées Françaises dans la Grande Guerre*, Tome V, Premier Volume, pp. 646-8.

went into action in May 1918 and by the end of the war around 3,000 had been built taking advantage of Renault's experience in car production line techniques. It proved to be highly successful with the return of mobile warfare. After the war many were exported to countries that used the model as the basis of fledgling armoured units. It remained in production throughout the 1920s and '30s.

Appendix VI

GQG Directive 2226 of 4 April 1917

D
irective 2226 was addressed by General Nivelle to the Headquarters of the British and Belgian Armies and the French Army Group Commands. It was intended to clarify what was expected of each Command during the imminent Offensive, taking into account the changed circumstances brought about by the voluntary German Army withdrawal to the Hindenburg Line. In translation it reads as follows.

I. General conditions of the Offensive

The objective to be attained remains the destruction of the main mass of the enemy forces on the Western Front.

The operations undertaken will therefore of necessity involve the following:
1. A prolonged battle in which our attacking armies will have to break through the enemy front and then beat the accessible enemy forces.
2. An intensive exploitation phase in which all the available allied forces will participate.

II. The Initial Offensives:

The initial offensives of the attacking armies will converge in such a way as to bring the combined efforts of the British Armies and those of the French Northern and Reserve Army Groups into a region of particular importance to enemy communications.
   a.   The British Armies.
   The attacking British Armies will undertake the task of breaking through the enemy front between Givenchy and Quéant. The breakthrough will be immediately followed by the breakout of the reserves in the direction of Cambrai and Douai and by a rapid lateral exploitation undertaken simultaneously to the north behind the Lens-La Bassée front and towards the southeast taking the Hindenburg line in reverse.
   On the right wing of the British forces the Fourth Army will link its movement to that of the French Northern Army Group (GAN) and co-operate in the latter's attacks.
   It is of the greatest importance for the development of the operations of the British attacking armies and GAN that the British Fourth Army ties down the maximum number of enemy forces on its front.
   b.   Northern Army Group.
   The GAN's mission is to pursue its offensive in a northeasterly direction, liaising with the British Fourth Army on the left and the Reserve Army Group (GAR) on the right.
   It will first attack the advanced enemy positions to the west and south of Saint-Quentin, then the Harly-Alaincourt front, in accordance with special orders from GQG.
   GAN will co-operative by all the means at its disposal with the attack of the French Sixth Army. It will agree with GAR on what will be required from it for this operation.
   c.   Reserve Army Group (GAR)
   The initial attacks of the GAR armies will take place on the front previously fixed. But because of the enemy's withdrawal to the Hindenburg Line they will have to be developed

mainly in the direction of Guise, Vervins and Hirson.

d.   Army Group Centre (GAC)

The Fourth Army will cooperate in the Reserve Army Group attack by taking the offensive on its front west of the Suippe river.

After having captured the Massif de Moronvillers it will push its left hand divisions northwards so as to run alongside the Suippe river, and prepare to develop operations in the direction of Vouziers and Attigny.

Its action will link up with that of the Fifth Army's right wing.

III. The Exploitation Phase

Following the breakthrough of the enemy front, achieved in accordance with the directions outlined above, the different groups of allied forces will immediately begin the exploitation of these first successes.

a.   The British Armies, resting their right on the Sambre river, will pursue their offensive following the general axis Valenciennes-Louvain.

Their left wing (Second Army), profiting from the weakness of the forces the enemy will then have in Flanders, will advance from the Ypres region in liaison with the Belgian Army.

b.   The mission of the Belgian Army will be to break the enemy front in the areas of Steenstraate and Dixmude, then advance as quickly as possible towards Roulers and Ghent.

Further north, the French 36th Corps will attack along the Belgian coast towards Ostend and Bruges.

c.   The GAN, and GAR [will be?]in the zone between the Sambre and the general line Berry-au-Bac – Château-Porcien – Sedan, and the GAC south of this line.

In all these armies, the exploitation operations must be conceived in an unconfined and audacious spirit.

In this connection:

The British Armies, having seized Cambrai and Douai, will have to advance towards Valenciennes and then Mons, Tournai and Courtrai, ceaselessly extending their operations northwards, recapturing occupied territory.

The first objectives of the Northern Army Group in the exploitation phase will be the rail lines from Hirson to Cambrai, Valenciennes and Maubeuge.

The GAR and GAC will first of all aim to capture the whole area known as "la Boucle de l'Aisne" and then the region between the Rivers Meuse, Sormonne and Oise.

Each Group must plan and organise ahead of time the rapid advance towards the enemy's lines of communication crossing their exploitation zone.

It is by the rapid advance of all our available forces and the rapid conquest of the most sensitive points in the resupply chains of the enemy armies that we must seek to disorganise them completely and precipitate their retreat.

Bibliography

Banks, Arthur, *A Military Atlas of the First World War*, Barnsley, Leo Cooper, 1997.

Barker, Stephen and Boardman, Christopher, *Lancashire's Forgotten Heroes: 8th Battalion East Lancashire Regiment in the Great War,* Stroud, The History Press, 2008.

Barton, Peter, with Banning, Jeremy, *Arras*, London, Constable & Robinson Ltd, 2010.

Bean, C.E.W., *The Australian Imperial Force in France 1917*, University of Queensland Press, St. Lucia, Queensland, 1982. (The Australian Official History)

Beaugier, Lieutenant Colonel, and others, *Les Armées Françaises dans La Grande Guerre, Tome V, Premier Volume*, Paris, Imprimerie Nationale, 1931 (The French Official History).

Bilton, David, *Oppy Wood*, Barnsley, Pen & Sword Military, 2005.

Bourne, J.M., *Who's Who in World War One*, London, Routledge, 2001.

Brumwell, P. Middleton, *The History of the 12th (Eastern) Division in the Great War, 1914-1918*, Uckfield, The Naval & Military Press, (reprinted: originally published 1923).

Bryant, Peter, *Grimsby Chums: The Story of the 10th Lincolnshires in the Great War*, Hull, Humberside Leisure Services, 1990.

Cave, Nigel, *Delville Wood*, Barnsley, Leo Cooper, 1999.

Cave, Nigel, *Sanctuary Wood and Hooge*, London, Leo Cooper, 1995.

Cave, Nigel, *Vimy Ridge*, London, Leo Cooper, 1996.

Charteris, Brigadier General J., *At GHQ*, London, Cassell, 1931.

Cherry, Niall, *Most Unfavourable Ground: the Battle of Loos 1915*, Solihull, Helion & Company Limited, 2005.

Christie, Norm, *For King & Empire: The Canadians at Vimy: April 1917*, Ottawa, CEF Books, 2000.

Clayton, Anthony, *Paths of Glory: The French Army 1914-18*, London, Cassell, 2005.

Congreve, Billy (Norman, Terry (ed.)), *Armageddon Road: A VC's Diary 1914-1916*, London, William Kimber & Co Limited, 1982.

Cron, Hermann, *Imperial German Army 1914-18: Organisation, Structure, Orders-of-Battle*, Solihull, Helion & Company Limited, 2006.

Doughty, Robert A., *Pyrrhic Victory: French Strategy and Operations in the Great War*, Belknap Harvard, USA, First Harvard University Press, 2008.

Edmonds, Brigadier General Sir J.E. (ed.), *History of the Great War Based on Official Documents: Military Operations France and Belgium: 1915, Volume II*, Nashville, Imperial War Museum Dept of Printed Books in association with the Battery Press, 1995.

Ewing, John, *The History of the Ninth (Scottish) Division 1914-1919*, Uckfield, Naval & Military Press.

Falls, Captain Cyril, *History of the Great War Based on Official Documents: Military Operations France and Belgium: 1917, Volume I and Volume I Appendices*, Uckfield, The Naval & Military Press Ltd in association with the Imperial War Museum Department of Printed Books, undated.

Farndale, General Sir Martin, KCB, *History of the Royal Regiment of Artillery: Western Front 1914-18*, London, The Royal Artillery Institution, 1986.

Farrar-Hockley, Anthony, *Goughie: The Life of General Sir Hubert Gough*, Hart-Davis, MacGibbon, London, 1975.

Farr, Don, *None That Go Return: Leighton, Brittain and Friends and the Lost Generation 1914-18*, Solihull, Helion & Company Limited, 2010.

Farr, Don, *The Silent General: Horne of the First Army*, Solihull, Helion & Company Limited, 2007.

Farrell, Fred A., *The 51st Division War Sketches*, Edinburgh, T.C. & E.C. Jack, Ltd, 1920.

Fox, Colin, *Monchy le Preux*, Barnsley, Leo Cooper, 2000.

Franks, Norman, Guest, Russell and Bailey, Frank, *Bloody April 1917*, London, Grub Street, 2017.

Gardner, Brian, *Allenby*, London, Cassell & Company Ltd, 1965.

Gillon, Captain Stair, *The Story of the 29th Division: A Record of Gallant Deeds*
, London, Thomas Nelson and Sons Ltd, 1925.

Girardet, Jean-Marie, Jacques, Alain and Duclos, Jean-Luc Letho, *Somewhere on the Western Front: Arras 1914-1918*, Arras, Editions Degeorge, 2003.

Gliddon, Gerald, *VCs of the First World War: Arras & Messines 1917*, Stroud, Sutton Publishing Limited, 1998.

Greenhalgh, Elizabeth, *The French Army and the First World War*, Cambridge, Cambridge University Press, 2014.

Hardy, Colin, *The Reconographers*, Solihull, Helion & Company Limited, 2016.

Hare, Major General Sir Steuart, *The Annals of the King's Royal Rifle Corps: Volume V. The Great War*, London, John Murray, 1932.

Hayes, Geoffrey; Iarocci, Andrew; Bechthold, Mike (eds.), *Vimy Ridge: A Canadian Reassessment*, Waterloo, Ontario, Laurier Centre for Military Strategic and Disarmament Studies and Wilfred Laurier University Press, 2007.

Haythornthwaite. Philip J., *The World War One Source Book*, London, Arms and Armour Press, 1999.

Hoyte, Lieutenant W.N., *10th(S) Battalion The Sherwood Foresters: The History of the Battalion during the Great War*, Uckfield, The Naval & Military Press Ltd, 2003.

Hughes, Peter, *Visiting the Fallen: Arras North*, Barnsley, Pen & Sword Military, 2015.

Hughes, Peter, *Visiting the Fallen: Arras South*, Barnsley, Pen & Sword Military, 2015.

Jacques, Alain and Mortier, Laurence, *La Bataille d'Arras*, Arras, Éditions Degeorge, 2014.

Jerrold, Douglas, *The Royal Naval Division*, Uckfield, Naval & Military Press Ltd (reprint of 1923 edition), undated.

Jones, Simon, *Underground Warfare 1914-1918*, Barnsley, Pen & Sword Military, 2010.

Jünger, Ernst, *The Storm of Steel*, London, Constable and Company Ltd, 1994.

Kendall, Paul, *Bullecourt 1917: Breaching the Hindenburg Line*, Stroud, Spellmount, 2010.

Liddell Hart, B.H., *History of the First World War*, London, Papermac, 1997.

Liddell Hart, Captain B.H., *The Tanks: the History of the Royal Tank Regiment, Volume One 1914-1939*, London, Cassell & Company Ltd, 1959.

Lloyd George, David, *War Memoirs, Volumes I and II*, London, Odhams Press Limited, 1934.

McCarthy, Chris, *The Somme: the Day-By-Day Account*, London, Brockhampton Press, 1998.

McKee, Alexander, *Vimy Ridge*, London, Pan Books Ltd., 1966.

Macksey, Kenneth, *Vimy Ridge 1914-18*, London, Pan/Ballantine, 1973.

Messenger, Charles, *Brief but Glorious: A Brief History of the 8th (Service) Battalion Royal Fusiliers 1914-18*, London, ONE, 2007.

Murphy, David, *Breaking Point of the French Army: The Nivelle Offensive of 1917*, Pen & Sword Military, Barnsley, 2015.

Neillands, Robin, *The Great War Generals on the Western Front*, London, Robinson Publishing Ltd, 1999.

Nicholls, Jonathan, *Cheerful Sacrifice: the Battle of Arras 1917*, London, Leo Cooper, 1990.

Nichols, Captain G.H.F., *The 18th Division in the Great War*, Edinburgh, William Blackwood and Sons, 1922 (reprinted by Naval & Military Press Ltd, undated.)

Nicholson, Colonel G.W.L., *Official History of the Canadian Army in the First World War: Canadian Expeditionary Force 1914-1919*, Ottawa, Queen's Printer, 1962.

O'Connor, Mike, *Airfields & Airmen: Arras*, Barnsley, Pen & Sword Military, 2004.

Passingham, Ian, *All the Kaiser's Men: The Life and Death of the German Soldier on the Western Front*, Stroud, The History Press, 2011.

Philpott, William, *Bloody Victory: The Sacrifice on the Somme*, London, Abacus, 2010.

Rawson, Andrew, *The Arras Campaign 1917*, Pen and Sword Military, Barnsley, 2017.

Reed, Paul, *Walking Arras: A Guide to the 1917 Arras Battlefields*, Barnsley, Pen & Sword Military, 2007.

Reid, Walter, *Arras 1917: The Journey to Railway Triangle*, Edinburgh, Birlinn Limited, 2011.

Rolland, Denis, *La Grève des Tranchées: Les Mutineries de 1917*, Paris, Editions Imago, 2005.

Sandilands, Lieutenant Colonel H.R., *The 23rd Division 1914-1919*, Edinburgh, William Blackwood and Sons, 1925, (undated reprint by Naval & Military Press Ltd).

Shakespear, Lieutenant Colonel J., *The Thirty Fourth Division 1915-1919*, Uckfield, The Naval & Military Press Ltd, (undated reprint).

Sheldon, Jack, *The German Army in the Spring Offensives 1917: Arras, Aisne and Champagne*, Barnsley, Pen & Sword Military, 2015.

Sheldon, Jack, *The German Army on Vimy Ridge 1914-1917*, Barnsley, Pen & Sword Military, 2013.

Sheldon, Jack and Cave, Nigel, *The Battle for Vimy Ridge – 1917*, Pen & Sword Military, Barnsley, 2007.

Sheffield, Gary and Bourne, John (eds.), *Douglas Haig: War Diaries and Letters 1914-1918*, London, Weidenfeld & Nicolson, 2005.

Snow, Dan, and Pottle, Mark (eds.), *The Confusion of Command*, London, Frontline Books, 2011.

Spears, Brigadier-General E.L., *Prelude to Victory*, London, Jonathan Cape Ltd, 1940.

Stewart, Lieutenant Colonel J. and Buchan, John, *The Fifteenth (Scottish) Division 1914-1919*, Edinburgh, William Blackwood and Sons, 1926 (reprinted by Naval & Military Press Ltd).

Strong, Paul and Marble, Sanders, *Artillery in the Great War*, Barnsley, Pen & Sword Military, 2011.

Tallett, Kyle and Tasker, Trevor, *Gavrelle*, Barnsley, Leo Cooper, 2000.

Uffindell, Andrew, *The Nivelle Offensive and the Battle of the Aisne 1917: A Battlefield Guide to the Chemin des Dames*, Barnsley, Pen & Sword Military, 2015.

Vale, Colonel W.L., *History of the South Staffordshire Regiment*, Aldershot, Gale & Polden Ltd., 1969.

Walker, Jonathan, *The Blood Tub: General Gough and the Battle of Bullecourt, 1917*, Staplehurst, Spellmount Limited, 1998.

Warner, Philip, *The Battle of Loos*, Ware, Wordsworth Editions Limited, 2000.

Watson, W.H.L., *A Company of Tanks*, Leonaur, Oakpast Ltd, 2009.

Wavell, Archibald (Field Marshal Lord), *Allenby, A Study In Greatness*, New York, Oxford University Press, 1941.

Williams, Charles, *Pétain*, London, Little, Brown, 2005.

Williams, J., *Byng of Vimy: General and Governor-General*, London, Leo Cooper/Secker & Warburg, 1983.

Wilson, Trevor, *The Myriad Faces of War: Britain and the Great War 1914-1918*, Cambridge, Polity Press, 1986.

Wynne, Captain G.C., *If Germany Attacks: The Battle in Depth in the West*, Westport, Connecticut, Greenwood Press, 1976.

Wynne, Captain G.C., *Landrecies to Cambrai: Case Studies of German Operations on the Western Front*, Solihull, Helion & Company Limited, 2011.

War Diaries: WO 95/ ... Series (consulted at The National Archives (TNA), Kew or online)

169	First Army
170	First Army
361	Third Army
362	Third Army
363	Third Army
519	Fifth Army
770	VI Corps (Third Army)
805	VII Corps (Third Army)
936	XVII Corps (Third Army)
1049	Canadian Corps (First Army)
1050	Canadian Corps (First Army)
1118	2nd Cavalry Division (Cavalry Corps)
1141	3rd Cavalry Division (Cavalry Corps)
1153	3rd Dragoon Guards (6 Cavalry Brigade)
1156	10th Hussars (8 Cavalry Brigade)
1156	1st Essex Yeomanry (8 Cavalry Brigade)
1297/1	2nd Division (XIII Corps)
1345	5 Brigade (2nd Division)
1348	2nd Oxford & Buckinghamshire Light Infantry (Ox & Bucks LI) (5 Bde)
1356	6 Brigade (2nd Division)

1371	1st Royal Berkshire Regiment (R Berks) (99 Brigade)
1378	3rd Division (VI Corps)
1417	8 Brigade (3rd Division)
1421	7th King's Shropshire Light Infantry (KSLI) (8 Brigade)
1422	1st Royal Scots Fusiliers (RSF) (8 Brigade)
1423	2nd Royal Scots (R Scots) (8 Brigade)
1424	8th East Yorkshire Regiment (8 Brigade)
1427	9 Brigade (3rd Division)
1429/2	13th King's (Liverpool) Regiment (King's) (9 Brigade)
1430	1st Northumberland Fusiliers (Northumberlands) (9 Brigade)
1431	4th Royal Fusiliers (RF) (9 Brigade)
1432	12th West Yorkshire Regiment (9 Brigade)
1433	76 Brigade (3rd Division)
1435	1st Gordon Highlanders (Gordons) (76 Brigade)
1436	8th King's Own (Royal Lancaster Regiment) (King's Own) (76 Brigade)
1436	10th Royal Welsh Fusiliers (RWF) (76 Brigade)
1437	2nd Suffolk Regiment (Suffolks) (76 Brigade)
1446	4th Division (XVII Corps)
1479	10th Brigade (4th Division)
1481/1	Household Battalion (10 Brigade)
1482	1st Royal Irish Fusiliers (RIF) (10 Brigade)
1483	2nd Seaforths (10 Brigade)
1484	1st Royal Warwickshire Regiment (Warwicks) (10 Brigade)
1491	11 Brigade (4th Division)
1495	1st Hampshire Regiment (Hampshires) (11 Brigade)
1496	1st Rifle Brigade (RB) (11 Brigade)
1498	1st East Lancashire Regiment (11 Brigade)
1499/1	1st SLI (11 Brigade)
1502/1503	12 Brigade (4th Division)
1505	2nd Essex Regiment (Essex) (12 Brigade)
1506	1st King's Own (12 Brigade)
1507	2nd Lancashire Fusiliers (12 Brigade)
1508	2nd Duke of Wellington's Regiment (Duke's) (12 Brigade)
1514	5th Division (I Corps)
1550	13 Brigade (5th Division)
1738	9th (Scottish) Division (XVII Corps)
1739	9th (Scottish) Division (XVII Corps)
1762	26 Brigade (9th (Scottish) Division)
1765	7th Seaforth Highlanders (Seaforths) (26 Brigade)
1766	8th Black Watch (26 Brigade)
1767	5th Cameron Highlanders (Camerons) (26 Brigade)
1768	10th Argyll & Sutherland Highlanders (Argylls) (26 Brigade)
1770	27 Brigade (9th (Scottish) Division)
1772	6th King's Own Scottish Borderers (KOSB) ((27 Brigade)
	9th Cameronians (Scottish Rifles) (SR) (27 Brigade)
1773	11th R Scots (27 Brigade)
	12th R Scots (27 Brigade)
1777	South African Brigade (9th (Scottish) Division)
1778	South African Brigade (9th (Scottish) Division)
1780	1st Regiment South African Infantry (SA Brigade)
1781	2nd Regiment South African Infantry (SA Brigade)
1784	3rd Regiment South African Infantry (SA Brigade)
1785	4th Regiment South African Infantry (SA Brigade)

1824	12th Division (VI Corps)
1848	35 Brigade (12th Division)
1850	5th R Berks (35 Brigade)
1851	9th Essex (35 Brigade)
1852	7th Suffolks (35 Brigade)
1853	7th Norfolk Regiment (Norfolks) (35 Brigade)
1854	36 Brigade (12th Division)
1856	11th Middlesex Regiment (Middlesex)(36 Brigade)
	7th Royal Sussex Regiment (R Sussex) (36 Brigade)
1857	8th RF (36 Brigade)
	9th RF (36 Brigade)
1858	37 Brigade (12th Division)
1860	6th The Buffs (East Kent Regiment) (37 Brigade)
1861	6th (Queen's Own) Royal West Kent Regiment (R West Kents)(37 Brigade)
1862	7th East Surrey Regiment (37 Brigade)
1863	6th Queen's (West Surrey Regiment) (Queen's) (37 Brigade)
1869	14th (Light) Division (VII Corps)
1896/1	7th RB (41 Brigade)
1896/3	7th King's Royal Rifle Corps (KRRC) (41 Brigade)
1898	42 Brigade (14th Division)
1904	43 Brigade (14th Division)
1906	6th King's Own Yorkshire Light Infantry (KOYLI) (43 Brigade)
1914	15th (Scottish) Division (VI Corps)
1935	44 Brigade (15th Division)
1937	9th Black Watch (44 Brigade)
1938	8th/10th Gordons (44 Brigade)
1941	7th Camerons (44 Brigade)
1943	45 Brigade (15th Division)
1944	11th Argylls (45 Brigade)
1945	6th Camerons (45 Brigade)
1946	13th R Scots (45 Brigade)
1947	6th/7th RSF (45 Brigade)
1950	46 Brigade (15th Division)
1952	10th/11th Highland Light Infantry (HLI) (46 Brigade)
	12th HLI (46 Brigade)
1953	7th/8th KOSB (46 Brigade)
1954	10th SR (46 Brigade)
2132	21st Division (VII Corps)
2152	62 Brigade (21st Division)
2154	1st Lincolnshire Regiment (Lincolns) (62 Brigade)
2155	12th Northumberlands (62 Brigade)
	13th Northumberlands (62 Brigade)
2156	10th Yorkshire Regiment (Green Howards) (62 Brigade)
2159	64 Brigade (21st Division)
2161	1st East Yorkshire Regiment (64 Brigade}
	15th Durham Light Infantry (DLI) (64 Brigade)
2162	9th KOYLI (64 Brigade)
	10th KOYLI (64 Brigade)
2163	110 Brigade (21st Division)
2164	6th Leicestershire Regiment (Leicesters) (110 Brigade)
	7th Leicesters (110 Brigade)
2165	8th Leicesters(110 Brigade)
	9th Leicesters (110 Brigade)

2190	24th Division (I Corps)
2217	73 Brigade (24th Division)
2218	2nd Leinster Regiment (73 Brigade)
2219	9th R Sussex (73 Brigade)
2311	30th Division (VII Corps)
2327	21 Brigade (30th Division)
2329	2nd Wiltshire Regiment (21 Brigade)
	2nd Green Howards (21 Brigade)
	19th Manchester Regiment (Manchesters) (21 Brigade)
2330	18th King's (21 Brigade)
2332	89 Brigade (30th Division)
2333	2nd Bedfordshire Regiment (Bedfords) (89 Brigade)
2334	17th King's (89 Brigade)
	19th King's (89 Brigade)
2335	20th King's (89 Brigade)
2337	90 Brigade (30th Division)
2339	16th Manchesters (90 Brigade)
	17th Manchesters (90 Brigade)
	18th Manchesters (90 Brigade)
2340	2nd RSF (90 Brigade)
2342/3	31st Division (XIII Corps)
2356/4	92 Brigade (31st Division)
2359/4	93 Brigade (31st Division)
2433	34th Division (XVII Corps)
2434	34th Division (XVII Corps)
2455	101 Brigade (34th Division)
2457/5	15th R Scots (101 Brigade)
2460	102 Brigade (34th Division)
2464	103 Brigade (34th Division)
2513	37th Division (VI/XVII Corps)
2528	63 Brigade (37th Division)
2528	4th Middlesex (63 Brigade)
2529	8th Lincolns (63 Brigade)
2529	8th Somerset Light Infantry (SLI) (63 Brigade)
2529	10th York & Lancs (63 Brigade)
2531	111 Brigade (37th Division)
2532	10th RF (111 Brigade)
	13th RF (111 Brigade)
2533	13th KRRC (111 Brigade)
2534	13th RB (111 Brigade)
2536	112 Brigade (37th Division)
2537	6th Bedfords (112 Brigade)
	8th East Lancashires (112 Brigade)
2538	11th Royal Warwickshire Regiment (Warwicks) (112 Brigade)
	10th Loyal North Lancashire Regiment (Loyals) (112 Brigade)
2534	13th RB (111 Brigade)
2536	112 Brigade (37th Division)
2845	51st (Highland) Division (XVII Corps)
2862	152 Brigade (51st Division)
2865/1	8th Argylls (152 Brigade)
2866	5th Seaforths (152 Brigade)
2867	6th Seaforths (152 Brigade)
2868/1	6th Gordons (152 Brigade)

2872	153 Brigade (51st Division)
2876	6th Black Watch (153 Brigade)
2879	7th Black Watch (153 Brigade)
2881	5th Gordons (153 Brigade)
2882/1	7th Gordons (153 Brigade)
2884	154 Brigade (51st Division)
2886/1	7th Argylls (154 Brigade)
2886/2	4th Gordons (154 Brigade)
2887/5	9th R Scots (154 Brigade)
2888/1	4th Seaforths (154 Brigade)
2933	56th (1 London) Infantry Division (VII Corps)
2947	167 Brigade (56th Division)
2951	168 Brigade (56th Division)
2954	1/12th London Regiment (Rangers) (168 Brigade)
	1/4th London Regiment (Royal Fusiliers) (168 Brigade)
2955	13th London Regiment (Kensington) (168 Brigade)
2958	169 Brigade (56th Division)
3079/3	185 Brigade (62nd Division)
3084/2	186 Brigade (62nd Division)
3088/2	187 Brigade (62nd Division)
3092	63rd (Royal Naval) Division (XIII Corps)
3094	63rd (Royal Naval) Division (XIII Corps)
3108	188 Brigade (63rd (RN) Division)
3112	189 Brigade (63rd (RN) Division)
3116	190 Brigade (63rd (RN) Division)
3727	1st Canadian Division (Canadian Corps)
3758	1 Canadian Brigade (CB) (1st Canadian Division)
3760	1st Canadian Battalion (1st CB)
3764	2 CB (1st Canadian Division)
3773	3 CB (1st Canadian Division)
3786	2nd Canadian Division (Canadian Corps)
3812	4 CB (2nd Canadian Division)
3820	5 CB (2nd Canadian Division)
3827	6 CB (2nd Canadian Division)
3838	3rd Canadian Division (Canadian Corps)
3864	7 CB (3rd Canadian Division)
3865	Royal Canadian Regiment (7 CB)
3866	Princess Patricia's Canadian Light Infantry (7 CB)
3866	42nd Canadian Infantry Battalion (CIB) (7 CB)
3867	49th CIB (7 CB)
3868	8 CB (3rd Canadian Division)
3870	1st Canadian Mounted Rifles (CMR) (8 CB)
3871	2nd CMR (8 CB)
3872	4th CMR (8 CB)
3873	5th CMR (8 CB)
3875	9 CB (3rd Canadian Division)
3877	52nd (CIB) (9 CB)
3878	43rd CIB (9 CB)
3879	60th CIB (9 CB)
3879	116th CIB (9 CB)
3880	4th Canadian Division
3895	10 CB (4th Canadian Division)
3898	44th CIB (10 CB)

3898	46th CIB (10 CB)
3899	47th CIB (10 CB)
3899	50th CIB (10 CB)
3900	11 CB (4th Canadian Division)
3902	54th CIB (11 CB)
3903	75th CIB (11 CB)
3903	102nd CIB (11 CB)
3904	87th CIB (11 CB)
3905	12 CB (4th Canadian Division)
3908	38th CIB (12 CB)
3908	72nd CIB (12 CB)
3908	73rd CIB (12 CB)
3909	78th CIB (12 CB)
3909	85th CIB (12 CB)

Index

Index of Formations and Units

General index